ORGANIZATIONAL BEHAVIOR IN SCHOOLS AND SCHOOL DISTRICTS

Edited by
Samuel B. Bacharach

PRAEGER SPECIAL STUDIES • PRAEGER SCIENTIFIC

Library of Congress Cataloging in Publication Data

Main entry under title:

Organizational behavior in schools and school districts.

 Bibliography: p.
 Includes index.
 Contents: Introduction and overview: Organizational
and political dimensions for research on school district
governance and administration / by Samuel B. Bacharach.
Design of the book—The Federal and state environment
of school districts: The effects of institutionalized
rules on administrators / by Brian Rowan. Response to
regulation, an organizational process approach / by
Lee S. Sproull. School systems and regulatory mandates,
a case study of the implementation of the Education for
All Handicapped Children Act / by Erwin C. Hargrove . . .
[et al.]—[etc.]
 1. School management and organization—United States
—Addresses, essays, lectures. 2. School districts—
United States—Management—Addresses, essays, lectures.
I. Bacharach, Samuel B.
LB2817.0723   379.1′5′0973   81-5138
ISBN 0-03-057669-5   AACR2

Published in 1981 by Praeger Publishers
CBS Educational and Professional Publishing
A Division of CBS, Inc.
521 Fifth Avenue, New York, New York 10175 U.S.A.

© 1981 by Praeger Publishers

123456789 145 987654321

Printed in the United States of America

ACKNOWLEDGMENTS

Many of the authors in this volume have had their research over the last few years sponsored by the National Institute of Education. This sponsored research has created a cross-disciplinary concern with the organizational analysis of schools and school districts. This edited book has emerged from this newly established network. In organizing the volume, I have tried to accentuate the scope of both the varied theoretical interests and the empirical research that is currently being conducted. Indeed, the impact of this research is only now coming to the surface, and it is hoped that this volume will draw attention to this new body of work.

In putting together this book, I have been greatly assisted by a number of individuals. First and foremost, I would like to thank my colleagues who saw the importance of the project and generously consented to contribute their work. Next, I would like to thank my own staff of personnel who gave generously of their time, common sense, patience, and, most importantly, humor. Rose Malanowski assisted in assuring the scheduling of this cumbersome process. She also critically commented on many of the chapters, consistently offering constructive advice. Stephen Mitchell helped to broaden this work and to assure the establishment of a primary integrative theme. Pamela Kline used her uncanny skills of organization to assure that what began as an idea mechanically translated itself into a book. Finally, I want to thank Carol and Bosch for not having torn the manuscripts that were strewn across the room.

Samuel B. Bacharach

DESIGN OF THE BOOK

Any research and analysis of school district governance and administration must take account of the central dilemma confronting school district administrators. This dilemma arises from the need to satisfy the political imperatives inherent in the notion of the school as a local democracy, while not compromising the administrative imperative of effectiveness and efficiency, which requires certainty and rationality in school administration. We believe that the political model that has been presented, by integrating the literature on community politics and complex organizations, is capable of organizing our understanding of schools so that we can directly address this dilemma and its consequences. Specifically, the political model highlights the two features of school district governance and administration that reflect the essence of the dilemma: the necessity of attending and adapting to external demands and constraints; and the necessity of maintaining control over the internal organization while succeeding in reaching effective decisions. The chapters in this volume are organized around these two features of school district governance and administration.

Traditionally, the primary environment affecting the school district has been that of the local community. As a consequence of increasing numbers of federal and state programs, however, other sectors of the environment now have a significant impact on local school systems. The effect of these programs on school administration is exacerbated either by their mandatory implementation or the increased reliance of local schools on external sources of revenue. In either case, it is essential that we understand the precise manner in which these programs impinge on local school systems. Three chapters in this volume (Part II) address this issue. Brian Rowan ("The Effects of Institutionalized Rules on Administrators") examines the growth of administrative staffs in school systems. His findings show that the growth of the administration is directly related to the increase in external programs, rather than a result of internal organizational factors. Lee Sproull, in "Response to Regulation: An Organizational Process Approach," presents a model of the process by which schools respond to federal programs, with particular attention paid to the role played by the superintendent in determining the school systems response. Her analysis suggests that how a regulation is interpreted has a major effect on the impact of the regulation. Finally, Erwin Hargrove and his associates ("School Systems and Regulatory Mandates: A Case Study of the Implementation of the Education for All Handicapped Children Act") use a case study to explore the organizational changes that must accompany program adoption if successful implementation is to come about. Their effort to develop an evaluation scheme highlights the fact that internal organizational processes must adapt to external demands and constraints if programs are to be successful. Taken together, these three chapters begin to document the specific impact that federal and state programs have on school district governance and administration.

The need to attend and respond to federal and state programs has not diminished the impact of the local community environment on the school system. School districts remain local democracies and school administrators must still attend to the demands of the local constituency. Three chapters (Part III) consider the relation of the community to school district governance and administration. Two of these are case studies of individual school districts. In "The Closing of Andrew Jackson Elementary School: Magnets in School System Organization and Politics," Mary Haywood Metz examines the closing of a successful magnet school in an urban system. Her analysis reveals the complexity of school closings, with federal mandates becoming mixed with community politics and individual personalities, resulting in seemingly objective decisions. Louis Smith, John Prunty, and David Dwyer return to Kensington, site of an earlier study, to provide us with a rare longitudinal analysis of change in schools. In "A Longitudinal Nested Systems Model of Innovation and Change in Schooling," they present a model that attempts to clarify conceptually many of the complexities of school district administration that they, like Metz, found operating in their case study. Much of the impact that the local community has on school district governance and administration results from attempts by local constituencies to have a say in the running of their schools. The final chapter in Part III, "A Theory of Decision Making in the Public Schools: A Public Choice Approach" by Jacob Michaelsen, uses recent developments in economic theory to outline an economic model of school district decision making. This model highlights the difficulty of achieving rational efficiency in a system that must confront political demands.

All of the chapters in Parts II and III on the environment of school districts reveal the impact of environmental factors, at both the federal and community levels, on the running of school districts. While this impact may be buffered by specialized administrative personnel or the perceptions of the superintendent, external forces do affect school district administration. It is this effect that makes up a significant portion of the political-administrative dilemma confronting school administrators. Another portion of this dilemma is revealed through an examination of the intraorganizational aspects of school district governance and administration. Here the focus shifts to those pressures that arise from within the school itself, pressures whose most apparent manifestations may be observed by considering the decision-making process and the control structures of school systems. The papers in Part IV of this book address these features of school systems.

The pressures that arise from within the organization usually reflect specific interest groups trying to achieve a voice over specific issue areas. In "Organizational Control in Educational Systems: A Case Study of Governance in Schools," E. Mark Hanson presents a model of control systems in education that is based on the notion of a group having a specific arena of interest over which it seeks control. Focusing on teachers and administrators, Hanson argues that while there is some consensus as to arenas of expertise, there are also overlapping areas over which control results from political negotiation. Two other chapters also focus on teachers' attempts to gain control or a voice in decision making. W. W. Charters explores the impact of team teaching on control in schools in "The Control of Microeducational Policy in Elementary Schools." By using a new methodology to compare control systems in schools with team teaching to those found in regular schools, he is able to pinpoint the stable and changing aspects of control over microeducational policy. The conditions under which involvement in decision making is sought and its effects on participants is explored by Daniel Duke, Beverly Showers, and Michael Imber in "Studying Shared Decision Making in Schools." They examine the interaction of opportunities for involvement and willingness to be involved for a variety of issues, making several recommendations for future research.

Teachers' demands for a voice in decision making or control over specific issues are based in large part on their expertise. In general, people seek control over areas in which they feel their expertise is applicable. In "Generalists versus Specialists," Stephen Kerr examines the recent trend toward increasing specialization of teachers, as opposed to the traditional generalist teacher. He notes that conflict between generalists and specialists affects numerous groups and assorted aspects of the school system, and he goes on to explore some of the ramifications of this trend. This chapter shows that it is not possible to assume that teachers, or any other group, act as a unit. Interest groups may form on a number of bases that must be empirically identified.

The proliferation of interest groups in schools makes it difficult to achieve the control that is normally seen as necessary to achieve organizational effectiveness and efficiency. In essence, the political nature of the internal organization hinders the development of a rational administration as much as the external political demands that arise in the environment. This means that a political analysis of school districts must consider external relations as well as internal organizational processes. The remainder of the chapters in this book (Part V) focus on the interaction of external and internal demands in school district governance and administration. In "Identifying Handicapped Students," Hugh Mehan and his associates present a case study analysis that shows how external demands, internal demands, and the bureaucratic control structure interact to defeat many of the educational goals and programs that everyone may agree are desirable. This chapter makes clear the necessity of integrating all of these factors.

The dilemma that arises from efforts to cope with political and administrative demands simultaneously falls most heavily on the superintendent. As chief school officer, it is his responsibility to resolve this dilemma. Martin Burlingame explores the strategies and tactics available to a superintendent. In "Superintendent Power Retention," he presents a series of rules for administrators to follow as they attempt to resolve the dilemma confronting them, even suggesting how to turn defeat into at least a moral victory. While the superintendent may bear the brunt of the dilemma, it should be apparent from the chapters reviewed above that no one in the school system is immune from the tension the dilemma creates. James Terborg and John Komocar present an outline of the impact of stress on all members of the school in "Individual and Group Behavior in Schools as a Function of Environmental Stress." Their analysis of factors that lead to stress and the variables that affect coping responses is consistent with the political model espoused here. They believe that an examination of stress can tell us not only how schools function as organizations, it can also pinpoint opportunities for creative change in school systems.

The political model of school district governance and administration was proposed in an effort to integrate and organize the diverse aspects of research and theory on schools, and to suggest new avenues of research. As previously noted, the model highlights two major features of schools: the demands and constraints imposed by the environment, and the internal organizational processes related to decision making and control. While all of the chapters reviewed above can be seen as addressing themselves to these features as well as other aspects of the political model, none of the research or theorizing presented was developed with a political model specifically in mind. While each of the chapters makes suggestions for future research that have implications for a political analysis of schools, none of them utilizes a political perspective as the basis for their suggestions. As such, this overview of the chapters utilizes the political model as an organizing device. In the final chapter, Samuel Bacharach and Stephen Mitchell present a plan for research that is based on the political model presented here. Focusing on the local teachers' union as an interest group, they outline several research questions that follow from a political perspective on schools. The chapter is intended as an illustration of the direction in which a political model of schools can take research on school district governance and administration.

CONTENTS

PART III: THE COMMUNITY ENVIRONMENT
OF SCHOOL DISTRICTS

Chapter

PART IV: THE INTRAORGANIZATIONAL
ANALYSIS OF SCHOOLS: DECISION
MAKING AND CONTROL

PART V: THE POLITICAL PERSPECTIVE:
THE SCHOOL DISTRICT AS A TOTALITY

PART I

INTRODUCTION AND OVERVIEW

1

ORGANIZATIONAL AND POLITICAL DIMENSIONS FOR RESEARCH ON SCHOOL DISTRICT GOVERNANCE AND ADMINISTRATION

Samuel B. Bacharach

Throughout the history of public education in the United States, in the public mind the local school district has been viewed as the embodiment of democratic values. It has the responsibility for inculcating in each generation of youth the moral values and the technical skills needed for participation in the larger society. However, discharging this responsibility creates a fundamental dilemma for school district administrators; they are caught between two conflicting imperatives: the need to satisfy demands for educational excellence and administrative efficiency, and the need to either satisfy or assuage the demands of local constituencies. In effect, school district administrators are frequently compelled to compromise, sometimes sacrificing educational excellence for political expediency, at other times sacrificing political responsiveness in the name of either administrative efficiency or educational excellence.

In recent years this dilemma has been exacerbated by declining enrollment, racial strife, taxpayers' suits, defeated budgets, unwieldy state mandates, declining test scores, and increasing school violence—factors that have created an atmosphere of turmoil

This material is based upon work supported by the National Institute of Education under Grant No. NIE-G-78-0080. Any opinions, findings, and conclusions or recommendations expressed in this publication are those of the author(s) and do not necessarily reflect the views of the Institute of the Department of Health, Education and Welfare. The author would like to thank Stephen Mitchell and Jonathan Reeder for working very closely on this chapter, thus assuring its completion.

and uncertainty for many school districts. In order to cope with their embattled environments, many school districts have discarded old models of organization and adopted new ones. In some instances, adopting new models has proven premature, for it has occurred without an adequate understanding of school districts' administrative structure and processes and the political and historical contexts in which they are embedded.

Any effort to advise school administrators as to how school districts should resolve the dilemmas engendered by these conflicting imperatives—one administrative, the other political—must take account of the school as an organization as well as a democratic institution. To date, achieving such an understanding has been hindered by the tendency, resulting from the reform movement, to separate politics from school district administration (Wirt and Kirst, 1972; Zeigler and Jennings, 1974). The result has been the growth of two separate bodies of literature, one focusing primarily on the school board, the superintendent, and the community, the other dealing with the school as an organization, primarily focusing on administrative relationships within the school. In the first section of this chapter, each of these bodies of literature will be reviewed briefly, pointing out their strengths and limitations. It will be argued that, taken separately, neither of these approaches is adequate for understanding the dilemma confronting school district administrators. The contention is that in order to gain an adequate empirical understanding of the complexities of school district governance and administration, it is necessary to merge these two disparate bodies of literature. If research is to be of any use to educational practitioners, it is crucial that the conceptualization of the school district that guides the researcher reflects the realities of school district processes. Neither the research on community politics nor the research on the school as a formal organization accurately portrays the dilemma school district administrators face in trying to satisfy political and administrative imperatives simultaneously. We believe that the tension resulting from these imperatives can best be represented by a theoretical approach that envisions the school district as a political organization operating within a political system. In the second section of this chapter, the elements in our political model and the relationships between them will be explicated.

UNIFYING TWO APPROACHES TO THE
STUDY OF SCHOOL DISTRICTS

From the colonial period until the mid-1950s, a prevailing sentiment among many academicians and practitioners was that education should be separated from politics. One administrative imperative of this widely held belief was that local schools should be autonomous from local government. Wirt and Kirst (1972:5) and Zeigler and Jennings (1974:3), among others, have summarized the rationale for this insulation of public education from urban politics. In American culture, a good education historically has been prized as an essential ingredient for worldly success. Consequently, the provision of this highly valued service should not be entrusted to politicians, for, in the popular mind, they epitomize the antithesis of the very moral ideals the local school system should be inculcating in its students.

At the turn of the century, this widespread belief about shielding education from the taint of local politics was institutionalized. As Wirt and Kirst (1972:6-7) have pointed out, the reform movement—particularly university presidents, faculty from departments of education, and influential members of the laity and school superintendents—had as one of its prime objectives the removal of the school system from the rest of the local urban government apparatus. In their efforts to restructure school systems, the reformers turned to industry and business for their organizational models. Such features of these models as centralization, efficiency, and expertise were deemed to be effective safeguards against unwarranted political influence. As Zeigler and Jennings noted, the reformers were successful in rendering school districts structurally autonomous from local government, especially with regard to personnel selection and finance. The consequence of the reformers' efforts was not only to strip local education of the egregious features of partisan politics but to render the study of school district governance and administration apolitical. The result, as previously noted, is the division of research on school districts into two distinct bodies of literature, one focusing on the school board, the superintendent, and the community, the other on the internal, administrative aspects of schools. We turn now to a brief review of these two bodies of literature.

The School Board, the Superintendent, and the Community

Despite the indictment that educational research has traditionally been atheoretical, apolitical, and self-serving, over the past 50 years isolated studies, especially those concerned with the composition of school boards, were fraught with distinctly political implications. For example, George Counts' (1937) landmark study revealed that city school boards were overwhelmingly comprised of business and professional men. Conversely, little or no representation was afforded women, labor, and minorities. Almost 25 years later, W. W. Charters (1953) in his review of 62 studies of school board composition corroborates Counts' basic allegation that members of the upper echelons are disproportionately represented on school boards. In his portrayal of Elmtown's school board, Hollingshead (1949:125) succinctly summarized this finding as follows: "Members of the school board had a highly developed sense of responsibility for the preservation of the economic power and prestige interests of Class I and II. Their sense of responsibility to the remainder of the community was interpreted in terms of these interests." As Callahan's (1962:19-46) insightful historical overview attests, Counts' study and subsequent research on school board composition sparked a whole debate as to the necessity of the board, the scope of its functions, its size, and the mechanisms needed to insure more democratic representation. Despite the explicit political emphasis of this research, it did not act as a stimulus for the development of a political model of school districts.

The main drawback to school board research in terms of constructing a political model of school districts is that it poses problems regarding the unit of analysis. Although the underlying assumptions are not always made explicit, school board researchers have implicitly created an image of the school district that does not conform to the empirical referent. These assumptions need to be articulated.

The first assumption is that the school board plays a pivotal role in school district governance. In effect, elected officials, despite their part-time, unsalaried status, are the main source of authority in the district. The main responsibility of their appointed counterparts—the superintendent and his staff—is to implement policy. Two alternative interpretations may be put forth. First, since the superintendent and his staff enjoy certain bureaucratic advantages, expertise, greater control over material resources, and immediate access to valuable information, the crucial decisions in a school district are made at staff meetings, not board meetings. The school board, consequently, rather than representing the public's interests, serves, to invoke Kerr's phrase (1964), as "an agency of legitimation."

The second interpretation holds that while the school board may play an active role in the formulation of school district policy, its strategies and tactics are not evident in public arenas such as school board meetings. As Vidich and Bensman (1968:176-78) have observed, in public meetings the school board attempts to conceal dissent by either presenting a united front or quarreling over the finer points of essentially "hearts and flowers" resolutions (Cistone, 1975:166). Put another way, ascertaining the social and economic status of school board members provides few insights as to how they govern. The immediate response to this problem is to make the necessary methodological refinements. Such a solution would entail observing informal meetings as well as formal ones and supplementing these observations with interviews; however, such refinements offer only a partial solution, for the problem is theoretical in nature. Discovering who wields authority in a school district—the board or the administration—is not synonymous with understanding how a school district is governed. To address the latter issue, other questions must be asked. To invoke Laswell (1936), to understand the governance of school districts requires addressing not only the question of who governs but related questions such as how, when, why, and with what effect. To conclude, until the 1960s, research on local school districts had been mainly apolitical in its thrust. What little political research had been done tended to focus on the school board, particularly its socioeconomic composition, thereby equating one component of the governing process with the entire governing process.

Beginning in 1960, educational research became distinctly more political; moreover, the various notions of politics that informed this research were not bounded by the previous limited, normative view that focused on the school board. This shift in emphasis by education researchers was precipitated, in part, by certain changes in the political environment of school districts. Previously, school district environments, as reflected in research and as empirical entities, appeared to be relatively harmonious. Essentially, school districts were deemed to reflect the moral and social values of the large community. Two explanations for this harmonious relationship may be adduced. The first explanation held that the socioeconomic composition of most communities was sufficiently homogeneous that there was a high degree of consensus concerning school district goals and the means by which these goals were attained. What differences existed were couched in stylistic terms and, therefore, could be readily accommodated. The second explanation, as expressed by Hollingshead earlier, held that community elites designated themselves as guardians of the public interest with respect to education and, consequently, assumed the responsibility for setting school district policy and overseeing its implementation.

Beginning in 1960, the prevailing harmony that blanketed the political environment of many schools across the nation, irrespective of its sources, began to dissolve. The precipitants of this dissolution of political accord were numerous and diverse; however, it is not the aim of this chapter to disentangle them systematically. Nonetheless, a short discussion of some of the main sources of dissolution will make the brief for the adoption of a political approach in school district governance more compelling. Industrialization, urbanization, desegregation, ideological debate engendered by the Cold War, technological advance, and the rapid growth of the welfare state were the main social forces in the post-World War II era that transformed the socioeconomic makeup of U.S. communities. As a result of these developments, many communities became, in social and economic terms, more heterogeneous. Concomitantly, the political climate in many U.S. communities changed. Albeit an oversimplification in the past, various groups within communities were willing to submerge their more parochial concerns in the interest of preserving the overall harmony. However, in the 1960s, community groups, especially disadvantaged minorities, became increasingly cognizant of the social and economic differences that separated people from each other, both in the larger society and within their communities. They also became increasingly confident that these differences could be minimized through political action. In effect, the pursuit of self-interest by community groups began to take precedence over the preservation of consensus.

This change in the political climate of many communities manifested itself in a number of ways. First, disadvantaged minorities began to bring pressure to bear on school districts and other institutions of local government to satisfy their demands. In response to these potentially disruptive activities, community elites began to initiate strategies designed to preserve the status quo. As various community constituencies began to vie with each other for scarce resources, school districts and other public institutions encountered more and more obstacles in aggregating demands and converting them into policies that were beneficial to all groups. As a result, public institutions, in order to carry out their policy mandates, had to abandon the traditional political strategies and adopt new ones. In many instances, the adoption of a new strategy would not suffice, for school districts and other public institutions simply lacked the resources needed to satisfy the demands of various constituencies. As a result, school districts began to request assistance from state and federal governments. To conclude, the social and economic changes that took place in the decades following World War II had politicized the environment of school districts. The old foundations of consensus had been undermined, and new ones awaited discovery. School districts consequently became embattled political entities, attempting to mediate the conflicting demands of such local and extra-local political groups and institutions as parents, teachers, minorities, teachers' unions, state departments of education, state legislators, faculties of state teachers' colleges, state and federal courts, and the federal education bureaucracy. While the 1960s did not mark the beginning of interest group politics in public education, it did signal its proliferation.

Students of schools and other public sector institutions such as Charters (1952) and Eliot (1959) recognized the implications that these developments had for school research and entered cogent pleas for the adoption of a political approach. Nonetheless, despite the consensus among educational researchers across disciplines concerning the theoretical utility of a political approach, there was little agreement as to the appropriate unit of analysis. Likewise, there is considerable disagreement concerning which model is best suited for a political approach. More than 20 years after Eliot (1959) had criticized educational researchers for overlooking the political dynamics of school districts, the debate regarding the appropriate unit of analysis remains unresolved. However, progress has been made on a number of fronts. First, there is agreement that a political approach should encompass the school district and its environment. Moreover, some researchers (for example, Wirt and Kirst, 1972; Thompson, 1976) have made a convincing case for using a systems model to analyze the political dimensions of various relationships that link the school district to its environment. However, consensus has yet to emerge as to which political dimensions should be analyzed. At the conceptual level, there is still considerable disagreement. To the degree that confusion exists at the conceptual level, the debate concerning the appropriate unit of analysis for a political analysis of schools continues.

In order to understand some of the considerations that informed the construction of the model of school districts and their environments, which is presented in the second section of this chapter, it is necessary to examine models used by other researchers. In the next section, models used by Corwin (1965), Zeigler and Jennings (1974), Wirt and Kirst (1972), and Thompson (1976) to study school districts and their political environment will be assessed.

Corwin depicts the school district as a dynamic organizational entity operating in a highly political environment. The community does not automatically cede autonomy to the school district. By the same token, the school district does not assert its autonomy unchallenged. The autonomy of the school district is continually being challenged by various groups in its environment. Corwin (1965:45) has characterized this dynamic tension between the community and the school as follows:

> It is not only the fact that outside groups seek to regulate the organization's [the school] goals and activities that is important, but also the fact that the official structure and informal strategy of the school commit it to a line of action, which either promotes or restricts

> adaptation . . . far from being permanent, goals are
> in a constant state of revision as the school resists,
> bargains and adjusts to environmental pressures.

Corwin's main contribution was to conceive of schools as complex organizations. In the preface of his A Sociology of Education, Corwin (1965:vii) distinguishes his organizational perspectives from other perspectives as follows:

> It is the distinctive task of sociology to deal with the
> structural and functional features of complex systems
> of organization, and it seems safe to assume that the
> principles of organization are as responsible for the
> character of American education as the more widely
> recognized psychology of the classroom on the one
> hand or the general institutional values on the other.

In examining the intricate relationships that bind the school system to the larger society, Corwin uses various concepts from the sociology of organizations and the sociology of the professions to make salient the political dynamics inherent in these relationships. Specifically, he identifies the key actors and the patterns of interaction in which they engage. His second contribution was to present conceptually a more differentiated image of the school's environment than had been depicted in previous research. It was differentiated in two respects. First, Corwin, using the Weberian concepts of class, status, and power, identified not only the sources of consensus but also the sources of conflict. Second, from his perspective, the environment of the school system was manifestly political. Since schools lacked the resources to satisfy the demands of all the groups in their environments, they were compelled to adopt a number of strategies to sustain the requisite level of consensus needed to govern effectively. Corwin's third contribution was to catalog and explain the "adaptive strategies" used by schools to accommodate various environmental pressures. Drawing on the work of Thompson and McEwen (1958), he identifies five adaptive strategies: passive adaption, coalition, cooptation, bargaining, and competition. In identifying these strategies, Corwin demonstrates how schools, when viewed as complex organizations, function in highly political environments. In effect, he has taken an important preliminary step toward developing a political model of the school system and its environment. The view of the school system put forth by Corwin is more comprehensive in its scope than previous ones, for the interactions between the school system and its environment are no longer equated with the deliberations that occur between the school board and the superintendent.

Two criticisms can be made of Corwin's work. The first involves his focus on adaptive strategies as the dynamic aspect of school politics. While the concept "adaptive strategies" provides a useful point of departure for conducting a political analysis of schools, the scope is limited and its capacity for discriminating between various phenomena is moot. We maintain that the concept of decision making is more inclusive and analytically more fruitful, for it is through decision making that these strategies are initiated. Second, concepts such as coalition, cooptation, and bargaining do not permit the researcher to distinguish conceptually between power, authority, and influence, yet these distinctions are central to a political analysis of schools.

Zeigler and Jennings attempted to determine whether the principle of representative democracy guided the governing process of local school districts. Consequently, they concentrated on three sets of relationships: the selection of board members, the responsiveness of board members to the policy preferences of its constituents, and the sources of conflict and cooperation between the school board and the superintendent. Using a comparative methodology, they examined various hypotheses regarding these relationships in 82 school districts. Their rationale for focusing on the relationship between the public, the school boards, and the superintendent is stated as follows (1974:12): "Our choice was to focus on the level at which most of the decisions with immediate and practical effects on the quality of educational programs of schools are made. Despite evidence pointing toward growing state and federal involvement, immediate control over school politics still resides at the district level."

Zeigler and Jennings' research was guided by the following assumptions. The authors, despite the assertions of Callahan (1962:30), Kerr (1964:35), and Iannaccone and Lutz (1970:231) that the superintendent has gained the upper hand in the deliberations between the board and the administration, maintain that the supremacy of the superintendent awaits empirical confirmation. To buttress this contention, the authors contend that the school board, by law and by tradition, still retains considerable authority over such policy matters as finance, reorganization, personnel, and renovation. Moreover, the board has the authority to review the superintendent's performance and if it proves deficient, dismiss him. Another assumption adopted by Zeigler and Jennings is that to the degree that schools are democratic institutions, the board plays a pivotal role in the representation process, for it is the mechanism "through which local control is exercised." The authors qualify this assumption by maintaining that representative democracy depends upon a high degree of citizen involvement. Specifically, if these requirements of representative democracy are to be satisfied in operational terms, Zeigler and Jennings contend that there must be a high level of turnout and competition in school board elections.

Regarding the first linkage in the governance process, the election of board members, Zeigler and Jennings found that active citizen involvement, a necessary condition for effective representative democracy, was for the most part absent in school districts. Specifically, school board elections were characterized by low turnout, low competition, minimal debate over the issues, and low incumbent turnover (1974:71). Regarding the second linkage, board responsiveness to constituents, the authors (1974:141–42) discovered that while responsiveness varied with issues from a correlation of .02 to one of .79, the overall responsiveness was quite "modest," $r = .27$. Thus, Zeigler and Jennings (1974:142) conclude that "overall potential for the representation of public will in local educational policy making systems is very uneven and very much issue specific. As such, the school district representational process resembles that for congressional districts and most probably for other units of representation as well." Given the fact that schools are perceived by the public as the embodiment of democratic values, the relative lack of school board responsiveness to constituent preferences provides an ironic contrast. Zeigler and Jennings (1974:246) attribute this relative lack of responsiveness to public apathy. "The public, while declaring it wants delegates rather than trustees, nevertheless scarcely exerts itself to instruct the delegates."

Regarding the third linkage in the governing process, superintendent–board relationships, Zeigler and Jennings (1974:250) conclude that in most school districts, the superintendent has become the central figure in policy making: "Boards are likely to become spokesmen for the superintendent to the community; their representational roles are reversed and the superintendent becomes the dominant policy maker. . . ." The authors attribute this development to three factors: the complexity of educational problems, the sheer size of school district bureaucracy, and the lack of consensus on many school boards, which leaves them vulnerable to manipulation by the superintendent. Conversely, they assert (1974:250) that the superintendent is least likely to emerge as the dominant policy maker in "small nonpolitical school districts" governed by a consensual elite.

The basic contribution of Zeigler and Jennings' work is twofold. In comparison with earlier research that focused on the composition of school boards, this research focuses on the interactions between the school board, the superintendent, and the public. Moreover, by adopting representative democracy as a standard of comparison, it permits an assessment of not only who governs the school

district but how it is governed. The second contribution of this research is that the authors, in applying a comparative methodology
to a national sample of school districts, can draw some generalizable inferences. Since Gross and his colleagues (1958) conducted
their research on the attitudes, perceptions, and role orientations
of a select sample of superintendents and school boards in Massachusetts, comparative research on school districts has been increasing (Bailey et al., 1962; Bloomberg and Sunshine, 1963; Crain et al.,
1968; Kimbrough, 1964; and Martin, 1962). However, the Zeigler
and Jennings study marks one of the few attempts to examine questions related to the governing of school districts on a national level.

The main drawback to Zeigler and Jennings' study is that it
equates board, superintendent, and community relationships with the
entire governing process, thereby leaving the question of the appropriate unit of analysis unresolved. Relying primarily on interviews,
the authors concentrated on the superintendent, the board, and the
public's perceptions of political participation, board responsiveness,
and the sources of board-superintendent consensus and conflict. As
a result, they failed to examine the consequences of this political activity for school district policy making. Investigating the perceptions
of consensus and conflict provides few insights into how consensus is
maintained and how conflicts are resolved. In effect, Zeigler and
Jennings overlook the main political processes that comprise the
governing process of school districts. Put more abstractly, if the
school district governing is divided into two processes—the acquisition of authority and the allocation of authority—then Zeigler and
Jennings concerned themselves with the former; whereas Corwin
focused on the latter. It should also be noted that if Zeigler and
Jennings' intention was to study the governing of school districts,
they should have supplemented their interviews with other methodologies such as case studies and questionnaires.

In an effort to resolve this dilemma regarding the appropriate
unit of analysis for understanding the politics of the school district,
Wirt and Kirst (1972) and Thompson (1976) have proposed the adoption of a systems framework, drawing on Easton's work (1965) for
the basic model. Wirt and Kirst put forth several justifications for
adopting a political approach based on a systems framework. First,
such a framework presents a clear delineation of how schools respond
to the demands in their environment. As a public service institution,
they must be responsive to societal demands, the demands of particular groups, and the demands of individuals.

A second advantage of using a systems model to study the political features of school districts is that, given its dynamic emphasis as
indicated by the terms "input," "conversion process," and "output,"
it affords the researcher the opportunity to examine the structural

and process components of the relationship between the school district and its environment, thereby avoiding the static bias of earlier models. Moreover, a systems framework, if properly applied, enables the researcher to specify conceptually which structures and processes are unique to school districts and which structures and processes are typical of all systems of government.

A third justification, which is implied by Wirt and Kirst (1975) and made explicit by Thompson (1976), is that the school system is a dynamic political entity that is constantly interacting with various other entities. Thompson (1976:20) attempted to characterize this relationship as follows:

> Educational policies, in turn, affect all of the other
> social systems. How a society answers the major ques-
> tions about education affects the economic, social, cul-
> tural and political conditions of a society. In essence,
> the social system interacts with numerous social sys-
> tems in the total environment. It is affected by the
> other social systems and in turn it affects the other
> social systems.

This notion of interdependence is particularly important for viewing the school district as a governmental unit embedded in a larger system of government. Traditional school research, imbued with the notion of local autonomy, which turn-of-the-century reformers sought to promulgate, often depicted, either implicitly or explicitly, the school district as self-sufficient. Moreover, the self-sufficient image of the school district reflected in the research is a relatively accurate portrayal of the relationship between the school district and its environment during the nineteenth century and early twentieth century.

Another justification for adopting a systems framework is that it permits the empirical examination of the openness assumption. By the very nature of their mission, school districts may be viewed as open systems. In the past 15 years, the nature and the scope of this openness have changed considerably. During this period school districts have increasingly been plagued by union strife, court-ordered bussing, a shrinking tax base, declining enrollment, inflation, and the proliferation of cumbersome federal and state regulations. As a result, school districts have had to appeal to extralocal institutions such as the judicial, the legislative, and the executive branches of state and federal government for assistance. Not only have these developments eroded the autonomy of local school districts, but they also have undermined the authority of the superintendent. As the school system has become more open, the superintendent has had to adopt new political strategies to accomplish the administrative objective. The following excerpt from an interview conducted by Wirt and Kirst (1972:87) with a former big city superintendent illustrates how these developments have altered the superintendent's role:

> It used to be that a superintendent, if he was at all successful, would have the feeling that he had the ability to mount a program and carry it through successfully. I think at the present time very few superintendents would be able to say honestly that they have this feeling. They are at the beck and call of every pressure that is brought to them. They have lost initiative. They don't control their own time. One of the problems today is that teachers are so well trained; they know as much or more in their own specialization than any administrator does. . . . There has been a change in the role of superintendent from one who plans and carries through to one who works with groups of people in joint planning and ultimate realization of something the group can agree on.

As a result of these recent developments, the school system's openness is no longer coterminous with the community it serves; instead, it extends to the state and federal levels. Cast in conceptual terms, the openness of the school system has vertical and horizontal dimensions.

A final advantage of a systems framework is that its scope is sufficiently broad and it therefore is congruent with the unit of analysis, the school district. Previous theoretical perspectives have been hampered by their relatively narrow scope. Hence, they have tended to focus on a component of the school district such as board-superintendent relationships, making it difficult to draw systematic inferences about the governance of the school district.

Despite the fact that the basic systems model as articulated by Easton has an overarching concern with how governmental systems transform inputs into outputs, systems models are not wholly immune to the biases that infected earlier theoretical perspectives. The apolitical bias, which haunted more traditional educational research, stemmed from the tendency to confuse the normative (that is, how the school district should be governed) with the empirical (that is, how the school district is governed). The adoption of a systems framework does not, a priori, preclude such confusion. Often such frameworks are sufficiently flexible that they provide the researcher with considerable discretion in the selection of specific concepts. Put another way, the systems framework, by specifying

the various relationships that bind the school district to the environment, affords the researcher a general orientation. For example,
concerning the transformations of inputs into policy outputs, there
are a number of conversion processes. A conversion process is a
generalized term, covering a multitude of activities within the
school district. Various conversion processes differ empirically,
depending on a host of factors such as the purpose of the process,
the participants, the strategies involved, the nature of the opposition encountered, and, most importantly perhaps, the policy issue
involved.

To illustrate, although Wirt and Kirst (1972) and Thompson
(1976) have presented a systems framework as the most efficacious
way to conduct an analysis of school districts, their notions regarding conversion processes are distinctly different, yet they both reveal some of the limitations of a systems framework. Wirt and
Kirst's discussion of what they term "the local conversion process"
exemplifies some of the conceptual problems posed by indiscrimi-
nately employing a systems framework. A systems framework
helps to clarify what the unit of analysis is in descriptive terms;
however, it does not supply the researchers with the concepts needed
to analyze structures and processes that comprise it. To make this
criticism more explicit, we will examine Wirt and Kirst's treatment
of process. In attempting to delineate the salient features of the
local conversion process in school districts, the authors (1975:55)
make the following observations regarding school professionals:

> School professionals retain greater influence on policy
> issues. . . . They define alternatives, produce re-
> search, provide specific policy recommendations and
> recommend the formal agenda. In these and many
> other ways, professionals generate subsystem pres-
> sures and information that shape the board's delib-
> erations and policy decisions. In Easton's frame-
> work, the school superintendent and his staff provide
> "withinputs" to the school board and all levels of the
> school bureaucracy.

The first inference to be drawn from this quotation is that a systems
framework is not needed to sensitize the researcher to the potential
influence that school administrators may wield in the policy-making
process. Second, while the influence of the superintendent and his
staff in the conversion process may be substantial, it may not be
consequential for all policy issues. For example, in the case of desegregation, Crain and his collaborators (1969:377-78) found that
the board, not the administration, was the influential body in resolv-

ing this question. This example suggests that the superintendent's influence on policy making may wax or wane, depending on the issue. Third, while the superintendent is purportedly a key participant in school district policy making, his participation is not, as Wirt and Kirst imply, synonymous with the process. What warrants scrutiny is how he participates. Does he invoke the symbol of his office or does he rely on professional expertise? Wirt and Kirst maintain that the superintendent and his administrative staff are influential, because they "define alternatives, produce research and provide specific policy recommendations." While this assertion may prove accurate, it does not provide clues as to how these activities confer influence on the superintendent and his colleagues. In order to avoid making a priori assumptions about the conversion process, Wirt and Kirst should have adopted decision making as the unifying concept.

As mentioned earlier, Thompson (1976) also adopted a systems framework that is a refinement of the model proposed by David Easton (1965). Its basic weakness is the failure to crystallize clearly the concept of process. The flexibility a systems model affords the researcher can engender conceptual confusion. A discussion of Thompson's conceptualization of process will illustrate some of the theoretical problems posed by the failure to specify the concept of process. The author (1976:32-34) defines the concept of process in a school system as follows: "An examination of how schools adapt to these forces [for example, structural, cultural, and situational] and how policies are made reveals four adaptive processes, namely identification, bargaining, legal-bureaucratic mechanisms and coercive mechanisms."

The most salient drawback to Thompson's conceptualization of these adaptive mechanisms is that as they are defined, they do not satisfy one of the criteria of a discriminating conceptual definition: mutual exclusiveness. Failure to satisfy this criterion in and of itself, albeit salient, is not grounds for discarding Thompson's conceptual categories. However, this drawback reveals some important theoretical issues that Thompson has either ignored or left unresolved.

For example, Thompson draws a distinction between legal bureaucratic and coercive mechanisms; however, some of the coercive tactics are sanctioned by law and some are, manifestly, illegal. To illustrate, disciplining striking teachers in some states is coercive but legal. By the same token, the initiation of the strike that provoked the application of such disciplinary measures is illegal. Yet Thompson (1976:34) labels both mechanisms as coercive. Distinguishing between the legal and the illegal activity of public sector organizations has theoretical as well as empirical significance. If a political analysis of schools and other public sector organizations is to be comprehensive, their legitimizing processes must be examined. A related question that merits attention is the criteria that organizations use to determine which illegal or unacceptable patterns of individual or group behavior should be redefined as legal or acceptable and which should retain their illegal status. For example, under the Taylor Law in New York State, school teachers do not have the right to strike. Only the superintendent can declare a strike. However, in some school districts, teacher walkouts of short duration are tolerated without applying formal sanctions; whereas in others, a walkout of any duration is greeted with punitive measures. An examination of school districts' legitimizing processes and their underlying criteria should provide some insight into how they deal with teacher walkouts and other activities whose legal status is subject to interpretation. Labor relations, desegregation, and financial aid, among the various problems confronting school districts, raise issues for administrators whose resolution is not neatly prescribed by law.

A second limitation in Thompson's treatment of process is that his use of the term "adaptive mechanisms" is sufficiently nebulous as to preclude a systematic investigation of various questions of organizational power, the main dynamic in any political process. Thompson implies that these adaptive mechanisms (that is, identification, bargaining, and coercion) are the collective property of the school system. However, it may be argued that school systems do not identify, bargain, and coerce; individuals or groups within school systems identify, bargain, and coerce. Thompson's use of the term "adaptive mechanisms," even when cast in a systems framework, does not contribute much to the debate regarding the appropriate unit of analysis. Furthermore, while this term implies the use of power, it provides few clues as to its sources, its manifestations, and its consequences. Yet addressing these questions is central to any political analysis of a school system. To answer these questions requires a unifying concept with an action orientation. Moreover, such a concept is useful in sorting out the key elements in the conversion process and it, therefore, provides a starting point for developing a systematic understanding of power in the school system.

To conclude, prior to 1960, research on relationships between the community and the school district tended to focus on the composition of the school board or superintendent-board deliberations, thereby equating one role or one component of the governing process. Beginning in the 1960s, political approaches that were broader in scope began to evolve. These approaches enabled researchers to examine the relationships between the school district and community groups and institutions as well as the various relationships that linked school districts to extralocal groups and institutions. Despite their political orientation, most models of school district governance and policy making were not amenable to empirical research. Based on this review, it may be inferred that there is a growing awareness among educational researchers concerning the political dimensions of school district policy making but a lack of consensus as to which middle-range concepts are most appropriate.

Schools as Formal Organizations

The conceptual and empirical results noted above in the review of the literature on the community, the school board, and the superintendent hint at the importance of the formal organizational aspects of the school for an understanding of those relationships. Thus Corwin (1965) draws on organizational theory for his model of governance, and Zeigler and Jennings (1974) conclude that the increasing complexity of school bureaucracies has resulted in an increase in the power of the superintendent vis-a-vis the school board. Further, systems analysis, with its emphasis on conversion processes, carries with it an implicit requirement to examine the nature of the intraorganizational factors that comprise these processes. A full systems analysis would also recognize the fact that inputs or demands may also arise from within the organization. Yet despite these apparent linkages between the community aspect of schools and the organizational aspects of schools, these areas remain as two separate bodies of literature. From the viewpoint of organizational theory, this separation is indeed surprising, insofar as the relationship between the organization and its environment, especially in terms of environmental effects on organizational structure, has recently come to the forefront of organizational sociology (Aldrich, 1979; Karpik, 1978). The net result is that when we turn to a consideration of schools as formal organizations, a pattern similar to that observed in the study of the community aspects of schools emerges: a limited research focus that does not allow us to view the dynamics of the administrative and governance process.

The impact of the reform movement extends beyond the separation of the community aspects from the organizational aspects of schools to the content of the research conducted on the school as a formal organization. As noted earlier, as part of the effort to de-politicize schools, educators turned to administrative theory for models of how to run their schools. Despite this, however, there has been little research undertaken based on organizational models in school districts (Bidwell, 1965). As a result, little is known about either the interrelationship between such structural variables as size, differentiation, routinization, communication, and decentralization, or their effect on the political processes of the school system. Further, what research has been undertaken suffers from the limitations inherent in the majority of organizational research to date. The most important limitation is a confusion of units of analysis, that is, should we analyze the organization as a whole, as a composite of individuals, or as a composite of groups?

An analysis of the organization as a whole assumes that the organization is a rational system of interdependent units functionally held together by a common goal. Attention is focused on organizational structure (that is, size, vertical and horizontal differentiation, role specialization, span of control, and so on) and work processes (that is, communication, interaction, centralization, and so on). Empirically, the appearance of a harmonious whole is enhanced through the use of aggregate data as the basis of analysis. Such a perspective assumes a uniform effect of structure and process across the organization, combining scores to create one measure of each variable for the total organization.

One of the limitations of previous structural research is its failure to depict organizations as dynamic entities subject to conflict and change. Structure has been reified in such a manner that it, rather than action, has become the focal point of analysis. Even where attention is paid to processes, they are conceptualized as if they were organizational structures. For example, various social control processes are simply referred to as organizational formalization; similarly, various power processes are subsumed under the broad category of centralization. Applied to school districts, this perspective reinforces the tendency to overlook the internal dynamics of schools as well as the effect of external relations on internal processes.

While educational practitioners generally adhere to the holistic and objective assumptions of the rational managerial perspective that underlies a structuralist approach, organizational theorists have recently turned to the analysis of school districts to propose an alternative perspective based on the individual level of analysis. This perspective is generally labeled the "loosely coupled systems" approach (Weick, 1976).

The twin assumptions of heterogeneity and subjectivity underlie this approach, that is, every individual is unique and has his own conception of the organization. Since strict adherence to the behavioral imperatives in these assumptions may result in organizational chaos, the question to be answered by adherents of this approach is how individuals coalesce into a larger unit capable of coordinated action. The answer is that coordinated action comes about when there exists a shared conceptualization of the organizational reality. Indeed, Weick (1969) defines organizations as the existence of an intersubjective reality that results in coordinated action. The argument, then, is that the coupling that enables coordinated action is a function of the rationality used to conceptualize the organization.

Individuals are "coupled" through variables that provide the linkages between two or more persons. The identification of these linking variables is a matter for research, although Weick (1976) suggests that technology, authority, interaction, and action are some possibilities. Which variables will be employed as linkages will vary with the context in which the coupling takes place. Within any single organization, this perspective requires that attention be paid to the pattern of coupling across the organization and over time. Attempts to explicate these patterns must include the identification of the mechanisms employed to enhance the probability of coupling. Such mechanisms may be largely symbolic (Edelman, 1971), and may include the use of sagas (Clark, 1974) and other efforts at legitimation (Meyer and Rowan, 1977).

While the concept of a loosely coupled system is epistemologically grounded in an individualistic perspective, research undertaken utilizing this approach has tended to make inferences about the entire structure of the organization as a whole. For example, Davis et al. (1976) show that superintendents do not perceive their program in the same manner as their principals, whose perceptions differ in turn from those of the teachers. The general conclusion drawn from this and similar studies (for example, Burlingame, Chapter 13 in this volume) is that the administrative aspects of the district are loosely coupled to the technical core of public education. The focus of this research is the conditions producing loose coupling between these two spheres. To the degree this coupling is a product of a political process, this perspective would appear to be in line with the approach we are proposing. To date, however, those researchers employing this perspective have not adopted a political framework to examine coupling, focusing instead on the looseness of coupling. Several pitfalls of this perspective can be noted. First, while it is based on a phenomenological perspective that implies a focus on the individual (and it has been explicated as such here), there is a tendency to use the model as a metaphor for the functioning of the organization. When this happens, the proponents of this approach are guilty of anthropomorphizing the organization. There is a danger that the metaphor becomes a replacement for research priorities, with exercises in conceptualization taking the place of empirical research. Second, there is a tendency to overemphasize the chaotic nature of action in organizations. Where the structuralists err in failing to consider the internal dynamics of organizations, the adherents of the loosely coupled systems approach fail to consider the structural constraints that impinge on the individual's cognitions and actions.

A third alternative is an organizational model that is based on the group as the unit of analysis; it envisions the work group as the primary focus for the study of organizations. This perspective affords an empirical middle ground between a concentration on aggregate and individual data by examining collectivities of individuals within an organization. To date, the potential of the group model has not been fully realized. The group has been seen as a relatively formal entity whose activities within the organization are passive and of little interest to the research. What attention has been paid to the group focuses on group autonomy, that is, with the group itself rather than the group's relationship with other work groups in the organization. Realization of the full potential of the group perspective requires that the dynamics of the group interrelationships become a focal point for future research. Properly conceptualized, a group model is well suited to an examination of the administrative and political imperatives that confront school administrators as they are expressed in various group interactions. None of the other perspectives (rational managerial or individualistic) is capable of doing this. We believe that the proper application of the group model can be achieved if it is embedded in a theoretical approach that considers the organization as a political system.

To conclude, research into the school as a formal organization suffers from a confusion as to the appropriate unit of analysis. While the majority of research adopts a perspective that considers the organization as a whole, a recent theoretical alternative has been proposed that adopts an individualistic perspective. We believe that a third alternative that focuses on the group best reflects the realities of school district governance and administration, while taking into account the benefits of the holistic and individualistic perspectives. What is needed is an approach to school districts that affords the researcher the opportunity: to adopt a holistic but integrated view of the school district; to use concepts that are amenable to comparative analysis; to examine the interorganizational and intraorganizational aspects of schools; and to emphasize the dynamics of organizational process.

Organizations as Political Systems

The earliest formulations of a political perspective of organizations may be found in the works of Gouldner (1954) and Selznick (1957). However, the most cited articulation of this perspective is contained in the work of Cyert and March (1963), who view the organization as a coalition of individuals, some of whom are additionally subsumed in subcoalitions. Drawing on the theoretical perspective of Cyert and March, Bacharach and Lawler (1980) have argued that if organizations are to be treated as active dynamic political entities, they should be conceptualized as follows: organizations should be viewed as political systems, both internally and in their external relationships; organizational participants should be conceived of as political actors with their own needs, objectives, and strategies to achieve those objectives; coalitions of actors emerge in organizations, identify collective objectives, and devise strategies to achieve their objectives; and their actions are constrained by organizational structures, technologies, and ideologies.

By viewing the organization as a political system, we are able to address both the political and administrative imperatives, taking full advantage of the research done by students of community politics and organizations without succumbing to their limitations. This perspective recognizes both the constraints imposed by structure and the informal aspects of the organization. It recognizes the importance of individuals qua individuals as well as individuals as members of groups. It also assumes that school districts are open systems. Most importantly, a political framework allows us to view school districts as dynamic entities.

From a political perspective, the dynamics of organizational processes may be best observed by focusing on the decision-making process. Decisions are the arena in which resources are distributed and through which individuals and groups are able to achieve representation, increasing the probability of reaching their objectives. Every individual or group can be expected to approach a decision with the objective of maximizing their specific interests or goals rather than the maximization of some general organizational objective. Every individual or group can also be expected to enter the decision arena with a different definition of the situation (that is, each will have a different view of who has authority, who has influence, or who should have authority to make a specific decision) that will affect the strategies and tactics they employ. Adopting this perspective requires that we view the organization as a system in which the main issue is the mobilization of power for either achieving or blocking the achievement of a particular task. Applied to school districts, this entails examining the behavior of various individuals or groups in the district as they attempt either to initiate or block decisions regarding policy issues.

We believe that a political perspective accurately reflects the realities of school district governance and administration. It addresses both the political and administrative imperatives confronting school district administrators, while providing the conceptual foundation necessary to explore the dynamics surrounding the resolution of the tension generated by these conflicting imperatives. Finally, school districts are an especially appropriate empirical referent for a political perspective because: they have identifiable critical decisions to make on a regular basis (for example, budget, personnel, curriculum, and so on); they are comprised of definable groups (for example, school board, teachers, superintendent, principal, and so on); they have some degree of prescribed interaction among groups for the accomplishment of goals; and they have a delimited organizational boundary based on a legally defined jurisdiction. The next section will examine the application of a political perspective to school districts in more detail.

ELEMENTS IN A POLITICAL ANALYSIS OF SCHOOL SYSTEMS

It has been argued that the adoption of a political perspective in the analysis of school districts provides a unified, comprehensive, and empirical approach to the study of school districts that directly addresses the dilemma arising from having to confront political and administrative imperatives simultaneously. In so doing, it also succeeds in integrating two bodies of literature on schools. While variables have been suggested that are crucial to such an analysis (for example, groups, decision issues, consensus on authority and influence, structure, technology, and so on), the model that guides the proposal has not yet been specified. In this section of the chapter, the concepts that comprise a political model of school systems will be defined and potential relationships between these concepts will be discussed.

Figure 1.1 provides a picture of the preliminary schematic model. It is not intended to be a path diagram. Each of the elements in the model is reviewed, explicating what each entails. In addition, the expected relationships between elements as suggested by the arrows will be covered in the text.

Environmental Constraints

The relationship between organizations and their environments has recently come to the forefront of organizational sociology. Theoretically, the primary emphasis has been placed on the effect of the environment on internal organizational structure. In this context, concepts such as heterogeneity and instability are frequently

FIGURE 1.1

A Preliminary Schematic Model for the Political Analysis of School Systems

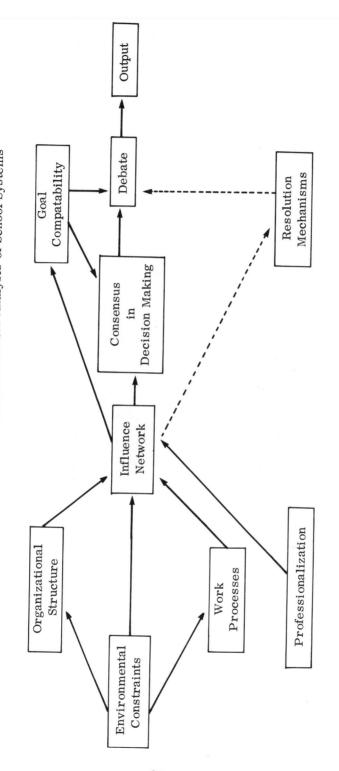

Source: Compiled by the author.

identified as environmental dimensions that, together with perceptions of uncertainty on the part of organizational members, have an
impact on internal organizational arrangements (Dill, 1958; Lawrence
and Lorsch, 1967; Duncan, 1972). Several studies support the general hypothesis that in more heterogeneous and differentiated environments, internal organizational structure will be more organic
(Blau and Schoenherr, 1971; Negandhi and Reimann, 1972). However, other work (Karpik, 1978) suggests that the relationship between environmental heterogeneity and organizational structure depends upon the degree of organizational permeability. It is possible
for the organization to buffer itself from its environment to such a
degree that there is no relation between environmental differentiation and organizational structure. Such contradictory findings make
the empirical test of this linkage a necessity.

There is little real consensus as to how the environment's relationship with the organization should be conceptualized or measured. Our political perspective suggests that the environment of
the school is best conceived in terms of political processes. Finally, it is necessary to consider schools in a historical perspective,
that is, current processes in schools are best seen as part of larger
historical processes.

Methodologically, the debate has centered on whether the environment is to be operationalized objectively (Pugh et al., 1969;
Blau and Schoenherr, 1971; Negandhi and Reimann, 1972; Downey
et al., 1975), or as perceptions of organizational actors (Lawrence
and Lorsch, 1967; Duncan, 1972). Whichever methodology is employed, the crucial factor would appear to be the specification of
the structures and mechanisms in the environment that produce uncertainty. It is necessary to understand the specificities of organization environments, in addition to their generalizable features.

While there are numerous dimensions of environmental heterogeneity that can be examined, our primary concern should be with
the political, economic, and social composition of school districts.
The social environment of the district is characterized by its ethnic
composition, racial composition, the educational level of its residents, and the average income of its residents. The political environment may be defined as participation in school board elections
or in budget referendums, political party affiliation of district residents, and the level of competition in school board elections. The
economic environment may be defined as the number of economic
establishments, budget level, tax rates, state aid, and federal assistance. We argue that the internal political workings of school districts may, in fact, reflect the instability of the general social,
political, and economic environment, or, more specifically, the
relative number and strength of organized interest groups in the

community vying for control over school decisions. To take full advantage of this perspective, it can be argued that the effect of the environment on particular groups should be the focal point of analysis. For example, it may be hypothesized that environmental uncertainty affects one particular group more dramatically than another.

The linkages between the environment and other elements in the political model operate in a number of ways. We have already seen that research in organizational sociology suggests that under certain conditions of permeability, an organization will adopt a structure congruent with its environment's heterogeneity. Other research suggests that the political ideology of the dominant coalition will affect the organization's structure (Aiken and Bacharach, 1978). In schools, Mitchell (1974) found that there were likely to be structural differences in the types of schools run by conservatives and liberals. Finally, the model suggests that environmental heterogeneity will affect the number and types of influence networks in the school district. The exact nature of these linkages in a school system remains to be tested.

Beyond the concern with the immediate task environment (as the composite characteristics of the school district) we also need to be aware of the effects of central government regulation and policy on the characteristics of schools and school districts. In the last 20 years federal and state governments have played an increasing role in the regulation and administration of local district policies. Therefore, the environment of schools and school districts has been broadened to include the legislated regulation and the policy expectations of federal and state governments. Specifically, we need to examine the mechanisms of linkage between these various levels of government and the processes of policy transference, policy supervision, and the institutionalization of federal and state mandates by local districts.

Bureaucratization of Schools and School Districts

In taking a look at organizational outputs there has been a tendency to draw a direct linkage between environmental characteristics and the outputs of organizations. For example, in the urban sociology literature (Mott and Aiken, 1971) characteristics such as revenue, population, size, and regulations have been directly linked to the outputs of cities. Similar analyses have been conducted on school districts. However, the impact of environmental constraints on the output can be understood only if we examine the internal workings of schools and school districts as intervening between environment and output. It is the internal characteristics of the district organization that will serve to transfer environmental constraints into district results.

It is the primary premise of a political analysis of organizations that the environment will constrain the bureaucratic structure of the organization that will, in turn, affect the political structure that will determine the level of political conflict, which serves as the primary predictor of output.

Organizations have often been cast on a continuum of magnitude of bureaucratization. In considering the level of school district bureaucratization we need to take into account three sets of variables: the nature of school district personnel; the nature of school and school district work processes; and the nature of school and school district structure. In considering school district personnel the primary concern should be with the degree of professionalization and level of specialization of organizational members. It is generally accepted that the more professional the personnel of an organization, the greater the expected autonomy of those personnel and the less susceptible those personnel are to any routinized, bureaucratic expectation. The point of reference of such professionals may well be their own socialized expectations both in terms of how work is done and what level of success is appropriate. The existence of professional groups in school districts may thus create a basis for active interest group politics that may be in direct conflict with the formal structures and processes of the districts. As such, one way to understand the impact of the environment on the effectiveness of school districts is to examine its impact on the professional compositions of personnel. For example, districts with lower revenue bases may not be able to afford highly professionalized personnel and as such may rely more on standardized work processes and formal structures to get the work done rather than relying on autonomous work groupings.

The bureaucratic structure of an organization may be understood in terms of its morphology. It will include such dimensions as division of labor, departmentalization, hierarchical division, and so on. Work processes, as distinguished from organizational structure, may be defined as the patterns of behavior associated with the conduct of organizational work. Essentially, work process variables depict the behavior of an actor in various aspects of his work. Among the dimensions included here are the degree to which an actor experiences autonomy in the conduct of his work, the degree to which he conducts his work in a routine versus a nonroutine manner, and the degree to which he observes the rules and regulations of the organization (Bacharach and Aiken, 1976). Bureaucratic structure and bureaucratic work processes are at times presented as mechanisms for enhancing organizational efficiency through the specification of the behavior, perceptions, and expectations of organizational members. However, at the same time these characteristics, in that they diminish autonomy, may stifle creative initiative on the part of the organizational members. Specifically, in school districts the bureaucratic imperatives may operate in direct contradiction to professional expectations. On the one hand, districts want to hire, if they can afford to, the most professional personnel. On the other hand, they tend to immerse professional personnel in a web of administrative bureaucracy. The need for administrative efficiency thus may emerge in direct conflict with the need to hire the most suitable personnel. In turn, environmental constraints may create a basic political contradiction. For example, if a community resource base allows for the employment of more highly trained teachers, it may at the same time demand an expansion of the administrative apparatus creating with the organization two parallel but contradictory expansions. Clearly, in this context, the best of all possible worlds would emerge in small and wealthy school districts.

Decision-Making Structure

The contradictions between the administrative apparatus and the composition of the district may be best tapped by examining the decision-making structure of the districts. Decision making is the primary arena in which coalitions of organizational actors with similar or different roles will attempt to politically affect organizational decisions. Three dimensions of the decision-making structure should be considered: the influence network, goal compatability, and consensus in decision making.

Our conceptualization of schools and school districts as a political system requires that attention be accorded to coalitions of organizational actors and to the interactions between these coalitions in the decision-making process. Networks may be defined as the patterned relationship of a given type among a set of people or among groups or suborganizations that form the total organization; hence, for the purposes of this study, the school system may be viewed as consisting of a number of networks. While other networks may exist, a comparative political analysis places primary emphasis on the examination of influence networks across school systems. Studies of decision making generally break the decision process down into four basic tasks: problem identification, information gathering, alternative generation, and selection of an alternative (Schein, 1965; Pounds, 1969). In the context of our political model, we are arguing that the completion of any one of these tasks in the decision process is affected by the influence network of the district. Thus how a problem comes to be defined as necessitating a decision, what information is gathered on the problem, what alternatives are generated, and which alternative is selected are all constrained by the influence network of the school district.

In identifying the sources of influence, linkages between key actors become critical. Methodologically, these may be identified through questions of interaction and communication. In identifying the linkages that comprise the influence network, it is important to keep in mind that time and energy are scarce resources for organizational members, and that not every issue on which a decision is made will be perceived as requiring involvement (March and Olsen, 1976); consequently the interaction and communication data that are collected should be issue specific. It is also important to remember that the influence network may extend beyond the organization into the environment. In this regard, the influence network is a useful concept for integrating inter- and intraorganizational analyses into a unified political analysis.

Conceptually, the influence network is affected by a number of other variables. First, the influence network is affected by the structure of the organization. As a school district becomes increasingly complex, the number of formal positions increases, thus enhancing the potential number of bonds between members. In effect, the resulting network configuration produced by such organizational complexity is pluralistic. Conversely, the relative lack of structural complexity in a school district would probably give rise to a monolithic network. Second, the influence network is affected by work processes. Here, the primary source of network complexity is the uncertainty in the roles of school district personnel. Thus it may be argued that the more autonomous the work activity, the less routine the work activity; and the less adherence to rules and regulations, the more ambiguity school district members experience in the conduct of their work roles. Such ambiguity when coupled with a high level of professionalization, as reflected in the relative lack of constraints in work activity, leads to more diversified influence networks. Since professionalization represents socialization by an external reference group, the greater the level of professionalization in a school, the more diversified the influence network. Finally, the environment of the school system will affect the nature and the scope of the influence network. A heterogeneous environment that is characterized by ethnic diversity and by conspicuous differences in income and education between various social strata gives rise to interest groups with competing sets of demands. To reconcile these demands, the school district network must adopt certain accommodative strategies that, in turn, increase its diversification.

Conversely, in a more homogeneous environment, the school district network will be confronted with fewer conflicting demands and,
therefore, its diversification will be less. Of course, these hypothesized relationships are intended to be illustrative not exhaustive.

The influence network may be described in terms of a number
of different dimensions. The first dimension is network size, which
may be defined as the number of individuals included in the influence
network. The second dimension in the influence network is connected-
ness. It refers to the degree to which any member of the network can
or cannot influence another member either directly or indirectly.
Thus an organizational system in which each of the members is connected directly or indirectly may be described as low in fragmentation; conversely, an organizational system in which connections—
either direct or indirect—are often lacking may be described as high
in fragmentation. The third dimension is the number of coalitions.
A coalition may be defined as a dense clustering of reciprocal relationships within any network. The fourth dimension—centrality—refers to the degree to which a coalition is the center of any network.
The fifth dimension refers to whether coalition membership is either
overlapping or mutually exclusive. Specifically, the distinction embodied in this dimension seeks to ascertain whether key actors belong to more than one coalition. The sixth dimension refers to the
degree to which the influence network coincides with the formally
specified authority structure. The seventh and final dimension concerns the question of dominant coalitions. It is designed to determine whether the same coalition prevails over different decision
areas.

The influence network, as specified by these dimensions, will
in turn affect other variables in our model. To illustrate, the influence network will affect the degree of goal compatibility in a district. Our model assumes that each actor or group of actors in the
school district attempts to maximize their goals and priorities by
having their views represented in policy decisions. The influence
network may either promote or thwart representation. In general,
the more pluralistic the influence network, the greater the degree of
goal incompatibility. Conversely, a monolithic influence network
leads to goal consensus. The influence network is also expected to
affect the degree of consensus achieved in decision making. Specifically, we are concerned with the degree of consensus concerning
perceptions of who has formal authority in a decision area and who
has influence in a decision area. We contend that a major source
of organizational political tension may be cognitive, resulting from
competing definitions of the political situation held by actors in different subgroups. With regard to decision making, organizational
actors, depending on their subgroup, will have different perceptions

as to who has the authority to make particular decisions and who has influence over particular decisions. Hence it may be argued that the nature and the degree to which these perceptions differ may affect the degree of consensus in the decision-making process. Finally, the influence network affects the resolution mechanisms used to handle debate over goal incompatibility or consensus in decision making. Regarding goal incompatibility, the influence network is a means of achieving coordination of the various goals held by actors in the district. The mechanisms used to achieve this coordination, therefore, are another important element in school district decision making that warrants investigation. The influence network can also be used to settle conflict over perceptions of authority and influence. Thus, for example, a person who is a member of several coalitions may be instrumental in resolving conflicts between coalitions. Where there is no overlapping membership, other conflict resolution mechanisms will be used. In a larger sense, this discussion has attempted to illustrate the analytic value of the concept influence network for examining political processes in the school system that heretofore have been ignored.

Goal Compatibility

Any analysis that purports to examine organizations as a composite of groups must place some emphasis on the issue of goal compatibility. Organizational actors have multiple goals. First, the school district can be seen as a vehicle for the attainment of an actor's personal goals (Cummings, 1977). The actor, as a member of an organizational subunit, also has specific task goals. Despite the importance of these goals in a political analysis of organizations, it is only recently that subunit goals have been studied empirically (Balke, Hammond, and Meyer, 1973; Huber, 1974; Kochan, Huber, and Cummings, 1976). Finally, while the notion of an overarching organizational goal has been widely attacked in the organizational literature, recent critiques have emphasized the importance of examining key actors' definitions of organizational goals (Campbell, 1977). A political analysis of school districts focuses on an actor's efforts to realize each of these goals (that is, personal, task, and organizational goals).

It has already been shown that goal compatibility is affected by the nature of the influence network. What remains to be discussed is how goal compatibility affects debate and consensus in decision making. While there has been a dearth of empirical literature on the subject, goal consensus, it may be argued, is an important predictor of conflict within an organization (March and Simon, 1958;

Schmidt and Kochan, 1972). It may be hypothesized that the degree to which organizational actors share the same goals, consensus regarding strategic decisions and work decisions is easier to achieve. In turn, it may be posited that the degree to which goal compatibility results in consensus, the more likely the management of conflict can be routinized. Conversely, it may be argued that where goal incompatibility exists, the scope and the impact of conflict will be greater. In extreme circumstances, if conflict of considerable magnitude and intensity persists unchecked it can challenge the very legitimacy of the school system. The most common manifestation of this political phenomenon is the dismissal of the superintendent.

Consensus in Decision Making

Since we are concerned with the decision-making process, identifying the power relationships is essential (March and Simon, 1958; Cyert and March, 1963; Thompson, 1967; March and Olsen, 1976); however, power relationships in organizational systems are multifaceted. For the sake of analysis, they may be broadly subdivided into authority and influence (Bacharach and Aiken, 1976, 1977; Bacharach, 1978).

Authority refers to the official decision-making power that resides in various positions in the organizational system. Indeed, it may be argued that due to its formal, structural properties, determining the locus of authority in organizations may be based solely on positional criteria that are contained in organizational charts. However, a careful reexamination of the concept of authority reveals an explicit cognitive aspect of Weber's original formulation, for it was Weber (1947:328) who delineated authority as resting on "the belief" in the legitimacy of the action. Therefore, within the context of organizations, for an actor to have authority, it is necessary for the actor as well as his or her superior and subordinates to recognize that he or she possesses power and that the use of such power is legitimate (Kochan, Schmidt, and DeCotiis, 1975). Thus, theoretically speaking, the structural phenomenon of authority is a consequence of cognitive consensus. Organizational actors do not obey the imperatives of structural authority unless there is consensus that this authority is legitimate. We may thus expect systematic differences in the patterns of behavior between superiors and subordinates depending on whether or not there is consensus concerning the distribution of organizational authority. If the cognitive nature of authority is stressed, and, in turn, if organizations are cast as stratified systems in potential conflict over the definition of the distribution of authority (that is, as political systems), the obvious question that arises is, in what type of organizations is there consensus or lack of consensus across interest groups regarding the distribution of authority? Thus consensus as to authority is one aspect of the variable "consensus in decision making."

By contrast, influence is the more elusive aspect of organizational power. Consensus about authority in the decision-making process taps only the most formal dimension of power relations in an organization. In any organization, the authority structure is supplemented by the influence process. The two do not always coincide; they may exist independently of each other. Therefore, the formal, structural characteristics of the organizational system do not always provide clues as to the sources of influence. Indeed, one of the fundamental dilemmas in the analysis of organizational decision making is the failure to explicate the distinction between the authority structure and the influence processes. For example, much of the debate over whether organizations are centralized or decentralized has been theoretically circumscribed because it is never clear whether organizational theorists are directing their attention to authority or influence. Some organizations may have a highly centralized authority structure but a dispersed influence process. Other organizations may have both a centralized authority structure and a centralized influence process. The distinction between authority and influence is crucial to a political analysis, for, as Gamson (1968) has pointed out, it is necessary to identify the sources of authority and the sources of influence.

By building on the work of previous theorists, several distinctions may be drawn between authority and influence (Bierstedt, 1950; Simon, 1953). Influence is conducted informally, whereas authority is conducted formally. Authority is the power to make the final decision, influence is the power to guide decision makers. Thus the scope of authority is well-defined, the scope of influence is more amorphous. The overarching distinction, however, is that authority as opposed to influence may be viewed in terms of zero-sum notions of power. While the number of people with influence in a decision-making process may continually expand, the number of actors who have authority over a particular decision at any point in time is limited and specified.

These distinctions between authority and influence become particularly important when considering the dilemma that the decision-making process poses for the higher echelons in schools. This dilemma stems from two potentially conflicting imperatives: the need for reliable information to facilitate decision making and the need to retain formal control over decision making. To make the proper decisions, higher echelons must avail themselves of all possible sources of information. To achieve this objective, they must involve actors from all levels in the organization in the decision-making process. Despite the need for information, however, they may be reluctant to permit such involvement if it is going to undermine their formal control over the decision-making process. One need only consider the debates concerning community control of schools in New York City to appreciate the reality of this dilemma. Decentralization of authority, while supplying the requisite information, represents a challenge to formal authority and, therefore, is not, by itself, a viable solution to the dilemma. The dispersion of influence provides a way out of this dilemma, for it allows higher echelons to obtain the necessary information without relinquishing their formal control. The dispersion of influence permits actors from all levels in the organization to make their expertise felt in specific decision areas, but the final approval of their recommendations still rests with the higher echelons. It is this distinction between authority and influence and its relevance for the administrative dilemma of higher echelons that previous research, by concentrating primarily on the decentralization of authority, has tended to overlook. Our variable "consensus in decision making" concerns both consensus on authority and consensus on influence.

We have already seen that consensus in decision making is a function of goal compatibility and the nature of the influence network. The linkage between consensus in decision making and conflict is based on the premise that within the context of our political model, a major source of tension may be cognitive, resulting from a discrepant definition of the political situation.

Conflict

One of the well-known limitations in theories of complex organization is the inability to explain the sources of intraorganizational conflict (Benson, 1977). One of the main foci of an intraorganizational analysis should be the sources of the internal change; hence, examining conflict facilitates the identification of these sources of change. Moreover, a political analysis of the internal dynamics of an organization that fails to consider conflict would be incomplete. For these reasons, conflict occupies a focal position in our model.

We are primarily concerned with the cognitive sources of conflict. It may be argued that such conflicts stem from disagreements over "official interpretations" of organizational goals, authority, and influence. The degree of cognitive consensus about goals, authority, and influence is indicative of the potential for conflict. To explore in more detail this potential, it is necessary to specify the linkages between the prevailing consensus and the degree to which the perceptions of organizational members concerning goals, authority, and influence diverge from the dominant or official view, and the degree to which such divergence translates into political behavior. As Aldrich (1979) has observed in his critique of Hirschman's thesis in Exit, Voice and Loyalty (1972), dissatisfaction among organizational members, in some instances, can result in inaction. Another consideration informing our examination of intraorganizational conflict is its focus. In most instances, conflict is related to a specific issue; hence, it is necessary to identify those issues that seem to provoke conflict. A proper identification should include the identification of such issue dimensions as importance, salience, duration, and impact. In contrast to issue-specific conflict, in some instances conflict exemplified by superintendent turnover, the electoral defeat of incumbents on the school board, racial strife, school closings, and labor disputes may be precipitated by a specific issue but evolves to the point where the legitimacy of the school system is being challenged. This example demonstrates the need to examine not only the sources of conflict but its consequences and the mechanisms used to resolve it.

The Outcome of Conflict

It may be argued that the greater the conflict, the lower the level of output. This interpretation assumes that conflict is not conducive to effective policy making. It may also be argued that the degree to which conflict in the school district has been institutionalized will serve to clarify the available policy options, thereby expediting the decision-making process and increasing the level of policy output. An empirical examination of the relationships between conflict and output should provide some insight into school districts' managing conflict. In the context of a political analysis, we also need to consider the mechanism of conflict resolution. The assumptions made by structural and management theorists about the holistic and cooperative nature of organizations have merit. As proponents of a loosely coupled systems perspective have observed, effective action in organizations requires cooperation and coordination. Even those who consider conflict as a positive factor recognize that it is a means to an end. Schools and school districts use a variety of mechanisms to resolve conflict. The issue in conflict determines, to a large degree, which mechanism is selected. For example, if it is a labor dispute, the intervention of a factfinder or an arbitrator may be required. If conflict centers on the question of building renovation, the advice of architectural consultants may be solicited. As the work of Bachrach and Baratz (1970) suggests, one

possible resolution mechanism is the nondecision. Potential controversial issues can be suppressed through inaction or delay. The basic
assumption underlying the model is that the choice of the resolution
mechanism will affect the duration and the outcome of the conflict.

Output

Output within a political analysis may be considered on two
levels. The first is to consider the immediate outcome of the conflict as an output. At the same time, we may focus on the school
district output by looking at such variables as the number of college
entrants, the number of dropouts, the number of employed students,
scores on standardized tests, innovations in classroom arrangements, organization, scheduling, and instructional methods. This
latter approach assumes that the administrative process directly affects the output of the school. However, as we noted in discussing
the loosely coupled systems perspective, there is some evidence to
suggest that the administrative policy process functions independently of the technical core on which most output measures are based.
The basic assumption is that the social and technical organization of
the classroom has the greatest effect on student performance. Empirically, the relation between these two levels of output, that is,
between specific policy decisions and district-level output, needs to
be examined. Exploration of the effect of policy decisions on the
social and technical organization of the classroom would appear to
be a fruitful avenue of approach to take in this regard.

CONCLUSION

This chapter has attempted to present a comprehensive but
integrated model of school district governance and administration
that can both organize current knowledge and suggest directions for
future research. In theoretical terms, it has sought to demonstrate
the analytic potential of concepts drawn from the fields of community politics and complex organizations for examining the structures
and processes that comprise school district governance and administration. As demonstrated by the range of studies in this volume,
the model affords the researcher considerable latitude; he or she
can focus on: the interorganizational relationships between the
school district and its environment; the intraorganizational dynamics
of the school district; or the relationships between interorganizational
and intraorganizational aspects of school districts. Methodologically, this model has two advantages. First, it is conducive to middle-
range research and hence promises to produce results of both theo-

retical and practical importance. Second, as again demonstrated by the range of studies in the volume, it is sufficiently flexible to not require a prior commitment to a single methodological approach. Theoretically and methodologically, therefore, the model affords the researcher considerable discretion. Most importantly, we believe that the model reflects the realities of school district governance and administration in directly addressing the dilemma that arises in schools from having to meet political and administrative imperatives simultaneously.

REFERENCES

Aiken, M., and S. Bacharach. 1978. "The Urban System, Politics, and Bureaucratic Structure: A Comparative Analysis of 44 Local Governments in Belgium." In Organizations and Their Environments, edited by L. Karpik. London: Sage Publications.

Aldrich, Howard E. 1979. Organizations and Environments. Englewood Cliffs, N.J.: Prentice-Hall.

Aldrich, Howard E., and Diane Herker. 1977. "Boundary Spanning Roles and Organization Structure." Academy of Management Review, April, pp. 217-30.

Bacharach, Samuel B. 1978. "Morphologie et Processus: Une Critique de la Recherche Intra-Organisationelle Contemporaire." Review de Sociologie du Travail 20:153-73.

Bacharach, Samuel B., and Michael Aiken. 1976. "Structural and Process Constraints of Influence in Organizations: A Level Specific Analysis." Administrative Science Quarterly 21 (December):623-42.

Bacharach, Samuel B., and Michael Aiken. 1977. "Communication in Administrative Bureaucracies." Academy of Management Journal 18:365-77.

Bacharach, Samuel B., and Edward J. Lawler. 1980. Power, Coalitions and Bargaining: The Social Psychology of Organizational Politics. San Francisco: Jossey-Bass.

Bachrach, P., and M. Baratz. 1970. Power and Poverty. New York: Oxford University Press.

Bailey, Stephen K. et al. 1962. Schoolmen and Politics. Syracuse, N.Y.: Syracuse University Press.

Balke, W. Hammond, K. and G. Meyer. 1973. "An Alternative Approach to Labor-Management Negotiations." Administrative Science Quarterly 18:311-27.

Benson, J. 1977. "Organizations: A Dialectical View." Administrative Science Quarterly 22:1-21.

Bidwell, Charles E. 1965. "The School as a Formal Organization." In Handbook of Organizations, edited by James G. March. Chicago: Rand McNally.

Bierstadt, R. 1950. "An Analysis of Social Power." American Sociological Review 15:730-38.

Blau, Peter M., and Richard A. Schoenherr. 1971. The Structure of Organizations. New York: Basic Books.

Bloomberg, J., and Morris Sunshine. 1963. Suburban Power Structures and Public Education. Syracuse, N.Y.: Syracuse University Press.

Callahan, Raymond E. 1962. Education and the Cult of Efficiency. Chicago: University of Chicago Press.

Campbell, J. 1977. "On the Nature of Organizational Effectiveness." In New Perspectives in Organizational Effectiveness, edited by P. Goodman and J. Pennings. San Francisco: Jossey-Bass.

Charters, W. W. 1953. "Social Class Analysis and the Control of Public Education." Harvard Educational Review 23 (Fall).

Cistone, P. 1975. Understanding School Boards. Lexington, Mass.: Lexington Books.

Clark, Burton. 1972. "The Organizational Saga in Higher Education." Administrative Science Quarterly 17 (June):178-84.

Corwin, Ronald G. 1965. A Sociology of Education. New York: Appleton-Century-Crofts.

Counts, George. 1937. The Social Composition of School Boards. Chicago: University of Chicago Press.

Crain, Robert L. et al. 1968. The Politics of School Desegregation. Garden City, N.Y.: Doubleday.

Crozier, Michael. 1964. The Bureaucratic Phenomenon. Chicago: University of Chicago Press.

Cummings, L. 1977. "Emergence of the Instrumental Organization." In New Perspectives in Organizational Effectiveness, edited by P. Goodman and J. Pennings. San Francisco: Jossey-Bass.

Cyert, Richard M., and James G. March. 1963. A Behavioral Theory of the Firm. Englewood Cliffs, N.J.: Prentice-Hall.

Davis, M. et al., ed. 1977. The Structure of Educational Systems. Stanford Center for Research and Development.

Dill, William R. 1958. "Environment as an Influence on Managerial Autonomy." Administrative Science Quarterly 2 (March):409-43.

Downey, H. Kirk et al. 1975. "Environmental Uncertainty: The Construct and Its Application." Administrative Science Quarterly 20 (December):613-29.

Duncan, Robert. 1972. "Characteristics of Organizational Environments and Perceived Environmental Uncertainty." Administrative Science Quarterly 17 (September):313-27.

Easton, D. 1965. A Systems Analysis of Political Life. Chicago: University of Chicago Press.

Edelman, M. 1971. Politics as Symbolic Action. Chicago: Markham.

Eliot, Thomas H. 1959. "Toward an Understanding of Public School Politics." American Political Science Review 52:1032-51.

Gamson, William. 1968. Power and Discontent. Homewood, Ill.: Dorsey.

Gouldner, Alvin. 1954. Patterns of Industrial Bureaucracy. New York: The Free Press.

Gross, Neal et al. 1958. Explorations in Role Analysis: Studies of the School Superintendency Roles. New York: John Wiley.

Hage, Jerald, and Michael Aiken. 1967. "Program Change and Organizational Properties." American Journal of Sociology 72 (March):503-19.

Hirschman, Albert O. 1972. Exit, Voice and Loyalty. Cambridge, Mass.: Harvard University Press.

Hollingshead, August B. 1949. Elmtown's Youth. New York: John Wiley.

Huber, G. 1974. "Multi-Attribute Utility Models: A Review of Field and Fieldlike Research." Management Science 20:1393-1402.

Iannaccone, L., and F. Lutz. 1970. Politics, Power and Policy: The Governing of Local School Districts. Columbus, Ohio: Charles Merrill.

Karpik, Lucien, ed. 1978. Organization and Environment: Theory, Issues and Reality. Beverly Hills, Calif.: Sage Publications.

Kerr, Norman D. 1964. "The School Board as an Agency of Legitimation." Sociology of Education 38:34-54.

Kimbrough, Ralph B. 1964. Political Power and Educational Decision-Making. Chicago: Rand McNally.

Kochan, T., G. Huber, and L. Cummings. 1975. "Determinants of Intraorganizational Conflict in Collective Bargaining in the Public Sector." Administrative Science Quarterly 20:10-23.

Kochan, T., S. Schmidt, and T. DeCotiis. 1975. "Superior-Subordinate Relations: Leadership and Headship." Human Relations 26:279-94.

Laswell, H. D. 1936. Politics, Who Gets What, When, How. New York: McGraw-Hill.

Lawrence, Paul R., and Jay W. Lorsch. 1967. Organization and Environment. Cambridge, Mass.: Harvard University Press.

March, James G., and Johan P. Olsen. 1976. Ambiguity and Choice in Organizations. Bergen: Universitetsforlaget.

March, James G., and H. Simon. 1958. Organizations. New York: John Wiley.

Martin, Roscoe C. 1962. Government and the Suburban School. Syracuse, N.Y.: Syracuse University Press.

Meyer, J., and B. Rowan. 1977. "Institutionalized Organizations: Formal Structure as Myth and Ceremony." American Journal of Sociology 83:340-63.

Mitchell, D. 1974. "Ideology and Public Policy Making." Urban Education 9 (1):35-59.

Mott, P., and M. Aiken. 1971. The Structure of Community Power. New York: Random House.

Negandhi, A., and B. Reimann. 1972. "A Contingency Theory of Organization Re-examined in the Context of a Developing Country." Academy of Management Journal 15:127-46.

Perrow, Charles. 1964. "A Framework for Comparative Organizational Analysis." American Sociological Review 26 (December): 854-65.

Pounds, W. 1969. "The Process of Problem Finding." Industrial Management Review 11:1-19.

Pugh, D., D. Hickson, C. Hinings, and C. Turner. 1969. "The Context of Organizational Structures." Administrative Science Quarterly 14:115-26.

Schein, E. 1965. Organizational Psychology. Englewood Cliffs, N.J.: Prentice-Hall.

Schmidt, S., and T. Kochan. 1972. "The Concept of Conflict." Administrative Science Quarterly 17:359-70.

Selznick, P. 1949. TVA and the Grass Roots. Berkeley: University of California Press.

Simon, H. 1953. "Notes on the Observation and Measurement of Political Power." Journal of Politics 15:500-12, 514, 516.

Thompson, James D. 1967. Organizations in Action. New York: McGraw-Hill.

Thompson, John T. 1976. Policy-making in American Education. Englewood Cliffs, N.J.: Prentice-Hall.

Thompson, J., and W. McEwen. 1958. "Organizational Goals and Environment: Goalsetting as an Interaction Process." American Sociological Review 23:23-31.

Vidich, A., and J. Bensman. 1968. Small Town in Mass Society. Princeton: Princeton University Press.

Weber, M. 1947. The Theory of Social and Economic Organizations. New York: Oxford University Press.

Weick, Karl. 1976. "Educational Organizations as Loosely Coupled Systems." Administrative Science Quarterly 21 (March):1-19.

Weick, K. 1969. The Social Psychology of Organizing. Reading, Mass.: Addison-Wesley.

Wirt, Frederick M., and Michael W. Kirst. 1975. The Political Web of American Schools. Boston: Little, Brown.

Zeigler, Harmon, and Kent Jennings. 1974. Governing American Schools. North Scituate, Mass.: Duxbury Press.

PART II

THE FEDERAL AND STATE ENVIRONMENT OF SCHOOL DISTRICTS

2

THE EFFECTS OF INSTITUTIONALIZED
RULES ON ADMINISTRATORS

Brian Rowan

During the past 50 years, school districts in the United States have evolved from simple organizations into relatively complex bureaucracies. One important aspect of this transformation has been the growth of district administrative staffs. In 1932, the earliest year for which records on the number of administrators in the public school system are available, there were only .23 local administrators per district. By 1970 that number increased to 6.8 administrators per public school district (Bureau of the Census, 1975:368-75).

This chapter considers two questions related to the expansion of educational administration: What has led school systems to add to their administrative staffs? and What are the consequences of administrative growth for the balance of control in school districts, particularly control over the core technology of education—the instructional process? Two approaches to these questions, both taken from organization theory, are considered below. In the discussion and data analysis I seek to show that one approach, which considers technological imperatives as a source of administrative expansion, does not fit well with existing evidence on the structure of educational organizations. I therefore turn to a second approach that

Work on this chapter was conducted at the Stanford Center for Research and Development in Teaching and was supported by the National Institute of Education (Contract No. NIE-C-00-3-0062). The views expressed here do not, of course, reflect NIE positions. I would like to acknowledge the helpful comments of John W. Meyer and W. Richard Scott.

focuses on the role of institutionalized rules and regulations in shaping the school administrative process.

The technological approach to administration is common among educators as well as organization theorists. At the turn of the century, for example, educators used it to justify the expansion of the educational bureaucracy. They argued that administrative growth was needed to make instructional work more efficient and effective, especially given the complex instructional problems facing modern schools (Callahan, 1962; Tyack, 1974). Ironically, critics of bureaucratic reforms in schools also use a technological approach. For example, a common argument is that the rise of large central administrative staffs has fostered rigid and constricting controls over teaching (Rogers, 1964).

The view of administration taken by many organization theorists corresponds quite closely to that of educators. In organization theory a common argument is that bureaucratic organizations succeed or fail on the basis of their ability to efficiently produce outputs. To achieve efficiency, administrators are thought to devote much time and attention to problems arising in their organization's "core technology" (Thompson, 1967). A simple theory of the causes and consequences of administrative growth follows from this standard social science view. The theory points to changes in the complexity of an organization's core technology as a cause of administrative expansion and sees increased technical controls resulting from this process.

One problem with applying this approach to educational organizations, however, is that arguments about the technological imperatives facing administrators are most suitable for organizations operating in output markets where survival depends on efficiency. A major point, developed below, is that public schools do not exist in this kind of environment. Rather, they operate in what Meyer and Rowan (1977) call a highly institutionalized environment where resource mobilization and organizational success depend on conformity to institutionalized norms and standards (Parsons, 1956). In the case of schools, such standards are institutionalized in the rules and regulations of legislative, professional, and judicial agencies, whose scope of authority over local educational affairs has been expanding. A cursory examination of the political economy of modern public schools illustrates the elevation of conformity over efficiency. Schools receive funding, not on the basis of how much learning they produce per dollar expended, but rather for following certification or curricular or other externally imposed requirements (Meyer and Rowan, 1978).

A different view of educational administration follows from the assumption that school systems exist in a highly institutionalized environment and mobilize resources through conformity. As external agencies come to hold the purse strings and define the rules of the game, administrative time and attention turn to the demands of conforming to externally imposed regulations. This has two results for administration and control in local educational organizations. First, as external demands for conformity increase, the work load of administrative personnel increases. This leads to administrative growth. Second, as administrators turn increasingly to the demands of conformity, they devote less time and energy to core instructional problems.

The view developed here is based on Meyer and Rowan's (1977) model of institutionalized organizations and is quite compatible with recent discussions of "loose coupling" in schools (March and Olsen, 1976; Weick, 1976) and the ways this is brought on by regulations in the environment (Meyer and Rowan, 1978). Meyer and Rowan (1977) argued that organizations regulated by institutional environments have formal structures that are shaped more by demands for institutional conformity than technical efficiency and that, as a result, their formal structures tend to be loosely coupled to technical activities. The argument made here is that school administrative staffs are structured by institutional controls, but as this shaping process continues, administrators tend to become decoupled from the instructional core. It is important to note that the institutional approach does not imply that instructional activities in schools go uncontrolled, for this is not the case (Davis, Rowan, and Stackhouse, 1976). Central district administrators, however, appear to exercise less control over classroom instruction as they become increasingly involved in the problems of institutional conformity.

These arguments will be developed further in this chapter. First, the technological approach to administration is reviewed and its failure to adequately describe educational administration is discussed. Next, the institutional approach is outlined. It not only makes clear why the technological approach is ill suited to educational organization, it also contains propositions about the effects of institutionalized controls on the administrative process in school systems. A final section uses data on a small sample of California school districts to demonstrate two theoretical points: increased controls by agencies in the institutional environment, rather than technical complexity, create administrative expansion in school systems; and institutionalized controls tend to decrease district controls over instruction.

THE TECHNOLOGICAL IMPERATIVE AND SCHOOL ADMINISTRATION

A concern for the impact of technology and technical problems on organization structure can be traced to the founding fathers of organization theory. Barnard (1938), for example, argued that organizations form when individuals are forced to cooperate on technological problems they cannot resolve alone. Weber (1946) argued that bureaucracies succeed or fail on the basis of technical efficiency. Recent work has carried on in this tradition. Thompson (1967) and Perrow (1970) made technology a central variable in their theories of organization structure, and much empirical work has been devoted to demonstrating the impact of technology on various properties of an organization's formal structure (Woodward, 1965; Rushing, 1968; Hickson, Pugh, and Pheysey, 1969; Pugh et al., 1969; Freeman, 1973; Tracy and Azumi, 1976; Van de Ven, Delbecq, and Koenig, 1976).

A simple causal model, shown in Figure 2.1, can be used to summarize the technological approach to bureaucratic administration. The relationships postulated here depend upon two central assumptions: that organizations are under pressure to be technically efficient, and that administrative personnel function to coordinate and control activities in the technical core.

FIGURE 2.1

The Technological Approach to Administration

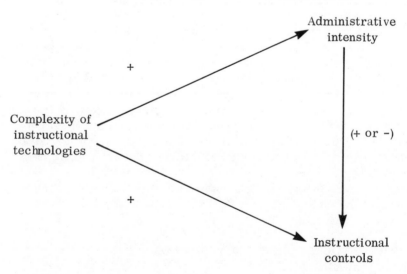

Source: Compiled by the author.

Given the assumptions above, three lines of theory have been used to explain the causal model shown in Figure 2.1:

One line of theory comes from studies of administrative intensity. As an organization's core technology becomes more complex, workflows within the organization become more interdependent and work becomes more specialized. This generates increasing problems of coordination and control and increases the work load of administrators. In order to handle this increased problem-solving load and maintain efficiency, organizations increase the size of their administrative staffs.

A second line of thinking can be found in the work of contingency theorists such as Lawrence and Lorsch (1967) and Thompson (1967). Again the assumption is that as an organization's core technology becomes interdependent, problems of coordination and control are increased. As a result, organizations must expend more "coordination costs" in order to maintain technical efficiency. This is done through the creation of formalized rules, committees, or increased informal consultations.

A third line of reasoning appears in discussions of the overall pattern of control in organizations (Blau and Scott, 1962; Corwin, 1974). Two patterns are possible in organizations dominated by the forces of efficiency. One is a reinforcement pattern. The idea here is that problem solving by administrators is one type of control and formalization or advice are others. If a reinforcement pattern of control is used, all patterns of control are used simultaneously. An alternative pattern is compensatory. One form of control can be used in place of another. For example, as administrative staffs expand, less formal controls will be needed. The reinforcement pattern predicts positive relations among administrative size and measures of formalization and consultation. The compensatory pattern predicts negative relationships.

Technology and Structure in School Systems

Have studies in educational organizations confirmed the technological approach to administration? One problem in answering this question is that many of the ways organizational technologies have been conceptualized—extent of mechanization, hardness of material inputs—are far more suited to analyses of manufacturing organizations than schools. Another problem is that instructional technologies are so diffuse that some observers have questioned whether schools even have a technology (Corwin, 1974). Jackson (1968), for example, found that teachers' discussions of their techniques were largely devoid of elaborate words and ideas, were conceptually simple, and tended to be based on intuitive rather than rational analysis.

Nevertheless, there are ways of conceptualizing the instructional process so that the technology-focused approach can be applied to school systems. In this chapter, instructional technologies within school districts will be classified by the degree to which they promote workflow interdependence. This concept is central to Thompson's (1967) discussion of the effects of technology on structure, and Pugh et al. (1969) reported positive correlations between "workflow integration" and measures of standardization, centralization, and control of workflow.

What impact have instructional technologies had on bureaucratization in American schools? The existing evidence does not support the idea that instructional technologies have a large impact. To begin with, it seems clear that as an historical account of the rise of the educational bureaucracy, theories based on changes in instructional technologies are of limited use. As Dreeben (1973) pointed out, teaching practices have, until recently, undergone little change. Moreover, traditional instructional technologies have very low levels of teacher, and even school, interdependence (Bidwell, 1965; Scott, 1975).

Nevertheless, in the 1970s, complex technologies were introduced into classrooms and schools. Unfortunately, little research has been done on their structural impact (Corwin, 1974). One exception is a line of research carried out at the Stanford Center for Research and Development in Teaching (Cohen et al., 1979; Davis et al., 1976). This research on classroom instructional technologies examined the impact of instructional complexity on the organizational structure of schools.

The results of these studies do not give strong support to technological approach. For one thing, measures of instructional complexity did not affect either the size of school administrative staffs or the patterns of formal control such as formalization and frequency of evaluation. This lack of effect of instructional complexity on administrative intensity and formalization stands in sharp contrast to findings in studies of manufacturing organizations where measures of technical complexity often show strong correlations to administrative intensity and formalization.

Nevertheless, it would be inaccurate to report that instructional complexity had no effect on instructional control. The main finding of these studies was that instructional complexity brought about team teaching and increased the amount of discussion between teachers and principals and teachers and specialists. Thus, the main effect appears to be on the patterns of discussion among school personnel rather than on the formal structure of schools or districts. In one sense, this result is not unexpected. To the extent that schools operate uncertain technologies of instruction, they approximate "organic" rather than "mechanistic" organizations (Burns and Stalker, 1961). Perrow (1970) and Galbraith (1973) pointed out that these organizations respond to technical complexity by developing more elaborate consultative relations among personnel.

Although the findings indicate a modest technological imperative in schools, a word of caution is needed. Charters (1973) studied two schools that differed in the extent to which instruction and staffing were differentiated. He found that discussions among teachers and between teachers and principals were more frequent in the technologically complex school. However, the level of task-related discussion in the complex and traditional schools did not differ. Moreover, the Stanford group found that teacher teams, where instructional control was presumably taking place, seldom sustained high levels of interaction. Over time the intensity of teaming tended to decrease.

Thus, the findings on the technological approach must be tempered by a caveat. The increased discussion spurred by instructional complexity may not be task-related and task-related discussion may take place very infrequently. In addition, it is clear that instructional complexity in classrooms has few effects on the formal structure of educational organizations. Complex instructional technologies had no effects on administrative intensity and did not bring about increases in either formalization or evaluation.

Administration and Instructional Control

The findings above suggest that the formal administrative system in educational organizations is insulated from instructional problems, which appear to be resolved informally through discussion and consultation. It therefore seems appropriate to ask whether administrators in school systems are primarily oriented to instructional issues. As we have seen, the technological approach implies they are, since a central function of administration is thought to be coordination and control of the technical core.

An interesting way to approach the issue of administrative concern for instruction is to examine the time allocations of educational administrators. Goodman (1976) studied school principals and found that, during the workday, about 17 percent of the principals' time was allocated to "instructional leadership," which he defined as program development and implementation, program evaluation, and staff evaluation. By comparison, 58 percent of the principals' time was allocated to "management" problems in the areas of personnel, finance, building and grounds, student record keeping and referrals, and contact with parents. Of the persons with whom principals had contact during the day, 17 percent were teachers, but over 70 percent of these contacts lasted less than five minutes. Approximately 9 percent of the principals' actions took place in classrooms.

Sproull (1976) studied the time allocations of managers of innovative educational programs. Her study included both district and school-level administrators. The results were similar to Goodman's (1976), especially with respect to the relative inattention devoted to the technical core. The composite manager in this study spent about 13 percent of his or her day attending to program planning, discussing, supervising, and monitoring.

These observational findings are reinforced by survey research. Meyer and Rowan (1978), for example, obtained questionnaire data from superintendents, principals, and teachers in San Francisco Bay Area school systems. Their findings also demonstrate that administrators pay infrequent attention to instruction and also show the weakness of the formal control system. Concerning direct administrative observation of instruction, 85 percent of the principals reported that they did not work with teachers on a daily basis, while about half the teachers indicated that they were observed by principals once a month or less. Moreover, school personnel overwhelmingly reported a weak system of formal controls. For example, only one of the 34 superintendents interviewed reported that the district office directly evaluated teachers. Other controls are also weak. For example, 93 percent of the principals reported that curricular guidelines are informal or general, as opposed to detailed. Only 4 percent of the principals reported that they were very influential in determining the instructional methods that teachers use.

A clear picture emerges from these studies. During their workday, administrators are often busy on tasks other than instructional management. In fact, instructional management appears to be a relatively minor part of their work load. In this light, the failure of instructional complexity to impact administrative components makes sense. Although problems of coordination and control are raised when instructional activities become complex, administrators do not attend to these problems. Even if they did, it appears they would have little authority to deal with them, since their influence over teaching and curriculum is weak and the formal controls available are vague and perhaps ceremonious.

EDUCATIONAL ADMINISTRATION IN THE
INSTITUTIONAL ENVIRONMENT

To understand why tasks related to technical efficiency play such an apparently minor role in educational administration, the nature of social environments must be discussed. Much of organization theory has been formulated for organizations existing in output markets. In this kind of environment, organizations are sponsored by investors who demand a reasonable financial return and who use a calculus of "formal rationality" (Weber, 1947) to judge returns. Additionally, consumers make purchasing decisions based on price and quality considerations, and this further encourages organizations to economize. Survival in output markets can be precarious (Aldrich, 1979) and is aided by the achievement of technical efficiency.

Market environments, however, are merely one type of modern social environment. Increasingly, a second type is being organized by collective social authorities such as legislatures and regulatory agencies. Meyer and Rowan (1977) called this type an institutional environment. It differs in two ways from markets. First, organization sponsors—in this case, legislatures or regulatory bodies—judge organizational performance on the basis of "substantive rationality" (Weber, 1947). The attainment of highly valued social goals is of utmost importance and superordinate to efficiency criteria. In addition, the exercise of purchasing power by consumers is often limited because institutionalized organizations are granted public monopolies or near monopolies. Organizations in institutional environments often face an existence far less precarious than their counterparts in competitive output markets (Meyer and Rowan, 1977), but in return for this privilege, they must sacrifice some autonomy. Their goals are set externally, as are the means of achieving these goals.

In an institutional environment, organizational success depends upon judicious conformity to external requirements. When required types of inputs are processed using sanctioned techniques to attain socially mandated ends, institutionalized organizations receive numerous benefits. One is legitimacy and the commitments of time and energy by participants that follow from it (Parsons, 1956; Meyer and Rowan, 1977). A second benefit is monetary resources. Schools that adopt certain institutionalized programs gain funding from legislative agencies. Finally, the use of institutionalized structures avoids sanctions. Schools that use certificated personnel, for example, avoid disaccreditation.

The power and complexity of education's institutional environment has been growing steadily, although nationally it remains decentralized.[1] In the next few sections, the effects of institutional controls on local school systems will be considered. First, it will be argued that the institutional environment is organized in a way that makes efficiency, especially in instruction, difficult to achieve. This explains why instructional technologies play such a minor role in structuring educational administration. Later, turning directly to the way institutional controls impact local school systems, the effects such controls have on administration and their control over instruction will be discussed.

The Institutional Environment and Barriers to Instructional Efficiency

According to the technological imperative, administrators pay attention to problems in their technical core because they are under pressure to run their organization efficiently. One problem with applying this perspective to all organizations is that pressures for efficiency are particularly strong only under some circumstances. First, Thompson (1967) pointed out that organizations with routine technologies can more easily develop a calculus of efficiency and use it to evaluate technical performance. Second, as Weber (1947) discussed, this calculus is most highly developed in organizations facing market competition.

The problem with applying the technological imperative to schools now becomes clear. The conditions promoting a concern for efficiency are, to a large degree, lacking in the current school system, as economists have pointed out. As do sociologists, economists point to two barriers to instructional efficiency. One is that instructional technologies are uncertain. Brown and Saks (1978) believe that this keeps educators from developing a calculus efficiency similar to the production functions used in industry. They also believe, however, that research can make instructional technologies better understood, and when this happens, instructional production functions will be developed. A second view is less sanguine. Michaelsen (1980) argues that production functions cannot be developed without pricing mechanisms that give educators incentives to make profits, and this is not possible as long as local schools continue to be monopolies.

The institutional approach echoes these themes with minor, but important, differences. Consider the theme of schools as monopolies. Michaelsen (1980) argued that local school monopolies take their profits in terms of internal inefficiencies. This is a powerful analogy if one wants to compare schools to more efficiently run organizations, but it is dangerous if used to condemn school personnel as greedy monopolists. The institutional approach aims for a sympathetic understanding of educational administration. From this perspective, it is necessary to point out that school personnel do not think in terms of profits and losses. Rather, the institutional environment forces them to think in terms of substantive rationality—how to attain important social goals even if it means being inefficient from the standpoint of formal rationality.

An example of how substantive rationality can impose "inefficiencies" on schools can be found in local adaptation to the institutionalized goal of "equal access to educational opportunity." Under this mandate, schools must process student inputs that are hard to work with and require additional processing and expense. Thus, no public school administrator can streamline operations to accept only students who are easy to work with and promise good returns, unlike profit-making hospitals where the selection of patient inputs is done with such factors in mind. Moreover, it is doubtful that many current administrators would want to take such steps. The goal of equal access is legitimate and takes precedence over efficiency.

The larger point is this: The institutional environment regulates both goals and means. Often institutionalized goals promote "inefficiencies," but educational administrators must attempt to meet these goals if they want funding and legitimacy. Moreover, even if administrators want to attain socially mandated goals in an efficient manner, their ability to do so is restricted by the regulation of means. As an example of this dilemma, consider an administrator who wants to place a deserving student in an underutilized special class but cannot do so because the student does not meet certain legal requirements. Again the institutional environment creates barriers to local efficiency.

Another barrier to the development of efficiency in school systems is the uncertainty of instructional technologies. Many reformers who want to employ efficiency criteria stress that concerted efforts must be made by educators to "discover" a clearer picture of how instructional technologies function. Social scientists (for example, Thompson, 1967) who argue that organizations strive for closure in their technical cores expect such discoveries as a matter of course. There are problems, however, with this view. One is that knowledge about technologies does not exist in some concrete way that can be discovered. Rather, it is socially constructed (Berger and Luckmann, 1967). Nor is there always a steady march toward rationalization. The social construction of technical knowledge can as easily lead to uncertainty as to certainty

(Meyer and Rowan, 1977). In fact, this appears to be the case in education. The extension of institutional controls often promotes uncertainties in local school systems and encourages personnel to resist technical rationalization.

Consider how institutionalized rules can create instructional uncertainties in local school systems. These rules are set at very high levels of the institutional system and are meant to regulate practices in many local settings. As a result, they are couched at a high level of generality. At the local level, this can be particularly frustrating (Wise, 1977) because local peculiarities often generate exceptions to the general rule. Thus, the institutional environment, by its very nature, can provide local systems with an incomplete and uncertain instructional technology.

Another tendency of the educational system frustrates reformers. The system often actively resists having its instructional technology rationalized. Sometimes resistance comes from the public, as in the 1920s when the "cult of efficiency" among educational administrators was rejected (Callahan, 1962). Pressures also often come from within the system. Recently, teachers, parents, and even educational psychologists have begun to attack the validity of standardized testing programs that could be used to rationalize instructional processes. Meyer and Rowan (1978) suggested several reasons why rationalized criteria for evaluating instruction might be rejected in American schools. Local populations might reject criteria that threaten to define their schools or children as incompetent, and local educators might resist efficiency criteria as long as institutional regulations make such criteria difficult to achieve.

What happens in organizations where efficiency criteria are unimportant, either because output competition is lacking or because the logic of substantive rationality is paramount? Studies by Pfeffer and Leblebici (1973) and Rushing (1976) suggest that administrative attention to problems originating in the technical core is diminished. Reasons for why this would happen in schools have already been advanced. School administrators do not particularly help their organizations by achieving internal efficiencies and, under some circumstances, may actually harm them, as when such efficiencies contradict institutionalized procedures and rulings. Moreover, by delegating authority for instruction to those closer to the line—teachers—administrators may actually increase the effectiveness of instruction, especially when institutional agencies provide local schools with uncertain and incomplete instructional technologies.

The Structuring of Administrative Processes
in School Systems

The argument thus far has explained why the forces of technology do not structure administrative time and attention in schools
and thus why the technological approach is ill-suited to educational
organization. An important question remains: What does structure the administrative process in local school systems? In this
section, it will be argued that the growth of institutionalized controls leads to increases in the size of local administrative staffs
but also leads to decreased instructional controls. Figure 2.2 depicts these assumptions as causal propositions.

FIGURE 2.2

Institutional Approach to Administration

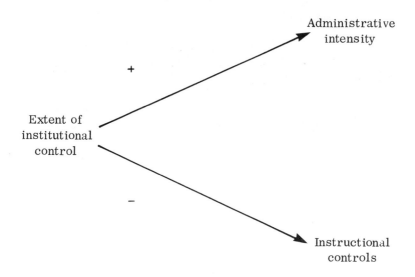

Source: Compiled by the author.

The first problem is to explain why administrative growth is related to the expansion of institutional controls. One simple explanation is that external rules often require the appointment of personnel to local staffs. For example, school systems that have programs for the mentally retarded are required by law to use certificated educational psychologists. Thus, schools with such programs have educational psychologists on their staff. Clearly, such specific external constraints on personnel appointments structure administrative staffs (see Freeman, 1979).

A more general approach to the problem, however, is to ask what the work load of administrators is and to find out what increases this work load, for as the work load increases, staff size increases. Here it is useful to turn to the studies of managerial time and attention discussed earlier. Goodman (1976) and Sproull (1976) suggest that a large proportion of a manager's day is spent keeping track of money, supplies, and people, and responding to external requests for information. Sproull's (1976) study suggests that these activities occupy nearly 40 percent of a manager's workday, while Goodman (1976) estimates that such functions might occupy nearly 60 percent of an administrator's day. Moreover, on issues such as personnel, scheduling, or finances, administrators appear to have assumed high levels of authority, especially when compared to their weak authority over instruction (Meyer and Rowan, 1978).

Regulations spawned by the institutional environment contribute to the work load of local administrative staffs. As regulators, agencies in the environment demand accounts from local systems. Have rules been followed? Have funds been expended as required? Have proper types of personnel been appointed and how have they spent their time? An example of how demands for accounting consume administrative time and attention can be found in "The October Report," which the State of California requires superintendents and principals to complete each October. This report deals solely with whether or not curricular and instructional rules are being followed locally. It asks administrators to report, among other things, the numbers and types of schools in the district and the grades in each; enrollment figures broken down by grade and by type of immigration visa held by students; length of the school term; the number of students who dropped out, were promoted, or were graduated and the requirements for graduation; the specific courses of study in grades 7 through 12; a list of all courses offered in grades 7 through 12; a list of courses in which topics such as venereal disease, fire prevention, first aid, manners, morals, citizenship, public safety, and accident prevention are discussed; how cumulative records of students are kept and transferred; whether the pledge of allegiance is said daily; the number of fire drills held yearly; and whether students are allowed to smoke on school grounds.

What is important to note about this report, in addition to its length, is that it is merely one of many such reports filed by districts. It does not even ask about personnel or finances, and it originates with only one agency of many in the institutional environment. It does, however, show why administrators in schools spend much of their time keeping track of people, money, and supplies. Institutionalized rules hold them accountable for such knowledge, and as the number of accounts they must file increases with new programs and regulations, their work load increases.

By affecting the work load of administrators, increased regulation contributes to the growth of administrative staffs in local school systems. It also has a second effect. As administrative time and attention are focused on documenting conformity, less attention is given to managing instructional technologies. Indeed, a common complaint of educational administrators is that they would like to be more involved in instructional leadership but don't have the time or are trapped by meaningless paperwork that wastes their time (compare Goodman, 1976; Sproull, 1976). Why do administrators let this happen?

Two ideas found in the literature on schools as loosely coupled systems can account for why increased institutionalized controls draw administrators away from duties concerned with instruction. One idea begins with the assumption that organizational participants have limited amounts of time and energy and must make choices about how to allocate these scarce resources (March and Olsen, 1976). The problem is to describe how such choices are made.

We can assume that administrators in schools are concerned with success and know the score—success in education comes by meeting demands for institutional conformity rather than instructional efficiency. Because administrators are working at full capacity (see Goodman, 1976) and have limited stocks of time and energy, they attend to problems having the larger payoff for their organization. This explains why administrators who want to exercise instructional leadership often don't. Duty forces them to attend to institutional details, and as these demands increase, administrators have less time available to be active in instructional programming, to tour the building and stop in classrooms, to talk to teachers about instructional problems, or to attend committee meetings about instruction.

If administrators do not have the time to become personally involved in regulating instruction, why don't they develop impersonal controls like formal policies and evaluations? One reason has already been suggested. Formal controls are an inappropriate mode of regulating an uncertain technology. In fact, since institutional rules often create uncertainties, formalized controls over instruction should decrease as external controls increase. There is another reason why formalized controls over instruction might decrease when instructional technologies are regulated externally. Meyer and Rowan (1978) argue that administrators actually avoid developing formal controls so that the inconsistencies between local practices and institutional rules are not discovered. This maintains the legitimacy of external rules, which can work only if local personnel are granted discretion, avoids the discovery of deviance by local personnel, who bend external rules to fit the local situation, and keeps up appearances of local conformity.

The larger point is that administrators deliberately decouple themselves from instructional demands. They do so because they lack the time and energy for instructional leadership and cannot use formal controls to compensate. In part, decoupling is designed to make a difficult situation more manageable. Loose coupling between administrative and instructional components prevents the discovery of local deviance and maintains the legitimacy of the local system's linkages to the institutional environment. Decoupling can also enhance the effectiveness of instructional operations. Since instruction is an uncertain technical activity, it is best controlled by those closest to the tasks involved—the teaching staff.

IMPLICATIONS FOR RESEARCH: AN EXAMPLE

The arguments presented above have clear implications for organizational research in school districts. They suggest an examination of relationships among four kinds of variables; measures of organizational technologies, environments, administrative staffs, and procedures for control. They also suggest that a specific pattern of relationships among these variables will be found in public educational organizations. In this section, these research implications will be illustrated by reporting findings from a study of school districts in the San Francisco Bay Area.[2]

The institutional approach to educational administration assumes that educational organizations are embedded in an institutional environment that reduces pressures for instructional efficiency. As a result, it predicts that the impact of instructional technologies on the administrative process in school systems is weak, especially compared to the impact of institutionalized controls. It also makes predictions about the consequences for local school systems of the trend toward increased control by professional, legislative, and judicial agencies. As institutionalized controls expand, the size of administrative components increases but controls over instruction decrease. Figure 2.3 summarizes these arguments in terms of a causal model. The parameters of the model will be estimated below, using multiple regression techniques.

FIGURE 2.3

Causal Model to Be Estimated

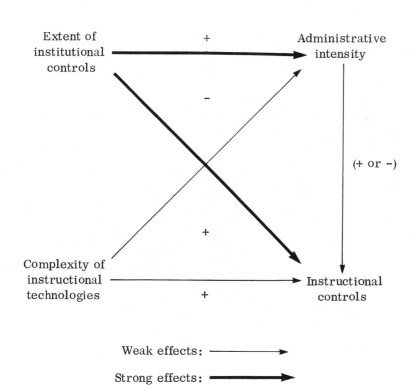

Source: Compiled by the author.

Before proceeding to the analysis, a brief discussion of the indicators to be used is in order. Of the four underlying theoretical concepts shown in Figure 2.3, the concept of technological complexity was the hardest to operationalize. Following Thompson (1967),

I searched for types of workflow interdependencies that existed among schools within a district. Two indicators were found. One indicator, called PROGRAM in the analysis below, was taken to reflect the extent to which schools existed in "pooled" interdependence. PROGRAM measures whether or not the elementary schools in a district operate using the same reading program. Those districts with a program were seen to have pooled interdependence among schools. A second indicator, called UNIFIED, was taken to reflect the existence of sequential interdependencies among schools in a district. In the Bay Area sample, some districts had only elementary schools, while others—the unified districts—had both elementary and secondary schools. I reasoned that administrators in unified districts faced the problem of coordinating a sequential interdependency, the flow of students from elementary to secondary schools. Obviously both PROGRAM and UNIFIED tap workflow interdependencies within districts imperfectly.

Other theoretical concepts were easier to operationalize. For example, the extent to which a given district was subject to institutional controls was measured by EXTFUND, the amount of special state and federal fundings per student. The size of a district's administrative component was measured by ADMIN, the number of Full Time Equivalent (FTE) administrators per student. In addition, there were two measures of instructional control: FORMAL, a summative index based on superintendents' responses to the questions of how explicit formal policies on curricular materials, instructional methods, and student progress reports were; and ADVICE, a variable based on superintendents' responses to how frequently they gave advice or information to principals. Unfortunately, ADVICE does not directly measure advice about instruction, but the indicator was included because it was the only available measure of the important informal mode of control within districts. One final variable, SIZE, was added to all analyses. SIZE was measured by the average daily attendance of a district.[3]

The first step in the analysis was to examine the determinants of administrative expansion in school districts. The institutional approach argues that institutional controls, measured by EXTFUND, have a larger impact on ADMIN than instructional technologies, measured by PROGRAM and UNIFIED. Table 2.1 reports the results of a multiple regression analysis with ADMIN as the dependent variable. In order to keep the number of regressors relative to the number of cases small, two equations were estimated, with one technology variable entered each time.

The results confirm the prediction that institutionalized controls are more important than the forces of instructional technology in promoting administrative growth, at least in this data. In each

equation, the standardized regression coefficients for the effect of
EXTFUND on ADMIN are large and statistically significant, while,
by comparison, the effects of PROGRAM and UNIFIED are small.
As expected, SIZE also affects ADMIN, with larger districts having
larger administrative staffs. [4]

TABLE 2.1

Determinants of Administrative Intensity
(N = 20)

	1	2
Constant	1949.12	2716.468
SIZE	.36*	.33*
	2041.102	1833.037
	(1433.931)	(1177.590)
EXTFUND	.68**	.73**
	174.056	185.460
	(52.891)	(53.566)
UNIFIED	.005	—
	23.687	
	(1014.095)	
PROGRAM	—	.16
		679.631
		(920.502)
	$R^2 = .42$	$R^2 = .44$

Note: First listing in table is standardized regression coefficient. Second listing is unstandardized coefficient. Third
listing (in parentheses) is standard error of estimate.
*p $\leq$ .10 one-tailed test.
**p $\leq$ .05 one-tailed test.
Source: Compiled by the author.

Table 2.2 turns to the development of formal controls over
instruction. Recall that the technological approach sees two determinants of formalization. One is the size of the administrative
component. If administrators use a reinforcement strategy of instructional control, ADMIN will have positive effects on FORMAL.

If a compensatory strategy is employed, administrative growth is a substitute for formal controls and ADMIN will have a negative effect on FORMAL. In addition, the technological approach predicts that PROGRAM and UNIFIED will have effects on FORMAL. The institutional approach takes a somewhat different perspective. First, since it views administrators as relatively unconcerned with instructional problems, it does not predict strong effects of ADMIN on FORMAL; but it does expect EXTFUND to affect FORMAL. As institutionalized controls increase, formal controls over instruction should decrease, especially since institutionalized controls raise uncertainties in the instructional core.

TABLE 2.2

Determinants of FORMAL
(N = 20)

	1	2
Constant	7.457	7.562
ADMIN	.29	.21
	.00015	.00011
	(.00016)	(.00016)
SIZE	.22	-.06
	.70864	-.1993
	(.96499)	(.7998)
EXTFUND	-.56**	-.35
	-.07958	-.0494
	(.04342)	(.0448)
UNIFIED	.37*	—
	.8737	
	(.6430)	
PROGRAM	—	.38*
		.9326
		(.5925)
	$R^2 = .27$	$R^2 = .30$

Note: First listing in table is standardized regression coefficient. Second listing is unstandardized coefficient. Third listing (in parentheses) is standard error of estimate.
* $p \leq .10$ one-tailed test.
**$p \leq .05$ one-tailed test.
Source: Compiled by the author.

The results in Table 2.2 indicate a modest technological imperative. For example, the effects of PROGRAM and UNIFIED on FORMAL are reasonably strong, especially given the small number of cases. Less strong are the positive effects of ADMIN on FORMAL, a result that contradicts the predictions of the institutional approach.[5] Nevertheless, there is strong support for the institutional approach in Table 2.2. As predicted, the effects of EXTFUND on FORMAL are negative and the coefficients are reasonably large. Thus, Table 2.2 gives modest support to both the technological and institutional approaches.

TABLE 2.3

Determinants of ADVICE
(N = 20)

	1	2
Constant	3.405	4.556
ADMIN	.39*	.37
	.00018	.00017
	(.00012)	(.00013)
SIZE	-.23	-.48**
	-.6103	-1.2734
	(.7240)	(.6543)
EXTFUND	-.74**	-.75**
	-.0878	-.0890
	(.0325)	(.0367)
UNIFIED	-.37*	—
	-.7415	
	(.4824)	
PROGRAM	—	.09
		.1890
		(.4847)
	$R^2 = .43$	$R^2 = .34$

Note: First listing in table is standardized regression coefficient. Second listing is unstandardized coefficient. Third listing (in parentheses) is standard error of estimate.
*$p \leq .10$ one-tailed test.
**$p \leq .05$ one-tailed test.
Source: Compiled by the author.

In Table 2.3, the effects of independent variables on ADVICE, a measure of informal controls, is shown. Again, the institutional approach predicts that EXTFUND has negative effects on ADVICE. The technological approach predicts that ADMIN, PROGRAM, and UNIFIED have positive effects on ADVICE.

The results in Table 2.3 give strong support to the institutional approach. The more a district is involved with state and federal fundings, the less superintendents are involved in giving advice to principals. As can be seen, the effects of EXTFUND on ADVICE are negative, and the coefficients are statistically significant. The results are difficult to interpret with respect to support for the technological imperative. On the one hand, it appears that the larger the administrative component, the more superintendents give advice, but the interpretation of this finding is unclear. It could be that superintendents with larger supporting staffs are free to dispense advice, while those with smaller supporting staffs are not. Or, the relationship could indicate a reinforcement pattern of control in which larger administrative staffs dispense more advice. It is worth noting that the technological variable having the strongest effects on ADVICE is UNIFIED, but its effects are in a direction opposite of that predicted. Further inspection of the table suggests an interpretation. It appears that larger organizations with multiple levels in the hierarchy create distance problems that prevent superintendents from exercising personal controls.

CONCLUSIONS

What can be said of the vitality of the two approaches to administration in educational organizations in light of the data reported here? Of the two approaches, the technological received the least support. Variables measuring the degree of workflow interdependence in districts failed to show effects on administrative growth in schools and had modest, and sometimes inconsistent, effects on measures of control. Nevertheless, there was some evidence of a modest technological imperative. Both PROGRAM and UNIFIED, the measures of technical complexity, had effects on the extent of formalization of instructional rules, and there was modest evidence that administrative growth might be connected to the expansion of instructional controls.

Compared to the modest and inconsistent effects of instructional technologies, the effects of institutionalized rules were robust and consistent. In five of the six estimated equations, effects were statistically significant even though the number of cases was small, and in every equation the effects were in the predicted direction.

Thus, the data lend strong support to the institutional approach. It is clear that increased institutional controls in education lead to administrative growth at local levels, and it is clear that institutional controls also lead to decreases in both formal and informal controls over instruction. Note also that the findings are consistent with other results on the effects of institutionalized controls on school systems (Freeman, 1979; Davis et al., 1976).

On the basis of these findings, it can tentatively be concluded that school districts resemble the type of organization Meyer and Rowan (1977) called an institutionalized organization. These organizations exist in, and are highly controlled by, powerful institutional environments composed of regulatory, legislative, and professional organizations. Meyer and Rowan (1977) argued that institutionalized organizations are highly structured by the rules of agencies in the institutional environment, and that this structuring process leads to loose coupling, especially between structural elements and ongoing technical activities. The results of this study appear to support this view of institutionalized organizations. Local school district administrative staffs appear to be structured by the demands of their institutional environments, but as these demands increase, internal coordination and control over ongoing instructional technologies are decreased, and district administrative components become loosely tied to school-level personnel and activities.

Thus, when schools are viewed as institutionalized organizations, one set of conditions leading to "loose coupling" (Weick, 1976) in educational systems becomes apparent. Beginning with Bidwell's (1965) discussion of loose structuring, organization theorists have been struck by the low levels of technical control over instruction in schools. Bidwell suggested that such loose structuring arises because bureaucratic rules in schools are inconsistent with the uncertainties of instruction and that teaching must therefore be buffered from such formal controls. The findings here suggest that this pattern is likely to continue as long as distant agencies in the institutional environment attempt to control local educational systems through highly abstract and formal rules.

The findings also partially explain the observations of Weick (1976) and Meyer and Rowan (1978), who see schools containing two separate and loosely joined subsystems; an instructional core and an administrative core. Although the findings do indicate some ways in which administrators are linked to instructional components, most notably through advice and consultation, these weak linkages are strained by time and energy demands connected to problems of institutional conformity. Thus, the data indicate that as institutionalized controls over local schools grow, the system becomes more loosely coupled.

Further research is clearly suggested by this study, especially comparative organizational research on schools. For example, I took the position that instructional technologies had weak effects on the administrative process because the institutional environment discourages a concern for technical efficiency. In part, this lack of concern, it was argued, is due to the fact that local schools are like monopolies. An obvious research question arises from this consideration. Are the effects of instructional technologies stronger in private schools that face market competition?

The question has merit above and beyond its scientific relevance. Answers to it might shed light on policy questions. For example, a voucher system in education has gained support in recent years. It seems clear that such a system would introduce competition into educational systems. Would this competition increase administrative concern for instructional affairs? Perhaps it would, and perhaps the costs of schooling might be lowered if a concern for efficiency were realized. A more interesting question is also relevant: If administrators did pay more attention to instruction and exercised more control over teaching, would schools be more effective?

There is reason to be skeptical. As Erickson (1977:5) points out, there is no trustworthy evidence that the school executive makes a profound difference in students' achievements. More of the variance in student achievement is associated with classrooms. Are we to turn to increased executive controls as an answer to instructional problems? The lessons of history, and the data presented here, show that local systems resist such controls and strive to loosely couple administrative and instructional components. Perhaps this is because the loosely coupled school system, with its flexible instructional core, is, despite its manifest shortcomings, an appropriate design for managing teaching and learning.

NOTES

1. The growth of external influence over local school systems is evident in the evolution of funding patterns in school systems. In 1930 the average American school district derived 82.7 percent of its funds locally, 17 percent from states, and less than 1 percent from the federal government. By 1970 local sources dropped to 52 percent, state sources increased to 40 percent, and the federal government contributed 8 percent to the average district's expenditures (Department of Health, Education and Welfare, 1975:34-35).

2. The data used in this analysis were collected in 1975 by researchers at the Stanford Center for Research and Development

in Teaching. Data were collected from a combined questionnaire and interview with superintendents in the San Francisco Bay Area. Details of sampling procedures can be found in Cohen et al. (1979). The original sample contained data on 27 districts, but because of missing data problems, only 20 districts are included in this analysis. Some properties of the data should be mentioned at the outset. Because the original researchers were concerned with elementary instruction, all indicators, including those of administrative size, funding, and procedures of control, refer only to elementary education in the districts.

3. In this analysis, SIZE is measured using the inverse of average daily attendance. The inverse of size was used for a number of reasons. One was that there was substantial multicollinearity between funding measures and enrollment figures. The use of the inverse reduced this multicollinearity and had very minor impacts on correlations of enrollment to other variables. In addition, use of transformed values of size allows Table 2.1 to be interpreted as a weighted least-squares solution appropriate given the pattern of errors observed. To interpret the table as a weighted least-squares result, the constant term should be read as the effects of enrollment on ADMIN, while the coefficient for SIZE becomes the constant. The ordinary least-squares interpretation and the weighted least-squares one, it should be noted, yield the same interpretation.

4. In this analysis, a measure of total district expenditures was substituted for technology variables to see if the effects of EXTFUND were simply reflecting the fact that richer districts had more administrators. Total expenditures did have a large and significant effect on ADMIN (beta = .46), and only slightly reduced the effect of EXTFUND on ADMIN (beta = .63).

5. It should be noted that when a measure of total district expenditures is substituted for measures of technology, the effects of ADMIN on FORMAL disappear (beta = .04). Thus the effects of ADMIN on FORMAL may be spurious.

REFERENCES

Aldrich, Howard. 1979. Organizations and Environments. Englewood Cliffs, N.J.: Prentice-Hall.

Barnard, Chester I. 1938. The Functions of the Executive. Cambridge, Mass.: Harvard University Press.

Berger, Peter L., and Thomas Luckmann. 1967. The Social Construction of Reality. New York: Doubleday.

Bidwell, Charles E. 1965. "The School as a Formal Organization." Handbook of Organizations, edited by James G. March.
Chicago: Rand McNally.

Blau, Peter M., and W. Richard Scott. 1962. Formal Organizations. San Francisco: Chandler.

Brown, Byron W., and Daniel Saks. 1978. Production Technol-
ogies and Resource Allocation within Classrooms and Schools:
Theory and Measurement. Chicago: Department of Education,
University of Chicago.

Bureau of the Census, U.S. 1975. Historical Statistics of the
United States. Washington, D.C.

Burns, Tom, and G. M. Stalker. 1961. The Management of Innovation. London: Tavistock.

Callahan, Raymond E. 1962. Education and the Cult of Efficiency.
Chicago: University of Chicago Press.

Charters, W. W. Jr. 1973. Measuring the Implementation of
Differentiated Staffing: A Comparison of Two Elementary
Schools. Eugene, Ore.: Center for the Advanced Study of Edu-
cational Administration.

Cohen, Elizabeth G., T. E. Deal, J. W. Meyer, and W. R. Scott.
1979. "Technology and Teaming in the Elementary School."
Sociology of Education 52:20-33.

Corwin, Ronald G. 1974. In Review of Research on Education,
edited by Fred Kerlinger and John Carroll, Vol. 2. Itasca, Ill.:
Peacock.

Davis, Margaret E., B. Rowan, and E. A. Stackhouse. 1976.
"Loose and Tight Coupling in Educational Organizations." In
The Structure of Educational Systems: Explorations on the
Theory of Loosely Coupled Systems, edited by Margaret R.
Davis et al. Stanford, Calif.: Stanford Center for Research
and Development in Teaching.

Department of Health, Education and Welfare, U.S. 1975. Digest
of Education Statistics. Washington, D.C.: National Center for
Education Statistics.

Dreeben, Robert. 1973. "The School as a Workplace." In Second Handbook of Research on Teaching, edited by R. M. W. Travers. Chicago: Rand McNally.

Erickson, Donald A. 1977. Educational Organization and Administration. Berkeley: McCutchan.

Freeman, John H. 1979. "Going to the Well: School District Administrative Intensity and Environmental Constraint." Administrative Science Quarterly 24:119-33.

Freeman, John H. 1973. "Environment, Technology and Administrative Intensity of Manufacturing Organizations." American Sociological Review 38:750-63.

Galbraith, Jay. 1973. Designing Complex Organizations. Reading, Mass.: Addison-Wesley.

Goodman, Samuel M. 1976. "The Principal's Leadership Role: Practice vs. Preference." Montgomery County Schools, Rockville, Maryland. Mimeographed.

Hickson, D. J., D. S. Pugh, and D. C. Pheysey. 1969. "Operations Technology and Organization Structure." Administrative Science Quarterly 14:378-97.

Jackson, P. W. 1968. Life in Classrooms. New York: Holt, Rinehart & Winston.

Lawrence, Paul R., and Jay W. Lorsch. 1967. "Differentiation and Integration in Complex Organizations." Administrative Science Quarterly 12:1-47.

March, James G., and Johan P. Olsen. 1976. Ambiguity and Choice in Organizations. Bergen: Universitetsforlaget.

Meyer, John W., and Brian Rowan. 1978. "The Structure of Educational Organizations." In Environments and Organizations, edited by Marshall W. Meyer et al. San Francisco: Jossey-Bass.

Meyer, John W., and Brian Rowan. 1977. "Institutionalized Organization: Formal Structure as Myth and Ceremony." American Journal of Sociology 83:440-63.

Michaelsen, Jacob B. 1980. "Assessing the Efficacy of Financial Reform in California." American Journal of Education 88:145-78.

Parsons, Talcott. 1956. "Suggestions for a Sociological Approach to the Theory of Organizations—I." Administrative Science Quarterly 1:63-85.

Perrow, Charles. 1970. Organizational Analysis: A Sociological View. Belmont, Calif.: Wadsworth.

Pfeffer, Jeffrey, and Huseyin Leblebici. 1973. "The Effect of Competition on Some Dimensions of Organization Structure." Social Forces 52:268-79.

Pugh, D., D. J. Hickson, C. R. Hinings, and C. Turner. 1969. "The Context of Organizational Structures." Administrative Science Quarterly 14:91-141.

Rogers, David. 1964. 110 Livingston Street. New York: Random House.

Rushing, William. 1976. "Profit and Nonprofit Orientations and the Differentiation-Coordination Hypothesis for Organizations." American Sociological Review 41:676-90.

Rushing, William. 1968. "Hardness of Material as an External Restraint on the Division of Labor in Manufacturing Organizations." Administrative Science Quarterly 12:267-95.

Scott, W. Richard. 1975. "Organization Structure." In Annual Review of Sociology, edited by Alex Inkeles. Palo Alto: Annual Reviews.

Sproull, Lee S. 1976. "Managerial Attention in New Education Programs: Some Preliminary Findings." Paper presented at Conference on Educational Organizations as Loosely Coupled Systems, Palo Alto, Calif.

Thompson, James D. 1967. Organizations in Action. New York: McGraw-Hill.

Tracy, Phalps, and Koya Asumi. 1976. "Determinants of Administrative Control: A Test of Theory with Japanese Factories." American Sociological Review 41:80-93.

Tyack, David B. 1974. The One Best System. Cambridge, Mass.: Harvard University Press.

Van de Ven, Andrew, A. L. Delbecq, and R. Koenig, Jr. 1976. "Determinants of Coordination Modes within Organizations." American Sociological Review 41:322-37.

Weber, Max. 1947. The Theory of Social and Economic Organization. New York: Oxford University Press.

Weber, Max. 1946. Essays in Sociology. New York: Oxford University Press.

Weick, Karl E. 1976. "Educational Organizations as Loosely Coupled Systems." Administrative Science Quarterly 21:1-19.

Wise, Arthur E. 1977. "The Hyper-rationalization of American Education." New York University Education Quarterly 8:2-6.

Woodward, Joan. 1965. Industrial Organization: Theory and Practice. London: Oxford University Press.

3

RESPONSE TO REGULATION:
AN ORGANIZATIONAL PROCESS APPROACH

Lee S. Sproull

As public sites where the nation's children are housed five days a week, and as instruments of social welfare, local school districts are an appropriate target for federal regulation "in the public interest." Despite the fact that the federal government is not constitutionally responsible for education, in recent years it has created regulations aimed at a host of local and school district practices (Williams, 1978; Wise, 1979). These practices include, for example, keeping pupil records (the Buckley Amendment), running girls' athletic programs (Title IX), maintaining special education classes (mainstreaming), providing access to programs (handicapped access), and staffing schools (racial balance teacher transfers). Although we are beginning to see analyses of how local districts respond to one or another set of federal regulations (Birman, 1979; Berman and McLaughlin, 1975; Dolbeare and Hammond, 1971; Herriott and Gross, 1979), there has been as yet no consideration of how local school districts cope with the totality of federal regulations facing them.

By federal regulation we mean any directive on the part of any federal actor intended to affect behavior within local school districts.

The work reported herein was supported by grant NIE-G-79-0018 from the National Institute of Education. I am grateful for assistance from Steven Andes, Virginia Connolly-Manhardt, and Maureen Mills. Pat Crecine and Pat Larkey provided helpful comments on an earlier draft of this chapter. Alice Young has been my collaborator in much of the work reported here.

A directive can be a law, an administrative rule, or a legal finding, issued by Congress, any administrative agency, or the Supreme Court. This extremely broad definition admits the widest possible scope for investigation and allows later narrowing and specification, if appropriate. Within this broad definition, federal directives can be categorized in a number of different ways: for example, by federal actor, scope of jurisdiction, intended beneficiary at the local level, intended locus of action at the local level (for example, classroom, counselor's office), or local behavior intended to be influenced (for example, hiring, pupil assignment). (Figure 3.1 displays examples of each of these categorizations.) Each of these dimensions, however, reflects a federal perspective; only to the extent that local officials find them meaningful will they be useful in understanding local response.

FIGURE 3.1

Alternative Ways to Categorize Federal Directives

Federal actor
Supreme Court
    Schoolhouse prayer decisions
    Brown v. Board of Education
Congress
    Family Educational Rights
    Education for All Handicapped Act (PL 94-142)
Administrative agencies
    Reporting and evaluation standards for Title I
    Nutritional requirements for school lunches

Jurisdiction
All school districts
    Family Educational Rights and Privacy Act
    Schoolhouse prayer
All school districts that receive any federal financial assistance
    Section 504
    Title IX
All school districts that receive particular program funds
    Reporting and evaluation requirements for Title I
    Nutritional requirements for school lunches

Intended beneficiary
All students and their parents
    FERPA
All handicapped students
    PL 94-142

All handicapped persons
   Section 504
All female persons
   Title IX
All minority students
   Brown v. Board of Education
   Lau decision

Intended action site
Central district office
   Comparability requirements for Title I
School
   Brown v. Board of Education
   PL 94-142
Classroom
   Schoolhouse prayer
   Bilingual instruction in Title VII classes
Counselor's office
   FERPA
   PL 94-142

Behaviors to be influenced
Personnel hiring
   Nondiscrimination against handicapped applicants (Section 504)
Pupil assignment to schools and classes
   Desegregation orders
   PL 94-142
Curricular decisions
   Lau decision
Expenditure patterns
   Title IX
Comparability requirements for Title I

Source: Compiled by the author.

The lack of comprehensive analysis of school district response to federal regulation is traceable to several factors. Until fairly recently, theories of response to regulation have been developed within the context of market sector organizations only. School districts and other public sector organizations have been invisible to these theorists. More pragmatically, local school districts themselves have not had the resources to analyze the impact of the federal government on their operations. Nor has the federal government had any coordinated program to monitor its effects on local school districts.

A program of research designed to understand how local school districts respond to federal regulation is important for at least three classes of reasons. The first has to do with intentionality. Every federal directive is constructed with positive intent; the constructor intends to prevent harm or to achieve some valued state. Without a theory of response to regulation, however, it is difficult to assess the conditions under which the intent of regulations is more or less likely to be accomplished. The second reason has to do with costs. Regulation is never cost-free, but without a theory of response to regulation it is difficult to estimate the actual costs of regulation. The third reason has to do with theory. Response to regulation should interest both organization theorists and political scientists, not just market sector economists. A program of research that piques their interest should encourage them to add their theoretical insights to the problem and to modify their theories to incorporate response to regulation.

This chapter introduces and illustrates some ways of thinking about school system response to regulation that are based on organization theory. It also describes actual school superintendent behaviors relevant to federal regulation. An organizational analysis of this problem seems appropriate both because organizations (school districts) are the target of regulatory activity and because organizational actors (school superintendents and their delegates) generate responses to such activity. The spirit of the chapter is exploratory and speculative. It is designed to suggest a way of thinking about a problem, to present some data relevant to that problem, then to explore implications of the data for extending the analysis.

The chapter is organized in four sections. The first sketches an organizational process view of response to regulation and suggests how the behaviors of school superintendents are important to this view. The second describes how data were collected from 25 school districts and their superintendents. The third section describes actual patterns of school superintendent behavior with respect to federal regulation. The fourth speculates on the significance of these patterns for organizational analysis.

RESPONDING TO REGULATION: AN
ORGANIZATIONAL PROCESS FRAMEWORK

From the federal perspective, every new regulation is issued with the best of intentions—in the service of, for example, due process, student rights, or equal protection. Each regulator typically wishes to affect a small class of behaviors at the local level. When a new regulation is promulgated, so the standard regulatory reasoning would have it, every district automatically notices and pays attention to it. Furthermore, every district uniformly understands its intent and implications. In addition, every district engages in the de novo problem solving, decision making, and implementation necessary to realize that intention.

This conventional formulation ignores three aspects of life in school districts or any other organizations. First, district personnel are busy running their districts; they have little time to spend scanning the environment for news of new federal regulations (Cuban, 1976; Hannaway and Sproull, 1979). Second, district personnel filter all incoming information—if they notice it at all—through their beliefs about past experiences and the nature of their organizations (March and Simon, 1958; Sproull, 1981a). Third, district personnel have available a small but stable set of routine performance programs that they draw upon when confronted with problems (Crecine, 1969; Gerwin, 1969). Whenever possible, personnel redefine a "new" problem to fit existing procedures (March and Simon, 1958; March and Olsen, 1976). This is the context within which response to regulation occurs. (See Sproull [1981b] for a more extensive treatment of these issues.)

How then are responses to regulation generated within this organizational context? Someone must actually notice or attend to the new regulation; somehow it must be interpreted for the particular local context; and it must be attached to a subset of routine performance programs. It is these processes then—and not the intent of the regulator—that become the primary determinant of response to regulation.

Attention

In order for a school district to respond to a new federal regulation or requirement, someone in the district must notice it, must attend to it. At one extreme a district could employ a full-time lawyer to read the Federal Register every day and the Legislative Digest and summary of Supreme Court decisions every week, looking for any and all directives having to do with local school districts. At the other extreme a district could follow an ignorance-is-bliss policy, avoiding all contact with and knowledge of federal directives (unless and until sued). A district's scanning procedures in part determine whether or not and how it will notice a new regulation. In addition to systematic and more or less formalized procedures for environment scanning, district officials may also use more idiosyncratic signaling devices to alert them to some federal requirements. Just as psychological theories of attention point to the importance of interrupt mechanisms in directing attention (Mandler, 1964; Norman, 1976), such mechanisms may have their counterpart in organizations. If so, district officials will have their own "red flags"—words or phrases that cause them to pay special attention to some regulations. Red flags also must contribute to how a district attends to regulations.

Interpretation

Even if two districts notice the "same" new regulation, their responses to it may vary because they interpret it differently. Understanding how a district constructs what a regulation means for its own circumstances entails understanding how people assign that regulation to various categories. For any new set of stimuli, categorizing is affected by how the perceiver organizes his mental representations of his world (Rosch and Lloyd, 1978). These categorizing processes are also often aided by social processes of consulting and coming to shared agreement (Berger and Luckmann, 1966). Thus we would also expect that ambiguous regulations would generate an appreciable amount of meeting and consultation.

Attachment

In order for a regulation actually to affect or change behavior it must become attached to some sort of procedure or routine that actually governs or produces behavior. Interpreting a new regulation sometimes involves attaching it to district standard operating procedures (SOPs). If an incoming regulation is categorized as "for the XYZ subunit" or "in Joe Smith's bailiwick," then the regulation has become at least loosely attached to a subset of district SOPs. "Routing" behavior would be evidence of this kind of attachment.

Attachment may also occur if implementing a regulation requires the use of or conflicts with one or more district procedures. Here we may expect to see tension between local ways of doing business and the requirements of the regulation. Thus attachment should not be thought of only as a smooth and nearly automatic process. It may involve substantial pullings and haulings to accommodate the local procedure to the regulation and vice versa.

Superintendent's Contribution

Superintendents can be key actors in all three of these processes. Because they represent their districts' legal administrative authority, they may be the initial recipients of new regulations. Their reaction will determine what attention, if any, these directives will receive by members of the school district. Superintendents often function as boundary spanners connecting their districts to external networks of other superintendents, professional associations, and so forth. These connections can influence the information districts have available when they try to interpret new regulations. Because superintendents oversee the daily work of the district, they can be instrumental in managing the processes by which regulations get attached to routine performance programs.

Obviously any superintendent's contribution to his district's response to regulation is an empirical question. We should like to know, first, if the superintendent has any involvement with federal regulations at all and, second, if so, what is the nature of that involvement? Does he participate in scanning? Does he have any personal red flags? How does he think about federal regulations generally? Does he ever get involved in interpreting particular ones? What is his contribution to meshing regulations with ongoing district work? Answers to such questions as these can help us assess the contribution of the superintendent in responding to regulation.

RESEARCH METHODS AND SAMPLE

The data reported in this chapter, collected by means of extensive open-ended interviews and observation, are from 25 school districts in one county in the northeastern United States.* The county includes a large urban industrial city and a wide range of surrounding communities and school districts, from working-class mill towns to highly affluent suburbs and exurbs. The sample districts as a whole had an average enrollment of 5,700 students and a per pupil expenditure of $1,828 in 1976-77. Sample districts have, on average, a slightly higher per pupil expenditure, slightly higher enrollment, and lower percent minority enrollment and federal funds per pupil than the nation as a whole. (See Table 3.1 for some characteristics of the districts.)

The modal superintendent in the district is white, male, in his fifties, with a doctoral degree in education. The sample super-

---

*These data were collected during the first phase of a multi-year research project. See Sproull and Young (1980) for more extensive documentation.

TABLE 3.1

Comparison of the Sample with Other Administrative Organizations in Education, 1976–77

	The Sample: 25 School Districts in One County	Districts which Declined to Participate: 21 School Districts	Total County Minus the One Large City	Total County: 46 School Districts and the Large City	State of Pennsylvania: 505 School Districts	United States: 16,271 School Systems
Average enrollment	5,712	2,666	4,189	5,528	4,306	2,738
Percent of minority	4.13	N.A.*	N.A.	N.A.	N.A.	14
Average per pupil expenditure	$1,828	$1,821	$1,825	$1,833	$1,852	$1,638
Average amount of federal funds	$256,908	$167,248	$212,078	$457,000	$714,646	$407,442
Average amount of federal funds per pupil	$44.98	$62.73	$50.63	$82.67	$165.97	$148.81

*Information not available.

Sources: Information taken from sample districts, local newspapers, Pennsylvania statistical Report on Education, Digest of Educational Statistics, and U.S. Statistical Abstract of 1978.

intendents are fairly new to their positions; half of them have been in their current position for three years or less. Eleven (44 percent) have previously held positions as federal coordinators, positions offering experiences that these superintendents believe stand them in good stead now.

SUPERINTENDENTS AND FEDERAL REGULATIONS

Daily Activity

Superintendents do encounter federal regulations during the course of their work and furthermore often find them troublesome. Eighty-five percent of the superintendents reported that they personally spent time on federal issues within the past week. Seventy-three percent could name ways in which the federal presence made doing their own job more difficult (see Table 3.2). Two major types of complaints about the intrusion of federal regulation into superintendents' work load predominate. First, 56 percent of the superintendents found managing the associated information flow burdensome. In this flow the superintendents function as brokers between the district and the federal government, processing paper about existing and new or changing requirements, attending meetings, and arranging for evaluations of federally funded programs. Second, 44 percent of the superintendents found the inflexibility of federal mandates troublesome. This inflexibility occurs in several interrelated forms: lack of recognition of local needs, inappropriate interference with local autonomy, and diversion of energy from more important matters.

One of the ways in which superintendents encounter federal regulations is through routine scanning procedures. All the superintendents in our sample report that they engage in relatively low-level passive scanning of incoming documents such as the Federal Register or circulars from the state department of education (see Table 3.3). They appear to scan routinely two kinds of documents: formal or legal announcements of new requirements from the federal or state government and interpretive materials. Their preference—both for learning about the existence of and for interpretations of new federal requirements—is for documents produced "close to home."

Superintendents report that the outcome of most of their scanning behavior is filing (assigning the label, "not worthy of any more attention") or routing (assigning the label "worthy of someone else's attention, but not my own"). Thus superintendent low-level "filing" decisions can determine whether or not a regulation receives any further attention in the district.

TABLE 3.2

Superintendent Contact with Federal Regulations

Federal Activity Engaged in During Previous Week	Number of Superintendents	Percent
Mainstreaming	7	27
Section 504	3	12
Title IX	2	8
Title IV	2	8
Title I	2	8
Gifted program	1	4
Paperwork, general	2	8
Meetings, general	2	8
Related to court order	1	4
None	4	15
Impact on Superintendent's Job		
Denies local autonomy	11	26
Extra paperwork and information processing	8	19
Financial drain	6	14
Extra meetings	4	10
Evaluations	2	5
Title I	1	2
Section 504	1	2
Title IX	1	2
Equal opportunity	1	2
Due process	1	2
None	6	14

Source: Compiled by the author.

Occasionally during scanning the superintendent notices a regulation that he considers worthy of further personal attention. Seventy percent of the superintendents described red flags that cause them to pay special attention and 50 percent described specific issues for which they take personal responsibility (see Table 3.4). Apparently if a superintendent encounters such phrases as "mandatory" or "must comply" or "the district must pay" during low-level scanning, he will be likely to place the associated requirement on his own agenda. He will also do this if the issue happens to be one in which he is personally interested or involved. For example, many of our superintendents reported that they automatically attended to equal opportunity directives themselves.

TABLE 3.3

Superintendent Sources of Information about Federal
Requirements and Regulations

Sources	Use at All	Best Existence	Best Interpretation
Written			
Intermediate unit	15	5	9
State officials	14	8	3
Professional publications	11	—	1
Federal Register	10	2	1
Federal officials	6	—	—
General news media	4	—	—
Internal district	1	—	—
Oral			
School officials	11	4	3
State officials	8	—	1
Intermediate unit	7	—	—
Fellow superintendents	4	1	1

Source: Compiled by the author.

Whether or not a superintendent takes personal responsibility for a particular regulation, he may become involved in trying to interpret what it means. Seventy-two percent of the superintendents could name a particular directive or requirement that was somewhat puzzling to them when they first heard about it. Forty percent (56 percent of the responses) described directives related to instructional programs; 28 percent (39 percent of the responses) described personnel rights directives (see Table 3.5). Interestingly, the list of puzzling directives includes both old and new interventions—for example, both Title I and handicapped access. Apparently experience and learning on the part of either the local districts or the federal government do not eliminate difficulties in interpreting directives.

TABLE 3.4

Superintendent Attention to Federal Regulations

	Number of Responses	Percent
Red Flags that Cause Attention		
Mandatory	11	34
Financial requirements	6	19
Deadlines	4	12
Impact district	2	6
Pet projects	1	3
Equal opportunity	1	3
None	7	22
Personal Projects		
Equal opportunity	5	18
Instructional only	3	11
Related to personnel	2	7
Anything new	2	7
Noninstructional only	1	4
Anything requiring board approval	1	4
All	1	4
None	13	45

Source: Compiled by the author.

TABLE 3.5

Directives Considered Puzzling by Superintendents

Dimension	Number of Responses	Percent
Instructional program	(10)	(56)
Title I	5	28
Mainstreaming	3	17
Votech	2	11
Personnel	(7)	(39)
Handicapped access	5	28
Equal opportunity	1	6
Title IX	1	6
Miscellaneous	(1)	(6)
Energy	1	6

Source: Compiled by the author.

In interpreting federal directives, superintendents consult with both written and oral sources, inside and outside the district. Much of the consultation system is shared by most superintendents in a given region and consists of interpretations from the state department of education, the regional intermediate unit, professional publications, and fellow superintendents. In our sample, these sources were named 80 percent of the time as providing the best interpretation of federal directives (see Table 3.3). In addition, 44 percent of the superintendents report discussing puzzling directives at staff meetings. Over one-third of the superintendents mentioned discussing mainstreaming and Section 504 directives in these meetings.

After consulting with others, superintendents resolve puzzling directives in one of three ways. Forty-six percent follow the interpretation constructed during consultation; 21 percent decide to do nothing and wait to see if the federal government will clarify its intentions; and 33 percent decide in the face of conflicting interpretations just to follow their own best judgment and plunge ahead (see Table 3.6). Obviously these differences in superintendent resolution strategies can result in adjacent districts' behaving completely differently with respect to the "same" regulation.

TABLE 3.6

Means of Resolving Puzzling Directives
Reported by Superintendents

Means of Resolving	Number of Responses	Percent
Consulted others	11	46
Intermediate unit	(2)	
Other school officials	(2)	
State officials	(3)	
Fellow superintendents	(4)	
Followed own judgment	8	33
Did not resolve	5	21

Source: Compiled by the author.

The superintendent's role in attaching regulations to district SOPs can be discharged through routing, mediation, or direct action. If a superintendent, during low-level scanning, routes a directive to a person responsible for procedures relevant to it, he can assume that the directive has become attached to those procedures. For example, 80 percent of our superintendents report that they automatically route all Title I directives to their Title I coordinator. (Obviously, however, it is necessary to investigate what the recipient of routed directives actually does with them. In these cases routing may be a necessary but by no means sufficient step for insuring that a directive actually affects behavior.)

Superintendents also engage in mediating between local administrative work and federal regulations. About 40 percent of the superintendents said that federal requirements produced difficulties for them in personnel hiring and assignment, budget construction and justification, and communicating with parents. Apparently one of the ways a regulation gets labeled as problematic is by being perceived as disruptive to or incompatible with local procedures. Part of the process of coming to understand what a regulation "really means" is coming to understand how it can be accommodated by local procedures. In these cases, superintendents often spend time in staff meetings interpreting and reinterpreting directives until they "fit" the local procedural structure.

If a directive does not obviously fall under the responsibility of one identifiable organizational subunit or set of routines, attachment or mediation is difficult. In these cases the superintendent may accept personal responsibility for directing behavior. For example, it may be the case that one reason superintendents report that they deal with equal employment opportunity issues themselves is because there is no one obvious person to whom they can be delegated. They are relevant to sets of hiring, supervision, and promotion procedures operated by at least three different subunits: those in charge of teachers, those in charge of support and maintenance personnel, and those in charge of administrators.

General Beliefs

All of the superintendent behaviors described above occur in the context of and affect the superintendent's general beliefs about the role of the federal government within his district. When superintendents are asked to describe the federal presence in their district, they tend to use the same set of categories they employ in

describing their districts generally. Ninety-two percent of the
sample use one or more of three general dimensions in describing
salient features of their district—financial position, instructional
program, and personnel (both staff and student) characteristics and
issues. These same dimensions reappear when superintendents describe the federal presence. They view the single most prominent
feature of the federal presence as programmatic; 68 percent of the
superintendents identifying the first thing that comes to mind or the
issue of greatest concern or the most positive effect of federal intervention mention such programmatic issues as Title I or Votech
or mainstreaming. A second set of responses is directed toward
financial implications—both the benefits of programmatic funds and
the costs of unfunded directives. A third is directed toward equal
opportunity or student and staff rights (see Table 3.7).

TABLE 3.7

Dimensions Employed by Superintendents in Thinking about
Federal Regulations: Responses to Four Questions

Dimensions	Question			
	First[a]	Negative[b]	Positive[c]	Encroach[d]
Programmatic issues	18	8	15	11
Financial issues	4	9	3	1
Equal opportunity issues	8	9	12	8
Information-processing burdens	6	17	—	—
Local control issues	8	18	—	7

[a]What is the first thing that comes to your mind when you
think about the federal presence in your district?

[b]In general, what do you think are the most negative effects
of federal intervention in your school district?

[c]In general, what do you think are the most positive effects
of federal intervention in your school district?

[d]Have there ever been any instances when you believe the
federal government has encroached upon matters that really should
be decided locally?

Source: Compiled by the author.

The two remaining general categories that seem to represent important dimensions about federal regulations suggest how superintendents perceive the nature of the relationship between local school districts and the federal government. The "federal presence" in a local school district is believed to impose two sets of high-level administrative costs apart from any specific programmatic or civil rights benefits it might offer. These are information processing burdens and local control issues. The category of information processing burdens includes complaints about both the volume of paperwork and printed matter and the problems of interpreting it. Someone, including the superintendent in our districts, must route incoming directives to the proper recipient, must attend to the problematic ones personally by invoking his personal information system, and must coordinate the outflow of information from the district back to those who have requested it.

Complaints about encroachments on local control appear to stem from two sources. The first is a concern expressed by some superintendents that federal regulations ignore or distort local goals and priorities. Federal interventions often "forget the average child," as one superintendent put it, yet the average child comprises the bulk of the student population and parents of average children represent the bulk of the district's taxpayers. A second source is mismatches between local and federal procedures. Superintendents who complain about "lack of flexibility" on the part of the federal government seem mostly to mean that federal timetables or selection, accounting, or reporting procedures do not match those of the local district. This mismatch between local and federal procedures may importantly contribute to difficulties districts face with respect to compliance.

Superintendents seem to distinguish between the substantive dimensions of federal regulation (program, finance, and staff and student rights) and the administrative dimensions (information burdens and encroachments on local control). This distinction allows them to justify actions that would be perceived as administrative noncompliance in the name of substantive action. Or as many superintendents are frank to admit, "We cheat all the time—in the interest of the kids."

DISCUSSION

To summarize the findings about school superintendent involvement with federal regulation, let us return to the three processes comprising response to regulation. Compliance does not occur automatically with the issuance of a new directive; regulations must be noticed, interpreted, and attached to SOPs. We have seen that the superintendent plays a role in all three processes.

Superintendents exhibit noticing behaviors through both routine scanning of internal documents and conversations with colleagues. Many of them devote personal attention to some subset of incoming regulations. They also trigger noticing behavior on the part of their subordinates by routing many other incoming directives to them. Important questions for further study here should center on interdistrict variations in noticing behavior: What causes some districts to be more aware than others of equally applicable regulations? What are the determinants and consequences of superintendent decisions to attend personally to some regulations and not others? What are the consequences of different routing decisions?

Superintendents are quite involved in local interpretations of federal regulations. Indeed their role in interpretation and in attaching regulations to SOPs is probably more important than their role as scanners. In many cases, the federal intent is not at all clear to local personnel. Apparently one common uncertainty requiring interpretation concerns federal regulations that conflict with local administrative work. In these cases, the superintendent usually engages in both internal and external consultation to resolve the uncertainty. Even interpretive consultation, however, does not always lead to resolution of the uncertainty. Over half of the superintendents in our sample report that their resolution strategy for puzzling directives was either do nothing in the hope that the federal government would issue a clarification or simply plunge ahead in the face of contradictory interpretations. Further work on the topics of interpretation and attachment should explore the existing local building blocks available for responding to regulations: Under what circumstances will superintendents invoke each of the three different strategies for resolving ambiguous regulations? What administrative procedures are perceived to be particularly vulnerable to federal influence?

In addition to their involvement in responding to any particular regulation, superintendents over time develop a set of general beliefs about the role of the federal government within their districts. These beliefs then form the context within which specific response activities occur. Superintendents appear to distinguish between substantive and administrative dimensions of federal regulation and find the administrative dimensions of information-processing burdens and interference within local control to be particularly troublesome. Important questions for further study with respect to superintendent beliefs about federal regulations should emphasize the consequences of alternative ways of categorizing regulations. Some federal interventions, for example Title IX or Section 504, are intended to affect a broad spectrum of behaviors in school districts. If these interventions are interpreted narrowly (as a result of an implicit category scheme that says regulations are either curricular or financial or civil rights), then the district behaviors potentially affectable by them will be equally limited.

This study illustrates an organizational process view of response to regulation. It highlights the importance of superintendent actions and beliefs with respect to noticing and interpreting federal regulations and attaching them to district routines. It also raises as many questions as it answers. Furthermore, it points to the need for understanding the actions and beliefs of other school district personnel with respect to federal regulations. The findings in this study bear upon three metaphors commonly employed in understanding how organizations adapt to external conditions. They do not necessarily undermine any metaphor, but rather suggest interesting empirical complications for each. We consider in turn the metaphors of objective environment, intentionality, and power/dependence.

A major implication of the objective environment metaphor is that observers of a particular condition external to an organization would report exactly the same phenomenon as would participants within the organization (Thompson, 1967; Aiken and Hage, 1968). This metaphor underlies analyses of organization/environment relations that apply the same measures of environmental features to all members of a set of organizations (Lawrence and Lorsch, 1969). Our findings suggest that an organization's understanding of its environment is mediated by what becomes attended to, how objects of attention become interpreted, as well as whether and where responsibility for follow-through becomes assigned. For example, if school district personnel are unaware that a particular regulation exists, let alone applies to them, the common external distinction between mandatory and voluntary regulations becomes meaningless. Or if two districts interpret the same regulation in totally different ways, common external understandings of what a regulation "means" become problematic. Thus, even if a common signal is sent to a group of organizations, there is no guarantee that a common recognition and interpretation of that signal will follow (Weick, 1969, 1977).

A major implication of the intentionality metaphor is that intention guides action (Simon, 1976). That is, participants decide what should be done, then proceed to fulfill those normative decisions through means/ends analysis. Our findings suggest a counterassumption—people do what they know how to do. Information that comes by way of standard channels gains the most attention. Directives that fit most easily into existing interpretations of what is expected, why, and through which means will be most heeded. Requests for action that are consonant with current patterns of delegation and ongoing programs are most likely to be honored. Thus, intention is in many ways an outcome, not a cause, of attention, interpretation, and delegation processes (March and Olsen, 1976).

A major implication of the power/dependence metaphor is that the holders of power will be able to impose their wishes upon those dependent upon them—in proportion to the degree of power and dependence involved (Jacobs, 1974). A corollary to this assertion applies to compliance theories of regulation: the greater the penalties and rewards used to enforce a policy, the greater the degree of compliance that will be obtained (Salancik, 1979). Once again, if local school districts do not perceive themselves to be dependent upon the federal government, either financially or perhaps politically, then objective measures of penalties for noncompliance become problematic. Attention, interpretation, and delegation processes mediate participants' perceptions of and reactions toward power and dependence; and the intention to comply with a regulatory directive becomes conditioned through these three processes.

The organizational process framework and findings about school superintendent beliefs and behaviors presented in this chapter should suggest some new ways for thinking about relationships between local school districts and the federal government. Both those who write regulations and those who study school districts should be able to use this work. It suggests that actually issuing directives—often considered as the end point by residents of Washington, D.C.—should be considered instead as the starting point for multiple response sets determined by different local conditions. It also suggests, for organizational theorists, that in addition to the conventional "objectives" variables we tend to use to describe local conditions—such as size, structure, and resource mix—we also need to understand local systems of beliefs and interpretations. These are not easy tasks, but the theoretical and policy rewards for so doing can be substantial.

REFERENCES

Aiken, Michael, and Jerald Hage. 1968. "Organizational Interdependence and Interorganizational Structure." American Sociological Review 33:912-30.

Berger, Peter L., and Thomas Luckmann. 1966. The Social Construction of Reality. Garden City, N.Y.: Doubleday.

Berman, Paul, and Milbrey McLaughlin. 1975. Federal Programs
Supporting Educational Change. Vol. 4: The Findings in Review.
Santa Monica, Calif.: The Rand Corporation.

Birman, Beatrice. 1979. Case Studies of Overlap between Title I
and PL 94-142 Services for Handicapped Students. Menlo Park,
Calif.: Stanford Research Institute.

Crecine, John. 1969. Governmental Problem Solving. Chicago:
Rand McNally.

Cuban, Larry. 1976. Urban School Chiefs under Fire. Chicago:
University of Chicago Press.

Dolbeare, Kenneth, and Phillip Hammond. 1971. The School
Prayer Decisions. Chicago: University of Chicago Press.

Gerwin, Donald. 1969. "A Process Model of Budgeting in a Public
School System." Management Science 15:338-61.

Hannaway, Jane, and Lee Sproull. 1979. "Who's Running the Show?
Managerial Interaction across the District/School Boundary."
Administrator's Notebook. Vol. 27, No. 9. Chicago: University
of Chicago Midwest Administration Center.

Herriott, Robert, and Neal Gross. 1979. The Dynamics of Planned
Educational Change. Berkeley: McCutchan.

Jacobs, David. 1974. "Dependence and Vulnerability: An Exchange
Approach to the Control of Organizations." Administrative
Science Quarterly 19:45-59.

Lawrence, Paul, and Jay Lorsch. 1969. Organization and Environment. Homewood, Ill.: Irwin.

Mandler, George. 1964. "The Interruption of Behavior." In
Nebraska Symposium on Motivation, edited by David Levine.
Lincoln: University of Nebraska Press.

March, James, and Johan Olsen. 1976. Ambiguity and Choice in
Organizations. Bergen: Universitetsforlaget.

March, James, and Herbert Simon. 1958. Organizations. New
York: John Wiley.

Norman, Donald. 1976. Memory and Attention, 2d ed. New York: John Wiley.

Rosch, E., and B. B. Lloyd, eds. 1978. Cognition and Categorization. Hillsdale, N.J.: Erlbaum.

Salancik, Gerald. 1979. "Interorganizational Dependence and Responsiveness to Affirmative Action: The Case of Women and Defense Contractors." Academy of Management Journal 22: 375-94.

Simon, Herbert. 1976. Administrative Behavior, 3d ed. New York: The Free Press.

Sproull, Lee. In press, 1981a. "Beliefs in Organizations." In Handbook of Organization Design, Vol. 2, edited by Paul Nystrom and William Starbuck. London: Oxford University Press.

Sproull, Lee. In press, 1981b. "Response to Regulation: An Organizational Process Framework." Administration and Society.

Sproull, Lee, and Alice Young. 1980. "Response to Regulation: An Analysis from the Perspective of Local School Superintendents." Carnegie-Mellon University, Social Science Department Working Paper.

Thompson, James. 1967. Organizations in Action. New York: McGraw-Hill.

Weick, Karl. 1977. "Enactment Processes in Organizations." In New Directions in Organizational Behavior, edited by Barry Staw and Gerald Salancik. Chicago: St. Clair Press, pp. 267-300.

Weick, Karl. 1969. The Social Psychology of Organizing. Reading, Mass.: Addison Wesley.

Williams, Mary Frase, ed. 1978. "Government in the Classroom." Proceedings of the Academy of Political Science 33.

Wise, Arthur. 1979. Legislated Learning. Berkeley: University of California Press.

4

SCHOOL SYSTEMS AND REGULATORY MANDATES: A CASE STUDY OF THE IMPLEMENTATION OF THE EDUCATION FOR ALL HANDICAPPED CHILDREN ACT

Erwin C. Hargrove   Virginia Abernethy
Scarlett G. Graham   Joseph Cunningham
Leslie E. Ward   William K. Vaughn

If the implementation of a federal social program is to be intelligently managed, it should be considered as a long-term and increasingly subtle process. Broad and sweeping regulatory strategies are necessary in the beginning to secure gross compliance with rules. For example, PL 94-142 (the Education for All Handicapped Children Act) requires school systems to identify at least 12 percent of the school population as handicapped, to set up procedures for diagnosing handicaps, and to provide an Individualized Education Plan (IEP) for each child. Insofar as possible, they are to be moved from institutions of confinement to schools, and from special education schools to regular schools. They are to receive supportive services from other social agencies.[1]

It takes some time and energy for federal and state governments to see that local school systems develop such procedures. Much of that time is given to field inspections in an effort to identify obvious lapses. The offenders are directed to mend their ways and comply with the law. Such government reports seldom suggest how this is to be done, they just say, do it.[2] Emphasis is upon trouble spots. Advocates ride herd on the regulatory agency with little tolerance for it or for recalcitrance or intractability at the grass roots.[3]

The research on which this chapter is based was supported by the National Institute of Education. The authors wish to thank Richard Elmore of the University of Washington, James Marver of SRI International, Ronald Corwin of Ohio State University, Fritz Mulhauser of NIE, and Jerome Murphy, Susan Johnson, and Louis Gomes of the Harvard University Graduate School of Education for helpful criticism.

The first phase of implementation can last a long time. It is perhaps never fully complete because of the great variety of circumstances and institutional capacities in a large nation. Gradually, however, a stable federal regulatory pattern emerges in which formal rules are supplemented by informal norms. For example, Paul Hill argues that federal authority in the implementation of Title I of the Elementary and Secondary Education Act has been effective because informal networks of state and local officials have been created whose careers depend upon the implementation of the law.[4] Formal rules would not suffice.

Eventually a second, and more difficult, stage of implementation begins. Formal compliance with the law is assumed and people begin to ask about the most effective strategies for achieving intended goals. This is a more subtle and difficult matter than counting, labeling, and reporting back that a lot of human processing has taken place. A great many ambiguities about what is best for those being served develop.

For example, PL 94-142 calls for placing handicapped children in the "least restrictive environment" permitted by their condition. This could mean "mainstreaming" mildly handicapped children into regular classrooms. However, the law also calls for identification of handicaps not previously diagnosed and the placement of such children in special classes if thought necessary. On the one hand they are to be mainstreamed and on the other hand they are to be set apart. The seeming contradiction can be reconciled if one thinks of it as successive steps in which the problems of children are first diagnosed, they are then set apart, and eventually mainstreamed. Or, they could be kept in regular classes and given support services. Or, they could remain in special classes. These are difficult questions of professional judgment to which there are no obvious first answers. It all depends upon what is best for the individual child.

It is possible to look at two schools that have different strategies for implementing 94-142 and not be sure if one is doing a better job than the other, or if both are performing well but in different, equally effective ways, or if one or both are engaging in bodily movements that have little to do with the welfare of the children in question. For example, how can an outside observer possibly know whether the number of children who could have been "mainstreamed" into regular classes in a given school have been, in fact, so treated? It would take a lot of study.

Federal and state governments can never know enough about local school systems to make such judgments.[5] In the second stage of implementation federal and state strategies should seek to foster the local institutional capacities to cope with their difficult and subtle delivery questions. They must first learn what institutional capacities are necessary and then ask how national and state actions might strengthen such capabilities.

It is sometimes hard for federal officials to accept this approach. They are more comfortable with rules, regulations, and compliance monitoring.[6] If the program has a strong regulatory aspect, they are also likely to believe that compliance with regulations based on the law requires uniformity across jurisdictions. They are reluctant to permit the exercise of discretion and variation for fear of noncompliance. Uniform rules and regulations from above, however, may actually engender a kind of pro forma compliance at the grass roots in which people go through the motions, forms are filled, bodies accounted for, and there is a fear that invention and experimentation will be taken as failure to comply.

The hard question is whether it is possible to so develop local institutional capacities that compliance becomes merely the first step in the search for effective service delivery. Federal regulatory agencies may have to pursue first and second stage implementation strategies simultaneously, depending upon the degree of development of institutional capacities in different states and communities.[7]

In the early years of a program no one, at any level of agreement, is likely to know the institutional capacities required to carry out the programs at the grass roots. This is learned by experience. Therefore, it is extremely important for all concerned to be watching, learning, and revising regulatory strategies accordingly. If the first stage of implementation is a top down strategy in which rules are imposed on localities, the second stage is a bottom up strategy in which rules are revised to foster elements of strength in local settings.[8]

We reserve for the conclusion of this chapter the question of whether federal agencies can be realistically expected to contribute to the development of local capacities.

RESEARCH INTO THE FUTURE

This is a case study of the implementation of PL 94-142 in a metropolitan school system that was very close to compliance with 94-142 at the time the law was implemented. This was only in part because there had been a comparable state law. There has been a long tradition of excellent special education programs in the school system and a long-term policy of locating mildly handicapped children in regular schools.

This study anticipates the second stage of implementation, as described earlier, because it shows the school system to be coping with two crucial questions. First, what constitutes effective implementation of 94-142? Second, what institutional capacities are required to carry out effective implementation?

Our research asks the same questions although for a different purpose. In the 1978-79 school year, we studied the school system and 16 elementary schools to ask how implementation was defined and what strategies were developed for achieving it. School officials were at first concerned to develop procedures and then to ask about the quality of those procedures. For example, were IEPs really being used in teaching? They have also gradually changed administrative structures and strategies in response to experience.

More conceptual questions were asked. What are the right criteria and measures for the effective implementation of the law in schools? What institutional capacities and strategies are required to achieve implementation? The research questions are therefore, by implication, operational questions. The methodological difficulties of research in defining and measuring implementation have their parallel in the problems faced by school officials in creating implementation.

This research into the experience of one exemplary school system may be of value in the development of implementation strategies at all levels of government for what was referred to earlier as the second stage. The metropolitan school system that was studied has already reached that stage.

The slippery phrase "effective implementation" has been used without defining it. By this is simply meant modes of implementation that are thought to be effective in helping children. They point toward success but do not guarantee it. Concern with such questions is a step beyond compliance with regulations. One must wait for evaluation of the progress of children to assess effectiveness. One could define implementation as the actions that are required by the law, for example, 12 percent of children who were identified and served. This is fine but it falls short of a search for effectiveness, which is also part of implementation. The flesh and blood people doing the implementing may care about effectiveness and this influences their actions, but they are also not sure what it is. So implementation is at least analytically distinct from results.

We regard this case study as something more than an examination of 94-142 in one setting. We hope that it may contribute to the development of theory about the institutional capacities required for effective responsiveness to regulatory mandates in social programs in general. Part of such theory would be insights about federal and state strategies that nurture such capacities.[9]

The School System

The system is organized into three separate school districts, each with a superintendent. The director of schools and the school board set policy. The three superintendents administer the schools. The functions of the central office under the director are to carry out professional development, technical assistance, and systemwide housekeeping, including financial management, personnel appointments, and transportation.

The department of special education is a staff office under the director of schools. Students in special education who are located in regular schools are the formal responsibility of the principals and their superintendents. The decisions about sending particular handicapped students to such schools or about the creation of classes for the handicapped within regular schools are shared between the central special education staff and the district office. In all cases, the line authority rests with the district.

We began our research with the exploration of authority patterns within this organizational web in order to discover how decisions about handicapped children were made. Such decisions are taken with reference to individual schools. Therefore, the second research step was to study 16 schools in order to understand the linkages with the larger system of authority and the factors within those schools that might influence outcomes. Nine elementary schools were chosen by stratified random sampling from the three districts. Four additional case study schools were chosen for specific reasons, and subsequently three more case study schools were added.

Historically the school system has been hospitable to special education. The director of schools initiated the development of a strong program during the 1960s. The growing staff was drawn in large part from the nationally prestigious department of special education of a local college of education. Faculty members have also been available for expert consultation.

The chief innovation of the special education division has been the resource room program. A special education teacher provides tutorial and small group instruction for both handicapped and "gifted" students in a resource room for a few hours each week. There are 58 such classes in the 90 elementary schools.

In recent years there has been a policy of shifting mildly handicapped children from self-contained classes for the handicapped to regular classes with other support services. About 80 percent of learning disabled (LD) children are in regular elementary and secondary classrooms with support services. Most of the remaining 20 percent are in regular schools in special classes. About

70 percent of the educable mentally retarded (EMR) are in special classes in elementary and secondary schools and most of the rest are in regular classes. Fifty-four percent of the deaf and hearing impaired children were in regular classes in 1978-79. Ninety-three percent of the visually impaired are in regular classes with support services.

These figures indicate that almost all of the mildly handicapped children (LD and EMR) are in regular schools. The special schools are reserved for the moderately and severely handicapped. Physically handicapped children are placed in regular schools with greater or less difficulty depending upon the disability.[10]

In 1972 the state legislature passed a law requiring the provision of a free appropriate public education to all handicapped children ages 4 to 21. The state law required that children be educated in regular classrooms to the maximum extent possible and armed parents with due process rights. However, the legislature failed to provide sufficient funds for the law to be implemented to any degree until an adverse court decision in 1974.

The historical pattern suggests that the Metro school system began to develop new special education policies quite independently of the stimulus of state or federal law. However, the passage of PL 94-142 did require some adaptations.

Top school administrators saw implementation as a training and technical assistance task. Principals and teachers had to be informed and persuaded that PL 94-142 could and should be acted upon as a part of their professional duties. The chief obstacles to implementation were foreseen as attitudes and money. It was thought that discussion was the best way to overcome fear and resistance and therefore workshops for all principals were conducted. Considerable resentment was expressed that neither federal nor state funds would fully cover meeting the requirements of the law. Leaving aside limitations on funds, top administrators foresaw no strong obstacles to implementation. They did not think in terms of providing incentives or involving sanctions as tools of persuasion. Education and professionalism would suffice.

During 1978-79 the five professionals in the central office of special education gave their primary attention to putting an IEP system in place in response to PL 94-142. The three special education consultants in the respective district offices were responsible for conducting the "staffings," which were meetings of a psychologist, teachers, and parents to consider the appropriate placement for a child who had been referred for special treatment. This multidisciplinary (M) team makes recommendations for the placement of each child to the central office where the actual decision is made.

There was some tension between the M teams and the central office because placements did not always match recommendations. Central administrators acknowledged this but pleaded the constraints of space, staff, and transportation, all of which cost money.

The salient problem was to reduce the long waiting list and get everyone placed. This was achieved in the spring of 1979. The general "staffing" procedures were also in place and working smoothly.

The distribution of responsibility between the central special education office and the three districts in regard to the implementation of special education policy has created an ambiguity about final responsibility. The director of schools has delegated responsibility to the three district superintendents, who rely on their directors of elementary education to work with school principals on implementation. However, this is only one of many tasks facing principals and elementary education directors. The primary concern expressed by the district office to principals therefore has been that each school comply with the formal requirements of the law, that is, identification of students with needs, staffings, and IEPs.

Neither the district superintendents nor the directors of elementary education hace developed measures for assessing the performance of schools on 94-142. Rather, success in regard to this policy is assumed to be a derivative of an implicit, but strongly held, model of a "good school." This is a school in which the principal exercises effective authority with teachers, there are good feelings and relationships among teachers, and there is a strong commitment by principal and teachers to the goal of individualization in education. We discern a congruence in the minds of administrators between a certain "progressive" model of education and the objectives of 94-142.

District officials look to the central special education staff for assistance with the technical problem of appropriate placement of children and the design of programs. The great bulk of the time of the central special education staff is spent in the schools working with special and regular teachers on the problems of particular children.

There have been no plans at the top or at the district level for monitoring the implementation of 94-142 in the schools or for evaluating the effects of change on children. The reporting requirements of the U.S. Bureau of Education for the Handicapped (BEH) are perceived as a mechanical exercise of compiling data about services. There is no plan to break such data down by schools to provide comparative snapshots of implementation across time. Monitoring and assessment were delegated to the districts.

However, the central office of special education has all the data necessary for a comparative overview, none of which is used for analytical purposes.

The very general orientation of the districts and the technical and specific approach of special education staff give great latitude to principals and teachers in regard to implementation. This is in part because of the ambiguity of administrative responsibility. It is also due to the fact that neither district nor special education officials think in terms of general criteria of evaluation by which schools might be compared and assessed. Indeed, it was argued that schools are unique and cannot be compared.

CRITERIA OF IMPLEMENTATION

Criteria and measures for the effective implementation of this law by schools are not obvious to even the most experienced eye once one goes beyond mechanical compliance. If a group engaged in field research finds it difficult to develop unambiguous criteria and measures, imagine the quandary of federal, state, and local administrators who must enforce and monitor implementation.

The research for this study focused on the central provisions of the law:

Identify all handicapped children in a given jurisdiction who are in need of special educational services and develop and implement educational plans for them.

Place all handicapped children in the educational setting that provides "the least restrictive environment" that their handicap will permit. (This is sometimes referred to as "mainstreaming" handicapped children by installing them in regular schools, perhaps even regular classrooms. However, many graduated combinations of the regular classrooms with special education, and within special education alone, are possible.)

Each handicapped child is to have an Individualized Education Program prepared for him or her by a team of teachers and specialists in consultation with parents. (This provision has legal teeth in that parents have the right to a hearing on the plan for their child and the recourse of legal action in case of dissatisfaction.)

We did not examine actions to move children from custodial institutions to special schools. Nor did we look at the five special education schools. Our interest was in the disposition of mentally and physically handicapped children in the regular schools.

CRITERIA AND MEASURES OF IMPLEMENTATION
FOR INDIVIDUAL SCHOOLS

The study searched for dependent variables, that is, definitions and measures of implementation that could be matched to school characteristics as independent variables. It is important not to jumble the two together because, of course, dependent variables are also, to some extent, school characteristics. This is because one is describing outputs—what schools do—rather than outcomes— the results of what they do.

Child Find

In ordinary schools the place for identifying children with handicaps is the regular classroom. The process of "referral" identifies candidates for help. Referral may be initiated by teachers, parents, a principal, or an outside agency. A psychological diagnosis then determines whether there should be a "staffing" in which a professional team meets with the parents to develop an appropriate placement for the child.

There are five possible outcomes from a referral:

□ Return of the child to the classroom with the conclusion that the referral was inappropriate.

□ Return of the child to the classroom with a diagnosis to help the teacher to serve the child.

□ Return of the child to the classroom with the assignment of special help, perhaps from a resource teacher or some other specialist.

□ Assignment of the child to a special education class in that or another school.

□ Return of the child to the regular classroom with no special help, when the child needs help.

All of these options except the last are compatible with the law, which asks that handicapped children receive the services they need. However, it is not obvious from observation which of the first four choices is best for any given child or succession of children.

A school that refers a large number of children for testing may be seeking to get rid of them because they are handicapped. Or, the teachers may be very alert to the needs of children. One cannot determine which is the case from referral rates alone. Such figures must be interpreted by knowledge of particular schools. For example, one school with a very low referral rate might appear from the figures to be disregarding the law, but a close look reveals that special education and other supportive staff are working with children who have problems without a formal referral and staffing process. They never leave the mainstream. Ranking by scoring would be misleading. The principal in question so resists the idea of stigmatizing through labeling that referring is discouraged and diagnoses are informal.

The referral rates of schools correspond, for the most part, with knowledge about the schools derived from interviews. All teachers were surveyed. A sample of regular and special teachers in each school was interviewed personally. All principals were interviewed at least twice. External views of each school were derived from directors of elementary education for each of the three districts, superintendents, school psychologists, central and district special education staffs, and representatives of advocate groups. A profile of each school was fashioned from these interviews. The numerical measures developed were explained by the profiles.

The referral level of a school is defined as the percentage of the total school population recommended for psychological or other diagnostic evaluation in a given academic year. Since there is no established standard for gauging a reasonable referral rate, a standard based upon the median referral rate for the 16 schools was developed.

The median referral level for the 16 schools is 5.2 percent of the total population of the school. This figure is almost identical to the average referral rate for all elementary schools in the total system being studied.* All of the schools in the study whose referral levels come very close to this average figure are given a score of 2 for appropriate child find. Two schools are substantially below the 5.2 percent figure, but because they keep and serve many special children in regular classes without referrals, they are given the high score. The two schools that deviate from the pattern were chosen because they are atypical in their approach to serving handicapped children and are therefore not treated as a part of the random sample.

Two schools have referral levels that are midway between the median level (5.2 percent) and the highest level (11.0 percent) and

---

*It is not known whether this single system average is typical of, higher than, or lower than other systems. However, the system under study does provide special education services to 14 percent of its school-age population, 2 percent above what BEH has suggested is the likely level of need nationally.

are given scores of 1 because of the high but not absurdly high referral levels. Qualitative information on both of these schools suggests that some overreferral is indicated in both cases.

The four schools whose referral rates are markedly higher than the median are given scores of 0, because overreferral is strongly indicated from qualitative information.

It would be a mistake for a school administrator to use the 5.2 median figure as the sole basis for judgment about school performance without further personal knowledge. A suspicious figure should be used as a warning sign to investigate. It would also be a mistake to impose a 5.2 requirement on all schools without further knowledge of particular situations.

Least Restrictive Environment (LRE)

The law does not require the placement of handicapped children in regular classrooms. Such mainstreaming is the final step in a series of legitimate moves, such as from an institution to a special school and from a special school to a self-contained special class in a regular school.

The ambiguity of mainstreaming is confusing. Children are to be referred out of regular classes, when necessary, but also moved in, when possible. Judgments about the appropriateness of such actions in any school are difficult. The law clearly encourages the placement of the maximum possible number of children in regular classes, even if they are enrolled in special classes; but how is one to know the "optimal" number of possibilities in a given school? These are professional judgments and such judgments vary widely among teachers and principals. One could ideally match schools with similar student populations to compare levels of mainstreaming, but no two schools are exactly comparable in that regard.

We can look for the presence or absence of a regular movement of children from self-contained to regular classes within a given school. A low level may reveal a reluctance to mainstream and a high level may indicate enthusiasm, but many records will be mixed and unclear, especially with such small numbers.

The interviews told us a great deal about interest in and willingness to mainstream handicapped children within each school. This was the primary basis for the ranking judgments. For example, two very similar schools with long histories of high academic standards have changed markedly in the demographic characteristics of the students since bussing began. Slightly less than half of the students in each school are minority children. One of the schools staffs out low-performing handicapped students (EMRs) and keeps the LD students in self-contained classes for the most part. The other keeps most of its handicapped students after staffings and mainstreams a greater proportion of students.

The quantitative measures developed as indexes for LRE were roughly congruent with such observations. There were two measures: All 16 schools were compared on staffing levels; then the five schools with only resource rooms and no self-contained classes were dropped and the remaining 11 were compared on the numbers of children who were mainstreamed. The first score is assigned to all schools and is assigned on the basis of the staffing level for each school, defined as the percentage of total population staffed to self-contained special education classes in or out of the school. The higher the level of such staffings the less the likelihood that the school is making an effort to serve mildly handicapped children in regular classes before resorting to self-contained placement. Use of regular classrooms with support services to serve children is one variety of least restrictive environment as described by 94-142.

The median staffing level for the 16 schools is 2.2 percent. All schools below that level or very near that level are assigned a score of 2 on this measure, with the exception of one school in which there is evidence that children are being kept in the mainstream without appropriate support services. The failure to provide needed services is as much a violation of LRE as the over-provision of self-contained services.

As in the case of measure no. 1, two schools are about midway between the median level and the highest level (5.5 percent) and are therefore assigned a score of 1. Three schools are given a score of 0 because of their markedly high staffing levels.

The second LRE score is applied only to those schools housing self-contained special education classes. This score is given on the basis of reported degrees of mainstreaming from special education classes in each school, defined as the number of children who go out of the self-contained class into the mainstream for some part of the school day. (Reports of mainstreaming for physical education [PE] and lunch are not included as a basis for this score, since all self-contained teachers report mainstreaming for PE and lunch except some of those at one school.) Schools in which high numbers of the total self-contained special education population were reported to be mainstreamed for some part of the day received a score of 2 on this item. Schools who reported some mainstreaming, but less than might be expected, given everything else we learned about them, were given a score of 1. Schools in which no appreciable mainstreaming was reported received a score of 0. This mark was justified by other knowledge about how the school functioned.

Quality of the Process of Individual Placements

If the psychologist judges that a child needs special help the question is presented to a multidisciplinary team that consists of the district special education consultant, the psychologist, regular and special teachers from the child's school or the principal, and the child's parents. A conclusion is developed about the appropriate services to be given the child. Because all staffings are the responsibility of the districts, it is only that part of the process that takes place within individual schools—that is, everything up to and including the decision to go to a staffing—that can be used to compare individual schools.

The comparative analysis of the schools suggested four analytic components that could be used to assess the general quality of this portion of the total process from school to school. These components reflect the process standards that are implied by 94-142. The components are: a high number of participants in the in-school process, a high degree of communication among participants in the process, multiple opportunities for parents to participate in the process, and a clear-cut search for service options other than special education within the school before a staffing is considered. The first three components are highly correlated but do not in fact collapse in every case. They are therefore maintained as separate components in order to give maximum range to the empirical variations among our schools.

Some elaboration of the meanings of the four components is desirable. The first, a high number of participants in the process, suggests that the greatest amount of available data on a child is being brought to bear upon the process leading to a decision as to whether or not this child should receive self-contained services. In schools where a high number of participants are indicated, school personnel other than the referring teacher, the principal, and the psychologist, such as a resource room teacher or other special education teacher, are usually included in the process. What is more, parents are likely to be used as a source of information about the child, not just as the granters of permission for the process to take place.

The second component is related to the first but is nevertheless distinct: a high degree of communication among participants in the process. This is indicated when the evidence suggests that participants in the process are engaged in a dialogue, characterized by a reciprocal pattern of communication rather than in a sequential pattern in which the various participants appear to have their say at distinct points in the process and then drop out altogether.

The law requires that parental permission be given before a child undergoes evaluation. Parents must also be informed of the evaluation results and give consent for the child to be sent to a staffing for self-contained placement. These minimal points of parental participation are insufficient to receive a high score on the multiple opportunities for parental participation component of this measure. Only those schools in which the evidence suggests that parents are substantially involved in the process at points before a final decision is reached receive credit for this item.

The fourth component, a clear-cut search for service options within the school, is important because some schools are much more inclined to search for service options within the school before considering a self-contained placement for a child. Objectively, some of our schools have considerably more resources and service options than other schools, but the easy availability of program options does not control performance on this item. Several schools, some with greater resources, some with fewer resources, clearly pursue available options before separation of the child is considered.

The point immediately preceding a formal referral is chosen as the beginning of the process because a prereferral search for service options and prereferral screening are quite visible in some schools. The process ends at the point at which a final decision is made as to whether or not a child should go to staffing for a self-contained placement. After that point, the districts handle the process until a staffing decision is formally proposed. Once the staffing decision is final, the central system completes the process by assigning a placement purportedly based upon the staffing recommendation.

The bases upon which scores reflecting the quality of this process at the school level were determined derived from a comparative analysis of interviews with school psychologists, principals, VE teachers, and regular and special teachers.

The schools ranking high on all components of this measure receive a score of 2. Those schools ranking high on only one or two of these components are given a score of 1. Those schools ranking low on these components are given a score of 0. Table 4.1 ranks the 16 schools according to the study's criteria and judgments. The numerical rankings reflect both quantitative data and qualitative judgments with the latter controlling in every case.

TABLE 4.1

PL 94-142 Performance, 1978-79

Performance		Child Find	LRE-1	LRE-2	Process	Total
High	A*	2	2	—	2	6
	B*†	2	2	—	2	6
	C*	2	2	—	2	6
	D[a]	2	2	2	2	8
	E†	2	2	2	2	8
	F[b]	2	2	1	2	7
	G†	2	2	2	2	8
Middle	H*	2	1	—	1	4
	I*	1	1	—	1	3
	J	2	2	0	1	5
	K	1	1	1	1	4
	L	2	0	0	1	3
Low	M	0	0	1	1	2
	N	0	0	2	0	2
	O[c]	0	2	0	0	2
	P[d]	0	0	1	1	2

*Highest possible total score is 6, since lack of special education classes makes LRE-2 inapplicable.

†These schools were selected for study because they are widely regarded as good schools with outstanding principals. Two of the three schools are viewed as having atypical approaches to serving handicapped children (schools E and G). For these reasons, it is highly likely that high performers are overrepresented in this sample as compared to their actual proportion of the population of schools in the system.

[a]Chosen because it is the only middle school in the system. The remainder of schools in the system follow the traditional elementary, junior high, high school pattern.

[b]Chosen because it houses one of two classes in the public school system for the trainable mentally retarded (TMR) in a regular elementary school. All other TMR classes are housed in special schools.

[c]Chosen because almost half of the school's population is handicapped.

[d]Chosen because it is a very small school as compared to most other elementary schools in the system. It also has a sizable special education population.

Source: Compiled by the authors.

The high-performing schools attempted to keep handicapped children in the school, to mainstream whenever possible, and there was no gross pattern of overreferral through fear or disdain or underreferral through neglect. Processes of consultation, among professionals and with parents, were highly collegial. The schools in the middle group tended to overrefer and send children away, showed limited interest in mainstreaming, and carried out staffing processes somewhat mechanically. The low performers were characterized by extreme patterns of under- or overreferral, virtually no interest in mainstreaming, and a very routine approach to staffing.

SCHOOL CHARACTERISTICS

Table 4.2 lists the independent variables one associates with the performance of schools. Information about these characteristics was developed through the survey and intereviewing process described earlier. The dimensions in Table 4.2 were explored through all these avenues, but they were sharpened considerably as a result of the research. It was the intention of the study to develop a composite picture of the authority structure of each school to see if this would be the key to the structuring and flow of all students, including the handicapped. The characterizations of schools describe behavior in general, not just actions in regard to 94-142.

TABLE 4.2

Independent Variables to Explain Differences in the
Performance of Schools on PL 94-142

The leadership style of principals
    Authoritative democrat
    Risk avoidant but orderly manager
    Authoritarian
    Laissez-faire
Relations among teachers
    Frequent sharing of tasks
    Separated and work alone
Programmatic structure
    Range of curricular options from few to many
    Range of support services from few to many

Source: Compiled by the authors.

Sixteen elementary schools were selected for study. Nine of the schools were chosen by a stratified random sample from the 91 elementary schools after all schools without special education programs were eliminated. The basis of stratification was the imputed authority style of the principal based upon a panel of informants. Three schools were chosen from each district. An additional four case study schools were selected because of specific characteristics, that is, model size, a middle school, a school with a high percentage of special education students, and one of two regular schools with trainable mentally retarded students. We subsequently added three schools that were said by a panel of informants to have exemplary principals.

It might be possible to disaggregate these indexes and score them quantitatively for the ranking of schools as was done with performance measures. However, school authority patterns are dynamic configurations that are not easily disaggregated. As a result we attempted to characterize each school through a profile based upon all available information. Dominant patterns and tendencies have been described.

The study infers that these are the important things about schools for the implementation of 94-142. This cannot be proven; our analysis is one of descriptive plausibility. We began with the idea that the leadership styles of principals might significantly affect the ways teachers interrelate with each other and work with students. We are aware of the ambiguity in the literature on leadership about whether leaders create authority patterns in others or adapt their styles to conform to established patterns. Therefore, the question was left open. In any case the identification of an authority pattern need not presume causation.

The initial conceptions of leadership styles were derived from the work of Lewin, Lippitt, and White as interpreted for political scientists by Sidney Verba.[11] Three possible "ideal types" of principals were conceived:

Democratic: Policies are developed through group discussion guided by the leader. Group members have latitude to show initiative in carrying out tasks.

Authoritarian: The leader determines policy and dictates the steps for implementation so that discretion by group members is limited.

Laissez-faire: There is minimal leader participation in a process of freedom of individual and group decisions. The leader takes part only when asked.

The experimental research on which these concepts are based has indicated that "democratic" leadership will produce more member satisfaction, more enthusiasm for the work, work of higher quality, and as much productivity as authoritarian leadership.[12] Authoritarian leadership may get a task done, but the group members neither internalize goals nor make suggestions to improve performance in the way that characterizes democratically led groups. The laissez-faire leader obtains the least on any of these dimensions from the group.[13]

The "participation hypothesis" asserts that democratically led groups are more likely to be able to incorporate change into their activity because, through discussion, they appropriate new goals as their own.[14] This idea matches findings about innovations in school curricula that relate the implementation of new curricula to participatory processes in which teachers incorporate new approaches into new routines.[15]

However, research has uncovered another variation in democratic leadership. Leaders may guide, persuade, and perhaps manipulate group opinion under the guise of participation. This may be due to the unwillingness of group members to accept full responsibility. It is also because of the difficulty of achieving consensus where opinion is divided. Therefore, the democratic leader may have to be "authoritative." Such leadership often gives the illusion of full participation even though the group is being guided in a predetermined direction. So long as the illusion is believed, the positive benefits that follow from the "participation hypothesis" accrue.[16]

Verba points out, and the research confirms, that it is extremely difficult to distinguish between democratic leadership that guides and presents choices in an open manner and that which manipulates. In any case, such leadership departs from the pure experimental model in which the group guides the leader more than or as much as it is guided.

We found no examples of this pure model in our schools. We did find, among teachers, a strong and dominant norm for what we call the "authoritative democrat."[17] Our surveys of and interviews with teachers revealed that they expect strength in principals because they want to be protected—from parents, advocate groups, sometimes from students, and from higher administrators; but they also want a principal who listens and respects their views. Such a leadership style contains elements of both persuasion and manipulation, as our studies show, and we have not attempted to disentangle these qualities.

We found few examples of the pure authoritarian type but did discover a type of principal who combines some aspects of authoritarian and laissez-faire traits. This is the leader who runs a tight ship, emphasizes order and stability, and prefers predictable routine over risk and innovation. Again, this nuance emerges from the character of schools and the desire for order and regularity. Most of the pure authoritarians seem to have disappeared.

For the same reason, the pure laissez-faire leader is rare. Principals must do more than ignore problems; but we did find some who seemed to do as little as possible.

In short, we began with the three experimentally developed types and revised them in response to the descriptive material developed by our research.

The other independent variables, relations among teachers and programmatic structure, were subjects for study from the beginning. We did not foresee any necessary relationships between them. However, we did think it likely that a principal with a "democratic" style would be found in schools with a high degree of collegiality among teachers.

Our inquiries pursued a number of other independent variables that did not prove to be important. The greatest surprise was to discover that advocate groups and parents have not been highly visible or active. Their efforts have focused on grievances in regard to individual children, and matters of general school performance and educational policy have been passed by.

HIGH-PERFORMING SCHOOLS

Seven schools fell into this category by our measures. In four the principals are clearly authoritative democrats. In all of these schools there is considerable collaboration among teachers. The four schools with principals who are authoritative democrats were chosen by methods other than that which selected the original sample of nine. One was chosen as a case study school because it had classes for trainable mentally retarded children. The other three schools were subsequently chosen in an effort to find principals who were regarded as exemplary by knowledgeable informants. A reputational method was used; criteria were not invoked to elicit responses. This suggests that these four high-performing schools are atypical of the school system in having "authoritative democrats" as principals and perhaps in the high performance on 94-142.

The other three schools share one characteristic. For different historical reasons, a high degree of common commitment to a mission has come to be shared by most of the teachers in each school. One of the principals was a good facilitator of this situation and the other two were neutral. In none of the cases was the principal a vital factor.

A variety of programmatic options is present in each of these schools. This appears to be a manifestation of the belief that all children, including the handicapped, should receive as individual a program as possible. The contrasting emphasis is upon standardization, whether toward a median or toward high academic achievement. The value we call emphasis upon individual development is too subtle to be set aside as a separate independent variable. Rather, it emerges from the words of principals and teachers. One cannot say whether it is a cause of collegiality or a manifestation of it.

The four principals whom we call "authoritative democrats" are all strong leaders in regard to 94-142 and other educational areas. One is the principal of an "open" school which prides itself on great flexibility in meeting the needs of individual children. Another is regarded as an exemplary principal because she has created a unified school in which half the students have disadvantaged backgrounds and the other half are children of university faculty members or their professional counterparts. The school offers a wide variety of programs. The other two principals see themselves as educational leaders and spend considerable time in classrooms with teachers. They are continually encouraging curricular experimentation.

These four leaders appear to both persuade and manipulate. Their teachers strongly support them and the excitement they generate. One gets the clear impression from conversations with teachers that these principals get what they want by planting ideas and building support for them—in short, through self-conscious strategies of leadership. There's no sense of the principal presiding over a town meeting of teachers. Each of these principals articulates a clear and strong sense of direction to teachers but they also listen and adapt to the ideas of others.

Handicapped children are made to feel at home in these schools because they are included in as many programs as possible. Every effort is made to keep them in regular classrooms, with support services, rather than refer them to special education. Mainstreaming from self-contained special education classes is encouraged. A commitment by principals and teachers to 94-142 is simply a manifestation of an individualized approach to education. The authority structures of these schools facilitate such an approach.

The principals of the other three schools were not described as strong leaders. A new middle school (grades 5 through 8) had been created in a previously black high school. White students are bussed. The district elementary director had worked intensively with the principal and teachers to ensure a unified faculty. For example, the teachers in each grade form a team that plans curriculum and activities. The special education teachers belong to these teams. The teachers registered a higher sense of shared responsibility for special students than for any other school. There was a strong leader in the wings in the form of the district director of elementary education who had conceived the curricular structure. The principal was regarded as an effective facilitator of these collegial arrangements.

The other two schools serve, respectively, a heavily disadvantaged population, white and black, and a lower-middle-class population. In both cases, for reasons which we do not understand, the teachers in these schools cooperate with each other a great deal. Special students are kept in regular classes whenever possible with help from support services. In the school with the large disadvantaged population, special education is only one of many services such as Title I, a full-time social worker, and several teacher's aides. The two principals were helpful facilitators but not dynamic leaders.

If more illustrative detail could be provided, the relationship between the free and open atmosphere of these schools and the flexible treatment of handicapped children would be clear.

PERFORMANCE IN A MIDDLE RANGE

Four of these schools are so alike that they can be characterized as if they were one school. Their principals emphasize order, regularity, control, and avoidance of risk. They are good managers who are less attentive to educational leadership than the "authoritative democrats." There is no evidence of efforts by these principals to foster general collegiality or specific sharing of tasks among teachers.

The general ethic in these schools is one of self-contained classrooms, whether special or regular, in which teachers have autonomy. The principals make important decisions without consultation. Flexible sharing relationships among teachers are not encouraged.

Each school has unique characteristics. One is so large that day-to-day management consumes the principal. The other three have transient and disadvantaged populations and face difficult educational tasks. Whereas some of the schools in our higher group have seen this as an opportunity, the principals in the second group are either passive and discouraged, in one case, or tightly in control to ensure order, in the other two cases.

In these schools standardization seems to be preferred to individualization, although this is difficult to document; however, these are perfectly adequate schools in which there is order and regularity. All are in pro forma compliance with 94-142, but none have stirred themselves to invent creative responses to that task as have our high-performing schools.

The fifth school stands alone. The principal is highly regarded as creative and appears to be an "authoritative democrat." However, there was resistance to taking self-contained special education classes in the building because of the strong academic values the principal and teachers share. Handicapped students would change the character of the school.

LOW PERFORMERS

There are only a few ways to succeed but there are many ways to fail. In one school the principal has a laissez-faire leadership style, the teachers do not collaborate, and opportunities for sharing and inventing are limited. In another school the principal is strongly committed to affective learning, opposed to labeling children, and is determined to create flexible programs for all children. However, the principal's style of leadership is arbitrary and inconsistent and there is so little disciplining of students that the school is in constant turmoil.

The principal of the third school is close to being an authoritarian—for example, the teachers must sign in and out. This principal does not believe that mainstreaming is part of the new law and a large number of children are referred out of the school through staffings.

The fourth school is one of the most interesting. By traditional standards it would be regarded as an excellent school. It has a long tradition of high academic standards and achievement scores are high. The principal is a strong and effective but open person. However, both principal and teachers are chiefly interested in having only the most mildly handicapped children in the school. There are several self-contained classes for those with learning disabilities. Few of these students are ever in regular classes. The principal believes that a learning disability requires intensive work and that, once corrected, the student should go into regular classes. The school strongly stresses cognitive achievement, even with LD children. The performance of this school suggests that 94-142 is not congruent with a traditional academic orientation. The high-performing schools could be characterized as more open to affective learning and individualization than to the objective standards of achievement stressed in this traditional school.

We have no method with such a small sample of assessing the relative importance of skillful leadership, collegial relations among teachers, and richness of programmatic alternatives for the positive treatment that handicapped children receive. Indeed, our findings suggest that these factors are often found together and certainly reinforce each other.

It may be safe to infer that a dynamic principal can infuse a school with new energy more quickly and easily than is the case with the introduction of new teachers or a new curricular structure. This is the belief of central and district administrators. They work with and rely on principals to improve schools. However, creative leaders are in short supply. Emphasis upon leadership in administration may cause a neglect of structural factors, such as curricular and teaching patterns, wich might facilitate broader implementation of systemwide goals.

In any event, uncertainty about the prerequisites of high performance makes it more difficult for central and district administrators to determine the most effective instruments for policy implementation.

The district directors of elementary education and the central special education staff see these 16 schools much as we do. The elementary directors work closely with principals, some of whom they think are less than adequate. We saw evidence of improvement in performance on 94-142 in three schools in 1979-80 as a result of such interventions. Such actions, however, are ad hoc, time consuming, and directed to individual schools.

The central special education staff work with schools primarily in regard to the problems of individual teachers and students. They have not worked closely with the elementary directors in assessments of individual schools.

Both groups deny the value of a standardized instrument to evaluate performance by which schools might be compared. This fact, plus the limited coordination between special and regular administrators, helps explain the great variation in school performance.

The overall picture that emerges is one of balance between hierarchy and discretion. Educational hierarchies are so loosely coupled that there is great discretion at each descending level. Goals are too vague to be easily operationalized so that discretion prevails. Leadership is by persuasion and indirection and higher administration must guide principals in most cases. Orders will not produce the desired results.

PRESCRIPTIONS

Before we return to the question of a more subtle federal role, we must ask what local implementation capacities and strategies a federal role might promote. The following suggestions as to what the Metro school department should do are perhaps generally applicable to school systems in the second stage of implementation:

District superintendents, and their staffs, plus the central special education staff, should develop a coherent implementation strategy. The chief ingredient would be regular conversations between representatives of each group to consider all the schools in each district as schools, that is, as whole entities. The task would be to identify strengths and deficiencies in performance on 94-142 and develop ways to strengthen school capacities.

Schools should be accorded different treatment depending on performance levels. Outstanding principals can be left alone but they are few and the selection of better principals is a long-term proposition that cannot be used as the key to improvement of a program. Every conceivable lever that can be used should be used. Place a particular special education teacher who knows how to lead regular teachers in a school requiring such leadership. Hold continuous workshops in schools in which teachers are not sharing tasks but could be brought together. Reward teachers who mainstream with aides if money permits.

Quantitative indexes are useful as benchmarks for success and as warning signs for lapses but they should be used sparingly. If they are invoked by administrators as quotas to be met, implementation will become mechanical and the game will have been lost.

The research office should track the performance of handicapped children over time to see if there is any relationship between high-performing schools, or implementation measures, and changes in children. It is possible that factors important for implementation, of the kind discussed here, are not the variables that explain improved performance of children. Simple variables affecting teaching, such as extra education for regular teachers, may be more important.

Use 94-142 as a fulcrum for moving more schools into the high-performing category in regard to education in general. Trends may be breaking down the isolation of teachers in self-contained classrooms and promoting support for team teaching, collective participation in educational planning, and greater educational leadership by principals. Both Title I or Elementary and Secondary Education Act (ESEA) and 94-142 are pushing in this direction.[18] Teachers are insecure about these trends and will need help.

Finally, to be realistic, it will take a long time and more than a handful of committed people to change a large percentage of 90 elementary schools, not to mention junior high and high schools.

If we assume that it would be desirable to engender practices of this kind in all school systems, but also recognize what a difficult and slow effort it will be, is there a realistic federal supportive role? We will first argue against such an idea and then qualify the argument:

The authority relationships within school systems that we regard as desirable are too intangible and subtle to be influenced by federal rules.

A federal regulatory role to ensure gross patterns of local compliance is realistic and no more should be asked.

Federal law and regulations should compensate for the weaknesses of national government by empowering local supporters of the law to demand performance from school systems. For example, the parents of handicapped children have legal standing in 94-142. Power is put at the bottom where it can be used.

It is not clear that factors favorable to implementation are the crucial factors for good teaching and improvement. A lot of effort could be wasted in blind alleys. It might be better to wait for evaluation findings to achieve a better economy of effort.

These are strong arguments. However, the federal government is a presence in the situation. There is a danger that if it confines itself to strictly regulatory activities, damage to local institution building may be done and opportunities missed.

Awareness of the need to develop local institutional capacities may make federal officials more aware of cross-currents caused by their own actions. For example, there are pressures to centralize decisions about the placement of handicapped children in some school systems in the belief that central control may avert lawsuits and the complaints of unions about differential practices in schools.[19] Regulatory goals, such as giving parents legal standing, may conflict with service delivery goals, which call for decentralization of decisions. Federal officials must find ways to plow both furrows at once.

As more is learned over time about the relation between implementation capacities and strategies and the welfare of children it may be possible for federal policy to strengthen these linkages. For example, the comparative efficacy of outside consultants, in-service training, and workshops for teachers on the willingness and ability of regular teachers to teach handicapped children can be assessed and federal funds and rules revised accordingly.[20]

However, it may very well be that the stimulation of creative leadership and new patterns of communication between teachers for changes in authority relations will be beyond the power of rational calculation to control in two ways. First, national bureaucracy is too remote to affect authority patterns through conscious design. Second, national policies will affect such patterns but in contradictory and uncontrollable ways by making incompatible organizational demands on school systems.

Loose couplings and missing links between and within levels of government are a fact of life and there is never quite enough human talent to make up the difference. It is ironic to see in our study that behind the formal hierarchy each level of authority is unsure of what is going on below or how to intelligently intervene. This dilemma extends all the way from Washington to the classroom.

The purpose of our research is to go beyond an understanding of 94-142 to ask how each level of authority might play its role in relation to the others more intelligently. The implicit model of the type of school system most conducive to the implementation of 94-142 is an organization in which decentralized responsibility for innovation is placed in the schools within a larger framework of accountability for performance to higher levels of authority. It is not clear whether federal action can effectively foster such patterns. Resistances to the decentralization of such responsibilities are common in school systems. Furthermore, there is no evidence that implementation of 94-142 in the manner described here will necessarily create better education for handicapped children. This chapter has only described a set of possibilities that may be good for children.

NOTES

1. Education for all Handicapped Children Act of 1975, 20 USC 1401.

2. Report on Program Administrative Review, Bureau of Education for the Handicapped, draft report for Tennessee, June 6, 1979.

3. Report on Federal Compliance Activities to Implement the Education for All Handicapped Children Act (PL 94-142), April 16, 1980. The Children's Defense Fund of Washington, D.C., appears to be the lead group in the coalition.

4. Paul T. Hill, "Enforcement and Informal Pressure in the Management of Federal Categorical Programs in Education," A Rand note prepared for the U.S. Department of Health, Education and Welfare, August 1979, N-1232-HEW, pp. 17-19.

5. Ibid., p. 10.

6. Erwin C. Hargrove and Gillian Dean, "Federal Authority and Grass-Roots Accountability: The Case of CETA," Policy Analysis 6 (Spring 1980): 127-49.

7. Mark L. Chadwin, John J. Mitchell, Erwin C. Hargrove, and Lawrence M. Mead, The Employment Service: An Institutional Analysis (Washington, D.C.: Urban Institute, 1977).

8. Richard F. Elmore, "Mapping Backward: Using Implementation Analysis to Structure Policy Decisions," Political Science Quarterly, Winter 1979-80.

9. The study of 16 elementary schools in 1978-79 that is the subject of this chapter was continued in 1979-80. Three junior high schools and three high schools were also added in the latter year.

10. These data were supplied by the research division of the Metropolitan School System.

11. Sidney Verba, Small Groups and Political Behavior, A Study of Leadership (Princeton, N.J.: Princeton University Press, 1961), pp. 202-25.

12. Ibid., p. 210.

13. Ibid., pp. 215-16.

14. Ibid., p. 206.

15. Paul Berman and Milbrey McLaughlin, Federal Programs Supporting Educational Change: The Findings in Review (Santa Monica, California: Rand Corporation, 1975).

16. Verba, op. cit., pp. 224-34.

17. The standardized survey of teachers produced this finding.

18. This idea was expressed to me by Professor Jerome Murphy of the Harvard Graduate School of Education.

19. Susan Johnson and Louis Gomes of the Harvard Graduate School of Education are doing interesting work on the forces pushing for increasing central control in school systems, particularly unions and threats of legal action.

20. Lois-ellin Datta illustrates this method of analysis in her reinterpretation of findings of the Rand Corporation "change agent" studies, "Damn the Experts and Full Speed Ahead: An Examination of the Study of Federal Programs Supporting Educational Change as Evidence Against Directed Development and for Local Problem Solving" (Washington, D.C.: National Institute of Education, December 1979).

PART III

THE COMMUNITY ENVIRONMENT OF SCHOOL DISTRICTS

5

THE CLOSING OF ANDREW JACKSON ELEMENTARY SCHOOL: MAGNETS IN SCHOOL SYSTEM ORGANIZATION AND POLITICS

Mary Haywood Metz

Andrew Jackson Elementary School[1] was located in downtown Heartland, one of the nation's 25 largest cities. In September 1975 it was transformed from a remedial school into a magnet school serving volunteers from all over the city on a racially desegregated basis. The school drew upon methods developed in its remedial days to accomplish striking successes with children who had had difficulty in other settings, and its methods and staff were equally effective with highly achieving children. Its varied students mixed freely on the playground as well as in the classroom and learned from one another's different strengths; the school was not only desegregated but integrated. The Diagnostic Learning Program,[2] which was Jackson's special academic approach, became known beyond the borders of the state and visitors came from near and far to learn how things were done at Andrew Jackson in Heartland.

At a school board meeting on August 1, 1978, however, the chairman of the Heartland school board's finance committee proposed—at 11:45 P.M.—that Andrew Jackson be closed in September 1978 and its students, staff, and program combined with those of another school in another building. His motion was the first public mention of such an idea. A half hour later, at 12:15 A.M. August 2, Andrew Jackson was closed by a vote of the school board.

Analysis and writing for this article were supported by a grant from the National Institute of Education, Project No. G-79-0017. Opinions stated are those of the author and do not necessarily represent National Institute of Education position or policy.

This chapter tells the story of Andrew Jackson School and asks how, with so much success in the areas public schools find most recalcitrant, it came to be so summarily closed. The answers involve organizational and political processes that are fundamental in the operation of the U.S. school systems. As a magnet, Jackson belonged to a category of schools with considerable policy relevance. I shall argue that the generalized processes that led to its demise bear upon other similar schools as well.

The events immediately precipitating the closing are simply told. Early in the summer of 1978, the Heartland City Council took out a full-page newspaper advertisement blaming high city tax rates on school costs that failed to decline with enrollments. In response the newly elected president of the school board pledged that the board would save $1 million through closing schools that summer. The schools the boards selected for closing were several black elementary schools with low enrollments, two elementary schools in white neighborhoods, and a black high school. No one made a concerted attempt to save the black elementary schools, but the neighborhoods of the white elementary schools organized to mount a campaign on their behalf. The neighborhood of the black high school came together under the leadership of a gifted orator to make a highly publicized and vigorous protest. Controversy raged throughout July.

The president of the board was determined to save the $1 million. As his colleagues began to reconsider closing the schools, he waged an intensive telephone campaign the weekend before the meeting of August 1, when final action was to be taken. At the meeting the board voted to close the black elementary schools, but gave the white elementary schools and the black high school a year of grace. The board had shown that it would close schools to save money, but it had also shown some consideration to the communities involved and avoided the appearance of precipitate action. Community resistance was defused, but the $1 million was not saved.

The chairman of the board's finance committee then moved that two "specialty schools," or magnet schools, be "transferred" from their current locations to buildings that each would share with another program, and that their buildings be closed in September. The action was taken.

One of these schools was Andrew Jackson. The transfer was actually the closing of the school since it was clear from the outset that it and the program with which it was blended would become a single school with a single staff, student body, and program. The Twelfth Avenue School, to which it was moved, was a new building with facilities and program designed for a Reading Center specialty. The board said nothing of how the two programs or staffs would be combined.

The school closed along with Andrew Jackson was a middle school for the "gifted and talented, " formerly housed at the Atlantic Avenue School. It was moved into a high school building that had been expensively remodeled in order to open in the fall as a special citywide high school for "the college bound." While the ages of the children dictated separation of programs, the action created a seven-year high school, even though the board had just enacted a policy to discontinue six-year high schools because of the negative effects of the broad age span.

The parents of Jackson and Atlantic coordinated their efforts in making a major protest of the board's action. One Atlantic parent instituted a lawsuit on the grounds that lack of notice in the agenda of the August 1 school board meeting that the schools were to be considered for closing constituted a violation of the state open meetings law. Parents intensely lobbied board members and their associates and arranged a few media events such as television coverage of a tour of the unfinished Twelfth Avenue building under the shelter of hard hats required by the construction company. Nonetheless, as soon as several board members who had gone on vacation returned to the city, the board reconvened with due public notice and reaffirmed its action of August 1 and 2 by a vote of nine to six. The Andrew Jackson and Atlantic schools were closed and their programs moved.

One third of Andrew Jackson's children did not move with the program, but found last-minute places in neighborhood public schools and parochial and private schools.

In the following pages, after brief methodological comments, I will describe the history and character of Andrew Jackson School. I will next analyze the reasons that parents objected to the transfer and then the political, organizational, and personal influences that came together in the board's action. Finally, I will consider the implications of this single case for our understanding of the organizational and political relationships between schools and school systems.

METHODOLOGICAL COMMENTS

My account of Andrew Jackson and the events surrounding its closing is that of an observer participant. Our older son was in the first grade at Andrew Jackson the year before it was closed. I became president of its Parent Teacher Organization (PTO) in May of that year, and in that capacity I particpated actively in the protest of its closing. I did so because parent leadership was sparse and I believed that the move would be seriously detrimental to the

individual children and to the overall character of the school program. My son did not go with the program to Twelfth Avenue; so
my personal involvement ended with the protest.

However, my analysis of the school's career and its closing
arises in part from research I am currently pursuing in three of
Heartland's citywide magnet schools at the middle school level.
One of these is the middle school for the gifted and talented, formerly at the Atlantic Avenue School. I had submitted a formal
proposal to do this research to the National Institute of Education
the April before Jackson was closed. Approval was given late the
following fall and I started work the following January.[3] The more
distant perspective that comes with passing time and my reflections
upon the three middle schools, where I do not have a personal stake,
have brought the events at Andrew Jackson into sociological focus.

In that light it is clear to me that Andrew Jackson's closing
was not an idiosyncratic and strange event, but rather an almost
predictable product of organizational and political processes that
Heartland shares with other cities. Despite some gaps in the story
that arise from the manner in which I learned it, it is one well
worth telling.

THE HISTORY AND CHARACTER OF
ANDREW JACKSON SCHOOL

The Setting: Heartland

The city of Heartland is a conservative city lying away from
the rapid beat of either coast. Originally established in the last
half of the nineteenth century, it was populated mostly with immi-
grants from a few countries in northern and eastern Europe. Its
neighborhoods until recently have had clear ethnic identities and
close social ties. They still retain some of this character. The
city is in many ways reminiscent of smaller communities. Strang-
ers are at ease and helpful in giving directions and passing the
time of day with one another in public places.

This friendliness, however, has not extended to Heartland's
black population, which has been strictly segregated in housing and
schools. Close ethnic ties have created ethnic exclusion. Heartland's school system has been built around the neighborhood public
school. Blacks have had little say in this system, as their recently
successful desegregation suit against it has clearly proved. Though
Heartland's population is 27 percent black, low for a major city, the
proportion of black children in the schools has been climbing
rapidly as white birth rates fall and white children leave the city,

while the number of black children remains steady or slightly rising.
At this writing the proportion of black school children is nearing
50 percent; it is higher in the elementary schools.

The History of Andrew Jackson School

The Andrew Jackson building was constructed of brick in the
1890s, on the fringe of downtown Heartland. In 1978 it was surrounded by a group of expensive new high-rise apartments and by a
school of engineering. Its neighborhood children had melted away
and the building had thus been available for special programs. Its
recent history started in the late 1960s when national concern over
the low performance of minority and poor children and the availability of special state money combined as incentives for the Heartland district to establish a set of Interrelated Language Skills
Centers. Jackson was one of these. It took fourth through sixth
graders who were reading at least two years below grade level.
State monies made possible class sizes of only ten and the purchase
of a great variety of materials. The staff, brought to Jackson to
work with this special population, hammered out a special approach
to their needs. They tested students extensively to discover both
what skills and knowledge they already possessed and what their
distinctive learning styles were; did they learn best through seeing
or hearing, through holistic or analytical approaches? The staff
then concentrated upon each student's greatest strengths and sought
to foster his or her confidence by building upon the successes he or
she could accomplish in areas of strength.   Other areas then followed in due course. When I became head of the PTO, the principal
and two others of the original staff met with me to acquaint me with
the history and philosophy of the school. They positively glowed
as they told of this period and of the successful careers of some of
their students.
    Times changed, however. Compensatory education lost its
sheen and the Interrelated Language Skills Centers lost their funding. This reduction was gradual; their number decreased and then
their character changed. In the summer of 1975, Jackson, which
remained alone, faced reduced funding and an uncertain future. A
new superintendent had just arrived in Heartland from the superintendency of a smaller system where he had gained notice for the
introduction of "specialty" schools with distinctive educational
approaches that drew volunteers for desegregation and innovative
education in one package. Heartland's schools were under suit for
desegregation and the decision was soon to be handed down.
Jackson provided the new superintendent a fortunate opportunity.

He got the agreement of the board to transform its program into a Diagnostic Learning Program, which retained some of the features of the old program. It would draw volunteering children of every ability level from all over the city, with quotas for racial balance. It would span the elementary grades from first through sixth. The earlier diagnostic approach and the rich and varied curricular materials were to be kept. There would be two classes of 26 children for each grade staffed by two regular teachers and a third "cooperating" teacher. So the effective ratio was 52 to 3 or 17.3 to 1, exclusive of administrative personnel.

The board approved this plan in August and the superintendent's intuitions proved right. Far more families, both white and black, volunteered than could be accommodated. The school had to hire primary-level teachers and develop an altered program in a month, but these tasks were accomplished and problems were ironed out with time. Staff and parents considered the program successful.

The following January the court ordered the city's schools desegregated but allowed the system to propose a method to accomplish student movement. The superintendent and board responded with a plan that gave "specialty" schools and voluntary integration the most attention. To the skeptics who questioned whether enough parents, especially white parents, would volunteer, the administration exhibited Andrew Jackson and an open education middle school, initiated by parents and staff, which had been run on a similar citywide, integrated, voluntary basis since 1972.

The court accepted the plan, a number of specialties were founded, and the goal of integrating one-third of the schools in the first year was reached. In the second year, with two-thirds of the schools to integrate, more specialties were established, and every parent of a public school child had to list three choices of school for the fall, only one of which could be the neighborhood school. Again the plan succeeded, two-thirds of the schools were desegregated with most children receiving their first choice and all but a handful finding a place in one of their schools of choice.

The school board had appealed the court ruling, however, and in the fall of 1977 a higher court sent the decision back to the Heartland judge for reconsideration in light of the Dayton decision, which questioned the necessity of a systemwide remedy unless systemwide intentional segregation had been proved. Desegregation in Heartland, about to face the last and most difficult third of its task, went into a holding pattern. The legal status of the system was blurred, but the administration declared its intention to keep the schools at least at their current levels of desegregation for the fall of 1978.

It was in this climate that the new Twelfth Avenue School, to which Jackson eventually was moved, neared the end of construction and began the process of enrollment of students. It is located in a poor black neighborhood in the part of the city where the city's black population is concentrated. A decrepit school had been demolished and the community demanded that a new building be built on that site. In the intervening time the court order had been handed down and it seemed that the new $5 million facility must be opened on a desegregated basis.

The building was designated as a Reading Center specialty elementary program. An energetic black woman was hired as its principal and given the second semester of the previous year to plan its program. During that spring of 1978, however, the system's push toward integration was lackluster. Publicity on the specialties for the 1978-79 year was limited to a bulletin sent home to the parents of current public school children, which gave each specialty a one-paragraph description written by the system's standing publicity department. Twelfth Avenue's description sounded as though reading would be stressed at the expense of other subjects and it suggested—though it did not state—emphasis on remedial problems. No separate brochure was issued and no special publicity campaign was planned. The system expected to draw 600 children on the basis of a paragraph, an unfinished building, and the efforts of a principal whose staff was not yet hired. In August, despite the principal's energetic work without pay through the summer and the help of an enthusiastic group of white parents, the school had drawn only about 250 children, two-thirds of them black. Andrew Jackson's 320 children would serve to fill the building, thus accomplishing at one time the savings of closing Andrew Jackson's building and of filling the expensive new Twelfth Avenue building on a more nearly desegregated basis.

Thus, in Andrew Jackson's ten-year history, it had three times served to solve a problem presented to top administrators or board members of Heartland without disturbing the ongoing life of the neighborhood schools that constitute the backbone of the system. In 1968 it was used to demonstrate the system's concern for improving the achievement of poor and minority children, without creating changes in ordinary schools. In 1975 it was used to demonstrate the viability of voluntary integration, while freeing the system of the expense of funding its original mission from local money. In 1978 it was used to solve the board's dilemma in finding schools to close to save $1 million and their embarrassment at the failure of voluntary integration when their efforts had slacked off and an expensive building been left unfilled. Andrew Jackson's building and its staff and children were a movable piece in a generally standardized and immobile system that could be brought to whatever boundary of the system was under scrutiny or attack from the environment of the system as a whole. Outside audiences could be satisfied and the majority of central office staff, school staffs, and parents and children be unaffected.

The Character of Andrew Jackson

Inside the school, the staff hired for the original remedial program took their mission seriously and drew sustenance from their successes. They remained when the school was expanded to become the Diagnostic Learning Program, and their style and concerns colored the new school, even as it served a broader clientele with larger class sizes.[4]

In the year before it was closed, Andrew Jackson served a genuinely diverse population. Its students were 50 percent black, 10 percent other minority, and 40 percent white. The social status of the population was diverse overall but heavier on the low end. The vast majority of parents, both black and white, were working class; 55 percent of the children qualified for free lunches. In the first year of its existence as a diverse school, several prominent families had sent their children to the school and a few of these remained. Participation by visibly high-status families trailed off as several specialty schools were opened.

The students' academic ability ranged from well above to well below grade level. Some children with very high abilities were in each class. In my son's class, one black and one white child entered first grade testing at the sixth grade level in reading. With Andrew Jackson's flexible program, these two children progressed in reading without feeling isolated or drawing negative comment from their peers. When I first came to look at the school, the principal told me that, while the school could be helpful to any child, he preferred to have average and below average children whose lives would be most affected by its benefits. The student population did contain a heavy concentration of such children. Principals of other schools and parents of children who had academic or social difficulties continued to perceive Jackson as a school that worked effectively with such children and to steer them to it. Thus, Jackson drew more than the city's average of children with academic or social problems. However, it also drew children whose parents were ambitious for them and parents who sought alternatives to a bad local school or a dangerous walk to get to school. They saw a bus ride to Jackson, often a very long ride, as an escape from the neighborhood to a safer or a more stimulating experience.

Jackson apparently generated unusual academic success with both its difficult population and its able students. The parents who called me after the closing told of children with severe academic or social problems in other schools who had caught up to average or above average academic skills and started to lead far happier, more cooperative lives after going to Jackson. Several of the parents drawn out to the meetings to deal with the closing were the parents of academically successful children. They also felt their children were well served intellectually and were making excellent academic progress. My own child learned a great deal and enjoyed doing it, as did his two best friends, one of whom had been formally diagnosed as "learning disabled."

Certainly Jackson's method of testing children to diagnose both their skills and their learning style and its low pupil-teacher ratio helped its academic success. Its social atmosphere was important, too, and more subtle in its effect. At first when my six-year-old happily told stories of battles on the playground between Spiderman and his enemies or Batman and the Joker's legions, I listened half attentively. Then one winter night when he told of the victory of his side, I asked how they knew who won. "We fight until one side doesn't have a man left standing," he said cheerfully. My middle-class eyebrows went up. I inquired of his friends' parents. "Oh yes, it's rough, I've decided not to ask what happens," answered one. I looked at my rather too sensitive six-year-old once again as he told these tales of warfare that left no visible bruises and conveyed obvious delight. The wars included not only his friends but a changing cast of characters of many hues and backgrounds. I decided to trust his judgment and the school's.

In the spring when the staff briefed me as president of the PTO, I asked about roughness on the playground. They agreed that the playground play was rough. Some children find it difficult to adjust at first the principal said; but soon they do, and they've acquired some self-confidence and self-reliance in the process. I gradually came to see that the staff's acceptance of rough and active (but not hostile)[5] playground activity was part of a pattern of accepting as legitimate the life style of tough and self-reliant poor children.

Jackson's children came in a rainbow of colors, yet when I asked my son to tell me about the children in his class he never mentioned their color. In mid-winter, when curiosity overcame me and I asked, he patiently answered my adult questions with careful descriptions, "light tan" or "dark brown about like Jim" (a neighbor). Though the reason might have been his young age, I think it was more that color was not a social category at Andrew Jackson. When he entered second grade and his brother entered kindergarten in the neighborhood white school, which was having difficulty adjusting to the addition of black children, both swiftly developed the category "black." Further, it was not long before the older asked, "Why are all the black kids at school bad except Jim?" It is my guess that not only did white children not learn to categorize children by skin color at Jackson, but that dark-skinned children did not feel they were a category apart who must stick together through solidarity against the teacher and other children.

Jackson's principal, Mr. Everett, was an imposing black man who saw his mission in helping children, especially children who started out with disadvantages. Half of his staff had been drawn to the school to work with children with low skills. They had experienced success with such children, and they had learned to work with the strengths the children brought with them rather than simply to decry their weaknesses. They apparently continued that attitude as the school became more diverse. With some self-consciousness they drew upon the strengths of street children to enrich the personalities and widen the horizons of more protected children. They used the academic abilities and enthusiasm of different children to involve those with fewer such skills in book learning.

Andrew Jackson's staff thus used diversity to increase the capabilities of all the children. Differences were perceived as legitimate and normal and each child progressed academically and socially from the point where he entered, learning from both peers and adults. The atmosphere of the school was a warm and happy one. The diversity of Jackson's mix and the large number of children with difficulties made this feat much more challenging than it appeared on the surface. [6]

Even in the midst of Jackson's success, a seasoned observer would have known that its life was likely to be short. The first and most serious of its difficulties lay in the fact that its low pupil-teacher ratio and extracurricular materials were funded out of state monies, which were gradually phased out, ending in the spring of 1978. The school system would have to pick up the total costs of its operation after that.

Given its high costs, Jackson needed political muscle. Despite its success with children, it lacked that muscle. Its mostly working-class parents had neither time, tradition, nor confidence for participation in parent activities at the school, let alone for monitoring or lobbying the central administration and school board. An idiosyncratic, but not uncommon, circumstance alienated most of the relatively few middle-class parents who might have helped.

When the school first drew a diverse clientele, it maintained the structure of a parent advisory committee often required where state or federal money is given with intent to reach a low-income population. At the first meeting of this group, so one parent told me, a lawyer from the city's leading law firm suggested that a black former state assemblyman active in city and school affairs become chairman of the group. No one objected and he remained unelected and unopposed through the succeeding three years. With many civic commitments, he had little time for Jackson, and he also had little sense for the delicate art of inspiring volunteer labor. He consistently arrived a half hour late at meetings, ran groups that ranged in size from 15 to 4 with Roberts' Rules of Order, used last names as a form of address, and often treated others' suggestions brusquely. Attendance, initially mostly of new parents, dwindled through the year of my participation. Though this man warned the group on at least two occasions that the loss of state money could imperil the program, he did not suggest concrete steps the group or individuals might take, and he took none himself. Since few parents could tolerate his regime for more than a year, there were no other experienced parents to mobilize systemwide support for the program. It was to change this pattern that a group of parents decided to found a Parent Teacher Organization and to hold formal elections for officers, thus allowing a change of regime with as much grace as possible. This beginning to parent activism was too little too late, however.

Jackson lost politically through its distinctive drawing patterns and inactive parents in another way. The school system makes public summaries of the standardized test scores of each school, which the newspapers publish. Jackson's scores were above the city average in reading for 1978-79 and slightly below the city average in math—to which it gave less emphasis. This record is if anything a sign of success, given the nature of the school's population. However, there is no readily available measure of the kind of student body each school takes in, and the central administration was critical of Jackson's scores, feeling that a visible and well-funded specialty school should do better. Mr. Everett, reversing his statement in our first conversation, told me that for the sake of the school's political standing it needed more students with high abilities and skills. Parents in citywide specialty schools with large concentrations from the middle class run their own recruiting campaigns, in which they especially seek out active parents and able children. I planned to organize such a campaign during the year I would have been president.

Jackson also could have obtained political muscle through its principal directly; but Mr. Everett did not carry weight with the central administration. There were several reasons for this. First, the program remained under the division of the administration

responsible for special education. The administrator charged with
tending to its needs and pleading its case in the central administration had little interest in it or understanding of it. The principal
had to work through him and so was often blocked at the start.

Some principals can evade such problems through informal
personal ties with persons in the central administration who can
praise the school's work at appropriate moments and plead its case
where necessary. Principals in the Heartland system who have such
ties often spend considerable energy cultivating them. Mr. Everett
did not have such ties, nor was it accidental to the history and character of Andrew Jackson that he did not. Mr. Everett was a black
in a system that had only very recently hired blacks at all. When
he first came to Heartland he had been told there were no teaching
openings, though he later found that there were for whites. He
found a career in youth work of another kind and returned to the
schools when increasing numbers of black children made the system
more willing to hire black adults. He was promoted to administration when the federal government put severe pressure on the system to change the lily-white complexion of its administrative ranks.
He thus was, along with other blacks, a latecomer with fewer informal ties. As such, he had been placed in a program that was
initially an ancillary undertaking, a sop to the disadvantaged.

Further, he had been placed in this elementary program even
though his credentials were in secondary education. A pragmatic
man who was willing to adapt to circumstances, he developed a
close working relationship with the curriculum coordinator. She
had a broad knowledge of elementary curricular materials and a gift
for working with a match of materials and children's learning styles.
Thus much of the technical aspect of the program was her invention,
and much of its success due to her work. However, she was less
suited to the exercise of successful direction over adults, and she
did not have Mr. Everett's warm and indomitable way with children.
Thus it was the combination of her curricular skills and his skills
in working with teachers and children as whole persons that made
an administrative contribution to the program's strength. When the
central administration wanted a representative of the school to discuss curriculum, they invited the principal. Unimpressed with his
grasp of elementary curriculum, at least some members of the
central administration's department of curriculum and instruction
concluded that his presence was not important to the success of the
program.

The school's history as a remedial school and the principal's
race both directly and indirectly served to undermine its influence
at the central administration building. Its history as a remedial
school, however, was an important ingredient in its success in

working with a diverse clientele; and the principal's race served simply through his appearance to increase the status and sense of belonging of the black children. It worked also through the chemistry of his experience and personality to make him someone who set the tone for Jackson's special capacity to draw out the strengths of its varied children so that each gained rather than lost from living in a diverse environment.

PARENTS' OPPOSITION TO THE CLOSING

According to the school board's action, the Diagnostic Learning Program was to be transferred to the Twelfth Avenue building. That new building was expected to have some advanced facilities—such as a news teletype written at the elementary level. When parents first contacted board members, expressing opposition to the move, some of them responded testily that they should hardly object to an improvement in facilities. Why then did the parents object?

The first reason lay in the manner of the decision and its implementation. The board and central administration had praised their own progressive steps in offering parents a range of different public schools from which they could make an informed choice on the basis of the particular needs of their child. Parents who had taken the trouble to make such a choice found it offensive to be given a new setting without warning at midnight a month before school was to open. Similarly, the administration immediately informed Mr. Everett that he would not accompany the program; but they had him sign their letter formally announcing the change to parents, which included the statement that "the entire staff" would move with it. This action suggested bad faith. Further, many parents believed Mr. Everett to be a crucial element in Andrew Jackson's success. His removal suggested that the administration was willing to change a great deal about the school in the process of "transferring" it.

The parents' second objection rose from their doubt of the realistic possibility of continuing Jackson's program in a new setting. The move meant the presence of two different specialty programs in one building. Questions to the administration were answered from the start with the statement that there would be a single program at the school. At first administrators were vague about the nature of that program, but as the lawsuit progressed and as parents impressed upon board members the difficulties of implementing the plan, private conversations between board members and the administration resulted in its announcing that the whole school would be run according to the Diagnostic Learning Program. This solution created a new set of problems for 250 parents who had signed up for the Reading Center specialty and for its principal who had spent the last eight months in intensive work planning and promoting the Reading Center program. Nor did it satisfy the Jackson parents, as few believed that a principal and half a staff unfamiliar with their program would or could implement it.

The parents' third objection concerned the availability of the building. When the Jackson teachers and parents were shown the building in small groups, carefully escorted past hazards and sheltered under hard hats, it was clear that only intensive overtime—eating up a good part of the school board's hard-won financial savings—could have the building anywhere near ready for September occupancy. Even then staff and students would have to step around workmen putting in finishing touches for many weeks to come. As events turned out, intensive overtime was used and one wing was ready for the lower three grades. The older three grades of children who had signed up for both schools spent the first two months of the year in the Jackson building while the second wing was prepared to the point where they could occupy it.

Finally, the parents objected to the fact that the Twelfth Avenue building was designed on an open-space plan. It contained six large pods, rooms large enough for 100 children. The only space that could be partitioned off was one small room intended for noisy activities. Thus children would be in a physical environment considerably different from Jackson's. Further, the large space was designed for team teaching, and at the least required the visual and auditory mixing of activities of different groups. Thus the architecture of the new building required that teachers who had not met previously and who had been hired for different programs form themselves into working teams between the first of August and the first of September. No special time or money had been set aside for the accomplishment of this task.

The open-space design of the Twelfth Avenue School also presented special problems because of the character of Jackson's children. There were about 15 learning disabled children, formally categorized but mainstreamed, for whom the multiple activities of such large spaces are particularly distracting. Parents of many of Jackson's other children who had had academic difficulties before coming to Jackson thought that the distractions of a large open space would be detrimental to their children. Parents of children with no special difficulties wished that they could at least see such a school in operation. It was difficult to know what level of noise and movement would in fact evolve in such large spaces, with which most were unfamiliar. Doubling the size of the student body in the new facility also seemed detrimental to many parents who had consciously chosen a small school for their children.

Interestingly, of all the parents I talked with, only two mentioned Twelfth Avenue's location in the inner city as a problem. Others may have thought of it and not mentioned it, but it is more likely that parents of children who had already attended Jackson were aware that they would spend essentially no time beyond the limits of the school and playground; the location was thus much less important than it would have been for children of high school age.

The parents, then, argued that the transfer of the Diagnostic Learning Program to Twelfth Avenue was not a transfer but the dismantling of an existing school and the establishment of a new one with some of the same people but with crucial differences that would foster unforeseeable consequences. Given the unreadiness of the building and the short time for moving and planning, one foreseeable consequence was considerable turmoil and confusion at the outset. They asked for a year's reprive while Twelfth Avenue had a chance to attract a full quota of students for its Reading Center and parents and staff from Jackson had a chance to seek a site more suitable for their children and the Diagnostic Learning Program.

THE BOARD'S REASONS FOR CLOSING
ANDREW JACKSON

In the course of the three-week attempt to get the board to grant Jackson a reprive, I and other Jackson parents talked with some of the board members who supported the move, with a few top administrators, and with board members who supported keeping Jackson open. Two of the latter were persons who had initially voted for the closure, including the chairman of the finance committee who had made the original motion. They were willing to tell us something of the discussions that had led to the decision. What follows is based on all of these discussions.

The Problem of Finance

The official reason given for closing Andrew Jackson was the declining elementary school enrollment in the total system and the need to save taxpayers' money by closing unneeded buildings. Because the Jackson building housed only 325 students and was old, it was one of the more expensive buildings to run.

Further, the empty seats in the new $5 million Twelfth Avenue building were an embarrassment at a time when the board had committed itself to close buildings. The argument was made that the Diagnostic Learning Program and the Reading Center were "compatible" and "similar," but no one said who had made this judgment or how he, she, or they had arrived at it, or whether there had been any consideration of moving other programs into Twelfth Avenue. It was said that moving Jackson would entail less cost than moving other schools because Jackson children were already bussed.

Since the Twelfth Avenue school was not ready for occupancy, a number of extra charges were incurred by the move, such as programming bussing of the upper grades of both schools twice for the two different locations, and overtime to speed the construction of the full building. It seems it was the appearance of saving money, more than the fact, that motivated the board.

Andrew Jackson's Site

Andrew Jackson's downtown site had recently increased in monetary value. Several development companies were planning major construction in the immediate area. Within 24 hours of the board's decision a number of these and some institutions in the area had publicly expressed interest in the land. Several board members had business and social ties that could have brought them into contact with persons interested in acquiring Jackson's land if the board should empty the school and sell the lot. Their arguments could have influenced the choice of a building to close and a program to combine with Twelfth Avenue.

The Politics of Equity and Magnet Schools

The board members who supported the closing of Andrew Jackson did not all have the same reasons. One group had strong reservations about the equity of magnet schools. The system had used much rhetoric about the voluntary character of its desegregation plan and its progressive provision of an array of specialty schools from which parents could choose. Over 80 percent of the children who "volunteer" to ride the bus out of their neighborhood are black children, most of them riding not to specialty schools but to white neighborhood schools that offer them a dubious welcome and no special facilities or innovative educational approaches. In many cases they leave their neighborhoods because their schools have been closed and reopened as specialty schools, sometimes with considerable physical improvements that the surrounding community had been unable to obtain through years of patient requests. Some liberal board members, both black and white, saw the specialty schools as havens of privilege for upper-middle-class whites.

Blacks were particularly angry over the elementary school for the gifted and talented, which was placed in a beautiful old building, the potentialities of which were realized when it was both rid of its rats and roaches and elegantly carpeted and painted—after its neighborhood black children were removed. Some board members may have moved the Atlantic middle school for the gifted and talented in part to let the graduates of this elementary school share some of the inconveniences of the total system. Because Andrew Jackson initially attracted some of the city's visible elite families, these board members may have seen its clientele as privileged and may have wished to make them also pay a price. A black board member who actively promoted the move spoke to me, though cryptically, of the need to create equity as a justification for the move.

The Desegregation Process

The only other black member of the board (whose mother taught at Jackson) expressed ambivalence, avoided the parents throughout the three-week protest, and then voted with the majority to move the school. A year later, he said at a meeting of parents from citywide schools that Jackson "should never have been moved." As we talked at some length after the meeting, he explained his vote as based on the necessity to keep Twelfth Avenue (and the high school to which Atlantic was moved) from becoming segregated schools. Once they opened with a large majority of blacks, he thought they would be nearly impossible to integrate. He blamed the situation on the lack of effort exerted by the administration in recruitment for those schools on a desegregated basis earlier in the year. He thought that if they were run as expensive showplace buildings for black children only, they would go far to reestablish the philosophy of neighborhood schools that ruled the city before the court order. For him, the principle of integration was worth the sacrifice of Jackson.

This argument is lent some weight by the fact that the board members most strongly defending Andrew Jackson and Atlantic were the two most politically adept of the white conservative faction. Both are realtors; both had staunchly opposed desegregation.

Even though one had supported Jackson actively from its beginnings, it is quite possible that their motives for defending Jackson and Atlantic included a desire to see Twelfth Avenue and the college-bound high school become examples of the difficulty of desegregating inner city schools and of the benefits of sending black children to elegant facilities in their own neighborhoods.

Internal Board Politics

The decision to close Jackson and Atlantic was also affected by internal board politics. Some members voted in order to express solidarity with or opposition to other members, rather than to affect Jackson or Twelfth Avenue. Three elements in the development of the board were important. First, in the crucial votes over desegregating the schools and appealing the court order the board had consistently split 8 to 7, with the conservatives who opposed desegregation in the majority. An intervening election and the issues of the two years succeeding the first appeal had blurred these lines slightly, but all but one or two board members were clearly identified with the liberal or conservative bloc. Second, shortly prior to the Jackson decision a board member who had made several unsuccessful tries for the presidency of the board managed to break a stalemated election by drawing support from both the liberal and conservative wings. He promised his supporters that he would be able to arrange traded votes and to deliver them passage of favorite issues if they would follow his leadership. This pattern of trading was new in the politics of the board and perhaps stimulated by a third change. The state legislature had voted to reduce the size of the board and to have the members elected by district instead of at large. Thus several board members were lame ducks and the rest were aware that they would shortly be acting as representatives of districts.

One liberal white board member who voted for the closings told a delegation of Jackson and Atlantic parents that he had traded his vote on the two schools for conservative votes on the handling of drugs in the schools, a matter he thought much more important. He advised the delegation, some of whom had been his campaign supporters, to go get more political power if they wanted his continuing support for their concerns.

The fact that the votes on Jackson and Atlantic followed the lines of the board's presidential election, splitting what had been a solid liberal minority and a solid conservative majority, also affected board members' emotional responses to reconsideration of their action. The liberals who favored the move saw resistance to it as engineered by wily conservatives who were their long-standing political opponents and sometimes bitter personal antagonists. Indeed, these conservative board members must have taken secret delight in seeing the liberal faction split and generally liberal, prointegration parents angry at the prointegration board members they had been supporting for years. Meanwhile their own conservative allies who voted to save money must have felt angrily betrayed.

Board-Administration Politics

Some board members argued that Jackson and Atlantic were chosen for closing as a deliberate slapping of the superintendent's hands on the part of the board. The superintendent considered both the Diagnostic Learning Program and the gifted and talented schools showpieces for display within and beyond the city. Several of the board members claimed that they were put in the awkward situation of voting to close schools in the summer preceding the closings because the administration had dragged its feet in making available the appropriate information earlier. The superintendent had not thought closings necessary and had not given them sufficient information upon which to make earlier decisions. This version of events is supported by the fact that conservative board members who generally support the superintendent (not the conservatives mentioned earlier) voted not to close Jackson and Atlantic even though they generally like to save money.

Not all members of the administration wanted the Jackson and Atlantic programs to remain where they were. At the very end of my involvement with Andrew Jackson, I spoke with a man active in recruiting for the Twelfth Avenue reading program in his role as a parent who also worked in the curriculum and instruction division of the central administration. He told me that the idea to close Jackson and move the program to Twelfth Avenue had circulated through the central administration lower echelons earlier in the summer, but he thought it had been dropped. The circumstances of the conversation prevented my questioning him thoroughly, but his statements make it clear that someone somewhere in the central administration suggested the closing of Jackson to one or more members of the board and made an argument for its benefits.

Ignorance of the Move's Effects

An important element supporting the board's decision to move Andrew Jackson, though not an active push toward it or conscious reason for it, was general ignorance of the nature of the Jackson program and of the implications of the move for it among central administrators and board members. During the half hour of formal discussion of the motion among the board on August 1, most of the time was spent on Atlantic. What time was spent on Jackson did not bring out the fact that Twelfth Avenue had open pods, a fact that board members once knew in approving plans for the school but that most we spoke with had forgotten. Most of the board members we talked with also thought of Jackson simply as a successful magnet and were unaware of its high proportion of students who had had difficulties elsewhere. The members of central administration who were making decisions for implementation were apparently unaware of the importance of the teamwork of the principal and curriculum coordinator to the successful administration of the school.

As a body the board did not consider obvious questions that arose immediately after the decision, not did many board members appear to have thought about them. If two programs were to share one building, would both or only one actually be run? Which of two principals would remain? It would not require any great act of the imagination to see that merging two programs, doubling the size of the student population, and choosing only one administrator would create a change in the character and quality of both original schools. The board could fail to answer these crucial issues and could fail to be aware of the physical differences in the schools with their exacerbation of the problems of combining programs, because the effect of their action on the life of either school was of minor importance to them. Their actions were based on political relations with taxpayers and with one another, and on requirements of the broad process of desegregation in the system as a whole. Jackson, Atlantic, Twelfth Avenue, and the high school and their staffs and children were counters that could be moved as they pursued these ends. Important considerations in the decision did not include the programs of the individual schools or the experiences of the children.

THEORETICAL IMPLICATIONS OF JACKSON'S CLOSING

What can we learn for a broader understanding of schools and school systems from the case of Andrew Jackson? In this section I shall argue first that the decision-making process itself provides one more case for the model of "garbage-can decision making." Second, I will review Jackson's total history as it reveals relationships between schools and school districts, providing us with a substantive look at the process called loose coupling and suggesting some more specific shape to that relationship. Third, I shall consider Jackson's closing in light not only of organizational but of political relations between schools and school districts. In that light it appears that magnet schools upset the political balance of school systems in ways that are acceptable in the first turmoil of desegregation, but that are likely to cause objections once desegregation is systemwide and somewhat stabilized. In fact the more successful a magnet becomes, the more it violates political accommodations and invites public attack.

The limited data on decision making given in the body of this chapter strongly recall the patterns of "garbage-can decision making" proposed by Cohen, March, and Olsen (1972) and elaborated by March and Olsen (1976). The decision to close Andrew Jackson and to transfer the Diagnostic Learning Program could not in any sense be described as a rational solution to a single problem. Rather, the decision-making process gathered to itself a range of problems reaching from the maintenance of momentum toward desegregation to the expression of personal enmities within the board. The solution satisfied its various supporters for various reasons. None of the parties even claimed it would improve education for the children directly involved—though some held the children would at least not be harmed.

Despite the variety of reasons for board members voting as they did, the fact that the closing was proposed and that it was acceptable to a majority of the board as a solution to their varied concerns was not a random event. On the contrary, though it would have been quite possible that two board members would have voted differently and saved the school, in retrospect the proposal that Andrew Jackson, with all its strengths, be closed was in keeping with larger organizational and political processes.

Let us consider Andrew Jackson's relationship to the organization of the Heartland Public Schools as a total system. It is clear the closing made no sense at all from the perspective of Jackson and its staff and students. The school was drawing adequate numbers of volunteers, and staff and students were bending their efforts to the business of teaching and learning. Desegregation had become integration. Parents were more than satisfied. In short, the move was in no way addressed to internal school problems.

Jackson's history from beginning to end, however, was one in which district-level decisions about the school were made to satisfy district-level needs, not school-level needs. It was first established as a remedial school to show that the Heartland district was "doing something" about students who were falling behind in achievement. Then, despite its successes in that mission, it was essentially closed three years before the events described here when the remedial program was discontinued and the school

was transformed into a citywide school for ordinary children in all
six grades. Its staff and its positive reputation were used as capital in launching a new program. The purpose of the new program
was to prove the viability of voluntary integration in the system as
a whole more than it was to serve the needs of the particular children attending. In the process the district was saved the expense
of funding the remedial program—now of less political importance—
out of local funds.

Not only did the district twice cut off programs the Jackson
staff had gotten to a point of some success and stability, the district
also did little to help them reach the accomplishments it later cast
aside. It funneled state money to the school for the purchase of a
wide array of learning materials and for low teacher-pupil ratios.
Otherwise the school prospered because of the skill, effort, and
caring of its staff. On the other hand, between summary execu-
tions, the central office and board also did little to interfere with
the programs. The staff and students were left alone to work out
their relations as they thought best.

Thus, on a day-to-day basis, Jackson's relations with the
Heartland district were an example of the loose coupling of which
much has been recently written in the educational literature (March
and Olsen, 1976; Weick, 1976). Neither the central office staff nor
the school board knew or cared very much about what happened at
the school so long as it continued to draw a desegregated group of
students and to generate parents who did not complain.

Loose coupling, however, is a description of daily or yearly
interaction, not an institutionalized relationship. The relations
between Jackson and the Heartland school district remained those
of subunit and whole in a formal bureaucracy. That relationship
gives the central office and the board unambiguous authority to alter,
transform, transfer, or discontinue the programs of the schools
that make up the system. The Jackson and Atlantic parents could
sue about the legality of making the decison to close the schools
without due notice. They could lobby and attempt rational persuasion. When the board reconvened with legal prior notice and then
reaffirmed their action, however, there was no doubt in any one's
mind that that action was formally legitimate and binding.

Thus, it is well to remember that legitimate authority need
not atrophy from disuse. School systems in the United States are
organized as formal bureaucracies with significant policy-making
power in the hands of the central office and board. Even where
much decision making is delegated by custom, it can be returned
to the central authorities at their pleasure. Thus, from the
schools' point of view, their relations with the central office might
be likened to those of farmers renting from a giant who owns vast

lands. The giant may spend most of his time sleeping on a distant mountain and he may have neither knowledge nor interest in the nature and success of their crops so long as they pay the rent. Though he wakes rarely, when he does, a simple stroll through his domains with gargantuan feet can wreak havoc among the delicate vines and plants nurtured through years of patient labor and natural growth. Much as the tenant may resent and dread these visits, he has no legitimate right so much as to post a "No Trespassing" sign, let alone to enforce it.

Of course, Jackson is not an entirely fair model for schools in general. Since Jackson was a special school, formed to solve district-level needs, it was the natural first target of attention when those needs changed. In fact, the system's triennial redefinition of Jackson's mission saved the neighborhood schools from its disorienting attentions.

Why should schools be loosely coupled even to the degree that they are? Two lines of reply seem relevant to the case of Andrew Jackson. First, observations from Waller's time ([1932] 1965) on have consistently found a disjunction between classroom activities and administrative control within the school. This has been explained (Dreeben, 1973; Lortie, 1977; Metz, 1978) on the basis of the technology of teaching. The variable character of children and the lack of clearly effective methods require teachers to adjust to new situations as they arise. Studies of a variety of kinds of organizations indicate that such situations breed formal or informal autonomy for those closest to the actual work of the organization (Lipsky, 1980; Perrow, 1967; Woodward, 1965). In schools this autonomy is weakly institutionalized, but in most it is nonetheless real.

Summaries of early studies of the relations between schools and school districts (Bidwell, 1965; Corwin, 1974) found the same pattern of informal autonomy for schools vis-a-vis their districts that classroom teachers have established vis-a-vis their principals. More recent studies (Deal and Celotti, 1980; Deal, Meyer, and Scott, 1975; Meyer et al., 1978) have underscored the looseness of this relationship as they found innovations started and supported at the school or even the classroom level. Systemwide administrators may be ignorant of practices in the schools, while school-level administrators vary in their statements of routine district policies. Such mutual ignorance of rules and activities at other levels implies a lack of significant contact and of regular enforcement of formal policies.

Since the needs of student clientele and the working style of teaching staffs will vary from school to school, it is reasonable to argue that such loose coupling allows each school to design its technology to suit its tasks and resources. It is important to remember, however, that bureaucratic authority continues to rest with the central office and board and to constrain activities that persons in schools know will not be acceptable to them.

Meyer and Rowan (1978) have argued that the loose coupling between schools and school districts also increases the responsiveness of the total organization to its unusually intrusive environment. They maintain that school systems are coordinated by certification and categorization of persons and activities. Thus school systems specify very exactly who is qualified to teach and who to study the fourth grade or high school trigonometry, but they control very loosely what happens in fourth grade or trigonometry classes or what the students know when they finish with them. This pattern is based upon a shared presumption that there exists somewhere a clear definition of the fourth grade and of trigonometry and that all properly certified people have a grasp of this definition. Thus, these units of study are commonly considered to be clearly defined, even standardized, activities that form building blocks in an educational career. The structured bureaucracy can thus administer the offering of these standard units without ever inspecting the daily agenda or the students' detailed skills and knowledge. Coordination occurs through certification, categorization, and a logic of confidence.

This form of control, Meyer and Rowan argue, allows a great deal of unofficial flexibility that enables schools to adapt to the pressures brought by their immediate environments. Since the adaptations are not changes in name but only in actual activity, adjustments at one school do not bring pressures upon another or upon the central structure to make comparable changes elsewhere. At the same time, the system as a whole can respond to pressures brought at the system level with changes in labeling and categorization that make it appear responsive but need not disturb the established daily activities of individual schools except through an occasional change in language. Thus the system is doubly responsive to its environment, while the diverse needs of individual schools and the mostly ritualistic activities of the central administration coordinate little enough not to interfere with each other.

According to this model it is possible to see each of the programs instituted for Jackson as a symbolic gesture toward system change that left the large numbers of ordinary schools untouched but allowed the system to claim responsiveness to demands made at the system level.

We can go a great deal further with Meyer and Rowan's model if we add to it political as well as organizational considerations. There is political weight in the categorical language of the schools and the assumption it breeds that the fourth grade or junior-level English is always the same. This myth is not a trivial one in American education. It claims that everyone who has finished the fourth grade—or graduated from high school—can be said to have substantially similar knowledge and skills, and that schools are substantially similar. One can go anywhere, especially within a single district, and get the same education. The impersonal bureaucracy, the systemwide curriculum guides, and the system-wide curricular and administrative supervision are all visible social signs that this equivalence exists. Textbook manufacturers and test designers add to this belief with their grade-level textbooks and tests that give grade-level scores. In a society that argues that education is the key to opportunity and that every child should have an equal opportunity, this standardization is important reassurance of such equality.

At the same time, however, it is an open secret that both within and between districts schools are anything but equivalent. They vary not only in their access to tangible monetary resources but in their supply of the subtler resources of good students and good staffs, and the even more intangible ones of high morale and common sense of academic and social purpose. Schools develop reputations as good or bad that are so widely shared that realtors can advertise houses according to their school attendance area and confidently expect adults to pay several thousand dollars more for a house that will allow their child to attend a fourth grade that is more equal than another.

In other words, the schools and the public simultaneously hold two contradictory beliefs. They believe in the reality of standardized units of work that are appropriate to given ages and commonly shared among schools. They also believe that some schools are much better than others, teaching more in knowledge, skills, and zest for inquiry, despite their standard labels. Edelman (1977) has argued that in political life such contradictory sets of beliefs are commonplace. We rely upon the set of ideas that is convenient to our current purposes or frame of mind with no sense of inconsistency.

If the relationship between schools and school systems is one defined in these contradictory ways, that fact goes far to explain the political relationships surrounding schooling. Thus the myth of standardization allows us comfortably to accept schooling as an open route to opportunity for the able and ambitious. At the same time, the belief in informal differences among schools allows us to seek a head start for our own child and indeed to have some say in the nature of that head start as we both select a school attendance area and work with teachers or with the school as a whole. At a more social level, politically powerful neighborhoods can demand more resources—especially less tangible resources—for their schools and politically powerless neighborhoods can be deprived of those resources while claims are still made that all children receive equivalent education.

Thus claims for standardization allow the fact of political competition for scarce resources without the appearance of it. At the same time, they do place some limits upon the inequity that can be practiced. Board members or administrators can, if they wish, limit the resources given to favored schools in the name of standardized and equal education. Representatives of less powerful schools can discover the resources available to others and demand some of the same.

The contradictions of this system have not gone unnoticed by representatives of the politically powerless, especially racial minorities. Over the last 15 to 20 years outcries have been increasing over the fact that all fourth grade completers and all high school graduates do not have anything like comparable skills and knowledge. Similarly, the intangible resources in better students and teachers, as well as in facilities and amenities, available to more powerful schools have been vigorously noted in many contexts.

Jackson's programs were designed to address just such complaints at the level of the whole Heartland system. First, Jackson was designed as a response to poor achievement among minority and poor children in central city neighborhoods. Then it was designed to address the far more thoroughgoing movement for desegregation.

Desegregation, especially in the north, is in part a tool to redress the imbalance discussed above. At issue is not simply the opportunity for a black child to sit next to a white child, but the opportunity for a black child to have access to equally good educational opportunities. If black children and white children sit in the same classrooms, then white parents who exercise political influence on behalf of their own children's education will benefit black children as well.

It is an irony of Jackson's history that, while directly benefiting mostly children of the politically powerless, both its first and second programs were designed to address political pressures for equal education in ways that would leave power differences in schooling for the bulk of Heartland's children untouched. Thus individual children with learning problems were drawn out for the original Jackson remedial program. However, the schools in whose primary grades their learning problems grew were not changed. Magnet schools, for which Jackson was a pilot, provide a method for desegregation with as much preservation of the status quo as possible.

When Heartland established magnet schools, it addressed first and foremost the problem of widespread or dramatically concentrated resistance among the public and parents. The example of Boston was fresh in everyone's mind, and Heartland is also a city of working-class ethnic neighborhoods. Magnets provided an ingenious solution to this problem. First, they drew attention away from the fact of the desegregation itself. The rhetoric used by system officials concentrated upon the variety of learning needs and styles among children, and the forward-looking character of the Heartland schools in providing parents an array of schools with different learning objectives and styles from which they might choose for their children. The few magnet schools were formally advertised and, as news, thoroughly covered by the press.

Thus it went less advertised and less noticed that black schools were closed or turned into magnets accepting only small numbers of neighborhood children so that many black children were forced to "choose" a school outside their own neighborhood. Nor could very many of them be accommodated in magnet schools. Instead they went to white neighborhood schools.

At the same time, those white families who are fearful of "forced bussing," were vastly relieved to find they did not have to leave their neighborhood schools but could leave that to other people who could do so voluntarily. They did have to accept black children, a few at first, then gradually more, into their own school. This fact was not emphasized and it seemed to them clearly the lesser of the evils that had appeared possible when the court ordered desegregation.

White parents who were willing to leave their neighborhoods (along with a matching number of blacks) were rewarded not only with feelings of moral rectitude but with special educational modes and lower student-teacher ratios and extra materials and programs.

The magnets proved in Heartland to be an effective solution to the short-term problem of desegregation. There was little public protest and aside from some difficulties with the complex bussing system, few problems that reached general public notice. Blacks got desegregation. Whites got to stay in their neighborhood schools if they wished or to go to schools that were officially labeled as superior if they were willing to ride a few miles.

I suggest, however, that Jackson's closing was an early sign in Heartland that magnets will face a difficult long-range future. While they solved the short-range problems of desegregation, they disrupted fundamental organizational patterns and changed political rhetoric to do it. They violated the pattern just described, first, in the system's official recognition that different children learn in different ways and at different rates and, second, in the logical consequence that schools should therefore take a variety of approaches to education. Administrators proclaimed formal differences among schools and among units of study within schools. Furthermore, magnets had to be less formally, but necessarily visibly, better schools. They had to have more resources in finances and staff, as well as imaginative programs, if they were to provide the reward to draw people away from their neighborhood schools. Though they were carefully labeled specialty schools— to suggest simple diversity—they still had to have an aura of superiority to exert the pull that the more common term "magnet schools" suggests.

These schools made public, official, and legitimate previously only informally recognized differences among schools. They thus openly raised the question of why some parents and children are offered services that are superior to those offered to others. At the beginning of desegregation, that question could be answered at least implicitly with the fact that superior services were an exchange for willingness to leave the neighborhood. Also the schools and services were open to every child in the city, with admission given by flexible racial quotas (25 to 50 percent black) and random selection in oversubscribed categories.

With time, however, those responses lost their persuasiveness. As the symbolic character of desegregation gave way to the daily realities experienced by children, a number of changes occurred. First, black families became restless with their continuing disadvantaged situation. Their children were the majority of those waiting in the winter snow on street corners and leaving home early and arriving home late because of transportation time. Their reward for those efforts was to attend neighborhood white schools where often children and teachers were unused to their physical appearance, their cultural styles, and their educational needs. Second, blue-collar white families began to resent even one-way desegregation as teachers complained of academic diversity, and as the fears of black and white children and of teachers, unalloyed by any significant preparation for desegregation, sometimes created edgy or hostile relationships. Since their children participated in desegregation in any case, riding a bus seemed a less fearsome prospect than previously, and less an act to be rewarded in others. Thus, as both these groups experienced pains from desegregation, they cast a baleful eye upon the magnet schools where other people's children received formal advantages for participating in the process. Further, more of the whites gathered the courage to volunteer their own children, only to find that the most popular schools were oversubscribed and many could not gain admission. For blacks, oversubscription was an even more serious problem.

At the same time, resources in the district as a whole are
dwindling. Enrollments decline, and with them state monies, while
inflation decreases the value of the tax dollar and the willingness of
the citizenry to bear increased taxes. The system has less money
with which to cope with routine needs at a time when desegregation
and its readjustments add new needs. At first the magnets helped
this problem with their eligibility for federal funds that covered
most of their special services; but those funds are temporary and
are fast shrinking—as did Jackson's state money for its special
missions before.

Jackson was closed in response to some of the first signs of
these forces that will increasingly attack magnet schools. The city
council's call for fiscal restraint by the schools and the board's
decision to save money by closing schools were harbingers of the
effects of declining enrollment and financial difficulty. The furor
that was raised over the proposed closing of the black high school
and the two white neighborhood elementary schools (which their
proponents pointed out were both formally desegregated with just
over 25 percent black students) signaled the increasing readiness
of both black and white community groups to express feelings of
grievance and demands for their fair share of resources. What
was more natural, then, than for the board to ask sacrifices from
the privileged parents and children attending magnet schools to
get them through this financial problem? That the majority of
parents and children at Jackson were racial minorities, working
class, and possessed of academic or social learning problems was
beside the symbolic point.

Events that have followed the closing of Jackson have been
consistent with this interpretation. The magnets do not want for
patrons. As whites as well as blacks learn that their relatives and
coworkers have been bussed without harm and educated to their
benefit in magnet schools, a wider group of whites have been willing
to patronize them. All but a handful had both black and white waiting lists for the fall of 1980. Twelfth Avenue and the middle school
for the gifted and talented had sizable ones. White neighborhoods
request magnets when their schools are considered for closing.
The privileges are worth the loss of "traditional" education.

Rhetoric at school board meetings, however, turns increasingly around issues of "equity" and these discussions often raise
magnet schools as signs of inequities to be dealt with. One of
Jackson's supporters said directly at the June 1980 meeting that as
long as specialty schools continue to draw parents there is no
reason for them to have more resources than other schools; their
extra resources were intended simply to get them started. In this
light, the lackluster efforts to recruit children for Twelfth Avenue

and the high school for the college-bound may have been a drawing back from advertising the special virtue of magnets. As I studied the three citywide middle schools from January 1979 to June 1980, I saw a steady withdrawal of staff positions and special resources. Most of this was not announced publicly and it was not in the interest of the schools to announce it to parents, but administrators and teachers agreed that it seriously corroded their capacity to offer the special programs that had been promised.

In part this phenomenon reflects an established pattern. When the special funds that support special programs are withdrawn the programs wither with them. In part it also reflects the political embarrassment that the magnets are becoming. They have created a new, formal, highly visible elite of schools and students. They are a far more open elite than the previous one, since they include racial minorities in substantial numbers and they are open to poor as well as affluent students. However, they violate the terms of formal equity through standardization and make inequality of resources and the exercise of political influence for privilege far more visible.

Advantaged schools thus more easily become a source of resentment in the system among those who do not share their privileges. Some individuals and school communities join in increasing pressures and competition to become part of the elite ranks, while others demand that equity be reestablished in the form of formal parity of resources across all schools.

The rhetoric surrounding the magnets makes profound educational sense. Children do learn in different ways at different rates. A variety of schools would meet their needs better than standardized traditional schools; but the myth of standardized courses and knowledge combined with loose coupling, which allows variation according to local educational and political resources, meshes with our social and political ambivalence over equality of opportunity. To tamper with it for the sake of buffering political resistance to desegregation was one thing. To tamper with it over the long run in the context of declining resources is quite another.

NOTES

1. All proper names used in this account are pseudonyms.
2. This name is also a pseudonym.
3. Naturally my participation in the same school system as an advocate for Andrew Jackson and as a researcher in the middle schools has created some role conflicts. I took the position of president of Jackson's PTO reluctantly, agreeing only because no

one else was available and the parent organization badly needed
strengthening. I did not want to be visible as an advocate of any
kind beyond the walls of Andrew Jackson if I were to be doing research in the wider system. I had not the slightest inkling of the
level of advocacy to which I would be called! It is to the credit of
Heartland's top administrators that though some have become aware
of my double identity, they have not in any way weakened the commitment to the research given by the system before my April 1978
application to NIE. However, it seemed it might strain this cour-
tesy, were I to question districtwide policy makers further about
Andrew Jackson for this study, since it is not included in my research design. I have therefore relied upon information on which
I already had notes or which was available in public documents.

In my work in the middle school, my experience with Andrew
Jackson has alerted me to issues I might otherwise have been slower
to see, and it has generally improved my rapport with both parents
and staffs in the schools—where these are aware of it. I have become a politically inactive parent, though my children are still in
the system. With half a year of field work still ahead of me, I have
waited to interview persons in the district administration until time
has softened my advocate's image.

4. My research in the middle schools has given me some
skepticism of the depth of parental knowledge of schools. The
reader therefore deserves a detailed account of the sources of my
knowledge of Andrew Jackson's internal affairs. I learned from the
conventional parental sources, from my child's accounts and behaviors, and from conferences and conversations with his teachers.
I also learned by helping in a different first grade room five or six
mornings during the first semester. I spoke with the other parents
who came to the small monthly meetings of the parent group. As I
helped to set up a network of telephone contacts on each bus route
to inform parents of late busses and to arrange food and hospitality
for each grade at a winter open house, I spoke to between 30 and
40 other parents on the telephone. After I became president of the
PTO I had several conversations with the principal and with some
teachers about the needs of the school that parents could meet.
After the closing I talked intensively with the principal and about
five teachers both separately and in groups about the nature of the
current program and the probable impact of the move upon it. I
met yet more parents at strategy meetings for the protest. Because
my telephone number was on a letter sent to all parents by the PTO
informing them of the move, I received many calls from parents I
had not previously known about the impact of the move on their particular child and about his or her prior experiences at Jackson.

5. A child with rheumatoid arthritis was constantly teased at his bus stop by the middle-class children who would not accept his unwillingness to run, jump, and throw snowballs, activities that caused him considerable pain. His mother told me that the principal quietly and successfully detailed some older children to see that he was not so teased on the playground at school.

6. I do not mean to imply that Jackson was the Garden of Eden. Teachers talked about students they could not reach either academically or socially. They got angry and some shouted at children who persistently disrupted group activities. There were some tensions and disagreements among the staff. Despite these ordinary mortal failings, the school still attained its positive social atmosphere and academic success.

REFERENCES

Bidwell, C. E. 1965. "The School as a Formal Organization." In Handbook of Organizations, edited by J. March. Chicago: Rand McNally.

Cohen, M. D., J. G. March, and J. P. Olsen. 1972. "A Garbage Can Model of Organizational Choice." Administrative Science Quarterly 17:1-25.

Corwin, R. G. 1974. Education and Crisis: A Sociological Analysis of Schools and Universities in Transition. New York: John Wiley.

Deal, T. E., and L. D. Celotti. 1980. "How Much Influence Do (and Can) Educational Administrators Have on Classrooms?" Phi Delta Kappan 61:471-73.

Deal, T. E., J. W. Meyer, and W. R. Scott. 1975. "Organizational Influences on Educational Innovation." In Managing Change in Educational Organizations, edited by J. V. Baldridge and T. E. Deal. Berkeley: McCutchan.

Dreeben, R. 1973. "The School as a Workplace." In Second Handbook of Research on Teaching, edited by R. M. W. Travers. Chicago: Rand McNally.

Edelman, M. 1977. Political Language: Words That Succeed and Policies That Fail. New York: Academic Press.

Lipsky, Michael. 1980. Street-Level Bureaucracy: Dilemmas of the Individual in Public Service. New York: Russell Sage Foundation.

Lortie, D.C. 1977. Schoolteacher: A Sociological Study. Chicago: University of Chicago Press.

March, J. G., and J. P. Olsen. 1976. Ambiguity and Choice in Organizations. Bergen: Universitetsforlaget.

Metz, M. H. 1978. Classrooms and Corridors: The Crisis of Authority in Desegregated Secondary Schools. Berkeley: University of California Press.

Meyer, J. W., and B. Rowan. 1978. "The Structure of Educational Organizations." In Environments and Organizations, edited by M. W. Meyer and Associates. San Francisco: Jossey-Bass.

Meyer, J. W., W. R. Scott, S. Cole, and J. K. Intili. 1978. "Instructional Dissensus and Institutional Consensus in Schools." In Environments and Organizations, edited by M. W. Meyer and Associates. San Francisco: Jossey-Bass.

Perrow, C. 1967. "A Framework for the Comparative Analysis of Organizations." American Sociological Review 32:194-208.

Waller, W. 1965. The Sociology of Teaching. New York: John Wiley. (Originally published in 1932.)

Weick, K. E. 1976. "Educational Organizations as Loosely Coupled Systems." Administrative Science Quarterly 21:1-19.

Woodward, J. 1965. Industrial Organization. New York: Oxford University Press.

6

A LONGITUDINAL NESTED SYSTEMS MODEL OF INNOVATION AND CHANGE IN SCHOOLING

Louis M. Smith

John J. Prunty

David C. Dwyer

Only on rare occasions are social scientists and educators able to make predictions and then check them out many years later. We are fortunate to have that opportunity. Over 15 years ago we studied the first year in the life of Kensington, an innovative elementary school.[1] The school building was new, with exciting architecture and open space. A faculty had been brought together from all parts of the country. The approach to curriculum, instruction, grouping, and administration was new, different, nontraditional. A number of events and conditions we observed then led us to forecast changes for Kensington in the years ahead. In Figure 6.1, from the original study, we saw incongruities between the community's vision of schools and Kensington's innovativeness. This disharmony meant increased external pressure for both Kensington School and the Milford District Central Administration. As we began to see personnel and policy changes, the handwriting on the wall seemed to read: "reversion to the old Milford type." Fifteen years later, we found our prediction to be true but overshadowed by what we found the "new Kensington" to be. Some of our initial observations on returning included:

▢ The school now had its fourth principal.
▢ While none of the original faculty is currently teaching at Kensington, a core group of a half-dozen has been here for 12–13 years.

Supported in part by National Institute of Education Grant No. G-78-0074, Kensington Revisited. The perspective expressed does not necessarily represent NIE or Milford School District policy or point of view, and no inferences should be made to that effect.

FIGURE 6.1

The Social Context of Kensington's Administrative Change

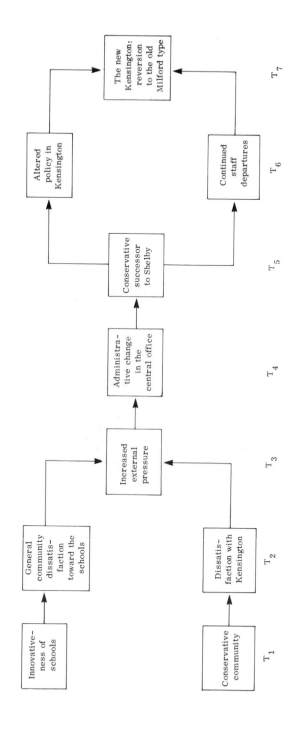

Source: Lewis M. Smith and Pat M. Keith, Anatomy of Educational Innovation: An Organizational Analysis of an Elementary School (New York: John Wiley, 1971), p. 16.

161

□ The physical plant has changed: the outdoor play shelter has been enclosed and made into a multipurpose room, several walls have been built between instructional areas, and barbed wire is strung on the perimeter of the roof.

□ Approximately 60 percent of the pupil population is now black in contrast to the previous 100 percent white.

□ The school is graded and teachers and children are identified by grade levels rather than the broad nongraded divisions (basic skills, transition, and independent study division).

□ Textbooks and dittoed worksheets are now widely used as instructional materials.

□ A special education program for learning disabilities occupies a teacher, a room, and several dozen children.

□ Corporal punishment is now part of a set of multiple approaches to discipline.

In short, our checking on a simple prediction made "unwittingly" years ago ensnared us in some of the most complex and exciting current issues in educational and social science thought.[2]

When we now ask when, how, and why these changes have come about we find a series of events—some fortuitous, others the result of decisions of men and women—related to changes in the Milford District, the county, the state, and the nation. Furthermore, we find that many of these changes are not Milford or Kensington innovations, that is, planned creative changes initiated by the district or the school. Rather, they are reactions and responses to factors originating in these multiple external contexts. As we sought to explain the changes in the school, we found ourselves drawn back in time and into more distant places. Kensington School's immediate geographic and social context is the Milford School District. It will not be surprising to see both the school and the district having interdependent histories. As we began exploring these histories, we found plots and themes that enmeshed with even more far-ranging contexts. It was as if Kensington's history were circumscribed by Milford's, and these two in ever widening temporal and spatial milieus. When we first conceived of returning to Kensington School, its 15-year history seemed to define our task. We found that we could not explain the changes in this once innovative school with such a narrow conception. Our notion of "longitudinal nested systems" is an effort to come to grips with the role of these interdependent contexts in shaping the school we found on our return visit. We have displayed this model in Figure 6.2, which is a simple grid with systems nested on the ordinate and the time line on the abscissa. What is missing are only the concrete events in the Kensington story, which shall soon appear in our

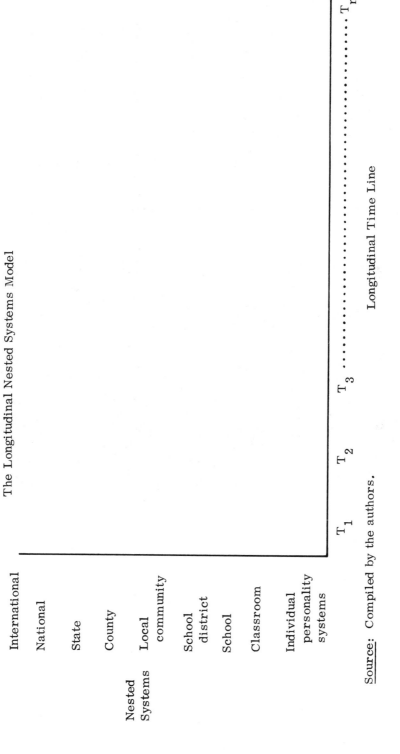

FIGURE 6.2

The Longitudinal Nested Systems Model

Source: Compiled by the authors.

163

historical narrative and later be displayed in our analysis. Our
conception of longitudinal nested systems is really an extension of
our efforts to account for policy and curricular efforts from several intensive inquiries in classrooms, schools, districts, and government agencies (Dwyer, 1981; Prunty, 1981; Smith and Geoffrey,
1968; Smith and Pohland, 1974; Smith and Dwyer, 1979; Smith, 1979;
Smith, In Process). In fact, the rudiments of our model were pre-
saged in our first study of Kensington when we noted:

> At a very concrete level, one of the most striking gen-
> eralizations is that the social environment has a number
> of discriminable parts. Each of these parts is a minia-
> ture social system in itself. These systems have inter-
> dependencies among themselves as well as with Kensing-
> ton (Smith and Keith, 1971:121).

We shall have more to say about this model of change and innovation
at the end of this chapter. We turn next to the Kensington story, in
search of the antecedents to the profound changes the school has
undergone and an understanding of the issues facing the school today.

THE KENSINGTON STORY

Introduction

We begin again the story of Kensington after a long absence.
Both nostalgia and excitement characterized our first return trip.
Some of these feelings were captured in our notes:

> Traveling up here raises all kinds of old images and
> feelings and thoughts of people that have been out of
> my life for years. . . . They're thoughts of the for-
> mer superintendent, the former principal, some of the
> teachers, the trips to and fro that went on for over ten
> months some thirteen years ago. . . . It's a very dif-
> ferent experience than any I've ever had before.
>   Larder Road is totally changed and it's now a
> highway. . . . I've just passed the school which is on
> my left. The flag is flying and the kids are out on the
> playground. . . . Everything else is totally built up.
> I can't get over all of the apartments, the new sub-
> divisions of small houses, the condominium type places

just everywhere. It really mystifies me (FN, 3/24/77).*

Reminiscence faded as curiosity was piqued and several years of work began. Our task was to chronicle the changes, subtle and glaring, that brought about the "New Kensington." We have found those changes extensive and complex, each composed of multiple, historical strands. Some of these were related intimately with the school building itself, the succession of principals, staff, students, and curriculum. Others were by important events and people outside the school and from many points in time. We now begin our story with the broader view, specifically, the changing Milford community and succession of superintendents and board of education membership that led to the creation of Kensington.

Milestones Along the Road to Kensington

Beginnings of the Milford Superintendency

In the early years of the century, Milford had only a single one-room rural school governed by a three-member Board of Education. In the 1920s the district grew in size and numbers, changed its status to a six-director board, began a high school, built an elementary school, the Attucks, for black children.

We choose to begin our story of Kensington in 1928, when the Milford School District was small and still mostly rural. In that year, Milford appointed its first superintendent of schools, Mrs. Claire Briggs. That event, though far removed in time from Kensington School, began the lineage of superintendents who acted to shape the district and its schools. Mrs. Briggs was important because she contrasted with the completely male-dominated administrations that followed her to present times. The historical record of the circumstances that led to her termination were problematical. Prior to her brief tenure as superintendent, 1928-30, she originated the new Milford High School and served as a teacher/principal. Her termination resulted from alleged conflicts with children, teachers, and the Board of Education. One member of the first high school

---

*FN refers to Field Notes. At other points we will refer to TI for Taped Interviews, SO for Summary Observations, and PD for Project Documents, the major kinds of data we have generated. For a more detailed account of our methodological approach, see Smith (1979).

graduating class (1931) in an interview described her personality as "forceful" and "abrasive." Another member of the class, with good humor, phrased his perceptions more metaphorically: "When she said 'frog,' you jumped." The board minutes stated the issue this way: "Our district is growing so rapidly and we are in the midst of a building program this year and we feel keenly the need of a man at the head of our school system" (PD, 1930). Thus, the responsibilities of the superintendent were changing rapidly in complexity and responsibility. They were considered too demanding for a woman by the early Milford board.

Only two superintendents filled the position between Mrs. Briggs and Dr. Spanman, who set the stage for Kensington in 1964. The first, Fred Grey, served between 1930 and 1935. He died suddenly and unexpectedly, a young man. Walter McBride followed him and held the office for 27 years. McBride, who had taken office during the Depression, was replaced in the post-Sputnik and Cold War era. The board replaced McBride amidst considerable strife and controversy. That story bears critically on Kensington, both on its origins and its reversion to the old Milford. We take up next with the controversy and conflict that had Milford hiring its fourth superintendent.

Ending of McBride's Tenure

When a general question arises about hiring a new superintendent, several subquestions come to mind. Why a new superintendent? Why now? and Why this particular individual? Each instance has its own special circumstances, and this seems true of the ending of McBride's tenure and Steven Spanman's joining the Milford District. At the request of a teacher, Ronald George, the president of the local Community Teachers Association, the National Education Association (NEA) interceded on McBride's behalf. Excerpts from a long memo and an accompanying letter provide a vivid introduction. The letter was directed to the president of the Milford Board of Education by the chairman of the NEA Commission on Professional Rights and Responsibilities. The critical substantive paragraph carried the tenor of the remarks:

> As emphasized in the statement, we hope you will recognize the need for deliberate action by both sides in the proposals made. The undignified treatment to which Mr. McBride has been submitted does not affect him as an individual alone—it is considered an affront to all the professional personnel in the school system. Under the circumstances the Board of Education has

nothing to lose and considerable to gain in finding a
solution to the situation that will remove a good deal
of the bitterness from the present conditions and make
possible an immediate step toward a more wholesome
administrative situation (PD, 11/29/61).

Several paragraphs from a report entitled "Treatment of Superintendent" underscore the problem, as seen by the NEA commission:

On April 7, 1961, three days after the election of three
men without previous board experience, the Milford
School District Board of Education unanimously agreed
that the Assistant Superintendent should report directly
to the Board on items concerning curriculum and certified personnel. Until this time, it has always been the
responsibility of the Superintendent of Schools to inform
the Board concerning such matters. It is a surprising
thing that an important decision of this nature, with such
severe overtones, would be taken by the Board without
more first-hand knowledge acquired by official contact
with the Superintendent over a reasonable period of time.

Three months later, on July 11, the Board, by
unanimous vote, requested the resignation of the Superintendent. The Superintendent refused to comply. In a
statement released at a subsequent meeting, the Board
President stated that the resignation had been requested
because the Superintendent "had failed to carry out
Board policies and procedures and had attempted to
thwart them at every opportunity." No specific examples of failures or resistance to Board wishes were
stated. . . .

It was not the purpose of this inquiry to determine whether or not the Superintendent was capable of
performing his total responsibilities. It appears to
many members of the professional staff and to many
citizens, however, that it is nothing short of tragic
for a man who has devoted twenty-six years of service
to the school system to end his career under extremely
embarrassing and unhappy conditions. No information
was presented from any source to indicate that there
had been any dramatic change in the personality of the
Superintendent or any abrupt loss of professional, mental, or physical ability that would warrant such con-
temptuous treatment of the chief administrative officer
of the school system . . . (PD, 11/61).

The commission developed several lines of argument that sketched out the breadth and depth of the problem and the serious nature of the conflict. They indicated multiple necessary aspects of an immediate solution that could at the same time prevent future conflicts of a similar nature. Those recommendations included:

□ Development of a Policy Manual applicable to all administrators, supervisors, and teachers.

□ One part would be "a set of approved personnel policies, including particularly a Fair Dismissal Policy." The latter would include written notice, an opportunity for improvement, and a hearing before final action.

□ Involvement of Board members, administrators, and teachers in the process.

□ Establish an office of Senior Consultant to the Board, equal in salary and coterminous with current contract.

□ ". . . secure the best qualified person available for the position of Superintendent of Schools. In view of the deep-seated emotions that have developed over the present situation, it would be well to endeavor to find someone who has not been in any way involved in the present difficulties" (our emphasis).

□ The new Superintendent should be "a man who will have the personality to win confidence, the background to develop a program of quality education, the integrity to stand for what he and his staff deem important as well as carry out the specific decisions of the Board, and the ability to win the cooperation and devoted efforts of all those responsible for the program of the public schools in Milford."

□ To increase the likelihood of securing an able successor the report suggested setting up an ad hoc committee of several prominent educators to study the district, screen applicants, and develop a short list of several candidates for the Board's final consideration (our emphasis) (PD, 11/61).

Eventually, agreement was reached between Superintendent McBride and the board that reflected the substance of the committee's recommendation. The superintendency was vacated and McBride was hired for the remainder of his original contract as a consultant to the district. One who worked with McBride commented that he was reassigned office space that amounted to not much more than a "broom closet." The resolution of this incident led to the search for the next superintendent.

To pause for a moment, we might review for emphasis several aspects of this controversy and its solution. First, there was the tremendous turmoil that existed over the replacement of the

superintendent. Second, the interplay between the Milford community, the Board of Education, and the district professional staff led
to the election of new board members. The new board initiated
change in policy, personnel, and administration. Their actions
further precipitated reactions by McBride, the community teachers
led by Ronald George, and so on. Third, the district teacher organization had become an important element in district affairs—
policy, personnel, and point of view. Fourth, an outside professional committee, the NEA commission, for the first time was influential in district affairs. Fifth, one of the commission's recommendations was to go outside the district for the next superintendent.
By seeking someone unconnected with the conflict, the possibility of
hiring an "inside candidate" was precluded. Sixth, by working with
a selection committee of outside consultants, a contemporary version of the national "old boys network," Milford was connected to
the men who selected, trained, and controlled careers and job placements of most of the major superintendencies in the country. And
seventh, the final contenders who emerged from the process were
bright, young, ambitious men with outstanding qualifications. Steven
Spanman was one of them—he was impressive and charismatic. For
those who like more homely metaphors, he was described as "a man
who could talk the birds out of the trees." He promised to bring a
quality education oriented to the future to the boys and girls of Milford.

From our theoretical perspective these key events in the transition from McBride to Spanman set the occasion for a number of
changes that were to occur in the Milford District and for the designing, building, and staffing of the Kensington School. The events were
to play a part four years later in Spanman's departure and in the
selection of his successor. We have found items such as these critical to understanding innovation and change in the Milford School District.

The Spanman Era: Lighthouse District (1962-66)

The close of the McBride era found the Milford District in a
pattern of expansion and growing complexity. The tone, however,
was optimistic. A majority of the board—but not all—sought a new,
young, dynamic superintendent to lead the parade. Steven P. Spanman, Ed.D., burst upon the scene ready and willing for a challenge,
a young man clearly on the move, a rising star.

Milford's community newsletters gave a fascinating view of
The Spanman Era. Spanman's editions provided a striking contrast
with the routine reporting of bus schedules, high school sports cal-
endars, homecoming events, and so on, of previous issues. His

sweeping headlines portrayed an educational utopia, down the road
and around the very next corner. In an early edition he urged his
staff to prepare for the future: "New ideas, new ways of living and
new technology require new and equally challenging ideas in education. Teachers must be aware of their added responsibilities because of these changes" (PD, 1962).

The impact of Spanman on the small Milford community was
nothing less than spectacular. In two short years he arrived, found
fertile soil for his ideas, and proceeded at a blinding pace to commit the district to a $1 million construction agenda, entertained na-
tional educational figures, placed the district in the national lime-
light, involved his teachers in an ambitious and exhausting in-service
program, altered the traditional district curriculum, and rallied
parents to his causes. As we indicated in the earlier account,
Anatomy of Educational Innovation (Smith and Keith, 1971), his pace
was too fast for many and his "parade" was left behind. An essential
part of that parade was the old Milford administrators. As an outsider, he was never able to rally them to his cause.

It remains speculation whether Spanman had read the handwriting on the wall—a shifting political and economic climate in the district—or whether opportunity knocked fortuitously, but, still only 35
years old, he was provided a glorious exit. He received an opportunity to spend a year with the National Foundation, a prestigious,
innovative educational organization. In the spring of 1966 the annual
school board elections appeared with their seasonal regularity. A
disgruntled board member, who had been faced down by Spanman
earlier, was joined by two new members, supporters of the earlier
McBride position, and the power shifted once again. One of Spanman's supporters on the school board who had the superintendent's
resignation in hand submitted it. Spanman never returned to Milford
and eventually moved on to a major city superintendency. Kensington,
of course, had been an integral part of the Spanman dream.

The Kensington School

> The setting was the Kensington School, a unique archi-
> tectural structure with open-space laboratory suites,
> an instructional materials center, and a theatre. . . .
> The program exemplified the new elementary educa-
> tion of team teaching, individualized instruction, and
> multi-age groups. A broad strategy of innovation—the
> alternative of grandeur . . . was devised and imple-
> mented. The intended outcome was pupil development
> toward maturity—a self-directed, internally motivated,
> and productive competence (Smith and Keith, 1971:v).

This encapsulated view of the setting captures the excitement and promise of the Kensington innovation. The story of its return to the "Old Milford," the traditional roots from which it sprang, begins in 1964, the first year the school opened under the principalship of Eugene Shelby.

Shelby had come to Milford the year before and remained at Kensington for just under two years. He left in March of the spring semester. In part, some of his problems while at the school are accounted for by the fact that he was viewed as a "deviant newcomer" to the district by other Milford principals and was therefore out of the communication and support network such a reference group provides. Within his own building, conflict during the first year developed with his staff over his professed preference for a bottom to top or democratic leadership style and the increasingly directive stance he developed. In our earlier study we characterized Shelby as "intensely analytical" and "passionate in the pursuit of rationality" and as one whose ego was involved in his work to the extent that his own ideas were seen as "more vital and more real and more ideal than anything else that might be arrived at." Other views of Shelby included his uncanny ability to "sell" his program and building. A staff member reflected that Shelby virtually "brainwashed parents" with the positive aspects of the program. In part, however, the larger Milford District remained unconvinced; but the image we are left with is of a man filled with a true belief in the new elementary education, coming to Milford an outsider and then leaving, relatively unchanged. In his own words, he "continued to pursue the holy grail" in education. His role in the Kensington story essentially ended midway in the spring of the 1965–66 school year as he left the district to begin another innovative school in a metropolitan school district.

Kensington, the school building Shelby opened, was truly a bold reflection of the philosophy and pedagogy it was to house. It was one of the first and most radically designed open-space schools in the nation. Inside, the class areas or "laboratory suites" surrounded a "perception core," a multimedia resource center. The laboratory suites each opened independently to the outside of the school and within to the perception core. However, no walls separated the suites from one another. Other unique areas included an "acting tower" and "children's theatre," a large aquarium, and a "covered play shelter" with a wall-less exposure to the outdoors. A "nerve center" was the central location for audio-visual and electronic equipment. The building further boasted wall-to-wall carpeting throughout, colorful contemporary furnishings, and air conditioning.

The staff assembled to formulate and implement the Kensington program was mostly young, bright, and new to teaching. Most were recruited from outside the district. However, at the end of the first year, all but three of these original faculty resigned. New staff were hired. At the end of the second year, 1965-66, 17 staff resigned. In effect, the end of the Shelby era and the beginning of the next saw an almost complete turnover of staff. Only two of the original staff remained after the second year.

Most of the children came from lower-middle-class families, many of whom had recently joined the suburban Milford community. The parents generally sought the better homes and schools that suburbia provided. Although data were limited even at that time, we sensed that many parents had high aspirations, perhaps unrealistically high, for their children. Those expectations were reflected in the parents' interest in the school. Some parents strongly supported the Kensington program, and others strongly opposed the new ideas and wished to see more traditional modes of schooling. Most parents, however, had vague ideas and understandings about the school. At various meetings parents asked pointed questions regarding the Kensington program. Their involvement and interest were encouraged; this was part of the Kensington plan.

The parents, students, staff, and principal were all to work cooperatively in the grand dream to reshape and revitalize elementary education and it was to happen in the specially designed Kensington School. According to Shelby's vision, Kensington's most general objectives were represented in changing "From" . . . "To" (Smith and Keith, 1971:34):

From	To
Passive, reactive pupils	Active, initiating pupils
Pupil followership	Pupil leadership
Restriction of pupils	Freedom for pupils
External discipline	Self-discipline
External motivation	Self-motivation
Group activities	Individual activities
Restricting pupil interaction	Encouraging pupil interaction
Teacher responsibility for teaching	Pupil responsibility for learning
Teacher planning	Teacher-pupil planning
Teacher evaluation	Teacher-pupil evaluation
Teacher as a dispenser of knowledge	Teacher as catalyst for inquiry
Teacher as controller of pupils	Teacher as organizer for learning
Identical roles for teachers	Differentiated roles for teachers
Closed, rigid social climate	Open, flexible social climate

The fact that Shelby had a vision, especially one formalized in a ten-page document, was an early point of contention in the new school. At least some of the staff welcomed an opportunity to democratically shape the program, an opportunity they believed would be available at Kensington. As with the principal, other staff members had their own ideas about the new elementary education. Subgroups formed both informally and formally among the staff as groups and committees met to discuss or develop the program. T-groups, breakfasts, and after-school meetings all became the forums for discussions, debates, and battles over differences in approaches to teaching methods, materials, pupil control, and staff organization. The disagreements, however, were focused by the institutional plan, Shelby's initial conception. The plan highlighted the individual process-oriented, flexible programs that Kensington would come to epitomize. Discipline was viewed as everyone's responsibility, as Shelby believed it should be in any democratic society. Yet the dream began to give way to grim realities. All was not ideal at Kensington. Generally, the staff began to feel a need for tighter administrative and teacher control of the program. However, even in this regard, misgivings were created as changes were handed down to teachers from Shelby rather than democratically developed. Other problems swirled around the late or nonarrival of materials, unclear student and teacher expectations, increasing tensions between parts of the central office and Kensington, and districtwide hostilities over the perceived "favored son" treatment that Kensington received. Clearly, significant problems existed that cast dark shadows over Superintendent Spanman's multiphase plan to extend the Kensington model to all of its elementary schools.

Finally, in February 1966 with the "dream" barely begun and the reality in a state of disarray, the Shelby era came to a close. The field notes captured the mood of Shelby's farewell party:

> As the people joked, the spirit was much more of we against them—the forces outside the community which were trying to stifle the school and trying to attack the principal. I had the feeling as I talked alone with John that the villain in the eyes of the teachers this year was the district, which wouldn't support the basic idea that the school was trying to convey. He talked most earnestly about "It's been a good idea and there were some unfinished things to be done yet" (our emphasis) (Smith and Keith, 1971:5).

This "true belief" remains with Shelby even to this day. His current perception is that the second year was far more successful than the first, that the district would not support the overall vision of Spanman and himself, and that the realization of the dream would have to come elsewhere.

The year 1966, then, saw both the Kensington principal and the "lighthouse" superintendent, Spanman, leaving Milford. Before continuing the Kensington School story, we must return briefly to the superintendent strand as the new appointee, Dr. Ronald George, again brought the winds of change to all of Milford's schools—but not with the same gale force as in the Spanman tenure.

Milford's Georgian Era: A Contextual Note (1966-present)

Dr. Ronald George quietly became superintendent of Milford on May 27, 1966. One of four candidates from inside the district, Dr. George was voted in on a split 4-2 decision by the board and offered a one-year contract. The new superintendent had taught elementary and junior high school in the district for a dozen years. Recently he had finished an Ed.D. at City University. That quiet inauspicious beginning was not really the beginning, however. Rather, we need to return to 1961-62, the year of turmoil when the board tried to force McBride's resignation and the Milford Community Teachers Association (CTA) for the first time became a major force in the district. Its leader was an outspoken young junior high school social studies teacher, Ron George.

As president of CTA, George's letter had brought the NEA Professional Standard Committee to Milford.

> Be it moved by the Milford Community Teachers Association that the Suburban County Teachers Association, the Midwest State Teachers Association and the National Educational Association be asked to set up a fact finding group which would study the current controversial situation existing between the Board of Education and the Superintendent of Milford School District.
>
> Such group to act as impartial fact-finder and to submit a report of its findings and recommendations to the Board of Education, the Superintendent, the Staff and the Community (PD, 1961).

A copy of the motion and an accompanying letter dated September 11, 1961 were sent to the president of the board. The letter indicated it had passed by an "overwhelming majority." It concluded with this sentence: "We trust that you will hear from each of these organizations soon and will accept this resolution in the spirit in which it is offered."

At the end of that year, George's activities had earned him a place in the board minutes, Item No. 4397, 1961-62. The minutes clearly indicated that the board had not taken George's actions in an entirely positive light.

> Mr. Henderson moved that junior high school teacher, Ronald George, not be re-employed for the school year 1962-63, because of his contemptuous attitude toward board members, his irrational behavior in public, and his totally unprofessional behavior. Mr. Obermeir seconded the motion. Messrs. Henderson, Obermeir, and Tompkins voting "yes" and Messrs. Wilkerson, Baskin, and Randle voting "no." The motion failed. (Tie vote on reemployment automatically fails.) (Board Minutes, Project Documents, 1962.)

Ron George was able to hold on, retain his position, and gain stature over the next few years through the teacher organization. The same board power shift that indicated the end of the line for Spanman created an opening for George. It is ironic that he was both instrumental in the process that led to the hiring of Spanman with the resultant liberal change in district agendas, and, as Spanman's replacement, became the leader of the district's conservative reconsolidation.

In effect, Milford's "back to the basics" period began earlier than did the national trend. The cluster of tighter control and discipline, self-contained classrooms, use of textbooks as curriculum, and assign, study, and recitation teaching methods were part of the mandate the new board presented to Dr. George. In an important sense, this wasn't a major problem because the majority of Spanman's appointments had departed. This meant, in effect, that those on Dr. George's Central Office staff were individuals, as was he, from the earlier McBride era. They were localists and traditionalists in the best sense of those terms.

The Spanman strategy for bringing change to Milford involved establishing a seed bed for innovation embodied by the Kensington School and staff. However, the Kensington innovation had not spread to the rest of the district, ostensibly because of Spanman's early departure. Also, considerable resistance to Kensington's innovative ways had emerged in the district as a result of objections to Kensington's perceived special treatment. Thus, the larger part of the district had not been much affected by Spanman's regime, and the conservative consolidation tended to be more of an accent of what was still in place rather than a shift in what was going on in curriculum, teaching methods, and discipline at Kensington School.

Kensington was the last school built in the Milford District.
Conflicts over bond issues and tax levies, while never disappearing
totally, took on a less pressing and emotionally charged quality.
The size of the district student body continued to rise but at a decreasing rate. The teaching staff was still riding on the salary increase of previous years, inflation was under reasonable control,
and the fact that purchasing power was gradually eroding was little
noticed.

In our view, some of the most important variables influencing
innovation and change in the Kensington School and the Milford School
District are demographic changes and especially population shifts.
They were important items even as they set problems Mrs. Briggs
"could not handle" early on in the district. They consumed the energies of everyone in the 1952-64 period of "population explosion."
Now, in the second half of Superintendent George's tenure, they have
influenced everything in the district. Specifically we would point to:
declining enrollments, changing racial composition, dropping socioeconomic status, and increase in single-parent families in apartments. In addition, and perhaps most critical for the Kensington
School has been pupil turnover or "in and out" figures as the District Central Office staff calls them.[3]

As outsiders, one of our perceptions is that many of the issues
embedded in the demographic analyses have not been pulled out,
highlighted, and addressed directly by the multiple subgroups that
make up the overall school district. We were struck by the difficulties in assembling into one clear overall set of graphs the major aspects of declining enrollments, racial changes, and "in and out"
figures. When "lumped together" they indicate the Milford District
now, since 1971-72 is profoundly different from Milford in 1925, 1952,
1962, or 1966; just as those points revealed other important if not
profound differences. The continuing story of the Kensington School
becomes an important case in point.

The Revisionary Decade of Principal Michael Edwards
(March 1966 to April 1976)

Michael Edwards was born and raised in neighboring Big City
and took his first teaching job with the Milford District in 1949 as
an elementary teacher. In 1956, at age 31, Edwards was promoted
to principal at Field School, where he served just under ten years.
Those who worked with him describe the last couple of years at
Field Elementary as a time when staleness and boredom were beginning to set in. Shelby's untimely resignation in February 1966
drew a half-dozen applicants for the position. Edwards was appointed to fill the vacancy. We were told that Edwards joyfully accepted his new position. As the last few months of school drew to a

close, the staff Shelby left behind rallied around the memory of their former leader. Edwards assumed the formal leadership but never gained that staff's allegiance. At the end of the school year, Edwards received 17 resignations from the teaching staff. Much of the summer was spent in interviewing prospective teachers. Edwards consciously assembled a staff to include new teachers and veteran staff, but selected mostly from within the Milford District. The new Kensington faculty was more experienced and more feminine than the one preceding. In 1980, 14 years later, we find that one-fourth of the teachers presently at Kensington began with Edwards in 1966. In all, one-half of the current faculty was hired by Edwards during his tenure.

We divide the ten-year incumbency of Michael Edwards into two segments. During the first six years, we find some modification of Shelby's vision. We also see an actualization of much of the original plan, and a period of community and school stability. During the final four years we find dramatic demographic changes in the district that affected Kensington and waged major challenges to Edwards' philosophy and plan for the school. The dream's final defeat came with Edwards' death in 1976.

The "Golden Age" (September 1966 to June 1972). Over 600 children arrived at Kensington in the fall of 1966. They were greeted by a new principal, a new teaching staff, and classrooms with textbooks. One of the teachers remembered that first encounter and some of the changes that had occurred over the summer:

> The kids were not allowed to make as many choices.
> [In Shelby's era] they were allowed to make choices
> all day long. And choices in important things such as
> "Do I want to go to math class today, or do I want to
> go out and play?"
> And I can remember talking to him [Edwards]
> about it, and he said, "Oh no, the kids will have
> class." . . . Once we said to the kids, "This is the
> way we're going to do it now, we're all new and this
> is what we've decided to do." There was nothing else,
> we did it that way. And the amazing part of this, the
> kids never said, or very seldom said, "But last year
> we . . . ." I always found that very amazing. [4]
> And another thing I remember is when I passed
> out textbooks, the kids were terribly excited: "This
> is my book?" "Yes, it's your book." "And I get to
> keep it all year?" "All year." They really liked that
> textbook that they could keep in their desk (TI, 1980).

The curricular modifications appeared to have been carried out swiftly and smoothly. They endured throughout Edwards' first six years. The district curriculum guidelines were followed to a greater extent than in Shelby's era. Teachers did more teaching, and students' learning activities were more scheduled and less independent. With these changes, the "perception core," where individualized learning materials were filed and used, took on a more library-like quality and was renamed "resource center." Changes notwithstanding, we are told that Edwards was enamored of much of what he saw at Kensington at the end of the Shelby era. The "continuous progress" philosophy that ignored grade levels, and instead referred to three "divisions"—basic skills, transition, and independent study—persisted throughout the Golden Age of Edwards. "Team teaching"[5] in large open space "suites" also continued. Each division was assisted by a teaching aide.

During Edwards' first six years there were changes in the physical plant, but these occurred more slowly than curricular change. A wall was constructed in the basic skills division, and the "covered play shelter" had its open northwesterly face sealed with brick. "The coldest place on God's earth," as a teacher put it, became a gymnasium and lunchroom. The "aquarium" was drained when carpet lint continued to clog the pumping system and the fish kept dying. Such physical changes, however, did little to alter the overwhelmingly "open" quality of the Kensington School. Visitors continued to flow through the building, but the principal who scheduled their visits was much more casual about the tour and program the visitors received.

Over and above the instructional and architectural change and continuities, we found major differences in the personality and leadership styles of Shelby and Edwards, which led to administrative realignment with parents, students, and staff. Ideologically Edwards and Shelby were both child-centered principals. Edwards' personality enabled him to implement the philosophy and put him more in synchrony with the community. He was able to diffuse much of the community disapproval that welled up in Shelby's time. A Mother's Club parent from the early Edwards period remembered her children's principal this way:

> Mr. Edwards was—how do I put it—just a very special person. Everyone respected him over there, and there were no personality conflicts or anything of the sort. He worked hard with the children, and the children respected Mr. Edwards. He had a way of talking to kids, and he could just say what he had to without using physical punishment or anything of the sort. We

worked with him quite closely with the Mother's Club
(TI, 1980).

Not by edict, but rather by example, Edwards' love of children became a model for teachers. As one teacher reminisced, "I think
all in all that his philosophy rubbed off on a majority of teachers
. . . that you can love a child and teach them. They don't have to
be punished." Edwards' nonpunitive approach to discipline, the
strength of this personal rapport, and a cooperative lower-middle-
class group of students made for few "problems." Students who
were referred to the principal for misbehavior found a soft-spoken
man who spanked only two children in ten years.

The staff division and conflict that marked Shelby's early tenure were changed drastically in Edwards' time. The new principal
allowed the teachers considerable autonomy in instructional matters.
The frequent faculty meetings, and late-night and weekend planning
sessions all but disappeared. One of the teachers reflected on a
happy and harmonious staff who worked hard under a considerate
and thoughtful leader: "The teachers got along together and we really loved each other. It was like one big happy family. It was really
a rare experience" (TI, 1980). In contrast to Shelby, who maintained an administrative aloofness from his staff, Edwards placed
little social distance between himself and his teachers. Parties,
banquets, celebrations, and general good humor were part of the
formula for a cohesive and hard working teacher-principal team,
as described by a teacher:

> We always had surprise parties for him and he got
> various things like a mop for a wig, and he was a
> practical joker, and all of us in turn were practical
> jokers. So this kept the morale of the staff going.
> Like the time we used a syringe and inserted green
> food coloring into his milk, because we knew he always
> ate cereal and it was St. Patrick's Day and there had
> been nothing pulled, I mean, he had made it through
> the whole day and it was lunch time. And when he
> started to eat, the whole staff was up there to see the
> green milk come out and you know, it was just some-
> thing everyone attempted to have a happy time, a
> good time . . . just pranks and fun and games. And at
> the same time everyone was working (TI, 1980).

In spite of the increased structure that came with Edwards,
we still see him as an innovator, but not of the "alternative of
grandeur" variety as his predecessor. Edwards encouraged the

faculty to try new ideas and experiment with curriculum. One of the innovations that arose in Edwards' early years was a special activities program where Friday afternoons had students and teachers involved in projects not available at other times. In what corresponds to extracurricular activities in secondary schools, students learned a variety of subjects such as pottery making, photography, stamp collecting, and auto mechanics. Edwards was not only supportive of teachers' ideas but also took the initiative to bring about change and self-renewal. As one teacher told us, "He was always searching for new things and better ways to do things." This proactive style had Edwards bringing speakers to the Kensington School, arranging and participating in workshops, and arranging for the Kensington faculty to visit other innovative schools for observation and interaction. At the end of what we have called the Golden Age, 1971-72, a small proportion of minority children were enrolled at Kensington. Anticipating changes in the student body, Edwards arranged for a workshop and consultation from a neighboring school district that had undergone racial changes.

The Stressful Conclusion (September 1972 to April 1976). The final four years of Edwards' decade were marked by the principal's failing health, dramatic changes in the racial composition of the community, and major challenges to Kensington's goals, procedures, and norms forged in the Golden Age. When school resumed in autumn of 1972, enrollments fell below the 500 mark, reflecting the more general trends within the school district and nation. The percentage of black children attending Kensington that year was just under 4 percent; four years later, 35 percent of the children at Kensington were black. As we look for the antecedents to the rapid change in racial composition, we find a tangle of determinants with far-ranging origins.

Singleton Terrace Apartments were constructed in a time of Suburban County expansion that had Milford building schools such as Kensington. What had been woodland and a golf course was developed into several apartment complexes. By Edwards' final year, there were some 1,600 apartment units within walking distance of Kensington Elementary School. These rental properties insured an itinerant population of school children. In 1974 a large federal housing project in Big City was closed and demolished, and over 2,000 families living in the inner city were displaced from a culture of poverty. Some of these families relocated near Kensington School. Other black families of more moderate income also moved from Big City with the general county expansion. Some bought homes in the once white subdivision of Kennerly Heights,[6] while others took up residence in the abundant apartment housing. Some of Kensington's

new black families were aided by housing subsidies, a policy re-
sented by some of the white community. The residential pattern of
black families in Milford had half the district integrated, and the
other half nearly all white.

The change in white/black proportions from 24:1 to 2:1 in four
years accounts, in the eyes of the staff, for many of the changes
that occurred in Edwards' last years, as well as the changes his
successors would make. One of the teachers remembered this
transition, the changes it wrought, and some of the mutual adaptation required of new students and the white faculty:

> Just the noise. All right, six years ago never would
> you have found this. If she and I were sitting in the
> classroom where we were visible, where we could be
> seen, our kids would not say a word. The worst thing
> I ever had happen in all the years that I taught before
> that year when things started changing was one of my
> boys—a very bright boy—got mad at another one, and
> put his books in the sink and ran water on them. That
> was the worst thing. . . . I never picked up a paddle
> until four years ago. That was not my way and I've
> taught kindergarten, first grade, you know, all the
> way through. The different language. . . . I remem-
> ber the first time we heard someone was "melling"
> somebody. "Melling," I thought, "Oh dear, how do I
> face this one?" I came to find out it was "messing
> with," you know, "bothering," you know, "upsetting."
>
> Maybe I build this up too much, okay, but I was
> confused. I didn't understand. I wanted somebody to
> help me. I wanted to know how I could keep teaching
> fifth grade reading when my kids were on first grade
> reading level. What do I do? . . . And then the fights.
> We were not used to that at all. And you'd be sitting in
> the classroom teaching when all of a sudden two of them
> would jump up and start going at it. One time I got be-
> tween two of them and I really got hit and it was the
> last time. I backed off and I said I would never do that
> again. . . . It would be interesting to look up some of
> the IQ scores. It used to be nothing for us to have an
> average IQ of 110 and now we're lucky if our average IQ
> in a classroom is 95 to 100. I don't like to go by IQ's,
> don't get me wrong, but it just used to fascinate me that
> there were so many bright kids. . . . The other thing
> was not listening. I could talk 'til I was blue and they
> would talk to each other or they would just simply . . .

they cannot look you in the eye at all. And this looking around would upset me so much . . . do I grab
their face and turn them around? Do I forget it and
not care whether they look at me? How do I handle
that? . . . I could not accept the fact that every
other word that came out of their mouth was, you
know, dirty. And I couldn't accept the fact that they
were so verbal and talked all the time. Not that I
couldn't accept it, just that I was having a very hard
time handling it. . . . I'm speaking more of the inner
city rather than just black (TI, 1980).

Teachers directly related changes in instructional format and
the building itself to their changing class groups:

Teacher A: In those first years I don't ever remember having a child who read below fifth grade level,
and having them at fifth grade level was rare. So now
all of a sudden you had this whole bunch that . . . you
had to revamp your whole thinking, you know, and you
couldn't teach them as a whole group. You had to revamp completely. Because those kids needed more
help and you knew right from the beginning that these
kids are never going to be up to grade level by the time
this year ends.
Teacher B: Yeah, that's sort of when the "divisions" and that all fell by the wayside I think.
Teacher A: And more and more teachers requested walls. That was the first thing they thought—
I say they thought "If I have two walls, one on each
side, it will be better" (TI, 1980).

During the time when Kensington teachers were struggling to
adjust to their changing classroom conditions, Edwards' health began to fail. Despite his illness, Edwards insisted he would see the
school through its trying times. He still believed that his philosophy
and program plan were sound. Yet, as a supportive principal, he
made compromises for teachers, such as the construction of the
walls teachers were requesting. One teacher remembered Edwards'
final days, and the supportive staff that closed ranks around the ail-
ing leader:[7]

We watched him die is what we really did. We watched
the man that used to run up the steps and run down the
steps barely be able to get up, and have a very difficult

time getting down. But never did he lose his finesse,
his class, his ability to make a decision, or uphold
someone, or to tell them they were wrong. . . .
And even when he was in the hospital . . . his only desire was to get back to this school, because this was
his school, this was his responsibility . . . and all
this time we had problems—we had classroom problems,
fights, knives, you know, we had problems. . . . We
didn't take them to him because he had enough problems.
So we learned, in essence, to fend for ourselves, to go
to different people to get the assistance that we needed.
I spent hours on the phone at night getting parental assistance. . . . We just protected . . . I don't think Central Office ever realized for years how sick the man
was (TI, 1980).

Subtle changes in the program occurred in Edwards' final
years. Grade levels replaced the continuous progress approach
and "transition rooms" between grade levels were employed to avoid
retaining low-ability students at grade level. Itinerant Special Services personnel were used to provide help for children with special
learning needs. One of the most significant curricular changes occurred in 1975 with the districtwide adoption of the McMillan Reading series. Its 36 achievement levels made for a more highly individualized approach to reading but at the same time increased the
number of instructional groups for each teacher and required more
preparation time.

The 1972 to 1976 years were difficult ones: difficult for the
group of minority students entering a suburban school, and difficult
for the white faculty unused to teaching black students and lower-
socioeconomic-status white students. Edwards struggled to the last
to uphold the philosophy and plan that had borne fruit in the Golden
Age. The principal held fast to his child-centered beliefs and maintained his soft-spoken, nonpunitive discipline style to the end.
Edwards' impact on the school, and the community's and district's
appreciation for his efforts, is perhaps best seen by a gesture made
shortly after his death. Kensington School was renamed the Michael
Edwards Elementary School. [8]

Marking Time: The Hawkins Years
(April 1976 to June 1979)

As we have indicated, the final three years of Edwards' tenure
were increasingly overshadowed by failing health. The image of the
teaching staff we piece together is much like a team pulling together,

taking up the slack, and getting the job done. All of this was at a time when the community and student population was changing and the teachers' confidence in tried and true instructional methods was being called to question. During these final months of Edwards' tenure, a veteran teacher, Miss Porter, was designated "assistant principal" to help with the tasks that Edwards was increasingly less able to perform. Upon Edwards' death, many of the Kensington faculty felt that Miss Porter would be the logical successor as principal. This, however, was not to be. A teacher made some brief recollections about her being passed over:

> There are no women principals in Milford, as I'm sure you're aware. There was one a long time ago when I first came down here, and she was relieved of her position and made a teacher in Field School. There's not been a woman principal in this district since that time (TI, 1980).

Kensington's new principal was a man named William Hawkins, who grew up in a small rural community and taught and principaled there before coming to Milford in the late 1950s.[9] Miss Porter continued in her "assistant" role, for the transition of leadership was too rapid to be smooth. Hawkins recalled the turbulence surrounding his succession of Edwards:

> One day Dr. George walked in and said, "I've come after you to go to Kensington School as Mr. Edwards' assistant. He's ill and I want you to go over there this morning." Mr. Edwards had gone to the hospital that morning and he died four days later. I never did even get to see him. So I took over cold here.
> I came in cold with the idea of trying to improve the discipline as they were having a great deal of calls from parents at the Central Office. They were having a lot of discipline problems with children fighting and things like this. So the first morning I come into the school, out in front on the circle out here and up on the hill, there must have been 150 kids playing right out in the streets where the cars were coming in. So I decided something had to be done quick. I called the Director of Elementary Education to come over and he came over that morning and we walked around the building and broke up three fights the first time around.
> I suspended three children I think that first week. And things began to cool a little bit. Every time I would

call a parent, practically, their theory was you've got to use a paddle up there at that school and I hadn't been used to doing that. So I tried to break up the situation and I began discipline and to control without it. But after a while, I finally decided that that was the way you had to do it, and the discipline problem was really the thing that bothered me when I came to this school. We don't have that much discipline problem— we do have some yet, we always will have I think. But anyhow, that was what I saw the day that I came over here (TI, 1979).

Underlying the behavioral differences of black children was the perception of attitudinal differences as well. Furthermore, and as Hawkins was aware, there were cultural differences too:

Attitude . . . attitude, I think that's the biggest one. These kids come in with the most horrible attitudes you've ever seen. In other words, if a teacher crosses their path, they may pout, they may bust the kid next door to them or something, you know, they really, really have an aggressive attitude when they get here.

Well, I have had conferences many times trying to figure it out myself and most of the time I get the story, "Well, I worked all my life, he was put out on the street to make it for himself early in life so that's why he developed that attitude. The kids picked on him when he was home, down in the city or wherever. The kids have always picked on him or her." It's not just boys, understand, I'm always saying "him," but it's boys and girls, too. I never say in any school I'd ever been, I never saw the boys—big boys, sixth graders, fifth graders—fight girls, but they would just as soon fight a girl as a boy.

We have a Black custodian—I called him in here, set him down and asked him a lot of questions about these kids. "Well, from knee high on," he says, "they've been taking care of themselves." He said, "The only way they know is to fight" (TI, 1979).

For Hawkins, administration of the Kensington School was complicated by the transient nature of the school's new families and the high turnover rate of pupils. Again, Hawkins commented:

All the areas I taught in were home areas and very
stable, . . . my home town was a small town that had
nothing but families that lived there for years. Raised
up there. McBride School was an area when I started
teaching over there in 1957.

And they were very stable there. When I was
principal over there, if we had four people to move in
and out during the year, it was a big number.

We have that many every week here. Well, I
know we registered two children yesterday morning,
so by the end of the week we'll register two or three
more. Maybe one or two will leave or something.
This is one of the big problems at this school—if the
children are here for a while, I find they fit in well
after they are here for six or eight months but there's
just so many of them that by the time you get some of
them fitting in well, there are probably ten more that
come in with behavior problems (TI, 1979).

The general and serious nature of the problem can be seen in
the 1978-79 year, for instance, when such turnover reached a peak:
49 children came new into the Kensington School and 102 left. Roughly that's 150 children in a school of 450, or one-third of the children
changed. In a class of 30 youngsters, seven of the originals will
leave and three will enter. Included in these changes were a handful of Vietnamese children. Their special needs were met mostly
by the classroom teachers; some special services were provided by
the district. The consequences on class routines, discipline, instructional groups, and knowledge of individual children appear
throughout our observations and interviews. The consequences on
schoolwide programs—band, musical festivals, mother's clubs—
also are apparent. The district problems in housing, staffing, ex-
penses of consumable materials, and so on, are also self-evident.
The cumulative effects of these changes are even more devastating.
In three to five years there is the equivalent of a completely new
population of pupils; and this doesn't account for enrollment changes
made in redrawing school boundaries as the shifts are uneven from
school to school nor the redrawing of boundaries when two schools
were closed at the beginning of 1975-76. In 1980 another elementary
school was closed.

In his candid manner, Hawkins spoke of a further problem he
related to the changing student population:

We have already, I believe, within this year referred
I would say 25 kids to Special District. And all the

children that we refer just about after they've tested them, come up with learning disabilities. There are more learning disabilities than you can imagine in a school of this size. . . .

Observer: Does the district do anything special about that flow of kids in and out?

Hawkins: No, I don't know if there is anything they could do. I mean we have to take them—we have to accept them if they live in the district, and we have to let them go if they decide to leave the district. So I don't know; the only thing that I could see, and I have suggested this many times, is to lower the ratio, and this is what I was talking about a while ago. This school and another school or two have this influx in and out so much that lowering the ratio in those type schools would be an answer to part of it. It wouldn't completely take care of it, but lowering the ratio to 20:1 would help.

Observer: What's the problem with getting that kind of solution implemented?

Hawkins: Money. The same thing with making changes. Most changes cost money. This district is a very poor district, operating on the same tax level they operated on in 1969. Here it is 1979. . . .

Observer: Tell me a little bit about how you handle the "in and out" problem in the sense you mentioned that you send out these procedures on discipline and rules and regulations. Are there other ways that you kind of work on that problem of 100 or 150 kids— have them flowing in and out of the school? Anything special?

Hawkins: No, nothing special, no. When they arrive here, we start testing them and of course we find out as quickly as possible where these children are in their progress and then start trying to meet their needs from that. That's almost a job in itself with as many children as we have and teachers just can't teach as many groups as there are in there. Although I strongly believe in individualization of their teaching, it's almost impossible to do. Now this year we have a 26:1 ratio (TI, 1979).

In short, the changes were novel, rapid, pervasive, and potent, and not all of the changes occurring during the Hawkins era were in response to community changes. New laws, policies, and opinions at the state and federal level also affected Kensington. One

example from the state level was the development and mandated use
of a basic skills achievement test by all public schools. Hawkins
felt the impact of the test on Kensington would be an overemphasis
or a narrowing of focus on just those basic skills. He also commented on a complication in Kensington's discipline procedure that
resulted from a state regulation that required a different procedure
regarding corporal punishment from that of Big City, from which
many of Kensington's new pupils came. Specifically, the variation
in procedure resulted in confused parents who thought the rights of
their children might be overlooked. Hawkins described the Kensington procedure:

> I have a small paddle. [I] bend them over and swat
> them on the seat. No place else. No kid is supposed
> to ever be hit anywhere else. There is another thing.
> These kids come out of the city, and up until last fall
> when the court said that they had the right to do it in the
> city, too, these kids were never [paddled]—they always
> thought Mom has to come and talk to the teacher. . . .
> Out here you don't need that. We are strictly on state
> law. . . . That was the thing we tried to get over to
> them, that there is a difference out here . . . when it
> comes to discipline of the children (TI, 1979).

A further demonstration of outside influence, this time from the
federal level, came during the Hawkins era in the form of an intervention by the Equal Employment Opportunity Commission (EEOC)
affecting the racial composition of the Kensington staff. During the
Hawkins era, Kensington's first black teacher was hired. The principal commented further:

> The EEOC caused us to start hiring black teachers
> I guess. I started asking for black teachers when I
> first came over here, but it didn't take the EEOC long
> until someone had reported us and now we have to hire
> one black teacher for two whites we hire.
> Observer: Is that out of the Central Office or is
> that out of this particular school or . . . ?
> Hawkins: That's in all of the hiring—that's out
> of the personnel office. I hired my first black teacher,
> Mrs. Perry, so I called her and asked her about this
> problem, and she said, "Well, how could I answer your
> question, because I was not raised like they are?"
> (TI, 1979).

This final remark illustrates the complicated nature of cultural, social class, and family influences and the ineffectiveness of a well-intended piece of legislation, at least in this instance.

One final set of factors influencing the nature of schooling we found at Kensington on our return visit was idiosyncratic to the principal himself. Hawkins was ending his career as an educator and planning early retirement. That knowledge greatly affected how Hawkins saw his role at the school and the actions he took while there.

> Two years ago next week, I had a heart attack and have been ill with this ever since—missed probably 40 days this year with being ill. So I have not been able to really put too much pressure on changing the situation around here and knowing that I would only be here for two years.
> . . . It takes vim and vigor to really make changes. You've got to really be able to prove to them that you believe in what you are doing (TI, 1979).

We have described the Hawkins years as "Marking Time." This third principal was a gentle, friendly man, beset with health problems at the end of his career. His roots were small town, rural, southern. He followed a principal who had stamped the school indelibly. Kensington and its immediate neighborhood had continued to change at a rapid pace during his brief tenure.

Jonas Wales and the Current Period of Traditional Stabilization (1979-present)

Like his predecessor Hawkins, Dr. Wales had previously served as a teacher and principal in a rural community. When Wales moved to Milford, he ended ten years as an educator and left tobacco fields, coal mines, and the bible belt behind. At age 35, Dr. Wales began teaching junior high mathematics in Milford at the time Kensington Elementary School was entering its second year in the Shelby era, during which time he met Ron George, the teacher across the hall. After a year with the Milford District, Wales resigned his post and transferred to an adjacent school district. For the next six years, while Kensington was in its Golden Age with Edwards, Wales continued to teach junior high mathematics outside the district. In 1972 he returned to Milford and resumed junior high math instruction for two years. While the Kensington School was entering the "Stressful Conclusion" of the Edwards era, Wales accepted a one-year contract to serve as principal at the Field School. The following year, 1975, marked the closing of Marquette and

Grant Schools and the return of both Wales and Hawkins to classroom teaching. When Edwards died in 1976, Hawkins succeeded
him while Jonas Wales continued teaching junior high math, three
years away from the principal position he would be the next to assume. When the Kensington faculty and Central Office staff met in
the Little Theatre for Hawkins' retirement party, Jonas Wales was
one among many dipping from the punch bowl and sampling the
sweets. Three weeks later, Wales formally assumed his new office.
Title I Summer School was in progress, enrollments were beginning, supplies needed to be ordered, and an unusual building needed
exploration. The teachers would be returning in seven weeks.

Several days of planning in late summer provided Wales and
the Kensington faculty a chance to informally interact. Formal in-
troductions came just before school opened with Wales' first faculty
meeting. It was a robust and outwardly confident man who addressed
the group of teachers. The new principal's brief speech projected
an image of teacher supporter, disciplinarian, and final authority.
Teachers also caught a glimpse of Wales' wit and sense of humor in
a couple of self-inflicted "whale jokes." Our observations of Dr.
Wales' birthday party the first week of classes captured the ease of
Wales' transition and acceptance. He arrived at school to find a
large sheet cake decorated with a blue whale leaping between icing
waves; underneath were the words "Happy Birthday Dr. Wales."
We recorded some of the festive ambience afterwards:

> One of the gifts was a framed picture of "Charlene
> Tuna" wearing long blonde hair and striking a sexy
> pose. The picture was signed "Charlene" with the
> message "To my favorite principal, Dr. Wales. I
> love you." Wales took this with delight and said that
> he would display it in his office. Another gift was a
> certificate worth one "atta boy." When one thousand
> of these were accumulated, Wales was to receive a
> prize. He was warned that if he received one "awshit"
> he would forfeit all his "atta boys." The new music
> teacher made a red paper crown for him that said
> "Birthday Boy" which he wore happily. He resisted
> cutting his birthday cake until a camera had been
> found. I was singularly impressed with the wit and
> congeniality of Dr. Wales in a new school (SO, 1979).

Dr. Wales' disposition meshed easily with the faculty social
system in ways reminiscent of the Edwards era:

> Immediately after the party one of the staff said,
> "Isn't it so nice!" referring to the humor and how

Dr. Wales took it. She began talking about Mr.
Edwards and told how the staff had done something
similar for him. The teachers gave Edwards a mop
toupee which he wore all that day. On another occasion they had given Edwards a different toupee with a
part down the middle. She alluded to the quality of the
humor then and the good feelings it created, and how
today's party was so similar. She was so pleased that
this had happened so early in the year (SO, 1979).

From the group of teachers who had silently borne the stress since
the last of the Edwards era, there was a collective "sigh of relief,"
as one teacher put it. Reciprocally, Wales regarded his staff as
highly cooperative, hard working, and competent. Later he commented to us:

I had talked to some of the people and after that I
recognized the fact that discipline was not as strict,
as tight, as regulated—whatever the word is—that I
would like it to be. And so one of the first things I
wanted to get established was that we were gonna have
discipline, and the kids were not going to be horsing
around in the classrooms. Teachers were going to
teach and discipline was a whole lot my category. So
I have taken quite a bit of time with discipline this
year for that reason. Because teachers should be
teaching and they can't do that if they've got problems
in the classroom. . . . Teachers are to teach. My
job as principal is to coordinate that and to alleviate
any problems that interfere with that and support them
in any way: materials, myself, whatever it takes to
support them in their teaching job. They're supposed
to be teaching. I'm supposed to be a helping person
who makes teaching easier (TI, 1980).

With Wales at the helm, we find the Kensington School align-
ing more with the Milford District policy and practices. Wales was
the first principal to actively participate in the superintendent's advisory committee and having a hand in district policy making. This
involvement with the broader district network provided greater con-
tinuity between the Central Office and Kensington School. Wales'
view of his liaison role was expressed to us: "I've always been of
the mind that the superintendent sets the tone for a district, and the
principal sets the tone for a building and the teachers set the tone
in the way it's going to be run in the classroom" (TI, 1980).

The nature of curriculum and teaching remained constant from the Hawkins era on through Wales' first year. Ability grouping, individualization, worksheets, "teaming," and traditional teaching were unchanged. There were small and subtle changes. One, a sign on a door inscribed "Nerve Center" was replaced by "Reading Room." This last piece of "jargon" from the Shelby era gave way to the functional realities of school life and the preferences of the new principal. By far, the most sweeping changes we noted in the Wales incumbency were in the realm of discipline. More suspensions from school were reported in Wales' first year than in the entire time preceding. Like his predecessors, Wales supervised the lunchroom to free teachers from an onerous duty. Unlike the principals before him, Wales' suitcoat was propped up in the back by a paddle in his back pocket as he walked among the tables in the gymnasium that was once the "covered play shelter." In the spring of 1980, Wales made a significant change in the administration of discipline. A detention program was instituted as an intermediary form of punishment between paddling and suspension. Wales' decision was a response to teacher requests and consistent with his notion of teacher supporter.

Kensington did indeed "tighten up" with Wales' appointment, but that is not to say that all aspects of the school were under his control. Another outside influence intruded on his domain. A recent federal law, Public Law 94-142, resulted in a rush of additional special services to handicapped students that combined with an already active Exceptional Services program within the school. Wales said:

> One of the concerns I had this year was the Special
> District Resource Room. Hadn't worked with this
> concept or anybody concerned with this. . . . I had
> a discussion with the Resource Room teacher personal-
> ly and I was given to understand that it was impossible
> for me to take anyone out of this program once they
> were in it (TI, 1979).

Some teachers also expressed concern with the disruptive influence of Suburban County Exceptional Children's Services. One teacher we talked with had two-thirds of her class receiving some form of special services. The effect was to complicate the task of teaching:

> Here's just one example: if these kids are out of the
> room at the time I'm having English class, okay, then
> it's either reteach to each one of those children when
> they come back or get one of the other students to work

with them which causes more noise problems, right?
It's hard enough trying to teach a whole group, but
trying to teach the same thing two or three times. . . .
Now I know somebody will turn around and say, "Well,
that's your job, that's what you're supposed to do";
well, maybe it is but the more they push on the classroom teacher, the harder I think it is . . . to teach.
We were talking about that this morning. Now when
there is an IEP conference plan, I think that's what
it's called, where you go and plan for the child's program, okay, the classroom teacher is expected to be
there and yet, for instance, with one youngster I have
nothing to do with his math, so why should I be there.
I don't mind being there but if it's scheduled at 8:00 in
the morning then I leave my children to come here an
hour or half hour early which I don't like to do, I like
to stay with them, right there; okay, I'm being selfish
again, but at the same time I don't think it's necessary
for me to be there (TI, 1979).

The new group of school counselors and Special Services staff requested a further change. To facilitate more private conferences
with students and parents, another wall was raised in Kensington.

Districtwide, the trend in declining enrollments made further
school closings in Milford certain. This would require reassignment
of principals. With Wales' low seniority, he and his staff worried
that he would be replaced. When notice was received that Wales was
to sign a two-year contract, another collective sigh of relief was
audible. The trend of traditional stabilization promised to continue.

THE LONGITUDINAL NESTED SYSTEMS MODEL

We have moved from an initial set of predictions into a lengthy
discussion of Kensington's history as it intertwined with other community, district, county, state, national, and even international
events. We also presented in the introduction a skeletal form of our
Longitudinal Nested Systems Model. We indicated that our conception formed around two dimensions, time and space. We are now
ready to flesh out that earlier conception with some specific events
in Kensington's history, demonstrating the use of the model and discussing its contributions to the study of change and innovation. We
also believe this approach extends the analysis of social systems in
education. As such it represents a fresh look at an often underemphasized or overlooked point. Some years ago, Homans (1975 [1941]:4)

simply but aptly stated the importance of such holistic views of inter-dependent systems:

> By studying any state of affairs as a whole, as the sum of its parts and something more, we are often able to understand it in a way we could not otherwise have done. This is a commonplace, but like many commonplaces is important and often forgotten.
>
> Perhaps it is pretentious to say that an attempt will be made to describe the social order as a whole. All that these words mean is an attempt will be made to consider not simply a few of the important aspects of society but rather as many as possible. The list cannot in fact be complete, partly because the records . . . are necessarily fragmentary and one-sided, and partly because different generations of scholars see with different eyes: the men of the present day cannot tell what the future will find they have overlooked.

The Model in Use

The general model we presented in the introduction was a simple grid. The nested systems were arranged hierarchically on the ordinate; the time line was constructed on the abscissa. The generic quality of the model is suggested by the possibility of inserting any set of nested systems on the vertical axis and any time line on the horizontal. In Figure 6.3 we insert the systems we have seen as relevant to Kensington and Milford and add a time line from 1910 when the first records of Milford appear. Into this we place some of the items and events from the stories we have told in our narrative. Simply, we are capturing instances of innovation and change, putting them into categories that are more general and abstract, and then arranging them to demonstrate their temporal relations. We contend that each such conceptual act adds clarity and depth to the Kensington story and improves our ability to think about our original problem: What happened at Kensington? The process has not only been enlightening in this respect but has expanded the initial conceptualization of the study by suggesting further fruitful avenues of inquiry. For example, as we view the Milford District story as an important influence on Kensington events, that story becomes significant in its own right. Now one of our guiding questions is not so much "How and why did this school change from 1964 to 1979?" but also "Why did the Kensington School appear at all in the Milford School District?"

FIGURE 6.3

Selected Events and School Personnel Arrayed on the Longitudinal Nested Systems Model

	1910	1920	1930	1940	1950	1960	1970
International				World War II (1939–45)		Sputnik (1957)	Vietnam War (1960s)	
National (USA)				Post-World War II Baby Boom (1945)	Supreme Court Desegregation Decision (1954)	NEA Intervention in District (1962)	Equal Education for Handicapped PL 94–142 passed (1975)
State (Midwest)				State Law for School Reorganization (1948)			Statewide Basic Achievement Testing (1978)
County (Suburban)				Reorganization of Suburban County Districts (1949–52)		County Services for Exceptional Children (1962)	CSES Involvement in Kensington (1978)
Local Community (several municipalities)						Population Shifts Land Development Extensive Building of Apartments	Community Receipt of Federal Housing Support Population Shifts (1975)
School District (Milford)	One-Room School (1910)	Six-Director Board (1925)	First Superintendent Appointed: Briggs (1928–30) / Grey's Superintendency (1930–35)	McBride's Superintendency (1935–62)	Marquette District Annexed (1949) / Massive School Construction: 10 Buildings (1952–64)	Spanman's Superintendency (1962–66)	George's Superintendency (1966–)
School (Kensington)						Shelby (1964–66) / Edwards (1966–76)	Hawkins (1976–79) / Wales (1979–)
Classroom						Building Walls (1966–)	
Individual personality systems						Charismatic Personalities (Spanman, Edwards)	

Source: Compiled by the authors.

In our first look at the Kensington School in 1964 we focused primarily on the school itself, limiting our comments about innovation and change to people and events connected directly with the school. Analysis of the community, parents, and district administrators was undertaken almost entirely from observations at the school or in meetings that intimately concerned the setting. Today we find that perspective insufficient to explain how Kensington has changed. This fact alone speaks to the increasing complexity of the setting and the methodology needed to understand it. Any issue we would begin to examine—administrative succession, discipline, curriculum, racial change, and so on—carried us into ever wider circles of inquiry.

The multiple categories of antecedents for the changes at Kensington most easily fell along geographical, political, and organizational lines: international, national, state, county, community, district, and school. In part, this captured the spread of the nested systems, but the narrative also indicates that we found much of the interaction between the systems to be typified by conflict, politics, and legal constraints. Each theme and strand we pursued developed as a twisted blend of these multiple systems. Those events that represented innovations—intentional, planned, creative alternatives— soon were entangled in other kinds of change growing out of personal and political interests, activities of other organizations, and forces emanating from larger systems.

A further look at one of the themes in our narrative, the significance of racial change at Kensington, will illustrate these points. One of the most dramatic changes in the Kensington School revolved around a whole series of "nested" national, state, and local events. As we indicated, education of students in Midwest State was segregated legally by race until 1954 when the Brown vs. Topeka Supreme Court decision was handed down. Following that was a ruling by Midwest State and a decision by the Milford School Board. The latter was phrased quite explicitly as noted in the Milford School Community Bulletin:

> Segregation to end in Milford Schools September 1, 1955.
>
> After a ruling from the Midwest State Attorney General and a ruling from the State Department of Education at Capitol City, the Board of Education of the School District of Milford has decided [our emphasis] that segregation in the Milford School District will end on September 1, 1955.
>
> The status of our schools will remain the same as in the past until September 1, 1955 (PD, 1954).

In a larger sense, the court decision and the multiple interrelated events of the deteriorating central city, problems in federally subsidized housing, and public attitudes toward education, school integration, and neighborhood schools led to the large demographic population shifts of the mid-1970s.[10] These, in turn, changed the Kensington School from a school with just a few isolated non-Caucasian youngsters to a school that is now approximately 60 percent black. The cultural, social, educational impact of that shift in population was dramatic.

We find a host of observations captured in the tangled impact: (1) The community consists of predominantly white neighborhoods, some integrated neighborhoods, and a few predominantly minority neighborhoods. (2) Over the years, there were several instances of school boundary changes in the district to balance pupil numbers. Despite those changes, one set of schools in the district remained mostly white, while others became 60-95 percent black. (3) There has never been a black person on the Milford Board of Education. In a recent election two blacks ran for the board. Both were overwhelmingly defeated. (4) Districtwide, there is one black administrator, an assistant principal. (5) Kensington School, in 1979-80, had two blacks, one counselor and one teacher on the professional staff. The teacher was moved to another school the following year because of recency of tenure and declining enrollments. (6) District policy has consistently followed a neighborhood school concept. (7) Kensington staff responded, in part, to their changing student population with more walls, more traditional curriculum and instructional styles, and tighter discipline. (8) Regarding the variety of emotional response to changes in racial composition, one commentator described Kensington positively as "sunkissed," a change for the better. The feeling of another was expressed by an analogy to Kubler-Ross' (1969) analysis of death and dying: Kensington went through stages of denial, anger, bargaining, depression, acceptance, and hope. For better or worse, we find these powerful metaphors. The phenomenon is not one taken lightly. In short, state and federal steps taken to integrate schools are in opposition to local housing patterns, and to continuing locally elected conservative boards, and are less of a priority than a number of educational policies regarding school organization and personnel.

The example of antecedents related to the racial changes at Kensington is only one of a more complex set. It is joined, as told in the narration with other strands such as inflation, PL 94-142, the "back-to-basics" movement, and state guidelines and local concerns over discipline. One more illustrative theme deepens our view of this tangle of strands. Our descriptive stories hinted at the checkered history of discipline in the district and at Kensington School.

Some of the very earliest items in the board minutes were actions taken regarding pupil misbehavior. Concerns over corporal punishment occurred early and the board articulated in 1925 a "no corporal punishment policy" and argued for school suspensions in serious cases and a hearing before the board. Over the years that policy was lost, new views appeared, and the district has wrestled long and hard with what is, in our view, a very complex and difficult practical problem. The initial Kensington policy articulated by Shelby, in its list of "from-to" aspects of its formal doctrine, was an attempt to move from "external discipline, external motivation, restricting pupil interaction, and the teacher as a controller of pupils to self-discipline, self-motivation, encouraging pupil interaction, and teacher as organizer for learning." We have noted that Dr. George's initial mandate from the board and his own predispositions and attitudes lay in the need for discipline and control as a precondition for pupil learning. Our narrative indicated the flow from Edwards to Hawkins to Wales in point of view.

In the spring of 1980, the continuing concern over discipline was reflected in Kensington policies of paddling, detention, and suspension devised by the staff and principal. These have been supported by the Central Office. Discipline was an issue in the recent board elections. One incumbent was described in a news account: "He said he had focused most of his campaign on quality education and discipline within the school system. 'I just believe in discipline,' he said. 'I think there has to be a re-emphasis on discipline in order to keep quality education'" (PD, 1980). The incumbent was returned to the board with over 5,000 votes. The losing members garnered less than 1,000 votes, less than one-sixth of the total. While a number of other issues were critically involved in the election, the point we would make here is the congruence in action across the classroom system, the building system, the multiple aspects of the district as a system, and finally to the Milford patrons' views represented in the annual school elections. We recognize that changes in discipline are but one of the differences we found at Kensington 15 years later. Again, our model helps to simplify the picture of the accumulating effects of actions from the nested systems. By examining the specific events recorded in the model in Figure 6.3 we can develop a more abstract version, Figure 6.4, which illustrates more general classes of actions or antecedents and a general flow of consequences from events in the world, nation, and state to community responses, to the district, and to the school.

In effect, we are back to Figure 6.1 and the prediction from 15 years ago, "The new Kensington: reversion to the old Milford type" (Smith and Keith, 1971:16). Now we can examine Figure 6.4 and see what we have learned. The first conclusion is that Milford has

FIGURE 6.4

A Longitudinal Nested Systems Portrayal of the Changes in the Kensington School

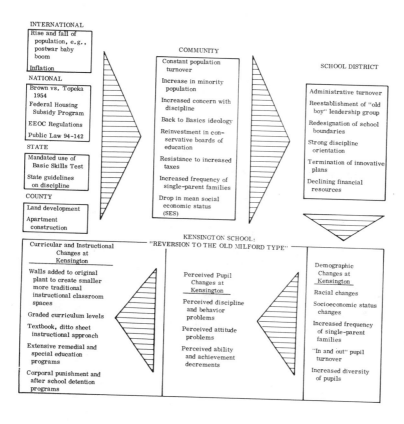

Source: Compiled by the authors.

changed and the return to the "old Milford type" is vastly more complicated than the label would indicate. Edwards did, in part, take Kensington that way, but he, too, was a maverick in Milford and was responsive to many of the original ideals of Kensington. Second, events in the larger systems, in which Kensington is nested, have their own integrity and dynamic, for example, 1954 was a major year. The consequences have been felt only in the last half-dozen years. Finally, and most particularly in the school, the "effects" seem much more interactive than linear. Demographic changes flow in and out of perceptual changes, which in turn flow back and forth from curricular and instructional changes as the various classes of actors in the school—principals, teachers, and children—interact over the years.

With this deepened view of the reestablishment of the "old Milford type" at Kensington and with a more intensive view of the Milford School District qua district and its history since the turn of the century, we are tempted to venture a further prediction. From even before Mrs. Briggs, the first superintendent, when an early attempt to establish a high school failed because of lack of awareness of state regulations, to her difficulties in a tax levy being rescinded because it conflicted with state rules, we find a lack of understanding of problems and concerns with state and federal involvement in education in Milford. The gradual acceptance of federal monies and federal regulations for buildings and school lunches appears in our longer account of the 1930s and 1940s. Today, the concerns in civil rights regarding women, handicapped, and minority education within and between school districts in federal monies for programs, and in multiple federal regulations, are very much a part of the school district. Milford—the community, the board, the administration—seems on a collision course with state and federal regulations. These events also seem to be increasingly a part of state and national politics in the 1980 elections. Candidates made issues and took stands about bussing, decentralization of low-income housing, and amount and kind of federal spending. Perhaps we shall have another opportunity to check our prediction. If so, part of the "next" Kensington story may be a tale of a district and the courts, localism versus state control of education versus federal control.

Contributions of the Model

We emphasize that the Longitudinal Nested Systems Model is not a theory of change or innovation in itself. It is a tool of inquiry and analysis. It offers a structure that helps us think through our data and a format in which our data can be arrayed for analysis.

This perspective has implications for both the metatheoretical and the theoretical levels of analysis. For example, it argues implicitly for a contextualist root metaphor rather than a formistic, mechanistic, or organic one (Pepper, 1942; Sarbin, 1977). Theoretically, it seems open to varied substantive theories, for example, organizational, political, or cultural. In this regard, as the Kensington and Milford stories unfolded and the Longitudinal Nested Systems Model arose, it provided an important understanding for another set of ideas that was dimly perceived in the initial proposal: "Cultural, organizational, and social psychological change theories: an educational test case." A competing theories notion struck us as a fruitful, future effort. What would result if we attempted to compare, to contrast, even to synthesize or extend various theories of change in light of the model? Visions of recent attempts at synthesis by House (1979) on innovation theory and Allison (1971) on policy theory danced through our heads. That agenda both entices and overwhelms us. For now we are satisfied to speculate about these possibilities and postpone the systematic effort and report on its outcome in future publications.

Further, the model helps locate our approach in relation to other social science studies of change and innovation in education.[11] First, we find ourselves examining increasingly long periods of time for relevant information in our inquiries. This differs from the snapshot variety of study that examines a brief, specific period. Second, our perspective involves a holistic view of events; we contend that one cannot understand an innovation or change in a system without considering the larger systems of which it is a part. Third, our model makes explicit a hierarchic arrangement among the nested systems. It highlights the direct and indirect "controls" one system may impose on another. Fourth, the longitudinal nested systems notion allows one to focus on parameters or "givens" of the field of action set by one system upon another. Fifth, it assumes some autonomy both analytically and practically for each system—perhaps less than some educational theorists imply and more than some educational practitioners perceive. Sixth, it builds upon a psychology of individual actors, involved in events or scenes, that cumulate into meaningful structures resembling plots in drama and literature (Kelly, 1955; Sarbin, 1977). Seventh, it includes a respect for the chance event, the fortuitous, the serendipic, which nature forces upon us in the form of health or illness, death, and luck or natural disaster. Finally, our conception aligns closely with the perspective of some historians but we differ from them, too, in that our longitudinal approach carries the time line to the present, the realm of contemporary events.

Our orientation leans us in the direction of storytelling as an important element in explanation of change and innovation. Yet we cannot concede the value of more abstract, conceptual forms of analysis. As such, we place ourselves in a debate commonly waged among historians, that is, how to best contribute to cumulative knowledge. Hexter (1971:151) described this diatribe as "storytelling" versus "scientific explanation":

> Historical stories are quite unlike scientific explanation sketches. The latter are thin; they have to be filled out with missing words and sentences formulating the missing implied laws and boundary conditions. But although historical stories omit a good many laws and conditions, too, and although some laws are rather hard to find even when one looks for them, those stories are not thin; by scientific standards they are often fat, egregiously obese, stuffed with unessential words quite useless for the purpose of adequate and satisfactory explanation.

Although the Longitudinal Nested Systems Model will not resolve the debate, it keeps us moving by providing a working solution to, if not compromise between, "storytelling" and "scientific explanation" and a way to begin to integrate more abstract concepts and theoretical generalizations into thinking about innovation and change in education. More generally though tentatively, we feel that our model may aid discussion of the place of values in educational thought (O'Connor, 1973; Hirst, 1973). We believe that that is at the heart of what is sometimes called practical reasoning (Schwab, 1969; Reid, 1978; Smith, In process). We believe one's viewpoint on the role of values in inquiry and policy making has major consequences for the models one builds in education and the practical decisions that must be made. We would argue that the Milford District was "caught" in its history in a variety of ways. We would also add that the district has forgotten some of its history. That lineage with the past could become an illuminative part of district discussion and debate, curriculum and teaching, and a new perspective on old problems. In that light, our model becomes one form of input into the "what-does-one-do-now" agenda of patrons, parents, pupils, teachers, administrators, and board members. We believe educational research and theory must deal with the questions of values and assist the practitioners through their quandaries. We see some of that begun in Fein (1971), Gittell et al. (1973), Rokeach (1975), and Peshkin (1978). The imperative in this area stems from wrenching issues in conflict today, to wit: the inherent conflict between such stances as "fraternity/community/

neighborhood schools," "equality/justice/affirmative action/desegregation," or "liberty/freedom/individualism/local control."[12] We have seen such divergent values in conflict at Kensington School and the Milford District. We know they are at issue elsewhere too. Our hope is that by telling the Kensington story, and proposing a way of looking at it, we will make a modest contribution to understanding and resolving of some of the complex problems that schools face in the 1980s.

NOTES

1. This account is in book form, Anatomy of Educational Innovation: An Organizational Analysis of an Elementary School (Smith and Keith, 1971).

2. A wider range of issues and research problems have emerged from Kensington School than we consider here. For example, our current efforts include tracing the consequences of the Kensington experience on its original faculty. That fuller account arises out of our current project, Lewis M. Smith, John J. Prunty, David C. Dwyer, and Paul F. Kleine, Kensington Revisited: A Fifteen Year Follow-up of an Innovative School and Its Faculty (National Institute of Education project. Final Report in progress).

3. In our longer report we are wrestling with alternative illustrations and metaphors for thinking about such problems. For instance, New Zealand has a practice of admitting children to school the day they turn five. The children go to a special "entering room" for initial socialization and later to permanent rooms. Is that a possible mechanism to handle the "in and out" phenomenon? Some countries such as Israel have elaborate immigrant induction centers. Do they know things useful to us?

4. Our interviews and field notes are full of perceptive observations such as these comments by one of the teachers. In our final project report, Kensington Revisited, we try to develop in some detail their meaning for curriculum, teaching, and schooling.

5. The term "team teaching" denoted a variety of teacher relationships but mostly a departmentalized instructional process where groups of teachers would specialize in certain areas and switch students. Generally they shared a common open space area, divided primarily by movable book cases and wardrobe racks.

6. Kensington School was originally named after Kennerly Heights and Singleton Terrace subdivisions.

7. Central Office staff who had known him for years as both friend and professional colleague dispute this view. From their perspective, the dilemma is when to relieve a long-term, esteemed

colleague when he wants to continue. How does one minimize the hurt to him and to the school?

8. For purposes of clarity we will continue to call the school Kensington, even though it has been renamed.

9. This rural southern background of Hawkins and a number of teachers at Kensington is part of a larger post-World War II migration to the Milford District as well as to other parts of Suburban County. It poses another kind of clash in the school and district.

10. Similarly, the postwar baby boom, new housing, and jobs in decentralized industry contributed to the expansion of the Milford District from three schools to 14 between 1950 and 1964.

11. Our investigation, Federal Policy in Action: A Case Study of an Urban Education Project (Smith and Dwyer, 1979) is a "history and analysis" also. It anticipates many of these ideas.

12. Whether the values and issues cluster in these ways seems an important analytical and empirical problem in its own right.

REFERENCES

Allison, G. T. 1971. Essence of Decision: Explaining the Cuban Missile Crisis. Boston: Little Brown.

Boorstin, D. J. 1978. The Americans: The Democratic Experience. New York: Random House.

Dill, W. R. 1962. "The Impact of Environment on Organization Development." In Concepts and Issues in Administrative Behavior, edited by S. Mailick and E. H. Van Ness. Englewood Cliffs, N.J.: Prentice-Hall.

Dwyer, D. C. 1981. "Ideology and Organizational Conflict: A Comparative Study of Two Educational Innovations." Doctoral dissertation, Washington University.

Fein, L. J. 1971. The Ecology of the Public School: An Inquiry into Community Control. New York: Bobbs-Merrill.

Geertz, C. 1973. The Interpretation of Cultures. New York: Basic Books.

Gittell, M. et al. 1973. School Boards and School Policy: An Evaluation of Decentralization in New York City. New York: Praeger.

Hatch, E. 1973. Theories of Man and Culture. New York: Columbia University Press.

Hexter, J. 1971. The History Primer. New York: Basic Books.

Hirst, P. H. 1973. "The Nature and Scope of Educational Theory (2) Reply to D. J. O'Connor." In New Essays in the Philosophy of Education, edited by Sir G. Langfeld and D. J. O'Connor. London: Routledge and Kegan Paul.

Homans, G. C. 1975. English Villages in the 13th Century. New York: Norton. (Originally published in 1941.)

Homans, G. C. 1974. Social Behavior: Its Elementary Forms (New edition). New York: Harcourt, Brace and World.

Homans, G. C. 1950. The Human Group. New York: Harcourt, Brace.

House, E. 1979. "Technology vs Craft: A Ten Year Perspective on Innovation." Journal of Curriculum Studies 11:1-15.

Kelly, G. 1955. The Psychology of Personal Constructs. New York: Norton.

Kubler-Ross, E. 1969. On Death and Dying. New York: Macmillan.

Kuper, Adam. 1973. Anthropologists and Anthropology: The British School 1922-1972. London: Aller Lane.

O'Connor, D. J. 1973. "The Nature and Scope of Educational Theory." In New Essays in the Philosophy of Education, edited by Sir G. Langfeld and D. J. O'Connor. London: Routledge and Kegan Paul.

Pepper, S. 1942. World Hypotheses: A Study in Evidence. Berkeley: University of California Press.

Peshkin, A. 1978. Growing Up American: Schooling and the Survival of Community. Chicago: University of Chicago Press.

Prunty, J. 1981. "A Participant Observation Study of a Public Alternative High School: An Analysis of Factors Influencing Organizational Effectiveness." Doctoral dissertation, Washington University.

Reid, W. 1978. Thinking about Curriculum. London: Routledge and Kegan Paul.

Rokeach, M. 1975. Beliefs, Attitudes, and Values. San Francisco: Jossey-Bass.

Sarbin, T. 1977. "Contextualism: A World View for Modern Psychology." In Nebraska Symposium on Motivation 1976. Lincoln: University of Nebraska Press.

Schwab, J. 1969. "The Practical: A Language for Curriculum." School Review 78:1-23.

Simon, H. A. 1962. "The Architecture of Complexity." Proceedings of the American Philosophical Society 106:467-82.

Smith, L. M. In process. Curriculum and Teaching: An Illuminative Evaluation Perspective. London: Croom Helm.

Smith, L. M. 1979. "An Evolving Logic of Participant Observation, Educational Ethnography and Other Case Studies." In Review of Research in Education, edited by L. Shulman. Chicago: Peacock Press.

Smith, L. M. 1978. "Science Education in the Alte Schools: A Kind of Case Study." In NSF Case Studies in Science Education, edited by R. Stake and J. Easley.

Smith, L. M., and D. C. Dwyer. 1979. Federal Policy in Action: A Case Study of an Urban Education Project. St. Louis: Washington University.

Smith, L. M., D. C. Dwyer, and J. Prunty. 1979. "Social Roles and Field Study Knowledge." Paper delivered at American Education Research Association (AERA), Boston.

Smith, L. M., and W. Geoffrey. 1968. The Complexities of an Urban Classroom. New York: Holt, Rinehart and Winston.

Smith, L. M., and B. R. Hudgins. 1964. Educational Psychology. New York: Knopf.

Smith, L. M., and P. Keith. 1971. Anatomy of Educational Innovation: An Organizational Analysis of an Elementary School. New York: John Wiley.

Smith, L. M., and Paul D. Pohland. 1974. "Education, Technology and the Rural Highland." American Research Association Monograph Series on Curriculum Evaluation, Vol. 7.

Weick, K. E. 1976. "Educational Organizations as Loosely Coupled Systems." Administrative Science Quarterly 21:1-19.

7

A THEORY OF DECISION MAKING
IN THE PUBLIC SCHOOLS:
A PUBLIC CHOICE APPROACH

Jacob B. Michaelsen

Theoretical work on organizational decision making has not
led to a comprehensive and well-supported analysis of how resources
are allocated and managed in school districts.[1] Yet such an analysis is essential to evaluating past and current efforts to improve
the schools and to planning new ones. With a well-tested model of
how decisions are made in the public schools, we should understand
better than we now do what changes in financial and governance
arrangements of the schools would lead to improved educational
processes and outcomes. This chapter sets out a theory of school
system behavior that, hopefully, will help to fill this gap and
thereby provide a sounder foundation for formulating public policy
toward the schools.

The theory of decision making in public schools developed
here is adapted from the public choice approach to modeling the
behavior of nonprofit organizations that has recently appeared in
the economics literature. This work brings microeconomic theory
to bear on organizational behavior in nonmarket settings, thus
promising to make this body of powerful analytic tools available for
the study of school district decision making. The defining characteristic of the field of public choice economics is its concern with

The research for this chapter was supported by funds from
the National Institute of Education (Grant No. OB-NIE-G-78-0212).
The analysis and conclusions do not necessarily reflect the views
or policies of that organization nor the views of Jay Chambers,
Daniel Duke, Robert Hawkinson, Michael Kirst, Henry Levin, and
John Meyer, who provided valuable criticism and suggestions.

the conduct of individuals when they pursue their purposes collectively. In it individuals are seen as seeking to advance their own interests in collective as well as individualistic contexts. Public choice theory seeks to discover how the configuration of property rights—those circumstances and arrangements that support self-interested action—constrains and directs productive activity when it is collectively organized. It is the existence of property rights in virtually all organizational settings that makes economic analysis applicable to organizations operating in the political arena.

The plan of the chapter is as follows. The first section provides a review of recent work by public choice theorists bearing on resource allocation and management decisions in organizations operating in nonmarket settings, focusing on the general theoretical features of this approach. The second section adapts these general features to the setting of the public schools with a view to developing specific hypotheses about the behavior of public school systems. Possible ways to test hypotheses drawn from the model are considered in the last section, together with a review of selected evidence bearing on these hypotheses collected by other investigators and some concluding remarks.

DECISION MAKING IN NONMARKET SETTINGS

Some Prior Considerations

In a paper on educational research and development (R&D) policy, John Pincus (1974) suggests some important features that should be contained in a fully integrated theory of how school systems behave. A consideration of his suggestions provides a useful point of departure for constructing such a theory. His method is economic: He characterizes public schooling as an industry, distinguishing an industry (external) structure in which schools are embedded and a bureaucratic (internal) structure in which decision making takes place. Pincus believes "a fully specified model of how school systems behave" would integrate both structures but he does not attempt this himself.

Because the public schooling industry is largely composed of local monopolies, he compares its industrial structure to that of privately owned utilities, finding both similarities and important differences between them. As with utilities, there are substantial impediments to competition for clientele among school jurisdictions. Schooling differs from these utilities in at least two important respects. First, the aims of schooling are ambiguous, "or at least there is no consensus about what priority should be given to various aims." Second, the technology of schooling is unclear; that is, "We don't know what the educational production function is, or even if there is one" (Pincus, 1974:114).[2] These two features must be kept at the forefront of our effort to model school system behavior.

Pincus turns from private utilities to nonmarket-oriented civil service agencies for relevant comparisons of internal structure. He notes especially the self-perpetuating character of public bureaucracies. Thus, "in a self-perpetuating nonmarket system, bureaucratic values become socialized and tend to dominate other criteria; or, in other words, the bureaucratic costs are the real costs of the system" (Pincus, 1974:120). His analysis of these costs is not systematic, being "a blend of evidence and speculation," though it is consistent with the public choice position that these costs stem from the disposition of property rights characteristic of public bureaucracies. Let us now turn to this approach to modeling these bureaucracies.

The Public Choice Approach

Public choice theorists, more than other analysts of modern bureaucracy, distinguish sharply between private, profit-seeking organizations and public, nonprofit bureaus.[3] Charles Wolf (1979) has recently noted that public understanding of organizational failure in market settings is so widespread and sophisticated that it has exerted substantial influence on public policy. Most notably, it has lent support to the growing government intervention in markets on behalf of the environment and of health and safety. In marked contrast, public understanding of the systemic deficiencies of nonmarket organizations is rudimentary at best. Hopefully, the argument developed here, which recognizes and builds on this distinction, will make a contribution to the development of a comparable understanding of nonmarket failure.

The budgets of private firms are derived from sales to customers who, when markets are competitive, can respond to unsatisfactory performance by the firm in two ways: they can attempt to influence the firm's behavior by voicing their complaints, thereby directly influencing the organization's decision processes, and they can turn to alternative suppliers.[4] Since the latter, exit option reduces the firm's budget and the exercise of voice presages the possibility of budget reductions, these options together place the manager of the firm under considerable constraint to attend to the demands of customers. In contrast, the public bureau is typically a monopoly that receives its budget as a block grant through a legislative process. Both because alternative suppliers are virtually nonexistent and exit does not affect budgets strongly, bureau clientele must rely mainly on the voice option. Voice, however, is a much less potent remedy for an organization's clientele when exit is not a possibility because the organization's budget is then much more secure. One way to view the public choice approach is as a theory of the behavior of modern bureaucratic organizations subject primarily to the constraints of clientele voice and, at most, only minimally to those of clientele exit.

The principal features of the public choice approach are as follows: (1) the separation of the factors determining the level and character of the bureau's activities into the traditional categories of demand and supply; (2) a theory of demand that incorporates the results of work on the economic theory of democracy and interest group politics and on the institutional arrangements of representative government including the congressional committee appropriations review process; (3) a theory of supply that recognizes the possibilities for self-interested action by bureaucrats who enjoy a monopolistic position relative to the bureau's sponsor—the body of elected officials—and the implications of depending on grants from taxes rather than on per-unit sales to satisfied customers for revenues; and (4) a model of the interaction of supply and demand that shows that the level and quality of the bureau's activities, the magnitude of its budget, and the ways in which it conducts its productive activity systemically fall short of optimality. This shortfall may be characterized as a twofold departure from efficiency norms. Compared to the level of output and costs of production that would obtain if the activity were conducted under a regime of competitive markets, the bureau's output is too large and its costs of production are too high; that is, the bureau is both allocatively and technically inefficient.

Allocative efficiency is a much more complex matter than technical efficiency. Overproduction by individual organizations will lead to an inappropriate mix of output at the macro level since, if the outputs of some units are excessive, those of at least some others must be less than optimal. It is also possible for the mix of output to be inappropriate at the micro level. To illustrate, individual school districts may meet reasonably well the needs of students who are easy to teach while neglecting those of students whose attitudes and behavior make them slow to learn. Put differently, it is possible for a bureau to produce the wrong output as well as too much output. We shall be concerned with inefficiency as a nonoptimal output mix at the organizational level when we turn to modeling school district behavior.

These departures from efficiency norms arise in the following way. The bureau faces an elected government, or sponsor; together they constitute a bilateral monopoly. The sponsor expresses the demand for the bureau's output as it is generated through its appropriations review processes and voting procedures in the budget it allocates to the bureau. This demand can be conceptualized by analogy to the traditional market demand schedule that shows the successive amounts of funding the sponsor would be willing to provide for the delivery of successive increments in the bureau's output. A cost schedule derivable from the technical knowledge of how inputs are transformed into outputs and from the prices of inputs is attributed to the bureau. Following standard price theory, the demand schedule slopes downward and the cost schedule slopes upward, the two intersecting at what would be a market clearing equilibrium level of output and budget were the activity conducted under competitive market conditions. As Orzechowski (1977) emphasizes, a key contribution of the public choice approach is to show why the level of output and budget are greater than this competitive standard.

The crucial factor leading to this result is the imbalance in bargaining power in favor of the bureau over the sponsor owing to the bureaucrat's superior knowledge of the bureau's cost schedule. Bureaucrats, like the managers of private firms, are assumed to act self-interestedly and hence will exploit this superiority. They do this by maintaining as much secrecy as possible about the bureau's cost schedules. Given the absence of alternative suppliers who could offer to produce demanded outputs for a smaller budget or provide the sponsor information on the costs of production, bureaucrats exploit the sponsor's relative ignorance by proposing excessive output and funding levels.[5]

Why is it in the bureaucrats' interest to obtain budgets and output commitments from the sponsor that exceed the levels the sponsor would choose had it the requisite knowledge to do so? The answer lies in the character of the managerial reward structure in public bureaus. In private firms, managers can be remunerated in ways that make it in their personal interest not to exceed optimal levels of output and budget. In public bureaus the gains from reducing costs and limiting output cannot, for the most part, be shared with managers in privately appropriable forms. Under these conditions, excessive budget and output levels lead to "profits" that are appropriable internally. These "profits" can enhance managerial prestige, insure social and physical amenities, and command the loyalty and cooperation of subordinates.[6] They do not, however, contribute to the efficient production of government services.

To use economic theory in this way requires a number of simplifying assumptions. Thus, output was taken as an unambiguous and, presumably, objectively measurable quantity. The requisite technology for producing this output was taken as existing independently of the needs and interests of participants and objectively knowable by, at least, some of them.[7] Bureaucrats were taken to be primarily self-interested, if not single-mindedly self-serving, leaving little scope for altruistically motivated action. From the perspective of positive economics, the simplifying character of these assumptions is of no particular significance. What matters is whether they lead to successful predictions of relevant behavior. Recent studies provide some evidence that public enterprises have excess operating budgets.[8] Since work in this field has just begun, a definitive judgment about the efficacy of the model with these assumptions is premature. However, if our interest is in the public schools where, as Pincus (1974) noted, ambiguous ends and uncertain means are of the essence, further inquiry into the appropriateness of these assumptions is timely.

Ambiguity about goals and the concomitant uncertainty about technology are probably inherent in all public enterprises. In contrast to a competitive industry where managers need only know how to run their organization profitably for the public's interest in efficient production to be served, in a public bureau an explicit plan or understanding of how to achieve optimality is necessary since there is no counterpart to automatic market forces to move an unwilling or unknowing bureaucrat toward it. Thus, the information required about what is in the public's interest to produce and how best to produce it is much more extensive in a public setting than a private one. Because of this, public managers may only infrequently, if at all, possess an authoritative plan capable of keeping the bureau's activities focused on producing the optimal output mix at least-cost.

A number of difficulties arise if an authoritative version of the bureau's purposes cannot be firmly established. Individual bureaucrats may come to have differing and inconsistent views about the bureau's goals. Moreover, some bureaucrats may act chiefly to advance their own interests. For both reasons some key decision makers may pursue mutually incompatible objectives, making it virtually impossible to achieve any version of the bureau's purposes efficiently. Such an impasse "leads even the most selfless bureaucrats to choose some feasible, lower-level goal, and this usually leads to developing expertise in some narrow field. The development of expertise usually generates a sense of dedication, and it is understandable that many bureaucrats identify this dedication with the public interest" (Niskanen, 1971:39).

In the absence of some powerful offsetting influence, the displacement of goals in public bureaus is likely to be pervasive.

Under such circumstances, the notions of efficiency we have considered lose precision. To be sure, the bureau's budget can still be larger than the sponsor would choose had it the means to offset the bureau's bargaining power; but the notion of efficiency requires a known technology and identifiable input and outputs. What the bureau will be shrouding in secrecy under pervasive goal displacement is not its cost schedules, as in the analogy to market supply and demand analysis, but rather the ways it uses its budget to hold together its activities in face of their potential and actual incoherence as an ensemble.

How useful can the public choice approach be in providing insights into organizational decision making under these conditions since this organizational incoherence makes the possibility of instrumental rationality questionable? Because this incoherence arises primarily from conditions and imperatives within the organization, economic analysis will prove useful in identifying the instrumental rationality underlying bureaucratic decision-making processes. We shall examine later, in connection with school district behavior, a view of this incoherence or "loose coupling" of activities that accounts for it in terms of imperatives arising primarily outside the organization that effectively preclude technical efficiency as we have defined it. For the moment we simply note the wide difference in perspectives on the sources of instrumental inefficacy in public bureaus.

If the activities undertaken by a bureau cannot be regarded as ordered by clear goals and a known technology, they must be ordered in some other way, for they are not conducted at random. They exhibit regularities that persist over time, capable of commanding the resources requisite for survival and growth. We now turn to an examination of what public choice theory offers for developing an understanding of how this orderly structure comes to be established and maintained.

In economic theory, productive organizations are taken to be instruments designed to advance the welfare of their owners. To understand the ways in which instrumental rationality informs the decision-making process in bureaus, it will be helpful to examine the relationship between it and its owners. Our procedure will be to investigate selected organizations along a continuum, identifying the consequences of the separation of de jure ownership from control as we move from the classic entrepreneur-managed firm to the public bureau as the limiting case of such separation. We shall find that as the degree of separation increases, the de jure rights of those who own become increasingly attenuated, being usurped, as it were, by the de facto rights of those who control. Viewed by the de facto owners, the decision-making process may display substantial instrumental rationality even though the organization may verge on incoherence from the perspective of the de jure owners.

It will be helpful to distinguish between the formal and the informal decision structure in any organization. [9] The former, typically explicit, displays attributes commonly associated with instrumental rationality. Thus it would establish priorities in accord with the interests of the de jure owners and call for systematic weighing of budget alternatives in terms of their consequences for these priorities. It would specify the selection of budgets that maximized the welfare of the owners. The latter structure is implicit. It interjects the interests of de facto owners into the decision-making processes. These two structures will usually exist side by side. To the extent that the informal structure is the effective one, actual decision processes will not display the attributes of instrumental rationality. Evidence of instrumental rationality in the informal structure will take quite different forms, as we shall soon see.

Let us begin with the classical entrepreneur under atomistic competition. Here there is no separation of ownership from control. The entrepreneur plans and controls the entire operation. Because he can supervise organizational processes closely, the formal structure is the effective decision-making structure. Given competition, both allocative and technical efficiency are achieved, the entrepreneur maximizes his or her returns, and the public obtain goods and services in the appropriate mix at least-cost.

Now consider a firm that is too large for any single person to exercise effective personal control over it. Consequently the owner must hire managers, thus separating ownership from control and thereby giving scope to the informal decision structure. Meckling and Jensen (1976) have shown that this separation introduces special agency costs; hired managers can be expected to use the informal decision structure to divert some resources to their own purposes. While competition limits their ability to do so, they retain some residual discretion and this, Meckling and Jensen claim, should be considered a necessary cost of doing business. When an agency is necessary, owners may use stock options or other profit-sharing schemes to provide incentives for managers to reduce agency costs. By permitting a fraction of those costs to be privately appropriated by management, the remainder can be kept from dissipation within the firm and thereby appropriable by the de jure owners.

If a firm is large enough to exert influence over market transactions, hired managers will have additional opportunities to divert resources for their own use. When competition is less than perfect, above-average returns are available to firms in the industry if they restrict output. This, of course leads the industry output to be less than optimal. De jure owners can capture the entire gain from the exercise of market power if technical efficiency is maintained. However, the informal decision structure, as with agency cost, makes it possible for the managers as de facto owners to appropriate some portion of the monopoly gains in the form of perquisites, larger staff, and, perhaps, a quieter life.[10] Again, profit-sharing schemes can help to keep this organizational slack from being entirely appropriated by hired managers. Nevertheless, it is clear that the separation of ownership from control can lead private firms to depart from efficiency norms. These departures are likely to be more severe the larger the organization and the less constrained it is by competitors.

Turning now to the monopoly public bureau, we find the separation of ownership from control to be virtually complete. While each member of the public possesses de jure rights in the bureau, none is in a position to exercise effective direct control as is possible in varying degrees in private firms. Public owners have no specific claim on bureau resources that could compensate them for the costs of oversight. Consequently, control must be exercised by elected representatives through the process of representative government if it is to be exercised at all. As with the firm, the hired managers, including all those with power to influence decisions significantly, become de facto owners. However, it is apparently not possible to devise counterparts to the profit-sharing scheme used in firms so that returns to de facto ownership can be enjoyed only internally.

Because de jure rights in the bureau are exercised, however imperfectly, only by elected representatives, all others who possess power to influence the bureau's decision-making processes in their favor—that is, who can effectively exercise voice—should be classed as de facto owners. As in the firm, this class will include hired managers but it may also include others who manage to make their voices heard. What determines who will possess the power to gain benefits from the bureau's resources?

To answer this question, for each group whose members share an interest in the outcomes of the bureau's decisions, let us posit schedules showing the cost and benefits of the effective exercise of de facto ownership rights.[11] I have already argued that the exercise of de jure right by the public at large is precluded by the excess of the costs of exercise over benefits, but both cost and benefit schedules may vary in magnitude among interest groups. Thus, for bureau employees who are connected closely to the informal decision structure, the cost of exercise will be relatively low. Because their major source of income is the bureau, benefits from effective exercise will be relatively high. While costs will generally be higher for nonemployees, benefits may be sufficiently high on particular issues to make possible their mobilization into effective groups.

We may now return to the question of how to understand the orderly patterns of bureaucratic activity in light of the argument that public bureaus suffer from pervasive goal displacement. Even though, from the perspective of the public's interest in efficient production in public enterprises, the ensemble of the bureau's activities may appear to verge on incoherence and disorder, from the perspectives of actual and potential de facto ownership groups, the norms of instrumental rationality may appear to rule. The regularities in the patterns of resources allocation and the management of the bureau's activities should be understandable as a reflection of the net benefits to the exercise of ownership rights for the de facto ownership group or groups. While this explanation may resolve the question of regularities in bureaucratic behavior under goal displacement, it raises another for the de jure owners who, not being well-served, may come to question the bureau's legitimacy. We will return to the matter of legitimacy later.

To summarize, the public choice approach to bureaucracy under representative government predicts systemic departures from efficiency norms in bureaucratic production. The source of these departures is the relation of bilateral monopoly between the bureau and its sponsor in which the bureau possesses superior bargaining power because of its special access to and control over information about its production processes. Because of the inherent difficulty these circumstances create for setting goals and monitoring performance and because bureaucrats are likely to exploit their position to advance their own interests, bureaucratic decision making will be marked by pervasive goal displacement. To understand the patterns of resource allocation and management that arise under such displacement, the notion of de facto ownership rights with cost and benefit schedules associated with their exercise was advanced. To develop suitable hypotheses about the relationship between these patterns and de facto rights, the institutional arrangements that characterize the particular bureau and its sponsor need to be taken explicitly into account. Let us then turn from these general considerations to an examination of the public school industry.

MODELING SCHOOL DISTRICT DECISION MAKING

State government remains the primary sponsor of public schooling in the United States, even though the federal government has been playing a growing role in the conduct of the schools. In adapting the public choice approach to modeling school district

decision making, I shall emphasize state government as the gener-
ator of the demand for schooling. The state expresses this demand
in two ways. First, it establishes an education code that sets out
the formal goals of school districts and establishes rules and regulations for their operation. The formal goals are of a sufficiently
high level of generality to command widespread assent, but too high
to provide direction for the day-to-day conduct of schooling. The
detailed rules and regulations are, in part, aimed at assuring conduct that advances these formal goals. They are also the product
of extensive and continuing efforts by educators and other employees
of school districts to protect and enlarge their de facto ownership
rights in the schools; consequently, they may serve as impediments
to realizing these formal goals. [12] In what follows we take the code
as given and focus on how the local district functions within its
constraints.

The state also grants school districts their budgets. Until
quite recently, budgetary determination took the form of rules
within which local authorities had some discretion over local tax
receipts and hence total expenditures. However, because of pressures for financial equalization among school districts, local discretion appears to be diminishing. It will be convenient in what
follows to assume full state funding of the school budgets. Under
this assumption, the school district does not propose a budgetary
total and, hence, cannot influence the size of its budget during the
recurrent budgetary process. However, the possibility of allocative
inefficiency still remains, for, as we have seen, the output mix at
the district level can still be nonoptimal. Of course, the possibility of technical inefficiency remains under full state funding.

Local governing boards do not appear in the formal public
choice model. In it elected officials serve on legislative appropriations committees that scrutinize the budgets and activities of
individual bureaus. However, these committees typically review
the appropriations of a number of bureaus and their members participate in and have responsibility for a wider range of activities
than these appropriations reviews. Because of their primary,
close, and ongoing involvement in school district decision-making
processes, it is appropriate to give these local governing boards
particular prominence in modeling school districts compared to
that accorded legislative review committees. Jay Chambers (1975)
has done this in his adaptation of the public choice approach to
school districts. His work provides an excellent point of departure
from which to develop a general model of school district decision
making that shows why the governing board's failure as a setter of
goals and as an evaluation of means is systemic.

Before turning to Chambers' work it will be helpful to see the form the main features of the public choice approach take in school districts. Table 7.1 shows the main groups that seek to influence school district decision making, their goals, and the principal factors that constrain their pursuit of them. It is of central importance that only the de jure ownership groups are in a position to consistently press for the advancement of broad public goals. Members of de facto groups may, of course, share these interests, but the shared private interests that make collective action feasible dominate the actions of these groups. The analysis that follows elaborates the relationships and interactions suggested by the table.

TABLE 7.1

Property Rights in School District Decision Making

Ownership Groups	Goals	Principal Constraints
De jure		
Local citizens	Efficient production of schooling benefits, public and private	Cost of exercising voice
School board	Act as trustees for citizens, maximize quality of programs	Resource base, de facto owners
De facto, employees		
Teachers	Control over conduct of work, avoidance of close supervision and evaluation	Site and central administration
Site administrators	Job security, advancement, enlarged resource base	Teachers, central administration
Central	Job security, advancement, enlarged resource base	Board, teachers, site administrators
De facto, nonemployees		
Parents	Enhanced private benefits for own children	Other de facto owners, cost of exercising voice
Special issue constituencies	Instatement of particular policies	Other de facto owners, cost of exercising voice

Source: Compiled by the author.

Chambers was not primarily interested in modeling school district decision making for this broad purpose. Rather he sought to understand salary differentials in the market for teachers. Interpretation of empirical results of wage and salary studies requires some assumptions about the motivations of the demanders of labor. When the demanders are private firms, the assumption of profit maximization is quite helpful. Typically, wage differentials are seen to reflect differentials in productivity. Profit is maximized by taking these productivity differences carefully into account in constituting the firm's labor forces. Recognizing that this interpretation of labor productivity becomes problematic in an industry that has an uncertain technology, Chambers proposed his model as a way to posit maximizing behavior by school districts as a basis for a stable structure of salary differentials keyed to variations in important teacher characteristics. It is this more limited effort we seek to generalize.

Consistent with the public choice approach, Chambers argued that substantial obstacles inherent in the structure of incentives in school districts as they are presently organized and governed virtually preclude overall instrumental rationality in the conduct of school districts. What then do school district managers maximize if they cannot maximize the welfare of the district's de jure owners? Chambers proposed that they maximize the quality of the district's activities as it is perceived, in the first instance, by the district's governing board. What is required to give this hypothesis empirical content is to show how the maximization of perceived quality can lead to regularity in teacher salary differentials across districts and, for our more general purposes, how it can be consistent with the maximization of the welfare of the district's de facto owners, which include, of course, the district's managers.

Beginning with the latter requirement, Chambers makes the connection between the maximization of perceived quality and the private interests of the districts' decision makers in the following way. He posits two main categories of district decision makers: trustees and high-level administrators. Relying on the extensive literature documenting the dominance of the governing board by the superintendent, Chambers (1975:10) argues that, under the superintendent's direction, school administrators

> will tend to avoid controversy and abrupt, drastic changes in policy, and they will manage the system in such a way as to promote the maximum amount of reliance and trust in their personal judgments concerning the operation of the school district in order to minimize the potential for conflict.

If they do this well, they can hope to persuade the governing board that the educational activities they manage and the policies and budgets they propose to support them, and which at the same time serve the interests of the de facto owners, possess the qualities the public's interest in the efficient production of school requires.

The maximization of perceived quality is, as it were, a public cover for the maximization of the private welfare of those who are in a position to influence the allocation and management of district resources. As we have seen, under pervasive goal displacement and the reward system characteristic of public bureaus, maximization of private welfare can create a potential problem of legitimacy, since the de jure owners' interests are inherently compromised. The public side of the maximization process, then, can be viewed as an effort by the school districts' managers to maintain and enhance legitimacy. While they create "images" of good schooling for public consumption, they do not do this out of whole cloth. To illustrate, characteristics of teachers that command salary differentials systematically across districts are likely to be those that have a common sense plausibility whether or not they contribute to student outcomes in proportion to the differentials they command. The district's manager must work with the materials at hand, some of which derive from widespread perceptions of the public about how things ought to work and some of which are of their own making. Whatever the sources of perceived quality, the major impetus for its creation arises from the self-interest of the employees of public school districts.

It might be supposed that the effort to sustain legitimacy in the face of the subordination of de jure ownership interests is undertaken in bad faith. To do so would be a mistake. As Niskanen (1971) has pointed out, the pursuit of displaced goals often leads to the development of expertise and a sense of dedication and, ultimately, to an identification of these lesser goals with the public interest. Individuals who have chosen careers in public education most likely have accepted the legitimacy of schools at the outset. Becker (1973) has argued that most persons have a strongly felt need to believe in what they are doing that leads them to dismiss or reinterpret dissonant evidence that might otherwise produce cynicism and bad faith.[13] If we accept this view, it is easy to understand why participants may not regard the creation of perceptions of quality as manipulative. At the same time it also becomes clear why the process is not likely to be altered by the selection of only "good" people to run the schools.

Chambers' characterization of school district decision making as dominated by the superintendent and high-level administrators serves his purposes adequately but is not sufficiently developed to serve more general ones. Other significant actors need to be identified and their interrelationships specified if we are to gain a full understanding of the systemic features of school district decision-making processes. We may begin by distinguishing two classes of actors: those persons employed by the district and all others. Within each of these broad classes, further important distinctions can be made. Let us turn first to district employees.

In most school districts both administrators and teachers "own" positions as tenured teachers. Only rarely do administrators own positions as administrators. Noncertificated employees do not possess tenure rights, though state law usually offers substantial job protection. Since these persons do not play a critical role in the analysis that follows, consideration of them is deferred to another time. We focus, then, on the relationships between teachers, site administrators, and central administrators and the way in which their de facto ownership rights influence critical decision-making processes.

The bundle of rights included in the ownership of a teaching position includes the right to the basic salary as long as student enrollments do not decline. Since competition from alternative suppliers is not a significant factor in enrollment decline, the budgetary base will depend primarily on demographic and other factors not closely related to individual employee or system performance. In addition to this claim on a position, teachers also possess the right to progress through the salary schedule without regard to individual merit.[14] Hence, salary will not depend on performance either.

These rights constrain the conduct of administrators in a number of important ways. Principals have very limited sanctions and rewards to support their efforts to direct the work of teachers. Because of this, teachers who do not wish direction can safely avoid it. Since the principal's tenure as supervisor depends in part on the support of his staff, the teachers become the principal's primary constituency. Principals and teachers then come to develop reciprocal expectations in which the former recognize and respect the principals' need to maintain their position vis-a-vis the central administration. This mutual accommodation extends as well between site and central administrators, since the latter are well aware of the constraints under which the former work and which condition their own scope of action. In the district hierarchy there is control up as well as down.

This system of mutual accommodation is a major determinant of the ways resource allocation and management in school districts falls short of efficiency norms. As we have seen, the movement toward interdistrict expenditure equalization takes the determination of total district expenditures outside local jurisdiction. As a consequence, allocative inefficiency in the form of excessive budgets will have its source in decision-making processes outside the school district.[15] However, allocative inefficiency in the sense of an inappropriate mix of activities at the local level will remain subject to local determination. Moreover, the existence of the de facto rights of employees will generally preclude sustained efforts to achieve technical efficiency.

The main ways allocative inefficiency arises within school districts is through the preparation and adoption of budgets and policies and the development and application of working rules. Budgets and policies generally go before the governing board for at least pro forma approval. Their preparation is largely in the hands of administrative staff who can often keep their full significance hidden. District employees, in contrast to outsiders, are likely to have a keen sense of how their interests will be affected by budget and policy proposals. Moreover, employees have relatively easy access to the internal processes by which such proposals are generated. Further, if nonemployees cannot express a clear consensus about such proposals, there will be little countervailing pressure to offset the voice of employees. As a consequence, the preferences and priorities of employees will be regularly reflected in budgets and policies at the cost of subordinating the needs and interests of students, families, and the public at large. However, there are occasions when the needs and interests of nonemployees gain prominence over those of employees. We shall consider the circumstances later under which this reversal is likely to occur.

In any school district, rules, procedures, and understandings develop that do not come before the governing board for scrutiny or approval. In many ways these will be less visible publicly than matters that must come before the board. Because of this, public access to their formulation is even more limited than for budgets and policies. We would expect employees to dominate discussion processes more fully in such matters than in those that come before the governing board. To place the issue of who dominates decision making in perspective, it should be noted that the issue arises only when interests conflict and they do not always do so. As Lortie (1975) observed, teachers gain significant rewards from working effectively with their students. Nevertheless, teachers have private interests and, like persons acting in other contexts, will pursue them within the constraints they face. We are concerned here to analyze the effects of this pursuit when interests conflict rather than what happens when interests are harmonious.

Turning to the question of technical inefficiency, in the absence of a well-understood educational technology, it will be quite

difficult to distinguish between excessive costs and the diversion
of resources to serve the interests of employees that we have just
discussed. Nevertheless, some useful things can be said about it
in connection with administrative practices. As we have seen, one
result of pervasive goal displacement is for individual bureaucrats
to select and pursue activities in accordance with their own preferences and priorities so that the ensemble of activities tends to
lack coherence from the perspective of the organization's de jure
owners. Under these conditions it will not be feasible to coordinate
closely the activities of the school district and keep them focused
on clear goals. Thus, the kind of tight coordination and control
characteristic of organizations with clear goals and well-defined
technologies will be absent from school districts—at least from
those in which dissension about goals is substantial. Tight coupling
of activities to each other and to the organization's goals can be
taken as a necessary, though not sufficient, condition for technical
efficiency.

A number of writers have commented on the "loose coupling"
that characterizes the conduct of school district decision making. [16]
They note, for example, that teachers have control over the allocation of their own energy and attention among tasks and students
within the classroom to an extent that is incompatible with the norms
of instrumental rationality. I have argued that this discretion and
the concomitant absence of supervision and evaluation stem from
the rights of teachers embedded in tenure and the nonmerit salary
schedule. These features are themselves ultimately the result of
the monopoly the public schools have over public funds for education. [17] I take this loose coupling then as a necessary consequence
of the systemic deficiencies of public school districts as a producer
of educational services. Later we shall consider a quite different
interpretation of loose coupling where I will propose a test to discriminate between these two views. [18]

I do not mean to suggest that the possession of de facto ownership rights makes employment in school districts ideal or even especially desirable. Because the power to divert district resources
to serve private interests and a personal or idiosyncratic notion of
the public interest is structural and largely implicit, it may be
taken for granted. Indeed it may not even be seen particularly as
power but as a prerequisite for effective public service. Moreover,
the parties to this system of mutual accommodation may find themselves at times in conflict—after all, resources are scarce. On
occasion, the exigencies of image creation may entail compromise
and constraint. In addition, the balance in the system changes over
time—witness the growth of collective bargaining—in ways that disturb existing patterns of allocation and management. If de facto

rights were transferable, individuals could make fine adjustments in their situations by engaging in appropriate transactions, but there is no market in de facto property rights. Returns can be taken in kind only within the overall resource constraints of the organization and with regard to the preferences and interests of other employees. Participants may then come to see themselves as victims of the system at the same time that they are its beneficiaries.

So far, the benefits accruing to district employees from exercising their ownership rights have been portrayed as greater than the cost of doing so for a wide range of decisions. This is likely to be true for the routine conduct of school and classroom activities that bulk large in the total school program. At the same time, the costs are likely to exceed the benefits of exercise for nonemployees in these areas for a number of reasons. First, the mobilization of nonemployees suffers from the perennial obstacles to organizing collective action outlined by Olson (1965). The tendency for individuals to ride free on the efforts of others is much more pronounced when the group on behalf of whom the action is to be taken is large and the members have weak interlinkages. The free-rider problem is much less severe for groups like employees, which have a continuous existence for other reasons. Second, these decisions are not highly visible to outsiders: at least they are much more visible, and their implications much more understandable, to employees than to nonemployees.

Nevertheless, there are other, less routine decisions for which the impact on nonemployees is substantial and highly visible. The benefit from the exercise of ownership rights by nonemployee groups on such issues as bussing for racial balance, school closings, and drastic alterations in school program may be substantial.[19] In such instances we may expect collective actions by nonemployee groups. Further, employees may find such actions to impact on their interest and can act accordingly to raise or lower the cost of effective action by outsiders. As important as such episodes may be for particular aspects of the district's operation, they are not likely to make heavy inroads into the fundamental diversion of resources toward serving employee interests caused by the monopoly character of public school districts under pervasive goal displacement.

To summarize, the unavoidable ambiguity of goals in public school districts and the concomitant technological incoherence provide the occasion for interested groups to propose specific budgets and policies to gain commitments of resources from governing boards, which, if the boards had to devise concrete objectives and plans on their own, would be hard pressed to give adequate direction to district administrators. In school districts, employee groups enjoy superior access to the decision processes that determine the day-to-day conduct of the district's activities. The absence of structures, automatic or administrative, to insure that the interest of employees coincides with the public's interest in the efficient production of educational services means that budgets, policies, and working rules will favor the private interests and personal interpretations of the public interest of employees over those of the de jure owners of the school district. Unless a clear consensus on district goals can be reached, the weak coordination and control of district activities denoted by the concept of "loose coupling" is inevitable. However inefficient the conduct of the schools may appear from a broad, public perspective, from the narrow ones of the groups that have successfully exercised their voice on budgetary allocations, policies, and working rules that affect them, it is highly likely that the benefits they receive are commensurate with the costs they have incurred to achieve them.

TESTING THE PUBLIC CHOICE MODEL

For the public choice approach to advance our understanding of how decisions are made in school districts, hypotheses derived from it must survive rigorous testing. Moreover, these hypotheses must perform better than alternatives. The available alternative hypotheses derive from less comprehensive views of the political context of the schools and focus accordingly on more limited aspects of school district decision behavior. Thus, the institutionalized organization model alluded to above offers a competing explanation of the genesis of goal displacement and the accompanying loose coupling of organizational activities. Because the particulars of this genesis are so central to the public choice model—the tendency toward the pervasive displacement of goals is the key factor in it causing school districts to depart from efficiency norms—it is highly desirable to determine which of these two models best predicts observable behavior. For that reason, this institutionalized organization model will be developed more fully before reviewing ways in which testing might proceed.

Meyer and Rowan (1977) have developed an analysis of the school district as an organization that operates in conformity with institutionalized myths and rituals that determine popular understanding of proper school practice. They see the gaps in the coordination and control of educational programs and other departures from the norms of instrumental rationality commonly observed, not as systemic deficiencies in need of correction, but as means school managers employ to maintain system legitimacy by conforming to proper practice. Attempts to institute close coordination and control and other techniques of rational management could violate popular understanding and hence lead, in their view, to a decline in the educational system's public support and thence to a decline in its effectiveness and possibly even to its dismantling. What is dysfunctional in the public choice model is essential for survival in this view of schools as institutionalized organizations. Whatever the ways in which these two approaches may complement each other, they differ strikingly in their analysis of the sources of loose coupling.

The implications of these two approaches for school district decision making differ substantially. In the public choice model, pervasive goal displacement in school districts, which is a consequence of the ambiguity characteristic of the organization's goals, makes the close coordination and control of district activities and educational programs infeasible. The divergence between the interests of the district's de jure owners and the interests actually served by the resulting patterns of resource allocation and management poses a potential threat to system legitimacy, which the district's staff work to offset by creating images of program effectiveness and quality. The key element in this scenario is the absence of consensus about school district goals. The model implies that were such a consensus to be established, close coordination and control—tight coupling—would be possible. Under certain conditions, which we shall examine below, it may be possible for the de jure owners to establish clear goals for the district and likely that they would do so. If this reasoning is correct, it should be possible to observe relatively tight coupling in such school districts.

By contrast, in the institutionalized organization model, loose coupling derives from sources external to the district. If myths about proper school practice determine the character of the coordination and control of district activities, the quality of coupling will not depend on the extent of consensus within the district about its purposes. Should the degree of consensus about district goals vary significantly among districts, we would not expect to find, following this approach, associated variation in the quality of district administrative practices or the efficiency with which resources are allocated and managed among districts.

Turning now to the ways in which these models can be tested, there appear to be at least three main approaches available. First, we can compare decision-making behavior across a sample of school districts in which one or more key behavioral determinants, such as the degree of consensus about goals, specified by the models vary significantly. Second, we can determine the extent to which the responses of school districts to changes imposed by state and federal governments that affect key operating variables specified by the models are consistent with the response behavior the models imply. Third, we can compare important characteristics of public and nonpublic schools that bear closely on the implications of the models for decision-making behavior. In what follows I shall propose tests to distinguish between alternative hypotheses about the sources of loose coupling that make use of variations in the extent of goal consensus among school districts. I will also review selected evidence collected by other investigators that illustrates the likely results of these approaches to testing models of school district decision making and suggest ways to devise tests along these lines.

Natural Cross-Section Studies

School districts vary in a wide range of characteristics such as location, size, racial composition, tax base, and the level and dispersion of family income. Recent work reported by Paul Peterson (1979) suggests that interdistrict variations of this kind may be associated with significant variations in the feasibility and hence extent of consensus on district goals. If so, analyses of decision-making behavior across districts that differ systematically in the extent of goal consensus may provide a means to test the implications of the public choice and institutionalized organization models of school district decision making.

Peterson found systematic differences in behavior between suburban and central city school districts that he attributed to differences in management objectives. He theorized that because suburban districts are committed to fostering the economic development of their communities, they provide the quality of education for which their constituents are willing to pay. Because families tend to select suburban residences on the basis of their incomes and demand for schooling, school programs tend to "reinforce and increase initial differences in child performances correlated with differences in the amount families pay for schooling" (Peterson, 1979:6). Thus, while substantial differences in quality may be found between suburban school districts, there is substantial homogeneity in family constituencies within each district.

In contrast to this, central city districts have quite heterogeneous constituencies. These districts, focused more on maintenance than development, tend to follow redistributive policies, parceling out resources evenhandedly and independently of differences in the family backgrounds and incomes of their students. The result of this redistribution, Peterson argues, is to diminish the initial differences in child performances that suburban districts enhance.

The evidence he presents on the relationship between property values, student performance, and expenditures in central city and suburban districts and his reinterpretation of the Coleman data support his hypothesis of a dual education system in metropolitan areas. Peterson found property values, student cognitive performance, and school expenditures in the Chicago metropolitan area to be positively correlated across suburban school districts. He failed to find a similar relationship across a sample of central city districts. These findings are consistent with the hypothesis that families get what they pay for in the suburbs but not in the central cities. Reworking the Coleman data, Peterson found evidence, contrary to Coleman's initial interpretation, for school effects independent of variations in family backgrounds. These school effects appear to be most pronounced for whites who live in the suburbs in contrast to a much weaker relationship for blacks who reside largely in the central city. He interprets this contrast as supporting the dual system hypothesis.

Peterson's dual system hypothesis is quite compatible with the public choice model advanced here. He sees the universalistic rules adopted for the allocation of school resources as a means central city school administrators have adapted to protect themselves from the pressures of diverse interest groups for special treatment. While these rules may enable school authorities to claim "that every pupil was being treated equally and fairly," equal educational opportunity is likely to require quite diverse treatment of students given the heterogeneity of backgrounds to be found in the central city. Given this heterogeneity, these rules are precisely the kind of behavior that insures the looseness of coordination and control we would expect to find under a regime of pervasive goal displacement. Central city districts, then, should display ample evidence of loose coupling.

Suburban districts have much more homogenous constituencies than central city districts and appear to deliver the level and quality of educational services their constituencies demand. This homogeneity should make possible a much clearer and more concrete specification of goals in the suburbs than is possible in the central city. If suburban governing boards can specify objectives for conduct with sufficient clarity and concreteness, they may be in a position to both specify the mix of educational services offered and insure the effective coordination and control of the districts' activities. To determine whether this is so, we can compare the internal decision processes of suburban and central city districts to determine the extent to which they differ with respect to the norms of rational management as identified by those who see the schools as institutionalized organizations that cannot adhere closely to these norms.

Response to Interventions

Legislative initiatives can provide opportunities to gain insights in how decisions are made in school districts, especially if these are designed to improve educational programs.[20] Cohen and Miller (1979) report findings on school site responses to Early Childhood Education (ECE) legislation in California that are worth reviewing closely because of the light they shed on the public choice model of school districts' decision making. Their main finding, which is quite consistent with the public choice model, is that when a school is faced with clear and measurable goals accompanied by significant sanctions for failure to achieve them, it moves toward a more sophisticated mode of coordination and control of classroom activities than the loosely coupled mode it previously followed. At the same time, the school falls short of adopting fully the norms of rational management the organizational theory literature prescribes. They point to this "shortfall" but do not attempt to account for it systematically. As I shall show, it too is implied by the public choice model.

The Early Childhood Education program was designed to improve instruction, especially reading, beginning in kindergarten and extending through the third grade. The state gave money directly to elementary schools that had submitted acceptable programs. A central feature of the program was the strict accountability demanded by the state. Schools with ECE programs were regularly inspected and rated in their success in reaching specified instructional objectives. Persistent shortfalls in performance led to the withdrawal of funds. Participants in the preparation of proposals and in the conduct of the program included parents as well as the principal and teaching staff. The prospective benefits of the program were sufficiently attractive to enough of the participants to call forth substantial and sustained effort in a number of California school districts.

Cohen and Miller (1979:1) note that an elementary school is "a simple organization typically lacking in strong hierarchical control and showing few sophisticated coordination mechanisms." Under these conditions instructional activities are planned and managed by individual teachers who need not have similar educational philosophies or instructional objectives and who may display widely different teaching practices. Evaluation of teacher performance is infrequent and has very little bearing on the formal sanctions available to principals. Principals are mainly concerned with managing the routine matters that fall outside the conduct of the classroom activities. In a word, the schools' activities are loosely coupled.

The introduction of ECE to a school introduces very clear and enforceable demands that require coordination and control techniques capable of mobilizing and focusing the time and energy of teachers, parents, and supporting resources in new and sophisticated ways. Cohen and Miller (1979:21) report that "ECE schools show more coordination requiring horizontal communication and mutual adjustment" than the non-ECE schools they studied. Further, failure to employ new coordination and control strategies led "to failure in the decision-making process (as judged by teachers)." Part of this failure stemmed from the difficulty many principals experienced in gaining the cooperation of their teaching staffs. The ECE program required considerable additional effort and surely some teachers were less than wholeheartedly committed to it. Cohen and Miller suggest that some principals were able to obtain the cooperation of their staffs by informally exchanging "resources, praise and personal instructional support." The formal organizational sanctions available to them were too weak to be effective.

Cohen and Miller also report that ECE has not led to systematic performance evaluation through hierarchic controls as the norms of rational management require. They are skeptical that accountability requirements of the kind employed in the ECE program will finally make the schools the instruments of public policy envisioned by those who designed the program. They conclude that "the lack of evaluation even under conditions of increased accountability and inspection of outcomes confirms the suspicion that schools are fundamentally 'different' [from organizations that adhere to the norms of rational management]" (p. 23). They do not, however, explore systematically the sources of this difference.

The failure of principals to engage in significant evaluation of teachers and to employ formal organizational sanctions on the basis of them instead of relying on informal exchanges to elicit cooperation is quite consistent with the public choice model. Consider that ECE programs are grafts onto a system in which the de facto rights of teachers in their jobs and in a nonmerit salary schedule remain unaltered. Were the ECE funds to be withdrawn, the regular, unaccountable program would continue unthreatened. Since ECE may provide some benefits to teachers as well as other participants, their active participation is likely as long as their de facto rights are not compromised and the benefits they receive are sufficient to offset the costs of accommodation to change.

To be sure, the Cohen-Miller study was not designed to discriminate between the public choice and institutionalized organization models of school district decision making. The findings they report are suggestive but hardly definitive. Nevertheless, the interpretation of them presented here suggests that it may be possible to use their approach to design studies of legislative interventions to test these models directly. Moreover, their empirical procedures provide some useful starting points for studying the characteristics of coordination and control systems in suburban and central city school districts.

Comparison of Public to Nonpublic Schools

Schools funded primarily by user fees and whose clients have easy access to alternative providers of educational services should behave differently from public schools in two important respects. The public choice model predicts that fee schools will provide a mix of services that more closely matches the needs and interests of its clientele and will produce these services at less cost than public schools. The institutionalized organization model makes all schooling subject to the influence of broad cultural myths and rituals. If the institutionalized rules dominate all schools, private and public schools should not differ systematically in the ways just described.

Evidence on differences in costs between public and private providers in industries such as air transport, garbage collection, and water supply tend to show public providers to be more costly. [21] However, in such industries output is relatively unambiguous so that the mismatch of output to client needs is not likely to be an important issue and, equally important, unit cost comparisons are feasible. At the very least, the ambiguous character of school outputs will make regression analyses of the kind employed successfully elsewhere quite difficult in the schooling industry. Nevertheless, evidence on the extent of goal consensus, the character of the coordination and control of school activities, and the attitudes of students, parents, and school staff in nonpublic schools can shed light indirectly on the accuracy of these predictions.

The British Columbia legislature has recently made available $500 per pupil to nonpublic schools. Donald Erickson et al. (1979) undertook an extensive survey of public and independent (nonpublic) schools just prior to the start of this new program to provide a baseline against which its impact on both kinds of schools could be judged. The research strategy they employed is based on models of school district decision making quite different from the public choice model advanced here. Even so, the survey findings provide a good deal of indirect evidence on the public choice model. We shall be concerned here chiefly with these findings.

The core of the baseline study was a questionnaire survey of parents, teachers, and students associated with independent and public schools in British Columbia. The survey centered on 37 factors believed to have a clear connection to the effectiveness of programs in the two kinds of schools. A summary of the survey findings follows.

> As compared with public school parents, independent school parents have a notably greater tendency to describe people at their schools as pulling together toward a common goal, and they similarly describe their schools as responsive to parents and acknowledging the need of parental help. As compared with the public school teachers in our sample, the independent school teachers have a greater tendency to see their schools as having a special, widely agreed-upon mission; to describe parent commitment, manifested in a willingness to help out, as high; to describe social relationships in the school as cohesive and supportive; to describe community involvement as extensive and highly valued by the school; to describe themselves and their colleagues as highly committed to the job and to each other; and to describe their work rewards as strong. As compared with their public school counterparts, students in independent schools express a dramatically greater willingness to help out in school functions, describe their teachers as much more committed, exhibit less prejudiced responses regarding minorities, less frequently attribute rewards and punishments in school to luck or injustice, are more conscious that their schools are in jeopardy, describe their schools as more "special," find their teachers and classes more attractive, express more enthusiasm for their school work, and exhibit more self-confidence (Erickson et al., 1979:164, 168).

While not definitive, these findings strongly suggest the absence of substantial goal displacement in independent schools. Indeed, the apparent consensus on goals and the shared commitment to achieve them is not surprising in light of homogeneity of the independent schools' constituency insured by voluntary association and selective admission. This homogeneity was also important in Peterson's suburban schools where goal displacement appeared to be less pronounced than in central city school districts.

This baseline survey is an interim report. As further work becomes available, new findings bearing more directly on the questions raised here may be reported. However, definitive resolution of these questions will require empirical work explicitly designed to test the implications of the public choice and institutionalized organization models in a comparative setting.

One possible way to compare the behavior of public and nonpublic schools follows directly from the line of argument presented above. Consider that selective student admissions policies, self-selection of staff, and the relatively low cost of selecting schools for which enrollment is not conditioned on residential location would make goals more focused and coordination and control of educational activities more effective in nonpublic schools. A comparative study of the extent of loose coupling in public and nonpublic schools should reveal a continuum along which central city schools display the loosest coupling and nonpublic schools the tightest, suburban schools falling in between. In some respects, such as the homogeneity of student populations, suburban schools may resemble nonpublic schools. However, these kinds of schools differ in important ways. Suburban schools are subject to more extensive state regulation, which can impede effective coordination and control. Moreover, suburban school teachers enjoy the security of tenure and the nonmerit salary schedule. The difference appears to justify the intermediate placement of suburban schools. To be sure, the crux of such a study is the measurement of the degree of coupling. However, if a satisfactory solution to the measurement problem can be found, a definitive test of the two models should follow.

Concluding Remarks

A central feature of the public choice model of school district decision making proposed here is the systemic character of the district's deficiencies as an instrument of public policy. The tests proposed above should help to establish a basis for assessing the promise of the public choice approach in the field of schooling. If the model gains acceptance as a reliable account of the salient tendencies of decision making in the schools, the larger, comprehensive analysis of public enterprise offered by the positive theory of public choice will become available for developing public policy to improve educational processes and to enhance school outcomes for students.

This chapter has not focused on the implications of the model for public policy toward the schools. A brief word on that subject may be useful. The central tenet of the public choice approach is that self-interest permeates political life just as it does the marketplace. Just as private enterprise may fall short of social optimality because of the limitations of self-interest, so also may public enterprise fail. Under the present mode of finance and governance of public schools, strategically placed individuals are led to divert resources to advance their own welfare at the expense of the school's clients and the public. The model implies that this structure of incentives, described above as a system of de facto property rights in potential, and often actual, conflict with the de jure rights of the larger public, can be altered only by significantly constraining or eliminating these de facto rights. Conversely, policy interventions that do not address the issue of incentive structures are not likely to have a significant impact on the schools. Since most policy interventions in the schools have not addressed the issue of incentives in a significant way, this is a large claim. Only time and much concerted research effort will tell whether it is a valid one.

NOTES

1. See Michael Kirst (1977) for a discussion of the current state of theory and evidence on decision making in the schools. While he finds current theories unintegrated and incomplete, he does not consider the public choice approach.

2. See Michaelsen (1980) for a discussion of educational production functions and their relation to standard economic analysis. The use of production functions in the analysis of markets makes it possible to account for technology without detailed knowledge of it. This ignorance does not impede the analysis because the necessary technical knowledge can be assumed to be embedded in the industry in ways that facilitate and insure its effective use. Embedded technical knowledge of this kind cannot be assumed in the schooling industry. Consequently, the analyst's ignorance poses special analytic problems as we shall see.

3. An early formal effort to model nonmarket organizations in the context of representative government using price theory was made by William Niskanen (1971). His work has been catalytic, eliciting responses that have filled a number of gaps in his original

model and moved the analysis in important new directions. Niskanen (1975) discusses these contributions and adapts his analysis to them. See also Margolis (1975) for a critique of the revised model.

4. See Hirschman (1970) for a provocative analysis of the means available to the various constituencies of modern organizations for protecting themselves from organizational failures.

5. The analysis here is the traditional one of bilateral monopoly, with one side having superior access to the relevant information. Niskanen (1975) fleshes this out considerably by showing how the sponsor can develop access to this information but argues that the bureau will nearly always retain a significant residual advantage due to this superior access.

6. Orzechowski (1977) shows that Niskanen's model is closely related to the behavioral theory of the firm developed by Cyert and March (1963) and Williamson (1964). The presence of slack and the ways in which decisions about its disposition are made is quite similar in both analyses.

7. Stockfisch (1976) argues that because knowledge about the bureau's production processes in the hands of outsiders can be used to reduce the bureau's budget, bureaucrats will guard it carefully. They might even avoid collecting important kinds of data. "One consequence of this behavior is that a bureau head may not be able to manage his organization even if he 'wanted' to" (p. 15). This loss of control may frustrate bureau heads at times but it keeps outsiders at bay.

8. See Niskanen (1975) and Borcherding (1977) for reviews of this evidence. Much of it is based on the comparative performance of public and proprietary organizations producing similar services. See note 21 for reference to three comparisons of this kind. Some of it pertains to comparisons between public and private, nonprofit organizations. Here the comparisons become more complex since in some instances, such as medical care, consumer choice is mediated by professionals and third-party payment schemes, and in others, such as schooling, it is not.

9. See Thompson (1974) for a discussion of this distinction in the context of modern organization theory.

10. The resources that make these appropriations possible appear as the organizational slack in the behavioral theory of the firm. See note 6 above.

11. Olson (1965) has provided a very useful analysis of collective action that is pertinent here. He notes that while the good sought is the private interest of group members, it is a public good with respect to the group. My analysis follows his discussion of the costs and benefits associated with undertaking collective action.

12. Levin (1974) notes the influential role educational professionals have had in the formulation of public school legislation. In his view, this dominance of the producers over the consumers of educational services "raises very serious questions about the ability of present political processes to reflect true social priorities in the educational arena" (p. 378).

13. Becker (1973) makes a fascinating case that the need to believe in the sense used here is one of the fundamental human motives, more basic, for example, than Freud's libido.

14. See Staaf (1977) for a discussion of salary schedules for teachers and administrators and how they reflect de facto ownership rights.

15. Following the public choice approach, excessive budgets result from strong representation of organized interest groups in the deliberative processes of representative government compared to that of the general body of voters and taxpayers. In jurisdictions in which referenda may initiate outside these processes, budgets could turn out to be less than optimal. For example, in California Proposition 13 was defeated in some local jurisdictions even though it passed by a wide margin in the state as a whole. The analysis presented here assumes that such referenda do not occur, though it could be modified to take account of them.

16. See, for example, Meyer and Rowan (1977), Cohen, March and Olsen (1972), and March and Olsen (1976).

17. West (1967) documents that up to the last quarter of the nineteenth century in New York State, schooling was provided by a substantial number of private and public schools dependent on tuition fees. Public schooling became a monopoly only after the legislature, strongly influenced by organized educational professionals, made public schools free and compulsory. The literature on the role of professionals in establishing nonmerit salary schedules and tenure is scant. In the absence of a satisfactory documentation on how these aspects of current teaching positions became established, we are constrained to treat them as a fait accompli.

18. Levin (1976) treats the school district as a political arena in which coalitions of interested groups act to influence the allocation of resources. His emphasis on coalition politics as an explanation of how decisions are made subordinates organizational issues such as loose coupling and its causes. The public choice approach allows for coalition politics among such groups but also addresses these organizational issues explicitly.

19. Boyd (1976) provides a very useful discussion of the kinds of issues around which various nonemployee groups may organize and seek to express their voice in district decision-making processes.

20. Legislation that changes funding levels without altering governance arrangements can provide such opportunities as well. The findings of Kirst (1977) and Smith (1977), for example, strongly suggest that school districts allocate unrestricted increases in funds according to preexisting priorities. Some evidence on the allocation of unrestricted decreases in funds is described later in the chapter. Michaelsen (1980) proposes tests of hypotheses about the effects of recent financial reform in California that did entail changes in school district governance.

21. See Davies (1971), Spann (1977), and Crain and Zardkoohi (1978).

REFERENCES

Becker, Ernest. 1973. The Denial of Death. New York: The Free Press.

Borcherding, Thomas E., ed. 1977. Budgets and Bureaucrats: The Sources of Government Growth. Durham, N.C.: Duke University Press.

Boyd, William L. 1976. "The Public, the Professionals, and Educational Policy Making: Who Governs?" Teachers College Record 77:539-77.

Chambers, Jay G. 1975. "An Economic Analysis of Decision-Making in Public School Districts." Rochester, N.Y.: University of Rochester. Mimeographed.

Cohen, Elizabeth, and Russell H. Miller. 1979. "Increased Accountability and the Organization of the Schools." Stanford, Calif.: Stanford University. Mimeographed.

Cohen, Michael D., James G. March, and Johan P. Olsen. 1972. "A Garbage Can Model of Organizational Choice." Administrative Science Quarterly 17:1-25.

Crain, W. Mark, and Asghar Zardkoohi. 1978. "A Test of the Property Rights Theory of the Firm: Water Utilities in the United States." Journal of Law and Economics 20:395-408.

Cyert, Richard M., and James G. March. 1963. A Behavioral Theory of the Firm. Englewood Cliffs, N.J.: Prentice-Hall.

Davies, David G. 1971. "The Efficiency of Public Versus Private Firms: The Case of Australia's Two Airlines." Journal of Law and Economics 14: 149-65.

Erickson, Donald A., Lloyd MacDonald, and Michael E. Manely-Casimir. 1979. Characteristics and Relationships in Public and Independent Schools: COPIS Baseline Interim Report. Center for Research in Private Education, University of San Francisco, and Educational Research Institute of British Columbia, Vancouver.

Hirschman, Albert. 1970. Exit Voice and Loyalty. Cambridge, Mass.: Harvard University Press.

Kirst, Michael W. 1977. "What Happens at the Local Level after School Finance Reform?" Policy Analysis 3:301-24.

Levin, Henry M. 1974. "A Conceptual Framework for Accountability in Education." School Review 82:363-91.

Levin, Henry M. 1976. "Effects of Expenditure Increases on Educational Resource Allocation and Effectiveness." In The Limits of Educational Reform, edited by Martin Carnoy and Henry M. Levin. New York: David McKay.

Lortie, Dan C. 1975. Schoolteacher. Chicago: University of Chicago Press.

March, James G., and Johan P. Olsen. 1976. Ambiguity and Choice in Organizations. Bergen: Universitetsforlaget.

Margolis, Julius. 1975. "Bureaucrats and Politicians, Comment." Journal of Law and Economics 18:645-59.

Meckling, William, and Michael Jensen. 1976. "Theory of the Firm: Managerial Behavior, Agency Costs and Ownership Structure." Journal of Financial Economics 3:305-60.

Meyer, John W., and Brian Rowan. 1977. "Institutionalized Organizations: Formal Structure vs. Myth and Ceremony." American Journal of Sociology 83:340-63.

Michaelsen, Jacob B. 1980. "Assessing the Efficacy of Financial Reform in California." American Journal of Education 88:145-78. forthcoming

Niskanen, William. 1971. Bureaucracy and Representative Government. Chicago: Aldine-Atherton.

Niskanen, William. 1975. "Bureaucrats and Politicians." Journal of Law and Economics 18:617-43.

Olson, Mancur, Jr. 1965. The Logic of Collective Action. Cambridge, Mass.: Harvard University Press.

Orzechowski, William. 1977. "Economic Models of Bureaucracy: Survey, Extensions, and Evidence." In Budgets and Bureaucrats: The Sources of Government Growth, edited by Thomas E. Borcherding. Durham, N.C.: Duke University Press.

Peterson, Paul E. 1979. "Developmental Versus Redistributive Policies in Central City and Suburban Schools." Paper presented at the Annual Meetings of the American Educational Research Association, San Francisco, April.

Pincus, John. 1974. "Incentives for Innovation in the Public Schools." Review of Educational Research 44:113-44.

Smith, James R. 1977. Predicting the Effects at the Local Level of State Educational Finance Equalization. Doctoral Dissertation, School of Education, Stanford University.

Spann, Robert M. 1977. "Public Versus Private Provision of Government Services." In Budgets and Bureaucrats: The Sources of Government Growth, edited by Thomas E. Borcherding. Durham, N.C.: Duke University Press.

Staaf, Robert J. 1977. "The Growth of Educational Bureaucracy: Do Teachers Make a Difference?" In Budgets and Bureaucrats: The Sources of Government Growth, edited by Thomas E. Borcherding. Durham, N.C.: Duke University Press.

Stockfisch, Jacob A. 1976. "Analysis of Bureaucratic Behavior: The Ill-defined Production Process." Rand Paper Series, p-559 1. Santa Monica, Calif.: Rand Corporation.

Thompson, Victor A. 1974. The Development of Modern Bureaucracy: Tools Out of People. Morristown, N.J.: General Learning Press.

West, E. G. 1967. "The Political Economy of American Public School Legislation." Journal of Law and Economics 10:101-28.

Williamson, Oliver. 1964. The Economics of Discretionary Behavior: Managerial Objectives in a Theory of the Firm. Englewood Cliffs, N.J.: Prentice-Hall.

Wolf, Charles, Jr. 1979. "A Theory of Non-Market Failures." Public Interest 55:114-33.

PART IV

THE INTRAORGANIZATIONAL ANALYSIS OF SCHOOLS: DECISION MAKING AND CONTROL

8

ORGANIZATIONAL CONTROL IN EDUCATIONAL SYSTEMS: A CASE STUDY OF GOVERNANCE IN SCHOOLS

E. Mark Hanson

This chapter suggests that the conceptual models we have devised to describe, analyze, and predict behavior and events in educational organizations are of low-grade quality and not extremely useful in helping us solve, or even cope with successfully, the many complex problems that confront our public schools.

In response to part of this problem, a basic goal of this research is to develop a conceptual model of school governance and decision making that highlights the semiprofessional/bureaucratic interplay. An ethnographic research methodology is used to study and diagnose the decision-making process of selected schools.

The data of the study suggest that a school is composed of multiple spheres of influence, each maintaining differing degrees of decisional autonomy, a semiprofessional/bureaucratic interaction, formal and informal power bases, coalitions that form and break apart under shifting environmental conditions (for example, placid to turbulent), a "contested zone," and a relatively informal "negotiated order," which serves, among other things, to link the various spheres of influence into a "loosely coupled system."

The study is significant because it challenges much of the conventional wisdom surrounding how our educational organizations function and draws into the field of education many useful concepts now found mostly in literature of management sectors outside of education.

This chapter was supported in part by an intramural research grant from the Academic Senate of the University of California, Riverside. Special thanks are given to Edith McKenzie and Michael Brown for their contributions to this work.

Management scientists do not have the luxury of treating theory like Cinderella's slipper, unique to a single organization; nor like The Old Woman's Shoe, encompassing every member of the family of organizations. In establishing a useful relationship between theory and practice, management scientists must develop reasoned "images of reality" that explain and predict behavior and events. These images of reality, usually called models or conceptual frameworks, should be sensitive to the unique features of an organizational type (such as schools) that distinguish it from other organizational types (such as business or industry). A need now exists to develop a "school specific" model of organization. Accordingly, toward that end the objectives of this research are as follows:

□ To diagnose the process of school governance and decision making in selected schools. Based on this diagnosis,
□ to develop a conceptual framework that depicts how the processes of governance and decision making function in schools. Specifically,
□ to develop a conceptual framework that gives special treatment to a relatively unique feature found in educational organizations: the professional-bureaucratic interaction of teachers and administrators.

Decision making is defined here as the process of making choices in organizations (Simon, 1957:4). Governance is defined as control over the decision-making process.

The professional-bureaucratic interaction is important to issues of governance and decision making because the teachers as professionals, or semiprofessionals if you will (Lortie, 1969), sense a legitimacy in claims of first allegiance to the norms of the profession and to their colleague group. In contrast, the administrators as officers of the bureaucracy—bureaucrats in Weber's (1947) use of the term—must be loyal to the organization that employs them (Corwin, 1974a:247). "In this instance," Lortie (1969:1) writes, "the several strands of hierarchical control, collegial control, and autonomy become tangled and complex." Helping to unravel these tangles is an important aspect of this research.

It is important to note that the term "bureaucrat" is used here in its original Weberian context associated with rationality and efficiency as opposed to the popular pejorative connotation of rigidity and inefficiency. Working in a similar research vein, Wolcott (1977: 118-20) narrows the focus a bit and speaks of school administrators as technocrats as opposed to bureaucrats.

CONCEPTUAL "IMAGES OF REALITY"

Since the study of organization and administration moved from an art to a science early this century, three proposed models (sometimes called traditions or schools of thought) have dominated the field of management: the classical hierarchical model, which tends to be a mix of bureaucratic theory (Weber, 1947) and scientific management (Taylor, 1923); the social system model, a derivative of the Hawthorne Studies (Roethlisberger and Dickson, 1939); and the open system model (Katz and Kahn, 1966). It is important to note that these models tend to serve both as guidelines for practitioners as they attempt to make organizations function effectively and efficiently and as conceptual frameworks or "lenses" used by researchers as they attempt to diagnose the complex sociotechnical relationships found in organizations.

The classic hierarchical model has probably been the dominant organizational framework used in trying to operate as well as analyze educational systems (Callahan, 1962; Griffiths et al., 1962; Anderson, 1968; Abbott, 1969). Clearly a school system has numerous characteristics that suggest it has roots in classical organization theory, such as: a well-defined hierarchy of authority (board of education to superintendent, to principals, to teachers), a division of labor (teachers, aides, counselors), a prescribed ordering of events (third to fourth to fifth grade), a body of rules and policies stipulating expected and prohibited behavior, an emphasis on disciplined compliance, and so on.

The second conceptual lens frequently used to understand issues of governance and decision making is the social system model, which emphasizes the makeup and operation of formal and informal groups that operate in a semiautonomous fashion in the internal environment of an organization. Issues of decision making are complicated by the fact that the informal social systems have their own sets of norms, expectations, objectives, and sources of power (Becker, 1961; Goslin, 1965; Getzels et al., 1968; Bates and Harvey, 1975).

The third conceptual lens has us trying to understand the operations of schools through the perspective of contingency theory (Lawrence and Lorsch, 1967, 1969; Derr and Gabarro, 1972; Tyler, 1973; Hanson and Brown, 1977), which is a derivative of open system theory (Herriott and Hodgkins, 1973; Bredo and Bredo, 1975). A distinctive feature of open system theory is the focus on the dependency relationships and exchanges between the organization and its external environment. Schools are supported by and in turn must support the social, political, and cultural demands of the community. As an open system, the school is seen as linking processes of input

(for example, human, material constraints, expectations), through-
put (for example, teaching-learning, reward systems, socialization),
output (for example, graduates, custodial control, behavioral changes,
romantic attachments), and feedback and renewal process (for example, information guiding decision making, financial support to renew
the cycle).

Contingency theory, on the other hand, concentrates its analytical focus on the adjustments internal to the organization (for example, differentiation and integration) as it seeks to modify procedures to meet the changing demands of the environment of the open
system. Thus, the contingency perspective stresses that the school
requires variability in organizational response capabilities to cope
with changing environmental needs and demands.

The brief sketch of these three often-used "images of reality"
highlights the fact that they are rooted in differing assumptions about
such critical issues as, for example, rationality and limits to rationality, authority and power, organizational control, incentives,
and the like. Allison (1969:690) helps give focus to the problem when
he writes that "conceptual models both fix the mesh of the nets that
the analyst drags through the material in order to explain a particular action or decision and direct him to cast his net in selected ponds,
at certain depths, in order to catch the fish he is after." Hence, if
educators use the wrong conceptual lens in description, analysis,
and prediction or use a "flawed" lens, they find themselves throwing
the wrong net into the wrong pond at the wrong depth and catching
fish they are not after (unanticipated consequences). Unfortunately,
we often see these unanticipated consequences emerge as, for example, innovations that fail, tension and conflict between teachers and
administrators, directives that are ignored, and the like.

THE PROBLEM

In response to growing concerns about our most-used images
of reality, various organization theorists have spoken out for the
need to rethink how our educational organizations work in the real
world. Griffiths (1977:4) speaks for many of us when he writes:

Clearly, the way in which people view themselves and
their relations to others in organizations has changed
to the point that the theories of administrative and organizational behavior we have been using are no longer
applicable. They do not describe organizational behavior, nor do they predict such behavior. They ignore the basic change in authority relationships that

has been underway since World War II and that ac-
celerated in the early 1960s.

In trying to describe and analyze "real world" school issues,
a fundamental problem exists when we look for help in our educational literature. Much of the literature that treats questions of
school organization utilizes adaptations of the business or industrial
models as the basic underlying conceptual framework. Also, much
work has been cast exclusively in a bureaucratic, social system, or
open system conceptual framework.

The continuing difficulty with these approaches is that when
used exclusively, they have serious limitations built into them by
the basic assumptions upon which they are structured. Although
none are uniquely suited to the educational organization, each has
its own valuable contributions to make.

Therefore, an important research step to take is to develop a
school-specific organizational model based on data drawn from field
studies. These data must then be analyzed by borrowing elements
from existing conceptual frameworks that then can treat the unique
characteristics of educational systems. For example, bureaucratic
theory offers elements as formal structure, rules of procedure,
hierarchy, and legitimate authority; social system theory offers elements as informal systems, coalitions, spheres of influence, power
centers, and interpersonal interactions; and contingency theory can
merge elements as the above into the context of variables influencing
the internal structural adjustments of a school as it responds to
changing environmental demands.

As the objectives section of this chapter points out, an intent
of this study is to make a move in the direction of a school-specific
model that will differentiate the unique characteristics of the educational organization from other organizational types.

RESEARCH DESIGN

The data of the research were drawn from studies of two elementary schools, one middle school, and two high schools found in
what will be called the Sherwood School District, which is located in
a large western city. The data were gathered using an ethnographic
"observer as participant" methodology (Lutz and Iannaccone, 1969:
108) in which the researchers could view natural situations in the
schools after establishing bonds of confidence with the educators
(Scott, 1965). The three researchers involved were viewed, to a
large extent, as impartial onlookers and questioners who could ask
questions regarding matters not usually discussed among colleagues

or authority figures. In this context, the researchers spent approximately six months gathering data at each of the three levels of schooling, covering a total time period of approximately two years.

Specific research questions, rather than the hypotheses more frequently used in quantitative designs, were developed to give initial focus to the study.

How do hierarchical control and collegial control work simultaneously in the same school setting?

How does the school provide for the simultaneous existence and interaction of two very dissimilar decisional environments: rational and programmed versus unencumbered and nonprescriptive?

How do administrative authority and teacher autonomy operate simultaneously in the same school setting?

What sources of power are available to administrators and teachers in making and carrying out their own types of decisions?

What are the limitations on administrator authority and teacher autonomy?

How are specific issues resolved when teachers claim autonomy over them and administrators claim authority?

Do all teachers in a school have the same degree of autonomy? If not, why not?

Under what conditions do teachers collaborate in making decisions and taking actions regarding their own interests?

What means do teachers and administrators have to protect themselves against encroachment on their autonomy?

The data-gathering process included intensive interviews (30 to 60 minutes each), direct observation (faculty cafeteria, classrooms, school meetings, and so on), and document analysis (minutes of meetings, correspondence, policy handbooks, and so on). With descriptive data available, the key to analysis was the emergence and identification of behavioral patterns in those data.

This chapter represents a synthesis of the "component part" studies reported elsewhere (Hanson, 1976; Hanson and Brown, 1977; Brown, 1976; McKenzie, 1977). Because of space limitations, the raw data are not reported here but are available in the original works. Other limitations exist. The teacher-administrator interaction was of primary importance; therefore, the roles of the central office officials, students, and noncertificated personnel were recognized but given limited attention. This is not a study of a school district, but of five schools that happen to be in a single school district. When the term "administrators" is used, it refers to the administrators at the school level (for example, principal, vice-principal) and not to the district-level administrators. An important study yet to be done would be to add in the role of the superintendent, with his central office personnel, and thus make the school district the unit of analysis rather than the school alone.

Also, detailed attention will not be given here to discussing differences between elementary or secondary levels; only processes common to educational organizations will be treated. All issues influencing school governance cannot, of course, be treated. Those issues central to the bureaucratic-professional interaction will be highlighted.

In a field study such as this, the vehicle of generalization is the conceptual model that emerges from the research. The model is then presented to the research community for testing, using other methodologies (for example, experimental) in other school-community settings.

AN OVERVIEW OF THE INTERACTING SPHERES MODEL

The key organizational characteristics of the model, referred to as the Interacting Spheres Model (ISM), that emerged from the data are illustrated in Figure 8.1. The key components of the model are as follows:

□ Problems emerge and decisions must follow as the organizational environment shifts from a placid to turbulent condition.

□ Problems must be resolved in a milieu of multiple interacting spheres of influence.

□ Each sphere of influence is shaped by the needs of a specific decision-making environment.

□ The dominant spheres of influence are those that surround the task needs of the semiprofessionals (teachers) and the bureaucrats (administrators), although the noncertificated personnel, parent groups, and so on, also have their own spheres of influence.

□ Specific decisions are formally or informally zones to different spheres of influence.

□ Each sphere of influence has a measure of decision-making autonomy (discretion) as well as identifiable constraints on that autonomy.

□ Formal and informal subcoalitions form and break apart within and between spheres depending on the character of the particular emergent decision to be made.

□ The formal and informal subcoalitions develop differing degrees of differentiation and integration depending on the issue at hand.

FIGURE 8.1

Interacting Spheres Model

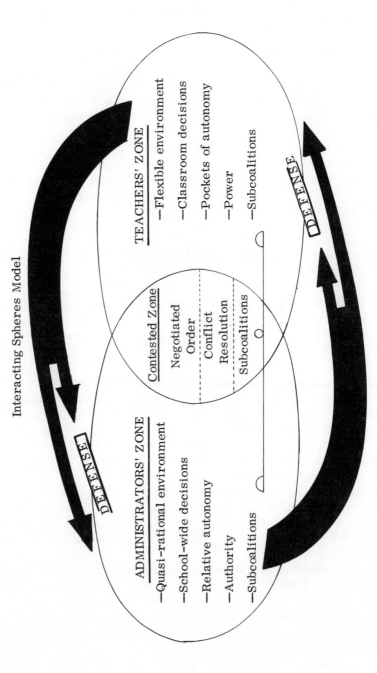

Source: Compiled by the author.

252

▫ Each sphere has a source of power enabling it to take action.

▫ Specific decisions that fall within more than one sphere of influence are in a contested zone.

▫ Decisions made regarding problems within a contested zone are the product of informal or formal negotiation, and a negotiated order emerges.

▫ The multiple spheres of influence that are linked together by the negotiated order form the basis of a loosely coupled system.

▫ Administrators have developed tactics to attempt informal interventions into the teachers' sphere of influence, and the teachers have developed defensive strategies to defend their sphere against such outside interventions.

▫ Teachers have developed tactics to attempt informal interventions into the administrators' sphere of influence, and the administrators have developed defensive strategies to defend their sphere against such outside interventions.

The researchers found that a key to understanding the processes of making decisions that give direction to schools was an understanding of the spheres of influence.

SPHERES OF INFLUENCE

The first few weeks of observation in each school would typically unfold as a confusing buzz of events, like static on a wireless. At any given moment in a high school, for example, we could find one administrator reviewing personnel files in the quiet of his office, a second being verbally abused by an angry parent, and a third chairing a crisis meeting of department heads, exhorting them to get out of the behavioral objectives because an accreditation visit is coming up shortly.

Some of the teachers would be found lecturing to their students in highly structured settings, while others could be found sitting under trees discussing the subject of the day. Students could be found, for example, studying in the library, smoking clandestinely behind the cars in the parking lot, listening attentively in the classroom, or just standing around looking bored.

Some very specific organizational patterns were immediately visible, such as busses coming and going, bells ringing on the hour, football players turning out for practice, lunches being served, meetings being called, roll being taken, and examinations being given. Other patterns took weeks to sort out, such as the struggle by teachers to gain extensive participation in the selection of new administrators, the drive to improve the testing program, or the struggle to obtain greater support and resources for specific academic programs.

We often saw teachers and administrators working together in a more or less collaborative fashion toward a more or less defined goal. However, we also saw these same groups at times taking their own leads and working in opposition to one another and often in defiance of established school policy and rules (for example, the rejection of team teaching through thinly disguised noncompliance).

In short, rather than finding a rationally planned and logically executed process of organization and administration controlled from the top of the hierarchy, we found a mixed bag of structured and unstructured activity, formal and informal procedures, and controlled and autonomous behavior. One of the first major research questions we had to treat was, "How is it possible that a school can function with such a set of seemingly coordinated as well as random activities and behaviors going on all at once?" Or, as one teacher so poignantly phrased the issue, "Is there really a method behind all this madness?"

Our data suggest that there is a method, and on reflection it appears quite reasonable and understandable. In all of the schools studied we discovered the existence of spheres of influence, or what might be called domains or decisional zones. Although among the many schools we studied the spheres differed in kind and content, they did exist. Visible spheres of influence were maintained at least by the noncertificated personnel (for example, secretaries, janitors, cooks), the school administrators, guidance personnel, teachers, students, parent groups, and central office officials. Each sphere maintained relative degrees of power, autonomy, decision-making discretion, legitimacy, and its own ill-defined tasks and objectives. The two dominant spheres of influence were maintained by the local school administrators and teachers and these two will become the central focus of this chapter.

The two dominant spheres of influence seem to be an organizational response to a fundamental decision-making problem found in schools. Cast in the form of a question, "How does the school simultaneously provide for at least two very necessary and distinct decisional environments, one of which supports a rational, programmed, and consistent environment while the other a personalistic, unencumbered, and flexible environment?" On the face of it, we might think that two such unlikely decision-making environments, one responsive to bureaucratic needs and the other to professional needs, could not live together under one roof without continuously creating insurmountable problems for one another.

In response to the question, our data fell into a pattern that supports a process identified by Lortie (1969:35-36) as decisional "zoning." Roughly speaking, each sphere of influence is built around and rooted in a decisional zone where either by formal delegation, informal assumption, or traditional dominion a specific group tends to control the choices that take place in that zone. Decisional zoning establishes conditions that influence the processes of governance and decision making in schools. Numerous researchers (compare Lortie, 1975; Pellegrin, 1975) have observed that the primary activities and responsibilities of administrators and teachers serve as the basis of zoning. The administrator's primary concerns revolve around schoolwide issues, while the teachers tend to devote their energies to the classroom. Bidwell (1965:976-77) writes that "the looseness of system structures and the nature of the teaching task seem to press for a professional mode of school system organization, while demands for uniformity of product and the long time span over which cohorts of students are trained press for rationalization of activities and thus for a bureaucratic base of organization."

A professional mode of organization that impacts on the governance process has some unique features that set it apart from a bureaucratic type. Professionals, for example, have authority limited to their narrow area of expertise, have autonomy over their own decisions, have higher loyalties to the values and expectations of their profession than to those espoused by the organization that employs them, control the admission, sanction, and evaluation of those who aspire to or are within the profession, and have stress placed on goal achievement, client orientation, and the uniqueness of the clients' problems rather than on technical efficiency, task orientation, and the uniformity of clients' problems (Blau and Scott, 1962; Corwin, 1965).

After examining our data, we found ourselves agreeing with Lortie (1969) when he characterized teachers as semiprofessionals rather than professionals. The school administrators are evaluators of teacher behavior and thus are required to intrude into professionally guarded areas of teacher expertise. Nor do teachers control the means by which new aspirant teachers enter the field, as do doctors and lawyers control entry into their fields (Hall, 1954).

It is important to note that the zoning process laid the basis for predictability between the teachers and the administrators. Although in each school the inclusive character of the zones differed to some extent, general understandings existed on the part of all parties (teachers, administrators, students, janitors, and so on) with regard to "the way we do things around here." New arrivals to any one school were quickly socialized through such means as faculty meetings, teacher handbooks, conversations with "old hands," and the like. Most of the school personnel admitted to the researchers that "after a few weeks around here, there are few surprises."

Hence, the existence of spheres of influence forms the basis of predictability between teachers and administrators and thus functions as a conflict-reduction mechanism that permits the tasks of schooling to be carried out more smoothly.

The existence of spheres of influence suggests the presence of decisional discretion or autonomy. The next research question becomes: "In the Sherwood Schools, what are the organizational characteristics that contribute to the presence of autonomy within a given sphere of influence ?"

AUTONOMY WITHIN SPHERES

According to F. E. Katz (1968:18), autonomy "refers to the independence of subunits of an organization from control by other parts of the organization or even by the whole organization." Autonomy, however, does not mean license. In the Sherwood Schools, the teachers and administrators were quite clear and articulate about those decisions upon which they felt they could act independently and those where they felt they needed to consult on or share the act of choice. Rather than "blanket and uniform autonomy" within the separate domains of teachers and administrators, it is more appropriate to speak of "pockets of autonomy," each differing in membership (for example, history teachers, football coaches), freedom from outside intervention, and levels and limits of discretion (for example, coaches have more discretion on the football field than history teachers in the classroom).

The degrees of autonomy within each sphere of influence in general, and within each pocket of autonomy specifically, were constrained by limits imposed, for example, by the state legislature (books must be selected from an approved list), the court system (no prayer in the classroom), the school board (individualized instruction is the only acceptable teaching mode), and the principal ("All teachers must be in the classroom by 8 A.M."). In some instances the limits to autonomy were fixed and inflexible, such as the requirement for teachers to take roll in each class, and at other times flexible and subject to interpretation, such as the degree to which behavioral objectives were actually used to guide classroom instruction.

Once all the formal constraints to autonomy were treated, the teachers still did not feel they had complete freedom to act in an unrestrained fashion. Their sense of the norms of the profession seemed to establish limits to acceptable behavior, in varying degrees of course, with teachers. Also, in the Sherwood Schools we found the principals to be significant forces in determining the scope of the teachers' autonomy. The principal is the one who usually interprets the directives and constraints coming down from the central office, the state legislature, the community, and so on.

School administrators also reported on a network of constraints that limited their own domains. These constraints ranged from the legal to the psychological variety. They spoke of limits placed by state laws, accreditation teams, budgets, district policy, community expectations, teacher needs, federal grant requirements, health and safety codes, court decisions, and the like.

APPLICATIONS OF POWER

Power is the ability of one unit to influence or impose its will upon another unit (Kaplan, 1964:13-14). Because a specific group has autonomy over a specific set of decisions does not necessarily mean that the source of that autonomy is some sort of power (Corwin, 1974b:257). The autonomy can be rooted in, for example, the isolation of the classroom or delegation from the principal. The school administrators were often seen actively protecting and nurturing the autonomy of teachers because the administrators seemed to be aware that through this autonomy the mission of the school was being carried out—"teaching kids."

However, the application of power also contributes at times to the source of teacher autonomy. French and Raven (1959) identify five bases of power, all of which were found operating in the hands of teachers and administrators in the Sherwood Schools. Illustrations of teacher power sources are as follows: legitimate power (sometimes called authority): derived from the hierarchy and directed mostly at students ("we will have a test on Friday"); coercive power: threats to go directly to the board of education or the newspapers with a complaint; expert power: specialized academic knowledge; reward power: expressions of praise or appreciation; and referent power: charismatic or friendship behavior with which others can identify.

In short, the researchers found that teachers and administrators tend to make decisions within what might be described as "protected pockets of autonomy." These pockets are incorporated in decision-making spheres of influence. The spheres and pockets of autonomy have limits placed upon them by a network of constraints. The sources of autonomy can be rooted in either the formal hierarchical structure, work-space isolation, or the informal application of power.

Given the existence of spheres of influence, the next research question becomes: "What are the types of decisions that are made by the bureaucrats and the semiprofessionals in their own domains?"

DECISION-MAKING CATEGORIES

The researchers identified five categories of decisions being made in the Sherwood Schools.

□ Allocation decisions: the distribution of human and material resources in the school.

□ Security decisions: the preservation of physical and psychological safety of faculty and students.

□ Boundary decisions: the determination of who controls the passage of materials, information, and people from one domain to another within the school or between the school and the community.

□ Evaluation decisions: the passing of judgment on the quality of performance (teacher or student).

□ Instructional decisions: the determination of classroom teaching-learning processes and content.

A close inspection of each category in the Sherwood Schools revealed that some decisions within a given category fell basically within the administrators' sphere of influence, others fell within the teachers' sphere, and others fell within the overlap area we called the "contested zone" (as illustrated in Figure 8.1). The material dealing with decisional categories reported in this section was drawn principally from the high schools, although the same categories were also found in the lower grades. Examples of the five categories, some of which had subcategories, are presented in Table 8.1. No attempt is made here to identify all the decisions found in each sphere; only a single example is presented as an illustration. (For a complete presentation of decisions in all categories, see Brown, 1976:Ch. 4).

Having examined categories of decisions, the research question becomes: "Do the teachers or administrators act in concert on decisions falling within their own sphere of influence?"

SUBCOALITIONS WITHIN SPHERES OF INFLUENCE

As depicted thus far, a school is made up of differing decisional environments that form the bases of spheres of influence. However, even within their own domains, the teachers or administrators in the Sherwood Schools typically were not observed as acting in concert. Instead, they could be seen acting in small groups (sometimes merging into larger groups) that would struggle to achieve some objective (for example, "We must improve our relations with parents," or "We need more bilingual teachers").

TABLE 8.1

Decision-Making Categories

Administrators' Sphere	Contested Sphere	Teachers' Sphere
	Allocation Decisions	
Budgeting: Schoolwide budget responsibility	Special project money utilization (for example, stoves versus football equipment)	Specific department spending (for example, books, field trips)
Scheduling: Use of school facilities	Master schedule preparation	Student placement in honors classes
Personnel: Classified or administrative employment	Certificated employment	Selection of department heads
	Security Decisions	
Protection: Use of police on campus	Campus supervision	In-class safety
Attendance: Legal attendance policies	Campus attendance control	In-class attendance procedures
Discipline: Campus discipline	Referred discipline problem cases	In-class discipline measures
	Boundary Decisions	
Represent school in community activities	Dealing with parents on campus	Teacher ties with union activities
	Evaluation Decisions	
Probationary teacher performance	Tenured teacher performance	Student performance
	Instructional Decisions	
Teaching-learning: Emergent crisis over controversial subjects	Large-scale innovation	Classroom instruction
Curricular decisions: Mandated subjects	Special programs (for example, bilingual, accelerated)	Course content

Source: Compiled by the author.

259

Providing insight into this perspective, Cyert and March (1963:27) wrote, "Let us view the organization as a coalition. It is a coalition of individuals, some of them organized into subcoalitions." The subcoalition members can usually be identified over a specified, relatively brief, period of time or for a particular decision. Over a more extended period of time, Cyert and March argue, we can usually identify certain classes of decisions that are treated by ongoing subcoalitions.

These subcoalitions seem to share with one another only those ambiguous goals that act as public flags with great symbolic value. Goals such as "to develop an awareness of the values inherent in our democratic society and loyalty to its underlying principles" serve as symbolic cement that holds the organization together. In an informal sense, however, the researchers observed the subcoalition members establishing their own priorities based on their own interpretation of dominant needs (for example, client, community, teacher, school). In any given school the researchers might observe, for example, one group of teachers trying to change the reading program, a second concerned with improving working conditions, and a third trying to block changes in the testing program. The impact on school policy and procedures by the different subcoalitions differed due to a number of variables, such as the alliances any given subcoalition could form, the extent of outside pressure existing in support or opposition to the goal of the subcoalition, the visibility of the issue, and the relative power of the subcoalition.

After identifying the presence of various subcoalitions in the Sherwood Schools, the researchers set out to understand the nature of the subcoalitions' organization and the roles they play in the decision-making process. Information concerning these issues are reported in the next section and will be drawn principally from the elementary school level.

FORMALLY ORGANIZED SUBCOALITIONS

At the elementary and secondary school levels, the researchers found formal and informal subcoalitions that were organized around long-standing "durable interests" ("We are always looking for ways to build strong community relations") or episodic "troublesome issues" ("It hit the fan last week regarding a reading assignment"). We found the subcoalitions generally had focus, task direction, an identifiable membership (although some members were rather fluid in participation), a rough but generally understood set of norms and expectations, a sense of legitimacy, sources of power, and a set of constraints limiting the arena of action.

At the elementary school level, for example, we typically found three types of formally organized subcoalitions: the lower-grade teachers, who were concerned primarily with the formation of student-role norms and social values; the upper-grade teachers, who were primarily concerned with the formation of basic skills; and the standing committees, such as the guidance committee and the student activities committee. At the elementary level there usually weren't enough administrators to form formally organized subcoalitions, but such groups could be found at the high school level. These formally organized subcoalitions played active roles in the lives of their schools, meeting more or less on a regular basis and making choices on issues that involved their specified decision-making domains.

INFORMALLY ORGANIZED SUBCOALITIONS

Gross and Trask (1960:173-74) have pointed out that:

> important value issues arise over such questions as the respective responsibilities of the home and the school, the definition of a "good education," the teaching of moral values, the school's obligations to typical and atypical children, and the questioning of the status quo. On each of these and other value questions, there may be contradictory points of view among school personnel and between school personnel and the community.

In the Sherwood Schools, informal subcoalitions could be seen forming around these "contradictory points of view." Unlike the formal subcoalitions, the informal systems had an ebb and flow quality about them. For a time an informal subcoalition would be highly visible, influential, and active; then it would drop from sight only to return again at a later date. Informal subcoalitions seemed to emerge where formal subcoalitions were unwilling, unprepared, unstructured, or unauthorized to serve as the advocate or problem-solving vehicle for a troublesome issue.

The researchers often observed teachers banding together in a small alliance to fight for or against such things as the implementation of a central-office-mandated instructional program, or an attempt by an outside teacher association to influence decision making at the school sites. At times subcoalitions would form and clash with one another on opposite sides of an issue. (For a more detailed analysis of formally and informally organized subcoalitions, see McKenzie, 1977:Ch. 4.)

The types of informally organized subcoalitions that played an active part in shaping processes of school governance and decision making are as follows.

Miniteams: These teams, usually composed of an informal alliance of two or three teachers, typically formed to treat a specific emergent problem or task and dissolved when it had been resolved or the participants tired of the effort. Miniteams were often observed doing such things as developing new curricular units, writing behavioral objectives, or pressuring the principal for more resources.

Administrative-oriented alliances: Frequently issues would surface that placed in direct confrontation a position held by the majority of teachers and a position held by administrators, such as a problem dealing with the appropriate use of teacher planning time, the unionization of teachers, or the need for increased articulation between academic programs. On those issues where administrators were taking a strong position, an alliance of administrators and those teachers who had aspirations of becoming administrators would often form as a temporary subcoalition.

Equal education opportunity subcoalitions: Each school had an informal subcoalition organized around an identification with special concerns about the ethnic minority communities. The subcoalitions became active when such issues arose as the need for subject materials treating black or Chicano history, the consequences of student tracking, or the importance of hiring more minority teachers.

Outerdirected teacher subcoalitions: A subcoalition of teachers would often emerge and become active when "outside" (for example, central office, districtwide, teachers' union) issues would emerge, such as salaries and benefits, teacher selection, teacher evaluation, or additional time demands on after-school activities.

Teacher-pedagogical alliances: Most schools had informal teacher alliances based on shared beliefs about teaching. These subcoalitions were organized around a philosophical-pedagogical orientation regarding what should be taught in schools and how it should be taught. Specifically, the researchers frequently encountered conservative-essentialist teachers banding together and arguing about such things as declining academic standards, the need for more basic education, and a stricter approach to student discipline. The liberal-progressive teacher coalition, on the other hand, pressed concerns pertaining to such things as the negative effects of "classifying" students through test scores, the need for "relevant and meaningful" educational experiences, and the importance of building a sense of self-discipline within the students (as opposed to externally enforced discipline).

Administrator-specialist-teacher alliances: Temporary alliances of specific teachers, administrators, and specialists would sometimes emerge. These alliances were typically formed as a base from which to influence the central office regarding problems that affected the whole school, such as a pending program funding cut, or the need to obtain additional specialized teachers.

The list of formal and informal subcoalitions identified here is not all-inclusive nor were these same subcoalitions found in every school. The significant point is that specific, identifiable subcoalitions representing specific interests were found in all schools. Some of these subcoalitions were relatively enduring while others formed and broke apart with the rise and decline of specific issues. Also, interestingly enough, specific administrators and teachers would at times form informal alliances that would bridge their own spheres of influence to tackle an emergent schoolwide problem.

With respect to the process of governance and decision making, the next significant question becomes: "How does the mix of formal and informal subcoalitions serve to retard or propel the school in its intended direction?"

DIFFERENTIATION AND INTEGRATION
OF SUBCOALITIONS

Open system theory, in contrast to classical hierarchical theory and social system theory, places special emphasis on the dependency relationship an organization has with its surrounding environment (Katz and Kahn, 1966). Contingency theory, an extension of open system theory, stresses that shifting external and/or internal environmental demands require an organization to be flexible enough to adapt its own structures and processes to meet the new demands (Lawrence and Lorsch, 1967, 1969).

Thus, as the environment of a school moves from placid to turbulent (Emery and Trist, 1965) on any given issue, such as declining reading scores, increased truancy, or decreasing tax revenues, a corresponding shift must take place in the school's activities to treat the requirements of the new trend. For example, when one of the high schools of our study detected a demographic shift in its community, and hence in the student population (open system theory), the content and procedures of the guidance program were modified accordingly (contingency theory) to provide the desired new services more effectively.

According to the precepts of contingency theory, if an organization is to have a capability to respond readily to changing environmental demands, it must be composed of subunits (for example, departments, subsystems, subcoalitions) that are both differentiated and integrated. Differentiated subsystems (subcoalitions) work on different problems or different parts of the same problem the organization has encountered. Each subsystem has its own tasks (for example, obtain federal grants, improve learning diagnostic capabilities), its own time frame (long-term, short-term), and its own structural characteristics (formal or informal sanctions, work norms).

Integration refers to the quality and intensity of the collaboration that exists between the subsystems that are necessary to achieve a relative unity of effort that facilitates a successful response to a changing environment. Close integration of subsystems usually requires such organizational characteristics as multidirectional communication channels, flexible leadership styles, decentralized decision making. Lawrence and Lorsch (1967) have found in their studies that those organizations that exhibit a high order of differentiation and integration among subsystems were more effective in adjusting their activities to meet the requirements of a shifting environment.

Only in recent years has contingency theory made its initial inroads into the field of education (Tyler, 1973; Derr and Gabarro, 1972; Hanson and Brown, 1977). The data of our research suggest that in schools where the subcoalitions are not integrated in any meaningful way, but tend to work against one another, the schools make minimal progress toward resolving their special problems. In one of the secondary schools, for example, two strong pedagogical alliances emerged among teachers of different pedagogical persuasions regarding a school policy permitting unstructured student time. The two subcoalitions clashed over the policy for such a period of time that a meaningful test of the concept was never carried out.

However, the researchers encountered many situations where the formal and informal subcoalitions became highly differentiated and integrated and responded successfully to a very intense environmental pressure. Such was the case with efforts to initiate an individualized instruction program. When the policy of implementing individualized instruction was announced, various formal and informal subcoalitions took charge of different parts of the task. One miniteam took a leadership role in developing behavioral objectives, a multicultural subcoalition worked on individualized learning experiences for minority group children, the specialists worked out student evaluation programs, the central office specialists held workshops for teachers, and parent groups were invited to participate in program planning and classroom activities.

In terms of contingency theory as it reflects on the implementation of the individualized instruction program, the various subcoalitions became highly integrated and differentiated. In fact, it might be said that the various subcoalitions joined to form a much larger coalition that drew together in a cooperative effort most of the administrators, specialists, and teachers.

It is important to note that the leadership roles of the principals typically played important parts in the levels of differentiation and integration of subcoalitions achieved in schools. The researchers concluded that those school administrators who were most knowledgeable about the informal coalitions and could work through them instead of against them tended to have the most success in implementing the new academic programs. These administrators were able to build a large coalition out of several smaller subcoalitions.

In sum, the researchers found that the teachers and administrators tended not always to act in concert within their own spheres of influence. They usually acted in the smaller groups we call subcoalitions. These coalitions, whether formally or informally established, were issue oriented and sometimes two subcoalitions would take different stances on the same issue (for example, examination procedures had one group of teachers working for improved standardized test scores and another for improved understanding of the material whether or not that reflected on the scores). Small groups would sometimes band together to form alliances on specific issues, and sometimes administrators and teachers would join in an alliance. The impact on the broader teacher or administrator sphere of influence was significant. The individual subcoalitions and alliances of subcoalitions gave the broader spheres of influence direction through a sort of cohesiveness on priorities, or lack of direction through fragmentation and infighting over specific issues.

Granting the existence of bureaucratic and semiprofessional spheres of influence in schools, the question becomes: "How are those decisions made where these two spheres of influence overlap?"

THE NEGOTIATED ORDER

The spheres of influence do not, of course, come as neatly separate entities. As Figure 8.1 illustrates, a considerable amount of overlap exists between the spheres and this area is referred to as the "contested zone." Table 8.1 illustrates the type of decisions that fall in the contested zone, ranging from setting the master schedule to campus supervision.

Key issues with respect to the contested zone revolve around such questions as: how decisions are made, how collaborative actions are structured, and how problems are solved. A process must be worked out that insures a relatively clear understanding by all parties regarding what must be done, who is to do it, and when. The process must insure minimum levels of conflict and thus insure sufficient order "to get the job done."

The hospital literature is useful in providing some insight into this important issue because hospitals also have a "contested" zone between professionals and bureaucrats. In a case study by Strauss et al. (1963) they write that in the contested zone "professionals and nonprofessionals are implicated together in a great web of negotiation." Thus when a problem flares up "a complicated process of negotiation, of bargaining, of give-and-take necessarily begins," and the authors refer to the outcome as the "negotiated order."

The negotiations in schools are informal rather than formal and virtually everyone participates when their interests are involved. When a troublesome situation arises for an individual or group, they seek to spin a network of negotiation around it. Teachers negotiated with administrators for a different approach to handling tough discipline cases, administrators negotiated with teachers for more parent contact, students negotiated with teachers for less homework, teachers negotiated with janitors for replacing a burnt-out lightbulb now instead of tomorrow, department chairpersons negotiated with office secretaries for typing a specific letter ahead of all the others waiting on the pile, and so on.

The agreements made in the contested zone were usually temporary and fragile, subject to renegotiation the next time the same issue surfaced. Because of the constant flow of small and large tasks that emerged in the contested zone, the teachers and administrators were constantly shifting their energies and efforts to new problems and negotiations that enabled them to get through each day. The end product of the ongoing negotiation process was to bring an acceptable degree of order and stability to a zone of potential disruption and discord.

LOOSELY COUPLED SYSTEMS

An additional concept that helps provide insight into the negotiated order is Weick's (1976) notion of loosely coupled systems. Weick (1976:3) writes that the concept

> intends to convey the image that coupled events are responsive, but that each event also preserves its own identity and some evidence of its physical or logical separateness. Thus, in the case of an educational

organization, it may be the case that the counselor's
office is loosely coupled to the principal's office. The
image is that the principal and the counselor are somehow attached, but that each retains some identity and
separateness and that their attachment may be circumscribed, infrequent, weak in its mutual effects, unimportant, and/or slow to respond.

As pointed out earlier in this chapter, the separate spheres of influence maintain degrees of autonomy and decisional discretion.
Thus, the spheres have at times loose coupling, which suggests they
are tied together weakly or infrequently with qualified interdependence.

The researchers observed that a large measure of the coupling
takes place in the contested zone of the school and the firmer (clearly established and agreed upon) the negotiated order the tighter the
coupling and vice versa. The researchers found that the tightness
in the intersphere coupling between the teachers and the administrators varies in specific situations, and frequently the memberships
of these two bodies find themselves acting in concert where they
might normally act with relative autonomy.

Primary situations signaling a tightening of the intersphere
coupling are as follows: when responding to legal decisions, such
as modifications in the language programs in accord with new state
laws; under conditions of crisis, such as the time the new sex education program in a secondary school came under fire from an active group of parents; in situations where outside evaluation is im-
minent, such as the pending arrival of an accreditation team; when
the potential for a negative community reaction exists, such as the
careful selection of instructional materials so that they do not offend
any ethnic population; and when time is extremely limited, such as
the approach of a federal grant application deadline.

Given the lack of a "command structure" bridging the semi-
professional-bureaucratic interface, the question becomes: "Are
the teachers and administrators willing to give one another complete
discretion of action in their own sphere of influence?"

INFORMAL MANAGEMENT BETWEEN SPHERES

The researchers found that just because the administrators
could not directly control many decisions and activities that fell
within the teachers' sphere of influence, by no means did the administrators give up trying to influence them indirectly. Administrators and teachers in all of the schools had developed what might

be called tactics of informal management, some of which were
direct and open while others were indirect and sub rosa.

Administrators Informally Managing Teachers

As an illustration of management tactics, some administrators
were very adept at manipulating the teachers' sense of an abstract
concept they called "professionalism." Administrators were often
heard telling teachers that "you should not do that because it is not
the professional thing to do," or "we must start doing (X) activity in
the classroom because it is best for kids," or "the parents want it."
When the teachers accepted the administrators' abstract definition
of the situation, then they were responding to informal control procedures. In other words, the administrators had devised informal
means of tightening the coupling between the spheres of influence.

Administrators from time to time informally influenced teachers by subtle and sometimes unsubtle reminders of the teacher evaluation process. Also, administrators generally were "keepers of in-
trinsic rewards." By selectively praising some teachers in open
gatherings of faculty members, the administrators were frequently
able to direct others seeking such rewards in a desired direction.

Teachers Informally Managing Administrators

Teachers in the Sherwood Schools were also observed using
informal tactics of managing administrator behavior. At times it
would be very undramatic, such as a single teacher asking the principal for additional resources for a specific class. At other times,
however, it could get very dramatic, such as when a group of teachers marched into the principal's office and demanded a greater voice
in the selection of new personnel and threatened to march down to
the central office and see the superintendent if they did not get their
way.

A common occurrence was for teachers to form coalitions
among subgroups and then take collective stands on an issue in faculty meetings. The sense of unanimity among teachers often made
a convincing impression on the administrators. Bridges (1970:12)
has captured the essence of the tactics of informal management with
his discussion of the administrator as a "pawn" of subordinates.
He describes three such conditions: pawn without his knowledge,
pawn against his will, and pawn by choice.

However, attempts at informal management between spheres
of influence were not always well received, and frequently the mem-

bers of each sphere found themselves actively protecting their domain from outside intrusion.

TEACHERS DEFENDING THEIR DOMAINS

As Figure 8.1 illustrates, the teachers often made conscious efforts to protect their sphere of influence. Corwin (1973:165) observes:

> The professional employee . . . denies the principle that his work always must be supervised by administrators and controlled by laymen. Because of his training, pressures from his colleagues, and his dedication to clients, the professionally oriented person considers himself competent enough to control his own work. Hence, he sometimes must be disobedient toward his supervisors precisely in order to improve his proficiency and to maintain standards of client welfare—especially if there are practices that jeopardize the best interests of students.

Depending on whether the teachers viewed the administrators' attempts at intervention as consistent with their own objectives, individuals and subcoalitions of teachers tended to form in support of or opposition to the intervention. Tactics of teacher resistance through argument typically fell into the following patterns: professionalism: "We know what is best for our kids"; past success: "I have been successfully using my technique for 15 years and see no reason to change now"; predicted failure: "We know several schools where that was tried and it didn't work"; planning time: "We would need considerable released time to prepare for this"; and added cost: "We would require a lot of expensive equipment for such a project."

One of the more interesting defensive tactics used by teachers the researchers called the "pocket veto." The concept of pocket veto is used because it becomes manifest through inaction, in other words, a lack of response to requests or mandates for action or change. Many teachers were magnificent in making it appear as though they were in complete support of an administrator's formal or informal intervention while all the time they were ignoring its every intent. It is important to note that these teachers typically were not lazy or incompetent; they genuinely saw themselves as the guardians of the classroom and had to hold the line against what they considered to be fads and "classroom gimmicks" that enjoy a short burst of popularity across the country and then fade away.

Corwin (1974a:228) identifies a wider range of tactics that have become associated with the teacher militancy movement, and they include "political lobbying, campaigns in school board municipal elections, public criticism of boards of education, day-to-day disputes with administrators, resignations, work slowdowns, professional holidays, mass resignations, withholding signed contracts, and blacklisting of uncooperative school districts."

ADMINISTRATORS DEFENDING THEIR DOMAINS

The researchers found that different school administrators used different protective tactics for defending their domains, but all did in fact employ some tactics. Administrators had one advantage over teachers in that administrators could directly say no to the teachers' requests. The formal hierarchic roles of administrators permitted that type of response. However, administrators seemed to avoid direct negative responses to the teachers' requests because administrators usually wanted to appear supportive of the teacher role whenever possible.

The administrators' tactics of defending their domains against a perceived outside intrusion attempt (for example, proposals, demands) fell into the following patterns: ignore it: decide not to decide and hope the proposal dies a natural death; delay it: leave the proposal off the agenda of the faculty meeting; study it: form a study committee and pack it with sympathetic members; buck it: pass the buck upward and claim the superintendent won't support such a proposal; or publicly support it: privately use a pocket veto.

As was the case with the teachers, in taking actions as these, the administrators were generally not seen by themselves, or the researchers, as unmotivated or self-seeking. They typically had in mind what they considered to be in the best interests of the school.

CONCLUSION

With respect to contemporary issues of school governance, Corwin (1974a:238-39) has observed:

Most administrators were trained in an era when the problems of classroom teaching could be reduced (so it was thought) to the psychology of individual learners and when the central administrative problems seemed to revolve around efficient internal management. The current generation of teachers, by contrast, has been

reared in a sociological era characterized by rapid
social change and group conflict. Administration
has become largely a matter of managing an increasingly complex balance of forces from outside as well
as from within the schools. Many school administrators still in positions of authority today are not
trained to cope with these problems.

Corwin's view adds to the argument that our conceptual frameworks are proving to be less than satisfactory in their utility toward
useful description, analysis, and prediction of behavior and events
in educational organizations.

As the introduction to this chapter points out, there is a need
to develop a school-specific organizational model that can treat the
features that make the school a unique organization. Toward that
end, the research reported here resulted in the construction of a
model that draws useful concepts and ideas from the three conventional frameworks of classical hierarchical theory, social system
theory, and open system/contingency theory. The principal area of
interest is the interaction of the administrators (bureaucrats) and
teachers (semiprofessionals).

The Interacting Spheres Model, as depicted in Figure 8.1,
suggests that school governance (control over the decision-making
process) and decision making take place within the context of multiple spheres of influence. The dominant spheres at the school level
are maintained by teachers and administrators (for example, principal, vice-principal).

Specific decisions, either by tradition, delegation, or assumption, are zones to the administrators' sphere or to the teachers'
sphere where action is taken with considerable autonomy. Where
the two spheres overlap (the contested zone) informal negotiations
take place to work out an acceptable, although temporary, accord.
The degree of coupling, from tight to loose, depends upon the
strength and durability of the agreements worked out for the contested zone as well as understandings regarding the spheres themselves. A tightly coupled school is one in which there is a high level
of agreed upon and coordinated activity between the spheres, while
a loosely coupled system is just the opposite.

Figure 8.1 also illustrates that at times teachers and administrators attempt, directly or indirectly, to intervene in the sphere
of influence of the other. Subtle as well as forceful tactics to this
end were identified. Also, teachers and administrators have worked
out subtle and forceful means of defending their spheres, such as the
use of the pocket veto or a strike.

Within the spheres of influence there are both formal and informal subcoalitions that have their own objectives, members, norms, sources of power, and senses of legitimacy. As the school's environment shifts between placid and turbulent, problem situations arise and different subcoalitions emerge to involve themselves in the ensuing decision making. Sometimes several subcoalitions become differentiated and integrated as they take on a problem, and at other times they directly or indirectly combat one another. At times administrator and teacher subcoalitions join forces in making decisions, and thus bridge the separate spheres of influence, while at other times they go their separate ways. The principal, by his or her awareness and skill, seems to be a key figure in whether or not the subcoalitions are moved toward differentiation and integration or whether they simply go their own ways.

Hence, school governance, defined as the control over the decision-making process, certainly is not the product of a hiararchy. Rather, school governance seems to have coalescent and disjunctive qualities at the extremes. At times control over decision making seems to be dominated by administrators or teachers or both (within their domains) or shared (in the contested zone). In this sense governance seems to be coalescent—the work gets done, differentiation and integration exist between subcoalitions, and there are few surprises. At other times, however, struggles between spheres and/or within spheres develop, differentiation and integration of subcoalitions is negligible, and limited unity, thus predictability, surrounds the decision-making process. In this context school governance seems to be relatively disjunctive with the consequence of being unable to respond effectively to the changing demands of the community.

Certainly, the complexities of school governance are enormous and also extend far beyond the range of this chapter. However, trying to understand issues of governance and decision making as a process taking place within an arena of interacting spheres of influence seems to be an encouraging approach to a complex problem.

REFERENCES

Abbott, M. 1969. "Hierarchical Impediments to Innovation in Educational Organizations." In Organizations and Human Behavior: Focus on Schools, edited by Fred D. Carver and Thomas J. Sergiovanni. New York: McGraw-Hill.

Allison, G. T. 1969. "Conceptual Models and the Cuban Missile Crisis." American Political Science Review 63, no. 3.

Anderson, J. G. 1968. Bureaucracy in Education. Baltimore: Johns Hopkins University Press.

Bates, F., and C. Harvey. 1975. The Structure of Social Systems. New York: John Wiley.

Becker, H. S. 1961. "The Teacher in the Authority System of the Public School." In Complex Organizations, edited by Amitai Etzioni. New York: Holt, Rinehart and Winston.

Bidwell, C. 1965. "The School as a Formal Organization." In Handbook of Organizations, edited by J. G. March. Chicago: Rand McNally.

Blau, P. M., and W. R. Scott. 1962. Formal Organizations. San Francisco: Chandler.

Bredo, A., and E. Bredo. 1975. "Effects of Environment and Structure on the Process of Innovation." In Managing Change in Educational Organizations, edited by Victor Baldrige and Terrence Deal. Berkeley: McCutchan.

Bridges, E. 1970. "Administrative Man: Origin or Pawn in Decision Making?" Educational Administration Quarterly 6, no. 1.

Brown, M. E. 1976. "A Contingency Approach to Educational Decision-making: A Case Study of Governance in the High School." Doctoral dissertation, University of California, Riverside.

Callahan, R. E. 1962. Education and the Cult of Efficiency. Chicago: University of Chicago Press.

Corwin, R. G. 1974a. Education in Crisis: A Sociological Analysis of Schools and Universities in Transition. New York: John Wiley.

Corwin, R. G. 1974b. "Models of Educational Organizations." In Review of Research in Education No. 2, edited by Fred Kerlinger. Itasca, Ill.: Peacock.

Corwin, R. G. 1973. "The School as an Organization." In The School in Society, edited by Sam D. Sieber and David E. Wilder. New York: The Free Press.

Corwin, R. G. 1965. "Professional Persons in Public Organizations." Educational Administration Quarterly 1.

Cyert, R., and J. G. March. 1963. A Behavioral Theory of the Firm. Englewood Cliffs, N.J.: Prentice-Hall.

Derr, B., and J. Gabarro. 1972. "An Organizational Contingency Theory for Education." Educational Administration Quarterly 8, no. 2.

Emery, F. E., and E. L. Trist. 1965. "The Causal Texture of Organizational Environments." Human Relations 18, no. 1.

French, J. R. P., Jr., and B. Raven. 1959. "The Bases of Social Power." In Studies in Social Power, edited by D. Cartwright. Ann Arbor, Mich.: Institute for Social Research.

Getzels, J., J. Lipham, and R. Campbell. 1968. Educational Administration as a Social Process. New York: Harper and Row.

Goslin, D. A. 1965. The School in Contemporary Society. Glenview, Ill.: Scott, Foresman.

Griffiths, D. 1977. "The Individual in Organization: A theoretical Perspective." Educational Administration Quarterly 13, no. 2.

Griffiths, D., D. Clark, R. Wynn, and L. Iannacone. 1962. Organizing Schools for Effective Action. Danville, Ill.: Interstate Printers and Publishers.

Gross, N., and A. Trask. 1960. "Some Organizational Forces Influencing the Role of the Teacher." Educational Horizons 38, no. 3.

Hall, O. 1954. "Some Problems in the Provision of Medical Services." Canadian Journal of Economics and Political Science 20.

Hanson, E. M. 1976. "Beyond the Bureaucratic Model: A Study of Power and Autonomy in Educational Decision-Making." Interchange 7, no. 2.

Hanson, E. M., and M. E. Brown. 1977. "A Contingency View of Problem Solving in Schools: A Case Analysis." Educational Administration Quarterly 13, no. 2.

Herriott, R., and B. Hodgkins. 1973. The Environment of Schooling: Formal Education as an Open Social System. Englewood Cliffs, N.J.: Prentice-Hall.

Kaplan, A. 1964. "Power in Perspective." In Power and Conflict in Organizations, edited by R. L. Kahn and E. Boulding. New York: Basic Books.

Katz, D., and R. Kahn. 1966. The Social Psychology of Organizations. New York: John Wiley.

Katz, F. E. 1968. Autonomy and Organization: The Limits of Social Control. New York: Random House.

Lawrence, P., and J. Lorsch. 1969. Developing Organizations: Diagnosis and Action. Reading, Mass.: Addison-Wesley.

Lawrence, P., and J. Lorsch. 1967. Organizational Environment: Management Differentiation and Integration. Boston: Harvard University Graduate School of Business Administration.

Lortie, D. C. 1975. School Teacher. Chicago: University of Chicago Press.

Lortie, D. C. 1969. "The Balance of Control and Autonomy in Elementary School Teaching." In The Semi-professions and Their Organizations, edited by Amitai Etzioni. New York: The Free Press.

Lutz, F., and L. Iannaccone. 1969. Understanding Educational Organizations: A Field Study Approach. Columbus, Ohio: Charles E. Merrill.

McKenzie, E. B. 1977. "Multiple Interacting Spheres of Influence: A Contingency Model of School Governance." Doctoral dissertation, University of California, Riverside.

Pellegrin, R. 1975. "Some Organizational Characteristics of Multiunit Schools." In Managing Change in Educational Organizations, edited by Victor Baldridge and Terrence Deal. Berkeley: McCutchan.

Roethlisberger, F. J., and W. J. Dicison. 1939. Management and the Worker. Cambridge, Mass.: Harvard University Press.

Scott, R. 1965. "Field Methods in the Study of Organizations." In Handbook of Organizations, edited by James G. March. Chicago: Rand McNally.

Simon, H. A. 1957. Administrative Behavior. New York: Macmillan.

Strauss, A., L. Schatzman, D. Ehrlich, R. Bucher, and M. Sabshin. 1963. "The Hospital and Its Negotiated Order." In The Hospital in Modern Society, edited by Eliot Freidson. New York: The Free Press of Glencoe.

Taylor, F. 1923. The Principles of Scientific Management. New York: Harper.

Tyler, W. 1973. "The Organizational Structure of the Secondary School." Educational Review 25, no. 3.

Weber, M. 1947. The Theory of Social and Economic Organization. Translated by A. M. Henderson and T. Parsons. New York: Oxford University Press. Free Press edition, 1964.

Weick, K. E. 1976. "Educational Organizations as Loosely Coupled Systems." Administrative Science Quarterly 21.

Wolcott, H. F. 1977. Teachers versus Technocrats: An Educational Innovation in Anthropological Perspective. Eugene, Ore: Center for Educational Policy and Management.

9

THE CONTROL OF MICROEDUCATIONAL POLICY IN ELEMENTARY SCHOOLS

W. W. Charters, Jr.

From the standpoint of the sociology of organizations, team teaching is one of the more interesting innovations in elementary education, especially as it is manifested in the Multiunit School Plan developed and advocated by Wisconsin's Research and Development Center for Cognitive Learning in the late 1960s and early 1970s (Klausmeier, Rossmiller, and Saily, 1977). Fully implemented, this plan would represent a radical alteration in the control structure of the elementary school. By the plan, grade-level teachers would be formed into small teams, or units, responsible for planning and conducting the instructional program of the pupils assigned to the unit. A new position would be established in the otherwise flat hierarchy of the school—that of unit leader. The leaders, appointed or elected from among the unit membership, would meet together with the principal on a regular basis to establish educational policy and coordinate unit affairs.

Funds for the preparation of this report as well as many of the analyses it contains were provided to the author through a grant from the Spencer Foundation. The study on which the report is based was conducted under contract with the National Institute of Education. I also wish to acknowledge the key contributions of my colleagues, Richard O. Carlson, John S. Packard, Kenneth E. Duckworth, Thomas D. Jovick, Richard H. Moser, Patricia A. Schmuck, and many others, without which the project could never have been launched or completed. Any views expressed herein are the author's own and should not be construed as representing those of colleagues or the position, policy, or endorsement of the funding bodies.

Implications for the school's decision-making system are two-fold. The plan would afford teachers an opportunity to have their voices heard, at least through representatives, on general matters of school operation and policy that ordinarily are the sole responsibility of administrators. In addition, it implies a major shift in the locus of control with regard to the intimate affairs of classroom instruction, away from the individual teacher, who ordinarily has enjoyed wide discretion in this domain, to the small working group of colleagues. Thus, the power of professionals collectively would be enhanced at the expense of both administrator discretion and individual teacher autonomy.

Two sociologically oriented studies appeared around 1970 lending empirical support to the redistribution of control over micro-educational policy that accompanies the team form of organization (Pellegrin, 1970; Meyer and Cohen, 1971). Both studies were comparative in design and relied on teacher responses to questionnaire items to characterize the decision process. Meyer and Cohen and associates at Stanford's Center for Research and Development in Teaching followed an approach reminiscent of Tannenbaum's (1968) work on control graphs, asking teachers to rate the "influence" of various parties in the school with respect to a number of classroom- and school-related issues. They found that teachers in eight team-organized open-space schools in the San Francisco Bay Area attributed substantially greater influence to teacher groups and less influence to the principal than teachers in a like number of conventional schools.

In the Pellegrin study, the reports of teachers in three Multi-unit schools in Wisconsin regarding their roles in making decisions about each of several instructional decisions were compared with reports of teachers in three control schools chosen from the same districts. Multiunit teachers more often reported group-made decisions on such matters as choice of teaching methods or selection of instructional materials, while teachers in the conventional schools more often said they had complete or nearly complete autonomy in making them. Tabulations of other items showed that Multiunit teachers attributed greater influence to teachers as a group on "how the school is run" than control school teachers. In only one of the three Multiunit schools, though, was the influence attributed to the principal adversely affected, and in all but this school principals were rated as exercising greater overall influence than collegial groups.

In 1974 my colleagues and I at the University of Oregon's Center for Educational Policy and Management launched a longitudinal investigation supported by the National Institute of Education to replicate the studies and to certify that these and still other findings (concerning work arrangements, faculty interaction, and teacher attitudes) were the consequences of the team form of school organization rather than antecedent to it, something that studies using a cross-sectional design could not establish.

Sixteen elementary schools that began implementing the Individually Guided Education/Multiunit School Plan in the fall of 1974 were studied just prior to implementation (April 1974) and data were taken again every six months through the next two school years (April 1976). Parallel measures, of organizational and teacher attributes, also were taken according to the same schedule in another 13 schools, typically in the same districts, that retained the conventional organizational form throughout the period.

The overall results of the investigation are given in the final report to the National Institute of Education (Packard, Charters, and Duckworth, 1978). Here I shall concentrate on the work we undertook to develop and apply a measure of the elementary school's control structure, featuring the additional analyses we have recently completed to portray more fully decision-making systems and their change.

CONTROL STRUCTURE: CONCEPT
AND MEASUREMENT

Control structure, as we use the term, concerns a particular class of decision made by personnel of complex organizations. These are decisions that have the intent of directly regulating the task performance of the organization's operatives (teachers, in the present case).[1] Our usage relates closely to the concept of authority, which addresses the question of who is accorded the right to direct the behavior of whom. In the Bernard-Simon view, on which we have drawn, authority represents the circumstance in which the decisions of one party, or body, are accepted as the premises for the actions of a second party, without his or her deliberation on the expediency of those premises (Simon, 1947).

Regulating decisions ordinarily are hierarchically ordered in complex organizations, such that higher-order decisions serve as constraints on the alternatives considered in lower-order decision-making processes. Higher-order decisions that have this guiding intent often are called policy decisions. We did not systematically pursue the decision structure through its hierarchic layering in our investigation, choosing rather to focus on the structure most directly impinging on the task performance of classroom teachers—on the "micropolicies" of educational governance, as it were.

To map a school's control structure from this perspective is to locate the individuals or groups formally responsible for various kinds of decisions and to specify the class of teaching personnel whose behavior is affected by them. We refer to the decision maker(s) as the input population and those whose task performance is expected to be governed by the decisions as the output population. The relations of the membership of the input and output populations define the control structure. As will be seen shortly, both components of the relationship are taken into account in classifying decision types.

Control structure is a regularized or patterned feature of organizations, widely acknowledged by the participants themselves. Indeed, they may take it so for granted that it is best seen by an outsider in the specifics of their behavior. Control structure does not concern particulars of the process by which those in the decision arena reach decisions nor the relative efficacy of the participants, if more than one, in affecting decision outcomes—just the question of who legitimately is in the decision arena and who is expected to be governed by the decision outputs. Nor does control structure concern the matter of compliance with decision outputs or the organizational mechanisms for assuring it, although the methodology of our study focused attention on outputs with which teachers had, in fact, complied.

It is vital in mapping the structure of control in schools to take account of elements of teachers' task performance that are not subject to direct organizational control through a decision process. While operatives in many productive enterprises have so little discretion in their task performance that the condition may safely be ignored, this is decidedly not true in teaching, where the wide latitude of the classroom teacher in carrying out his or her instructional functions is considered the hallmark of the occupation (Lortie, 1969, 1975; Pellegrin, 1976). The control of the educative process in an important sense rests in the hands of teachers, individually, not collectively—an extreme form of decentralization. The decisions a teacher makes in the course of instruction are binding on no one's task performance but his or her own. Thus, a key trajectory of the change expected to be associated with team organization of the school is the replacement of individual discretion by collective decisions—of autonomy by control.

Decision Types

The relation of the input to the output population memberships gives rise to a variety of means for the systematic classification of decision types. A desideratum for our study was a classification system sufficiently abstract to apply equally to schools differing in hierarchic levels, official positions, and the presence of faculty sub-units, thus not begging the very questions to be examined empirically, but not so abstract that it failed to represent the phenomena expected to change with the advent of Multiunit organization. One dimension of obvious relevance to the measure of collegiality of the control structure was whether or not teachers affected by a decision were among those making the decision, that is, whether or not the input population contained <u>any</u> members of the output population. If it did not, the structure would be nonparticipative. Another dimension concerns whether or not the input population were comprised exclusively of teachers affected by the decision (some or all of the output population members), which, if it were, would represent a collegial decision. (The pure case of collegiality would be the complete identity of the two populations.)

Pure and intermediate types can be formed of these two considerations, and in other ways as well. One could, for instance, consider the comparative size of the input and output populations—the few making decisions for the many, the many making decisions for the few, and so on. Our present purposes were served, though, by considering the positions of personnel who were included in the input population—whether they were other affected or unaffected teachers in the school, the school's principal or other administrative officer, or personnel or agencies outside the school. These several classification principles permitted the specification of five decision types, including the boundary condition of discretion.

Outside or Type O: a structure in which neither the school's principal nor any teacher affected by the decision (the output population) is a member of the input population. Responsible agencies for decisions of this type ordinarily were central office personnel of the school district, such as curriculum supervisors, directors of elementary education, and the like, or legislative or regulatory bodies of state government.

Principal Alone, or Type P: a structure in which the principal of the school is the sole agent responsible for reaching the decision; no member of the output population is included in the input population. The principal's decision may be directed toward the work behavior of all teachers within the school, a subset of teachers, or an individual teacher.

Shared, or Type S: a structure in which at least one member of the output population joins other, unaffected personnel in comprising the input population. Nonteaching members of the input population in this type normally include the school's principal, although they alternatively may be personnel from outside the particular school.

Collegial, or Type C: a structure in which the input population is composed exclusively of teaching personnel within the school. The decision-making body could be a teacher committee, the members of a unit, the faculty as a whole, a group of unit leaders without the principal, and so on. It is broader than the pure type of collegiality noted earlier, in that some teachers of the school, unaffected by the decision, may not be among the decision makers, but empirically speaking, there were so few of these "impure" decision types in schools of the study that we did not hold them apart.

Discretion, or Type D: the limiting condition in which a teacher reaches an individual decision regarding task performance that governs no one's behavior but his or her own. Strictly speaking, discretion is not part of the school's control structure, in that it invokes no interpersonal processes and entails no organizational provisions for its enactment.

Decision Issues

There was reason to believe that the control structure for educational decisions would vary with the substantive issues at stake. In choosing areas of teacher task performance to probe, we thought it important to concentrate on areas susceptible to change with the advent of team organization. We might have examined a few global issues selected on a priori grounds but decided, instead, to probe a rather large number of specific issues, intending subsequently to locate groupings empirically.

The general arenas that guided the search for specific issues of decision were the following: curriculum scope and balance, methods of instruction, availability and use of instructional materials, methods of reporting pupil progress to parents, methods of responding to student misbehavior, and grouping students for instruction. Through extensive pretesting we developed an inventory of topics in each area with respect to which decisions might have been made. The list of topics guided the flow of our data-gathering procedure.

Control Structure Interviews

The basic data we used in assessing the school's control structure at each data-taking wave were obtained through a rather complex, two-stage procedure that involved first the distribution to selected informants a self-administered questionnaire, followed then by an interview of the informants that probed the information supplied by the questionnaire in considerable depth. The procedure had the purpose of obtaining evidence that a practice or event within each subarea was actually present in the classrooms or school and then of eliciting information concerning how decisions were made about it and whose behavior was intended to be governed by the decision—that is, the identities of the input and output populations. A detailed account of the procedure is available in a working paper by Packard and Carlson (1976).

The control structure interviews were subcontracted to an experienced survey organization, the Institute for Survey Research of Temple University, to assure professional training and supervision of the personnel responsible for conducting the rather intricate interviews. The interviewers, recruited from the locale of the schools in which they interviewed, were trained together both in large groups and on an individual basis. They were supervised not only with respect to their conformity to the standard procedures but also on the basis of the data they returned. Many of the interviews were recorded on audio tapes, which were spot checked regularly by field supervisors. The Institute was also responsible for coding, keypunching, and storing the basic data on magnetic tape, using standard practices of quality control at each step in the process. The tapes were delivered to the Oregon researchers for data analysis.

Respondents were chosen by our own staff for interviewing by the Institute's survey personnel. Our entire measurement approach was based on the premise that in-depth information concerning the school's control structure could more dependably be obtained from a few intimately knowledgeable individuals than from the pooled responses of a random, or otherwise unselected, sample of the staff. We viewed interviewees as informants rather than the respondents of the normal survey research approach. In the first wave of data collection, however, a random sample of no more than eight teachers was drawn for interviews in each school, since at that time we had no information on which to choose respondents for their knowledgeability. Thereafter, we chose teachers who had been with the school for more than a year or two and who, according to information we had been able to assemble, were centrally situated in the social and political fabric of the school. In the Multiunit schools the unit leaders almost invariably were among them. We were able to reduce the number of interviewees to four or five teachers per school by this selection process. The interviews themselves lasted anywhere from 45 minutes to 90 minutes in the first data-taking wave, gradually becoming shorter with subsequent waves as informants, or at least the informants who had been interviewed before, became familiar with the line of questioning.

Data Reduction

The raw data furnished by the Institute for Survey Research enabled our staff to specify the decision type, as defined above, associated with each specific practice or event that informants reported in response to probings of interviewers. These specifics were numerous indeed, running to several hundred in a given school. The detailed data were subjected to intensive analysis in order to reduce redundancies and establish general characteristics. The analysis proceeded through a number of steps, beginning with the elimination of rarely occurring events and grouping the rest into obviously identical classes. Thirteen areas of decision issue common to all the schools were identified in this way, and subsequently these were grouped into three general "domains" on grounds of similarities in profiles of their decision types. These are listed in Table 9.1. The step-by-step procedures by which the groupings were established is documented in a technical report by Jovick (1978). More will be said about the domains later in the chapter.

TABLE 9.1

Decision Issues Listed by Domain

Instructional Processes Domain
    Lessons presented in each subject taught.
    When and how long each subject is taught.
    Instructional materials available in school.
    Textbooks actually used in teaching.
    Instructional materials actually used in teaching, other than
      textbooks.
    Methods used in teaching.
    Frequency and methods of reporting pupil progress to parents,
      other than regular parent conferences and report cards.
    Disciplinary practices used.
Deployment of Pupils and Teachers
    Grade-level composition and number of pupils in class.
    If more than one group or class is taught, the number, grade-level
      composition, and selection of pupils in groups.
Systemic Decisions
    Subjects taught by teacher.
    Textbooks available to teacher.
    Frequency and methods of reporting pupil progress to parents:
      report cards and regular parent conferences.

Source: Compiled by the author.

THE SUBJECT SCHOOLS

The schools of the study were selected after an extensive search by the research staff, first to locate schools planning to switch to the Individually Guided Education (IGE) Plan in the fall of 1974 and agreeable to participation in a long-term study, and then to find conventional schools in the same districts whose staffs would volunteer to serve as controls. Thus, sampling was purposive rather than representational. All schools lay east of the Mississippi River, principally in the New England, Mid-Atlantic, and Border states. Some were inner city schools serving low-income families, others were in affluent and not-so-affluent suburbs, and still others in small communities of rural America. Most, but not all, were public schools; four parish schools of a Roman Catholic diocese were included. The public schools were located in 12 different school districts, one of them among the larger districts of the United States, with 135,000 students, while the smallest district enrolled 2,500 elementary and secondary students. Per-pupil expenditures of the districts ranged from $460 to $1,440 in 1974 dollars.

The elementary schools were heterogeneous with respect to size, structure, and other circumstances. They ranged in size from a faculty of eight serving 200 students to one of nearly 30 serving 800 students (median = 13 classroom teachers, 362 pupils). The grade organization varied substantially within the sample: several included the seventh and eighth grades, a few were essentially primary or middle schools, and about half offered kindergarten programs. Most of the schools had a traditional corridor-classroom architectural design, but a few included open-space areas, typically as additions to older buildings.

Most of the schools had a full-time building administrator, and a number also had assistant principals—either full-time appointees or classroom teachers who served part-time in that capacity. Principals in the Multiunit schools were more likely to be female than their nonunitized counterparts, were younger, had fewer years of administrative experience, and had been in their present principalship a shorter length of time.

Teaching staffs of the two sets of schools were alike in sex distribution (92 percent female) and educational attainment (modally, bachelor's degree plus credits toward the M.A.). However, teachers in the Multiunit schools were younger and less experienced than those in nonunitized schools and somewhat less traditional in their educational views, according to measures we took of teacher belief systems.

The systematic difference between the two sets of schools (after the first measurement period, of course) was the presence or absence of formal faculty teams, or units. The number of units in the Multiunit schools ran from two to seven, depending on faculty size; unit membership typically consisted of three, four, or perhaps five grade-level teachers. The units were active entities in most schools, meeting weekly or more often, especially during the first year. Leaders of the units usually were appointed by the principal. With a few exceptions no special perquisites were associated with the position, such as released time or salary increments. It was our general impression from various pieces of evidence that the leader position did not become an especially consequential one in most instances, other than affording the leaders the opportunity to meet with the principal in the so-called Instructional Improvement Committee—that is, the faculty cabinet. In about half of the schools, the cabinets became key arenas of coordination and governance, but in other schools, after an ambitious start, they seem to have withered away. The Multiunit schools were distinctive, too, in their efforts to install curriculum and instructional reforms supposedly along the lines of IGE, but the particular innovations they sought to introduce were as various as the schools themselves.

DECISION ISSUES AND DOMAINS

The bar graphs in Figure 9.1 represent the percentage distributions of the five decision types, defined earlier, for each of the 13 decision issues listed in Table 9.1. These data are for the 13 conventional schools measured at T_1. Since the Multiunit schools were still in their supposedly conventional mode at T_1, too, it might have seemed logical to include them in the data. We found, however, that the Multiunit schools as a group had higher percentages of collegial (Type C) decisions over most of the decision issues even before reorganization, a fact for which we had to correct in analyses for the main body of our report. We speculated that this may have been the result of the planning and training workshops that occurred in some of the schools in anticipation of unit formation in the following fall. In any event, the data in Figure 9.1 exclude the "experimental" schools in order to provide a more representative description.

The bar graphs show marked differences in decision structure for the various issues, ranging from issues where teachers had nearly unfettered autonomy to those predominantly implicating the principal, either as the sole agent or jointly with the staff and on to issues where the responsible parties lay predominantly outside the school and perhaps the school district. Interestingly, collegial decisions (Type C) were by no means absent from these conventional schools. They could have come about through the deliberations of faculty

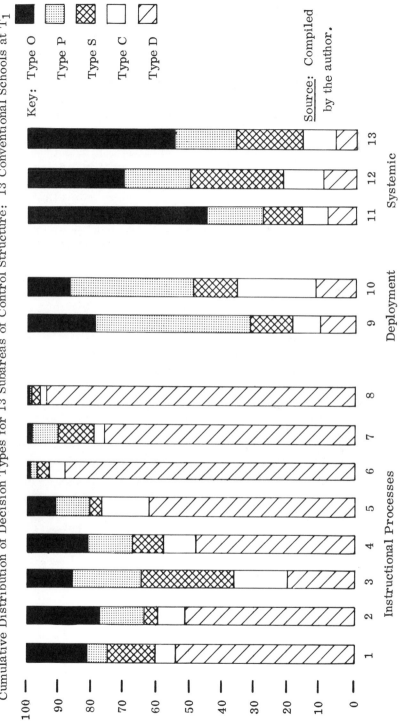

FIGURE 9.1

Cumulative Distribution of Decision Types for 13 Subareas of Control Structure: 13 Conventional Schools at T_1

Key: Type O
     Type P
     Type S
     Type C
     Type D

Source: Compiled by the author.

287

committees or as informal arrangements among teachers who worked closely together in the instructional program.

Before describing the groupings of the issues it is worth making some overall observations regarding the 13 issues. For one thing, the results document definitively the wide latitude of choice of the individual teacher behind the classroom door. At the heart of the delivery of educational service—the core technology of the teaching craft—decisions were firmly in the hands of professionals (Lortie, 1969, 1975; Pellegrin, 1976). Modes of interacting with pupils, the particular style of teaching and lesson planning, the scheduling of instruction, and the choice of instructional materials were predominately discretionary. Interactions with parents, too, were left largely to the discretion of teachers—at least those interactions that went beyond the standard reporting procedures established by the district. Discussions in the literature regarding "centralization" versus "decentralization" in educational organizations infrequently take into account the extreme level of decentralization that already exists at the micro level of educational policy.

While the individual teacher in these conventional schools had considerable freedom once the classroom door was closed, he or she had far less to say about how that class was formed in the first place. It was the school's principal or other administrator who dominated decisions concerning which pupils would be taught by which teachers. Apparently colleagues could get together occasionally to achieve regroupings of pupils assigned to them or to work out informal "turn-teaching" patterns, such as we observed in certain schools. Those decisions would be reflected in Area 10 of the figure, but such regroupings would normally occur within the context of the overall structure established predominantly by the principal (Area 9).

One feature of the display in Figure 9.1 is especially illuminating in regard to the control, or lack of it, by upper-level policy makers. We separated our questioning about instructional materials into two parts: decisions concerning the selection (adoption) of textbooks and other instructional materials and decisions concerning their actual use in the classroom. Considering the rather high levels of discretion on actual use, the lesson is clear: schoolwide or districtwide adoption of materials did not mean, ipso facto, that the materials would find their way into classroom instruction.

The argument of teacher discretion, however, should not be carried too far. As we noted earlier, we did not systematically examine the manner in which decisions higher in the authority system had the effect of limiting the range of alternatives within which choice could be exercised. For instance, the seemingly broad range of choice teachers had with respect to disciplinary practices was certainly constrained by legal considerations, ethical principles, as well as school-district policy. In the same way, teachers' apparent freedom in the use of textbooks must surely have occurred within important bounds—bounds established by prior or even contemporaneous adoption policies of the school, district, and state. Some upper-level decisions have an indirect effect on the issues we studied. Decisions reached at budget-making time concerning discretionary funds allotted to faculty members could seriously modify the teacher's freedom in the use of instructional materials. "You are free to select any materials you want during the year as long as they don't cost more than $25.00." Such layerings of decisions bearing on the teacher deserve closer investigation than we gave them.

A final observation regarding Figure 9.1 concerns school size. Although we do not display the data, we can say that decisions made by the principal alone (Type P) were systematically higher in the larger than the smaller schools. We used 15 classroom teachers as the dividing point. This was true in virtually every one of the 13 decision areas, although they were not as notable in the instructional processes domain as in the others. Elevation of the Type P percentages often, but not universally, was at the expense of Type S decisions. Said differently, more sharing of decisions occurred in the smaller schools. It makes intuitive sense, at least, to expect the principal of a school with 8, 10, or 12 teachers to be less removed from the faculty than the principal with a staff of 20 or 30 teachers.

The data analyses on which we will hereafter report were based on clusters of the decision issues rather than on the 13 separately. Through several statistical procedures we grouped issues whose decision structures followed reasonably similar configurations (Jovick, 1978). The groupings were not altogether empirically based, since we were guided in part by the purposes of the larger study and the matters to which our measures needed to be sensitive. The three groupings we identified are suggested in Table 9.1.

The first grouping, or domain, included issues dominated by teacher discretion (Type D decisions), covering such matters as when and how long subjects are taught in the classroom, the particular lessons that are presented, teaching methods, and disciplinary practices. We call this the instructional processes domain. The second domain concerns issues as to which teachers are to teach which classes or groups of pupils and how such classes are formed—issues in which the building administrator ordinarily plays the leading role (Type P decisions). We refer to this as the domain of pupil and teacher deployment. The third domain, called the domain of systemic decisions, includes issues relating to the school's curriculum, textbook adoption, and the procedures for reporting pupil progress to parents. Decisions in this domain characteristically are made outside the given school (Type O)—by school boards, upper-level administrators, or in some instances by state authorities. In very small districts, with only one or two elementary schools and no central office staff to speak of, or in some of the parochial schools of the sample, resolution of some of the systemic decisions may actually come to rest in the individual school rather than outside it.

SCHOOL VARIATIONS IN CONTROL STRUCTURE

We were interested in getting beneath the aggregated data of Figure 9.1 to an understanding of the similarities and differences on a school-to-school basis. While the 29 schools of the study (now counting the "experimental" schools) were highly heterogeneous in many respects, we thought that a few universal patterns of control structure might emerge if sought in an appropriate way.

Most of our analyses for the main report of the study had been confined to collegial decisions. Specifically, we treated the percentage of Type C decisions as a school score, sometimes aggregating over both the instructional processes and the deployment domains and sometimes holding the two apart. We made little use of decisions in the systemic domain, since we had little reason to expect that such decisions made outside the school in the school district or beyond would be sensitive to the kind of innovation we were examining, which implicated just one of the schools in the district.[2] (We will continue to exclude decisions of the systemic domain in what is to follow.) The ipsative character of the percentage distributions for the five decision types precluded using more than one decision type at a time in the multiple regression analysis on which we relied, even though we had some clear expectations concerning the impact of the Multiunit innovation on other aspects of the decision structure.

In particular, we expected that team organization would have the effect of increasing Type C decisions in the instructional processes domain at the expense of individual discretion, or Type D decisions, while in the deployment domain we anticipated that Type C decisions and/or Type S decisions would grow at the expense of Type P decisions, reflecting what some would call participatory decision making.

Multidimensional Scaling

We employed the statistical technique of nonmetric multidimensional scaling as the tool for examining configurations of decision structures, comparing one school to the next at one point in time or the same school from one time to the next. The procedure as we used it takes a measure of profile similarity between pairs of schools and searches for the simplest way of displaying the similarities and dissimilarities among schools in geometric space. We had access to the computer program developed by Guttman and Lingoes called MINISSA-I(M).[3] A school's profile consisted of ten points, whose elevations were the percentages of decisions of Types D, C, S, P, and O for the instructional processes domain and for the deployment domain in a given data-taking wave. To be concrete, Figure 9.2 shows the profiles for two control schools measured at T_1. The profile for School 35 is close to the average for all schools at that time, reflecting the high level of discretion in the instructional processes domain and the dominance of Type P decisions in the deployment of students and teachers. School 16, a smaller one with a staff of 12 teachers, also displayed considerable discretion in the instructional processes domain but notably higher Type C decisions and lower Type P decisions in the deployment domain. We used D^2 as the measure of profile similarity (or, more accurately, dissimilarity). This measure squared the difference between the percentages at each point and summed the squared values over the ten. We took the square root of the sum of the squared deviations in order to keep the values reasonably small. Two schools with identical profiles would have a D^2 of 0; the theoretical maximum D^2 that could be obtained between a pair of schools is 200, but rarely did we observe values larger than 100. The D^2 between the schools in Figure 9.2 was 45.5.

The scaling program seeks an order in the similarity-dissimilarity scores of all pairs of schools in the analysis, determining how well the array of scores can be represented in a two-, three-, or n-dimensional space. A coefficient called Kruskal's stress is one of the numerical values that expresses the goodness of fit of the original D^2s in the space of a given dimension. Generally stress decreases as the dimensionality increases, indicating a better and better fit. The cost of increasing the dimensionality to achieve a better fit, however, is high and in an important respect defeats the purpose of the scaling technique, which is to reduce complex numerical data to graphic form for easy visual interpretation. One experiences difficulty in envisioning and interpreting values in three-dimensional space, and the task becomes much harder in spaces of higher order. In the present case, we have limited our presentation to two-dimensional depictions, suffering stress coefficients as high as .18. (Coefficients of .05 or lower are generally regarded as desirable.) Most of our analyses were also conducted for a three-dimensional solution and our interpretations will take their results into account.

FIGURE 9.2

Illustration of Profiles in Two Decision Domains, T_1

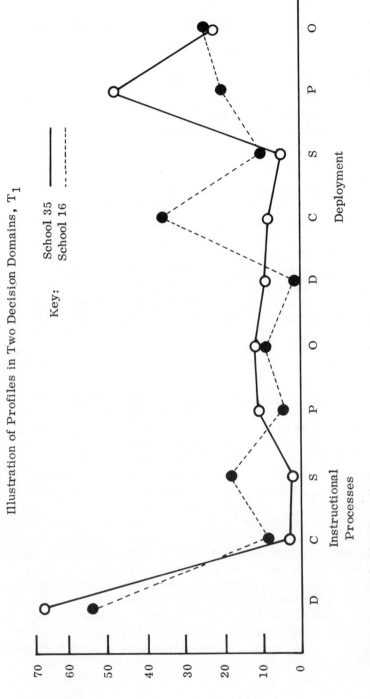

Source: Compiled by the author.

The MINISSA-I(M) program produces a diagram in which schools whose profiles are similar, as estimated by an iterative procedure, are plotted near one another and schools whose profiles are dissimilar are plotted far apart. The coordinates of the diagram are arbitrary and may hold little meaning, or they may be suggestive of particular dimensions along which the profiles vary, especially if stress is low and one is willing to rotate the axes visually. Our efforts to interpret the results will depend on internal analysis. That is to say, we refer back to the original control structure profiles of the schools closely clustered to detect the unique characteristics of their configurations, sometimes examining profiles of remote schools to clarify the distinctive features. An interactive computer routine facilitated the process of making the profile comparisons.

Patterns of Profiles

Figure 9.3 displays the two-dimensional solution of profile similarities and differences for all 29 schools at the first data-taking wave. We have distinguished between the "experimental" and "control" schools by representing the former as circles and the latter as squares. In addition, we show the larger schools (15 or more classroom teachers) as double-walled circles or boxes. The stress coefficient for the two-dimensional solution was .178, the highest of all we encountered. Stress for the three-dimensional solution was considerably lower, .094.

The most prominent observation in the figure is the absence of clearly distinctive groupings of schools. Rather, the schools appear quite evenly spaced in Quadrants I and II, with a few outliers in Quadrant IV. Examination of the third dimension indicated further diversity. Thus, the four schools in the upper-right corner of Quadrant I separated into two dissimilar configurations when the third dimension was considered. While a number of pairs of schools with similar profiles could be identified, there was but one larger grouping with configurations reasonably close together. These were the five schools on the far right of Figure 9.3, excluding School 17, whose profile proved to be discrepant in the third dimension. They were alike in that they had somewhat elevated percentages of collegial decisions in the instructional processes domain, somewhat higher proportions of Type P decisions in the deployment domain, and slightly depressed percentages of Type S decisions in both domains. One would find it difficult to detect anything other than slight differences between the profiles for these schools and the average profile across all schools. It was the single outliers that displayed marked de-

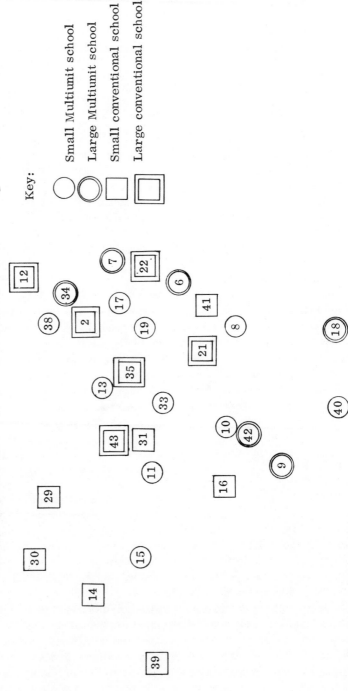

FIGURE 9.3

Smallest Space Solution (two dimensions) for 29 Schools at T_1

Key:

○ Small Multiunit school

◎ Large Multiunit school

□ Small conventional school

▣ Large conventional school

Source: Compiled by the author.

partures from the norm. School 39, on the far left, for instance, was set apart from the others by the unusually high percentages of decisions made outside the school in both domains. School 18, near the bottom right, was distinctive by virtue of the unusually high proportion of instructional process decisions made by the principal alone. School 30, in the upper left, and to a lesser extent school 29, displayed unusually high proportions of shared decisions in both domains. In short, we found in this analysis one strong overall pattern of decision structure, with a few major but idiosyncratic departures from it. The picture was one of continuities, not of three or four distinct groupings.

While we attach little significance to it, it is interesting to note that all of the larger schools fell on the right of the diagram. It could imply simply that the left to right dimension of the figure reflected the level of Type P decisions, which, as we commented earlier, was associated with school size. Detailed inspection of the profiles lent sustenance to that implication.

Profiles after Two Years

In Figure 9.4 we show results of the analysis at the end of the second year of effort on the part of the "experimental" schools to implement the IGE/MUS innovation. The stress coefficient for the two-dimensional analysis, shown in the figure, was .104 and .061 for the three-dimensional solution. The effect of the innovative organization on decision making is patently clear: All but two, perhaps three, of the Multiunit schools are further right on the horizontal dimension than any conventional school, all of which are clustered in Quadrant III.

Internal analysis of the profiles showed unequivocally that the horizontal dimension reflects the elevation of Type C decisions in one or both decision-making domains. In Figure 9.5 the profiles of School 38, the Multiunit school, and School 39, the conventional school, are compared (the D^2 between them was 118.4). Both schools, incidentally, were in the same school district. The profile for School 39 was similar to the general pattern of conventional schools—high teacher discretion in the instructional processes domain and a high level of principal-made decisions in the deployment domain. School 38, on the other hand, had an extremely high elevation of collegial decisions, especially in the deployment domain, virtually excluding the principal's participation. The Type C decisions in the instructional processes area were only moderately high for this school. Other comparisons we made along the horizontal dimension yielded parallel results: To the left were schools in which

FIGURE 9.4

Smallest Space Solution (two dimensions) for 29 Schools at T$_5$

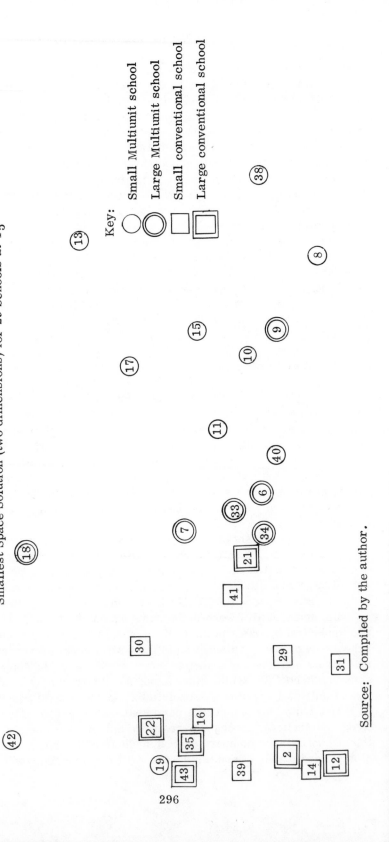

Key:

Small Multiunit school

Large Multiunit school

Small conventional school

Large conventional school

Source: Compiled by the author.

296

FIGURE 9.5

Control Structure Profiles for Two Contrasting Schools at T_5: School 38 and School 39

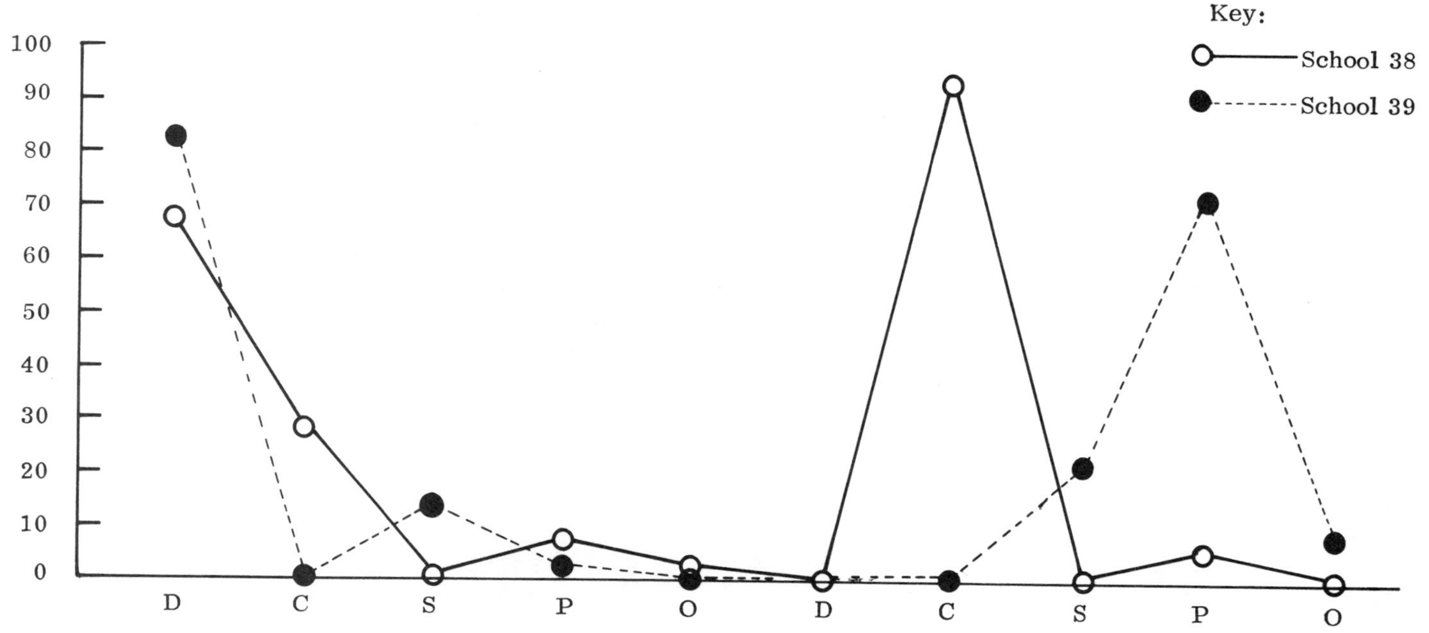

Source: Compiled by the author.

297

collegial decisions were all but absent, and to the right were schools in which collegial decisions were prominent, either in the deployment domain or in both.

The vertical dimension (as well as the third dimension) did not yield so readily to general interpretation. However, if only the schools in the right two quadrants are investigated, running from School 8 at the lowest level and up through 9 and 10 to 13 to the highest level, there is a consistent increase in Type C decisions in the instructional processes domain. Type C deployment decisions remained steadily high in that progression. The profile for School 13 is worth displaying, since it comes as close as any school to epitomizing the control structure under the Multiunit plan. In Figure 9.6 we contrast it with School 14, the conventional school in the same district that was remote from it, in the lower left corner (D^2 = 119.2).

The distinction for the Multiunit schools on the vertical dimension deserves further comment. Assumption of decisions concerning the intimate details of classroom instruction, as would be indicated by the location of schools in Quadrant I, would be a direct confrontation with the autonomy that Lortie (1969) and others suggest teachers so jealously defend. Control of deployment decisions, whether by colleagues or by administrators, would be less of a threat. Perhaps it is no accident that most of the Multiunit schools ended their second year of implementation in Quadrant II rather than Quadrant I. It is further notable that even in School 13 individual teachers still exercised substantial discretion in the instructional processes domain.

The same observation we made about the absence of discrete clusters of schools in Figure 9.3 applies nearly as well to Figure 9.4. Continuities are more prominent among the schools than discontinuities. One cluster of schools just left of center in Quadrant III, consisting of Schools 41, 21, 23, 33, 6, and 40 (but not 7, which was discrepant in the third dimension) were notable only for their moderation. That is, they varied hardly at all from the average profile for all schools. Another cluster at the far left, consisting of Schools 16, 19, 35, and 43 (but not 22) were similar not only in the absence of Type C decisions but in the high elevations of discretion in the instructional processes domain, coupled with low levels of Type P decisions. They also showed high elevation of Type S decisions, oddly enough. Other groupings could be pointed out, but as before these would consist of two or possibly three schools that shared some particular anomaly, such as being subject to inordinately high levels of decisions outside the school. A few distinct types did not stand out.

FIGURE 9.6

Control Structure Profiles for Two Contrasting Schools at T_5: School 13 and School 14

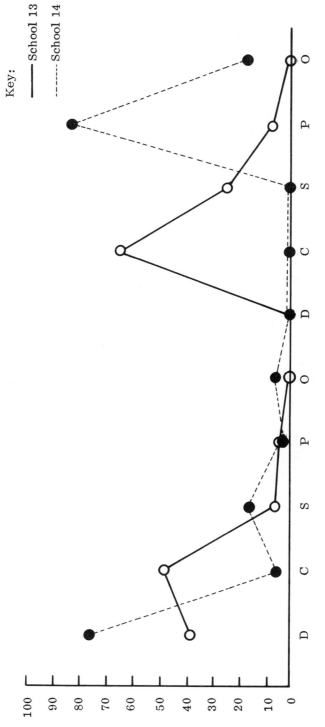

Key:

———— School 13

------- School 14

Source: Compiled by the author.

THE STUDY OF CHANGE

The general observation of increase in collegial decisions in most of the Multiunit schools had been confirmed earlier using standard analysis procedures. In those analyses the percentages of Type C decisions alone were treated as scores and a multiple regression approach to the analysis of covariance demonstrated significant overall increases among the Multiunit schools after taking account of their higher scores before implementation began (Packard et al., 1978:Ch. 4). What the standard analysis could not show, however, was the manner in which the Multiunit schools reached their destinations or what aspects of their control structures suffered as collegiality increased. We mentioned earlier our suspicion that they may have followed a few common trajectories—that in the instructional processes domain collegiality gained at the expense of discretion and in the deployment domain a shift occurred toward collegial or shared decisions with a loss in decisions made by the principal alone. We were interested to learn, too, what had happened in the three Multiunit schools that seemed in Figure 9.4 to have remained on the left of the horizontal (collegiality) dimension along with the conventional schools.

We put the profile analysis and multidimensional scaling procedure to a novel use to discern the trajectories of change. Specifically, we calculated D^2 values between every pair of Multiunit schools in a 48 by 48 matrix, where the profiles for the 16 schools were entered three times—at T_1 before implementation began, at T_3 after one year of implementation, and at T_5 after two years. The full matrix was submitted for scaling by the MINISSA program and a two-dimensional map of the estimated location of the schools was printed. Although the stress coefficient was fairly high (.140), suggesting that higher orders of dimensionality would be necessary for a better fit, we decided not to proceed beyond the second dimension; with the time element included, the data were complicated enough to interpret as it was.

We show first, in Figure 9.7, results of the parallel analysis we made for the 13 control schools. Our interest was to suggest the meanderings of decision structures from year to year under supposedly normal conditions. With the comparatively high stress coefficient of .159, interpretation of the two dimensions was not readily apparent, although the vertical dimension seemed to reflect the magnitude of Type S decisions, with the higher proportions toward the top, and the horizontal dimension of Type P decisions, with the higher proportions on the left. More importantly, the amount of movement of the schools from year to year was surprisingly great. A few changed hardly at all, but the movement in others was dramatic.

FIGURE 9.7

Smallest Space Solution (two dimensions) for 13 Conventional Schools at T₁, T₃, and T₅

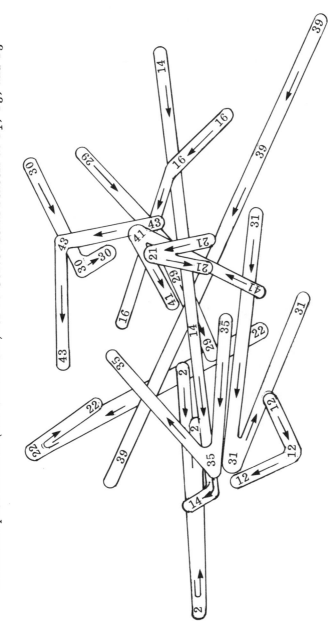

Source: Compiled by the author.

School 39 is a case in point. This small eight-teacher school began with a control structure in which Type O decisions were uncommonly high in both domains and changed to one in which Type D decisions were unusually high in the instructional process domain and the principal became the dominant decision maker in the deployment domain. School 14 took a rather similar path between the first and second year. In general, there seemed to be a considerable amount of "noise" in the system.

As we will see, the diagram for the Multiunit schools had a similar element of meandering about it, and we became concerned that the changes in decision structures were, indeed, little more than expressions of unreliability of the measuring process. We undertook some additional analyses to check this disturbing possibility. We made the appropriate calculations to allow a determination of whether the profiles for the same schools from one year to the next were significantly more alike than the profiles for different schools in a given year. We carried the analysis a step further. We asked the same question about between versus within profile similarities using measures taken six months apart in the same year—T_2 to T_3 and T_4 to T_5. We expected, of course, that the measures in the same school year would be more stable (that is, lower D^2 values) than measures spanning a full year. For these analyses we used the original D^2 computations for school pairs. The relevant calculations are given in Table 9.2.

TABLE 9.2

Mean Values of D^2s for Conventional Schools

	Wave(s)	Mean	Standard Deviation	Number
Different schools, same wave	1	48.8	13.66	78
	2	60.3	18.22	78
	3	53.6	16.63	78
	4	57.5	19.37	78
	5	41.2	10.30	78
Same school, different waves	2–3	34.9	17.05	13
	4–5	39.5	12.50	13
	1–3	45.5	14.49	13
	3–5	33.7	15.03	13

Source: Compiled by the author.

The numbers reveal that the mean D^2s for pairs of schools within a given data-taking wave (78 such pairs) ranged from 41 to 60, depending on the wave. Their mean was 52. The mean D^2s for the same schools from one measurement period to another, with one exception, were below 40, indicating a greater similarity of their profiles. Since the standard deviations were rather large, we conducted formal statistical tests of the differences, comparing the between-time means for the same schools with the within-time means, pooled for the applicable data-taking, by use of $\underline{t}$ tests. Three of the four comparisons were statistically significant beyond the .05 level, as Table 9.3 shows. The nonsignificant comparison was between T_1 and T_3, a full year apart. Although the effects were not strong, the data offer an indication that we are studying more than the vagaries of unreliable measurement.

TABLE 9.3

Significance Tests for Comparisons of D^2s

Comparison	Mean	Standard Deviation	$\underline{t}$
Waves 2 and 3			
Same school	34.9	17.05	4.3284*
Different schools, pooled	57.0	17.71	
Waves 4 and 5			
Same school	39.5	12.50	1.9859*
Different schools, pooled	49.3	17.49	
Waves 1 and 3			
Same school	45.5	14.49	1.2912
Different schools, pooled	51.2	15.37	
Waves 3 and 5			
Same school	33.7	15.03	3.1283*
Different schools, pooled	47.4	15.14	

*Significant beyond .05 level, 167 degrees of freedom (df).
Source: Compiled by the author.

ODYSSEYS OF THE MULTIUNIT SCHOOLS

Figure 9.8 displays the movement of the Multiunit schools through the three points of observation one year apart. The axes of the two-dimensional space, insofar as we could discern them without a three-dimensional solution, were similar to the dimensions in Figure 9.4. The main axis running horizontally from left to right indicated increasing proportions of collegial decisions, especially in the domain of pupil-teacher deployment. Accompanying this increase were decreases in the same domain of both shared decisions and decisions by the principal alone. Variations in the instructional processes domain did not help to define the horizontal axis. As before, the vertical axis was less readily interpretable. There was a suggestion that it implicated Type C decisions in the instructional processes domain, increasing as one moved upward in the diagram, but only in the center and right. The nature of the vertical dimension on the left was obscure without reference to a third dimension.

If we had expected a few simple trajectories of change among the Multiunit schools, the results in Figure 9.8 certainly disconfirmed that anticipation. The best that can be said is that the net movement for the majority of schools from T_1 to T_5 was toward the right of the diagram—toward higher proportions of collegial decisions. That much, though, had already been learned from previous displays and from earlier numerical analyses. It was also the case that the larger schools demonstrated less movement than the smaller ones, a fact we had noted in our initial investigation (Packard et al., 1978).[4]

The deviant cases that displayed net retrogressions between T_1 and T_5 were interesting to observe. School 18, before implementation began, had a control structure characterized by an unusually high proportion of Type P decisions and unusually low teacher discretion in the instructional processes domain, and collegial decisions in the deployment domain were much higher than principal-made decisions. The principal who was a key sponsor of the Multiunit plan left the school for another position during the summer before implementation began. By the end of the first year, the structure had shifted primarily in the deployment domain by a substantial drop in collegial decisions and an increase in principal-made decisions. Type P decisions in the instructional processes domain remained high and teacher discretion rather low. The school ended its attempt to implement the IGE/MUS plan at the end of that year (one of the two that did so, School 11 being the other), and at the end of the second year the decision structure changed again. The structure in the instructional processes domain continued to display high

FIGURE 9.8

Smallest Space Solution (two dimensional) for 16 Multiunit Schools at T_1, T_3, and T_5

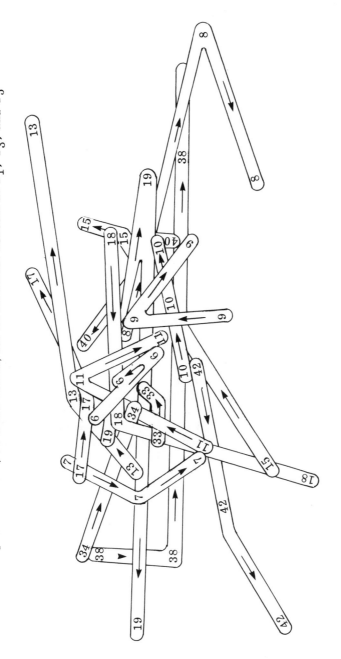

Source: Compiled by the author.

Type P decisions, even higher Type S decisions, and extraordinarily low teacher discretion. Type S decisions rather than Type P decisions dominated the structure of the deployment domain.

School 42, which also lost its principal—in this case by death during the first year of implementation—did not alter the decision structure in the instructional processes domain through the three time periods. It continued to manifest unusually high levels of teacher discretion. The alterations came mainly in the systematically increasing level of shared decisions in the deployment domain. School 19 showed a curious pattern of advance and retreat. Beginning with a pattern notable mainly for an overrepresentation of Type P decisions in the instructional processes domain, Type C decisions increased substantially, especially in the deployment domain, by the end of the first year; by the end of the second year, for reasons we have not discerned, Type C decisions dropped dramatically to be replaced by an uncommonly high proportion of Type S decisions in both domains.

We could continue to recount the odysseys of other schools, but their causes and consequences cannot be deciphered without reference to other data of the study, which we shall not attempt to introduce here. We can ask, however, whether the evidence indicates that the trajectories of change toward a collegial decision structure occurred regularly at the expense of certain other decision types or at the expense of Type D in the instructional processes domain and Type P in the deployment domain. We used selected schools to answer the question—schools that made prominent gains toward the right of Figure 9.8. These are Schools 10, 13, 15, and 17 at all three waves and Schools 8 and 19 for waves 1 and 3 and School 38 for waves 3 and 5. Our procedure was to tally the increases in Type C decisions from wave to wave and the decreases in Type D decisions through the same waves in the instructional processes domain. Part of the question will be answered if the Type C gains in the aggregate are offset by the Type D losses. For the deployment domain we tallied gains and losses in Type C, Type S, and Type P decisions, expecting that the gains in Type C and/or Type S decisions would be offset by losses in Type P decisions.

Table 9.4 summarizes the results of the tabulations. The figures show that the aggregate gain in collegiality (91.8 over 11 comparisons) was considerably larger than the aggregate loss in individual discretion in the instructional processes domain (-56.9). The remainder must have come from the other three decision types. In the deployment domain, the large gain in Type C decisions of 342.3 in these selected schools clearly was not offset by the loss in Type P decisions (-144.0). Moreover, contrary to expectations, the Type C gains were accompanied by losses, not gains, in Type S decisions as well. In sum, neither the discretion of individual teachers nor the power of principals acting on their own was substantially affected by the growth of collegiality in these Multiunit schools.

TABLE 9.4

Changes in Specified Decision Types Associated with Gains in Type C Decisions, for Seven Selected Multiunit Schools (11 Comparisons)

Domain	Total Change
Instructional processes	
Type C decisions	91.8
Type P decisions	−56.9
Deployment	
Type C decisions	342.3
Type S decisions	−69.7
Type P decisions	−144.0

Source: Compiled by the author.

CONCLUSIONS

Our purposes in this chapter have been several. We have sought to emphasize, for one thing, the importance of investigating the control of educational policy at the micro level—"where the rubber meets the road," to resort to a colloquialism. It is the issue of who decides what with regard to the transactions between teachers and pupils, which, after all, is the heart of the educational process. It is a level of analysis that generally is ignored in the grander studies of the politics of education, where questions regarding the making of federal, state, or local policies are at the forefront and concerns about the responsiveness of school district administrators or boards of education to external demands occupy attention. Harbingers of concern for the control of micro policies of education have come most prominently from educational research undertaken by sociologists of organizations who attend to the standing of teachers in the organizational hierarchy, by students of the teaching occupation, and by investigators of educational innovations, who so readily identify the classroom teacher as the saboteur of attempts to alter educational policies, practices, and structures unless exceptional efforts are made to enlist their collaboration. From this micro perspective we have sought to underscore empirically the pervasive decentralization of control of who teaches what to whom and how.

The case can be carried too far, of course, as we mentioned earlier. While it is currently popular in some quarters to characterize education as a loosely coupled system, there is no serious analyst who argues that it is an uncoupled system. No one argues that occurrences in the classroom are unrelated to occurrences in neighboring classrooms, directives, decisions, or leadership from the administrative hierarchy, or broader policies, practices, and pressures from the school board, the community, and beyond. The concept of loose coupling, as applied to education, came as a corrective to the view commonly held by scholars (and others) not intimately familiar with the U.S. educational system that it was a tightly coupled system. A basic issue we hoped to address, or at least open to inquiry, was where the couplings, loose or otherwise, resided. That we were unable, through our methodology, to trace upward the layers of constraints on lower-level decisions is not to deny the issue's significance.

Another purpose of the chapter has been to describe our conceptualization of control structure. We have narrowed the concept so that it applies specifically to decisions taken by one or more individuals deliberately to affect the task behavior of one or more individuals. Not only does this render the concept more precise, focusing it on the concept of authority or, in other terms, legitimate power, and separating it from the more diffuse concept of influence, but it opens to investigation various aspects of the relationship between the so-called input population and the output population. In the present study we have exploited only limited features of the relativity of the two populations. We have not, for instance, treated the issue of their relative sizes.

We have also attempted to illustrate a methodology—profile analysis and multidimensional scaling—that is especially suitable to the kind of data we collected. The data are, at best, weakly ipsative and, as we have employed them here, strongly ipsative. At the most fundamental level of analysis, we classified a specific issue for decision into one of five types. The more decisions classified in one type, the fewer there were to be classified in the other types. Thus, the frequencies of decision types were not independent of one another. This fundamental methodological decision, incidentally, committed us to a conception of power as a zero-sum game, one we are willing to defend conceptually. Others such as Tannenbaum (1968), who claim their data demonstrate that total power in an organization can shrink and expand, fail to realize that the possibility for it to do so is built into the basic methodology by which the data are taken, which in turn is dependent, wittingly or unwittingly, on their definition of power. The issue is a matter of conception, not of empirical demonstration. In any event, nonmetric multidimensional scaling constitutes a reasonable analytic approach to categorical data expressed as percentages when one is interested in the relative performance of the categories. Use of the procedure to map changes in percentage distributions through time is, to our knowledge, a unique application and deserves further experimentation. In certain analyses that we have not reported here, we employed the tactic of introducing "marker" profiles—fictitious data representing pure cases of specific types of control structure or of change in control structure. These we had hoped would aid in the interpretation of the dimensions of the program output, but limitations in the capacity of local computer facilities frustrated our efforts to test the idea adequately.

It is undoubtedly ill-advised to end a chapter in a negative tone, but two matters have haunted us in our investigation of the control of microeducational policies, one methodological and one substantive. On the methodological side, we have come to recognize that our measurement process and the data reduction procedures that we followed are essentially unreplicable. Collection of the raw data through in-depth interviews with knowledgeable informants was an expensive business and the manner in which we and the subcontracting survey institute processed the extensive information from the interviews would require more than a simple coding manual to explain. More direct and easily repeatable measurement procedures must surely be devised without succumbing to the shortcomings of the usual survey instruments, where "scores" of the informed respondents are treated as equal to the "scores" of the uninformed.

On the substantive side, hindsight has advised us that the control structure of an elementary school is not all of one piece. We do not have in mind that decision issues have different structures, for which we have accounted and clearly is the case, but rather that sectors of the school differ in the exercise of control. Our earliest recognition of this fact came in connection with the school's kindergarten program (where one existed). Detailed analyses of disparities in informant reports of a school's decision-making system revealed that many of the "disagreements" implicated reports by the kindergarten teachers. The "disagreements," we believe, were not that at all but differences in the manner, or extent, of control over their classroom activities. There is also reason to believe that control processes differed between the primary grades and the intermediate grades, differing further in the seventh and eighth grades of the sample that included them. Unfortunately, we have no means for checking on the possibility, since we began the data-taking process on the assumption that the school, not separate sectors of the school, was the relevant level of investigation.

Even using the "average" control structure of a school, however, substantial differences could be discerned and an important level of policy analysis has been proposed for further study.

NOTES

1. This definition is considerably narrower than Etzioni's (1965), which refers to any means used by an organization to elicit desired performance, not just authoritative directives, and includes the processes for certifying compliance. It is also more sharply drawn than in Tannenbaum's (1968) formulation, which equates control with the diffuse concepts of social influence and power.

2. We were surprised to discover that the incidence of Type C decisions increased significantly in the systemic domain as well as in the others, a fact we traced specifically to the adoption of textbook materials. Apparently, teachers in the Multiunit schools were given latitude here, perhaps reflecting their choice in the selection of the IGE materials.

Generally speaking, though, decisions in the systemic domain were found to reflect district characteristics. A one-way analysis of variance of Type O decisions, using the school district as the grouping factor, demonstrated that the district accounted for a significant part of the school variance, estimated at 68 percent. The same cannot be said for decisions in the other two domains; the district accounted for virtually none of the variance in Type D decisions in the instructional processes domain or Type P decisions in the deployment domain. These varied from school to school regardless of the district. Further analyses of the systemic domain suggested that Type O decisions were inversely related to both district size and district wealth, although the analyses were limited by the small number of districts available for investigation.

3. See Subkoviak (1975) for a general discussion of multidimensional scaling. The specific reference to the program as well as background information on its development is Roskam and Lingoes (1970).

4. The mean D^2 values for profiles from T_1 to T_3 and from T_3 to T_5 was 33.2 for the large schools and 51.7 for the small schools, a difference that was statistically dependable beyond the .01 level (t = 2.8002, with 30 df). No such difference in movement of small and large schools appeared among the conventional set—at least not a statistically dependable difference.

REFERENCES

Etzioni, A. 1965. "Organizational Control Structure." In Handbook of Organizations, edited by J. G. March. Chicago: Rand McNally.

Jovick, T. D. 1978. "Approaches to Data Analysis in Project MITT: Creating Indices from the Control Structure Interview through Data Collapsing and Multidimensional Scaling." Working Paper for MITT Project, Center for Educational Policy and Management, University of Oregon, Spring.

Klausmeier, H. J., R. A. Rossmiller, and M. Saily, eds. 1977. Individually Guided Elementary Education. New York: Academic Press.

Lortie, D. C. 1975. Schoolteacher: A Sociological Study. Chicago: University of Chicago Press.

Lortie, D. C. 1969. "The Balance of Control and Autonomy in Elementary School Teaching." In The Semi-Professions and Their Organization, edited by Amitai Etzioni. New York: The Free Press.

Meyer, John, and Elizabeth Cohen. 1971. The Impact of the Open-Space School upon Teacher Influence and Autonomy: The Effects of an Organizational Innovation. Technical Report No. 21, Stanford Center for Research and Development in Teaching.

Packard, J. S., and R. O. Carlson. 1976. Control Structure in Elementary Schools. Eugene: Center for Educational Policy and Management, University of Oregon.

Packard, John S., W. W. Charters, Jr., and Kenneth E. Duckworth. 1978. Management Implications of Team Teaching: Final Report. Eugene: Center for Educational Policy and Management, University of Oregon. (Eric Document access No. Ed 161 153.)

Pellegrin, R. J. 1976. "Schools as Work Settings." In Handbook of Work, Organization, and Society, edited by R. Dubin. Chicago: Rand McNally.

Pellegrin, R. J. 1970. Some Organizational Characteristics of Multiunit Schools. Technical Report No. 8, Eugene: Center for the Advanced Study of Educational Administration, University of Oregon.

Roskam, E., and J. C. Lingoes. 1970. "MINISSA-I: A Fortran IV(G) Program for the Smallest Space Analysis of Square Symmetric Matrices." Behavioral Science 15:204-05.

Simon, Herbert S. 1947. Administrative Behavior. New York: Macmillan.

Subkoviak, J. J. 1975. "The Use of Multidimensional Scaling in Educational Research." Review of Educational Research 45: 387-423.

Tannenbaum, Arnold S. 1968. Control in Organizations. New York: McGraw-Hill.

10

STUDYING SHARED DECISION MAKING
IN SCHOOLS

Daniel L. Duke
Beverly K. Showers
Michael Imber

In recent years, some experiments with shared decision making have attracted considerable attention. Terms such as "workplace democracy" and "power equalization" have begun to appear with greater frequency in the literature on organizations as some businesses have attempted to increase worker involvement in determining both the environment of the workplace and their own functions therein. Similar developments are occurring in the public sector as well, particularly in schools. Teacher unions and associations often have demanded and sometimes have won a substantial voice in determining certain aspects of educational practice. Schools and districts across the country have experimented with different types of shared decision-making schemes involving parents, students, teachers, and other interested constituencies. This chapter will explore some of the issues involved in studying shared decision making in schools and present a report of one such study. It will begin by discussing some of the issues we faced prior to the design and implementation of our own empirical study.

Much of the empirical work in this chapter was supported by the National Institute of Education and conducted under the auspices of the Stanford Institute for Research on Educational Finance and Governance. The authors wish to thank the following individuals for their contributions to this chapter: Jean Bartunek, Edwin Bridges, Michael Kirst, and James March.

DESIGNING A STUDY: SOME PRELIMINARY CONSIDERATIONS

"Shared decision making in schools" is a topic that is broad, complex, and relatively unstudied. As such, we realized that one necessary precursor to meaningful inquiry was a narrowed focus. We needed to choose certain specific subtopics and questions for detailed examination and to select, define, and analyze key terms and concepts that would be used in our study. We sought to develop a conceptual framework, one that would serve as a basis for identifying specific research questions and data collection schemes; inform decisions concerning which aspects of shared decision making to focus on and which to ignore; and facilitate systematic collection and useful organization of data.

Choosing Subtopics and Questions

In selecting specific subtopics and questions for detailed consideration, we recognized that while such choices may be made on the basis of previous research findings, personal knowledge or interest, or demands of supporting agencies, they often appear arbitrary to consumers of research. Our investigation was prompted by a special interest in the role of teachers in school decision making. This decision, however, does not suggest that we felt the involvement of administrators, parents, students, and communities was unimportant. Similarly, we chose to look at decisions whose impact was schoolwide, reserving for others the tasks of examining classroom, district, state, and national educational decisions.

Next, we selected two broad questions for examination: What opportunities for shared decision making are available to teachers? To what extent do teachers take advantage of these opportunities? Our rationale for this choice derived from the belief that answers to these questions could shed light on a variety of organizational issues including teacher morale and job satisfaction, distribution of authority in schools, and school effectiveness.

Analyzing Terms and Concepts

Our next task focused on the need to be able to recognize and classify instances of shared decision making in schools, particularly those that include teachers. We considered shared decision making to be any process in which more than one individual or role group is involved in making a decision. We defined "decision-making involvement" as physical presence during the decision-making process or the opportunity to provide input during any phase of decision making. In other words, we considered anyone who was present with the right to provide input or consulted when a decision was deliberated to have been involved in the decision. (It should be noted that a variety of other terms—including participation and commitment—have been used to describe phenomena similar to what we call involvement [Bartunek and Keys, 1979; Palches, 1970; Vroom and Yetton, 1973]. We reject these terms because they tend to connote more than mere physical presence or input.)

In order to be able to determine just who has been involved in a particular decision and to what extent, we next sought to identify the phases or components that are usually included in making a decision. We expected that in many instances of shared decision making, some individuals would be involved in one or more components but excluded from others. Furthermore, we felt that some components might be found usually to have greater impact on ultimate decisions than others and that it would be interesting if teacher involvement tended to be limited to more or less influential components. Our analysis of the decision-making process, particularly as it typically operates in schools, yielded five components: deciding to decide (agenda-setting), determining guidelines, gathering information, designing choices, and expressing preferences.

Table 10.1 presents a comparison of our scheme with several other published analyses.

Deciding to Decide

The first component of decision making—deciding to decide—is one of the least understood. It is uncertain, for instance, how many decisions result from spontaneous factors and how many decisions are premeditated, with a person or persons consciously determining that a specific decision needs to be made. While the initial step in formal decision making does not necessarily have to be deciding to decide, it is likely that much formal decision making begins in this manner. During this phase a problem in need of a decision is identified. Problems generally are situations that impede or threaten the organization's capacity to achieve its objectives.

When students of organizations speak of initiatives and initiating behavior—characteristics typically associated with effective executives and leaders—they are referring to the act of deciding to decide. Individuals in a position to determine or influence the determination of whether or not a decision will be made can exert considerable control over the decision-making process, even when

TABLE 10.1

Models of Decision Making

Duke, Showers, and Imber	Alexander[a]	Dill[b]	Janis and Mann[c]	Simon[d]
Deciding to decide	Perception of a need for a decision	Agenda-building	Appraising the challenge	Intelligence
Determining guidelines	—	—	—	—
Gathering information	—	—	Surveying the alternatives	—
Designing choices	Development of alternatives	Search	—	Design
—	Evaluation of alternatives	—	Weighing the alternatives	—
Expressing a preference	Choice of preferred action	Commitment	Deliberating about commitment	Choice
—	Implementation of preferred action	Implementation	—	—
—	—	Evaluation	—	—

[a]Ernest R. Alexander, "The Design of Alternatives in Organizational Contexts: A Pilot Study," Administrative Science Quarterly 24, no. 3 (September 1979): 382–404.

[b]William R. Dill, "Decision-Making," in Behavioral Science and Educational Administration, ed. Daniel E. Griffiths, The Sixty-third Yearbook of the National Society for the Study of Education (Chicago: University of Chicago Press, 1964).

[c]Irving L. Janis and Leon Mann, Decision Making (New York: The Free Press, 1977).

[d]Herbert A. Simon, The New Science of Management Decision (New York: Harper & Row, 1960).

316

they are not involved in other phases. For example, in schools where the agendas for faculty meetings are established by the principals, they can place selected issues before the faculty while withholding others, thus controlling the range of decisions in which teachers can share.

Determining Guidelines

The second phase of the decision-making process—determining the guidelines on which decision making will be based—also can have great impact on the entire process. In fact, we believe that the first two phases of decision making generally are the most critical.

Guidelines concern what course of action for reaching a decision will be followed by a group of decision makers. Guidelines may delimit the broad range of options from which a choice must be made, specify the type or amount of information needed to reach a decision, cover the rules governing how a decision will be made, or indicate the time frame within which a decision must be made. When a principal asks teachers to decide between three possible textbooks for ninth grade English, he or she is creating a guideline by limiting in advance the range of options.

Gathering Information

The third component of decision making involves gathering any information deemed necessary to enable participants to reach a decision. Information may come from within or outside the organization, and it may be shared through written documents, closed deliberations, or open hearings. The amount of input into the decision-making process can vary greatly from one situation to the next. Iannaccone (1964:229) writes that the "quality of decision-making in an organization is related to the amount of relevant information available concerning the issues under consideration." Cyert, Simon, and Trow (1971), Galbraith (1977), and Janis and Mann (1977) propose a number of methods for improved decision making that are based directly or indirectly on upgrading the quality of information available to decision makers. An example of the importance of information for school decision making concerns the evaluation of teachers for tenure. If a teacher has been observed only a few times during the probationary period, it is doubtful that sufficient data exist to make an informed decision. In addition, if those who observe the teacher are unfamiliar with the subject matter being taught and if they have made no effort to secure the opinions of specialists, the quality of the tenure decision-making process and of the decision it produces becomes even more dubious.

Designing Choices

The fourth phase of decision making—one that frequently depends heavily on the quality of the information available to decision makers—involves the designing of choices or alternatives. A choice may represent a proposed strategy, solution, person, or other response to a given problem, often the one identified in the first phase of the decision-making process. Choices may address one of the following decisional questions: who, what, where, when, how, or how much. Simon (1960) has written extensively on the design phase of decision making. He notes that the act of designing possible courses of action actually encompasses a number of small decisions, a fact that makes this phase quite complicated to study. An example of the design phase of decision making in a school context is when a teacher committee responds to a state mandate to establish high school proficiency standards by drafting several possible sets of graduation requirements to be submitted to the entire faculty.

Expressing a Preference

The final act of deciding—expressing a preference—often represents the least complicated phase of the decision-making process, particularly when a voice is the means of achieving resolution. Where other means are used, however—for example, decision by consensus—the process can become more complex and problematic (Janis, 1972). The act of deciding may range from one person unilaterally making a choice to a group of people casting secret ballots on which they have ranked several preferences. It is important to remember that actually expressing a preference is only the final phase of a complex process involving a preliminary commitment to decide, a set of guidelines on which decision making is based, certain information from within or outside the organization, and a designed choice or set of choices.

Finally, to complete our conceptual framework, we used our knowledge of the workings of schools to develop a typology of school-level decisions (see Table 10.2). While we did not expect to encompass every conceivable school decision in our typology, we felt that our effort would be useful in directing our school-based

TABLE 10.2

Types of Organizational Decisions

1.0 Instructional Coordination	6.2 Determining criteria for
1.1 Determining activities for	selecting personnel
multiple classrooms	6.3 Selecting personnel
1.2 Determining activities for	6.4 Determining criteria for
teaching teams	removing personnel
1.3 Selecting instructional	6.5 Removing personnel
materials for more than	6.6 Assigning and reassigning
one classroom	personnel

1.0 Instructional Coordination
  1.1 Determining activities for multiple classrooms
  1.2 Determining activities for teaching teams
  1.3 Selecting instructional materials for more than one classroom

2.0 Curriculum Development
  2.1 Determining curriculum outcome or goals
  2.2 Selecting curriculum content
  2.3 Selecting an organizational format for content

3.0 Professional Development
  3.1 Determining professional needs and goals
  3.2 Planning professional development activities
  3.3 Determining preservice needs and goals
  3.4 Planning preservice educational activities
  3.5 Selecting professional development personnel

4.0 Evaluation
  4.1 Selecting methods for evaluating curriculum, programs, professional development activities, teacher effectiveness, etc.
  4.2 Determining how to react to evaluation results

5.0 School Improvement
  5.1 Determining areas in need of improvement
  5.2 Planning school improvement
  5.3 Identifying resources for school improvement

6.0 Personnel
  6.1 Determining personnel needs
  6.2 Determining criteria for selecting personnel
  6.3 Selecting personnel
  6.4 Determining criteria for removing personnel
  6.5 Removing personnel
  6.6 Assigning and reassigning personnel

7.0 Rules and Discipline
  7.1 Determining school rules
  7.2 Determining consequences for rule-breaking
  7.3 Resolving conflicts concerning student behavior

8.0 General Administration
  8.1 Determining how to allocate space
  8.2 Determining how to allocate time (scheduling)
  8.3 Determining school calendar
  8.4 Determining how to allocate resources
  8.5 Settling employee grievances
  8.6 Determining public relations priorities
  8.7 Approving extracurricular activities
  8.8 Determining organizational rewards
  8.9 Determining budget
  8.10 Determining student placement

9.0 Policy making
  9.1 Determining how policy is to be made
  9.2 Determining local goals for education
  9.3 Determining how to comply with external mandates, legislation, etc.
  9.4 Determining rules for employees
  9.5 Determining program priorities

Source: Compiled by the authors.

observations toward potential instances of teacher involvement and in categorizing those instances. Subsequent field studies have supported our belief that almost all decisions made in schools fit into the categories listed in Table 10.2.

DATA COLLECTION

Once we had achieved a preliminary understanding of the phenomena we wished to study, we were able to begin a search for relevant data. We looked first at the work of others—organizational theory literature dealing with shared decision making and previous research on school organization. While some of these sources provided important insights, we came away with a renewed sense of the paucity of conclusive findings and of the need to generate our own data. We therefore initiated intensive case studies of the decision-making activities of five public secondary schools in an urban area of northern California. The five schools selected for case studies were chosen because they purported to provide formal opportunities for shared decision making. These opportunities are summarized in Table 10.3.

Three schools possessed School Site Councils, groups consisting of teachers, administrators, and parents that were mandated as part of California Assembly Bill (AB) 65, an omnibus school improvement bill. Schools receiving AB 65 funding were expected to administer funds through School Site Councils, which possessed the authority to decide a wide range of issues from professional development to some policy making. No one role group was permitted to have more than half the members of a council.

Procedures for selecting teacher members varied from school to school. At School A, one teacher from each of the three learning community units was elected by peers. A fourth member was elected at large from a pool of faculty volunteers. The council at School B had six teacher members, one elected by teachers from each of the six preparation periods. Teachers on School C's council were nominated by chairpersons from each department and then elected by department members.

A Program Improvement Council and Unit Councils existed at only one school. These bodies are essential parts of the governing structure of schools participating in Individually Guided Education, a broad-based school improvement program emanating from the University of Wisconsin and adopted by thousands of schools across the nation.

TABLE 10.3

Decision-Making Groups by School

| | School | | | | |
	A	B	C	D	E
SSC	Y	Y	Y		
PIC	Y				
AS	X	X	X	X	X
Departments	Y	Y	Y	Y	Y
DCC				Y	
EFP			Y	Y	Y
UC	Y				
PRC		Y			
Entire faculty		Y			
Decision groups with teacher members	4	4	3	3	2

Notes: Y = Decision-making groups with teacher members.
SSC = School Site Council.
PIC = Program Improvement Council.
AS = Administrative Staff.
DCC = Department Chairpersons Council.
EFP = Advisory groups for externally funded programs
(for example, Teacher Corps, Title I, and so on).
UC = Unit Councils.
PRC = Preparation Period Representative Council.
Entire faculty = operating as decision-making group.
Source: Compiled by the authors.

All five schools possessed a formal Administrative Staff
Council and departments organized by subject. Teachers were not
represented in any of the former bodies. Departments were pre-
sided over by chairpersons—typically teachers with released time
and sometimes a salary increment. Department chairpersons were
appointed by the principal in all schools except School D, where
they were elected by teachers in each department. Decisions made
at department meetings generally were limited to curriculum and
evaluation issues.
    Three of the schools received external grants other than
AB 65 school improvement funds. One of the conditions for accepting

these grants (Teachers Corps, ESEA Title I) was the creation of an advisory group consisting of school and community members. These groups dealt primarily with policy making and resource allocation.

Three other decision-making bodies were identified in the sample schools. School D had a Department Chairperson Council, which met regularly with the principal. A Preparation Period Representative Council was periodically convened at School B. Finally, School B was the only school that utilized the entire faculty as a decision-making body. Faculty meetings at the other schools were called solely for the purpose of making announcements and sharing information.

The schools in the sample thus were characterized by a variety of opportunities for teachers to become involved in decision making. It remained to be determined what specific kinds of school-level decisions actually were handled by these groups. Table 10.4 indicates the number of each broad type (from Table 10.2) of decision in which teachers and administrators were observed to be involved during 1978-79. The administrator column represents decisions made solely by administrators.

The actual number of decisions observed at each school varied little ($\bar{x}$ = 52.4; range = 46 to 62). However, the patterns formed by types of decisions made and persons involved in making them were distinctive for schools, reflecting not only different concerns and priorities at each school but different divisions of responsibilities with regard to decision making. For example, teachers at School A participated in seven decisions related to evaluation, while teachers at the other four schools participated in no evaluation decisions. Evaluation issues were a top priority at School A, and a special task force of teachers worked several months on an evaluation plan for the entire school program. Teachers at Schools A, B, and C were involved in many more administrative decisions than their counterparts at Schools D and E because administering AB 65 funds necessitated decisions concerning budgets and resource allocation. This suggests the types of decision-making bodies that exist in a given school can have a profound effect on the types of decisions made at that school.

Decisions in which teachers were involved ranged from three to eight out of the nine decision types listed in Table 10.2, and the total number of decisions in which teachers were involved ranged from 8 at Schools D and E to 39 at School A. Simply presenting data on between-school variations in the number of school decisions in which teachers participated, however, does not indicate much about the true position of teachers in the school authority structure. To get such information, it was necessary to obtain an indication of

TABLE 10.4

All Decisions Monitored for 1978-79 Academic Year by School

Decision Types*	A		B		C		D		E		Totals
	Teachers	Administration	Teachers	Administration	Teachers	Administration	Teachers	Administration	Teachers	Administration	
Instruction coordination	2	1	1	1	1	2	0	3	1	2	14
Curriculum development	3	1	3	1	1	0	0	3	0	0	12
Professional development	6	3	3	1	1	3	0	0	0	0	17
Evaluation	7	1	0	0	0	3	0	0	0	3	14
School improvement	5	1	6	0	13	0	0	0	0	2	27
Personnel	0	0	3	0	0	2	0	3	3	15	26
Rules and discipline	0	0	1	0	0	3	1	9	0	4	18
General administration	8	4	14	5	9	7	2	8	2	15	74
Policy	8	3	7	1	1	0	5	20	2	13	60
Subtotals	39	14	38	9	26	20	8	46	8	54	
Percent	74	26	81	19	57	43	15	85	13	87	
Totals	53		47		46		54		62		262

*See Table 10.2 for a breakdown of decisions included under each category.

Source: Compiled by the authors.

the importance of the decisions in which teachers did and did not participate. Conceivably, for example, participation in making one budget decision could have been more significant than participation in 20 minor curricular decisions.

IMPORTANCE OF DECISIONS

Decision inventories for each of the decision-making groups were presented to the principals in June 1979. Principals were asked to identify the most important decision made during the year and to explain their choices (see Table 10.5).

At Schools A and B, teachers participated in 80 percent and 91 percent, respectively, of decisions that principals cited as important. These high percentages contrasted with those in the other three schools, where principals acknowledged that teachers participated in relatively few important decisions. Not surprisingly, these findings were consistent with the attitudes expressed toward teacher decision making by the principals during previous interviews. The findings also were reflected in the perceptions of principals' attitudes expressed by our teacher informants. Principals at Schools A and B viewed, and were perceived by teachers to view, school decision making as a joint enterprise. Both principals felt free to lobby for their positions on an issue, but they abided by the will of the majority. Decision making at Schools A and B was more cooperative than adversarial, possibly because of highly formalized procedures for decision making.

The principal at School C believed school decision making was his prerogative because responsibility for the success or failure of the school was attributed to him by both the central administration and community members. Teachers at School C reported that the principal seldom asked for their input. When their input was requested, it seemed to have little influence on outcomes. Teachers also reported a top-down decision-making process in the district, a process seemingly confirmed by the low rate of policy decisions made at School C (of 60 policy decisions made at the five case study schools, only one was made at School C). Since School C was located in a different district than the other four schools, there is some reason to suspect that certain between-school variations in decision making may derive from central office differences.

The principal at School D believed decision making was inseparable from his role as "school leader." He regularly received teacher input from a council of department chairpersons, but he regarded the group primarily as a vehicle for disseminating

TABLE 10.5

Decisions Cited by Administrators as Important

Decision Types	A		B		C		D		E		Totals
	Teachers	Administration	Teachers	Administration	Teachers	Administration	Teachers	Administration	Teachers	Administration	
Instruction coordination	0	0	1	0	0	1	0	0	0	1	3
Curriculum development	0	0	0	1	0	0	0	1	0	1	3
Professional development	0	0	0	0	0	1	0	1	0	0	2
Evaluation	2	0	0	0	0	0	0	0	0	1	3
School improvement	1	0	3	0	1	0	0	0	0	0	5
Personnel	0	2	0	0	1	3	0	0	0	1	7
Rules and discipline	0	0	0	0	1	0	0	1	0	1	3
General administration	1	0	3	0	0	2	0	3	0	1	10
Policy	4	0	3	0	1	0	1	5	2	3	19
Totals	8	2	10	1	4	7	1	11	2	9	55
Percent	80	20	91	9	36	64	8	92	18	82	

Source: Compiled by the authors.

administrative decisions. At the end of the study, decision-making processes at School D were being renegotiated because the teachers felt the need for greater influence over schoolwide issues.

The principal at School E viewed decision making as his domain but felt an obligation to seek and follow teacher advice. Much of the teacher input at School E was informal in that it did not occur at prearranged, regularly scheduled times but instead during chance encounters between the principal and individual teachers. Unlike teachers at School D, many teachers at School E felt they were able to influence the decisions that most directly affected them. Occasionally, when issues of importance to the entire faculty arose, faculty meetings were called for discussion and decision making.

As indicated earlier, the reasons provided by the principal of School A for his choice of important decisions reflected his support for shared decision making. Decisions identified as most important (eight out of ten were teacher-made decisions) were chosen because teachers, by these decisions, were "demonstrating understanding of organizational goals and administrative needs," "assuming responsibility," "demonstrating independence, "involving other faculty members," and "developing policy in areas of evaluation and staff development that would streamline future decision making."

At School B, where teachers were involved in 10 out of 11 of the important decisions, the principal identified decisions as important because teachers were "setting priorities," "increasing cooperation between school and community," "creating policy in areas where the law was ambiguous," and "improving the instructional program."

The principal at School C chose seven of his own decisions as most important compared with four in which teachers were involved. The decisions selected as important reflected an emphasis on managerial tasks; for example, personnel assignments, centralization of secretarial services, computerizing of scheduling, attendance, and student records. The principal also attributed to teachers an appreciation for his decisions that may have been fallacious. For example, his unilateral decision to implement student instruction in how to take tests was perceived by the principal as universally supported by the faculty. In reality, when the teachers were interviewed, they were either noncommittal about the program or stoically resigned to the additional work. They felt the principal actually was interested in raising test scores primarily to enhance his reputation.

At School D, the principal identified 12 decisions as important, 11 of which he had personally made. Most of the decisions set rules teacher and student behavior. These decisions were considered important because they "got people on task," "clearly defined responsibilities," and "provided structure."

The rationales provided by the principal at School E for his choice of "important" decisions reflected his humanitarian concerns. Decisions were judged important if they "boosted teacher morale," "lightened the supervisory work of teachers," "showed respect for parents," "protected students from misplacement in special programs," "made teachers more secure," and "provided students with greater opportunities for academic achievement." Despite these teacher- or student-centered concerns, the principal made most of the decisions he judged to be important without the involvement of others.

The case studies of decision making in the five schools create a picture of considerable between-school variation—variation in terms of the types of formal decision-making opportunities available to teachers, the types of decisions actually made, and the importance of these decisions as judged by principals. Such variation—particularly in a small sample of purportedly similar schools— belies the notion that public schools are essentially identical organizations in terms of decision making and the distribution of authority. It is probably a mistake for researchers to push generalizations too far about all schools being similarly "bureaucratic" or "hierarchic." These labels are likely to conceal important between-school differences.

EXTENT OF TEACHER INVOLVEMENT

Up to now we have been concerned with the opportunities for teachers to be involved in school-level decision making and the types of decisions that were actually made during a particular school year. Where opportunities for teachers to make decisions exist and where decisions are, in fact, made, it can easily be assumed that teachers have been involved. Such an assumption underlies much of the research on shared decision making in schools. As a result of our interviews with teachers, however, we have strong reason to believe that many teachers choose not to become involved in school decision making, despite the existence of opportunities to do so.

Interview data from random samples of ten teachers at each school indicate that 36 percent of the teachers declined some or all of the decision-making opportunities with which they were presented. An additional 27 percent reported not being involved because they felt no opportunities for shared decision making existed. This

latter finding was quite surprising, since we knew that such opportunities did exist. Thus, over half the teachers with whom we
spoke claimed to have been uninvolved or less involved than they
could have been. Furthermore many of the remaining 42 percent
indicated that their involvement had yielded little satisfaction.

What factors might account for this lack of teacher enthusiasm for shared decision making? We identified four possible
reasons, including lack of teacher confidence, lack of teacher interest, trust in administrators, and belief that the costs of involvement would outweigh the benefits.

Lack of Confidence

The basic argument here is that teachers do not take advantage of decision-making opportunities because they do not feel they
have appropriate skills or knowledge to contribute. Using Bandura's
(1977) terminology, they lack the perceived self-efficacy necessary
for active involvement.

Showers (1980), in an investigation of the relationship between
teacher self-efficacy and participation in school decision making,
found a positive, though nonsignificant, relationship between perceived self-efficacy and rates of decision-making behavior among
teachers at four secondary schools.

In a study of architects that may have implications for
teachers, Blau (1979) reports that "decision power" is related to
professional skills. She goes further to point to organization size
as a critical variable. Architects in large firms have fewer opportunities than those in small firms to engage in a variety of
tasks and develop diverse skills. As a result they tend to have less
decision power. It can be argued that little of the content of conventional teacher training is concerned with the acquisition of
skills or content related to school decision making. In addition the
process by which new teachers are inducted (socialized) into the
profession seems to reinforce the image of the teacher as a classroom leader, but not a school leader. Teachers who wish to engage in school decision making learn to seek positions as administrators.

Several studies indicate, however, that teachers can be
trained to function effectively as school decision makers. Seeman
and Seeman (1976) provided opportunities for teachers to refine
their problem-solving skills when dealing with schoolwide concerns
and actually discovered posttraining changes in student attitudes.
Bartunek and Keys (1979) utilized a contingency model to guide their
efforts to train teachers as school decision makers. Beginning with

the assumption that there was not one "best" way to make decisions, they trained teachers to match particular strategies with particular situations. The training led, in general, to higher levels of teacher involvement, suggesting that involvement may be a function, at least in part, of skill acquisition and confidence.

Lack of Interest

Apathy can be confused with acceptance by those trying to account for inactivity. This confusion is manifested in the area of decision making by the notion of zoning. Originally Barnard (1938) spoke of a "zone of indifference, " or a set of decisions in which subordinates were sufficiently uninterested to permit superiors to make them without challenge or complaint. Others (Bridges, 1967; Kuntz and Hoy, 1976; Simon, 1976) changed Barnard's term to "zone of acceptance. " What has been lost in the debate over terminology is the fact that indifference and acceptance may be prompted by quite different factors.

An individual may not care at all about a certain decision. Even if he does not trust the decision maker, the decision itself is of such low importance that he remains unconcerned. On the other hand, he may care a great deal about the decision but possess sufficient trust or faith in the person making the decision to decline involvement. We find it useful to treat these two separately. The following section will consider the matter of acceptance—or what we call trust.

In Table 10.2, nine areas of school decision making were identified. Obviously, teachers are not equally interested in every decision area, however. This observation has been confirmed in several studies (Alutto and Belasco, 1972; Carson, Goldhammer, and Pellegrin, 1967; Conway, 1976; Lortie, 1975). Lortie suggests that any concern that cannot be related directly to classroom instruction and students will not tend to generate teacher interest.

Saying that some teachers avoid involvement in school decision making because of lack of interest leaves several questions unanswered, however. For example, is indifference really a defense mechanism to compensate for teachers' perceived lack of self-efficacy? Is it a reaction to the advent of collective bargaining? In the latter case, teachers may feel sufficiently protected by their professional organization that they do not worry about safeguarding their interest through direct personal involvement in school decision making. Again additional research is needed in order to understand teacher behavior more clearly.

Trust in Administrators

In the last section we suggested that some teachers may avoid involvement in school decision making because of trust in the principal rather than apathy. In studying teachers' professional zone of acceptance, Kunz and Hoy (1976) found that their perceptions of principals' leader behavior were related to their willingness to accept directives. The professional zone of acceptance of teachers was significantly greater for principals rated high on scales of consideration and initiating structure (using the Leadership Behavior Description Questionnaire). Interestingly, principals rated high on consideration but low on initiating structure had teachers with a significantly narrower zone of acceptance. The implication could be that a quality like trust or consideration is necessary, but insufficient alone to cause teachers to leave decisions to the principal.

Other factors that Kunz and Hoy found were statistically related to the breadth of the professional zone of acceptance included teacher sex (females tended to be more accepting of directives than males) and educational background (teachers with graduate degrees tended to be more accepting of directives than those without). This research tends to substantiate the notion that involvement is an extremely complex construct, which can vary within individuals over time and between individuals and which is subject to a variety of influences, including situational factors and background characteristics of participants.

Costs and Benefits

It is conceivable that a teacher interested in a particular decision possesses the confidence to contribute and lacks sufficient trust in the principal to leave it up to him, yet still avoids becoming involved because he considers the potential benefits of involvement to be outweighed by the costs. The belief that behavior is to some extent a function of perceived benefits and costs has been well-expressed by exchange theorists. March and Simon (1958), using somewhat different terminology, convey the same basic idea when they propose their model of employee participation. Employees receive certain inducements (benefits) from the organization in return for certain contributions (costs). As long as these factors are relatively balanced, employee participation is expected. March and Simon's conception of participation is somewhat broader than decision-making involvement, however.

THE COSTS OF INVOLVEMENT

Of the four proposed explanations for the relatively low levels of teacher involvement reported in the case studies, the costs/benefits approach was judged the most promising to investigate and the least well understood. March and Olsen (1976:45) have written, apropos of organizational decision making: "A rational theory of attention allocation considers the gains and the costs of attention. Many theories of participation exclude a consideration of the costs of participation, the opportunities thereby foregone. . . . Some people will not be there by choice, they have better things to do."

We identified five potential costs and three potential benefits of teacher involvement in shared decision making. The costs included increased time demands, loss of autonomy, risk of collegial disfavor, subversion of collective bargaining, and threats to career advancement. The benefits were feelings of self-efficacy, a sense of ownership, and advancing the cause of workplace democracy.

Increased Time Demands

Time spent participating in one activity is time not spent on some other activity. Specifically, for teachers, time devoted to participating in decision-making processes is time not devoted to "teaching" activities—preparing and leading classes, grading papers, counseling students, advising extracurricular activities. If teaching activities required only a fixed expenditure of time, it would be possible for teachers to choose to spend time on school decision making in addition to other professional activities. By its very nature, however, teaching is a job in which there is always more than can be done. Teachers commonly complain that they do not have sufficient time to accomplish all that they wish. In other words, the time they deem available for all job-related activities (time not spent on personal activities) is already insufficient. For teachers to choose to devote some of their scarce professional time to participate in school decision making, they would have to view such participation as more rewarding than the performance of a teaching activity. There is reason to believe, however, that most teachers view teaching activities—especially working directly with students—as the most rewarding aspect of their job.

Lortie (1975:196) offers support for the contention that teachers consider their primary benefits to derive more from classroom work and contacts with students than other professional activities:

"It is of great importance to teachers to feel they have 'reached' their students—their core rewards are tied to that perception. . . . Other sources of satisfaction (for example, private scholarly activities, relationships with adults) pale in comparison with teachers' exchanges with students and the feeling that students have learned."

It is true that often new programs in which shared decision making is a primary component promise to produce improvements in classroom outcomes. Over the years, however, teachers have grown suspicious of these claims. Teachers have frequently discovered that innovations called for ever-increasing commitments of out-of-class time and yielded too little in the way of demonstrable classroom benefits (Duke, 1978). Thus, teachers might not view participation in school decision making as a particularly desirable activity unless they judge that a specific shared decision-making scheme has great potential for improvement of classroom life and student outcomes.

Loss of Autonomy

In addition to concern over time expenditures, teachers might fear that shared decision making may cost them a measure of autonomy. On the surface, perhaps this contention appears odd. Teacher involvement in school decision making, after all, is supposed to represent a means by which teachers can gain a greater voice in determining how schools are run. In reality, though, individual teachers—long accustomed to a relatively large measure of self-determination in their self-contained classrooms—might sense that autonomy could be jeopardized as more decisions were shifted to a group setting. In other words, teachers as a group might gain influence as a result of shared decision making, but the power of individual teachers might be compromised. Support for this argument comes from the literature on professionalism. Myers (1973:17), for example, writes that "the autonomy of the practitioner to follow his own dictates rather than being constrained by a superior, or even colleagues, is a basic characteristic of professionals" (emphasis added). Shared decision making could be regarded as a step backwards by some teachers who seek full professional status.

Furthermore, many of the new thrusts toward more collaborative school decision making have called for the active involvement of parents, community members, and students as well as teachers. For example, a number of recent federally and state funded programs have mandated the establishment of school site councils and advisory boards with varied constituencies. Thus, teachers face the prospect of sharing their traditional authority over classrooms with nonteachers as well as colleagues. No longer would teachers be protected from the community by school administrators. School site management exposes them to direct review and criticism by laymen. These factors might cause some teachers to view loss of autonomy as a potential cost of involvement in decision making.

Risk of Collegial Disfavor

Goode (1979) maintains that the respect of a person's peers is one of the most desirable benefits an individual can gain in contemporary society. Teachers may have reason to fear that involvement in school decision making is not a pathway to collegial respect. Some teachers have been observed to be suspicious of colleagues who identified too closely with the school authority structure.

One reason that efforts by individual teachers to exercise leadership or become involved in school decision making could stimulate unfavorable reactions from colleagues is the fear that such action might lead to cooptation by the administration. This fear might not be completely unwarranted. The delegation of authority to subordinates has long been considered a basic means by which managers maintain control (March and Simon, 1958:40-41). In reality, it is probably easier for administrators to control the behavior of influential teachers when they are part of the legitimate school authority structure than when they remain outside it.

Subversion of Collective Bargaining

A primary way in which contemporary teachers have exercised influence while remaining outside the traditional school authority structure has been through involvement in teacher associations and unions. The advent of collective bargaining for teachers in many states has meant that teachers potentially can exert an impact on working conditions and school policy without joining school advisory councils or risking administrative cooptation. Some concern exists among union leaders that any extensive involvement of individual teachers in shared decision making at the school level could jeopardize the collective bargaining position of teachers at the district level. Conceivably, some administrators may regard shared decision making as a means to circumvent the yearly negotiations process and keep school decisions under their direct supervision. It is noteworthy that the American Federation of Teachers has opposed many efforts to decentralize educational decision making, such as school site budgeting and community involvement in policy making. *

Because of the belief that a strong profession is one in which all members share a common professional identity, many teacher organizations also have resisted efforts to establish differentiated staffing, multiple wage scales, and merit pay—each of which could provide concrete inducements for greater teacher leadership and involvement in school decision making. As a result of their successful fight to maintain a single wage scale for teachers in the same district, teacher organizations have largely prevented school administrators from exercising control over teacher behavior through the manipulation of economic rewards. Efforts to decentralize decision making and to involve teachers as individuals rather than as representatives of a united profession thus could be regarded as threats to the current position of strength enjoyed by teacher organizations.

Threats to Career Advancement

A final reason why involvement in school decision making might be perceived by some teachers as costly is a concern that such participation could jeopardize their opportunity to get a more desirable position or become an administrator. School administrators are often selected from the ranks of classroom teachers. It is conceivable that some teachers would believe that keeping an orderly classroom and maintaining a low profile are important factors in determining which teachers are seriously considered for administrative openings. Anderson (1968:30) has noted this possibility in his analysis of school bureaucracy:

> Since effective teaching performance is difficult to measure, rewards and promotions must be based on seniority and on the judgment of superiors to a greater extent than in other professions. A teacher concerned about his career will minimize his areas of individual responsibility when there is any possibility of incurring the displeasure of his superiors. Minimizing responsibility is a way of protecting oneself and ensuring a favorable report by supervisors and principals.

---

*Our appreciation to Michael Kirst of Stanford University and to Roslyn Herman of the New York State Unified Teachers for this information.

Involvement in school decision making could increase the likelihood that a teacher might become known as a troublemaker or a malcontent. Teachers who seek career advancement might simply avoid such situations and bide their time until an administrative opening appears.

THE BENEFITS OF INVOLVEMENT

Not all teachers refuse to become involved in school decision making or manifest cynicism about their involvement. Some teachers expect to derive important benefits from participation in shared decision making. We speculated that teachers might see at least three benefits resulting from shared decision making: feelings of self-efficacy, a sense of shared ownership, and advancement of workplace democracy. What might seem to be an obvious benefit—monetary remuneration—was not listed. Our knowledge of California schools suggested that few provided financial incentives for teachers involved in school decision making.* Thus we did not predict that teachers would mention economic gain as a benefit of school decision making.

Feelings of Self-Efficacy

"Feelings of self-efficacy" refers to the perceptions people form of their competence to perform specific tasks, and judgments of personal efficacy are based partially on performance accomplishments. A teacher who serves on a committee that develops and recommends a new curriculum might feel efficacious if he or she contributes to what they consider an improved course for the students. Their satisfaction is likely to increase if their committee's curriculum is actually adopted and to increase again if students seem to enjoy and learn from the new curriculum.

It is important to note that while involvement in decision making may provide a vehicle for increased feelings of self-efficacy, involvement alone would probably not be enough to produce these feelings. A person who is involved in a decision-making process but who exerts no influence over the outcome of the process is unlikely to derive feelings of self-efficacy as a result of the

---

*Interestingly, in the one school we heard about in which teachers were offered remuneration ($10.00 per hour) to participate in school site council activities, the teachers rejected the offer.

experience. (In fact, the opposite result might well occur.) Only if the participant is able to have a real impact on the outcome of the decision-making process is involvement likely to be regarded as satisfying.

Ownership

Besides added confidence in one's ability to control his or her environment, shared decision making conceivably contributes to an individual's feeling of being part of a collective enterprise. The notion that one has a stake in the future of an enterprise sometimes is referred to as a feeling of shared ownership. Such a feeling might be considered a distinct benefit, since it can combat the destructive forces of anomie and alienation. Braverman (1974) argued that worker involvement in workplace decision making promised to reverse the degradation of work that has characterized twentieth-century employment.

Workplace Democracy

Related to the concept of shared ownership is the notion of workplace democracy (Duke, Showers, and Imber, 1979c:4-8). Workplace democracy is the doctrine that workers have a basic right to participate in the making of decisions that affect the utilization of their labor. Some teachers may derive satisfaction from exercising what they believe to be their right to participate in deciding how their time and energy will be used on the job. Furthermore, it is conceivable that some teachers would regard as beneficial any opportunity to engage in shared decision making, since it would serve to advance the general cause of worker rights. For these teachers, involvement in shared decision making would be beneficial, more so if they felt their involvement actually made a difference.

ASSESSING PERCEIVED COSTS AND BENEFITS

Having identified some of the potential costs and benefits of shared decision making that might be important to teachers, we designed an interview form that asked teachers to rate each cost and benefit on a scale of 1 (insignificant) to 7 (major). Since no pretense was made that the list of five costs and three benefits was exhaustive, room was provided for teachers to list additional costs or benefits and rate them.

Thirty-minute meetings were scheduled with each of ten teachers at the five sample schools. The same person conducted all of the interviews and collected all of the ratings. Each session was taped and later transcribed for analysis. The procedure called for the interviewer to ask the teacher what he or she perceived to be the costs and benefits of involvement in school decision making. Once the responses to this open-ended query had been recorded in the blank spaces on the rating sheet, the teacher was asked to rate the prespecified five costs and three benefits. Again the ratings were written down by the interviewer, this time using the 1 to 7 scale. Table 10.6 gives the means and standard deviation (by school) for the teacher ratings of the five prespecified costs.

TABLE 10.6

Teacher Ratings of Potential Costs of Shared Decision Making

		School					
		A	B	C	D	E	Total
Time	$\overline{X}$	3.67	4.80	6.11	4.90	5.09	4.92
	S.D.	2.12	1.81	1.36	2.28	1.92	2.00
Loss of	$\overline{X}$	1.33	1.40	2.44	3.10	1.50	1.96
autonomy	S.D.	.50	.70	2.12	2.28	.97	1.61
Risk of collegial	$\overline{X}$	1.88	2.50	1.44	2.30	2.27	2.10
disfavor	S.D.	1.83	2.01	.72	1.95	1.68	1.69
Subversion of collective	$\overline{X}$	2.00	2.40	2.61	1.30	3.40	2.36
bargaining	S.D.	1.41	1.65	2.06	.67	2.55	1.86
Threats to career	$\overline{X}$	2.75	1.00	1.67	1.78	2.00	1.83
advancement	S.D.	1.91	.00	1.66	1.56	2.24	1.70

Note: The ratings are based on a scale of 1 (insignificant) to 7 (a major cost).
Source: Compiled by the authors.

The data suggest that most teachers do not perceive these factors as potentially very costly, with the exception of time. In other words, loss of autonomy, risk of collegial disfavor, subversion of collective bargaining, and threats to career advancement generally were not perceived to be important reasons for avoiding shared decision making. On the other hand, the supporting interviews did reveal that particular costs were definite sources of concern for some teachers.

In discussing their responses with the interviewer, 20 percent of the teachers worried that shared decision making might lead to a reduction in their professional autonomy. Of the teachers, 26 percent said that they might encounter negative reactions from their colleagues; 24 percent indicated that the recently won right (in California) to bargain collectively could be jeopardized by shared decision making. The potential threat to career advancement posed by shared decision making was emphasized by 12 percent of the teachers. A teacher at School B put it very succinctly: "If you're highly motivated to move on—become an administrator—you learn to clam up, keep your mouth shut. It can work wonders."

Table 10.6 shows that many teachers regard time as a major consideration in thinking about shared decision making. In fact, even before being shown the rating scales, 80 percent of the teachers singled out time as a definite cost. This response from one teacher from School B was illustrative: "As a teacher I find myself very involved with my students, my class, and it is very hard to find time during school to meet. I don't think it's fair to the kids to take that time away from them, especially when we don't have a prep period."

During the interviews some teachers mentioned costs we had not anticipated. Four teachers indicated that shared decision making meant greater responsibility, including sharing the blame for bad decisions. Seven teachers expressed concern that shared decision making typically resulted in "rubber-stamping" administrative desires. Eight teachers commented on the emotional costs accompanying shared decision making. These costs encompassed feelings of frustration, energy loss, disillusionment, and powerlessness. Two individuals commented on their belief that shared decision making actually yielded lower-quality decisions than less democratic processes.

While none of these additional costs seemed to concern more than a few individuals, they did constitute legitimate personal issues. They also help to illustrate the complexity surrounding a study of teacher perceptions. Clearly teachers cannot be characterized by a single set of perceptions of school decision making (or probably any other issue).

Table 10.7 gives the means and standard deviations of teacher ratings of the three prespecified benefits.

TABLE 10.7

Teacher Ratings of Potential Benefits of Shared Decision Making

		School					Total
		A	B	C	D	E	
Self-efficacy	$\overline{X}$	6.22	5.70	6.00	4.50	6.37	5.77
	S.D.	.83	1.57	1.07	2.67	1.41	1.67
Ownership	$\overline{X}$	6.38	6.33	5.75	4.75	6.56	5.97
	S.D.	1.06	1.00	1.67	2.43	.73	1.55
Workplace	$\overline{X}$	5.83	6.63	6.29	3.86	6.50	5.82
democracy	S.D.	1.17	.52	.76	1.95	.84	1.51

Note: The ratings are based on a scale of 1 (insignificant) to 7 (major).
Source: Compiled by the authors.

The majority of teachers who were interviewed felt that shared decision making had some potential benefits. With few exceptions, they rated the potential benefits of involvement at or near the high end of the scale after having tended to rate the costs near the low end. Also, the teachers mentioned several additional benefits that we had not anticipated. Nineteen respondents expressed the belief that higher-quality decisions resulted when teachers were involved. Only ten teachers, however, actually stated that they felt shared decision making led to greater effectiveness or improved student outcomes. A teacher at School D made the following case:

> I think that teachers are in a position to know more
> about certain things than people outside the classroom.
> Teacher involvement would result in better decisions
> and more workable ones. We have experienced ad-
> ministrative-type decisions that were passed on.
> They just wouldn't fly, that's all. We could have
> told them in the beginning it wasn't the way to go.

Seventeen respondents contended that teachers are more likely to comply with decisions if they are involved in making them. Nineteen teachers felt that shared decision making stimulated closer relations among faculty members. Twenty teachers, or 40 percent of the sample, indicated that involvement in school decision making could enhance an individual's chances for career advancement. Finally, three teachers said that such involvement helped create a greater appreciation of the complexities of running a school.

INVOLVEMENT MAY NOT MEAN INFLUENCE

The analysis of the perceived costs and benefits of involvement raised a question rather than answering one. Almost all the respondents gave low ratings to the prespecified costs and high ratings to the prespecified benefits of shared decision making and listed many more additional benefits than costs. Time was the only cost of great consequence to most respondents and it generally was not regarded as an insurmountable obstacle to involvement. Why, then, did a large portion of the teachers refrain from taking advantage of opportunities for shared decision making?

One reason that emerged from a reanalysis of the interviews was that, for most teachers, involvement in shared decision making did not seem to make much of a difference. Sixty percent of the respondents made some mention of the fact that they had no real influence over the outcomes of shared decision making. Typically they felt that the principal or central office personnel actually made the important school decisions. Shared decision making might be regarded as worthwhile in theory, but in reality it was viewed with skepticism as an attempt by administrators to create the illusion of teacher power.

We thus realized that shared decision making could not be clearly understood unless involvement was separated conceptually from influence. Many researchers who study organizational decision making, however, have neglected to distinguish carefully these two constructs (Bartunek and Keys, 1979; Palches, 1970; Vroom and Yetton, 1973). In some cases, involvement and influence are treated as if they are synonymous. In others the implication is that the two are highly correlated. However, it is both logically possible and practically conceivable for individuals to be involved in a decision-making process without being influential or influential without being involved. In the latter case, consider the parish priest who exerts great influence over the local decision to modify sex education in the high school, but who is not a member of the curriculum review committee or the board of education. As for the former case, we have shown that some principals create the appearance of teacher involvement without actually permitting teachers to make the final decision.

What, exactly, is this phenomenon called influence? Involvement is relatively easy to isolate. According to the earlier definition, a person who attends a gathering at which decisions are made is involved—but what does the researcher of influence look for when conducting a field study?

Bell (1975:24) defines influence as a communication intended to affect the action of an individual in the absence of sanctions. Such a definition ignores, however, the possibility that influence can be exercised without any exchange of verbal or symbolic expression, but simply by virtue of a person's position or status (Pellegrin, 1976:358). Bacharach and Aiken (1976:623) contend that influence is an organizational process, rather than an organizational structure, and that it is one of two forms of power, the other being authority. Bell (1975), on the other hand, argues that influence, authority, and power are all distinct. Johnson (1975:16) provides a more operational definition, while distinguishing between participation and influence. For him, participation represents active involvement or consultation in the process leading up to a decision. Influence, on the other hand, is the act of basically making the decision. Mowday (1978:146) supports this distinction between involvement and influence and, like Johnson, sees influence in behavioral terms.

What all of these researchers overlook, though, is that influence, by the very ways we employ to study it, is a perception, rather than a process or a communication. We learn about the presence or absence of influence by asking those involved in decision making to indicate who or what guided them toward a particular preference. When teachers are asked who influenced a particular school decision, they, in fact, rarely cite themselves.

Teachers often assume that they lack the status, authority, power, or training to be influential. March (1955) has observed that people who accept such an assumption actually are being influenced by the assumption, not by a superior. If teachers perpetuate the belief that involvement in school decision making is futile, then it may be teachers, not administrators, who are determining the unilateral nature of school decision making.

The preceding observation does not mean that some administrators do not purposefully try to separate involvement and influence. Encouraging involvement while withholding influence can serve as a potent mechanism for maintaining control. Several organization theorists have commented on the cooptation process, whereby administrators create the appearance of shared decision making in order for leaders of the rank and file to be brought within the administrative sphere of influence, where their concerns and gripes can be more effectively monitored (Bidwell, 1965:1015; March and Simon, 1958:54; Mulder, 1971:34; Palches, 1970:28). It would appear from our research that teachers, too, may be aware of the possibility of cooptation and that this awareness causes some to avoid opportunities for shared decision making.

SUMMARY

In this chapter, as with others in the book, it has been assumed that decision making is an important focus for the study of school organization. One reason why decision making is important concerns its impact on other phases of school operations. We subscribe to Galbraith's conceptualization of organizations, with decision processes serving as one of five central and interrelated dimensions (1977:31). As the model in Figure 10.1 indicates, decision processes can influence, and in turn be influenced by, organization structure, tasks, people, and reward systems. Structure encompasses such factors as division of labor, departmentalization, and the distribution of power. Task subsumes the elements of diversity, difficulty, and variability and is, in turn, governed by organization goals. The "people" dimension covers training, selection, and promotion processes. Reward systems include the basic compensation system and the bases for promotion. Much can be learned about these elements of school organizations by studying decision-making processes. To understand school decision making, it is crucial to determine who is involved in the process and the extent of their involvement. In addition, it is important to know who is not involved and the reasons why. We propose that involvement is dependent on the presence of both organizational opportunities for involvement and the willingness of organization members to become involved. For an individual's level of involvement to be high, both factors must be high; neither alone is sufficient to account for involvement. Support for this argument was provided in a study by Showers (1980), in which teacher participation in school decision making was positively related to both opportunities for collaborative decision making and level of teachers' perceived self-efficacy with respect to decision-making competence.

Addressing issues of involvement and noninvolvement in school decision making promises to inform a variety of current concerns, including teacher confidence and interest in particular decisions, organizational trust and zones of acceptance, the perceived benefits and costs of involvement, and prevailing influence patterns. Students of school organization need to consider how these factors may be related to each other. For example, are teachers apathetic toward school decision making in part because of the low probability that their involvement will yield actual influence? An understanding of such relationships likely will require the use of concepts from various disciplines, including psychology, social psychology, organization theory, and political science.

FIGURE 10.1

Galbraith's Concept of Organization Design

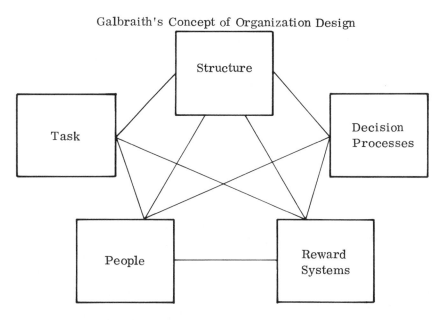

Source: Jay R. Galbraith, Organization Design (Reading, Mass.: Addison-Wesley, 1977).

For those committed to studying school decision making, there are several possible foci for the near future. We need to know the extent to which involvement and influence vary within individual schools over time and between schools. What organizational conditions are related to the increase or decrease of shared decision making in different schools? Where within- and/or between-school differences in decision making exist, it will be important to determine whether such differences are related to differences in outcomes such as teacher job satisfaction and student achievement.

Determining the relationship between teacher involvement and school outcomes clearly will be a key to the future of shared decision making in schools. To date most of the research on shared decision making has been conducted in industrial and commercial organizations. Of this type of research, Lammers (1967:206) writes:

There seems little doubt that forms of leadership that allow for direct participation (either by the individual alone or by the individual as a member of his colleague group in contact with his superior) often do contribute

> to the productivity and morale of the employees con-
> cerned. Even if such "power raises" make subor-
> dinates not more satisfied but simply less dissatis-
> fied, such leadership practices as delegation of
> authority, consulting one's men, or making decisions
> jointly with one's subordinates have been shown to
> lead to more effective goal attainment in terms of
> the . . . objectives of both the upper and lower ranks.

A later, more comprehensive review of the literature is less optimistic, however (Srivastva et al., 1977:173):

> The situation is not as simple for performance find-
> ings. . . . Autonomy alone cannot account for the
> differences in performance reported in the field ex-
> perimental studies. In fact, participative manage-
> ment studies, which manipulated only autonomy, show
> the lowest percentage of totally positive performance
> results. In the correlational studies autonomy is
> found to be an important variable in its possible ef-
> fects on performance, but several studies found a
> negative relationship between democratic supervisory
> style—clearly an autonomy-relevant variable—and
> performance. . . .

It is difficult to generalize the findings from industrial and
commercial organizations to schools. For one thing, the intended
outcomes of schools are much less clear than those of profit-making
organizations. Perhaps this fact explains, in part, why so few studies of school decision making have attempted to gather data on student outcomes. In fact, we located only one such study (Seeman and
Seeman, 1976). It reported that a small sample of teachers who
were more involved in school decision making had students with
more favorable attitudes toward their school, learning, and themselves. Interestingly, individual variables, such as teacher experience and attitudes, did not correlate with student outcomes.
   Most of the studies that treat school decision making as an independent variable attempt to relate it to teacher, rather than student, outcomes. Vavrus (1978) has done a competent job of reviewing these studies, as part of a dissertation in which he found a positive relationship between teacher involvement in decision making
and job satisfaction. Palches (1970) came up with similar findings
for English and social studies teachers. Carpenter (1971) looked at
schools with different decision-making structures and found that
teacher job satisfaction was greatest where there were the fewest

"layers of authority" above them. In an evaluation of the Teacher
Involvement Project, a federally funded program designed to establish teacher decision-making groups in San Jose, California, schools,
Emrick and Peterson (1978) found that participants listed the following benefits of their involvement: improved staff morale, increased
communications with administrators, more efficient use of meeting
time, better sense of professionalism and job satisfaction, and protection of teacher interests. Bridges (1964), in a study of 28 elementary schools in a Midwest district, reported that teacher attitudes toward their principals were more favorable where opportunities for shared decision making existed.

The positive relationship between involvement in school decisions and teacher outcomes is by no means firmly established, however. Schmuck, Paddock, and Packard (1977) found that job satisfaction was slightly greater among teachers in schools where collaborative decision making did not occur regularly. Mohrman,
Cooke, and Mohrman (1978) conducted a study in which teachers reported that greater job satisfaction resulted from involvement in
making certain kinds of decisions but not others. Conway (1976),
in a study of 166 nonrandomly selected secondary school teachers,
discovered that teacher perceptions of school organization varied
according to whether they were involved less than, more than, or
as much as they wished. Deal, Intili, Rosaler, and Stackhouse
(1977) indicated that the presence of school site councils in a sample
of California elementary schools did not seem to produce greater
teacher collaboration or coordination, even though teachers constituted roughly half of each council.

Despite the fact that most of the preceding studies looked at
small, nonrandomly selected groups of teachers, they do provide
some practical basis for further investigations. Coupled with our
own studies, this research suggests that under certain circumstances, shared decision making may be useful as both a dependent
and an independent variable. The model in Figure 10.2 indicates
one possible set of relationships that may merit systematic testing.

The model suggests that involvement is a function of two antecedents: the available opportunities for school employees to be involved and the willingness of employees to be involved. Decision
making generally yields decisions, among other things. These decisions, in turn, generate certain consequences that are proposed to
relate to the effectiveness of school employees and their attitudes
toward work. These two factors not only constitute potential influences on each other, but they also may impact on the antecedents of
future decision making, thus creating the possibility of a circular
effect. The extent to which employee effectiveness is positively affected by a shared decision probably contributes to the likelihood

FIGURE 10.2

Antecedents and Consequences of Shared Decision Making

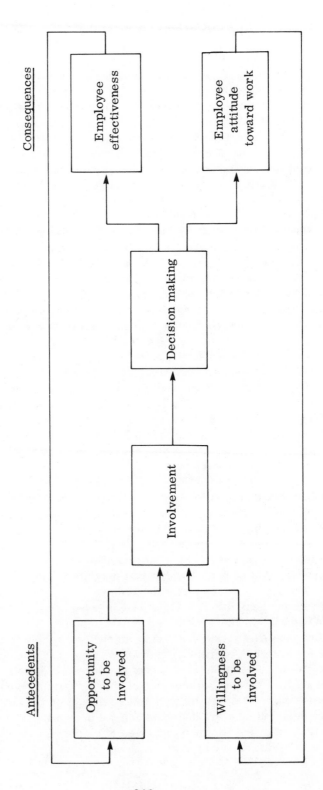

Source: Compiled by the authors.

that more opportunities for shared decision making will be available. In addition, the extent to which employee attitudes toward work are positively affected by a shared decision is hypothesized to influence the future willingness of employees to become involved.

It now would be useful to locate schools where shared decision making is perceived to be working well or to set up experimental situations in which teachers are involved in making school-level decisions and conduct longitudinal research on the relationship between teacher involvement and school outcomes. Failure to demonstrate a strong and consistent positive relationship, of course, would not necessarily mean that shared decision making should be abandoned. An argument could be made that teachers have a right to be involved in school decision making, regardless of the outcomes. However, demonstration of such a relationship clearly would further the cause of teacher leadership at a time when concern over low morale and job dissatisfaction among teachers is growing.

REFERENCES

Alutto, Joseph A., and James A. Belasco. 1972. "A Typology for Participation in Organizational Decision Making." Administrative Science Quarterly 17, no. 1 (March):117-25.

Anderson, James G. 1968. Bureaucracy in Education. Baltimore: Johns Hopkins University Press.

Bacharach, Samuel B., and Michael Aiken. 1976. "Structural and Process Constraints on Influence in Organizations: A Level-Specific Analysis." Administrative Science Quarterly 21, no. 4 (December):623-42.

Bandura, Albert. 1977. "Self-Efficacy: Toward a Unifying Theory of Behavioral Change." Psychological Review 84, no. 2:191-215.

Barnard, Chester I. 1938. The Functions of the Executive. Cambridge, Mass.: Harvard University Press.

Bartunek, Jean M., and Christopher B. Keys. 1979. "Participation in School Decision-Making." Urban Education 14:52-75.

Bell, David V. J. 1975. Power, Influence and Authority. New York: Oxford University Press.

Bidwell, Charles E. 1965. "The School as a Formal Organization." In Handbook of Organizations, edited by James G. March. Chicago: Rand McNally.

Blau, Judith R. 1979. "Expertise and Power in Professional Organizations." Sociology of Work and Occupations 6, no. 1 (February):103-23.

Braverman, Harry. 1974. Labor and Monopoly Capital. New York: Monthly Review Press.

Bridges, Edwin M. 1967. "A Model for Shared Decision Making in the School Principalship." Educational Administration Quarterly 3 (Winter):49-61.

Bridges, Edwin M. 1964. "Teacher Participation in Decision Making." Administrator's Notebook 12, no. 9 (May).

Carpenter, Harrell H. 1971. "Formal Organizational Structural Factors and Perceived Job Satisfaction of Classroom Teachers." Administrative Science Quarterly 16, no. 4 (December):460-65.

Carson, R. B., K. Goldhammer, and R. J. Pellegrin. 1967. Teacher Participation in the Community: Role Expectations and Behavior. Eugene: Center for the Advanced Study of Educational Administration, University of Oregon.

Cohen, Michael D., James G. March, and Johan P. Olsen. 1972. "A Garbage Can Model of Organizational Choice." Administrative Science Quarterly 17, no. 1 (March):1-25.

Conway, James A. 1976. "Test of Linearity between Teachers' Participation in Decision Making and Their Perceptions of Their Schools as Organizations." Administrative Science Quarterly 21, no. 1 (March):130-39.

Cyert, R. M., H. A. Simon, and D. B. Trow. 1971. "Observations of a Business Decision." In Management Decision Making, edited by Richard M. Cyert and Lawrence A. Welsch. Baltimore: Penguin Books.

Deal, Terrence E., Jo-Ann Intili, Jean A. Rosaler, and Ann Stackhouse. 1977. The Early Childhood Education Program: An Assessment of Its Impact and Implementation. Stanford, Calif.: Stanford Center for Research and Development in Teaching.

Dill, William R. 1964. "Decision-Making." In Behavioral Science and Educational Administration, edited by Daniel E. Griffiths. The Sixty-third Yearbook of the National Society for the Study of Education. Chicago: University of Chicago Press.

Duke, Daniel L. 1970. "Toward Responsible Innovation." Educational Forum 43, no. 3 (March):351-72.

Duke, Daniel L., Beverly K. Showers, and Michael Imber. 1979a. "Teacher Involvement in School Decision Making: An Examination of Between-School Differences." Stanford, Calif.: Institute for Research on Educational Finance and Governance.

Duke, Daniel L., Beverly K. Showers, and Michael Imber. 1979b. "Teachers and Shared Decision Making: The Costs and Benefits of Involvement." Stanford, Calif.: Institute for Research on Educational Finance and Governance.

Duke, Daniel L., Beverly K. Showers, and Michael Imber. 1979c. "Teachers as School Decision Makers." Stanford, Calif.: Institute for Research on Educational Finance and Governance.

Emrick, John A., and Susan M. Peterson. 1978. "Final Report: Follow-up Evaluation of the San Jose Teacher Involvement Project." Los Altos, Calif.: John A. Emrick & Associates.

Galbraith, Jay R. 1977. Organization Design. Reading, Mass.: Addison-Wesley.

Goode, William J. 1979. The Celebration of Heroes: Prestige as a Control System. Berkeley: University of California Press.

Iannaccone, Laurence. 1964. "An Approach to the Informal Organization of the School." In Behavioral Science and Educational Administration, edited by Daniel E. Griffiths. The Sixty-third Yearbook of the National Society for the Study of Education. Chicago: University of Chicago Press.

Janis, Irving L. 1972. Victims of Groupthink. Boston: Houghton Mifflin.

Janis, Irving L., and Leon Mann. 1977. Decision Making. New York: The Free Press.

Johnson, Rudolph. 1975. "The Relationship between Teacher Collaboration and Teacher and Principal Influence and Participation in School Decision Making." Doctoral dissertation, Stanford University.

Kunz, Daniel W., and Wayne K. Hoy. 1976. "Leadership Style of Principals and the Professional Zone of Acceptance of Teachers." Educational Administration Quarterly 12, no. 3 (Fall):49-64.

Lammers, C. J. 1967. "Power and Participation in Decision-Making in Formal Organizations." American Journal of Sociology 73, no. 2 (September):201-16.

Lortie, Dan C. 1975. Schoolteacher. Chicago: University of Chicago Press.

March, James G. 1955. "An Introduction to the Theory and Measurement of Influence." American Political Science Review 49, no. 2 (June):431-51.

March, James G., and Johan P. Olsen. 1976. "Attention and the Ambiguity of Self-Interest." In Ambiguity and Choice in Organizations, edited by James G. March and Johan P. Olsen. Bergen: Universitetsforlaget.

March, James G., and Herbert A. Simon. 1958. Organizations. New York: John Wiley.

Moeller, Gerald H. 1964. "Bureaucracy and Teachers Sense of Power." School Review 72, no. 2 (Summer):137-57.

Mohrman, Allen M., Robert A. Cooke, and Susan Albers Mohrman. 1978. "Participation in Decision Making: A Multidimensional Perspective." Educational Administration Quarterly 14, no. 1 (Winter):13-29.

Mowday, Richard T. 1978. "The Exercise of Upward Influence in Organizations." Administrative Science Quarterly 23, no. 1 (March):137-56.

Mulder, Mark. 1971. "Power Equalization through Participation?" Administrative Science Quarterly 16, no. 1 (March): 31-38.

Myers, Donald A. 1973. Teacher Power. Lexington, Mass.: Lexington Books.

Palches, Peter G. 1970. "Perceived Participation and Perceived Predictability as Determinants of Teacher Satisfaction with Decision-Making." Doctoral dissertation, Stanford University.

Pellegrin, Roland J. 1976. "Schools as Work Settings." In Handbook of Work, Organization, and Society, edited by Robert Dubin. Chicago: Rand McNally.

Roberts, Karlene, Charles L. Hulin, and Denise M. Rousseau. 1978. Developing an Interdisciplinary Science of Organizations. San Francisco: Jossey-Bass.

Sarason, Seymour B. 1971. The Culture of the School and the Problem of Change. Boston: Allyn and Bacon.

Schlechty, Phillip C. 1976. Teaching and Social Behavior. Boston: Allyn and Bacon.

Schmuck, Patricia, Susan Paddock, and John Packard. 1977. Managements Implications of Team Teaching. Eugene: Center for Organizational Research and Management, University of Oregon.

Seeman, A. Z., and M. Seeman. 1976. "Staff Processes and Pupil Attitudes: A Study of Teacher Participation in Educational Change." Human Relations 29, no. 1 (January):25-40.

Showers, Beverly K. 1980. "Self-Efficacy as a Predictor of Teacher Participation in School Decision Making." Doctoral dissertation, Stanford University.

Simon, Herbert A. 1976. Administrative Behavior, 3d ed. New York: The Free Press.

Simon, Herbert A. 1960. The New Science of Management Decision. New York: Harper & Row.

Srivastva, Suresh et al. 1977. Job Satisfaction and Productivity. Kent, Ohio: Kent State University Press.

Vavrus, Michael Joseph. 1978. "The Relationship of Teacher Alienation to School Workplace Characteristics and Career Stages of Teachers." Doctoral dissertation, Michigan State University.

Vroom, Victor H., and Philip W. Yetton. 1973. Leadership and Decision-Making. Pittsburgh: University of Pittsburgh Press.

11

GENERALISTS VERSUS SPECIALISTS

Stephen T. Kerr

Teaching has become increasingly specialized over the past decade. Where most teachers once saw themselves as consummate generalists, there have now emerged numerous specialized roles in education of the handicapped, of the disadvantaged, bilingual education, in student personnel services, and in school support services. Occurring as it did during an era of declining enrollments, this redistribution of educational roles has led to strains between specialist and generalist teachers and among teachers, administrators, and community groups.

The intent here is to examine the development of educational specialism and its impact on school organization. Evidence of role conflict among generalist and specialist teachers is combined with data from a study of referral patterns to suggest some of the problems generated by increasing specialization among educators. In addition, results from surveys of administrators, parents, and community leaders indicate that, while some creative ways of dealing with those problems have been developed, there is still a variety of complex issues awaiting more adequate treatment.

The concluding section proposes that conflict-creating difficulties may lie primarily in three areas: definition of specialist services, organization of specialist services, and ways of implementing

The activity that is the subject of this chapter was supported in whole or in part by the National Institute of Education, Department of Health, Education and Welfare. However, the opinions expressed herein do not necessarily reflect the position or policy of the National Institute of Education, and no official endorsement by the National Institute of Education should be inferred.

those services. In each case, the tension between administrative demands for efficiency and the political demands of the various interest groups involved illustrates serious potential problems for schools and school districts over the coming decade.

SPECIALIZATION: KEY TO PROFESSIONAL POWER?

Who Are Specialist Teachers?

It will be convenient here to describe as a specialist any educator whose work in the school system is not primarily to communicate a specific body of knowledge but rather to deal with particular student problems or conditions that impede learning, to aid students in noncurricular applied areas, and to encourage interaction among students, parents, other teachers, and school administrators. Using this definition, the following types of educational specialists may be distinguished: Special education teachers include teachers of the mentally retarded, learning disabled, physically handicapped, emotionally or behaviorally disturbed, and gifted. Teachers of the disadvantaged include reading and math specialists, together with bilingual education teachers. The group of student personnel staff is diverse; it takes in counselors, school psychologists, and school social workers. School support educators include librarians, media specialists, and curriculum specialists. Paraprofessional aides are also specialized but have more limited responsibilities. Secondary subject matter teachers will not be considered specialists here.

In order to add a touch of reality to the discussion, it may be interesting to create and follow two hypothetical educators—Conway Klassraum, a recently certified fourth grade teacher, and Selena Specialisti, a school psychologist with a new certificate. The concerns Conway and Selena hold about their work in schools and their interaction with each other provide a microcosmic glimpse into the day-to-day working world of classroom generalists and the new class of educational specialists.

Conway decided to enter teaching after discovering that he enjoyed working with children. A graduate of the school of education at the state university, his image of a good teacher is of a caring individual who knows his charges and helps them in any and all ways. His student-teaching experience was with a teacher who shared that view. At no point in his training did Conway work intensively with other teachers or with specialists. A contributing factor in his decision to enter teaching was his conviction that, in spite of current oversupply, there would always be a demand for good classroom teachers.

Selena came to education as a career somewhat later than Conway; her undergraduate degree is in psychology. Her original desire to work with handicapped and problem children grew out of an interest in the developmental problems many of them face. Her image of a good educator is of a competent professional, up to date on the latest methods and procedures for dealing with her charges. Her internship was in a special school at which she worked with other specialists and special education teachers. Her decision to enter education was somewhat influenced by an awareness that new laws and funding procedures would likely make jobs in her field easy to come by for many years.

The Growth of Specialism

Numerous studies have demonstrated rapid growth in the number of specialized teachers over the past decade. The National Survey of the Pre-service Preparation of Teachers (NCES, 1978; Morra, 1977) questioned, among others, 3,600 students in their final year of preservice training. The questions asked in this survey ranged over career expectations, aspirations, and their perceptions of the job market. This study outlined a number of changes: while only about 9 percent of teachers in 1972-73 indicated an intent to specialize, the figure had risen to about 21 percent by 1975-76 (Morra, 1977:100).

Data collected at five-year intervals by the National Education Association (NEA) provide further evidence of the trend toward specialization. At the secondary level, special education teachers made up only 0.03 percent of all teachers in 1961 and 0.04 percent in 1966. By 1971 the figure was 1.1 percent and it had risen to 3 percent by 1976 (NEA, 1977:6, 21). Elementary teachers working in a departmentalized setting (as opposed to self-contained classrooms) increased from 5 percent of all teachers in 1961 to 20 percent in 1976. Specialists in math, language arts, and special education made up almost one-third of those departmentalized teachers in 1976.

Immediate and future demand for various sorts of educators has been assessed in a number of recent national studies. A convenient measure of current demand is the number of unfilled, funded vacancies school districts have at any given time. Using this measure, Goor, Metz, and Farris (1978) found that 35 percent (3,238/ 9,245) of all vacancies in 1977 were in fields related to special education. Of these, about one-half were openings for teachers of the learning disabled. Bilingual teachers were also in short supply.

An Iowa study of employment among education graduates found that only 10 percent of special education certificate holders were

employed in nonschool jobs—the lowest ratio of any teaching specialty. A more recent study in Illinois found 88 percent of those certified in special education to be employed, again a figure much higher
than for generalists (Lawlis, 1979:3).

Implications of Specialization for School Organization

Practitioners in specialty areas usually assert that their particular service or expertise is both beneficial to the social order
and most efficiently provided by recognizing their group as best
qualified to deliver that service. Before turning to a closer examination of this argument, it may be useful to see how our hypothetical
friend Selena would express it.

Selena claims that the role of the school psychologist is increasingly important. Federal and state laws mandate assessment
of students using an increasingly complicated array of tests that
only the school psychologist is qualified to administer. Accurate
measurement of student abilities is critical, for much depends on
careful interpretation of the outcomes. Also, design of treatment
plans for handicapped children necessarily requires much insight
into psychological processes—insight the school psychologist is in a
unique position to provide. Leadership skills available to the school
psychologist through her training in group processes are also necessary in dealing with both multidisciplinary assessment teams and
parents. (Other specialists—counselors and social workers, for
example—might also lay special claim to some of these skills—but
let Selena tell her own legend.) The school psychologist, therefore,
is not only a worthy contributor to the task of educating the school's
youth, but also arguably the one most qualified to take the lead in a
wide variety of specific decisions on educational problems.

In the United States, the medical profession so successfully
convinced the public of the value of medical specialism using this
rationale that the proportion of generalist to specialist medical doctors reversed itself over the course of 40 years (Stevens, 1971:181).

The effects of specialization, however, may not always be
beneficial. In recent years, critics of specialism have argued that
the rationale of efficiency commonly advanced in support of professional differentiation may be flawed. Problems that develop when
services are provided through specialists, they have claimed, may
outweigh the advantages that specialized practice confers. Since
this argument developed first with respect to medicine, and since
that argument is critical to the further development of this study, it
is worthwhile to outline here some of the criticisms that have been
leveled against medical specialism in particular.

Problems of Medical Specialism

In recent years, medicine has increasingly come under attack because specialized services that seemed efficient to physicians did not meet public expectations for health care. Criticism of medical specialism has ranged from proposals for reform from within (for example, McKeown, 1976; Mechanic, 1976) to demands for radical restructuring of the entire health care system (Carlson, 1975; Illich, 1975). Illich (1977:23) has been most bitter in his critiques of specialism, noting that "the bodies of specialists that now dominate the creation, adjudication, and satisfaction of needs are a new kind of cartel."

In particular, the critics have focused on four problems of medical specialism: reductionism in diagnosis and health care sometimes means that the patient is treated as a "bag of symptoms" to be dealt with, rather than as a whole person whose problems may not be easily attributable to a single identifiable cause; specialists' certification, licensure, and professional autonomy, based on claims of arcane particular competence, may intimidate laypersons and keep them from seeking the information they need to make informed choices about their own care; at the same time, public confidence in the abilities of specialists to apply a "cure for anything" may lead to unreasonable demands for specialized services, and governmental response to such demands may lead to further bureaucratization and fragmentation in the quality of service offered (see especially Gilb, 1966; Ritzer, 1975); finally, maldistribution of personnel may result from the need for specialists to have a large population base and a constant stream of referrals from other practitioners (for example, Stevens, 1971).

Another problem medicine has experienced in specializing— referral—has affected not so much consumers of medical care but physicians themselves. As all forms of practice become more interdependent, the process by which physicians direct patients from generalist to specialist and back again becomes critical. Referrals come to define a physician's economic position (through their quantity), but they also play an increasingly important role in defining doctors' "dignity and career success—their very identities as physicians" (Friedson, 1975:85). Changes in number and distribution of specialists have thus brought with them conflicts about referrals (see also Hirsh, 1977; Shortell and Anderson, 1971).

The potential problems for education inherent in increased specialization, then, are numerous. Generalist-specialist conflict, especially over who is to do what with which children, is a critical problem, as is decreased teacher interest in and responsibility for individual students.

EVIDENCE OF CONFLICT AMONG
GENERALIST AND SPECIALIST TEACHERS

Journals, newsletters, and other ephemeral materials of specialist groups are a source of interesting data on how specialists see themselves in relation to their generalist colleagues. The title of an article by Maitland (1976), "Whose Child Is He—Yours, Mine, or Ours?" aptly illustrates the problems that at least some specialists and teachers encounter in figuring out who will do what with children in the school. Similar problems of conflict between generalists and specialists were described in more detail in a study by Weatherley and Lipsky (1977; see also Weatherley, 1979) of the implementation of an "education for all" act in Massachusetts.

Other specialist fields have also published comments about conflict between their practitioners and educational generalists. Counselors have complained that teachers do not understand what counselors do (Bauer, 1976; Betts, 1970; Pine, 1975; Quinn, 1969). Teachers and educational technologists have argued over the place that the expertise of the latter group should have in the classroom (Selden and Bhaerman, 1970; Heinich and Ebert, 1976). In a 1977 study, Cohen and others investigated how reading specialists and teachers worked (and didn't work) together; they found minimal interaction between the two groups, and only 20 percent of teachers reported receiving any service other than out-of-class instruction to students from the reading specialist on a weekly basis.

More information on generalist-specialist interaction is found in commentaries calling for role expansion. Many of these have been issued by the specialist groups, and they usually suggest that the role of that group be expanded to include new responsibilities. Often, the sort of expansion proposed would result in an improved position for the specialist in question vis-a-vis other educators. Counselors, for example, have been urged to consult with teachers about general school problems and engage in organizational development work (Murray and Schmuck, 1972). A new role for media personnel has been seen in encouraging communication among teachers in the school (Kerr, 1978). Psychologists have been exhorted to deemphasize the technical nature of their work and focus more on "helping approaches" (Maroldo, 1972).

THE POSITIONS OF NATIONAL ORGANIZATIONS
ON GENERALIST-SPECIALIST INTERACTION

Evidence that generalist classroom teachers perceive at least a potential threat to their position in the rise of specialists can be seen in a resolution passed by the NEA in 1978. The resolution pertained to PL 94-142, the Education for All Handicapped Children Act; while the resolution supported the intent of the law, no fewer than 16 qualifiers were appended, among them the following:

f. The classroom teacher(s) must have an appeal procedure regarding the implementation of the program, especially in terms of student placement.

o. All teachers must be made aware of their right of dissent concerning the appropriate program for a student, including the right to have the dissenting opinion recorded (NEA, 1978:213).

McDonnell (1977; McDonnell and Pascal, 1979) reported a dramatic surge in the number of professional issues that figured in collective bargaining negotiations during the 1966-71 period. Among these, the use of teacher aides and special education assignment, two issues related to specialization, showed increases of 612 percent and 723 percent, respectively. Such issues were predicted to become more prominent in coming years as financial resources become scarcer and "bread and butter" demands thus become less realistic.

Cautions have also been voiced about the possibly destructive effects of a "micro approach" to educational program accreditation and certification by numerous separate professional organizations. Such an approach, warned Koff and Florio (1977:37), could lead to "the education profession becoming a collection of societies or groups each in search of a professional identity."

Separate certification for specialists, however, continues to be an important target for specialist organizations (for example, AECT, 1977). Important national organizations have also urged that admission procedures and criteria be individualized by field (for example, Arnold et al., 1977:23; Rebell, 1976:18-19). The picture that these various reports paint is not an especially encouraging one. Examining the attitudes our hypothetical friends Conway and Selena hold about each other as colleagues may illustrate the problems more clearly.

Conway, the classroom teacher, sees his job as working with children on all the great and small problems of learning and growing. Any contact he has with other educators (specialists, administrators) in the school he regards as a distraction from that primary goal. He regards himself as competent to deal with most student difficulties. When Conway notes a student in class who seems to have real problems, he will sometimes send the child to Selena for testing. On the few occasions when a child is recommended for special placement,

Conway willingly complies. When the placement decision results in a child's working partly with Conway and partly with other specialists, however, Conway has felt disturbed both by the paperwork such placement generates and by problems the child has in returning to his class. Conway also resents that Selena is paid a higher salary than he is.

Selena, for her part, is confused by the seeming ambivalence of Conway toward her work: Using her services in some cases, he goes along with her recommendations only begrudgingly in others. She sees her efforts contributing to the overall success of the school's educational program and wishes that Conway and his fellow classroom teachers would more willingly share their students' problems with her. Selena is especially concerned that the classroom teachers do not really accept her and her role as necessary parts of the educational program of the school.

REFERRAL AMONG GENERALIST AND SPECIALIST TEACHERS

Why Study Referrals?

The actual work that educators do each day—teaching classes, working with individual students, or administration of programs—does not necessarily throw one educator into contact with another. In the case of generalist and specialist teachers, the only situation in which they must work with each other is when a student is referred, first by the generalist to the specialist, then, often, back to the classroom teacher. Referral, therefore, is probably the best issue to choose as an indicator of sources of strain in the relationships between generalist and specialist teachers.

Three administrative units with fundamentally different patterns of organization for specialist services were chosen for analysis in this study: a group of several small rural school districts offering specialist services cooperatively; a suburban district with centralized specialist services; and a large urban district with varied programs. For purposes of this chapter, the rural cooperative will be identified as "Evergreen," the suburban district as "Fillmore," and the urban district as "Weston." (None of these names is the actual name of the district in question.)

Following selection of districts and obtaining their agreement to participate in the study, samples of generalist and specialist teachers and relevant administrators were identified. A total of 66 educators eventually took part in the interviews.

Further discussion of the results of this study will focus on these four areas: agreement on appropriate grounds for referral; methods for dealing with areas of disagreement; perceived importance of and ways of following up on referrals; and perceived student reactions to being referred. (Data presented here are drawn from Kerr, 1979).

Agreement on Grounds for Referral

Overall, the generalist teachers interviewed in this study said they agreed with specialists on what appropriate grounds for referral are. Comments such as "It's cut and dried," "I've never had a referral rejected"; or "We just follow the [state] guidelines [for determining eligibility]" abounded. There were, however, some undercurrents in the responses. One recurring point was that the official state guidelines do not allow enough flexibility to help all children really needing special attention: "We agree on helping children with problems"; "Limits on the number who may participate [in a remedial reading program] force me to help many without documentation"; "We agree on what we want to do, but not about the guidelines"; "When a child does not meet requirements, I proceed as if they had and do whatever I can . . . for them"; "Teachers refer from human need and specialists use impersonal test scores to judge."

Only a few teachers felt that they disagreed more often than not: "Criteria for program placement leave many grey areas"; "We shouldn't wait until a student falls three grades behind to help him." Only 5 of 24 classroom teachers felt that there was this level of disagreement between themselves and specialists. No strong differences among districts appeared, though teachers in Weston made a strong distinction between their general approval of the Child Development Center (CDC) services (which use psychologists, social workers, counselors, and paraprofessional aides; such programs are located in individual schools) and their somewhat less positive evaluations of regular services available from central district offices.

Specialists' responses were somewhat less sanguine about the question of teacher-specialist agreement about grounds for referral. Indications of this could be seen in their generally longer and more qualified answers to the question. Overall, about half claimed that agreement exists and the other half found serious problems. A number of specific concerns stand out in specialists' replies.

First, there is the issue of "dumping." "Behavior problems with kids who test 'at level' are always a source of disagreement," noted one Weston specialist; one of his colleagues recalled "a student referred for being 'low in reading' who was really just disruptive."

A Fillmore specialist commented, "It's easy to confuse a student's ability with his disciplinary problems." Others who have investigated the way in which special services are provided have also noted this problem (for example, Kritek, 1979).

A second problem concerns the conflict specialists feel between the need to work within precise state guidelines and a desire to provide services. An Evergreen specialist noted that "I want to help students and not be bothered with legal issues and paperwork," but a colleague saw a need for a "strict formal process." Some specialists were forthright about the role their own judgment plays: "If I feel a student shouldn't be in the program, I'll test him fully, and he must qualify on each test. But if they do need it, I'll fudge the results." Another commented: "I usually get my say on who's in the program and who's not."

Differing levels of "teacher training, personal growth, and 'levels of consciousness'" were cited by other specialists as sources of disagreement. Some felt that time would take care of these problems as teachers gradually become aware of program criteria and procedures.

Specialists in Fillmore expressed the highest level of agreement with their generalist colleagues, while the most disagreement seemed to be in Evergreen (perhaps reflecting the physical separation of specialists and teachers in this multidistrict consortium). Comments in Weston reflected the greater diversity of problems in a large urban district.

Administrators tended to see disagreements over referrals either as resolvable through recourse to legal criteria ("Most cases are fairly obvious," "It's spelled out by law"), as cases of personality clash between specialist and classroom teacher, or as "borderline cases" in which any resolution is difficult ("Disagreement comes over the problems that are more subjective"). In dealing with disagreements, administrators seemed about evenly divided over whether they would accept the specialist's or the teacher's assessment; most, however, did claim that they would seek the best solution for the child.

No major differences among districts were notable, except that the administrators in Weston schools tended to see the CDC specialists not as members of a special, separate program, but rather as part of the regular school staff.

Dealing with Disagreement

Teachers indicated some feelings of frustration when asked how they would deal with conflicts over referrals. Most said they would simply continue working with the child in class as best they could ("I'd tough it out in the classroom"). Others would consult informally with specialists to try to get some help. Only a few indicated they would have the principal mediate such a dispute or that they would collect evidence to try to present a stronger second case. One teacher saw parental involvement as an effective tactic to use in such a case.

Specialists' responses to this question were somewhat defensive; many felt they had a right to protect their limited time and resources, and that they had a responsibility to tell teachers this ("I try to get the teacher on my side; I sell my program"). Others said they would stress legal requirements; but many said they would work outside of legal and official channels to get some help for a child needing it.

Administrators focused on two approaches: increasing teacher understanding of rules and criteria for providing services, and working out programs through informal consultations.

Following Up on Referrals

Almost all teachers interviewed for the study said that following up personally with specialists was "very important," "vital," or "extremely important." Most also felt that they went out of their way to keep lines of communication open with specialists. A few noted occasional problems ("Often there is not feedback," "I sometimes have to ask for more information"). Only two teachers expressed disinterest in following up on student referrals ("I worry about how a person does in my room and this is what counts").

Responses by specialists were quite similar to those of teachers, but with some differences in tone. Again, there was general agreement that follow-up is very important and that it occasionally doesn't happen to the extent that it should. Specialists, however, seem somewhat more "guilty" in their comments, with many taking blame on themselves for not staying in touch with teachers: "I would like to do more follow-up, yet I'm limited by time." Lack of time was the reason most commonly cited for this problem. Specialists also stressed the verbal and informal nature of feedback more than teachers did; perhaps this is because this sort of discussion of a child's problems is so different from the "paper shuffling" in special programs about which many of them complain bitterly. Only a single specialist indicated that giving feedback was unimportant.

Administrators saw feedback as important, but there was also a more removed feeling to their comments. Most felt that teachers and specialists were following up adequately, and that informal

meetings were more common and more important than formal ones.
Curiously, only one administrator mentioned encouragement of com-
munication between generalist and specialist as part of his own job.
Others seemed to assume that such communication just happens:
"They stay in contact by being in the same school. "

In sum, educators find follow-up on referred students desirable but sometimes fairly difficult to accomplish. Some reported
real problems with giving or receiving feedback, but most seemed
satisfied with the informal nature of that feedback. There was minimal evidence of possessiveness or of animosity between teachers
and specialists. A few generalists, however, did feel they should
be consulted more about the development of student individualized
education plans (IEPs) ("I see that student more than anybody; I
could help more!") Some specialists felt that teachers "have an
'out of sight, out of mind' attitude about referrals. "

How Do Students React to Being Referred?

Educators' observations about how students themselves react
to being referred were varied and interesting. This was one of the
few questions for which responses seemed to vary by district; it was
also one to which educators in all three groups responded at length.

Teachers in Fillmore were unanimous in seeing no problems
for students who were referred. In Weston, however, teachers
noted a number of difficulties: students who miss planned class activities feel left out; some teachers indicated that their generalist
colleagues occasionally made negative comments about a student's
"having to work with a specialist"; others saw problems with "head
clearing" or "gear shifting" for students who have to make midday
transitions. In Evergreen, some teachers felt there were no problems for students, while several others noted difficulties because
of peer pressure and pejorative labeling of students as "queer" or
"weird. "

Specialists in the Fillmore district (where teachers saw no
student problems with transitions) were generally positive, but several discussed difficulties—unwillingness of teachers to take students back into regular classes, students getting "out of practice"
with group teaching methods, and so on. In Weston, several specialists mentioned the problem of recidivism among students who return
to regular classes too early; others noted the general difficulty that
transitions seem to cause students. In Evergreen, a number of
specialists noted the "stigma" that is attached to special education,
the possible development of negative self-images among special education students, and problems with "role playing" (a student's paying

attention and working in a resource room, but reverting to old behavior patterns in a classroom).

Administrators in Fillmore did not see major student problems
stemming from referrals. They assumed that regulations and laws
mandating teacher-specialist interaction and student monitoring
would prevent any problems. In Weston, the CDC program seemed
to administrators not to cause problems with student transitions:
"Staff are present with regular teachers in the classroom," noted one
administrator. Others also commented that the visibility and integration of specialist services made transitions much easier than was
the case with the regular, centralized district program.

Why are there these differences among districts? Fillmore's
perceived lack of problems with student transitions may be due to the
district's relatively small size (6,700 students) and location of most
specialist services in individual schools. In Evergreen, a cooperative of districts, students may have to travel further and thus experience more problems in referral. In Weston, educators saw
some problems, but also seemed genuinely to like the CDC program
for putting specialists and teachers in close touch with each other.
The variety in types of problems noted is also interesting—all students apparently do not find it easy to make a switch from one teacher
to another, day after day, while some older students (junior high
level) seem to find it difficult to view special students as peers. The
problem of recidivism and its potential ill effects on students was
also seen as an important one.

What sort of composite picture of generalist-specialist relations emerges from these educators' responses to questions about
specialization? Selena and Conway can summarize the problems as
they perceive them.

Conway doesn't see particular difficulties in defining which
students he should refer to Selena for special consideration. Selena,
however, is concerned that Conway sometimes sends her students
who are really just hard to control in class. Selena is also angry at
state and local officials for trying to define too precisely which students she may and may not help. She would be much happier if she
had more leeway within which to exercise her professional judgment.

Dealing with conflicts over referrals is difficult for Conway.
He'd rather just try to do whatever he could for a child in his class
than to argue about the need for special treatment or services.
Selena sometimes feels that teachers expect too much of her and
that she's right to turn down some referrals. Both Conway and
Selena would try to circumvent the official rules and procedures if
they felt that would be most productive for the child.

Conway and Selena both emphasize the value of staying in touch
about a student's progress once a referral has been made, but Selena

in particular often finds it hard to do so. Her time is so fragmented that she can't follow up regularly.

Conway sees occasional problems for his students who are referred. It's difficult for some to make the transition from working with a specialist back to the routine of his classroom. Others are labeled as oddballs by their peers. Selena sees these problems too, but she also worries about recidivism among students who are cycled back into regular classrooms too soon.

In summary, Conway and Selena do not disagree over their roles in a major way, but they do complain about various facets of their working relationship. They also perceive students' needs somewhat differently, perhaps an unavoidable consequence of their different training and different administrative supervision. In particular, the common pattern of centralizing specialist services or having specialists move itinerantly among several school buildings appears to create a psychological, as well as a physical, gulf between generalist and specialist educators. Local, state, and federal programs have thus far not been aware of this gulf, or have not been willing to bridge it because of the cost increases such a change would entail.

ADMINISTRATIVE PATTERNS FOR SPECIALIST SERVICES

Educational administrators have been conscious for some time of the possibility of fragmentation in service that increasing specialization provides. Consequently, there have been more than a few administrative proposals for the organization of specialist and generalist services.

Many studies have noted that teachers tend to be virtually autonomous in their classrooms and little interested in working cooperatively on student problems (Lortie, 1975; Miles, 1967). Consequently, administrators have been urged to foster greater interaction among teachers in a school. While many of these proposals have dealt with generalist-generalist interaction, the principles involved have sometimes been applied to generalist-specialist exchanges (for example, Carter and Lynch, 1977; Goldman and Moynihan, 1972; Oakland, 1976). Such commentaries, however, are generally normative recommendations rather than empirical reports.

One major organizational effort to encourage productive interaction involved educational research and development workers from different specialty areas, together with a group of classroom teachers. Several factors were found to contribute to positive interaction:

opportunities for joint work created by the organization; administrative efforts to create "ideal type" roles that include elements from several different fields; and the elimination or minimization of status differences among specialists and generalists (Salmon-Cox and Holzner, 1977). Other studies have shown teacher-teacher or teacher-generalist interaction positively related to teacher confidence and interest in pupil management, curriculum, and novel teaching methods (Cohen, 1973; Johnson, 1976).

Programs of pre- or in-service education designed to improve interaction among teachers have also been developed to cope with the problem. A teacher "self-study" program, for example, urged teachers to record their feelings of satisfaction and frustration based on their work with colleagues and specialists. Simply sharing these observations among themselves became a very rewarding experience and one that led to increased empathy and understanding (Flatter and Koopman, 1976; see also Kelman and Wolff, 1976). In a similar experiment in medical education, participants also found that sharing perceptions in this manner led to an "enhanced sense of community" among specialists from different fields (Boyer, Lee, and Kirchner, 1977).

Individual case studies of how to make generalist-specialist interaction more productive have focused on a variety of factors: precise role definition for the parties involved (Gifford, 1978; Central, 1978); increasing the amount and quality of information flowing among teacher, specialist, and administrator (Westbrook, 1977); and the use of "in-basket" exercises to train specialists (Arikado et al., 1974).

PARENTAL INVOLVEMENT AND SPECIALIST SERVICES

The focus here on political and administrative aspects of school governance suggests that parents' reactions to specialization in the schools may also be important to consider. In U.S. education, after all, the client is not only the student but also the student's parents, who (in theory, at least) are entitled to some say in the content and method of that student's treatment in the educational system. Parental involvement in educational decision making is a value of long standing in this country, and so it makes sense to look at the ways in which parents have and have not been included in planning and carrying out specialist services in the schools.

In the study conducted by the National Committee for Citizens in Education (NCCE) (Salett, 1979:4), investigators found a good deal of parental approval for the way in which specialist services were provided: "Over two-thirds of responding parents felt adequately informed about the IEP and felt that the IEP generally fit their children's needs. Only five percent refused to approve their children's IEPs." The problem of general lack of parental involvement in the development of plans for their children led NCCE to propose district-wide advisory councils, mandated parental involvement in IEPs, and delay in preparation of IEPs until after initial parent-staff meetings.

A number of reports and studies have noted the difficulties parents may have in working with educational specialists. Teachers' use of jargon has been denounced as obfuscating (Rutherford and Edgar, 1979:4). Parents also have indicated feelings of inadequacy in confronting what they feel to be the superior knowledge and ability of specialist teachers (Morra, 1979; Progress, 1979:93). This should not obscure the fact, however, that passage of PL 94-142 in 1975 was due largely to increased parental militancy in demanding expanded specialist services (Sarason and Doris, 1979).

Many have championed the case for early parental involvement in decisions on special education. Wandler (1978) urged school psychologists to analyze test results jointly with parents and to solicit their comments on the data. Among other specialist groups, counselors frequently have been urged to go to the community through Parent-Teacher-Student Association (PTSA) meetings and other forums to discuss their programs (Nelson, 1974; Quenon, 1977).

At least a few studies have demonstrated empirically that parental involvement may have an effect on children receiving specialist services. Hill (1977) found that academic performance improved with more parent participation in deciding program content. A practicum on parent-teacher planning for child management was rated highly by 96 of 108 participants (Adreani and McCaffrey, 1974).

These various studies of parental involvement provide a mixed picture. On the one hand parents are eager to be involved in any planning affecting their children's future; on the other, feelings of inadequacy and inferiority may prevent them from becoming involved. While there has been intensive activity on the part of a minority of parents with regard to the special services their children use, the majority have yet to come in regular contact with specialists.

THREE KEY AREAS OF GENERALIST-SPECIALIST CONFLICT

Several issues emerge from the foregoing discussion of specialist services in school districts. These issues illustrate uniquely the conflict that schools may face between administrative demands for efficiency and political imperatives sensed by the various interest groups involved in making decisions on the shape of specialist services.

Defining Specialist Services

In the first place, attempts to define who a specialist is or what specialist services ought to be offered show that precise descriptions are rarely achieved. The roles of some specialists are less easy to identify specifically than those of classroom teachers as they involve dealing with a wide variety of academic and nonacademic student behavior. Delineating one specialist role from another is also sometimes difficult, and such distinctions as those among psychologist, counselor, and social worker often seem to depend mostly upon the interests and skills of those occupying the position. This confusion leads to two sorts of problems: conflict between generalists and specialists, and conflict between specialist groups and school districts.

Disagreement arises between generalists and specialists if roles are poorly defined. The specialist, whether because of separate certification or pay determined by a separate salary schedule, is often seen as an outsider, sometimes as a nonteacher by classroom generalists. Thus, attempts to define specialists' roles more precisely via such administrative devices as certification and salary schedules may actually be counterproductive in a political sense if they generate uncertainty and conflict in the working relationships of the educators affected.

In the broader arena of collective bargaining negotiations, relatively small specialist groups may find that their concerns are ignored by union representatives oriented toward the interests of the classroom teacher. In this way, the administrative advantages of a "united teaching profession" are seen to outweigh the political interests of diverse, but small, interest groups.

Conflict between specialist groups and school districts has focused most often on the definition of the specialist's position vis-a-vis other educators. Some districts, for example, have placed counselors on "classified" salary schedules (along with secretaries, janitors, and bus drivers) instead of certified schedules. Similarly, some districts have hired regular classroom teachers lacking specialist certification into positions supposedly requiring such certification. Neither of these moves, certainly expedient administratively, has been politically acceptable to specialist groups.

Organization of Specialist Services

Another key area of decision making in which politics and administration clash is that of how specialist services are to be organized. Specialist services are expensive, so there is frequently an administrative imperative to contain costs by centralizing services or sharing them with nearby districts. While this may result in immediate savings, the physical distance imposed between specialist and generalist frequently also translates into psychological distance. In the study of referrals discussed earlier, generalists and specialists who worked together in the same building were uniformly more positive in assessing each other as colleagues than were educators working in different parts of the district or in different districts. While the issue of physical location has not surfaced often in local negotiations regarding specialist services, it may do so increasingly in the future as educators come to realize the problems associated with physical placement.

Another problem in organizing specialist services is how to involve the clients of the system—most often parents. Formal procedures for parent involvement are included in such legislation as PL 94-142 and related state laws. Most of these spell out a particular administrative sequence in which decisions regarding a child's placement are to be taken. The steps are detailed and specific, with the obvious intent of both making the process flow freely and protecting the interests of all those concerned. In fact, the sequence is often short-circuited in order to save time, with consequential limits on parental involvement. That many parents are dissatisfied with the way the system actually operates testifies to the potential for political conflict here.

PROBLEMS OF IMPLEMENTING SPECIALIST SERVICES

Once specialist roles are defined and organizational patterns determined, programs must be actually carried out. Here, too, problems may develop. The findings on referral discussed above indicate that prescribed routines may break down in the face of local perceptions (for example, a student "clearly needing" services whose test scores do not fall within prescribed bounds, or one whose behavior leads a teacher to "dump" the student on a specialist). Administrative procedures may thus yield in practice to a kind of low-level negotiation for service among specialist and generalist.

Another arena in which this dilemma may increasingly come to be apparent during the next several years is that of documentation. Because categorical monies, both federal and state, usually fund specialist programs, record-keeping requirements are often more stringent than would be the case for local programs. Thus, attempts to hold such programs accountable lead also to exasperation with "unnecessary" record keeping on the parts of specialist educators involved. Given national concerns about overregulation by government, attempts to curtail paperwork and to make one form do the job of many may be expected over the next decade.

CONCLUSION: LINKAGE AND BUREAUCRATIC PROFESSIONALISM

Perhaps the single most important question in implementing specialist programs is simply how to encourage productive interaction among generalist and specialist teachers. Both sides have testified to feelings of ignorance about what the other does, and both have also indicated that they feel misunderstood by their counterparts. These fears and concerns, combined with the long-standing tendency among educators to think of themselves as omnicompetent in dealing with their charges, create real barriers to working together.

How might these barriers be overcome? The experience of successful programs and the responses of educators reviewed here suggest a new model for educational training and daily practice, a model based on internal linkage. I propose that this model may be of immediate practical benefit to educators in their attempts to cope with burgeoning specialization; additionally, the model may be more appropriate for education as a bureaucratized, personal service profession than that offered by medicine or other established professions in their present state of development.

Under an internal linkage model, improvements in training, the organization of educational work, and supervision would allow educators to work much more closely together than is now the case. Training would include a major focus on cooperative interaction. Daily teaching would provide for many more opportunities for joint or collaborative work by teachers, specialists, and administrators. Information and record systems would be designed both to promote the flow of useful information and to encourage swift decision making. District, state, and federal policies would emphasize small-scale programs for providing specialist services.

The implications of such a model for separate groups of educators deserve further consideration. Classroom teachers, for example, would be trained at a much earlier point in their careers to work jointly with specialists. Student teaching would necessarily include work with a variety of specialists. In actual school situations, teacher and specialist would work together in a single building. Physical arrangements would intersperse specialists' offices among classrooms. In-service programs would clarify expectations that generalists and specialists hold for each other. Local education organizations would expand to represent the concerns of both specialists and generalists.

Specialists would also receive careful training to prepare them for cooperative work with classroom generalists and with other specialists. Part of this training would parallel that generalists receive—earlier and more frequent experience working with counterparts. Other training would focus on improving communication among specialists, generalists, administrators, parents, and students. For some specialists (counselors, social workers, psychologists) such training would be naturally related to present curricula. For others, it might concentrate particularly on reducing reliance on jargon. Programs would certify "general specialists" in several specialty fields to serve small schools or rural areas for which the full complement of specialists would otherwise be prohibitively expensive or require overly centralized services.

For administrators, an internal linkage model would mean a stronger role facilitating contacts among generalists and specialists. Here again, both pre-service and in-service training could be valuable for the administrator. More importantly, administrators themselves would need to accept the responsibility for developing interaction among school staffs and accept also the prospect of being evaluated on their ability to bring such interaction about. Further, administrators would need to participate in a major effort to decentralize planning for specialist services and in making rules more flexible and responsive.

Community members would also have a new role to play. In the past, community members most involved in defining the scope of specialist services have been those whose children were service consumers (of, for example, special education or counseling). The perception of specialist services as separate and distinct from "regular" school offerings was thus reinforced, as was a sense that particular community interest groups "owned" those specialist services. Wider involvement of all sorts of community groups in the definition of specialist services could be productive in breaking down that possessiveness.

The trick, then, is how to preserve the advantages in application of knowledge to social problems that specialization provides while reversing the process of fragmentation that has accompanied specialization under the medical model of solo professionalism.

Assuming that specialization in education is here to stay, we may as well "get good at it." The internal linkage model proposed in outline form here could help to accomplish that. It might also provide a model of professional specialism more appropriate to late-twentieth-century conditions of bureaucratic control in other developing professions than does the compartmentalized model education has inherited from medicine. What is called for to effect the scenarios limned above is nothing less than a radical restructuring of educational training and educational roles.

REFERENCES

Adreani, A. J., and R. McCaffrey. 1974. Improving Child Management Practices of Parents and Teachers. Maxi I practicum. Final report. ERIC ED No. 106 729.

AECT (Association for Educational Communications and Technology). 1977. Guidelines for Certification of Media Specialists. Washington, D.C.: ACET.

Arikado, M. S. et al. 1974. The Elementary School Consultant. An In-basket Simulation Exercise. Toronto: Institute for Studies in Education. ERIC ED No. 140 484.

Arnold, D. S., G. Denemark, E. R. Nelli, A. Robinson, and E. L. Sagan. 1977. Quality Control in Teacher Education: Some Policy Issues. Washington, D.C.: American Association of Colleges for Teacher Education (AACTE) and ERIC Clearinghouse on Teacher Education, May.

Bauer, P. F. 1976. "Territorial Rights: Implications for the Pupil Personnel Worker." Journal of the International Association of Pupil Personnel Workers 20:104-07.

Betts, D. 1970. "Let's Communicate." The Balance Sheet 51, no. 6:254-55, 277.

Boyer, L., D. Lee, and C. Kirchner. 1977. "A Student-Run Course in Interprofessional Relations." Journal of Medical Education 52:183-89.

Carlson, R. J. 1975. The End of Medicine. New York: John Wiley.

Carter, D. G., and P. Lynch. 1977. "A Model Design for Organic Adaptive Teams." Planning and Changing 7, no. 4:61-69.

Central Midwestern Regional Education Lab. 1978. "Encouraging Staff Teamwork." Reporting on Reading 4, no. 2. ERIC ED No. 153 177.

Cohen, E. G. 1973. "Open-Space Schools: The Opportunity to Become Ambitious." Sociology of Education 46:143-61.

Cohen, E. G. et al. 1977. Teachers and Reading Specialists: Cooperation or Isolation? Stanford, Calif.: Center for Research and Development in Teaching, Stanford University.

Flatter, C. H., and E. J. Koopman. 1976. "An In-Service Self-Study Program: The Forgotten Key to Educational Success." Journal of Teacher Education 27:116-18.

Freidson, E. 1975. Doctoring Together. New York: Elsevier.

Gifford, I. 1978. "Developing Channels of Communication." Paper presented at the annual meeting of the International Reading Association, Houston, May. ERIC ED No. 157 035.

Gilb, C. L. 1966. Hidden Hierarchies: The Professions and Government. New York: Harper & Row.

Goldman, S., and W. Moynihan. 1972. "Strategies for Consultant-Client Interface." Educational Technology 12:27-90.

Goor, J., A. S. Metz, and E. Farris. 1978. Teacher and Administrator Shortages in Public School Systems, Fall, 1977. Fast Response Survey System Report No. 4. NCES Report No. 78-244. Washington, D.C.: National Center for Education Statistics.

Heinich, R., and K. Ebert. 1976. Legal Barriers to Educational Technology and Instructional Productivity. Final report. NIE Project No. 4-0781. Bloomington: University of Indiana.

Hill, E. B. 1977. "Building Cooperation between Resource and Elementary Classroom Teachers in Modifying Independent Work Habits." Paper presented at the annual meeting of the Council for Exceptional Children, Atlanta, April. ERIC ED No. 139 162.

Hirsh, H. L. 1977. "Duty to Consult and Confer." Legal Medicine Manual 3:257-58.

Illich, I. 1977. Toward a History of Needs. New York: Pantheon.

Illich, I. 1975. Medical Nemesis: The Expropriation of Health. New York: Random House.

Johnson, R. 1976. Teacher Collaboration, Principal Influence, and Decision Making in Elementary Schools. Technical Report No. 48. Stanford, Calif.: Center for Research and Development in Teaching, Stanford University. ERIC ED No. 126 083.

Kelman, E., and G. Wolff. 1976. "Data Feedback and Group Problem Solving: An Approach to Organizational Development in Schools." Psychology in the Schools 13:421-26.

Kerr, S. T. 1979. Specialization among Educators: Power, Efficiency, and the Medical Analogy. Final report. NIE Project No. 8-0614; Grant No. NIE-G-78-0166. Tacoma: University of Puget Sound, December.

Kerr, S. T. 1978. "Change in Education and the Future Role of the Educational Communications Consultant." Educational Communication and Technology Journal 26:153-64.

Koff, R. H., and D. H. Florio. 1977. "Accrediting Professional Education: Research and Policy Issues." In Professional Relationships: Reality and Action. AACTE yearbook, 1977 (Vol. 1). Washington, D.C.: AACTE.

Kritek, W. J. 1979. "Teacher Concerns in a Desegregated School." Paper presented at the annual meeting of the American Educational Research Association, San Francisco, April.

Lawlis, P. J. 1979. Surplus or Shortage: The Employment Outlook for Teachers in Illinois. Normal: Placement Service, University of Illinois, October.

Lortie, D. C. 1975. Schoolteacher. Chicago: University of Chicago Press.

Maitland, G. E. 1976. "Whose Child Is He—Yours, Mine, or Ours?" Journal of Childhood Communication Disorders 8, no. 1:15-26.

Maroldo, G. K. 1972. The Way of the Dinosaur: Will School Psychologists Become Extinct? ERIC ED No. 119 030.

McDonnell, L. M. 1977. "NEA Priorities and Their Impact on Teacher Education." In Professional Relationships: Reality and Action. AACTE Yearbook, 1977 (Vol. 1). Washington, D.C.: AACTE.

McDonnell, L. M., and A. Pascal. 1979. Organized Teachers in American Schools. NIE Report No. R-2407-NIE. Santa Monica, Calif.: RAND Corp.

McKeown, T. 1976. The Role of Medicine: Dream, Mirage or Nemesis? London: Nuffield Provincial Hospitals Trust.

Mechanic, D., ed. 1976. The Growth of Bureaucratic Medicine. New York: John Wiley.

Miles, M. 1967. "Some Properties of Schools as Social Systems." In Change in School Systems, edited by G. Watson. Washington, D.C.: NEA.

Morra, F. 1977. The Supply and Demand for Beginning Teachers, Past, Present and Future. Washington, D.C.: Lewin and Associates. ERIC ED No. 157 864.

Morra, L. 1979. "Case Study Views of the Implementation of the Least Restrictive Environment Provisions of P.L. 94-142." Paper presented at the annual meeting of the American Educational Research Association, San Francisco, April.

Murray, D., and R. Schmuck. 1972. "The Counselor-Consultant as a Specialist in Organizational Development." Elementary School Guidance and Counseling 7, no. 2:99-104.

NCES (National Center for Education Statistics). 1978. The State of Teacher Education, 1977. NCES Report No. 78-409. Washington, D.C.: NCES.

NEA (National Education Association). 1978. NEA Handbook, 1978-79. Washington, D.C.: NEA.

NEA. 1977. Status of the American Public School Teacher, 1975-76. Washington, D.C.: NEA.

Nelson, R. C. 1974. "Reaching Parents and the Community."
Elementary School Guidance and Counseling 9, no. 2:143-48.

Oakland, T. 1976. "An Interaction Model for Special Education and
School Psychology." Paper presented at the annual convention of
the Council for Exceptional Children, Chicago, April. ERIC ED
No. 142 028.

Pine, G. J. 1975. "School Counseling: Criticism and Contexts."
Paper presented at the annual meeting of the American Personnel
and Guidance Association, New York, March. ERIC ED No.
110 877.

Progress toward a Free Appropriate Public Education. 1979. A
Report to Congress on the Implementation of PL 94-142. Washington, D.C.: Office of Education.

Quenon, B., ed. 1977. Growing Up Is Very Hard to Do: Benefits
of an Elementary Counseling Program. Coloma County Schools,
Mich.: Michigan Elementary School Counselors Association.
ERIC ED No. 158 176.

Quinn, P. F. 1969. "Rapprochement—The Teacher and the Counselor." School Counselor 16:170-73.

Rebell, M. A. 1976. "The Law, the Courts, and Teacher Creden-
tialling Reform." In Licensing and Accreditation in Education:
The Law and the State Interest, edited by B. Levitov. Lincoln,
Neb.: Study Commission on Undergraduate Education and the
Education of Teachers. ERIC ED No. 131 043.

Ritzer, G. 1975. "Professionalization, Bureaucratization, and
Rationalization—The Views of Max Weber." Social Forces 53:
627-34.

Rutherford, R. B., and E. Edgar. 1979. Teachers and Parents:
A Guide to Interaction and Cooperation. Boston: Allyn & Bacon.

Salett, S. 1979. Congressional Testimony: Public Law 94-142.
Columbia, Md.: National Committee for Citizens in Education.

Salmon-Cox, L., and B. Holzner. 1977. "Managing Multidisci-
plinarity: Building and Bridging Epistemologies in Educational
Research and Development." Paper presented at the annual meeting of the American Educational Research Association, New York,
April. ERIC ED No. 135 760.

Sarason, S. B., and J. Doris. 1979. Educational Handicap, Public Policy, and Social History. New York: The Free Press.

Selden, D., and R. Bhaerman. 1970. "Instructional Technology and the Teaching Profession." Teachers College Record 71: 391-406.

Shortell, S. M., and O. W. Anderson. 1971. "The Physicial Referral Process: A Theoretical Perspective." Health Services Research 6:39-48.

Stevens, R. 1971. American Medicine and the Public Interest. New Haven, Conn.: Yale University Press.

Wandler, J. 1978. "Interpreting Test Results with Parents of Problem Children." School Guidance Worker 33, no. 4:35-38.

Weatherley, R. 1979. Reforming Special Education. Cambridge, Mass.: MIT Press.

Weatherley, R., and M. Lipsky. 1977. "Street-Level Bureaucrats and Institutional Innovation: Implementing Special Education Reform." Harvard Educational Review 47:171-97.

Westbrook, J. W. 1977. "Total Staff Involvement in Curriculum Decision Making." Paper presented at the annual meeting of the American Association of School Administrators, Las Vegas, February.

PART V

THE POLITICAL PERSPECTIVE:
THE SCHOOL DISTRICT
AS A TOTALITY

12

IDENTIFYING HANDICAPPED STUDENTS

Hugh Mehan
J. Lee Meihls
Alma Hertweck
Margaret S. Crowdes

School districts, like other public organizations, are frequently caught between two conflicting imperatives (Bacharach, Chapter 1 of this volume). On the one hand, there is the need to satisfy the demands for professional excellence. On the other hand, there is the need to satisfy the demands of various administrative responsibilities. These competing imperatives are a central focus of this chapter. They are discussed in terms of the decision-making processes involved in identifying and placing handicapped students in the special education programs in one particular midsize, suburban school district in California (henceforth called "the Coast District").

There is no greater demand for professional excellence among educators than in their decision-making activities. We found that

Our thanks to Sam Edward Combs, Elette Estrada, and Pierce J. Flynn for assisting in data collection, and to Delphia Cox for help in statistical compilation. Norma Allison, Jackie Mitchell, and Mitchell Rabinowitz also assisted this research; their help is greatly appreciated. We would also like to express our appreciation to the students, teachers, parents, and administrative officials of the Coast School District for facilitating the conduct of this research, and to Phil Davies, John Kitsuse, and John Van Maanen for helpful comments on earlier drafts of this chapter.

Support for this work was provided by the National Institute of Education, Grant No. 8-0497 (UCSD No. 3433). The statements expressed are solely the responsibility of the authors.

decision making in the Coast District was routinely constrained because education is bureaucratically organized. These routine, institutionally provided constraints on the search for and placement of students in special education programs were intensified and complicated because educators also had to satisfy the demands of recently enacted federal legislation concerning the education of handicapped students. The way in which the rationality of decision making is constrained by practical circumstances and legal mandates is the topic of the second section of this chapter. The impact of the mundane activities that constrain decision making in educational settings leads us to reconsider the commonly accepted view that educational identities, like "handicapped students," are a characteristic of students' conduct.

The adaptations that this district made to the institutional and legal constraints on decision making is the next topic addressed in the third section. The innovative manner in which the Coast District resolved the conflicts generated by these competing imperatives—the one administrative and the other professional—is described.

The institutional practices deployed by the school to satisfy the demands of these conflicting imperatives provide us with an opportunity to speculate on the model of schooling that emerges from our work (fourth section). In particular, we examine the assumptions about human information processing and social organizations that are built into the handicapped student education law and discuss the dialectical relations between federal policy and local organizations.

We begin the chapter by providing some background information about the origins of our case study, including our theoretical and methodological approach.

THE CONTEXT OF THE STUDY

The main issue addressed by this study is the influence of schooling on students' careers. Like researchers on education from many disciplines who have gone before us, we are interested in the ways schools makes a difference in the lives of students who attend them.

Our original plans for investigating this issue were to study the educational decision making associated with the placement of students into a variety of educational programs. However, PL 94-142, The Education for All Handicapped Students Act, was enacted at about the time the study was to begin. The implementation of this law in the Coast District transformed the study from a general study of educational decision making to a specific study of the "referral process" mandated by this recently enacted federal law.

This coincidence (like so many other serendipitous events in social science research) turned out to be fortuitous. It provided us with a unique opportunity to see how a local agency implemented a recently enacted federal law (see Attewell and Gerstein, 1979). This law is particularly important, sociologically speaking, as it seems to have been informed by social science research on "labeling," especially the stigmatizing effects of mislabeling (Goffman, 1963; Mercer, 1974). The law is also important because it is so specific in its provisions. For example, it specifies the population to be served and the components and temporal parameters of the placement process in great detail.

Public Law, Students' Careers, and
the Referral System

Under normal circumstances, students progress through school in a regular sequence. They enter school in the kindergarten, and at the end of each year are promoted to the next higher grade. Not all students follow this routine career path through school, however. Under unusual circumstances, students are removed from their regular classrooms during the school year and are placed in a variety of "special education" programs.

These special career paths have been a long-standing feature in U.S. public schools. Recently, federal legislation has formalized the procedures involved in placing students in special education programs. Public Law 94-142 was enacted to integrate handicapped individuals into the mainstream of American life. This act mandates a free and appropriate public education for all handicapped children between the ages of 3 and 21, and sets up a system of federal financial support to states who implement the law. Funds are supplied to each school system for each child who is enrolled in a special education program, until the number of students reaches 12 percent of the school population, after which no funds are available.

The major purpose of PL 94-142 is "to assure that all handicapped children have available to them . . . a free appropriate public education which emphasizes special education and related services designed to meet their unique needs." [Sec. 601(c)]. What constitutes an appropriate education for a handicapped child is embedded in the six leading principles of the act: zero reject, nondiscriminatory evaluation, individualized education programs, least restrictive environment, due process, and parental participation.

In order to describe the decision-making process involved as students are referred from "regular" elementary school classrooms and are considered for placement in one of a number of "special"

educational programs, or are retained in the regular classroom,
we followed the progress of students' cases through the special education referral system mandated by PL 94-142. A given case has
the potential of progressing through a number of major decision-
making points. The key decision-making points are referral, appraisal, assessment, reappraisal, evaluation, and placement.
These decision-making points are identified by ? in Figure 12.1.

Research Methodology and Its Theoretical Underpinnings

Many research techniques have been employed to follow the
progress of students' careers through this referral system. Data
have been gathered by reviewing official school records, by field
observations, by videotaping selected decision-making events, and
by interviewing people who participated in these events. The information gathered from this combination of documentary analysis,
interviewing, and observation provides us with a varied and systematic basis for analyzing the decision-making process concerning
student careers.

The records of all 2,700 students in the Coast District were
reviewed. These records provided us with such baseline information as age, grade, sex, and other demographic information, as
well as the official referral reason, date of referral, the person
making the referral, psychological assessment information, educational test results, dates of test administration, and final disposition of all referrals in the district.

The data gleaned from the school records give us general information about the products of the referral system—the educational
facts of the referral process if you will. Our interest is to describe
the institutional practices that constitute those educational facts.
To this end, we conducted a more micro, constitutive analysis of the
school district. This phase of the analysis includes field observations of daily educational practice, interviews with a number of
school personnel, and a detailed analysis of videotapes from a
smaller number of events at the referral, assessment, and placement phases of the referral system.

Contributing to the continuing dialogue among researchers in
the ethnographic tradition (broadly conceived), our study has been
guided by research techniques developed in micro- or constitutive
ethnography. The scope and definition of ethnography has varied
considerably, and opinions and practice differ on many details (see,
for example, Sanday, 1979; Erickson and Shultz, 1980; Hymes,
1980; Brice-Heath, 1981). These variations spurred serious re-
thinking of the many aspects of ethnographic research and led us

FIGURE 12.1

Referral Process as of August 1, 1979

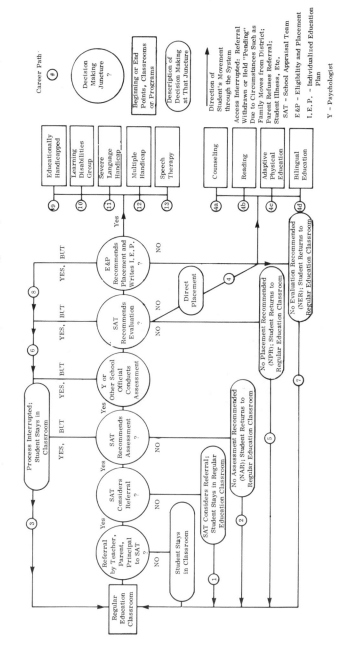

Source: Compiled by the authors.

385

(as they led others) to go beyond an uncritical narrative of cultural detail and focus on a deeper analysis of our recorded observations, developing the very theses (as well as new ones) that guided our research. Research, after all, is re-search, a statement about the reflections of our searches.

We are pressing for an ethnographically informed theory concerned with the wider educational and sociopolitical context of the classroom and the school. Microethnography has been associated with the fine-grained analysis of the minute details of face-to-face interaction in a small number of educational events. This association developed, in part we are sure, because as microethnographers were developing their theories, refining their research techniques, and acclimating educators, students, and parents to the use of audiovisual equipment, they concentrated on a small number of events. For the most part, the social organization of an event within one educational setting was described separately from events within other educational settings within the school, or without comparing events inside and outside of school.

Microethnography is not just a research technique; it is informed by a theory (Erickson and Shultz, 1980; Mehan, 1978; 1979; McDermott et al. , 1978). The theory is concerned about the ways in which the enduring and stable features of our everyday lives are assembled in social interaction. One place that these interactional processes can be located in the educational realm is in face-to-face encounters between people—for example, teachers and students— but that is not the only place. Social structures are also assembled when educators work autonomously—filling out forms—writing reports, or when a group of educators in the form of a committee works on a textual or documentary representation of previous face-to-face encounters (Cicourel, 1975). An underlying theme of this project is to demonstrate that the interactional or mutually constitutive theory informing microethnography has application across situations and in broader contexts.

In order to describe how we are linking the structuring of interaction that unfolds in face-to-face and person-to-text encounters with the broader educational and sociopolitical context, it may be helpful to borrow a popular metaphor. We started with a wide-angle lens and "zoomed" in on micro contexts (for example, classrooms, testing sessions, committee meetings), and progressively focused on the setting in order to capture the features considered most salient. Then, without editing out the larger sociopolitical and educational issues, we "zoomed" back out into the larger context, carrying with us those new insights we had gained into the microcontextual features.

SOME PRELIMINARY OBSERVATIONS

A total number of 141 "first time" referrals were processed through the referral system during the 1978-79 school year.[1] The classroom teacher was listed in the school records as the person making all of these referrals. We must not confuse the official referral agent of record and the people involved in the decision to refer. We simply cannot determine the number of times parents and teachers or principals and teachers conferred before the teacher filled out the official referral forms.

The average enrollment of this district was 2,781. This means that 5.0 percent of the students in this district were referred during the school year in which the study was conducted.

The various "career paths" through the referral system are depicted in Figure 12.1. Table 12.1 summarizes the number of students' cases that traversed these paths. The most-well-traveled path is from the classroom through referral, appraisal, assessment, and placement into a "learning disabilities" program. A total of 36 students (25.7 percent of referred students) were placed in this program. The "LD" Group, as it is sometimes called, is a pullout program, that is, students spend part of their school day in their home classroom and another part of their day in a special educational program.

The next most represented educational decision is career path No. 5, "no evaluation recommended." A student achieves this educational designation when his or her referral is considered by the School Appraisal Team, educational assessment is recommended and conducted, but upon reappraisal of the case not enough reason is found to warrant its further consideration. Instead, the student is retained in the regular classroom. A total of 28 cases (20 percent) traveled this career path through the system.

A formal decision was not reached on a significant number of cases because the referral process was interrupted for a variety of reasons. A total of 29 cases (20 percent; see career paths 3, 6, and 8) fell into this category. The consequence of all of these interruptions is that the student is left in the regular classroom by default, as it were.

The final points on the career paths are similar in their consequences for students' lives. There are two main decision outcomes generated by the system: retain in a regular educational program, or place in a special education program. A student can achieve the status of a regular education student by design or by default. That is, a formal decision to retain a student in a regular classroom can be reached, or the system is interrupted in such a

TABLE 12.1

Career Paths through the Referral System

Career Path	Description	Number	Percent
1	Child referred, case never considered by SAT; child remains in classroom	1	0.7
2	SAT considers case, no assessment recommended; child remains in classroom	19	13.6
3	Process interrupted at appraisal phase; child remains in classroom	24	17.1
4	SAT considers case at reappraisal phase, makes direct placement (Adaptive P.E. = 1; Bilingual = 3; Reading = 1; Counseling = 6)	11	7.9
5	SAT considers case, recommends assessment; assessment conducted, no evaluation recommended, child remains in classroom	28	20.0
6	Process interrupted at assessment or reappraisal phase; child remains in classroom	4	2.8
7	E&P considers case, no placement recommended; child remains in classroom	1	0.7
8	Process interrupted at evaluation phase; child remains in classroom	1	0.7
9	E&P considers case; recommends placement in Educationally Handicapped Classroom	7	5.0
10	E&P considers case; recommends placement in Learning Disabilities Group	36	25.7
11	E&P considers case; recommends placement in Severe Language Handicapped Classroom	3	2.1
12	E&P considers case; recommends placement in Multiple Handicapped Classroom	2	1.4
13	E&P considers case; recommends placement in Speech Therapy	3	2.1
Total		140	99.8

Source: Compiled by the authors.

way that the student remains in his classroom because the case is not closed. Special education programs can be grouped into "whole day," also called "self-contained," classrooms and "pullout" programs. The programs in the first group are considered the more extreme placements, while the programs in the second group are considered less extreme. The least severe placement of all is "counseling." In such cases, parents are encouraged to seek advice from a professional psychologist outside the district.

The "career paths" in Table 12.1 are collapsed into these Regular and Special Education Placement categories in Table 12.2. This table shows that 56 percent of the cases referred to were resolved, either by design or by default, as regular education placements. The remaining 44 percent of the students were placed into one of three types of special education programs. It is interesting to note that 62 percent (49 of 78) of the cases in the regular education category were not "placements" at all, but came as the result of interruptions in the referral system. The great majority (63 percent) of special education cases were placed into the less severe, "pullout" programs, while 27 percent of special education cases were placed into self-contained classrooms.

TABLE 12.2

Types of Placements

	Total	Percent
Regular Education		
Remains in classroom by decision	49	
Remains in classroom due to interruption in process	29	
Total regular ed	78	55.71
Special Education		
Counseling	6	
Pullout programs[a]	41	
Self-contained programs[b]	15	
Total special ed	62	44.28
Total referral cases	140	100.00

[a]Pullout special education programs are LDG, Speech Therapy, Reading, and Adaptive Physical Education.

[b]Self-contained programs are: EH, SLH, MH, and Bilingual Programs.

Source: Compiled by the authors.

These are the basic facts about the products of the referral process in the Coast District during the 1978-79 school year. We now turn our attention to the referral process itself. We will describe some of the institutional practices that are responsible for the distribution of students into these educational categories. Our investigation of decision making repeatedly led us to a number of factors that constrained the rationality of the referral process. These forces are the main topic of the following section.

CONSTRAINTS ON DECISION MAKING

There are a number of forces that impinge upon the referral system in such a way as to influence the identification, assessment, and treatment of children who are found to be in need of special education services. Some of these constraints on educational decision making are the direct result of federal and state legislation. Others are the consequence of the way in which this particular district has chosen to implement federal and state legislation; still others are the unintended consequences of organizational arrangements within this district.

We collect these constraints under the heading of "practical circumstances." These circumstances are "practical" in that they make their appearance day in and day out. They seem to be an inevitable part of the everyday routine of the education of students in an institution organized in a bureaucratic way. These constraints are "circumstances" in that they seem to be beyond the control of the people involved. They do not seem to be the personal responsibility of any one particular individual.

Thus, practical circumstances are the sedimentation from the actions of several individuals, some of which are taken in concert, others of which are taken autonomously, some in face-to-face encounters, others with textual or documentary representations of face-to-face encounters. The courses of action that educators take in response to these practical circumstances often have significant consequences. For example, they contribute to the construction of different educational career paths, or biographies, for students. However, the participants involved in this educational decision-making process do not necessarily plan to make educational services available to students differentially. Our daily observations, interviews, and discussions showed that educators were honest and genuinely concerned for the welfare of students in their charge; they were not trying to discriminate against any children. Nevertheless, special education services were made differentially available to students in the district. Differential educational opportunity seems to be more of an unintended consequence of bureaucratic organization than it is a matter of individual or collective intentions.

These practical circumstances impinge upon the referral process at each of the key decision-making points discussed above (Figure 12.1). Our discussion of their impact will follow the course that cases take through the system, from referral to appraisal, to assessment, to reappraisal and placement.

Referral

Informal Screening Practices

The public law governing special education (PL 94-142) and the local school district's policies state that once referrals are made, they will be immediately sent to the School Appraisal Team (SAT) (see Figure 12.1). We discovered via observation and interviews that the principals at two sites (Riverview and Woodview) had instituted some informal screening and scouting procedures. Instead of serving as record keepers and conduits of information from teachers to committees, it was their practice to discuss referrals in detail with referring teachers. Not only did they determine the facts of individual cases, but they made informal assessments. The Riverview principal in particular encouraged teachers to refer students whom he thought needed special help and discouraged teachers from making referrals that he thought were problematic. This principal also "went scouting" for referrals. He made regular visits to classrooms. If he saw a child who looked like he needed special help, he encouraged that student's teacher to make a referral.

These informal practices influenced the referral system in a number of ways. First, it suppressed the overall number of referrals. Cases that in the opinion of the principals did not seem appropriate were never forwarded to the SAT.[2] Second, in a manner analogous to "plea bargaining," it increased the efficiency of the placement process. Since only "clear-cut cases" were being forwarded to the appraisal team, cases were treated more quickly. Furthermore, the initial recommendation was ratified by constituents further into the system.

The influence of these informal practices on the speed of treatment is visible in Table 12.3, which shows that cases from Riverview and Woodview were completed much more quickly than they were completed at other schools. The influence of informal practices on the efficiency of treatment is visible in Table 12.4, which shows that Woodview and Riverview had a higher placement rate than the other schools that did not prescreen cases.

TABLE 12.3

Processing Time from Referral to Placement Meeting

School	Average Number of Days to E&P
Woodview	57
Islandia	74
Riverview	64
Midvale/Pleasant Valley	79

Source: Compiled by the authors.

TABLE 12.4

Referral and Placement Rates

	Islandia	Midvale/ Pleasant Valley	Riverview	Woodview	Totals
Average enrollment	762	561	662	796	2,781
Total referrals	36	25	33	47	141
Referral rate (percent)	4.7	4.4	5.0	6.5	5.0
Total placements	15	10	14	24	63
Placement rate (percent)	42	40	42	51	45

Source: Compiled by the authors.

Changes in Administrative Procedures

Administrative procedures, written to facilitate bureaucratic operations, were found to modify the very system they were intended to facilitate. Two notable trends emerged in the early months of our study. It soon became apparent that there were more cases being referred into the system than could be easily handled by existing special education personnel. Perhaps in reaction to this first trend, there was a movement toward more formalized reporting practices.

In the years preceding the study, and for the first half of the year that we observed in the district, the procedures for reporting referrals varied from school to school. Teachers in some schools wrote handwritten letters, while at others, they filled out mimeographed forms designed by the principal. As teachers became more aware of the referral system and its possibilities for dealing with children for whom they needed assistance, referrals increased at the school site level. This increased the varieties of forms in which referrals were made. Since referrals were transferred to the district level, it soon became apparent that there were wide variations in reporting procedures.

During the late fall, the director of special education introduced a uniform reporting procedure. Referrals were to be reported on a five-page form, which included a "face sheet," with information about the student's background, grade, age, and so on. The next four pages were a check sheet of symptoms observed by the teacher in the classroom. This new referral form was distributed by the central office along with extensive descriptions of the characteristics of children with certain learning disabilities to serve as guidelines.

A series of in-service workshops on the new referral procedures and the defining characteristics of special education children were also held during the winter months. These workshops served to augment the formalized reporting procedures in instructing the teachers concerning the information they were to supply on the forms. They also served to inform teachers about the types of children who should be referred. An additional topic of discussion during these workshops was in-class help for children having difficulties, which possibly had the result of diverting many children from the referral system.

As far as we can determine, the introduction of these new procedures had countervailing influences. On the one hand, it seems, based on our field observations and interviews with teachers, that these new procedures may have flattened the upward trend in referrals. Teachers complained that the new forms were too complicated, "too much of a hassle." On the other hand, the dissemination of information about special education students' characteristics and in-service workshops about symptoms may have had a "pygmalion" or "abnormal psychology syndrome" effect. The abnormal psychology syndrome is that which affects students taking courses in clinical psychology for the first time. As instructors discuss the symptoms associated with schizophrenia, neurosis, psychosis, and the rest, students discover evidence of these disorders in their own behavior. In an analogous fashion, teachers provided with a list of the symptoms associated with "learning disabilities" may now find evidence of these symptoms in their students' behavior. In this way, the presentation of a category or a concept provides a means to find a behavior to collect under it. Instead of the behavior of the children being the impetus to categorize, and thereby treating the behavior, the category becomes a procedure to search for and locate the behavior.

Another change in administrative procedures particularly influenced the referral system. The school psychologists came to the realization in March that the referral system was overloaded. They counted their case load and plotted it against the weeks remaining in the school year. They determined that it was practically impossible to process the number of students in the period of time available. After this information was reported to their supervisor, the director of pupil personnel services circulated a memo throughout the district, telling principals and teachers to refer only severe and obvious cases.

We are not proposing a simple, linear, unidirectional causal connection between institutional arrangements and student outcomes. Instead, we find that the institutional order of the school operates in interconnected ways. As a consequence, we are not suggesting that modifications in procedures such as the introduction of new forms and instructions to curtail referrals had a direct effect on the referral process. Furthermore, because of the interconnected nature of the institutionalized order of the school, such changes are not readily apparent in statistical arrays of the referral process. Nevertheless, there was a significant decline in the number of referrals throughout the district within a month after the new referral forms were introduced, in-service workshops were held, and the directives to curtail referrals were circulated. The average number of referrals from July to March was 13 a month. There were 13 referrals in April, and only 4 in May and 3 in June, or an average of 7 a month (see Figure 12.2). We interpret these figures to be a consequence of the combined influence of changes in administrative procedures.

Although we cannot propose a simple, direct causal connection, it is clear that changes in administrative procedures have

FIGURE 12.2

Number of Referrals in District by Month

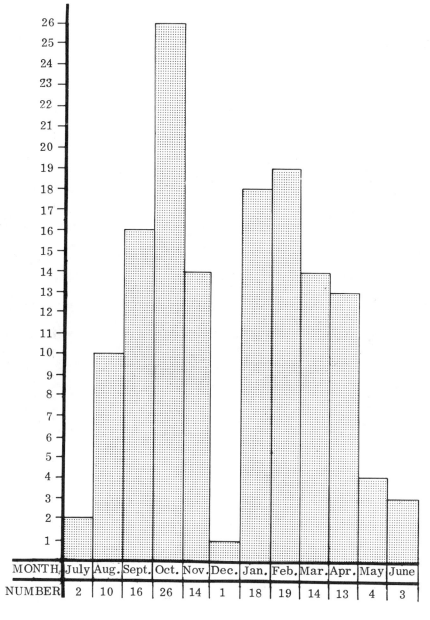

MONTH	July	Aug.	Sept.	Oct.	Nov.	Dec.	Jan.	Feb.	Mar.	Apr.	May	June
NUMBER	2	10	16	26	14	1	18	19	14	13	4	3

Source: Compiled by the authors.

consequences for the careers of students. Consider the case in which a teacher diagnoses a "reading problem" in a student in September or October. That child potentially can become a "special education" student, because the district has institutional arrangements in place to appraise, assess, and evaluate that student. Now consider the case in which that same student was not identified by his teacher until May or June. Like the students in Catholic schools in Riverside County studied by Mercer (1974), it is not possible to be a "special student" in the absence of institutionalized practices for their recognition and treatment. Designations like "educationally handicapped," "learning disabled," "normal student" are presumably reflections of the characteristics of the students; but these designations are influenced by the calendar and work load, which are institutionalized arrangements. These designations, then, are to be found in the institutional arrangements of the school as much as they are to be found in the characteristics of the students.

Competition among Special Programs

This district, like other modern districts, has established a wide variety of programs to assist students with special needs. Chief among the programs in this district were the bilingual program and the special education program. Presumably designed to complement each other by helping students with different problems, we became aware of occasions when these programs wound up in competition with each other.

Two of the schools in the district (Islandia and Midvale) had extensive bilingual programs for Mexican-American and Anglo students. These programs operated on a voluntary basis. While popular among Mexican-American parents who wanted their children to learn English, these programs experienced some difficulty in recruiting students from among the Anglo population. The personnel associated with these programs wanted to maintain an equal balance of Anglo and Mexican-American students in bilingual classrooms. This concern had unintended consequences for the identification and assessment of special education students. Teachers reported receiving resistance from their administrative superiors when they wished to refer Anglo students out of bilingual classrooms. The reason given was that removal of Anglo students would disrupt the ethnic balance of the bilingual programs.

We have suggested that the very designation of students as "special" was influenced by the calendar and work load. Now we have the case of that definition being influenced by the student's original classroom assignment. The Anglo student assigned to a bilingual classroom does not have the same opportunity to be identified as a special student, and to receive the assistance that presumably comes with that designation, as does a student who is assigned to a regular classroom. This inequality in educational opportunity is not a function of genetically endowed intelligence (Jensen, 1969, 1980; Herrnstein, 1974), "cognitive styles" (Bereiter and Engleman, 1972), or social class backgrounds (Coleman et al., 1966; Jencks, 1972; Bowles and Gintes, 1976); it is a consequence of unintended institutional arrangement, such as classroom assignment.

Mexican-American students in bilingual classrooms were also unlikely to be designated as special education students, but for different reasons. Previous studies of students in special education programs show an unequal ethnic distribution (Mercer, 1974)—ethnic students are overrepresented in special education classrooms. We did not find evidence of this unequal ethnic distribution in this school district. Table 12.5 shows that the number of students in special education classrooms is equivalent to the distribution of ethnic students in the district.

TABLE 12.5

The Ethnic Status of Referrals

	Percent of Students in District	Percent of Students Referred
Minority students	15	16
Majority students	85	84

Source: Compiled by the authors.

One account of this fact can be called "the Mercer effect." School district personnel are well aware of social science findings about the mislabeling of minority students and have instituted procedures to equitably serve students from different cultural backgrounds. Perhaps school officials in being overly sensitive to charges of mislabeling have produced these underrepresentations in special education classrooms.

Another unintended consequence of the operation of this district cannot be overlooked when reviewing these distributions. When we observed in bilingual classrooms we were often struck by the behavior of some of the students. It seemed to us their behavior was

more serious than that of some of the students who had been referred.
When we queried teachers about this discrepancy, they acknowledged
the accuracy of our observations. They went on to explain that they
did not refer Mexican-American students to special education programs because they did not believe that the district had adequate resources to test bilingual students or to help them outside the bilingual program. Because of their language expertise, teachers in
bilingual classrooms thought they were better equipped to teach students in their own classrooms than were the special education teachers in their special classrooms.

We are not interested in challenging the accuracy of these reports. Whether or not the district had adequate facilities for bilingual students in its special education classrooms is not the issue.
The quality of services for bilingual students is not a matter of fact;
it is a matter of belief. The teachers believed that their students
would be better served in their classrooms than in special classrooms. We are interested in the consequences of these beliefs,
however. As a consequence of teachers' actions based on these beliefs, bilingual students had a differential opportunity to be defined
as special students than did their nonbilingual counterparts.

The Introduction of a New Program

The laws governing special education require school districts
to provide educational opportunity to all students by whatever means
that are necessary. If facilities to educate students are not available within the district, then the district must supply the funds
necessary to educate students outside the district.

In the year before this study started, the district sent two students who had multiple physical handicaps to a special school outside
the district. A budgetary analysis conducted in the fall of the year
determined that, for the amount of money being spent on transportation and tuition of these two children outside the district, a teacher
and portable classroom could be purchased for use within the district. Within the year following the introduction of this new program,
the number of students with multiple handicaps rose from two to
eight. One explanation for this sudden and dramatic increase is that
there are simply more students with multiple physical handicaps.
That explanation defines "handicaps" as students' characteristics.
An alternative explanation that we have come to accept considers the
institutionalized practices of identifying handicapped students. In
order for students to be designated as members of educational categories, there must be institutional arrangements for their location,
identification, and assessment. A physical handicap is the product
of a social process, the realization of institutional practice. A

student cannot be physically handicapped, institutionally speaking, unless there are professional practices available for that determination.

Appraisal

After a referral has been made, it is sent to the SAT. This team is composed of teachers, a site administrator, and a number of educational specialists. There were a number of practical problems that plagued the organization and conduct of SAT meetings that influenced the referral process and, hence, the careers of children being considered for special education.

The seemingly simple act of scheduling committee meetings often posed insurmountable problems. Finding a time that was convenient for teachers, specialists, and administrators was challenging. If meetings were held during school hours, then teachers needed to find a way to be in two places at once. One way in which teachers secured release time was to turn their classroom over to an aide or a student teacher for the duration of the SAT meeting. Another was to try to obtain a substitute teacher. Neither of these solutions proved to be very satisfactory to all concerned. Teachers were reluctant to leave their classrooms in the hands of paraprofessionals, and if they did, they became impatient at prolonged discussions. Sometimes teachers left meetings before discussions were completed, reporting frustration because the referral case was not completed, and anger because regular classroom activities were disrupted. Principals were unwilling or unable to spend money for substitute teachers. In response to these practical problems, some schools resorted to scheduling meetings before and after school hours—early in the morning and late in the afternoon. This solution was not very satisfactory either, because it prolonged days, fatigued teachers, and seemed to lead to a general malaise. Some teachers reported they felt like just trying to get such meetings over with, an attitude that is not conducive to careful and reasoned discussions of complicated cases.

Scheduling meetings in this district was especially difficult because of the year-round school calendar. Often the consideration of a particular case had to be postponed because one or more of the required committee members would be "off track." If often seemed that the problem was compounded because, as soon as one participant would return, another would go off track. An information gap was created because the attendance of specialists varied from meeting to meeting.

Yet another factor complicating the scheduling of placement meetings is the "itinerant" status of the school psychologists. The district employed two school psychologists; one psychologist had two schools to service while the other had three. This work load distribution meant that the psychologists could be at certain schools only on certain days, which reduced the number of times available for conducting meetings. This particular scheduling problem became exacerbated when one of the psychologists left the district, and the one remaining psychologist had to rotate among all five schools until a replacement could be found.

As a consequence of these scheduling problems, especially postponed meetings, the appraisal of cases was delayed, which meant the final determination about the children involved was also delayed. These delays were so pervasive that sometimes children did not receive the necessary special education services for five months after they were referred officially to the SAT,[3] and occasionally they were placed so late that remediation had to be postponed until the next school year.

Teachers' attitudes were affected by these time delays. A recurrent theme that appeared in our teacher interviews was a negative attitude about the special education program. From the point of view of the teacher who refers a student in September, but doesn't have a special program designed for that student until April, this is an understandable feeling.

ASSESSMENT

Time Constraints

A common problem influencing the referral process was the amount of time it took to complete an assessment. Time was especially a problem for newly identified children. We asked the school psychologists to keep a diary of their activities associated with the assessment of an individual child. They reported that it took approximately 80 hours to "work up a case," in the best of circumstances. However, for reasons to be described below, it was never possible to prepare a case in one or even two batches of time. The work load was spread over a considerable stretch of time, which meant that even under the best of circumstances, it could take up to a month to prepare an assessment.

Circumstances were seldom favorable, however. Records often had to be obtained from another district, a private counselor, or a hospital. Parents were difficult to contact, and their permission is necessary to begin any formal classroom observation that involves working with the referred child on a one-to-one basis or individualized intelligence testing. Families often moved from one residence to another within the district, or moved in and out of the district, further complicating the problem of coordinating with parents.

These time delays interrupted the smooth processing intended by federal law. For practical purposes, the child who has been referred stays in the classroom—and these students stay in the classroom for a long time, often not having their case decided by the end of the school year. Such students are technically classified as "regular students," although this status is conferred upon them by administrative default, not by active decision making. (We have identified these students by tracing "interruptions" in the normal referral system; see paths 2, 6, and 8, in Table 12.1.)

Availability of Human and Material Resources

The itinerant status of the school psychologists interacted with the natural, normal time constraints associated with the processing of cases to produce a substantial impact on the assessment of children. Each school psychologist had only enough time available to spend one day a week at a given school site. This scheduling limitation had a major impact on the way in which students were processed by the school psychologist and other school specialists. On a typical day the school psychologist would arrange to assess a number of students at a given school. She would secure permission to administer tests from parents in advance and make arrangements with teachers to remove students from classrooms for individualized assessment. If all went well, the school psychologist might administer tests to as many as four children in one day at a particular school.

However, this optimal arrangement was seldom realized in practice. Students were absent, the parent's permission slip was misplaced or not returned on time; students' glasses were left at home; a teacher scheduled a filmstrip or a field trip or special activities without informing the school psychologist. These and a host of other practical matters often disrupted the school psychologist's carefully arranged plans.

Just as the itinerant status of the school psychologist dictated the construction of a tight schedule in the first place, so, too, it constrained the school psychologist's response to constraints imposed on her by disruptions in this carefully planned schedule. If one student was absent or on a field trip, the school psychologist could not simply turn to the next student on her list of those requiring testing from that school. Records were maintained at a central office. This meant that the school psychologist would have to drive from the school to the office just to get the necessary forms, then spend more time reviewing the case before administering tests.

Since the school psychologist could not simply go to the next child on her list, she had to wait a week until she cycled through the school again, which compounded the problem. First, it meant that the child who was supposed to be scheduled for a certain test was delayed until the next available slot; and since that first child was delayed, the child who should have been tested in the second's slot had to be bumped to yet another time slot. This cascade resulted in delays throughout the referral system. For this reason alone, it is not surprising that the length of time it took to process a child from the date of referral to the end of assessment averaged 52 days.

Another set of factors that compounded the assessment activity concerned the availability, or rather the nonavailability, of material resources. Not only were the school psychologists required to travel between schools in the district; they were also required to share office space with many other educational specialists at the school site visited. They shared offices with the speech teacher, the reading specialist, and sometimes the nurse. Under optimal conditions, the room in question would be set aside for the psychologist on the day that she was scheduled to visit a certain school; but the seemingly inevitable misschedulings, unexpected meetings, and just plain mistakes often resulted in the cancellation or postponement of testing sessions. This scheduling problem, combined with the problems associated with absenteeism, resulted in incredible time delays—delays that were, for all practical purposes, beyond the control of the school personnel involved.

A concomitant problem arose because testing material was not always available when needed. Coast is a small but rapidly expanding school district. Educational testing materials were apparently purchased when the district was smaller and serviced by one psychologist. As a consequence, each psychologist did not have a full battery of materials available for educational assessment. This situation was exacerbated by the financial condition of this district and others in the state in the wake of Proposition 13. Still uncertain of the impact of this tax-cutting initiative, districts were often reluctant to expend large sums of money. Fiscal policy had tangible consequences as different testers often needed the same testing materials at the same time. These conflicts caused the cancellation or postponement of one testing session to accommodate another. This delay contributed to the cascade effect described above; the child who could not be tested on a certain day could not simply be tested the next day. The itinerant status of the psychologists and the unavailability of work space and testing materials made it necessary to postpone the testing of that student until the psychologist cycled through the school again.

Placement

Placement meetings had all the problems associated with the SAT meetings described above, and had additional complications. The federal regulations informing special education required three specific participants at eligibility and placement (E&P) meetings: the child's teacher, parent(s) or legal guardian, and "a representative of the public agency, other than the child's teacher who is qualified to provide or supervise the provisions of special education." This was usually the school principal.

The Coordination of Schedules

The major difficulty was getting several busy people together for a meeting. The problem of coordinating schedules was compounded since the E&P meeting was held at the district office and not the local school site. The scheduling of meetings was especially a problem because of the need to include parents. They often had to take time off from work, arrange for child care, or did not express an interest in special education, all of which influenced their attendance at meetings.

As a consequence of these practical constraints, meetings were held at odd times, or those convenient to parents, which meant before and after school. As was the case with SAT meetings discussed above, the solution of one problem created other problems. When meetings were scheduled to accommodate parents, teachers could not come, or meetings were quickly scheduled when someone became available.

These vagaries in scheduling, not student characteristics, influenced the placement and treatment of students. It also influenced the perceptions of teachers and other personnel concerning the efficacy of the entire referral process. During our interviews, it was not uncommon for a teacher to express exasperation at the seemingly calculated practices of calling E&P meetings at the last moment, or canceling and rescheduling meetings.

Legal and Fiscal Incentives to Search for Students

The public law governing special education (PL 94-142) has specific guidelines concerning the population to be served. Testimony offered and reports written at the time the law was being considered by the Congress indicated that 12 percent of the school-age population was expected to be in need of special education. One interpretation of such reports is that the 12 percent figure is an estimate, a best guess of the special education constituency. The U.S. Office of Education (USOE), in its first report to Congress on the implementation of the law, found that, on the average, the states appeared to be serving 7.4 percent of the school-age population. The states varied from 5.2 percent to 11.5 percent (USOE, 1979). School districts and state agencies have been criticized for not "reaching" that number of students (Jones, 1979). It seems that the 12 percent figure is not an estimate at all but is to be treated as a compulsory figure.

The compulsory thrust of the law has consequences for the organization of education at the district level. There is an incentive to place students in special education programs in order to meet legal guidelines. Under circumstances such as these, students become "special" not because of their educational abilities or disabilities but because of an institutional response to legal mandates.

Coast District did not have 12 percent of its population in special education programs at the time of an audit by the state agency charged with the responsibility for monitoring special education. Special education teachers reported to us that they were given strong recommendations to find the children in order to meet the quota, or suffer the consequences of being found not in compliance with the law.

The legal incentive to search for special education students is reinforced by financial incentives. School districts are provided funds from state and federal governments for each student in school. The amount of funding is calculated on the basis of the "average daily attendance" (ADA) of the district. Coast District was reimbursed at the rate of $1,335 per student in regular classrooms. This ADA rate increased to $2,374 per student for pullout programs like Limited Disability Group (LDG), and to over $3,000 for Multi-Handicapped (MH) programs.

This difference in funding for regular and special education serves as an incentive to increase the number of students in special education. As we indicated above, the increased amount of ADA funds was sufficient to convince the district to provide special services to its multiple handicapped students with its own resources, rather than transport them outside the district to a special school.

Near the end of the year in which we conducted observations in the district, a new school was opened. When the students who transferred from other schools within the district were sorted out, and transfers from other districts were reassigned, there was a significant shortage of students in special education programs. Instead of the required 11 for educationally handicapped (EH) and 25 for LDG, there were 8 and 12, respectively. Special education teachers complained that there were not enough children in their programs. They were afraid that the district would lose some of its special education money as a consequence of this discrepancy. The reduction in funding would mean the loss of special classroom aides, a decrease in special equipment, and reduction of special salaries. As a consequence, the staff at the new school searched for students who would qualify for special programs.[4]

Disincentives to Place Students

Just as there is an incentive to locate and place students in special education programs in order to receive the maximum state and federal support, so, too, there is a disincentive to find too many special education students. There are not unlimited ADA funds for special programs. A funding ceiling is reached when 12 students are placed in an EH classroom with one teacher, 25 with an LD teacher, and 6 with a Severe Language Handicapped (SLH) teacher for ages 3-8 and 8 for an SLH teacher for ages 9-20. No additional money is provided if more students than that are assigned to a particular teacher.

These financial and legal matters constrain placement decisions. Committees take the number of students already assigned to special education programs into account when making final placements. Thus, many students with certain qualifications or characteristics are more likely to be placed in a special education program when it is short of students than when that same program is full of students. This means a learning disability is often a function of the calendar and is not the inherent characteristic or quality of the student.

Institutional Practice and Handicapped Students

We have described a number of mundane activities that occur every day in schools and other bureaucratically arranged organizations: concerns for budget and work load, equipment and personnel shortages, excessive work load, and shortage of time. Examined individually, these activities and concerns seem innocuous and of no particular consequence. When taken together, however, these mundane activities become a family of practical circumstances that operate at a structural level to constrain the decision making involved in identifying, assessing, and placing students in regular and special education programs.

The routine bureaucratic practice of prescreening teachers' referrals, discouraging referrals from certain classrooms and at

certain times of the year, changing administrative reporting procedures, and the rest, structures students' identities by constraining access to certain educational programs. That is, student identities are constructed by the institutional practices of the school.
This means that a designation like "learning disabilities," "mentally gifted minor," or "average student" is a feature of institutional practice, more so than a characteristic of children's conduct (see Buckholdt and Gubrium, 1979).

This institutional practice view contrasts with the view that there is a real world of troubled children "out there," waiting to be identified, assessed, and treated. The institutional practice view of disability does not separate the problems of children from the process of their discovery or procedures for their assessment or treatment.

The institutional practices that construct students' identities are a particular form of "social practice" (Garfinkel, 1967; Mehan and Wood, 1975) or "cultural practice" (LCHC, 1980). To "practice" social life is, literally, to work at its construction and maintenance. Practice constitutes social life; it is not a poor reflection of some more ideal state of affairs. Practice encompasses both people's ideals (including their interpretation, theories, and other beliefs) and people's application of those ideals in concrete situations of choice and practical action.

In looking at educators, we find them engaged in this construction work. Their work has a repetitive and routine character. The mundaneity of the character of their work should not overshadow the drama of its importance, however. We find educators "doing testing," "doing counseling," "doing decision making." The notion of work, signaled by the purposive use of the unwieldy gerund "doing," stresses the constructive and fluid aspects of institutional practice. From such practice, educational facts are assembled. Once assembled they are detached from the modes of their production. Once detached, they seem to take on a life of their own.

Ideological Implications of the Search
for Handicapped Children

In the seventeenth century, scientists concluded that the collapse of bridges proved that bridges could not be built. The reasoning that leads to that conclusion is comparable to the reasoning used by educators who place the blame on children for the failure of the educational system. That is, the children are seen as failing, not the educational system. Instead of placing the burden on children, and viewing them as the source of the problem, we have been looking at the institutional practices that serve as the foundations on which the programs are built, that is, the social construction of special education and the practice of identifying handicapped children.

By legal definition, referred students who are subsequently placed in special education programs are handicapped. The Education for All Handicapped Children Act (Public Law 94-142) is explicit in its definition. Handicapped children are: "mentally retarded, hard of hearing, deaf, orthopedically impaired, other health impaired, speech impaired, visually handicapped, seriously emotionally disturbed, or children with specific learning disabilities who by reason thereof require special education and related services" [Sec.4(a)(1)]. This indicates that a child is in the special education classroom because (s)he is educationally handicapped; (s)he is educationally handicapped because (s)he is in special education.

The correspondence theory of meaning (Ogden and Richards, 1934) inherent in this legal definition equates children with rows of file cabinets or jars with labels attached, telling us what's inside. Our research indicates that children and educational labels are not related by correspondence principles. Instead of a simple matching of label with child, intricate institutional practices of identifying, diagnosing, and treating children in a variety of situations structured the meanings of labels used in the school. Instead of a stable set of meanings, invariant across settings, we found institutionally structured labels to be situationally determined and they varied according to the context in which they appeared. Labels like "handicapped," "learning disabled," or "regular student" mean something different on different occasions within the school. The intricacy of these institutional practices makes it important to look further at the language used to communicate labels.

Labeling is perpetuated by mythic discourse. If someone in everyday life calls you a "dummy," or a "genius," or tells you "you're crazy," "insane," or "brilliant," then you have been labeled—at least for the moment. On the surface, that is, the banal level of everyday cliché, one often hears: "It's just an expression," or "It's only a myth." The cliché belittles the power of mythic discourse, although it is doubtful that the use of labels in everyday life will have significant influence in the long run.

When a child in public school is officially labeled "educationally handicapped" or "learning disabled," however, the label becomes a social fact about the child. Institutionalized labels are not just for the moment; they have consequences for the long run. The label becomes an object with a fixed meaning for the institution, albeit a social product of its own practices. In this state, the label can collapse into a signification, a category, a metaphor. That is, referred children are restricted and limited by the boundaries established by mythic discourse.

Much like the story of the five blind men who touched an elephant and related five different renditions as to what it was, five individual children who have all been identified as belonging to one educational category, for example, educationally handicapped, may have been placed there for five different reasons. The 15 students who went into self-contained special education programs (see Table 12.2) were referred for different reasons. The EH or LD or SLH label does not automatically inform educators about the child's individual characteristics. The child who is placed into an LD program may have similar educational "needs" to those of a child in the regular education classroom. The diversity among children's needs is as great as the diversity among schools and their individual programs. An increasing number of children are being labeled handicapped and consequently placed into "special" classes. A child who has been diagnosed as having poor reading comprehension or who has poor peer relations is as likely to be placed into a special education program as a deaf child or a child with multiple physical handicaps. "Legally," the labels tell us the institutional needs of children. For example, in the case of the LD child, how much time will be spent in the regular classroom and how much time in the special education class. More importantly, however, the official and legal labels do not tell us much about the referred child's individualized education program (IEP). Unfortunately it is the institutional label of EH or LD that follows the child throughout his or her career in school, rather than the IEP.

On the surface, referral reasons are considered merely descriptive, such as "slow learner" or "poor peer relations," but they are, in fact, attributive and stigmatizing ascriptions that invoke certain previously established traditional and institutional standards of evaluative judgments. The teacher's original label of "referred" student carries with it throughout the rest of the process an underlying pattern for the decision maker to explain and verify the student's identity in terms of the preestablished label "referred." For example, the student's possession of one learning disability trait (for example, poor reading comprehension) may carry a more generalized symbolic value, so that educators may automatically assume that the student possesses other stigmatizing traits allegedly associated with it, or at least other identifications are made. For instance, a student who displays poor reading comprehension may be presumed to have other "academic deficiencies," have poor peer relations, have emotional and psychological anxieties, come from a home where either the parents push too hard or don't care enough, and so on. This kind of "prospective reasoning" (Schutz, 1962;

Cicourel, 1973) assumes a constant relationship between an individual event and general occurrences. At the E & P committee placement meeting, "retrospective reasoning" (Shutz, 1962; Cicourel, 1973) mediates and decision makers rely heavily on inference, producing several "because" motives by taking the present information or label (for example, EH) and formulate it in terms of a past situation. For example, "Kenny scored low on the block design test because he is educationally handicapped." Such package deals of retrospective-prospective thinking place the burden on the child, rather than upon the teachers, testers, school, or society. This form of reasoning generates distorted syllogisms like: "Men die. Grass dies. Men are grass." Or, one that actually comes from our study: Marc has trouble with personal relationships. Learning disabled children have poor peer relations. Marc is learning disabled."

INSTITUTIONAL ADAPTATIONS TO LEGAL MANDATES

The expressed purpose of PL 94-142, and Assembly Bill (AB) 1250, its counterpart in Coast District's state, is individualized instruction—locating the best learning environment for the student with special education needs. In order to insure that school districts achieve these goals, specific requirements are mandated by the law. Notable in this regard are: the composition of decision-making groups identifying, assessing, and placing special education students; the need to obtain parents' informed written consent for special education actions; a specific sequence of events in which the steps in the referral process are to be carried out; and a time frame in which the referral process is to be completed.

The temporal parameters, personnel requirements, and informed consent obligations dictated by the passage of the law have created practical problems for school districts. The Coast District, like other districts, had to create new working arrangements in order to conform to these new requirements. This was not simply a matter of matching previously established operating procedures to new problems. The new law forced districts to develop entirely new ways of operating. In the case of the Coast District, it was often impossible to meet the legal requirements of PL 94-142 with the human and material resources available.

Nevertheless, students were somehow identified, somehow assessed, and somehow placed; the referral system was constantly active. That is, the district adapted to the requirements of the law. The adaptations that the district made to the constraints imposed by the law within the practical circumstances that seem to be inherent in institutionalized educational practice are the topic of the following discussion.

Creative Bookkeeping

The law requires school districts to conform to a rigid time schedule during the referral process. Once a child has been referred (usually, but not necessarily, by a teacher), the appropriate special education staff has 15 school days in which to assess the student's needs to develop an assessment plan and notify and send the assessment plan to the student's parents. Once informed consent is received from the parents for assessment, an eligibility and placement meeting must be held within 35 days, wherein an appropriate educational program is outlined for the student. Within 20 school days of the E&P meeting, the student must be enrolled in the prescribed special education program. That is, the school district has 70 school days in which to identify, assess, and place a student in a special education program.

For the variety of practical reasons described in the second section of this chapter, it was extremely difficult for the school district to complete a case within the time limits imposed by the law. The lack of adequate staff, the itinerant status of the school psychologists, the unavailability of material resources, the difficulty in obtaining records from other districts and permissions from parents, and other factors all contributed to considerable time delays.

The school district responded to this constraint on its operating procedure in creative ways. Perhaps the most creative concerned bookkeeping practices. It turns out that 15 working days is not long enough to process a referral from the teacher through the principal to the SAT, develop an assessment plan, and notify the student's parents. The backlog of cases and problems in simply scheduling a meeting often delayed the first presentation of a case to an SAT for weeks, and that action was preliminary to the construction of an assessment plan, the real heart of the initial referral process.

The district responded to this time constraint in a manner reminiscent of the procedure used in the U.S. Senate to complete business near the end of a session; the clock was stopped on this phase of the referral process. Instead of dating a referral form on the day that a teacher filled it out, the form was not dated until the day it was actually presented to an SAT meeting. This practice cut weeks from the amount of time a student's case was in the referral system. For example, if a case was scheduled to be discussed at an SAT meeting on the first Monday of the month, but had to be postponed because previous cases were not completed, the postponement was not part of the calculation of time in the referral system. The clock did not start on the case until it was actually heard by the committee. Even with the introduction of this innovative bookkeeping practice, the amount of time required to process a case through the referral system from referral to placement was longer than the time frame specified by law.

The practice of "stopping the clock" was made possible by the institutional equivalent of the enactment of "performative speech acts." According to Austin (1961), a "performative" is a speech act that by its very utterance accomplishes a social action. For example, saying to another person "I promise" accomplishes the act of promising. Likewise, under the proper circumstances—that is, with the right people present, and at the right time and place— saying "I do" ratifies a marriage, and saying "I'm sorry" accomplishes an apology.

In effect, educators in this district made a technical distinction between "teacher notifications" and "official referrals." Teacher notifications were the reports made by the teacher or other school official to the SAT about a student who needed special help, and official referrals were those same reports dated on the day the case was actually presented to the SAT. There was no substantial difference between the two reports, save the date stamp on the forms. Thus, the performative act of date-stamping was functionally equivalent to saying "I do." Just as the one transforms a single person into a married one, the other transforms an informal teacher notification into an official referral. This technical distinction was evident in the contrast between educators' everyday discourse and their official texts. On the one hand, for official record keeping and documentary purposes, educators, especially those in executive positions, were careful not to refer to a case as a referral unless it had been duly considered by the SAT. On the other hand, educators, especially those teachers who initiated the referral process, talked often, and at great length, about students as "referrals," including those for whom they were considering requesting special help, those for whom they had filled out forms, and those who had been considered by official committees.

This device of distinguishing between referrals in text and in discourse also points out yet another way in which the identity of a child is determined by institutional practice. Regardless of his classroom behavior or academic performance, a "student" is not "a referral student," institutionally speaking, until the date has been stamped on his case.

Formalized Informality

This informal method of dealing with constraints on operating procedure was complemented by a formalized method of delineating between less serious and more serious special education cases. It is practically impossible for all the children referred to be assigned to special education programs within the district because there are just not enough spaces available. Coupled with this unavailability of resources are financial reasons not to place students in programs outside the district. In addition, professionals (teachers, psychologists, other specialists) are expected to "handle" problems arising within their areas of expertise.

The temporal constraints just discussed, a system with too many students and too few resources, fiscal incentives, and professional ideology combined to contribute to the construction of an alternative method of processing referral cases. Students of organizational life (for example, Dalton, 1959) might predict that these educators, faced with very strict rules, would develop informal methods of solving problems. When we first saw the constraints under which the educators were trying to operate in this district, we, too, expected to see the development of informal practices, such as unofficial discussions, surreptitious classroom visits, clandestine decisions in teachers' lounges.

We were wrong, however; rather, we were not right enough. Instead of adopting informal methods of circumventing rigid legal requirements, the educators in this district built informal procedures right into the formal system. A Child Guidance Team was formed at each school site. This team was composed of a special education teacher, the nurse, the principal, and the reading teacher. Under this system, when a teacher identifies a child as having a learning difficulty, the case is referred to the Child Guidance Team, and not directly to the SAT. It is then the responsibility of the Child Guidance Team to evaluate the merits of the case.

It is important to note at this point that an "official referral" has not been declared. While an unofficial teacher notification exists in everyday discourse, this everyday discourse has not been transformed into official texts. Therefore, the requirements to "start the clock" and to obtain parental permission before conducting assessment do not apply.

If the Child Guidance Team concluded that some sort of evaluation seemed to be warranted, then the special education teacher, nurse, or reading specialist was dispatched to make "unofficial" assessments, classroom visits, and child interviews. The results of these informal assessments were reported to the Child Guidance Team. Based on this preliminary and informal information, the Child Guidance Team either referred the case to the SAT or recommended that no further action be taken on the case.

The degree of formality is the interesting aspect of this district's response to legal requirements to operate within certain time constraints. Instead of circumventing the law by informal means, this district made an informal component the first stage of a highly formal bureaucratic system.

The introduction of the Child Guidance Team into the referral system requires reformulation of the referral process. Figure 12.3 modifies Figure 12.1 to show this innovation.

Placement by Available Category

The construction of an individualized education plan for students with special needs is envisioned in theory by some special educators, advocates (such as the Council for Exceptional Children), and parents as a sequential process in which the child is identified as a candidate for special education through screening or by a teacher, the child is referred for assessment (with parental permission), and once assessment is completed an eligibility and placement meeting is held. That is, the process should proceed from "referral" to "placement" as depicted in Figure 12.1.

During placement meetings, the goals and objectives for the child's education are agreed upon, the services to be provided to the child are spelled out, educational criteria are specified, and a written plan is prepared, which is then signed by the parent. Just as there are statutes mandating a certain order of events in the referral process, it is our understanding that the law implies a certain temporal order for the conduct of the placement meetings:

1. The child's present level of performance would be determined by members of the committee who have information about the child.
2. Goals and objectives would be written based on the discrepancy between the child's actual and expected levels of performance.
3. The parents' rights to educational services, and the range of available services, would be explained.
4. The committee would reach a decision about the appropriate placement for the child based on those goals and objectives.

In practice, this sequence of events was not followed. The E&P meetings that we observed did not have that temporal order. The actual order of events was the following:

1. The presentation of information by committee members (same as 1 above).
2. The placement decision (4 above).
3. The explanation of parents' rights (3 above).
4. The writing of goals and objectives (2 above).

FIGURE 12.3

Referral Process as of August 1, 1980

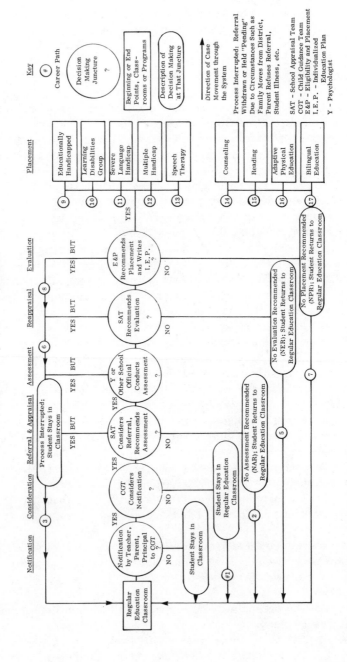

Source: Compiled by the authors.

The variation between the expected and the actual order of events in placement meetings suggests that the goals and objectives for the individual child were not written first and then the services suggested to meet these goals. Instead, placement was selected in the context of available services.

The occurrence of the explanation of parents' rights after the placement decision, but before the goals and objectives were written, was particularly telling in this regard. The following was typical of the statements read to parents during placement meetings:

> District Rep: Mrs. Ladd, if we, um, after evaluating Shane find that, um, we don't have the proper placement, the classroom available, appropriate placement for Shane, you can request—or you have rights to private school and you can request that. We've made the decision that we do have a class available for Shane to go into.

This statement indicates that the availability of an educational program had been previously determined, which effectively forecloses discussion of educational alternatives.

The "placement" column in Figure 12.1 presents the range of possibilities for special education within the district; but this range of possibilities was not presented to parents during placement meetings. At most, the possibility of placement in one or two closely related programs was presented, for example, an LDC or an EH placement. Even then, the possibilities were not presented as alternatives being weighed equally in the balance, but one was presented as the preferred option, and the other as a secondary consideration. For example:

> Case Carrier: Does the committee agree that the, um, learning disabilities placement might benefit him?
>
> Principal: I think we agree.
>
> Case Carrier: We're not considering then a special day class at all for him.
>
> Special Education Teacher: I wouldn't at this point.
>
> Many: No.

One could conclude from this discussion that the LDC placement was previously considered. This placement outcome was not so much a decision reached in this meeting as it was a ratification of actions that took place at previous stages in the decision-making process.

In fact, the ratification of early decisions was a general feature of E&P meetings. We found that considerable preplacement planning preceded the formal placement meeting. The reappraisal meetings identified in Figure 12.1 often served this purpose. They were occasions to prepare the paperwork needed in the placement meeting. The preplanning saved considerable time during placement meetings that were attended by several highly paid professionals with busy schedules. The reappraisal meetings were also viewed as an opportunity for the staff to reach a consensus before meeting with parents. The consensus could be either a gentle way of informing the parent of the child's problem or a defensive strategy for dealing with a parent aggressively seeking expensive service outside the district. The fact that only one of the 54 cases brought before E&P committees did not result in a special education placement is further evidence that at least some members of the committee had some ideas where the child would be placed very early in the referral process (see career path 7 in Table 12.1).

This ratification of decisions reached at earlier stages or events in the referral process is similar to the process by which a person becomes transformed from a "normal person" to a "mentally ill patient" (Goffman, 1961; Scheff, 1966). The process of the construction of mental illness starts when a person presents himself or herself to a public medical person. The entrance of a specialist into a situation that has been defined as "something wrong with someone here" establishes the presumption of a defect within the individual. This presumption is reaffirmed as the person, now a patient, goes through successive stages of the psychiatric intake process until, finally, the staff and patient alike accept the definition.

The equivalent process operates in the school context. The presumption is initiated by the classroom teacher, who often has only a general notion that a student "is in trouble" or "needs help." This original, rather general attribution establishes the presumption of a defect within the student. This attribution becomes refined as more and more institutional machinery is applied to the case, until, finally, by the placement meeting, only a parent's refusal to sign the IEP is likely to change the assumed placement.

This ratification of decisions between successive events or stages in a diagnostic process is similar to what Elstein et al. (1978) found within one particular diagnostic event. They report that doctors tend to confirm a particular hypothesis about the cause of a disease early in the diagnosis of a patient, well before most of the data have been obtained. Instead of weighing evidence to eliminate a number of possibly competing hypotheses, doctors take steps that tend to confirm the hypothesis generated early in the diagnosis, thus ratifying positions developed earlier.

CONCLUSIONS

The observation that individual education plans and placement decisions were rarely developed in the manner implied by law could be taken as an indictment against a school district for maliciously failing to comply with federal and state laws. Before such a conclusion is reached, we need to examine the assumptions about human information processing and social organizations that are built into the law, and to examine the relations between federal policy and local practice.

Cognitive and Organizational Limitations
on Rationality

In prescribing a particular temporal sequence for decision making, and by presuming that placement decisions would be made by considering the full range of placement possibilities, the law is assuming that school districts are rational organizations. The origins of this "rational model" (Benson, 1977) are in Weber's (1947, 1958) analysis of bureaucracy. Parsons' (1932) delineation of the means-end schema in terms of scientifically rational criteria further refined this model.

There is an "optimizing" strategy inherent in the rational model. It has the goal of making the best decision by maximizing the positive consequences and minimizing the negative consequences. However, a wide range of evidence is accumulating that indicates human beings rarely adopt this maximizing decision-making posture. One set of accounts explains the gap between the ideal rational model and real practice as a limitation in human information processing capacity. For example, Simon (1976:xxviii) says that people "have not the wits to maximize."

People do not maximize because "determining all the potentially favorable and unfavorable aspects of all the feasible courses of action would require the decision maker to process so much information that impossible demands would be placed on his resources and mental capacities" (Janis and Mann, 1977:22). While attempting to acquire the degree of knowledge needed to anticipate alternative outcomes, the decision maker is likely to be overwhelmed by information. "So many relevant variables may have to be taken into account that they can not be all kept in mind at the same time. The number of crucially relevant categories needed for rational decision making usually exceeds the limits of man's capacity for processing information in immediate memory" (Miller, 1956:95). Handicapped by the shortcomings of the human mind, the decision maker's atten-

tion, asserts Simon, "shifts from one value to another with consequent shifts in preference" (Janis and Mann, 1977:22).

Thus, one account for the gap between the ideal model and
real practice is a cognitive limitation, a failure, really, of the individual decision maker. The decision maker viewed from the cognitive point of view is depicted as working alone, or in isolation.
He makes mistakes and errors because he can't keep enough information in his head, or because he is inundated with too much information. Nevertheless, there is a glimmer of hope in the cognitive
characterization, based on the view of the perfectability of this "imperfect" (Watkins, 1970) or "reluctant" (Janis and Mann, 1977) decision maker. Errors imply corrections: If people make mistakes,
mistakes can be corrected.

While we would agree with proponents of rational theories of
organizations that there is a gap between the rational model of decision making and the actual day-to-day practices of identifying,
assessing, and placing students in this school district, we would
disagree with them about the reasons for this gap. From the point
of rational theories of organizations, this school district, like many
other social organizations, would be viewed as "pathological" (March
and Olsen, 1976) because individual decision makers are failing to
consider a wide range of alternatives, carefully weigh evidence, re-
examine alternatives, and so on. From our point of view, the gap
between the real and the ideal is not a matter of individual cognitive
limitations. What the rational organizational theorist posits as individual failures or cognitive limitations seem to us to be features
inherent in the organization of social groups. People do not act
irrationally because they lack cognitive capacity. Organizational
features arrange for decision making to take place in the way we
have observed.

We find educational decision makers to be acting rationally,
given the constraints they face. The educators are operating in
contexts that make it impossible to conform to the tenets of the
rational model. The litany of practical circumstances presented in
this chapter suggests that school districts do not have the unlimited
access to the unlimited resources presupposed by the rational model.
Given these limitations, "optimizing" does not seem to be the optimal strategy for decision making in organizations. The rational
model requires decision makers to consider the combination of all
possibilities, in all their consequences. A certain fastidiousness
is required when trying to consider all the alternatives, which can
blind the decision maker to an appreciation for the most important
factors that need to be taken into account. Furthermore, the rational
model assumes that all factors have an equal weight—but they may
not. In dealing with comparable problems, prior experience may

tell the decision maker that it is best to be highly selective, and to pay attention to a few, salient alternatives, which (s)he knows well in advance, instead of painstakingly computing the combination of all possibilities. As Watkins (1970:206) says: "A well known obstacle to computerizing chess is the lack of any known way to program a computer to concentrate on interesting developments: like the ideal decision maker of normative theory, the computer prefers to survey the entire board and take every possibility into account."

Thus, in accounting for the gap between ideal and real, we are more likely to find fault with the rational model of decision making itself than we are with the individual decision makers. Because the features that account for this gap are social or organizational, not psychological or cognitive in locus, they are not "errors to be corrected"—at least not by trying to improve an individual's memory, retrieval, or sorting skills. Improvements in decision making, if they are to come at all, will come from changing the constraints on decision makers, not by modifying human information processing capacity.

Government Policy and Local Practice[5]

There are two major positions concerning the impact of government policy on local organizations. Pressman and Wildavsky (1973) present the view that government policy becomes ineffectual in the face of local exigencies. Original policy intentions are diluted because power is diffused among multiple decision makers at the local level.

Attewell and Gerstein (1979) challenge this position. While agreeing that many government policies fail, they disagree that the source of the failure has to do with the complexities of implementation at the local level. They find fault with the policies themselves: "the failure of local efforts is seen to flow systematically from the structure of policy making, especially insofar as contradictory efforts, embodied in policy, undermine crucial resources that local agencies require in order to gain the compliance of their clients on a day to day basis" (Attewell and Gerstein, 1979:311).

We would like to examine these two positions in light of our case study, while keeping in mind that the structure of the federal law we are observing being implemented is not the same as those described by Attewell and Gerstein or Pressman and Wildavsky. For example, the policy studied by Attewell and Gerstein is much more specific in its regulations than the Education for All Handicapped Children law. These differences make strict determinations about either of these theories based on our case study risky. Nevertheless, some comparisons are in order.

If we approach the issue of the efficacy of the law by considering the broad goals of providing more equal educational opportunity for greater numbers of handicapped children, then we would have to conclude that the law has been somewhat successful. However, if we consider the more instrumental definition of more educational opportunity for handicapped children—that local school districts should have identified and be serving 12 percent of the school population—then we would have to conclude that the law has not been successful, at least not yet.

The next issue concerns the reason for this discrepancy. Is it because of failures at the local level, as Pressman and Wildavsky suggest, or is it due to the policy itself, as Attewell and Gerstein suggest? The evidence from our case study does not allow us to make a clear-cut distinction between the two interpretations. We find elements of both and reasons to exclude aspects of each argument.

We have certainly uncovered ample evidence of what Pressman and Wildavsky call "local exigencies." These "practical circumstances," which are the inherent features of the presentation of education in a bureaucratic mode, make the day-to-day conduct of regular education difficult, to say nothing of the implementation of a federal law for special children. While these bureaucratic arrangements certainly impinge upon the identification, assessment, and treatment of special education students, we do not have the evidence to conclude that these practical circumstances lead to mistakes in information processing that, in turn, cause the implementation of the law to fail. Nor do we observe the "diffusion of power" that Pressman and Wildavsky talk about as a source of failure to implement federal policy.

We also see some but not all elements of the Attewell and Gerstein analysis of the discrepancy between federal law and local pressure. Attewell and Gerstein (1979:311) say: "under certain specifiable conditions, federal policy can be seen to directly determine local program behavior even down to the microscopic level." Many of the daily activities of educators in this district, including their practices of "searching" for special education students, curtailing referrals at the end of the year, "creative bookkeeping," and "formalized informality," were the direct result of the district's attempts to implement the law. These, then, are definite places where sociopolitical forces that shape federal policy subsequently influence the practical realm of daily, organizational life.

We certainly see evidence of "contradictory interests embodied in policy" (Attewell and Gerstein, 1979:311) concerning the Education for All Handicapped Students law. There are contradictions within the law itself, as districts are told, on the one hand, to seek "least restrictive environments" for their special education children, involve parents in decision making, and then are told, on the other hand, to process students within a specified period of time, and use local resources to provide an appropriate education. The advent of PL 94-142 comes at a time when academic and psychological evaluation is being severely criticized and questioned as a reliable device to evaluate mental abilities and scholastic achievement. A related concern is the charge that certain ethnic groups have been inordinately represented in special education programs, and have been incorrectly labeled. In addition, the law comes on the heels of the Bilingual Education Act, which, in many cases, addresses the same population of students. In attending to the provisions of the law, school personnel must strike a delicate balance between children's right to be "normal" and their rights to be "exceptional," which has inherent contradictions. Thus, not only must the school district deal with contradictions within the law itself, but they also must deal with the relationship between this and other laws and respond to social movements, such as the protest against evaluative devices.

Attewell and Gerstein (1979:318) go on to say: "program responses to governmental regulation is a progressive displacement of organizational goals, away from therapeutic aims per se, toward an increasing concern with the manipulation of clinic practices in order to look good to outside agencies, particularly to powerful surveillance and funding agencies." We are not sure that we saw the "displacement" of organizational goals, as much as we saw the transformation of organizational practice in order to complete work at the local level, and thereby meet the demands of federal policy. What we have termed "creative bookkeeping" and "formalized informality" was not so much the substitution of one organizational goal for another, as it was manipulation of daily practice to achieve two goals simultaneously: the identification and education of special education students, and the compliance with federal guidelines concerning processing time and informed consent.

We found, as did Attewell and Gerstein, that there was an obvious concern among the people at the local level to meet the requirements of the federal policy. The motivations for this concern with compliance, however, seem to be different among educators than those that Attewell and Gerstein suggest exist among drug-law enforcers. The educators did not seem to conform with federal policy for "presentational reasons" (Attewell and Gerstein, 1979:326), that is, "to look good." Rather, their motivation for compliance was fear of reprisal, either in the form of a lawsuit brought by an irate parent[6] or in the form of governmental sanction.

In sum, we find elements of both the Pressman and Wildavsky and the Attewell and Gerstein interpretations in the manner in which the Coast District is implementing federal (and state) policy. This mixture of elements leads us to conclude that the gap between federal policy and local implementation is not a simple matter of either "local exigencies" or "the structure of federal policy."

Attewell and Gerstein overemphasize the degree of "coupling" (March and Olsen, 1976; Weick, 1976) between federal and local levels, and underestimate the adaptability of local organizations. In attempting to meet the demands of federally imposed policies, they say local agencies must substitute instrumental goals for loftier ones, which results in dysfunctional arrangements at the local level. This view implies that local agencies are powerless in the face of sweeping federal legislation to which they must comply.

If Attewell and Gerstein overemphasize the degree of fit between federal and local agencies, then Pressman and Wildavsky overestimate it. To Pressman and Wildavsky, local agencies are not just "loosely coupled" (March and Olsen, 1976; Weick, 1976) to federal agencies, they are completely uncoupled; that is, they enjoy a more or less autonomous position in relation to higher level government policies.

We would like to suggest that government policies are neither fully implemented at the local level (at least not according to the letter of the law), nor are they summarily circumvented by local implementers. The local agency, in this case a school district, institutes practices to implement the law, which thereby modifies the law. These modifications, rather than leading to a dysfunctional adaptation, as Attewell and Gerstein suggest, lead to a functional adaptation for those who must put the law into practice at the day-to-day, face-to-face level of interaction. Our observations show that governmental mandate indeed influences those at the microscopic level of everyday action, but people are not powerless in the grasp of federal laws. While people at the local level have a certain flexibility in action, due in part to the "loose coupling" between federal and local agencies, they do not have the power to render federal law impotent by circumvention.

These opposing views do not seem to consider features of diversity (or flexibility) that Pressman and Wildavsky see as a deterrent to the implementation of federal laws, and adaptation, which Attewell and Gerstein see as dysfunctional. Faced with federal and state mandates, educators in local school districts must attend to the formal policies and procedures outlined in the laws for identifying, assessing, and placing students in special education programs. However, the processes by which these goals are accomplished are negotiable within a given school system. The basic letter of the law must be, and will be, adhered to, even if in a perfunctory way. However, these processes of negotiation are not as accountable to federal agencies as are the products of the process. These informal process mechanisms can even be translated into flow charts, official descriptions of procedure, and rhetorics of compliance, which give every indication that the district is strictly adhering to the federal requirements and guidelines. These practices of formalizing the informal emerge from attempts to informalize the formal, that is, to translate federal mandates into everyday terms and practices that educators can work with. The repacking of the informal, practical methods back into formal mechanisms and rhetorics is not a matter of deception on the part of local agencies. It is a realistic method of dealing with internal contradictions within the law, its relation to the policies, and the need to conduct education on a daily basis.

While Attewell and Gerstein maintain that the implementation of laws fails because government policies make them fail, and Pressman and Wildavsky maintain that the implementation of laws fails because of extended central control at the local level, we come to a different conclusion. The findings of our study thus far seem to indicate that the implementation of federal policy succeeds, and succeeds all too well perhaps, at least at the surface, textual level where the technical requisites of the law are to be met. It is not as clear, however, whether this success in the textual realm is matched by success in the realm of everyday discourse, that is, in daily educational practice, where equal educational opportunity is to be provided to all handicapped students.

NOTES

1. One of these cases lacked sufficient information to process. For the most part we will consider 140 cases in our analysis. Sixteen additional cases were considered during this year. These were referrals from special education teachers, suggesting that students were ready for "mainstreaming" or a modification in their indidualized assessment plan. The "replacement" of students in regular classrooms is beyond the scope of this study, and these cases will not be considered in the following discussions.

2. Unfortunately, the consequences of this observation do not appear in the statistical information presented in the tables of this chapter. The absence, or nonoccurrence, of a referral cannot be shown as figures on a table or points on a graph. The consequences of this informal screening procedure are but one of the many to be discussed in this chapter and in our subsequent work concerning the problems involved in the uncritical use of official statistics (Kitsuse

and Cicourel, 1962). Just as in the case of unreported crimes, official records of referrals and placements do not reflect the day-to-day negotiations that constitute the determination of a special or normal student.

3. We said "referred officially" in this sentence on purpose. As we will discuss in a following section, the district distinguished between the date a teacher identified a student for referral and the date it was officially considered in the referral system.

4. This practice is not unique to this district. Inquiry into practices in another large metropolitan area of the state revealed a much more blatant search for special education candidates. Part-time personnel were hired in that area for the express purpose of a mass screening for special education children. Pressure was so great upon testing personnel to pursue testing to the point where a problem was located, that one psychological tester refused to continue on ethical grounds.

5. This is the title of a recent article by Attewell and Gerstein (1979), which stimulated many of the ideas in this section.

6. A lawsuit filed in the U.S. District Court, March 24, 1980, exemplifies this contradiction. The parents of a handicapped boy have sued the San Diego Unified School District, charging that his educational rights have been violated because the district took 18 months to process his case and place him in a special home for handicapped youngsters at school expense. The suit charges that it took two years of administrative hearings and a final appeal to the State Superintendent of Education before the student was placed in a special school after the district had determined that there were no educational facilities available within the district. (Los Angeles Times, May 26, 1980.)

REFERENCES

Apple, M. W. 1979. Ideology and Curriculum. London: Routledge & Kegan Paul.

Attewell, P., and D. R. Gerstein. 1979. "Government Policy and Local Practice." American Sociological Review 44:311-27.

Austin, J. L. 1961. Philosophical Papers. London: Oxford University Press.

Benson, J. K. 1977. "Innovation and Crisis in Organizational Analysis." Sociological Quarterly 18:3-16.

Bereiter, K., and S. Engleman. 1972. Teaching the Disadvantaged Child in the Preschool. Englewood Cliffs, N.J.: Prentice-Hall.

Bowles, S., and H. Gintes. 1976. Schooling in Capitalist America. New York: Basic Books.

Brice-Heath, S. 1981. "Ethnography in Education: Toward Defining the Essentials." In Ethnography and Education: Children In and Out of Schools, edited by P. Gilmore. Philadelphia: University of Pennsylvania Press.

Buckholdt, D. R., and J. F. Gubrium. 1979. Caretakers. Los Angeles: Sage Publications.

Cicourel, A. V. 1975. "Discourse and Text." Versus, September-December, pp. 33-84.

Cicourel, A. V. 1973. Cognitive Sociology: Language and Meaning in Social Interaction. London: Penguin.

Coleman, J. S., et al. 1966. Equality of Educational Opportunity. Washington, D.C.: U.S. Government Printing Office.

Dalton, M. 1959. Men Who Manage. New York: John Wiley.

Elstein, A. S., L. S. Shulman, and S. V. Sprafka. 1978. Medical Problem Solving. Cambridge, Mass.: Harvard University Press.

Erickson, F., and J. J. Shultz. 1980. Talking to the Man: Social and Cultural Organization of Communication in Counselling Interviews. New York: Academic Press.

Garfinkel, H. 1967. Studies in Ethnomethodology. Englewood Cliffs, N.J.: Prentice-Hall.

Goffman, E. 1961. Asylums: Essays on the Social Situation of Mental Patients and Other Inmates. Garden City, N.Y.: Anchor Books.

Goffman, I. 1963. Stigma. Englewood Cliffs, N.J.: Prentice-Hall.

Herrnstein, R. J. 1974. I.Q. in the Meritocracy. Boston: Little, Brown.

Hymes, D. 1980. "Educational Ethnology." Anthropology and Education Quarterly 11, no. 1:3-8.

Hymes, D. 1979. "What Is Ethnography." In Ethnography and Education: Children In and Out of Schools, edited by P. Gilmore. Philadelphia: University of Pennsylvania Press.

Janis, I., and L. Mann. 1978. Decision Making. New York: The Free Press.

Jencks, C. 1972. Inequality. New York: Basic Books.

Jensen, A. R. 1980. Bias in Mental Testing. New York: The Free Press.

Jensen, A. R. 1969. "How Much Can We Boost I.Q. and Scholastic Achievement?" Harvard Educational Review 39, no. 1:1-123.

Jones, P. R. 1979. "Can Old Dogs Be Taught New Tricks?" Journal of Education 161, no. 3:23-39.

Kitsuse, J., and A. V. Cicourel. 1963. "The Use of Official Statistics." Social Problems 11, no. 2:131-39.

LCHC (Laboratory of Comparative Human Cognition, University of California, San Diego. 1980. "Intelligence as a Cultural Practice." In Handbook of Intelligence, edited by W. Sternberg. New York: Cambridge University Press.

March, J. A., and J. P. Olsen. 1976. Ambiguity and Choice in Organizations. Bergen: Universitetsforlaget.

McDermott, R. P., K. Gospodinoff, and J. Aron. 1978. "Criteria for an Ethnographically Adequate Description of Concerted Activities and Their Contexts. Semiotica 24.

Mehan, H. 1979. Learning Lessons. Cambridge, Mass.: Harvard University Press.

Mehan, H. 1978. "Structuring School Structure." Harvard Educational Review 45, no. 1:311-38.

Mehan, H., and H. Wood. 1975. The Reality of Ethnomethodology. New York: Wiley Interscience.

Mercer, J. 1974. Labelling the Mentally Retarded. Berkeley: University of California Press.

Miller, G. A. 1956. "The Magic Number Seven Plus or Minus 2: Some Limits on Our Capacity for Processing Information." Psychology Review 63:81-97.

Ogden, C. K., and I. A. Richards. 1934. The Meaning of Meaning. New York: Harcourt & Brace.

Parsons, T. 1959. "The School as a Social System." Harvard Educational Review 29:297-318.

Parsons, T. 1932. The Structure of Social Action. Glencoe, Ill.: The Free Press.

Pressman, J., and A. B. Wildavsky. 1973. Implementation. Berkeley: University of California Press.

Sanday, P. 1979. "The Ethnographic Paradigm(s)." Administrative Science Quarterly, December, pp. 527-38.

Scheff, T. J. 1966. Being Mentally Ill: A Sociological Theory. Chicago: Aldine.

Schutz, A. 1962. Collected Papers I: The Problem of Social Reality. The Hague: Martinus Nijhoff.

Simon, N. 1976. Administrative Behavior. New York: The Free Press.

USOE (U.S. Office of Education). 1979. Progress Toward a Free Appropriate Public Education. First Report to Congress on the Implementation of PL 94-142. Washington, D.C.

Watkins, J. 1970. "Imperfect Rationality." In Explanation in the Behavioral Sciences, edited by R. Borger and F. Cioffi. Cambridge: Cambridge University Press.

Weber, M. 1958. "Bureaucracy." In From Max Weber: Essays in Sociology, edited by H. Gerth and C. W. Mills. New York: Oxford University Press.

Weber, M. 1947. The Theory of Social and Economic Organization. Translated by A. M. Henderson and T. Parsons. New York: The Free Press.

Weick, K. 1976. "Educational Organizations as Loosely Coupled Systems." Administrative Science Quarterly 21:1-19.

13

SUPERINTENDENT POWER RETENTION

Martin Burlingame

I seriously doubt that honesty is the best policy for superintendents who wish to retain power. It may well be that honesty does work well if there are agreements about goals sought, means used, roles of participants, and historical precedents—but superintendents know well that schools as organizations lack these characteristics. As superintendents in the field know all too well, there are numerous conflicts over goals, means, roles, and the past.

Our academic image of the school as an organization, and our scholarly images of educational leadership and administration, have been abruptly altered. The 1970s saw James G. March and others describe educational organizations as "organized anarchies."[1] These authors popularized to the scholarly community concepts such as "ambiguous and conflicting goals," "unclear technologies," "fluid participation," "uncertain history," and "loose coupling." Schools were seen from this perspective as organizations in which what happened at one level or in one subunit had almost no impact on other levels or subunits. Attempts to generate clear and specific goals produced either debilitating conflicts or deliberate neglect, to create specified technologies occasioned either enthusiastic support or subtle insubordination, to achieve consensus often resulted in even greater balkanization, and to fulfill goals of distant planners unaware of the realities of schools guaranteed a sad farce. Such scholarly descriptions also had major implications for those who are responsible for training the future leaders and administrators of schools.

This chapter seeks to examine some of the implications of those newer views about educational organizations for those who train and those who act as school superintendents. The chapter begins with three major propositions about schools as organizations.

These propositions, in turn, lead to a discussion of the importance of mystification and cover-up. These processes are viewed as neutral—neither good nor bad but available. Against these more generic propositions, the third and longest section details six hierarchic rules for superintendent power retention. These rules lead to the final section analyzing the martyrdom of superintendents.

THREE PROPOSITIONS

The literature of the 1970s suggests the general usefulness of three propositions about schools as organizations.

Proposition 1

While individuals know what they are about in their specific roles, for example, classroom instruction, schools as organizations do not know what they are about. [2]

My first point is that while individual teachers, students, and principals know what they are doing in their individual roles, there is no collective sense of purpose or mission that dominates schools as organizations. The actors in the school are busy pursuing those activities and goals, such as classroom instruction, they see as important. In that sense, each has some understanding of what he or she is doing, of why she or he is doing it, and where it leads. However, these autonomous and rational actors have only the weakest of images of what the total pattern of organizational intentions looks like, let alone means. The school itself is like some lower-order organism, lacking a brain and a central nervous system that integrates multiple acts. The individual actors within the system, however, have brains and central nervous systems but are afflicted with organizational myopia.

Proposition 2

Since most individuals know what they are about in schools, individual actors in schools stress participation, not examination.

Fernandez, for example, notes that field data of anthropologists based on extensive discussions with actors (in this case, members of a Fang reform religious cult) "remind us of the fact of variation in the individual interpretation of commonly experienced phenomena."[3] Fernandez argues that these variations in interpretations of key religious symbols suggest that often in social interaction "participation" is more important than "thought." Most social settings stress agreements to act in certain ways when confronted by social stimuli. These agreements not only insure "smooth coordination of interaction"[4] but also maintain high levels of social consensus. Put in terms of schools, agreements among actors to play roles such as teacher or student appropriately facilitate social action.

Those agreements that aid social consensus also mask disagreements about the larger meanings of such acts—what Fernandez calls "cultural consensus." Fernandez suggests that while members of the Fang reform religious cult exhibit strong agreement about social consensus—about the value of participating with others in the prescribed roles of cult activities—closer examination would find marked differences among actors in their understandings of the larger cultural meanings of cult activities. A fine-grained examination of the participants' espoused cultural ends would disclose sharply different conceptions of the nature and hierarchy of ends to be achieved. Fernandez writes: "Where high social consensus is evident further attempts at the achievement of cultural consensus may be felt to pose . . . too many uncertainties and threats to the cohesiveness already established."[5] Participation along the lines of socially understood and accepted roles facilitates social cohesion not only by masking differences in larger cultural meanings but also by inhibiting those who might seek to examine possible differences.

Through immersion and participation in a stream of commonplace activities, teachers, students, and administrators achieve and maintain "social consensus." These actors subvert both "insiders" and "outsiders" who might expose what may well be major conflicts in "cultural consensus" if they illuminated differing goals held within a single group. I would agree with Fernandez's conclusion that as academics

> we may tend to overlook the obvious fact that there are many situations in which ignorance is institutionalized and in which social consensus, the so-called existential continuum of uninterpreted interaction, is more highly valued. We may always be too persuaded by the Cartesian premise and overlook a widespread postulate, "I participate therefore I am!"[6]

Immersion in the life of the school (not detached reflection about the life of the school) is honored by most actors in schools.

Proposition 3

The actions of individual actors and the stress on participation become the stuff of organizational sagas and fictions.

In his analysis of the development of three colleges (Reed, Antioch, and Swarthmore), Clark found organizational sagas.[7] He argued that

> an organizational saga is a collective understanding of unique accomplishment in a formally established group. The group's definition of the accomplishment, intrinsically historical but embellished through retelling and rewriting, links stages of organizational development. The participants have added affects, an emotional loading, which places their conception between the coolness of rational purpose and the warmth of sentiment found in religion and magic.[8]

These sagas authenticate the purposes that individuals pursue by supporting both their commonalities with others (loyalty) and their minor deviances (breaking new ground as the founders did), thus creating a sense of cultural consensus. These sagas also facilitate social consensus by highlighting the accomplishments and rewards to be earned for those who participate. In this manner sagas serve to constrain those who seek to change the paths of organizations; but if those who seek change do realign organizational goals, new sagas soon develop to justify such changes.

Dubin has noted that organizations also seem to have "fictions."[9] Some of these organizational fictions serve to deal with unknowns—past, present, and future. For example, the history of U.S. education often suffers from fictions about past events. Other fictions disguise the true or emphasize the false. Dubin notes that if the truth is unsettling, "by a kind of silent agreement among members of the organization, this truth is clothed with a fiction."[10] In schools, for example, if teachers know that many students are not achieving at the level anticipated, teachers may suggest a "fiction" that students are not motivated. In contrast, he comments: "Fictions that emphasize the false are characterized by a more deep-seated reluctance to face up to the truth and are more aggressively oriented toward hiding the truth."[11] Such fictions may suggest that although teachers have different styles, they seek the same goals or that (vastly different) families really all want the schools to do the same things to and for their (vastly different) children.

These three propositions illuminate not only the conditions of schools as organizations but also the problems superintendents face as they seek to retain power. Superintendents must diligently seek to control both the internal reality and the public image of schools. In a very real sense, however, superintendents can control neither the internal reality of what goes on in schools nor the public images of schools. Under these conditions of relative powerlessness, superintendents become not only involved in processes such as mystification or cover-up but also become practitioners of tactical rules for survival.

MYSTIFICATION AND COVER-UP

Retention of power by superintendents depends heavily on mystification and cover-up.

Mystification

Our three propositions jointly suggest we should talk about mystification as a process that provides possible public rationales for private individual actors. These intended rational actors do not publicly describe and analyze their private activities, but they do join social groupings within schools that legitimate participation and hinder (if not downright block) analytic examinations, and they do help create generally shared sagas and fictions. These creative acts, however, produce neither a coherent and singular set of sagas or fictions nor a hierarchy of goals. Instead, they produce families of sagas, fictions, and goals, each bearing some common characteristics but also bearing sharply differing idiosyncratic features.

Moreover, we should anticipate that these public products of mystification should deal particularly with issues that are best kept private—ambiguous and conflicting goals, unclear technologies, fluid participants, uncertain history, and loose coupling. These public sagas and fictions should cloud those private issues that might be uncovered by critical examination, should dwell heavily on the values of private participation ("you don't understand because you've never taught subject X or grade Y"), and should help make a private world filled with possible uncertainty, conflict, and tension at least livable, if not always comfortable.

By dealing with these private quandaries the process and public products of mystification impregnate the school with what Weber would call traditional authority. It is an authority based upon the awareness of the common values of a culture, and of the social importance of those common valuings. The potential for cultural dissensus is avoided by the willingness to participate—to accept conventional roles and meanings, and to avoid examining conventions for fear that they might not be adequate.

Mystification thus takes on the shape of deliberate self-fulfilling prophecies about the school that each teacher knows if critically examined may not work, but that must be sustained by group members publicly if there is to be any likelihood for the prophecy ever to be achieved. Each member of the school faculty, therefore, must say that some greater public purpose can be fulfilled, even though each may privately doubt the possibility of accomplishing this goal, for example, the schooling of disadvantaged children. Most traditional authority is derived from sagas proclaiming that at one time the prophecy was fulfilled, the goal achieved. By simply continuing to participate, by both doing what they intend and acting "as if" they see public collective goals being fulfilled, actors increase the likelihood that some larger social good may be achieved accidentally (probabilistically).[12] Critical public examination, in contrast, would reveal significant differences among actors on both individual intentions and goals and small group intentions and goals. Such examinations by individuals are deliberately suppressed or are done only privately.

Cover-up

No matter how well mystification may operate, two problems can always be anticipated. First, individual teachers simply do their jobs as they see fit. While this heightens individual rationality, it means that in a larger sense the school is a crazy quilt of purposes. Superintendents, and others, forced to explain simply and clearly to public audiences what "the school" is doing, simplify, and hence cover up, the complexity and potential conflict of the school. Second, the environment doesn't cooperate—unanticipated events simply "goof up" the best laid cover-ups. What was a trivial and unimportant issue yesterday may well be critical today. Or the significant and all-consuming passion of society on Friday is seen as inconsequential by Monday. Priorities are unstable as the environment shifts and trembles. (One could imagine a school administrator as an individual trying to thread a needle in an earthquake—with someone changing both thread and needle every second.)

On the first point, the opportunities for individual teacher differences are myriad. We shall mention only three possibilities: the overenthusiastic pursuit of a single way of fulfilling a role requirement ("zealot"), the overly critical examination of the process and products of mystification ("cynic"), and the overresponsive or underresponsive reaction to the environment ("faddist" versus "old-liner"). In each of these cases, the rampant stress on teacher "equality" and "autonomy"[13] not only protects other teachers from the possible consequences of such extreme error-making but also insures that some individualistic error-making will occur. Being "lonely" is an essential part of working in schools because loneliness insures that collegial interactions about the core technology are infrequent. Loneliness facilitates the capabilities for individual actors to ignore what others are doing and to pursue diligently the particular means or ends they see as important at that moment.[14]

For those who are forced to represent the school to the public, for example, principals or superintendents, the teacher norms of autonomy and equality mean that what goes on in the school is driven by the interests of individual teachers and students. When pressed to explain why different teachers do different things to and for students, representatives must fall back on a rhetoric of either mystification or cover-up. This rhetoric suggests that those who are doing the work are motivated by a common sense of purpose, are well-trained and certified by knowledgeable experts, and are clearly in command of the situation. This rhetoric emphasizes the supposed influence of the superordinate administrator on subordinate workers, the purported acceptance of a hierarchy of goals by all school personnel, and the imagined close linkage among actors in the system, for example, fifth grade teachers prepare students for sixth grade activities. The cover-up makes the school appear to be a superbly rational, highly programmed machine with almost endless adaptation to input inconsistencies, near limitless capacities in reshaping and redesigning the conversion process, and close to perfect uniformity in schooling outcomes.

This cover-up rhetoric also benefits another purpose. The public stress on the rationality of the larger institution permits teachers and administrators who simply wish to participate to repair to a conventional, convenient, and acceptable way of talking about what they do. For those who participate—probably the bulk of teachers and administrators—the larger public image of corporate rationality provides a handy way of fitting larger purposes to what they say they do. This linkage means that actors can participate without inquiring deeply into either the validity or the reliability of the means or goals espoused. In contrast to those who see themselves as zealot, cynic, faddist, or old-liner, participants may feel less lonely and more collegial because they feel grounded on common purposes and understandings now in vogue. By not examining what they are doing, those who participate are able to make rational their actions as a significant and integral part of a larger set of beneficent activities.

Hence, cover-up activities not only make rational the larger organization to the environment but also provide rationalizations for internal participants. This cover-up activity provides an important element of self-fulfillment to the culture of those who work in schools. The larger sense of public purposes that cover-up activities "create" implies that various actors can "accept the assumption that the organization is effective."[15] Privately believing they are effective may in fact heighten the public effectiveness of teachers.

Cover-up activities also are necessitated by a second major factor—the environment. The constant shifts in demands from a highly segmented and differentiated environment (better, "environments") force administrators and teachers constantly to justify what they are doing. This constant pulling and hauling to stay current produces a vocabulary filled with images of wars between "us" and "them" and a frenetic set of activities in which brief, but frequent, meetings predominate.

One tactic used to lessen the negative consequences of this constraint struggle over priorities is diverting resources to create favorable public images.[16] Athletics, music, drama, or community-service activities all drain some resources from vital educational areas to generate (hopefully) more positive images of the school. While the costs of such activities may seem high to some (gyms larger than libraries or carpeted athletic field but tile floors in classrooms), the argument that larger public benefits exceed these educational costs usually carries the day.

The more general tactic used to cover up most problems generated by environmental demands is the redefinition of the "old" to fulfill the "new." This verbal sleight-of-hand allows the magical transformation of "exams" into "competency-based tests" by the simple stroke of a pen. "The conscious relabeling of routine activities to meet the new demands of publics" may well be the best definition we have in education of "implementation."

Such a redefinition of implementation seems justified on two counts. First, the very nature of the core technology of education—teaching—seems to be individual work.[17] The upshot of the studies of educational implementation conducted over the last decade, for example, provide support for this proposition. We are confident that teachers tacitly "know" what they are doing, what will or will not "work" for them, and what criterion or criteria they use to "evaluate" their work. Efforts by outsiders to introduce "new" ideas are successfully thwarted time and time again as teachers use their tacit knowledge to "select," "adapt," or "totally ignore" what they wish of the new. There is, much literature suggests, no reason to believe that there are controls ("brain," "central nervous system") that determine what all the elements in the school do. Rather, we have in schools a colony of individually purposive cells that are not linked by a brain or a central nervous system but by saga, fiction, custom, and slogan. In this highly differentiated colony, nonetheless, we can anticipate (by chance expectations) that some teachers are actually fulfilling the newest mandate or demand. All administrators have to do is to point to these "innovators," and then suggest that other teachers are moving slowly toward this newest of educational panaceas.

Second, the elaboration of "new" goals may well pull some of those who chose to participate to these new or to some slightly different goals. This pull occurs because of pluralistic ignorance[18] or deliberate ignorance.[19] The argument from pluralistic ignorance would suggest that while each teacher privately knows that the rhetoric of the administrator is fraudulent, in public each teacher can make only supportive statements. Since teachers do not know that other teachers truly believed the rhetoric to be false, they would make sincere individual efforts to try and perhaps to achieve a rhetorical goal no individual privately thought possible. (In these nationalistic days following the 1980 Winter Olympics we might rename this phenomenon the "American hockey team effect.")

Moore and Tumin have explored carefully the positive benefits of deliberate ignorance. They have noted, for instance, that "traditional behavior depends in part upon ignorance of alternatives."[20] In this sense, the socialization of teachers and administrators to their roles "serves to protect the traditional normative structure . . . through reinforcing the assumption that deviation from the rules is statistically insignificant."[21] If we link the willingness of many educators simply to participate, the extensive amount of pluralistic ignorance found in schools, and the substantial role of deliberate ignorance in creating lack of awareness of deviancy, we have created a rationale for covering up. "Covering up" permits autonomous individual teachers to be linked to greater social purposes or to trivial relabelings.

In sum, mystification and cover-up are essential devices superintendents and other school people use to adjust and to control tensions created by internal conflicts, external problems, or internal-external quandaries. As such, these devices are essentially neutral—they are neither good nor bad. They are available, nonetheless, to good or bad people.

In general, however, superintendents neither give nor receive advice about power retention in terms of mystification or cover-up. In contrast to these more generic processes, the usual advice is given in the form of "war stories." Six rules for power retention have been distilled from such stories.

A HIERARCHY OF TACTICAL RULES

Superintendents who wish to retain power should use the following hierarchy of rules.

1. Act like a superintendent so that others can know how to act.
2. Anticipate that ignorance will produce more positive than negative outcomes.
3. Stifle conflict by denial, bolstering, and differentiation.
4. Provide simple solutions for human problems, complex solutions for technical problems.
5. Don't decide—help or hinder others to decide.
6. If you must decide, make the second best decision.

Two caveats. First, these rules are arranged hierarchically. That is, try Rule 1, then Rule 2, and so on. Second, further theoretical and research work on "war stories" will undoubtedly create pressure to expand the number of rules and alter their hierarchic structure. Nonetheless, those committed to bridging the theory-practice gap ought to keep the total number of rules at less than 10—and definitely not let them expand to 13 in number. Equally, those seeking to help practitioners also will retain the hierarchic structure of these rules, and perhaps will generate seven rules.

Rule 1: Act Like a Superintendent So That
Others Can Know How to Act

One critical element in the retention of power by superintendents is the willingness of most actors simply to participate in social situations. We may well suggest in light of Fernandez's work[22] that superintendents retain power at least partially by immersing themselves and fellow actors in a stream of activities accentuating social consensus. These activities may well constitute the ritualistic events of opening school, speaking to parent groups, holding teacher in-service day conferences, and giving diplomas at graduation. These, and other ceremonial events, invite actors to play their role with zest and confidence without examining any larger meanings. These scenes—scenes in which all participants play their roles with exactness, confidence, and enjoyment—subvert examination by "insider" or "outsider" about possible differences among actors. Whatever conflicts that might exist about ends and goals ("cultural consensus") are squelched before they ever emerge.

This account by the anthropologist Fernandez fits well with the sociological analysis of Mills.[23] He suggested that "men discern situations with particular vocabularies, and it is in terms of some delimited vocabulary that they anticipate consequences of conduct."[24] These vocabularies not only are useful for structuring what the situation is but also for "interpreting actions and language as external manifestations of subjective and deeper lying elements in individuals."[25] Returning to the vocabulary of Fernandez, this common vocabulary and assignment of motives facilitates social consensus and hinders examination of possible problems in cultural consensus. Since various social settings have different vocabularies of motives, participants can ascribe to other actors "motives" as ways of explaining why actors behave as they do. These common motives, or, more precisely, the assertion by others that actors possess "vocabularies of motives appropriate to their respective behaviors,"[26] enhance social consensus.

Again, superintendents seeking to retain power should seek to have ascribed to their actions motives appropriate to the role in that situation. They should appear "learned," "judicious," "honest," and "reasonable" in situations. Superintendents should play such roles in scenes to emphasize that others must use these and other words from an appropriate vocabulary of motives. These situated actions and vocabularies of actions promote the smooth coordination of interaction (social consensus) without raising any issues of larger meanings (cultural consensus).

In sum, the first general rule of superintendent power retention is to act like a superintendent, thus enabling others in acting out their appropriate roles. Anticipate that commonly experienced events may be viewed from a myriad of individual perspectives— those who joyfully participate with the most superficial grasp of the situation and motives to those who see the situation and its vocabulary of motives in a common and uncritical way to those who delve deeply into the larger meanings of the situation and seek to "achieve logico-meaningful integration of high order."[27] Expect that most actors will be willing to participate, and that social consensus will heighten resistance to those who seek to critically assess the nature of cultural consensus.

Rule 2: Anticipate That Ignorance Will Provide More
Positive Than Negative Outcomes

The second major rule of superintendent power retention is an extension of the Fernandez-Mills thesis. Simply, this rule anticipates that most people will not know what others think privately, only what others say publicly. People will then seek to fulfill public expectations in spite of private doubts.

This rule rests upon the important values of pluralistic ignorance. Pluralistic ignorance is the social science argument that individuals misperceive the views of their peers.[28] While each teacher as an individual <u>privately</u> may believe that the public rhetoric of the administrator about the successes and goals of the school is fraudulent, in <u>public</u> teachers can make only supportive statements. Since teachers as individuals do not know exactly what other teachers truly believe, they assume that others may well share the views of the administrator. These individual teachers may even go so far as to change their public behavior to conform to the espoused public goals and image of success. What no individual believed to be important or worthwhile privately became a public outcome; what no individual believed achievable privately became a public success.

Ignorance not only creates the possibility of success but also strengthens the possibility of success by increasing redundancy and by permitting deviancy. Landau, for one, has argued for redundancy in human systems because it "is a powerful device for the suppression of error."[29] If we were to engineer a school as a tightly coupled, linear system in which at each specific moment each child learned a specific item, for example, $9 + 9 = 18$ while $9 \times 9 = 81$, then if for <u>any</u> reason a child, a teacher, children or teachers, a school, or a school system missed that moment, the entire system would short-circuit. All those future learnings depending on knowledge of $9 + 9$ or 9×9 would not be possible. (As an extreme example, suppose we taught <u>only once</u> in a student's career that some sentences do not need nouns.)

Landau suggests that those who argue for tightly coupled, linear, and extremely efficient human systems are committed themselves to "a form of administrative <u>brinksmanship</u>. They are extraordinary gambles. When one bulb blows, everything goes. Ordering parts in series makes them so dependent upon each other that any single failure can break the system."[30] The repetitive or cyclical nature of many school courses, for example, American history, increases the likelihood of redundancy.

Pluralistic ignorance also permits deviance. The large amounts of private work and thought in schools accentuates opportunities to try out "new" ideas—even if sometimes they are only reinventions of the wheel. The general ignorance of school faculties about the actions of individual classroom teachers means that standards for evaluating individual behavior will be weak. Scott, for example, hypothesized that "when social ties between groups are weak and tenuous, the standards used to evaluate behaviors which deviate from the ideal are lax, and when social ties are strong and enduring, standards for evaluating such actions are strong. "[31]

Moore and Tumin further suggest that "deliberate ignorance" (their term) "serves to protect the traditional normative structure . . . through reinforcing the assumption that that deviation from the rules is statistically insignificant. "[32] Thus, ignorance facilitates redundancy and deviancy—useful by-products not only for administrative survival but also educational success. More importantly, these theoretical and empirical claims suggest the wisdom for power retention of "expecting" ignorance to produce positive benefits.

Certainly, though, we should expect ignorance also to provoke conflict. What Rule 2 suggests is that administrators should anticipate ignorance to work for them. When ignorance fails, wise administrators should anticipate conflict. They then should turn to Rule 3.

Rule 3: Stifle Conflict by Denial, Bolstering, and Differentiation

The appearances of conflict, or of any symptom that suggests conflict is probable, requires more elaborate tactics. These tactics may be found in the works of social psychologists concerned with individual belief structures. Abelson, for example, discusses ways that individuals can resolve "conflicts between one belief and another, or more generally, conflicts within a belief structure. "[33] By analogy, organizations such as schools face similar problems in conflicts between one goal or another, between one technology and another technology, means-ends chains, and among various possible hierarchies of goals. More generally, superintendents face complex problems involving potential or actual conflicts. Because of the high possible costs of conflict, superintendents seeking to retain power are always willing to explore in more depth ways of managing conflict.

Abelson begins by noting that "there are innumerable inconsistencies in anyone's belief system which may lie dormant and unthought about. "[34] The press to participate (Rule 1) and to anticipate the positive benefits of ignorance (Rule 2) capitalize on the fact that dormant and unthought-about inconsistencies produce no conflict. When conflicting elements do become salient, Abelson argues there are four modes of resolution: denial, bolstering, differentiation, and transcendence. (The fourth mode needs to be incorporated into the discussion of a different rule. More about transcendence in Rule 5.)

The modes of resolution operate differently, but all work because there are only three possible sources of conflict. Conflict occurs when two positive elements are related negatively, a positive and a negative element are related positively, or two negative elements are related positively. These three possible ways of conflict may happen, for instance, between two different goals, two different technologies, two differing means-ends chains, or two different hierarchic orderings of goals. An example may help clarify this point. A superintendent might believe that academics are good (positive) and athletics are good (positive), but that if you have one, you cannot have the other (related negatively). Such a possible dilemma might be "lived with" for a long time, but the dilemma would surface "when the intensity of affect toward the objects is strong and when the dyad is often salient (that is, often present in thought)."[35] Such conditions might occur if declining student enrollments force the superintendent to contemplate cuts in academic or athletic programs.

When confronted with a belief dilemma, Abelson argues that the initial response is denial.

> Denial refers to direct attack upon one or both of the cognitive elements or the relation between them. The value felt toward the object, whether positive or negative, is denied, or the opposite is asserted; or the sign of the relation between the elements is explained away, or the opposite is asserted.[36]

Returning to our example, our puzzled superintendent might deny that athletics are a positive benefit to students. Athletics would then be made a negative element, and budget cuts would be made in that program. Or, the superintendent might deny that the relation between academics and athletics is negative. They could be seen as mutually beneficial (a positive relation), thus the superintendent might seek to cut budgets in other areas, for example, music.

Many times denial will not be adequate. If denial does not succeed in balancing and thus resolving the dilemma, the next response is bolstering. "The mechanism called 'bolstering' consists of relating one or the other of the two cognitive objects in a balanced way to other valued objects, thereby minimizing the relative imbalance in the structure."[37] Our harried superintendent, again, might argue that athletics should be viewed negatively because of numerous consequences such as the high costs involved for the few who do participate, the high incidence of injuries, and the drain of time and energy for students. These objections help drown out the imbalance in the dilemma. When used with denial, bolstering becomes a strong mechanism for reducing conflicts. Together they permit individuals to argue initially that elements or relations should be changed through denial of an element or of a relation, and then to bolster this argument by bringing additional material to the discussion. Bolstering does not necessarily eliminate the imbalance; it usually provides additional cognition elements to support the direction of the denial.

The third mechanism, differentiation, does not "preserve the cognitive elements,"[38] but in differentiation "an element may be split into two parts with a strong dissociative relation between the parts."[39] To return one final time to our example, the superintendent might differentiate between revenue-producing and nonrevenue-producing sports. This differentiation might be used to bolster the solution that academics and revenue-producing sports are compatible (positively related) in times of limited funds. Abelson points out that there are a "large number of dimensions along which objects can be differentiated. They may be differentiated according to the internal content of the object, the object as viewed in a social versus a personal context, the object as it is versus the object as it will be, etc."[40] Again, our superintendent might differentiate athletic events as important social benefits for the community from the high costs for the few individuals actually involved, and thus bolster the needs for more funds for athletics as a benefit to the community at large.

In contrast to lonely individuals and their attempts to resolve dilemmas in their belief systems, the settings of complex organizations provide ready-made catalogs of solutions. First, members have been socialized into the roles appropriate to the organization. These processes of adult socialization[41] and of role-making[42] provide individuals with denial, bolstering, and differentiation tactics "appropriate" for the role. Superintendents learn from significant others, for example, peers, professors, or parents, how superintendents in general resolve dilemmas. Second, other organizational members create "organizationally appropriate" dilemma resolutions. Educators, in general, bolster dilemma resolutions with appeals to the "benefit for children." As educators discuss carefully means or muddle through to resolutions, the ebb and flow of events illuminate certain tactics as more worthwhile than others. Such tactics work because they create the fewest difficulties, demand the least distortions, or reduce conflict to the lowest level.

Finally, Abelson suggests that a hierarchy of resolution attempts exists: "denial, bolstering, denial, differentiation. . . ."[43] In light of Rule 1, this hierarchy may need amending when applied to organizational role occupants. The very first attempt should be "participating without examination," or "unexamining." Unexamining should occur until such time as intensity and salience force the superintendent to invoke higher-order resolution mechanisms such as denial.

To recapitulate: Organizational role occupants, for example, superintendents, use basic resolution techniques to reduce dilemmas in goals, means, means-end chains, or goal hierarchies just as individuals use basic resolution mechanisms to reduce dilemmas in their belief systems. These resolution techniques are not only available to specific role occupants but also are combined in differing ways in organizations. We should expect, for instance, different denials, bolsters, or differentiations in elementary schools than we would find in secondary schools. Each organizational setting should provide a catalog of specific resolution techniques available to organization members.

Rule 4: Label All Problems as Professional/Technical, Not as Valuative/Human; Provide Complex Solutions for Technical Problems, Simple Solutions for Human Problems

If the resolution mechanisms of Rule 3 fail to solve the problem, wise superintendents invoke Rule 4. Rule 4 requires superintendents to force a dichotomy on problems—valuative/human or professional/technical—but to stress that "all" problems are professional/technical.

A number of researchers have noted the tendency for school superintendents to stress that educational problems are professional/technical and complex. Eliot, for example, has written:

> The thoroughly defensible assumption that school teaching and school administration are the specialized tasks of persons with professional training and status leads inevitably to a professional distrust of lay interference. This distrust has been accentuated by the frequency with which lay demands have conflicted with the convictions of the educators, seeming to them to be destructive of the very purposes of education. [44]

In his historical analysis of the forces that shaped the administration of public schools, Callahan found that most superintendents from 1900 on used scientific management techniques to solve problems. These techniques, Callahan argued, provided guidelines to a superintendent so that by a study of <u>local considerations</u> he meant a study of the per-pupil costs and pupil-recitation costs. His scientific determination of <u>educational value</u> turned out to be a determination of <u>dollar value.</u> His decisions on what should be taught were made <u>not on educational, but on financial grounds.</u> [45]

Finally, Martin wrote that educators seek

> to maximize internal issues, concerning almost a monopoly both of credible data and of sound point of view. Such issues—course of study, equipment needs, class size, teaching methods, library purchases, discipline, and so on—relate to precisely the professional areas in which the bureaucracy is presumed to be the most and laymen least competent. That schoolmen prefer to concentrate on internal problems is not a matter of wonder, for that is where they are most at home. They can dominate the conversation so long as they can limit it to technical subjects. [46]

These authors are only a minute sampling that support the proposition that superintendents retain power to the extent they are able to define problems as technical/professional.

This line of findings can be described in more abstract terms, which explore the relations between argument and suggestion, expertise in different types of groups, and efforts to overcome persuasive efforts. Much of the evidence rests upon studies done with small groups by social psychologists.

Cole attempted to separate the influence of "rational argument" from "prestige-suggestion" as factors influencing judgment. [47] In an experiment he asked students to judge the quality of some paintings. These art objects were of the same artistic value, but Cole manipulated the situation so that four different conditions existed: some students were given rational-sounding arguments for their favorites; an art professor presented her selections and also presented arguments for which painting was the best; and Cole discussed the paintings, pointing out which painting the art professor had liked, but providing no supporting arguments.

Cole found that peers with arguments and the art authority with arguments consistently produced the largest change in student opinion. The use of the art authority without argument ("prestige-suggestion") was less effective at shifting the opinions of students than were peers or the art authority with arguments. Cole concluded that experts gained that advantage when they were allowed to present arguments justifying their position. The use of an expert without presentation of an argument was much less effective. Cole did not test one question of interest: What was the impact of peers with arguments and authorities with arguments when they disagreed on which art object (in this case) was the best?

However, Gerard produces evidence that sheds some light on this question.[48] In a complex social experiment, he created conditions that generated four different types of groups. These groups differed on whether they were told all members were about equal in ability and skill (homogeneous) or were told they differed on ability and skill (heterogeneous). Again, the experimenter had created groups actually about equal on ability and skills. He also created differing conditions of social pressure (high versus low) by suggesting a postexperiment activity for the so-called high groups.

In contrasting these four different groups (homogeneous-low pressure; heterogeneous-low pressure; homogeneous-high pressure; heterogeneous-high pressure). Gerard found that both heterogeneous groups created "experts." In contrast to homogeneous groups, the high pressure heterogeneous groups created experts who were "expected" to find the correct issue and position on a controversial social issue. These high pressure heterogeneous groups also tended to greater group subdivision, that is, experts talked to experts, and minority members visited with minority members. Pressures arose to agree with experts in both the low and the high pressure heterogeneous groups, with greater pressure in the high group. In contrast, the homogeneous groups (even under high pressure) displayed tendencies toward uniformity and resistance to group subdivision.

These experiments by Cole and Gerard provide some insight into relations between superintendents, school boards, and communities, and why expertise may be so vital to the superintendent. Cole's findings suggest that when dealing with situations in which individuals must make decisions, these individuals look first to what they believe to be "rational" arguments, regardless of source, and then to "prestige-suggestions"—unsupported expert views. Experts are advantaged when provided the opportunity to present evidence and reasonable claims, and even further advantaged when the problem is in their area of expertise.

Both of these conditions are present in the school board setting. The superintendent comes with the aura of authority (much like the art professor evaluating art objects), and can enhance this authority by providing rational arguments for opinions given. School board members who have either no rational arguments or who offer unsupported opinions are at a severe disadvantage in challenging expert opinion.

If the superintendent does face a challenge, the homogeneity or heterogeneity of the school board may be critical. With a homogeneous board, we could expect strong pressures either to reduce differences between superintendent and board or to exclude the superintendent (as expert) from deliberations. With a heterogeneous board, we could expect the board to split into experts and minority members. These minority members become "swing votes" to be courted by experts who undoubtedly seek to provide both rational arguments and prestige suggestions.

This line of speculation is partially supported by Bowers' finding that moderate levels of group conflict enhance information sharing. [49] He found that personal commitment to an initial position motivated individuals to defend their choice by presenting all information available (extent) and to present their choice in as cogent a manner as possible (quality). Too little conflict or too much conflict suppressed both the extent and the quality of information sharing.

These experiments suggest why superintendents seek to make all educational disagreements technical issues. By discussing problems where rational argument is paramount, and where disagreeing groups may be heterogeneous, school experts gain distinct political advantage.

Equally, school leaders deliberately seek to communicate with the board and the public in ways that structure into the situation not only the information to be transmitted but also how the sender wishes the information to be interpreted. [50] Not only do superintendents wish to make "rational arguments" but they also wish to be seen as the single best source of rational arguments. In contrast to community interests, which may be heterogeneous and labeled as conflicting and self-serving, school leaders structure settings to support their expertise ("technical reports," "long-range planning documents," "standard operating procedures for management") and to enhance the perceptions of others of their role as experts. Wise superintendents wishing to retain power regulate the communication flow between board, public, and their offices to serve this dual purpose; to control information and to enhance their expert status.

Finally, Shaw suggested an important addition to this discussion. In a group experiment he found that "increased information, increased ranges of ideas, etc., probably lead to increased effectiveness when the task can be solved by logical procedures, whereas increased information is curvilinearly related to effectiveness when the task can be solved only by consensual procedures." [51] In a technical/professional problem, the quest for more information appeared reasonable, indicated high levels of involvement, and accentuated the positive worth the individual finds in group membership. With a valuative/human problem, however, too much information made informants appear uncommitted and uncertain; limited information in valuative/human problems made informants appear reasonable, committed to an alternative, and certain. Hence, superintendents may lose control when confronted by valuative/human problems.

McGuire provides additional insights into why superintendents may lose in such situations.[52] McGuire examined four different lines of research that explored reasons for resistance to persuasion: behavior commitment, anchoring beliefs to other cognitions, inducing resistance, and prior training.

The behavioral commitment approach to resistance to persuasion emphasizes various ways of acting that commit people to their beliefs. Resistance is increased, for example, if individuals make public announcements of their beliefs or actively participate in activities on the basis of the belief. A school board member, for example, who announces strong opposition to the closing of a neighborhood school and who states this at PTA meetings, argues this position in the public hearings, and gives interviews to newspapers supporting the maintenance of this school will be difficult, if not impossible, to persuade by expertise (or any other method) available to the superintendent.

The anchoring approach argues that resistance to persuasion is enhanced by linking a belief to other accepted beliefs, to accepted values, and to valued sources and reference groups. This approach emphasizes the importance of the pattern of beliefs individuals hold. Returning to Gerard's research on homogeneous and heterogeneous groups dealing with problems, we might suggest that homogeneous groups link the belief in the equality of all members to the importance of the total group reaching consensus. Such situations may arise, for instance, on school boards where all members are of the same occupation (farmers) or see themselves as professionals (lawyers, doctors, business leaders). In these circumstances, expertise of superintendents will be blunted by patterns of beliefs and values.

The third approach to understanding resistance to persuasion accentuates the creation of resistant states of mind. For instance, persuasion is reduced when individuals feel anxiety about the issues, when aggressiveness is induced into the discussion of beliefs, when issues of self-esteem are raised, or when individuals have been preconditioned to an ideological position. These conditions, for example, might be met in discussion about the values of extracurricular activities, such as Title IX athletic equity for boys and girls. Male members of the board might resist expert opinions that these Title IX activities are important to everyone involved because of their anxiety about the impact of sports on feminine stereotypes such as motherhood, their distress over the hostile attitudes of "pushy" feminists or "women's libbers," their concerns over male self-esteem if they bend to the influence of women, and other preconditionings as males in our society about the proper roles of women.

A final general approach to resisting persuasion is to provide prior training. Training might include efforts to analyze false or misleading advertising, to assess the various techniques for personally attacking individuals and thus discrediting their arguments, to understand the acceptable limits of generalizations, and to study the logic of argumentation. Such training creates individuals suspicious of how persuasive arguments are structured, how information sources are used, how data are marshaled, and how conclusions are reached.

These four different tactics for resisting persuasion provide insight into how superintendents and school boards handle valuative/human issues. Issues such as desegregation, reallocation of resources, sex equality, or grade-to-grade promotion criteria touch on issues that board members and community groups may see as reflecting important values. If this is the case, we can anticipate individuals taking strong public stands, linking these issues with other important beliefs, creating emotional scenes of confrontation, and attempting to point out how opponents are seeking to falsely persuade the remainder of the community. If the community is divided on the issue and if the pressure for a decision is great (Gerard's heterogeneous-high pressure situation), we could anticipate the development of two competing groups of experts seeking to influence others. If the community is homogeneous in its support of or opposition to the position of the expert, we could expect consensus and efforts to incorporate the expert. If the expert maintains a minority position, we could anticipate eventual dismissal.

Hence, we may now summarize the importance of expertise assumed by superintendents. Such an assumption creates conditions of political advantage if the expert is able to create or to interpret situations so that problems are seen as technical/professional. These conditions accentuate the rational arguments of the expert educator. If the board or community is divided (heterogeneous) about an issue, the school leader moreover can choose to play the expert role and persuade others in the importance of supporting the claim that the problem is technical. The superintendent can then use expert opinion to downgrade the opposition's arguments. If opponents attack the superintendent under these conditions, they must turn to other educational experts.

If the community, however, defines the problem as valuative/ human, the superintendent gains advantage by providing a very few alternatives and by supporting one of these alternatives (reasonably). This posture of simplification suggests to others that the superintendent is reasonably committed to an alternative, and certain. If, however, such a course of action appears likely to endanger superintendent power retention, apply Rule 5.

Rule 5: Don't Decide—Help or Hinder Others to Decide

Rule 5 enunciates the principle of power retention that not deciding is an important decision as well as a means of retaining power.[53] Further, this rule suggests that superintendents can either help or hinder others to decide.

This rule rests heavily on the work of Thompson and Tuden.[54] They developed a fourfold table of decisions and appropriate social structures. Thompson and Tuden argue that certain decision styles—for example, computation, compromise, judgment, or inspiration—are determined by beliefs about means and ends. These decision styles, in turn, are most appropriately housed in certain types of organizational structures, for example, bureaucratic. The two major dimensions of decision styles are: agreement or disagreement on the dimension of "beliefs about causation" (means); and "preferences about possible outcomes" (ends). Where agreement exists among all parties on both means and ends, the appropriate decision style is computational and the appropriate social structure is bureaucratic. Disagreements about means and agreements on ends characterize majority decisions found appropriately in collegial structures. Agreement about means but disagreement on ends dictates a bargaining decision style housed in representative structures. Finally, disagreements on both means and ends characterize an inspiration decision strategy found in an "anomic social structure" where charismatic leaders may prosper.

Following this analysis, Thompson and Tuden indicate that "a major proposition of this essay is that usually an organization adopts one of the four strategies—computation, collective judgment, compromise or inspiration—is its dominant strategy, and bases its structure on that strategy."[55] Returning to Rule 4 for a moment, the strategy implicit in that rule could now be restated in the Thompson and Tuden framework. Superintendents should press all problems into the technical/professional category because in this category they can be treated as problems with agreement on both means and ends. This agreement dictates a computational decision strategy (in which expertise is useful) and a bureaucratic social structure (in which decisions of the leader are efficiently and effectively implemented by followers). In valuative/human problems, other decision styles and organizational structures would be more appropriate—and superintendents would lose power. Under such conditions, Thompson and Tuden's final suggestion seems even more appropriate for superintendent power retention. They suggest "the general proposition that an important role for administrators is to manage the decision process, as distinct from making the decision."[56]

While it seems clear that these authors intend for administrators such as superintendents to manage the decision process to good ends, management could also hinder. Thompson and Tuden would suggest that a wise superintendent determines if agreement or disagreement exists on means and ends, proposes the appropriate decision strategy, and develops the appropriate social structure. The appropriate analysis of agreements and disagreements, strategies and structures would facilitate decisions being made by others. A less wise, more manipulative superintendent might seek to confuse others about agreements or disagreements on means and ends, might proffer the least appropriate decision strategy, and might suggest an inappropriate social structure. For example, a superintendent might "see" (accurately) that the community and the board want academic test scores increased (agreement on ends), but various groups in the community and members of the board disagree about methods (disagreement on means). Under these conditions, the appropriate strategy would be majority, and the appropriate structure would be collegial. However, our superintendent, intent upon retaining power, might suggest to board and community alike that they disagree not only about means (which they really do) but also ends (which they really do not). The superintendent would then propose that the appropriate decision style should be "bargaining" (when it really should be "majority") and the best social structure for this should be "open meetings" (an "anomic structure" inappropriate in this situation).

One aside before moving on to Rule 6. Readers may have noted in Rule 3, and again here in Rule 5, that these discussions have avoided "transcendence" and "charisma." The reason for this exclusion is modest—we have little empirical information supporting this dilemma resolution technique or decision strategy as a way of retaining power. The research literature suggests they are means of acquiring power, but that the retention of power depends upon elaborating this new belief system through denial, bolstering, and differentiation, better known as the "routinization of charisma."

Rule 6: If You Must Decide, Make the
Second Best Decision

If superintendents seek to retain power, Rules 1 through 5 suggest they should avoid making decisions. As a last resort, some situations require that superintendents do decide. In those cases, Johnson has found that "an executive should make decisions which have the least uncertainty and which generate the least amount of interpersonal friction. Such a decision is frequently not the most appropriate but is only second best."[57] Second best decisions help maintain the status quo on several dimensions: interpersonal relations, group membership, and both internal and external relationships of the organization.[58] Equally, the selection of second best decisions reduces the likelihood of "highly visible errors,"[59] which may cause those who evaluate superintendents, for instance, to make negative judgments. Second best decisions insure, therefore, that the superintendent's decision-making profile is low. For superintendents who wish to retain power, the lower the better.

RECAPITULATION: RULES AND THEIR RATIONALES

These six rules as elaborated provide a manual for superintendents who wish to retain power in school districts. Furthermore, these rules are hierarchically ordered: apply Rule 1, then Rule 2, and so on. As a rule fails in a specific situation then, and only then, is the next higher rule brought into play. Simply, in all situations Rule 1 should be applied initially; any deviation from this hierarchic order will cause mischief for superintendents. This also implies that Rule 1 is the most important of the rules for superintendents wishing to retain power.

Some may suggest that these rules present a cynical view of educational leadership—one that fits with mystification and cover-up. A more appropriate ("correct") view suggests that superintendents ought to pursue relentlessly educational excellence. They should prod communities and this nation toward higher educational goals. In this pursuit of excellence these superintendents should be willing to sacrifice themselves as "symbolic martyrs" to the higher cause of education.

While attractive, such a view is premised upon the contentious proposition that most of those who work in education are seriously flawed. The brand of leadership espoused by these rules, in contrast, is based upon an inherent belief in the normal distribution of educational outcomes—16 percent failures, 68 percent average, and 16 percent successes.[60] Our mystifying, cover-up, and role-bound administrator wisely plays the odds—some 84 percent of outcomes will be reasonably good. Put another way, a "good" superintendent anticipates that following these rules provides opportunities for average teachers working in average schools with average students to produce average or better outcomes 84 percent of the time.

We should be very sensitive to the fact that "average" often seems pejorative and debilitating. It should not be so when applied to superintendents wishing to retain power. The proper understanding of average outcomes helps superintendents in two ways. First, when superintendents seriously scan their work situations a keen sense of averageness heightens sensitivity both to mediocrity and to excellence. Knowing what most can do helps superintendents as they examine the extremes. They may then seek to eradicate mediocrity by radical means, for example, surgery. They may also wish to accentuate excellence as a way of skewing the average and the mediocre toward excellence (Rule 2). With averageness as a template, superintendents are able not only to discern extreme strengths or weaknesses but also to create a priority list of those problems that <u>must</u> be dealt with immediately. By being able to put off average problems until tomorrow, they can attack those situations of mediocrity that are dangers to the system. Averageness fixes the limited amount of time and energy of superintendents on important problems, not on <u>all</u> possible problems.

Second, the notion of average leads superintendents to be humble about their efforts to change school systems. Humility is induced not only by a sense of the enormous amount of energy needed to move <u>most</u> of the school system but also by the awareness that most others are doing their jobs. If superintendents truly do view the work environment, they will see that others may be playing their individual roles to the hilt: If superintendents truly do look they may find that most are zestfully immersed in the ongoing life of the schools. To dabble with other workers simply because they are average may upset the beneficial results of "social consensus." Hence, Rule 1 highlights the value of playing a role well so that others may play their roles on "average," if not better.

Anticipating that such conditions lead most often to "good" outcomes means that superintendents wisely see their work as primarily symbolic. They stand as the representatives of important institutions, protecting those who really do the work of the institution—in this case, teachers and students—from disruptive influences. One of the chief disruptive forces can be superintendents who may seek to reshape their school system. By avoiding this tendency to disrupt, by following closely Rule 1, administrators make stable, and thus enrich, the world of workers. By casting symbolic shadows that often mystify and cover up, superintendents retain the power of the office, permit their workers to achieve the real work and goals of the organization, and help the distribution of educational outcomes to be normal.

These rules underscore a third important point. Educational leadership depends upon an absolute sense of optimism. This optimism is based on the assumption that average and conventional individuals (most teachers and most administrators) who use average techniques and who seek rather conventional goals are able as a collective to produce unusually good results. There is something almost magical about the generally good results that occur in U.S. education. It is enough to make one believe that the whole is greater than the sum of the parts, or that pluralistic ignorance is blessed.

Such results occur, I would argue, because sloppiness is built into the educational system. This sloppiness manifests itself, first, in the great amounts of redundancy that occur. Landau, for one, has argued that redundancy is important in human systems because it "is a powerful device for the suppression of error."[61]

A second form of sloppiness values deviancy. As noted earlier, pluralistic ignorance and deliberate ignorance provide "cover" for possible deviancy. In this sense, the large amounts of individualism in schools accentuate opportunities to try out new ideas. Lacking sanctions to control behaviors means that deviancy may provide creative new options or simply reinforce redundancies for students. Not knowing or not being evaluated may provide constant stimuli to creativity—creativity that might be squelched by evaluations by veterans who "know" that a "new" idea is really an "old" bromide.

These and other sources of organizational sloppiness suggest that sagacious educational leaders often leave well enough alone—anticipating that what is happening today may well change for the better tomorrow. This sense of cock-eyed optimism rests on the genuinely held belief that those who don't like teaching simply get out—and those who have stood the test of time are generally adequate, if not slightly above average.

Sloppiness, however, also lets educational leaders strike forth with bold new ventures. Our person from La Mancha may tilt with any windmills he or she chooses, just so long as she or he remembers that not all will join in this venture. A symbolic attack, nonetheless, through the "magic" of pluralistic ignorance, may produce very real results. Equally, when viewed from a distance, the charge may fail—but hidden within the dross may well be nuggets of success. These steps forward—even though they may seem smaller than any great leap forward—may be important. For example, Marz has noted that efforts to use sophisticated management

techniques such as management information systems often fail.[62]
While the techniques are initially adopted because they appear to
be "magical" cures to bureaucratic uncertainty, these new rituals
simply don't work. However, these failures often produce valuable
benefits. Older, entrenched division heads may be replaced or
central authorities may gain power, for instance.

The other essential element of educational leadership is an
understanding of the nature of uncertainty. We need to distinguish
two differing senses of the concept. In analyzing the nature of uncertainty in medical practice, Davis suggested that we must "distinguish between 'real' uncertainty as a clinical and scientific
phenomenon and the use to which uncertainty—real or pretended,
'functional' uncertainty—lends itself in the management of patients
and their families by hospital physicians and other treatment personnel."[63] When the physician is certain and the prognosis is given
the patient, Davis suggests we have "communication." On the
other extreme, if the physician is uncertain and the prognosis is
not given the patient, we have an admission of "real" uncertainty.
Between these two options exist opportunities for "dissimulation"—
functional reduction of patient uncertainty to enhance the physician's
"reputation and livelihood,"[64] or "evasion"—the physician is certain but the prognosis is not given the patient because this enhances
the management of the patient and family by the physician.

In education much of our uncertainty is "real"—we are unable,
for various reasons, to overcome what Campbell and Stanley label
factors jeopardizing internal and external validity.[65] Factors such
as history, maturation, and selection as well as representativeness
all help create the aura, and the fact, that much of educational activity is truly uncertain. We are constant victims to significant
shifts not only in our subjects but also in the environment—shifts
that disrupt whatever certainty we seemed to possess at any one
moment.

The educational leader's belief in uncertainty is a faith driven
by the sense that tomorrow will be unlike today. Those activities
today that produced major victories, if applied tomorrow may result in crashing losses. Equally, a strategy that fell on deaf ears
today may bring cheers tomorrow. Significant victories in the
environment, sudden breakthrough discoveries by colleagues, or
smiles of approval by former foes must be treated as moments to
be treasured, but not hoarded. Real uncertainty, grounded on a
sense that change is ever-constant, implies that efforts to create
routine, to make permanent, or to develop standard operating procedures will always be thwarted by fate—fate in the guise of changing environmental conditions, insensitive peers, or too creative
others. To administrators, real uncertainty seems best translated

into the most famous of Murphy's Laws: "If anything can go wrong, it will." To be summed up (sadistically) in Murphy's Philosophy: "Smile . . . tomorrow will be worse."

Yet rarely are administrators faced with dramatic shifts. Rather, most administrators face a daily existence that produces minor crises—incremental movements best measured in terms of inches, not feet or yards. It is against the "ordinariness" of administrative work—the infamous alligators in the swamp that attack the administrator's posterior—that we must compare most issues of uncertainty. In ordinariness the problem is not one of reacting to major shifts in the environment but rather one of striving to find larger, emerging patterns in a mosaic of commonplace events. The maintenance of sensitivity becomes the bane of most school administrators. It becomes easy, downright seductive, to engage in the helter-skelter of activities without pausing for reflection. There is always the luxury of simple participation.

The crux of the problem generated by reflection about patterns that may be emerging is scale. Just how long a ruler must be used to measure the timeliness of the shape that may be emerging? Is it one month, one year, one decade, one generation, or one nation's history? What are the patterns of relationships that exist between obvious short-term and long-range outcomes? Nagged by quandaries such as these, retreating to moment-by-moment problems seems a sane gambit.

Yet optimism and uncertainty are sides of the same coin. Combined they suggest an inherent wisdom in believing in a normal distribution of educational events—some 68 percent will be adequate with 16 percent failures and 16 percent successes. The optimistic but uncertain administrator wisely plays the odds—some 84 percent of the time reasonably good results will occur. Under these conditions the wiser course is to be optimistic—things will generally turn out all right. Equally, wisdom implies uncertainty. Our base of knowledge is too weak to engineer success, even if our subjects and the environment both were kind enough to be still for a moment. Unfortunately, neither has the patience of a two-year-old child.

Optimism and uncertainty, nonetheless, create the groundwork for tension between educators and publics. Not only do educators and publics quarrel about the goals of education, the needs of educators to be able to protect uncertainty often crystallize into conflicts. At a general level these conflicts take the form of struggles about professional autonomy. Professional autonomy legitimates optimism, redundancy, deviancy, self-fulfilling prophecies, and real uncertainty. This press for professional autonomy aims to guarantee educators the room they need to fulfill the optimism inherent in the normal distributions of educational outcomes. Put another way, the price professionals ask of the public is one of 16 percent "failure" versus 84 percent "adequacy." To help maintain this sort of distribution pattern, administrators mystify and cover up.

MARTYRDOM

When this pattern is no longer acceptable to publics, administrators face the likelihood of martyrdom. More precisely, we should speak of "symbolic martyrdom." We shall examine this particular notion from the perspective of the superintendent, although it can happen at the other administrative positions to be found in education. Symbolic martyrdom occurs when the incumbent superintendent is in conflict with the school board and community about a major policy issue, for example, school closings, desegregation, collective bargaining strategy. The superintendent offers his or her resignation to the board, claiming that this dramatic move is prompted by his or her concern for the good of the schools and the entire community.

Such a "selfless" act, nonetheless, provides three important benefits for superintendents. First, in this gesture of martyrdom, professionals are able to control their destiny even though they may well be aware of the awesome power of the board and the community. By choosing to leave before "others" remove them from office, superintendents assert the free will of autonomous professionals. While clearly recognizing the limitations imposed by public control, the act of martyrdom asserts the even grander vision of moral authority held by resigning superintendents.

Second, the act of martyrdom is a part of the professional's constant struggle to make the school system better. Whether fought for teachers, for the improvement of conditions, or for students, issues pale before superintendents' commitments to educational improvement. While superintendents may win some and may lose some, in these battles superintendents must capture the flag of a better tomorrow. If a battle goes against superintendents, the act of symbolic martyrdom permits a victory for the office even while signaling a defeat for the individual. By underscoring that the ever-present forces of evil—"those who oppose improving educational services for children"—must be battled, the act of resignation simultaneously signals the weakness and limitations of a single superintendent while asserting the purity of the office. No shame is felt by those who retreat today so that they may fight tomorrow—in a different site.

Finally, the act of symbolic martyrdom provides important cohesiveness to the professional community. The complete identification of the individual martyr to improving the whole society through education of the future generation not only enhances the prestige of the office but also builds an important image of heroism for fellow superintendents. Those witnessing the symbolic demise sympathize with the tragic loss of a comrade, assist in finding a new position in a better community, and feel anointed by the goodness of their colleague. They now have a legitimate, vivid, and heroic image of the price they may be called upon one day to pay for the improvement of American education. Their peer "has not died in vain"; they are able to rededicate themselves in his memory to the noble profession they have chosen. Hence, symbolic martyrdom legitimates the assignment of important descriptors to the role. Superintendents, as all martyrs, are "selfless," "inspired," "wise," "visionary," and "heroic."

For members of the school board and community, symbolic martyrdom also has three consequences. First, the act of resignation helps soothe community tensions. The act of symbolic martyrdom may "short-circuit" tensions before they erupt as conflicts that might result in nearly irreversible cleavages among various community factions. The act of resignation may not only introduce ambiguity about who is to blame for "this mess" but also direct positive community action to the future resolution of the problem.

Second, the departure of the superintendent quiets discussions about unwillingness to act as the board and community wished. A close analysis of the entire situation might uncover a morass of conflicts of interest, intrigue, and petty hostility. The superintendent's public departure forestalls, and frequently forecloses, the airing of dirty linen. This act of civility and discretion—more the behavior of a Southern gentleman than a Yankee carpetbagger—dampens discussions about the superintendent as incompetent to manage conflict, unwilling to clean up "that" can of worms, or too stubborn (or too stupid) to listen to community sages. Martyrdom permits forgiveness, as well as strengthening a begrudged public image of the moral worthiness of superintendents.

Finally, the act of symbolic martyrdom enhances the power of the incoming superintendent with the board and the community. The position of the board and community is now one in which they must decide what they want done. The creation of this rationale ("mandate") for the successor weakens the bargaining power of the board after hiring. By being precisely clear about what they want, the board allows the new superintendents to reassert certain prerogatives. New superintendents claim they can accomplish these priorities only if they are given certain concessions. All other assessments by the board are now considered irrelevant while new superintendents work their way through their "mandate." Those who follow in the footsteps of martyrs are themselves seen as good—at least for a couple of months.

Hence, the actions of the board may help the community find ways to see itself with a larger image of improving its schools. All should now see that boards and communities ought to improve their schools, ought to work with good educators, and ought to continue to hire superintendents who are capable of symbolic martyrdom. Communities, then, ought to avoid superintendents who are "selfish," "routine," "dull," "common," and "average." To provide contrasts between "average" and "good," communities need martyrs—once in a while. Martyrdom must remain a rare event if it is to provide important consequences for all participants. Too much martyrdom wears thin. Hence, we should anticipate that mystification and cover-up are the more frequently used tactics of school administrators.

Standing in stark contrast to these successful maneuvers is the fatal flaw of school administration: "success." The worst possible administrative behavior is to believe that what you did as an administrator really "caused" a good outcome. While it is safe, and comforting, to believe that you as an administrator may have helped in part or by accident to create a scenario that may have worked this time, any self-congratulations beyond that point became exceedingly dangerous.

The logic of this claim is straightforward. First, an administration rarely controls enough resources to "cause" teachers to do exactly what that administrator might wish/want/demand. Second, left to themselves, teachers will produce average or "adequate," and occasionally "good," results. Third, even if the administrator could structure a situation so that teachers were cowed into behaving a certain way, the administrator could not know what the outcomes would be (real uncertainty) and could not control environments long enough to insure the program was ever put into effect. These conditions all suggest that what fundamentally happens in schools is beyond the direct control of the administrator. Indirectly, nonetheless, the administrator can: first, select "good" teachers; second, provide what teachers appear to want anticipating that this may facilitate their work; and third, hardly ever deny teachers the opportunity to explore options presented by their teaching situations or the environment. What this suggests is that wise administrators are optimistic—anticipating that good things will happen—and opportunistic—highlighting the happy mix of individuals, techniques, and times that may produce good results.

In this kind of world, a good administrator acts more like a gardener than a computer programmer. Instead of believing that a single set of instructions will always produce a good output, the administration knows that the particular weather of this season, and a particular seed and fertilizer, mean that this year's rose was better than last. Good administrators and good gardeners know that what they do is strongly influenced by forces beyond their control. Unfortunately, both often fall prey to believing that what they did "caused" the results. They often erroneously immediately follow this "success" with efforts to design more successes by programming and structuring the forces around them. In education "success" means concerted efforts to create formulas, for example, "leadership kits,"[66] "teacher-proof materials," "fool-proof instructions," which end up completely missing the factors that initially produced success. We should find wisdom in another of Murphy's Laws: "Every solution needs new problems."

I do not wish to suggest that administrators are never successful or never have successes—they do—but I do wish to point out that wise administrators do not seek to replicate success. Instead, they adjust in two ways. First, they recognize that a successful outcome can be a "fluke"—a statistical outlier that may never happen again. Second, they behave in ways that permit them to examine closely the configuration of events that produced success. This examination looks both to find patterns and to explore accidents. The examination is sensitive to the likelihood of these events ever coming this way again. By these means, administrators are able to examine the constructive roles of mystification, cover-up, tactical rules, and martyrdom, and to be wary of the destructive role of success.

SUMMARY

I seriously doubt that honesty is the best policy for school superintendents who wish to retain power. The deliberate uses of mystification, cover-up, tactical rules, and martyrdom are the best policy. These, and other administrative tactics, are successful because average teachers do their job, rhetorical slogans about educational goals are privately doubted (if thought about) but are publicly effective (in general) and real uncertainty is a source of both optimism and concern.

Real uncertainty generally (and fortunately) works to the advantage of those who see administration on average as a creative task much like growing beautiful gardens. Real uncertainty also continuously whets the appetites of those who wish to know and to

understand education. What we must never forget is that real uncertainty is at the heart of the greater success of educational administrators—the fulfillment of larger social purposes by groups
of individuals who in private may doubt that they can achieve much,
but who in public produce adequate or better results most of the
time. What good administrators do is to capitalize on public successes while they isolate "cynical" individuals so that private doubt
never spreads. By keeping teachers lonely, good administrators
help produce adequate or better group results. To obtain such a
public good, they mystify, cover up, follow tactical rules, and
suffer martyrdom. For administrators, it is simply all in a day's
work.

NOTES

1. See, for example, Michael D. Cohen, James G. March,
and Johan P. Olsen, "A Garbage Can Model of Organizational
Choice," Administrative Science Quarterly 17 (March 1972):1-25;
Michael D. Cohen and James G. March, Leadership and Ambiguity
(New York: McGraw-Hill, 1974); James G. March and Johan P.
Olsen, Ambiguity and Choice in Organizations (Bergen: Universitets-
forlaget, 1976); and Karl E. Weick, "Educational Organizations as
Loosely Coupled Systems," Administrative Science Quarterly 21
(March 1976):1-19.
2. See Martin Burlingame, "Some Neglected Dimensions in
the Study of Educational Administration," Educational Administration Quarterly 15 (Winter 1979): 1-18; and Martin Burlingame,
"Protecting Private Realities by Managing Public Schools: Mystifi-
cations, Cover-up, and Martyrdom," Presentation at the 1980
American Education Research Association (AERA) Meeting.
3. James W. Fernandez, "Symbolic Consensus in a Fang
Reformative Cult," American Anthropologist 67 (1965):906.
4. Ibid., p. 922.
5. Ibid.
6. Ibid., p. 925.
7. Burton R. Clark, "The Organizational Saga in Higher
Education," Administrative Science Quarterly 17 (June 1972):179-84.
8. Ibid., p. 178.
9. Robert Dubin, "Organization Fictions," in Human Relations in Administration with Readings, ed. Robert Dubin, 3d ed.
(Englewood Cliffs, N.J.: Prentice-Hall, 1968), pp. 493-98.
10. Ibid., p. 496.
11. Ibid.

12. This argument parallels the argument about "wise men" made in Karl W. Deutsch and William G. Madow, "A Note on the Appearance of Wisdom in Large Bureaucratic Organizations," Behavioral Science 6 (January 1961):72-78.

13. Dan C. Lortie, "The Teacher and Team Teaching: Suggestions for Long-Range Research," in Team Teaching, ed. J. T. Shaplin and H. F. Olds (New York: Harper & Row, 1964), pp. 270-305.

14. In contrast, information about the status hierarchy of the system or about working conditions may move quickly through the system. See Mark Hanson and Flora Ida Ortiz, "The Management Information System and the Control of Educational Change: A Field Study," Sociology of Education 48 (1975):257-75.

15. W. Keith Warner and A. Eugene Havens, "Goal Displacement and the Intangibility of Organizational Goals," Administrative Science Quarterly 12 (1968):544.

16. Charles Perrow, "Organizational Prestige: Some Functions and Dysfunctions," American Journal of Sociology 66 (January 1961):335-41.

17. See, for example, Ann Lieberman and Lynne Miller, "The Social Realities of Teaching," Teachers College Record 80 (September 1978):54-68.

18. John S. Packard and Donald J. Willower, "Pluralistic Ignorance and Pupil Control Ideology," Journal of Educational Administration 10 (May 1972):78-87.

19. Wilbur E. Moore and Melvin M. Tumin, "Some Social Functions of Ignorance," American Sociological Review 14 (1949): 787-95.

20. Ibid., p. 791.

21. Ibid.

22. Fernandez, "Symbolic Consensus," pp. 902-29.

23. C. Wright Mills, "Situated Actions and Vocabularies of Motive," American Sociological Review 5 (December 1940):904-13.

24. Ibid., p. 906.

25. Ibid., p. 913.

26. Ibid., p. 906.

27. Fernandez, "Symbolic Consensus," p. 908.

28. See the following: Packard and Willower, "Pluralistic Ignorance," pp. 78-87; John H. Kautsky, "Myth, Self-Fulfilling Prophecy, and Symbolic Reassurance in the East-West Conflict," Journal of Conflict Resolution 9 (March 1965):1-17; and John W. Meyer and Brian Rowan, "Institutionalized Organizations: Formal Structure as Myth and Ceremony," American Journal of Sociology 83 (September 1977): 340-63.

29. Martin Landau, "Redundancy, Rationality, and the Problem of Duplication and Overlap," Public Administration Review 29 (July/August 1969):347.

30. Ibid., p. 354.

31. Robert A. Scott, "Deviance, Sanctions, and Social Integration in Small-Scale Society," Social Forces 54 (March 1976):612.

32. Moore and Tumin, "Some Social Functions," p. 791.

33. Robert P. Abelson, "Models of Resolution of Belief Dilemmas," in Problems in Social Psychology: Selected Readings, ed. Carl W. Backman and Paul F. Secord (New York: McGraw-Hill, 1966), p. 136.

34. Ibid.

35. Ibid.

36. Ibid., p. 137.

37. Ibid.

38. Ibid.

39. Ibid.

40. Ibid., p. 138.

41. Orville G. Brim and Stanton Wheeler, Socialization After Childhood: Two Essays (New York: John Wiley, 1966), pp. 60-66 especially.

42. George Graen, "Role-Making Processes Within Complex Organizations," in Handbook of Industrial and Organizational Psychology, ed. Marvin D. Dunnette (Chicago: Rand McNally, 1976), pp. 1220-25 especially.

43. Abelson, "Models of Resolution," p. 138.

44. Thomas H. Eliot, "Toward an Understanding of Public School Politics," in Governing Education: A Reader on Politics, Power, and Public School Policy, ed. Alan Rosenthal (Garden City, N.Y.: Doubleday, 1969), p. 7.

45. Raymond E. Callahan, Education and the Cult of Efficiency: A Study of the Social Forces That Have Shaped the Administration of the Public Schools (Chicago: University of Chicago Press, 1962), p. 73.

46. Roscoe C. Martin, "School Government," in Rosenthal, Governing Education, pp. 287-88.

47. David Cole, "'Rational Argument' and 'Prestige Suggestion' as Factors Influencing Judgment," Sociometry 17 (November 1954):350-54.

48. Harold B. Gerard, "The Effect of Different Dimensions of Disagreement on the Communication Process in Small Groups," Human Relations 6 (1953):249-71.

49. Joseph L. Bower, "The Role of Conflict in Economic Decision-Making Groups: Some Empirical Results," Quarterly Journal of Economics 79 (May 1965):263-77.

50. John T. Dorsey, "A Communication Model for Administration," Administrative Science Quarterly 2 (December 1957):317.

51. Marvin E. Shaw, "Some Effects of Varying Amounts of Information Exclusively Possessed by a Group Member Upon His Behavior in the Group," Journal of General Psychology 78 (January 1963):78.

52. William J. McGuire, "Inducing Resistance to Persuasion: Some Contemporary Approaches," Advances in Experimental Social Psychology 1 (1964):191-229.

53. For an elaboration of this line of argument, see Thomas J. Sergiovanni, Martin Burlingame, Fred D. Coombs, and Paul W. Thurston, Educational Governance and Administration (Englewood Cliffs, N.J.: Prentice-Hall, 1980), pp. 354-72.

54. James D. Thompson and Arthur Tuden, "Strategies, Structures, and Processes of Organization Decisions," in James D. Thompson, Peter Hammond, Robert W. Hawkes, Buford H. Junker, and Arthur Tuden, Comparative Studies in Administration (Pittsburgh: University of Pittsburgh Press, 1959), pp. 195-216.

55. Ibid., p. 205.

56. Ibid., p. 209.

57. Russell J. Johnson, "Conflict Avoidance Through Acceptable Decisions," Human Relations 27 (January 1974):79.

58. Ibid., p. 77.

59. Ibid., p. 82.

60. See Meyer and Rowan, "Institutionalized Organizations," for this "logic of confidence."

61. Landau, "Redundancy," p. 347.

62. Robert H. Marz, "Myth, Magic, and Administrative Innovations," Administration & Society 10 (August 1978): 131-38.

63. Fred Davis, "Uncertainty in Medical Prognosis, Clinical and Functional," American Journal of Sociology 66 (July 1960):41.

64. Ibid., p. 47.

65. Donald T. Campbell and Julian C. Stanley, Experimental and Quasi-Experimental Designs for Research (Chicago: Rand McNally, 1966), pp. 5-6.

66. Thomas J. Sergiovanni, "Is Leadership the Next Great Training Robbery?" Educational Leadership 36 (March 1979): 388-94.

14

INDIVIDUAL AND GROUP BEHAVIOR IN SCHOOLS AS A FUNCTION OF ENVIRONMENTAL STRESS

James R. Terborg
John Komocar

Schools and school districts are particularly vulnerable to changes in social, economic, political, and legal demands. Whereas all organizations are to some degree dependent on these forces in the broader environment in which they operate, schools seem more dependent on and closely connected to outside pressures than are most other organization types. Bond-issue elections for additional revenue, parental demands for accountability, unexpected changes in state funding formulas, and court orders for integration are just a few examples of some critical dependencies schools have on their environments.

Research and theory in organizational behavior, however, have contributed little toward understanding how environmental changes external to organizations affect the attitudes and behaviors of participants inside organizations. Attempts to relate macroorganizational theory to microorganizational theory are few (Roberts, Hulin, and Rousseau, 1978). Yet meaningful relationships would seem to exist between changes in organizations' environments and patterns of behavior displayed by members of organizations.

The goal of this chapter is to outline the beginnings of a middle-range theory on individual and group behavior in schools that encounter

This chapter was prepared with support from Grant No. NIE-G-77-0043 from the National Institute of Education, James R. Terborg, Principal Investigator. We would like to thank Thomas Drabek, Charles Hulin, Joseph McGrath, Charles O'Reilly, and Karlene Roberts for helpful comments throughout various stages in the preparation of this chapter.

drastic changes in their environments. We will begin with a brief discussion of middle-range theories as applied to organizational research. This will be followed by a review and description of some organizational characteristics of schools that make them a unique organization type. Next we will introduce the concept of stress and describe the stress cycle. The stress cycle then will be applied to educational organizations. The chapter will conclude with a statement of working hypotheses and some suggestions for future research.

MIDDLE-RANGE THEORIES

Organizational theory and research is diverse, difficult to summarize, seemingly impossible to integrate, and often not practical enough to apply. There are several explanations for this. Organizations are complex social-technical systems that defy simple description and prescription. Organizations are studied from different paradigms and methodologies reflecting the disciplines of psychology, sociology, economics, political science, and education. Organizations are researched at different levels of analysis reflecting individuals, groups, and organizations, but rarely are all three levels researched simultaneously. As a result, we have developed simplified models that focus primarily on either micro or macro aspects (Roberts, Hulin, and Rousseau, 1978). Or we have erred in the opposite direction with contingency theories based on open systems notions, which state that everything is related to everything else.

In reaction to this growing divergence in the organizational literature, Weick (1974) and Pinder and Moore (1979) have promoted the utility of middle-range theorizing (see Merton, 1968) to organizational theory. According to Pinder and Moore (1979), middle-range theories of organizations differ from general theories of organizations in that middle-range theories are developed to deal with specified aspects of organizational phenomena as opposed to broad and general issues. The objective is to select a particular relationship of interest and to investigate that relationship within the confines of certain assumptions. Because different assumptions may guide research on the same phenomenon, it is possible that conflicting results and conclusions can be reached. This does not mean, however, that one set of results is to be preferred over another. Rather, it expands our knowledge of the phenomenon as investigated.

In one sense, critical experiments between competing middle-range theories of organizations may be difficult to design and this could be judged as a shortcoming. Taken another way, however, middle-range theories of organizations recognize complexities inherent in organizational behavior and deal with complexities through systematic reduction of topics of interest and/or acceptance of certain guiding assumptions. In the physical sciences, for example, much has been learned about the properties of light, even though one set of assumptions led to the study of light as particles whereas another set of assumptions led to the study of light as waves. The result was not the emergence of a general theory of the properties of light, but the development of limited but more accurate theories of light under certain conditions.

Returning to our discussion of organizations, there are several requirements that must be satisfied prior to the development of an organizational middle-range theory. First, specific organization types must be identified and described. The present work does this by focusing attention on schools as one type of organization. Second, a definable set of concepts must be chosen for inclusion in the theory. The present work does this through use of stress and the stress cycle. Finally, it may be necessary at times to specify unique research strategies and tactics. The conclusion of this work will discuss methodological implications associated with the study of individual and group behavior in schools that are experiencing environmental stress.

SCHOOLS AS ORGANIZATIONS

A major shortcoming of research on schools, as conducted by organizational behavior researchers, has been the treatment of schools as if they were similar to other organization types such as private industry or government (Blumberg, 1977). In this section some salient characteristics of schools as organizations will be discussed.

As previously noted, schools and school districts are especially vulnerable to changes in the environment (Bidwell, 1965; Miles, 1965; Newman and Wallender, 1978; Freeman, 1979). Schools are pluralistic organizations serving the needs of pluralistic social environments (Meyer and Rowan, 1978). Changes in local taxation, state funding formulas, population densities, birth rates, laws concerning integration, and parental demands for competency testing can have rather direct effects on the operation of schools.

Schools and school districts are characterized by a lack of consensus concerning organizational goals and measurement of goal achievement (Miles, 1965; Hills and Mahoney, 1978; Meyer, Scott, Cole, and Intili, 1978; Pfeffer and Salancik, 1974; Newman and Wallender, 1978; Salancik and Pfeffer, 1974). Schools operate in environments where there is little knowledge of cause and effect, a general lack of information, and a variable time span of discretion. Although traditionally the rate of environmental change has been slow, this may no longer be accurate.

Variability in input is another characteristic. Besides being dependent on outside agencies for funding, schools have little control over the number of students and the homogeneity of student needs (Carlson, 1965). Although large school districts can establish magnet schools for particular areas, schools in general have little impact on their inputs.

The importance of the school board as a force in the environment should not be overlooked (Bidwell, 1965). School board membership often consists of people who have little formal training in education. Consequently, when the board operates in a managerial rather than a fiduciary capacity, there is increased likelihood of conflict between professional school administrators and the school board.

Several writers also have discussed the "disconnectedness" of schools as compared with other organizations (compare Meyer et al., 1978; Meyer and Rowan, 1978; Weick, 1976). Meyer and Rowan (1978) observed that structure is loosely linked with technical work activity and that technical work activity is loosely linked with its effects. Weick (1976) used the term "loosely coupled" to depict the lack of functional relationships among subunits within the school. With the exception of certain activities such as scheduling, space, and hiring, which tend to be centralized and bureaucratic, the activities of separate systems within the school have little impact on each other (Meyer and Rowan, 1978).

Several writers have reported that schools are characteristically slow to adopt innovations. There is a built-in resistance to change (Miles, 1964; Sarason, 1971). This may be important when excessive demands are made of the organization. If historically schools have resisted innovation in educational practices, then why would we expect to find receptivity to changes brought about by outside interventions such as integration or competency testing? During periods of organizational munificence, there are solutions for most problems and each unit can function separately. When slack is reduced, however, units may become "tightly coupled." There no longer are solutions to most problems and changes in one area may now have rather severe consequences for other areas.

Finally, it has been suggested that schools and other nonprofit organizations tend to operate as political systems (Cohen and Gadon, 1978; Newman and Wallender, 1978; Pfeffer, 1978). In a political system, means and ends are primarily determined by the manipulation and management of resources, power, and authority. Because schools are dependent on government and public will for funding, and because school boards and school administrators may differ in expertise and opinion concerning the operation of the school, there is potential for considerable bargaining, influence, and counterinfluence at this level.

In summary, there are several characteristics of schools as organizations that must be considered if a middle-range theory is to be developed. Schools are vulnerable to environmental pressures and are easily accessed by constituents. Schools are composed of professional people with strong commitments to their careers who have a history of being autonomous and loosely coupled. School board members usually are not trained in educational procedures yet they have considerable potential to impact day-to-day operations. Schools traditionally have been slow to adapt to changes and to innovate. Finally, the possibility of political behavior that may involve a considerable number of participants is strong under certain conditions.

THE CONCEPT OF STRESS

Having described the nature of the specific organization type to be investigated, Pinder and Moore (1979) suggest that the next step in the development of a middle-range theory is to select particular relationships of interest and to identify relevant parameters and processes. We use the concept of stress for this purpose. Specifically, we are interested in externally induced stress and not in stress that originates from within the organization. Although external stress may result in internal stress, our initial attention is directed to stress in the environment. This brings the concept of stress in line with other environmental factors such as turbulence, uncertainty, and complexity. In contrast to these factors, stress research conducted at different levels of analysis provides a mechanism whereby macro concepts might be integrated with micro-level behavior. This promotes consolidation of otherwise segregated hypotheses.

The Definition of Stress

It is important to provide a clear and unambiguous definition of stress because stress has been operationalized in different ways and this inconsistency contributes to the diversity of results in stress research. We believe stress is best described as an interaction between the focal system and the environment. McGrath (1976:1352) states: "There is potential for stress when an environmental situation is perceived as presenting a demand which threatens to exceed the person's capabilities and resources for meeting it, under conditions where he expects a substantial differential in the rewards or costs from meeting the demand versus not meeting it."

Haas and Drabek (1973:251) use the organization as the focal system when they define stress as "the organizational state or condition indicated by the degree of discrepancy between organizational demands and organizational capacity." The key notions are an imbalance between some external force on the system and the capacity of the system to respond. Furthermore, this imbalance must be in an area where failure to remove the imbalance is judged to be of considerable importance.

A more general way of thinking about the types of environmental forces that fit within the stress concept has been proposed by Haythorn (1970). Environmental forces can have a demand function in that they compel or require certain sets of responses. These demands can be positive for the general state of the system or they can be negative. Second, forces can have a constraint function in that they preclude or prevent certain sets of responses from occurring. These constraints can be either positive or negative for the long-term state of the system. Finally, environmental forces can have a potentiality function where new sets of responses are permitted or are now possible, even though a specific response is not required or prevented. It is important to note that stress does not always lead to deterioration of the system. Stress can have positive effects too.

For the purpose of this chapter, stress is defined to exist when some environmental force produces a demand, constraint, or opportunity that creates an imbalance with regard to the system's current capacity to respond, and when this imbalance is judged to be of considerable importance such that failure to respond in some way is not desirable. This imbalance results from a change in environmental forces, from a change in the system's response capacity, or from both. This imbalance can be something that occurs suddenly, with or without warning, or it can be the accumulation of gradual changes such that failure to respond is no longer an acceptable response. Haas and Drabek (1973) referred to this time frame factor in their use of the terms "chronic" and "acute" stress.

Although it could be argued that this definition and conceptualization of stress is too general to be of much utility, one value of such a definition is that it allows several concepts to be subsumed within the stress framework. This is important given the general validity of the stress cycle found at different units of analysis—individual, group, organizational, and community. For example, several writers in organizational research have used basic notions of stress as developed here to describe other conditions that could usefully be studied when placed within the stress framework. Consider the concept of organizational slack. March and Olsen (1976:87) define organizational slack as "the difference between existing resources

and activated demands." Although in this work and in the preceding
works of Cyert and March (1963) and March and Simon (1958) propositions were developed concerning the effects of organizational slack
on the behavior of groups and individuals in organizations, these
propositions lack a unifying mechanism that integrates the notions
of slack to other related areas. Crisis is a second term closely
connected to stress research. Fink, Beak, and Taddeo (1971:16-17)
define crisis: "A human system (individual, group, organization,
or other) is assumed to be in a state of crisis when its repertoire of
coping responses is not adequate to bring about the resolution of a
problem which poses a threat to the system." Similarly, Mulder,
Ritsema, and de Jong (1971:21) define organizational crisis as "a
situation in which goals are at stake that are of high importance to
the system when the probability that these [necessary] goals will be
advanced is [too] small." The similarities between these definitions
of slack and crisis to the proposed definition of stress suggests that
these concepts merit consideration within general stress research.

Some Problems with Stress

Many problems exist with the stress concept and these are
discussed by McGrath (1970, 1976) and Haas and Drabek (1970, 1973).
First, a common metric is needed for measuring the degree of imbalance between some environmental force and the response capacity
of the system. Otherwise, stress research becomes ipsative and
ideographic. Second, measures of responses to conditions defined
as stressful show little convergence. This is especially evident in
research on human physiological changes. Third, attempts to define the existence of a stress condition by the set of responses stress
is hypothesized to produce is methodologically weak. Fourth, stress
may occur for several different reasons and these may happen singly
or in combination. Finally, different types of imbalance may produce different perceptions of stress for different parts of the system.
Nevertheless, the concept does appear to be useful at least for now,
and meaningful research can be designed that is sensitive to the problems mentioned.

THE STRESS CYCLE

One of the values of stress research to the development of a
middle-range theory is the existence of the stress cycle. The stress
cycle refers first to the process of response following the occurrence
of a change in the relationship between environmental demand-

constraint-opportunity forces and the response capacity of the system, and then to structural factors that affect the response process. Thus, through consideration of the stress cycle, it is possible to identify particular sets of responses that merit attention, the nature of exchanges between and among parts of the overall system that is in a state of stress, the temporal sequence of these responses and exchanges, and the structural conditions that facilitate, inhibit, and in other ways shape the progression of the response process itself.

The stress cycle to be described is seductively simple. Yet it has been proposed by researchers looking at different units of analysis and has been supported with empirical data. The following discussion is based on the work of Fink, Beak, and Taddeo (1971), Janis (1971), Kahn (1970), Lazarus (1966), McGrath (1970, 1976), Mileti, Drabek, and Haas (1975), and Selye (1956).

The stress cycle starts when something happens "out there" that presents a system with a demand, a constraint, or an opportunity for response. This class of events can collectively be called the environmental stress event. Second, there is recognition of the stress event by the focal system or by a part of the focal system. Through an appraisal process, the focal system attends to the stress event and evaluates the consequences of the stress event. Third, depending on the outcome of this appraisal process, some set of responses is emitted. If the stress event is judged to be of considerable consequence for the normal functioning of the system, then some set of responses will occur in direct reaction to perceptions of the stress event. This can be referred to as the response process. Fourth, there are consequences of the response process. Depending on how these consequences are perceived, the system either responds again in relation to the stress event, or the stress event loses its motivational properties and the system returns to a steady state. This steady state may be similar to or different from that which existed prior to the stress event. Once the stress event has been successfully dealt with, there is a stabilization process of readjustment to the new steady state.

THE STRESS CYCLE APPLIED TO
EDUCATIONAL ORGANIZATIONS

Being guided by notions of the stress cycle, it is possible to identify several sets of variables that can be incorporated into the study of individual and group behavior in educational organizations that are experiencing conditions of environmental stress. These variable sets are presented in Figure 14.1. The figure should be viewed as a listing of salient variables that merit study as the stress cycle unfolds. It is not intended to depict a complete formal model.

FIGURE 14.1

Framework for the Stress Cycle with Examples of Salient Variables

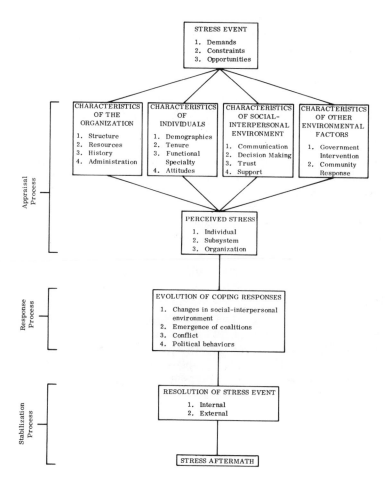

Source: Compiled by the authors.

Stress Event

First, at the top of the figure is placed the stress event. Consideration of the nature of the stress event can be complex, but as stated by Haas and Drabek (1973), the concept is useful if somewhat abstruse. Major considerations are the source or sources of the imbalance, the degree to which the imbalance could be described as chronic or acute, and the scope or severity of the imbalance. Sources of imbalance refer to the degree of changes in demands, constraints, and opportunities, or to changes in some combination of these. The distinction between chronic and acute stress deals primarily with the degree to which the imbalance is unexpected. Finally, scope refers to the severity of the imbalance, the degree to which the imbalance affects the entire system or only parts of the system, the degree to which the imbalance can be controlled, and the time frame of the imbalance. Consequently, the stress event is best conceptualized as continuous rather than discrete, and as consisting of multiple components.

In educational organizations, the imbalance created by the stress event can occur in several ways. It is important to specify some of these so that environmental stress can be identified independent of the effects it is supposed to produce. First, there can be changing patterns of funding at local, state, and federal levels. These changes can occur gradually or suddenly. Second, declining or accelerating enrollments can create an imbalance. Although this factor would usually be gradual, rapid shifts in population can occur. Third, government intervention such as bussing and equal employment in hiring can impact on the day-to-day as well as long-term functioning of the school. Fourth, changes in public attitudes toward education and in concern for demonstrated accountability should be considered. Fifth, factors dealing with teacher unionization are relevant. The possibility of unionization, choice of a particular union as the bargaining agent, and the occurrence of teacher strikes over wages, benefits, and teaching conditions could classify as stress events. Finally, disasters such as floods, fires, earthquakes, and tornadoes could damage the physical structures of schools and communities such that considerable disruption results.

These are just a few factors that could be listed. The important point is that schools as nonprofit organizations, dependent on public funding, and as pluralistic organizations, serving several environments, are in many ways vulnerable to factors that can create an imbalance and that can be incorporated into a study of environmental stress.

Appraisal Process

The appraisal process represents the next state in the stress cycle. This refers to factors that influence how the stress event is recognized, perceived, and evaluated by the system as a whole and by parts of the system. The appraisal process is important for human systems such as individuals, groups, organizations, and communities. It represents an important area where a stress-strain analogy from engineering would not be applicable. A bridge does not sense or recognize the load placed on it and a bridge does not respond as an active system that can exert counterpressure on the load. The importance of the appraisal process should not be underemphasized.

Relevant factors in the appraisal process for educational organizations are: characteristics of the external environment in which the school exists, characteristics of the school as an organization, characteristics of individuals who are members of the organization, and characteristics of the social-interpersonal environment of the organization. These factors will be discussed separately. It should be realized, however, that they can and do interact.

With regard to the external environment and the appraisal process, the perceived beneficence of the environment by organizational members may be important. If the environment historically has come to the aid of the school, then the stress event may be evaluated as less likely to have considerable effects on school functioning. Second, if the environment is perceived to possess necessary resources, the stress event also may be evaluated as less severe. Anxiety over an upcoming bond issue might be affected by local economic conditions. We would expect less anxiety in growing industrial communities than in communities where factory closings are commonplace. Third, the presence of public and elected official concerns over the importance of the stress event for the school should be considered. For example, there may be community efforts to raise contributions for the continuation of a threatened varsity athletic program, but there may be no such activities for art, music, and drama programs. In such instances we might expect different perceptions of the stress event among faculty in physical education and music.

We now turn to characteristics of schools as organizations and discuss how this affects the appraisal process. Based on the work of Hall (1977), Lawrence and Lorsch (1967), Pondy (1967), Thompson (1967), and Pfeffer (1978), we chose the organizational dimensions of complexity, centralization, and formalization as structural factors that will impact on how organizational members evaluate the stress event. Complex school districts, with considerable horizontal and vertical differentiation, may foster the formation of particularistic goals and values for unit members. Goal incompatibility is more likely to occur in highly differentiated organizations. Problems associated with communication and coordination also increase with complexity. Finally, in complex organizations and in loosely coupled organizations, the stress event may be localized within particular units rather than spread across the organization as a whole.

Centralization refers to the locus of formal control within the organization. It includes such factors as the locus of decision-making authority, the hierarchy of authority, autonomy, and participative decision making (Ford and Slocum, 1977). High centralization facilitates the degree to which top administrators can coordinate and mobilize activities and values of participants. In cases where quick action must be taken, high centralization is preferred (Hall, 1977). Centralization also would affect communication. Consequently, under situations of acute stress, centralization might be especially important for the transmission and accuracy of information concerning the reception and evaluation of the stress event. Errors and rumors could be more easily traced, monitored, and changed. But, as Pfeffer (1978) noted, centralization also could interfere with decision making because of information overload.

Finally, formalization refers to the degree to which rules and procedures are specified and adhered to (Ford and Slocum, 1977). Formalization and centralization are alternative forms of coordination and control. High formalization is functional when problems can be anticipated and procedures can be designed to deal with them. Thus, the existence of a procedure for dealing with school closings and teacher layoffs should affect the perception of a stress event that deals with declining enrollments. High formalization, however, is dysfunctional for reacting to unprogrammed situations (Hall, 1977). The degree of formalization may be more important for understanding perceptions to acute stress rather than to chronic stress.

It follows that organizational structure may affect the degree to which individuals believe that the organization can respond to a severe imbalance because structure affects the process of communication and information flow, member interactions, and the parameters that specify rules and procedures.

A second characteristic of the organization deals with the quality and experience of top administration. Newman and Wallender (1978) state that charismatic leadership and influence based on expertise rather than on formal authority are important in nonprofit organizations that include many professionals as members. This would apply to schools. Similarly, Mulder et al. (1971), Rosenbaum and Rosenbaum (1971), and Wynn (1977) report that leadership is especially important during crisis situations. We do not mean to consider traditional social-psychological factors of leader behavior such as consideration and initiating structure. Rather, we mean the role of administrators as resource allocators, decision makers, and system planners. There is little research on this aspect of administration, so it is difficult to present a list of factors that would denote quality administration. The impact of administration, however, regardless of whether the administration is good or bad, would probably be greatest during periods of stress and in organizations that are centralized, formalized, and not complex.

Finally, two other important factors at the organization level are organizational resources and organizational history. Availability of internal resources that can be reallocated may affect perceptions of stress to the extent that these resources are known to participants. Also, the history of the organization in dealing with past stress events may be relevant.

Characteristics of individuals who are members of the organization are a third factor important for the appraisal process. Knowledge of individual characteristics may be identified using the notion of frame of reference. As defined by Smith, Kendall, and Hulin (1969), frame of reference states that a person evaluates some situation or object on the basis of past experiences, perceptions of available alternatives, and expectations of future conditions. Demographic variables such as age, sex, marital status, number of dependents, and level of education may be surrogate measures for frame of reference. Knowledge of individual tenure, level in the organization, and functional speciality are other relevant factors. Given a budget cut, we might expect a person with tenure who is head of the high school mathematics department to perceive less stress at the individual level than a recently hired untenured teacher who is in the elementary education art program. Other individual characteristics include beliefs concerning professionalism, organizational commitment, and personal and organizational goals and priorities. Corwin (1973), in a study of curriculum changes in schools, found professionalism and personal goals to be especially relevant for understanding individual reactions to change.

The final factor that is relevant for the appraisal process is the nature of the social-interpersonal environment of the organization. This refers to perceptions and behaviors of organizational members concerning norms of appropriate behavior within the organization, past history of interpersonal exchanges, potential for future interaction, and the state of current interpersonal functioning. Relevant characteristics include such things as interpersonal trust; group and organizational cohesion; mode of informal decision making; distribution of power; communication frequency, openness, and accuracy; supportiveness; and degree of unresolved or latent conflict.

For example, if organizational members describe the social-interpersonal environment with terms like distrust, rigid, manipulative, competitive, covert, and overly emotional, we might expect a greater perception of stress to a proposed budget cut or a school closing and greater likelihood of destructive conflict behaviors and unsanctioned influence attempts than if organizational members described the social-interpersonal environment with terms like supportive, collaborative, open to new alternatives, cooperative, and honest.

The social-interpersonal environment also may affect the manner in which attributions are made about the stress event. Kilmann and Thomas (1978) proposed an attribution analysis in terms of conflict, but it also is relevant to the evaluation of a stress event. First, attributions can be made to process factors or to structural factors. Process deals with the temporal sequence of behaviors and exchanges. Structure deals with conditions that influence behavior. Second, attributions can be made to internal factors or to external factors. Internal factors deal with characteristics of individuals or parties involved. External factors deal with characteristics of outside agencies or people outside the organization. Not all stress events can be classified on both dimensions. For example, a natural disaster that destroys a school building would be a structural attribution that is external, but it is difficult to identify the outside party or parties involved. A teachers' strike, however, could be attributed to internal process factors such as friction between the teachers and the school board, or to external structural factors such as lack of funds due to a change in the state school funding formula. Part of the appraisal process involves ascertaining the "cause" of the stress event.

In summary, the perception of stress is the result of the stress event and characteristics of the organization, the external environment, the social-interpersonal environment, and of individuals. Also, as shown in Figure 14.1, the appraisal process must be examined from the perspectives of individuals, units within the system, and the entire system itself.

Response Process

The manner in which schools as organizations respond is perhaps the most interesting aspect of the stress cycle for the development of a middle-range theory relating environmental stress to intra-organizational functioning. During nonstress periods, behaviors settle into routines. An outstanding characteristic of many educational organizations is their stability and not their change. Although some degree of conflict over problems, solutions, and decisions may occur, and participants may vary according to issues and involvement, intraorganizational functioning might best be characterized as routine and stable. The stress event has potential to change this. Demands, constraints, and opportunities now exist and this is expected to disrupt the status quo.

Generally speaking, response patterns to environmental stress can be classified into two types. One type is functional in that it leads to successful coping with the stress event. Successful coping is defined as anything that leads to a relatively permanent restoration of balance between the system's capacity to respond and the demands, constraints, and opportunities currently in force on the system. The second type of response is dysfunctional to the extent that the imbalance is not removed. The continuation of an imbalance would lead to the eventual destruction of the system. The distinction between functional and dysfunctional response patterns should, however, be thought of as lying on a continuum rather than as two discrete response patterns.

The major determinants of a functional response are: the degree of past cooperation among parties involved, the degree of an organizationwide sense of cohesion, the belief that all participants share a common threat that can be minimized through joint efforts, and the belief that a clear solution agreeable to all parties involved can be reached (compare Deutsch, 1973; Hamblin, 1958; Janis, 1963; Katz and Kahn, 1966; Lott and Lott, 1965; March and Simon, 1958; Sherif, 1966; Stein, 1976; and Thomas, 1976). To the extent that these conditions exist or can be made to exist soon after the stress event occurs, we would expect to find honest collaboration and a minimum of conflict over issues that result from the stress event.

Complex organizations, however, are made up of individuals who have had different socialization experiences and training, belong to different formal and informal groups, have different goal priorities and outcome preferences, have different personalities and human relations skills, and are differently motivated to preserve and enhance their own self-interests and the interests of the groups to which they belong (Cyert and March, 1963; March and Olsen, 1976; Pfeffer, 1978). Consequently, the opportunity for conflict may be enhanced by the stress event (March and Simon, 1958; Walton, Dutton, and Cafferty, 1969).

Related to the issue of conflict is the emergence of political behaviors involving power and coalition formation. Decisions concerning how to cope with the stress event are likely to focus on questions of who gets what, when, where, and how (compare Salancik and Pfeffer, 1974; Pfeffer, Salancik, and Leblebici, 1976; Hills and Mahoney, 1978). Individuals and groups may be more likely to engage in behaviors designed to maintain or enhance one's position when no single solution to the stress event exists. Here, we might expect to find the formation of self-interest groups or coalitions with members who share common perceptions and values (compare Dalton, 1959; Gamson, 1968; Katz, 1964; Pfeffer, 1978; Stein, 1976; Thomas, 1976). Once formed, these self-interest groups or coalitions may then engage in power struggles or political behaviors that are inappropriate for the functioning of the organization as a whole. Research from a variety of disciplines suggests that these power struggles may be related to other determinants of dysfunctional response patterns. Some of these determinants are: distortion of communication, suspicion, polarization of opinions, reduced time perspectives, emotional behaviors, and other behaviors designed to enhance one's own position relative to others (compare Deutsch, 1973; Dalton, 1959; Gamson, 1965; Katz, 1964; Hermann, 1963; Laumann, Marsden, and Galaskiewicz, 1977; March and Olsen, 1976; Mulder et al., 1971; Pettigrew, 1973; Smart and Vertinsky, 1977). What might result from this is that win-lose orientations will develop, alternative or integrative solutions will not be considered, and the most powerful coalition or coalitions will advance their position at the expense of the other parties involved and possibly at the expense of the organization or constituents of the organization.

The notions of conflict and political behavior, and of functional versus dysfunctional responses to organizational growth as opposed to decline, deserve some attention. The preceding discussion primarily has focused on the stress event as a constraint. Rapid growth of a school district, however, can create a severe imbalance just as rapid decline can create a severe imbalance. Here, however, the objective may be more like empire building than survival. Coalitions may form around issues concerning the allocation of new resources rather than around the allocation of scarce resources. This aspect of behavior in organizations has received little attention. Although there may be many solutions to a variety of problems, expectations are raised. Win-lose situations could develop such that subunit or individual self-interests are maximized at the potential expense of the major goals of the school, the students, and the community.

In summary, the response process represents a period of increased activity among organizational members. These activities may be functional to the extent that balance between the system's response capacity and the demands and constraints placed on the system is restored. These activities may be dysfunctional to the extent that balance is not restored or that new problems are created resulting from destructive conflict and political behavior. Finally, both functional and dysfunctional response patterns in schools can occur regardless of whether the stress event places constraints on current functioning, as in a drop in state and community funding, or whether it places demands for increased output, as in growth resulting from changes in population densities.

Stabilization Process

The stabilization process is the final stage in the stress cycle. As a result of internal or external forces, some more or less final decision or solution will be implemented. To the extent that this restores balance to the organization–environment exchange, the stress event will lose motivating properties. This is followed by stress aftermath. Stress aftermath is characterized by a stabilization of the social–interpersonal environment, with possibly new interpersonal relationships of day-to-day activity patterns. These patterns may be quite dissimilar from what existed prior to the stress event. Characteristics of the organization also may have changed. Preventive coping in terms of formalized rules and procedures for dealing with future stress events may be developed, resources may be stockpiled, and the composition of organizational membership may be altered due to hirings and layoffs. The organization in essence has negotiated a new equilibrium level.

The importance of the stabilization process is that it prepares the organization for the next stress event, and it lays the groundwork for working through new patterns of exchange during the equilibrium period. It should not be assumed that the stabilization process and stress aftermath are periods of inactivity. The organization is not dormant but is functioning under a new set of demands, constraints, and opportunities.

WORKING HYPOTHESES: A SUMMARY
OF THE CHAPTER

Several writers from the areas of conflict, organizational behavior, and education have stated the need for descriptive work on processes of the type discussed in this chapter (compare Corwin, 1969; March and Olsen, 1976; Sarason, 1971; Thomas, 1976). The development at this time of detailed propositions would be unwise given the absence of general descriptive knowledge. Nevertheless, it would seem useful to summarize this chapter with the presentation of some general working hypotheses. The first ten hypotheses make general statements about relationships between stress events and

organization reactions. The last eight hypotheses focus more specifically on the nature of schools as organizations. These working
hypotheses are offered so that research can be designed in a meaningful way with attention toward developing a middle-range theory
of environmental stress and behavior within schools.

The first two working hypotheses (H1 and H2) note the dynamic
and reciprocal nature of relationships between and among systems:

H1: Organizations and subsystems within organizations adapt
to and create environments such that demands, constraints,
and opportunities are in balance with response capacities.

H2: Imbalance among environments, organizations, and subsystems within organizations occurs when demands,
constraints, and opportunities exceed in either direction
current response capacities.

The third working hypothesis emphasizes the need to consider
both micro-level factors and macro-level factors, and the notion
that environmental forces can have different effects on different
parts of the organization:

H3: Within the organization, individual perceptions of the
severity of stress for the individual, the unit in which the
individual works, and the organization as a whole will be
a function of individual characteristics, social-interpersonal environmental characteristics, organizational characteristics, and other forces in the external environment.

The next four hypotheses consider structural factors that influence the impact of leadership, the likelihood of innovative solutions, and the likelihood of implementation of solutions:

H4: Top administrators, whether competent or incompetent
with regard to the stress event, will have the greatest impact on the organization's response to the stress event
when organizational structure is simple, high on centralization, and high on formalization. They will have the
least impact when organizational structure is complex,
low on centralization, and low on formalization.

H5: The likelihood that diverse and innovative solutions to the
stress event will be proposed will be greatest in organizations that are complex, low on centralization, and low on
formalization, and least in organizations that are simple,
high on centralization, and high on formalization.

H6: The likelihood of successful implementation of a chosen course of action will be greatest in organizations that are simple, high on centralization, and high on formalization, and least in organizations that are complex, low on centralization, and low on formalization.

H7: The most effective response to the stress event will occur when top administration is able to change organizational structure such that the likelihood of both innovation and implementation is maximized.

The next three hypotheses pertain to possible system responses to the stress event:

H8: Perceived stress will be related to the magnitude of disturbance in the social-interpersonal environment. This could be indexed by changes in the perceptual and behavioral nature of the social-interpersonal environment, communication frequency and accuracy, emergence of coalitions, individual participation in decision making, and task-related activities.

H9: Disturbance in the social-interpersonal environment will be beneficial to the state of the organization to the extent that: a single solution to the stress event is seen as acceptable to influential parties, the stress event is perceived as a threat to the entire organization and not limited to specific subsystems or individuals, and an organizationwide sense of unity is achieved in terms of few opposing coalitions, shared values and goals, open communication, consideration of short- and long-range time perspectives, and an integrative solution is developed.

H10: Disturbance in the social-interpersonal environment will be dysfunctional to the state of the organization to the extent that: no single solution is seen as acceptable to influential parties, the stress event is perceived as a threat to specific subsystems or individuals, coalitions form around outcome preferences, influential people have incompatible outcome preferences, influential people belong to opposing coalitions, and opposing coalitions do not share common communication links.

The final eight hypotheses pertain more directly to schools as a particular organization type:

H11: Schools experience more severe and more frequent environmentally induced changes in demands, constraints, and opportunities for new action than do other organization types.

H12: Schools, in contrast with other organization types, control, coordinate, and assign resources more through rituals and institutionalized decision rules than through functional demands or evaluation of individual and subgroup output value.

H13: Schools, in contrast with other organization types, are highly differentiated and loosely coupled.

H14: Schools, as differentiated loosely coupled social systems, will display considerable heterogeneity in perceptions and appraisals of the stress event across different subgroups and different age/tenure classifications. This will result in the formation of cohesive identifiable cliques designed to protect self-interests.

H15: Schools, as differentiated loosely coupled social systems with little history of systemwide participation in problem solving, will be more likely to display dysfunctional response patterns than functional response patterns to stress events.

H16: Schools, as institutionalized loosely coupled social systems, will be swift and effective in responding to environmentally induced stress focused at the level of a particular subgroup. However, schools will be slow and ineffective in responding to environmentally induced stress focused at the entire system as a whole.

H17: Schools, characterized by a high degree of institutionalization, a low degree of objective evaluation of individual and subgroup output value, and the existence of relatively independent and particularistic subgroups, will base resource allocation decisions stemming from the stress event on subjective-emotional appeals and power rather than on objective-rational appeals and cooperation.

H18: Schools, characterized by a high degree of institutionalization, a low degree of objective evaluation of individual and subgroup output value, and the existence of relatively independent and particularistic subgroups, will be more likely to carry over latent conflict to the stress aftermath stage than to remove latent conflict effectively during resolution of the stress event.

SUGGESTIONS FOR THE CONDUCT OF RESEARCH

Current theorizing about organizations has focused attention on dynamic processes involving environments, organizations, and various levels of subsystems within organizations. The ideas presented in this chapter reflect this trend.

Research methodologies, however, have not been fully developed that deal efficiently with the involved complexities. Problems of aggregation are not easily solved. Static designs yield data that fail to capture reciprocal processes. The analysis and interpretation of change are often ambiguous. The purpose of this section is to comment briefly on some methodological issues that relate to the study of environmental stress and individual group behavior in schools as organizations.

First, stress, as a characteristic of the environment, must be operationalized independent of the effects it is hypothesized to produce. We suggest that initial focus be directed to more obvious sources of changes in demands, constraints, and opportunities such as anticipated but rapid shifts in enrollments, school closings, changes in state or local funding, forced bussing and desegregation, and natural disasters that destroy school buildings and equipment. Although it will require considerable front-end work to gain access to schools during these periods, we believe the effort is justified.

Second, it is almost a necessity that longitudinal designs be employed. Because of the dynamic nature of the stress cycle and because stress is thought to interrupt ongoing behavior (Weick, 1970), we must collect data that accurately depict the richness and variability of the behavior.

Third, logistical and analytical problems associated with sample size and units of analysis are not dismissed easily. For example, one attempt to study the effects of environmental stress on intraorganizational behavior would be to conduct massive attitude survey studies that include 30, 40, or more schools or school districts. In this way, effects of organizational structure could be examined as well as individual behavior within specific organizations— but this approach would be very time consuming and expensive and it creates numerous other problems that need not be specified here. Campbell (1977) suggests consideration of simulations or case study methods as possible alternatives. Although these procedures have problems (see Bouchard, 1976), case studies are useful for hypothesis generation (see Pettigrew, 1973) and simulations can be designed that allow for limited tests of theoretical relationships on the stress cycle (see Drabek, 1969). Participant observation in a single school during the stress event is a third consideration. This approach could produce rich descriptions of events, but the ability to test theoretical propositions concerning structure, for example, would be difficult.

We suggest consideration of a compromise approach. The objective would be to conduct field research on a small number of organizations with reliance on the use of a taxonomy of organization characteristics and a carefully planned assessment package. It is a variation of the N = 1 case study approach using time series designs with nonequivalent no treatment control groups. The first step is to select a small number of organizations that vary meaningfully on theoretically relevant organizational characteristics. This is where a common taxonomy of organizations would be useful. The next step is to select organizations that differ on some environmental factor of concern. The third step is to collect data over an appropriate time period. To the extent that patterns of relationships change as a function of organizational characteristics and environmental forces, and that data from several methods and sources converge, then reliable and valid conclusions can be drawn from studies that use a minimal number of organizations. For example, the effect of declining and increasing enrollments in school districts could be studied by carefully selecting school districts on the basis of size, location, structure, and by selecting them on the basis of rate of growth and decline. The effects of complex versus simple organizational structure and growth versus decline could be studied in depth over time using as few as four school districts. Also schools experiencing growth and decline could be compared with other organization types such as hospitals that are undergoing similar changes in demands.

The fourth and final point to be discussed concerns the empirical study of behavior in organizations under stress. A methodology is needed that adequately describes changes in the social-interpersonal environment. Organizations are social systems. People are joined by a variety of relationships and exchanges that pertain to such things as communication flow, affect, task-flow dependencies, influence, power, evaluation, and opinion. The richness of these exchanges needs to be fully described and understood. One possible and promising solution to the study of such relationships could be the use of network analysis to supplement data from surveys, interviews, and observation (see Tichy, Tushman, and Fombrun, 1979).

CONCLUSION

The purpose of this chapter was to consider factors that might be important for understanding how individuals and groups in schools respond to environmental stress. A considerable body of literature was reviewed and an attempt was made to develop the beginnings of a middle-range theory linking organization environments to organization member behaviors. The concept of stress and the process of the stress cycle were judged to be useful in this attempt at integration.

Schools as organizations were chosen for emphasis because of the particular vulnerability schools have to changes in environmental demands, constraints, and opportunities for action. In addition, schools possess characteristics that amplify the appraisal process, the response process, and the stabilization process within the stress cycle. Schools seem to operate as institutionalized organizations that are loosely coupled (Meyer et al., 1978). Although this may be functional for localized adaptation to localized stress, it would seem to be dysfunctional for systemwide adaptation to systemwide stress.

Dissensus on goals, absence of objective criteria for resource allocation, built-in resistance to change, and a history of autonomous functioning among professional people who have strong career commitments are characteristics that describe schools as organizations. These same characteristics are relevant for understanding behavior according to the stress cycle. These characteristics combined with the fact that schools are vulnerable to their environments make schools especially good organizations for study.

Although research on environmental stress will be difficult to do, we believe that much can be learned. Stress disrupts routine operations and presents opportunities for new behaviors. It is during these periods that considerable knowledge about organizational functioning and about schools as organizations can be acquired.

REFERENCES

Bidwell, C. E. 1965. "The School as a Formal Organization." In Handbook of Organizations, edited by James G. March. Chicago: Rand McNally.

Blumberg, A. 1977. "A Complex Problem—An Overly Simple Diagnosis." Journal of Applied Behavioral Science 13:184-89.

Bouchard, T. J. 1976. "Field Research Methods: Interviewing, Questionnaires, Participant Observation, Systematic Observation, Unobtrusive Measures." In Handbook of Industrial and Organizational Psychology, edited by M. D. Dunnette. Chicago: Rand McNally.

Campbell, J. P. 1977. "On the Nature of Organizational Effectiveness." In New Perspectives on Organizational Effectiveness, edited by P. S. Goodman and J. M. Pennings. San Francisco: Jossey-Bass.

Carlson, R. O. 1965. "Barriers to Change in Public Schools." In Change Processes in the Public Schools, edited by R. O. Carlson, A. Gallaher, M. B. Miles, R. J. Pellegrin, and E. M. Rogers. Eugene: Center for the Advanced Study of Educational Administration, University of Oregon.

Cohen, A. R., and H. Gadon. 1978. "Changing the Management Culture in a Public School System." Journal of Applied Behavioral Science 14:61-78.

Corwin, R. G. 1973. Reform and Organizational Survival. New York: John Wiley.

Corwin, R. G. 1969. "Patterns of Organizational Conflict." Administrative Science Quarterly 14:507-20.

Cyert, R. M., and J. G. March. 1963. A Behavioral Theory of the Firm. Englewood Cliffs, N.J.: Prentice-Hall.

Dalton, M. 1959. Men Who Manage. New York: John Wiley.

Deutsch, M. 1973. The Resolution of Conflict: Constructive and Destructive Processes. New Haven, Conn.: Yale University Press.

Drabek, T. E. 1969. Laboratory Simulation of a Police Communication System Under Stress. Columbus: College of Administrative Science, Ohio State University.

Fink, S. L., J. Beak, and K. Taddeo. 1971. "Organizational Crises and Change." Journal of Applied Behavioral Science 7:15-37.

Ford, J. D., and J. W. Slocum. 1977. "Size, Technology, Environment and the Structure of Organizations." Academy of Management Review 2:561-75.

Freeman, J. 1979. "Going to the Well: School District Administrative Intensity and Environmental Constraint." Administrative Science Quarterly 24:119-33.

Gamson, W. A. 1968. Power and Discontent. Homewood, Ill.: Dorsey Press.

Haas, J. E., and T. E. Drabek. 1973. Complex Organizations: A Sociological Perspective. New York: Macmillan.

Haas, J. E., and T. E. Drabek. 1970. "Community Disaster and System Stress: A Sociological Perspective." In Social and Psychological Factors in Stress, edited by J. E. McGrath. New York: Holt, Rinehart, & Winston.

Hall, R. H. 1977. Organizations: Structure and Process. Englewood Cliffs, N.J.: Prentice-Hall.

Hamblin, R. L. 1958. "Group Integration during a Crisis." Human Relations 11:67-76.

Haythorn, W. W. 1970. "Interpersonal Stress in Isolated Groups." In Social and Psychological Factors in Stress, edited by J. E. McGrath. New York: Holt, Rinehart & Winston.

Hermann, C. F. 1963. "Some Consequences of Crisis Which Limit the Viability of Organizations." Administrative Science Quarterly 8:61-82.

Hills, F. S., and T. A. Mahoney. 1978. "University Budgets and Organizational Decision Making." Administrative Science Quarterly 23:454-65.

Janis, I. L. 1971. Stress and Frustration. New York: Harcourt, Brace, Jovanovich.

Janis, I. L. 1963. "Group Identification under Conditions of External Danger." British Journal of Medical Psychology 36:227-38.

Kahn, R. L. 1970. "Some Propositions toward a Researchable Conceptualization of Stress." In Social and Psychological Factors in Stress, edited by J. E. McGrath. New York: Holt, Rinehart & Winston.

Katz, D. 1964. "Approaches to Managing Conflict." In Power and Conflict in Organizations, edited by R. L. Kahn and K. Boulding. New York: Basic Books.

Katz, D., and R. L. Kahn. 1966. The Social Psychology of Organizations. New York: John Wiley.

Kilmann, R. H., and K. W. Thomas. 1978. "Four Perspectives on Conflict Management: An Attributional Framework for Organizing Descriptive and Normative Theory." Academy of Management Review 3:59-68.

Laumann, E. O., P. V. Marsden, and J. Galaskiewicz. 1977. "Community-elite Influence Structures: Extension of a Network Approach." American Journal of Sociology 83:594-631.

Lawrence, P. R., and J. W. Lorsch. 1967. Organization and Environment. Cambridge, Mass.: Harvard University Press.

Lazarus, R. S. 1966. Psychological Stress and the Coping Process. New York: McGraw-Hill.

Lott, A. J., and B. E. Lott. 1965. "Groups Cohesiveness as Interpersonal Attraction: A Review of Relationships with Antecedent and Consequent Variables." Psychological Bulletin 64:259-409.

March, J. G., and J. P. Olsen. 1976. Ambiguity and Choice in Organizations. Oslo: Universitetsforlaget.

March, J. G., and H. A. Simon. 1958. Organizations. New York: John Wiley.

McGrath, J. E. 1976. "Stress and Behavior in Organizations." In Handbook of Industrial and Organizational Psychology, edited by M. D. Dunnette. Chicago: Rand McNally.

McGrath, J. E. 1970. Social and Psychological Factors in Stress. New York: Holt, Rinehart & Winston.

Merton, R. 1968. Social Theory and Social Structure. Glencoe, Ill.: The Free Press.

Meyer, J. W., and B. Rowan. 1978. "The Structure of Educational Organizations." In Environments and Organizations, edited by M. W. Meyer. San Francisco: Jossey-Bass.

Meyer, J. W., W. R. Scott, S. Cole, and J. K. Intili. 1978. "Instructional Dissensus and Institutional Consensus in Schools." In Environments and Organizations, edited by M. W. Meyer. San Francisco: Jossey-Bass.

Miles, M. B. 1965. "Planned Change and Organizational Health: Figure and Ground." In Change Processes in the Public Schools, edited by R. O. Carlson, A. Gallaher, M. B. Miles, R. J. Pellegrin, and E. M. Rogers. Eugene: Center for the Advanced Study of Educational Administration, University of Oregon.

Miles, M. B. 1964. "Educational Innovation: The Nature of the Problem." In Innovation in Education, edited by M. B. Miles. New York: Columbia University Press.

Mileti, D. S., T. E. Drabek, and J. E. Haas. 1975. Human Systems in Extreme Environments: A Sociological Perspective. Boulder, Colo.: Institute of Behavioral Science.

Mulder, M., J. R. Ritsema, and R. D. de Jong. 1971. "An Organization in Crisis and Non-crisis Situations." Human Relations 24:19-41.

Newman, W. H., and H. W. Wallender. 1978. "Managing Not-for-Profit Enterprises." Academy of Management Review 3:24-31.

Pettigrew, A. M. 1973. The Politics of Organizational Decision Making. London: Tavistock.

Pfeffer, J. 1978. Organizational Design. Arlington Heights, Ill.: AHM Publishing Company.

Pfeffer, J., and G. R. Salancik. 1974. "Organizational Decision-Making as a Political Process: The Case of a University Budget." Administrative Science Quarterly 19:135-51.

Pfeffer, J., G. R. Salancik, and H. Leblebici. 1976. "The Effect of Uncertainty on the Use of Social Influence in Organizational Decision Making." Administrative Science Quarterly 21:227-45.

Pinder, C. C., and L. F. Moore. 1979. "The Resurrection of Taxonomy to Aid the Development of Middle Range Theories of Organizational Behavior." Administrative Science Quarterly 24:99-118.

Pondy, L. R. 1967. "Organizational Conflict: Concepts and Models." Administrative Science Quarterly 12:296-320.

Roberts, K. H., C. L. Hulin, and D. Rousseau. 1978. Organizational Science: Strategies for Research and Theory Development. San Francisco: Jossey-Bass.

Rogers, E. M., and R. Agarwala-Rogers. 1976. Communication in Organizations. New York: The Free Press.

Rosenbaum, L. L., and W. B. Rosenbaum. 1971. "Morale and Productivity Consequences of Group Leadership Style, Stress, and Type of Task." Journal of Applied Psychology 55:343-48.

Salancik, G. R., and J. Pfeffer. 1974. "The Bases and Use of Power in Organizational Decision-making: The Case of a University." Administrative Science Quarterly 19:453-73.

Sarason, S. B. 1971. The Culture of the School and the Problem of Change. Boston: Allyn & Bacon.

Selye, H. 1956. The Stresses of Life. New York: McGraw-Hill.

Sherif, M. 1966. In Common Predicament: Social Psychology of Intergroup Conflict and Cooperation. Boston: Houghton Mifflin.

Smart, C., and I. Vertinsky. 1977. "Designs for Crisis Decision Units." Administrative Science Quarterly 22:640-57.

Smith, P. C., L. M. Kendall, and C. L. Hulin. 1969. The Measurement of Satisfaction in Work and Retirement. Chicago: Rand McNally.

Stein, A. A. 1976. "Conflict and Cohesion." Journal of Conflict Resolution 20:143-72.

Thomas, K. 1976. "Conflict and Conflict Management." In Handbook of Industrial Organizational Psychology, edited by M. D. Dunnette. Chicago: Rand McNally.

Thompson, J. D. 1967. Organizations in Action. New York: McGraw-Hill.

Tichy, N. M., M. L. Tushman, and C. Fombrun. 1979. "Social Network Analysis for Organizations." Academy of Management Review 4:507-20.

Walton, R. E., J. M. Dutton, and T. P. Cafferty. 1969. "The Management of Interdepartmental Conflict: A Model and Review." Administrative Science Quarterly 14:73-84.

Weick, K. E. 1976. "Educational Organizations as Loosely Coupled Systems." Administrative Science Quarterly 21:1-19.

Weick, K. E. 1974. "Middle Range Theories of Social Systems." Behavioral Science 19:357-67.

Weick, K. E. 1970. "The 'ess' in Stress: Some Conceptual and Methodological Problems." In Social and Psychological Factors in Stress, edited by J. E. McGrath. New York: Holt, Rinehart & Winston.

Wynn, R. 1977. "Intra-Organizational Conflict in Schools." Paper presented at the Annual Meeting of the American Association of School Administrators, Las Vegas, February.

15

INTEREST GROUP POLITICS IN SCHOOL DISTRICTS: THE CASE OF LOCAL TEACHERS' UNIONS

Samuel B. Bacharach
Stephen M. Mitchell

Declining enrollment, racial strife, taxpayers' suits, defeated budgets, unwieldy state mandates, declining test scores, and increasing violence have created an atmosphere of turmoil and uncertainty for many local school districts. This environmental turbulence has resulted in a proliferation of studies intended to provide some answers as to the causes of these environmental problems as well as to suggest some solutions. The scope and focus of these studies are diverse, yet they all share one common conceptual and methodological problem: the question of the appropriate unit of analysis in the study of local school districts.

As noted in Chapter 1, prior research on the administration and governance of school districts has utilized three different units of analysis: the organization as a whole, the individual, and the group. We contend that the group model, when embedded in a larger theoretical framework that views the school district as a political system, is capable of absorbing the insights of the other perspectives while avoiding their limitations. More importantly, we feel that the group perspective most accurately reflects the realities of school district administration we have observed over the last two years while conducting research into school district governance and administration.

To elaborate, the utilization of a political perspective with a specific focus on the group as the unit of analysis considers the structural factors that dominate the rational managerial perspective (which considers the organization as a whole) as objective constraints on individual and group action within an organization. It is clear that the size of the organization, the number of functional departments, the degree of formalization, the channels of communication, and so on, will affect individual and group behavior. By focusing on the group as the primary unit of analysis, however, we are sensitized to the differences in cognition and action that occur across groups within an organization, something not possible within the strict confines of the rational managerial perspective. Insofar as differences in cognition and action across groups contribute to the dynamics of organizations, this approach also sensitizes us to the organization as a dynamic entity. Further, as noted in Chapter 1, in considering school districts as political organizations, it is important to draw from both the literature that analyzes schools as organizations as well as the literature that examines the community politics of school districts. That is, we must take account of the school as an organization, as well as a local democracy. We believe that the political perspective we are adopting, which allows us to focus on groups within the formal organization as well as those groups that arise in the community, best approaches the complexities of school district reality. Specifically, it enables us to account for both internal and external sources of pressure on the school district. Because of this, our approach is well suited to an analysis of the dilemma that arises from school district administrators having to meet administrative and political imperatives simultaneously.

In this chapter we will pursue the concept of the group as the appropriate unit of analysis for the investigation of school districts. To do so, we will focus on the local teachers' union, presenting a series of research questions that we believe typify the type of research agenda a political perspective utilizing the group as the unit of analysis entails. In so doing, we hope to address some important substantive issues concerning local teachers' unions while demonstrating the utility of a political analysis of school systems.

THE LOCAL TEACHERS' UNION AS A
COALITION OF TEACHERS' INTEREST GROUPS

While school districts are comprised of many groups, a strategic point of departure for a political analysis is teachers' interest groups and the local teachers' union. Due to their sheer numbers and professional training, teachers have been an integral part of local school district governance and administration. In New York State, in the past 20 years, teachers have gradually emerged at the state and local levels as a formidable political force in the formulation and implementation of education policies. This rise to political prominence by teachers in New York State may be attributed to their unionization. Beginning in the early 1960s, the economic plight and working conditions of many teachers began to worsen. Moreover, a growing number of teachers began to accept the idea that some kind of collective action was necessary if their social and economic status was going to be ameliorated. Furthermore, the traditional teachers' association had proven inadequate as a political vehicle for effecting social and economic redress. Hence, as a result of their deteriorating economic and social circumstances, the need for collective action, and the inadequacy of the traditional teachers' organization, teachers and their associations increasingly began to accept the notion of unionization and began to apply the tactics embodied in this notion to their interaction with local school district administrations and state officials. The trend toward unionization in New York State was given considerable momentum by the passage of the Taylor Law in 1967. Specifically, this legislation endowed the teachers' union with considerable legitimacy and added political leverage as teachers obtained the right to collective bargaining. During the course of our present research, a theme frequently expressed by school district administrators, school board members, union officials, and teachers stressed that in order to understand the administrative dilemmas and policy-making process of local school districts, it is necessary to examine the nature of the local union and the activities it undertakes. Within this context any empirical examination of the administrative and political workings of school districts as organizations must pay attention to the role of the teachers' union.

A RESEARCH AGENDA

Given the importance of studying local teachers' unions, we must now consider what research questions within a political perspective will reveal the significant dimensions of union activity and impact. Although the teachers' unions in most of the districts we have studied share the same affiliation, there is considerable variation between school districts in ways in which the teachers' union operates. Keeping in mind the arguments we have made thus far and drawing from our experience in the field, there are five research questions that appear to highlight the major dimensions affecting union activity.

Question 1: Under What Conditions Does the Local
Teachers' Union Serve as the Main Representative
for Various Teachers' Interest Groups?

It should be evident that the issues in which a specific local teachers' union becomes involved depends, in large part, on the predisposition and attitudes of the members of that union. On the surface it would appear that teachers in a given school district constitute a monolithic interest group with common goals and a similar orientation toward the union and the union's role in the school district. This monolithic image is bolstered by previous research, the high percentage of union membership, and the continuous expansion of agency shops, all of which imply that teachers are a homogeneous group. A serependipitous finding that emerges from our current research is that even given membership in a union, teachers in a given school district are often divided into various informal interest groups. Across school districts, the number and composition of teacher interest groups exhibit a high degree of variation. Some may be small and homogeneous, while others are large and heterogeneous. Moreover, some of these informal groups have frequent recourse to the union as the main mechanism for articulating their demands, while other groups of teachers do not. In our current research, this distinction has been made particularly salient. To wit, in our conversations with local union presidents, a source of frustration that was cited again and again was that in a given district some groups of teachers regularly availed themselves of union support, while other groups made only infrequent claims on the union for assistance. Still others were manifestly hostile to the union. While not evidencing the frustration of local union presidents, superintendents also made the same observations. It is evident that in certain school districts, different teachers' interest groups are more likely than others to have recourse to the local union. These differences may occur by department, subject matter, grade, and so on. Two illustrations will lend support to this observation. In one school district in our current study, the elementary school teachers as a group have chosen to operate independently of the union, pursuing their interests by dealing directly with the school board and the administration. The second illustration concerns the physical education department in one school, which, in an active effort to prevent cutbacks in the athletic budget, enlisted the support of a community group (a local booster club) without the aid of the union.

It is important to note that in casting the question in these terms, we are shifting away from the conventional research question of which teachers choose to become involved in local unions and which teachers do not. We believe that advances that unions have made in the last decade, the institutionalization of labor-management relations, and other factors such as the growth of agency shops, make the question of membership an interesting but moot point. Based on our studies, it is unusual to find a school district where membership is below 80 percent, with most locals approaching

approaching 90 to 100 percent membership. The fact is that local teachers' unions in our sample area are no longer fighting for recognition or membership, they are an established part of school district life. The question we are asking is under what conditions or for what issues do teachers decide to turn to the union as their representative?

The decision to work through the union reflects, in part, a recognition of powerlessness on the part of the individual. It is a recognition of the fact that groups, especially organized groups, wield more authority and influence than most individuals (Coleman, 1973). The local teachers' union is no exception. For its part, the union "successfully mediates on behalf of an individual when it provides him with the influence of an organization through which to voice and subsequently gain satisfaction of his demands" (Zeigler, 1967:55). We assume that the decision to work through the union reflects a utilitarian decision based on self-interest. The question we are posing here is under what condition will that decision be in favor of union activity. [1]

Coleman (1966) argues that the decision made by an individual to engage in a collective action will depend, in part, on the resources that the collectivity can bring to bear over a wide range of issues. Specifically, an individual may engage in collective action on one issue for which he has little interest in order to utilize the resources and power of the collectivity in an area in which he does have an interest. This means that we must consider the entire range of issues for which the union serves as a representative, as well as the resources the union is able to bring to bear on these issues. Following Coleman's (1966; 1973) line of reasoning, we can expect the union to serve as a representative for those issues in which no teacher has sufficient resources or power to achieve his self-interest acting alone or as part of an interest group. For local teachers' unions, "organization provides the effective means for teachers to decide among themselves. It alone serves as a framework through which they can participate with administrators and board members on an equal basis" (Rosenthal, 1969:7). Thus the perception of the union as a viable coalition for the achievement of teachers' interests will depend, in large part, on the perceived power of the union.

Drawing on these arguments concerning the power of collectivities and from our current research, we expect that for those issues or areas in which there is consensus among the teachers that authority and influence are vested in the school board or administration, the union will be turned to for representation. In those areas where there is a consensus among teachers that authority and influence resides with lower level personnel, there is a high probability that the teachers will utilize other avenues of representation.

A fruitful avenue of approach to the question of when the union will serve as the teachers' representative is through the concept of social exchange, with particular emphasis on dependency theory. Utilizing this approach requires that we focus on the decision the teacher must make as to whether or not to turn to the union. We assume that the teacher will perform a subjective cost/benefit analysis and will select the tactic that provides him or her with the most benefit at the least cost. Three possibilities can be considered: the teacher can work alone, the teacher can work as part of an interest group, or the teacher can work as part of the union.[2]

Our primary focus in this chapter is on the political activity of groups. Therefore we are more concerned with the second and third possibilities than the first. Specifically, we need to identify the dimensions that determine when the union (a coalition) will be seen as a more viable approach to an issue than an interest group. For example, suppose that the school administration is considering adopting a policy that would prohibit probationary and noncertified personnel from extracurricular duties such as leading the drama club or newspaper. Assume that for some of these teachers, the extra income from these positions is highly desirable (the value of the outcome is high), and that there are no comparable secondary jobs available (the number of alternatives is low). Further, these teachers realize that they have little power over the administration as individuals. They must then decide whether to work together as an interest group or to work through the union (this is a choice of tactics). It may be the case that many of these positions have been held by probationary or noncertified personnel in the past, and that without them the programs would cease to operate. The teachers may therefore decide that they can make a reasonable argument as an interest group. Alternatively, it may be the case that the union has played a role in the past in determining who receives extracurricular duties, and this may be seen as a more viable option. In either case, one of the major determinants in the decision will be the sanctions the other party can bring to bear . (Both Coles, 1969, and Rosenthal, 1969, have shown that the sanctions available to the administration are a major determinant of the level of teacher militancy.) To continue with the example, if the teachers work as an interest group, given their probationary and noncertified status, it may be possible for the administration to threaten their jobs. These sanctions may not be considered as likely should they decide to work through the union. Thus we see that in reaching a decision on tactics, the major dimensions to be considered are the value of the outcome, the alternatives, and the possible sanctions.

Since the cost/benefit analysis the teacher undergoes in deciding whether to work through an interest group or through the union is subjective, we must also consider a number of factors that are likely to influence the perception of the situation, thereby affecting one of the dimensions noted above. Included here are the variety of variables that have been related in prior research to union membership and militant activity. We believe that these variables affect attitudes that color the teachers' perception of the situation, thereby affecting the decision on whether to work through the union. As Zeigler (1967:135) notes, "the greatest roadblock in the way of union efforts to organize teachers is . . . the attitudes of the teachers themselves." In general, past research has found that: males are more likely to favor unions than females; high school teachers are more likely to be prounion than elementary teachers; teachers from large schools are more likely to be prounion than teachers from small schools; large classes lead to prounion sentiments; poor students lead to prounion attitudes; the principal's attitudes affect teachers' views of the union; and younger teachers tend to be more prounion than older teachers (Alutto and Belasco, 1976; Coles, 1969; Corwin, 1965, 1971; Fox and Wince, 1976; Rosenthal, 1969; Zeigler, 1967). As working hypotheses, we expect all of these relationships to hold, that is, prounion attitudes will result in teachers working with the union as opposed to working alone or through interest groups.

Variables related to group cohesiveness are also likely to affect the teachers' perceptions of the utility of working with the union. Coles (1969) found that social support and the teacher's reference group were factors influencing union membership, while Zeigler (1967) found that group power was related to union activity. Drawing on these findings, we expect that the higher the percentage of membership in the union, the more likely the teachers are to work through the union. One qualification is necessary, however. We expect that this relationship will be strongest in local unions where members are satisfied with the activity of the local, and where factionalism within the union is not a problem. That is, the greater the cohesiveness of the union, the greater the probability that the teacher will decide to work through the union. These relationships will be strongest for those teachers who consider their fellow teachers as their primary reference group.

The satisfaction felt with the local union will be determined, in part, by the degree of success the union has enjoyed in the past. Zeigler (1967), Coles (1969), and Rosenthal (1969) all cite the importance of success in gaining union members. We expect, therefore, that the more successful the union has been in the past, the greater the probability that teachers will turn to the union as their representative.

Question 2: How Does the Local Teachers' Union Insure
the Involvement of the Various Teachers' Interest Groups,
or, How Does It Maintain Intracoalitional Solidarity?

In our first research question we attempted to outline some of
the factors that would lead teachers to turn to the union as a viable
coalition for the expression of their interests. We argued that this
decision was based on a subjective cost-benefit analysis that was
influenced by the teachers' perceptions of the union and its role in
the school district. In this question, we are expanding our focus
to consider what processes and mechanisms are available to the
local union to generate and sustain intracoalitional solidarity. Thus
we are concerned with actions the local union can take to insure that
the union is seen as a viable coalition for the expression of teachers'
interests. In brief, the processes and mechanisms for generating
and sustaining involvement and commitment among union members
can be examined under the following headings: dissatisfaction,
communication, union leadership, normative mechanisms for
coalition mobilization, balancing of issues, and a continuum of involvement. We will consider each of these in turn:

Dissatisfaction

Research on teachers' unions indicates that dissatisfaction,
either with job conditions or prestige, is one of the primary reasons
for joining unions (Coles, 1969; Rosenthal, 1969; Zeigler, 1967).
The same suggestion is made in the literature on union organizing
in which isolating the sources of workers' dissatisfaction is considered one of the first steps toward achieving union representation
(Mitchell, 1978). In terms of our first research question, being
dissatisfied would cause teachers to seek to redress the condition
and achieve a state of satisfaction. The implication of this is that
the level of dissatisfaction among union members is directly related
to the probability of the union being seen as a viable coalition for
the expression of teachers' interests. The higher the level of dissatisfaction among union members, the greater the probability of
the union emerging as a viable coalition. From the union's point of
view, it is crucial that it be aware of the teachers' dissatisfaction
so that it can present the union as a vehicle for achieving satisfaction.

A union may consciously create a sense of dissatisfaction
where none existed. Dissatisfaction occurs when a person's
achievements in reality fall below their expectations. By attempting to raise the expectations of their members, unions are capable
of generating dissatisfaction. This can be done through a thorough
knowledge of the administrative practices of the school district,
especially in comparison to other districts. Armed with knowledge

of a practice that is inconsistent with practices of other districts or unfair to teachers, the union may be able to create dissatisfaction where a prior lack of knowledge prevented any dissatisfaction from being felt. In a similar manner, one of the goals of a union is to educate its members or potential members as to their rights under the law. Given the complexity of the Taylor Law and the Education Law in New York State, it is unlikely that any untrained individual could fully understand the legal aspects of union activity and school district administrative responsibilities. We have found that it is not uncommon to find school administrators who are either ignorant of certain aspects of the law or who act in conscious violation of certain statutes. Under these conditions, knowledge of the law becomes a union tool. Again, by providing information that was previously unavailable, the union may be able to create a sense of dissatisfaction. In those cases where the union provided the information, it seems likely that the teacher would continue to rely on the union to redress the newly created dissatisfaction.

We should also note that it is the duty of the local union to police their contract, that is, to make sure that the administration fulfills all of the provisions of the contract. Based on our field observations, we believe that the degree to which local unions police their contracts varies widely across districts. We expect that unions that maintain a close watch over the fulfillment of their contract would be able to isolate more sources of dissatisfaction and therefore would be able to generate more involvement in the union.

Kerchner (1979) labels this phase interest articulation. In this period, information control, that is, information exchange and expansion, becomes the primary mechanism for coalition mobilization. Information is used to identify or generate dissatisfaction, which increases the likelihood of coalition mobilization. For the union, the ideal condition is to pinpoint several target areas that are sources of dissatisfaction for the majority of teachers. In that case, we are concerned with the use of universal information that is of use to the majority of the union members. Creating a sense of unity or commonality in dissatisfaction greatly eases the burden placed on the union. In considering information control, however, we must realize that all information will not be of use to all groups. Evidence suggests that where there is high turnover, a heterogeneous working group, or a population generally characterized by low prounion sentiments (see question 1), the probability of creating this sense of commonality is diminished (Coles, 1969; Mitchell, 1978; Zeigler, 1967). In these cases the union may have to rely on information that is interest group specific, that is, information that addresses the dissatisfactions of a specific interest group rather than the entire membership. Such an appeal would seem to be much more tenuous than one based on common dissatisfactions. This would be true insofar as the strength of numbers adds legitimacy to the union's position. It may also be the case that one teachers' group may feel that another group's source of dissatisfaction is not a proper union matter and may withdraw their support should the union decide to represent that case. The conditions under which the union will rely on universal as opposed to interest group specific information, as well as the consequences of employing either form of information, need to be investigated.

The viability of any local union rests on its ability to generate a perception of the union as the central coalition for the alleviation of teacher dissatisfaction. This means that the union must be able to convince teachers that they will be able to best carry the interests of the teachers through to the interest aggregation phase of bargaining and decision making (Kerchner, 1979). Thus the union not only must be aware of dissatisfaction, it must be able to make the teachers feel that the union has the authority, influence, and access to alleviate the dissatisfaction.

Communication

In this context, the importance of communication between the union and its members for insuring the viability of the union as a coalition becomes critical. By communication, we refer to conditions that enhance or constrain interaction among the various groups of teachers. For example, in some schools there is very little communication between school buildings within the school district. Within specific schools, there is considerable variation in the degree of communication across grades and subject areas. Adequate communication is essential to interest group articulation and coalition mobilization. We believe that the organization of the local union is the primary determinant of communication within the union. It is the mechanism in which communication occurs and through which teachers' predisposition to act can be channeled into action. We must inquire whether or not the union is organized to be a viable communication mechanism.

Despite the importance of the organization of the local union, it has received little attention in the literature. In our current research, we have observed a great deal of variation concerning the structure and workings of the local union across school districts. The extent and content of this variation, as well as its effect on union activity, need to be examined. Among the issues that should be empirically studied are:

□ The organizational structure of the local union. Here we are concerned with the nature of the hierarchy and the division of labor. How many officers does the local have and what are their duties? What committees does the local have, how often do they meet, what are their duties? How are their members selected?

□ What is the nature of local union meetings? Three types of meetings can occur: building meetings, district meetings, and regional meetings.[3] The content and the frequency of these three types of meetings deserve attention.

□ What mechanisms, aside from meetings, does the union use to keep its members informed and to obtain their input? Does it conduct surveys of members? Does it have a suggestion box? Are the union leaders accessible to members? Does it have a newspaper?

We believe that these questions concerning the mundane, practical aspects of running a local union are crucial to an examination of the union as a political entity in the district. They represent the dimensions on which the viability of the union's communication mechanism rests. The fact that they have been unexplored by prior research only increases their importance.

Union Leadership

Research on teachers' unions (Coles, 1969; Rosenthal, 1969) and on union organizing in general (Mitchell, 1978) stresses the importance of leadership in the development and maintenance of a successful union. The union leadership plays two complementary and potentially conflicting roles. The first is to lead, that is, to provide goals, strategies, and tactics for the membership to rally around (Rosenthal, 1969). The second is to represent the interests and needs of teachers and their interest group, a task that requires being in touch with the members' feelings and desires. The problem of leadership is one of maintaining consistency between these two tasks. The leader should lead in a direction in which the members desire to go.

In part, the two tasks confronting the union leadership are related to the elements of information control outlined above in the "Dissatisfaction" section of this question. In this case, however, we are concerned with dissatisfactions related to the union and union activity. Thus, balancing the two tasks confronting union leadership requires that the leaders obtain input from union members, while also keeping the membership informed of union activities.

Obviously, many of the structural devices utilized to enhance communication are relevant to this issue. Our concern here, however, is with the use of these mechanisms by leadership. Research suggests that the interaction of individual variables with structural constraints has a significant impact on union effectiveness (Freeman and Medoff, 1979; Glassman and Belasco, 1976). While we speak of the union as engaging in some activity or having some effect, we realize that it is the leaders of the union acting through the structure of the union and with the authority of their position that directs union activity. It is the leadership's use of the structure for communication and administration that maintains the union as a viable coalition. Because of this, a study of teacher unions as political systems must consider the predispositions and attitudes of the union leaders regarding their role.

In general, we would expect that a significant portion of the members' satisfaction or dissatisfaction with the union hinges on the role of the building representative and his relation with the local president. Does the building representative act as a representative of interest groups within the building or as a representative of the union and union policy? While the chances are good that the leadership fulfills both these tasks, the question then becomes when does one task take precedence over the other? Overall, it is likely that the degree to which the union can induce various groups to present a united front on a given issue is, to a large degree, contingent on fulfilling both of these tasks, while maintaining rapport between the leaders themselves. It is also evident that aside from these tasks, the leadership must be able to maintain an efficient administrative apparatus, a problem that relates directly to the structure of the union and the leaders' use of it.

Thus far in our discussion of union leadership, we have focused on the tasks confronting union leaders and the leaders' use of the union structure to achieve these tasks. We have argued that the leadership must allow for the expression of members' dissatisfaction with the union and its activity. In this regard, we must also consider the mechanisms available to members to change the leadership of the union. What are the procedures for electing presidents and other officers, the length of the officers' terms, the degree of competition for union positions, and the general turnout for union elections? By focusing on union elections, one could gather additional evidence on the members' attitudes toward their union leaders and, ultimately, the union itself.

Normative Mechanisms for Coalition Mobilization

Creating a perception of the union as the best representative for teachers essentially involves generating involvement and commitment among teachers. These are objective signs of union success, much more so than raw membership percentages. Zeigler (1967) found that the majority of union members are apathetic, with the active minority generally constituting 15 percent of the membership. While our field observations indicate that the activity of members increases during contract years or when key issues arise, the true test of a union's strength comes from its ability to generate involvement regardless of the issue under discussion. Several mechanisms are cited in the literature on union organizing to generate commitment and increase involvement (Mitchell, 1978), and it is worth exploring the degree to which local teachers' unions employ these mechanisms. Organizationally, committees are one means of generating involvement. Other mechanisms such as songs, slogans, picnics, and awards are also means of insuring commitment and involvement.

Balancing of Issues

We presented the normative mechanisms noted above, as well as the mechanisms related to dissatisfaction, communication, and union leadership as if they were generalized devices for increasing intracoalition solidarity. We realize, however, that intracoalition solidarity will also depend on the nature of the issues facing the school district, the various teachers' interest groups, and the union. In some instances, the very nature of the issue may have little appeal for the union and it will choose not to involve itself, leaving the teachers' interest groups no option but to go it alone. In other instances, an issue such as a school closing or a school board election will be of mutual concern to the union and the teachers' interest groups. Such an issue will permit the union to emerge as the focal point for collective action.

It would appear that one of the key factors determining which issues will be pursued by the union is the degree to which organizational interests predominate over self-interests (Rosenthal, 1969). By organizational interests, we mean the selection of issues based on what they can do for the union as an organization. On this basis, we would expect unions to pursue only those issues in which they have a reasonable chance of succeeding or in which a victory would add substantial prestige or legitimacy to the union. Issues selected on the basis of self-interest, in contrast, are those in which the union gets involved solely on the basis of helping an individual teacher or group of teachers, regardless of the effect of this involvement on the legitimacy and reputation of the union itself. Thus we can delineate two types of issues in which the local teachers' union may become involved: primary union issues and interest group specific issues. Primary union issues are those that are relevant to the majority of union members or that affect the possibility of the union serving as a viable coalition. Involvement in primary union issues is based on organizational interests. Interest

group specific issues are selected on the basis of self-interest.
They affect a specific group of teachers rather than the majority
of the membership or the union itself. Undoubtedly, the union engages in both types of issues. What needs to be examined is the
balance that is struck between the types of issues and the conditions
affecting the balance.

A Continuum of Intracoalition Solidarity

Thus far, we have been considering the various means the
union may employ to ensure that teachers turn to the union as its
main representative, and some of the factors effecting the use of
these various mechanisms. The trend of the argument has been to
emphasize the importance of generating involvement and commitment in union members to insure intracoalition solidarity. In
closing this section, we would like to outline a continuum of intracoalition solidarity. The location of a local union on this continuum
will depend upon the success the union has in utilizing the various
mechanisms presented above. We are interested not only in the
location the union occupies on this continuum but also in the changes
in location that occur over time or across issues.

At one extreme, we have a local union with a highly involved
and committed membership that shows a high degree of intracoalition solidarity. Under these conditions, a "narrowing of vision"
can occur (Bacharach and Lawler, 1980). In brief, narrowing of
vision means that the union will adopt a hard-line, no-compromise
approach to issues at the expense of flexibility and adaptation. This
may also lead to the adoption of more militant tactics. The factors
that lead to a narrowing of vision are the same factors that result
from success in generating commitment and involvement. Specifically, narrowing of vision occurs where there is high constituency
involvement, representatives are held accountable to members,
some degree of formalization of constituency-representative relations is present, and where representatives are loyal to the group
(Bacharach and Lawler, 1980). These are the very factors that will
result from the union's successful use of the mechanisms outlined
above to generate involvement and commitment among its members.
Should this occur, the potential exists for a hard-nosed and militant
union.

In the middle of the continuum, we encounter those unions that
do not fully succeed in generating involvement and commitment
among their members. A narrowing of vision is unlikely under
these conditions. There probably will be a substantial number of
apathetic members. Union leaders will be more able to follow their
own inclinations in running the union. The potential exists for a

more flexible stance, one that allows for compromise. In general, we expect the majority of unions to fall in the middle of the continuum.

At the other extreme of our continuum, we find those unions that fail to generate a sense of involvement and commitment in their members. As a result, there is little evidence of intracoalition solidarity. This will occur where the union has not succeeded in utilizing the mechanisms presented above, that is, where the dissatisfaction members feel with their jobs or the union has not been addressed, where there has been a failure in communication, where the union leadership has been unable to lead in a direction the members see as desirable, where normative mechanisms have not been employed, or where there has been an inability to balance primary union issues with interest group specific issues. Under these conditions, we may expect to see a turnover in union leadership, factionalism in the union, and possibly an attempt to alter the local's state and national affiliation. All of these events are likely where the union is not seen as a viable coalition, that is, where individual action or interest group action will predominate over activity in the union.

Question 3: What Is the Relationship of the Union with Other Key Groups within the District and Outside the District, or Who Is Involved in the Unions' Intercoalitional Mobilization?

The first two research questions addressed the conditions that facilitated the union being chosen as a viable coalition for individual teachers or teachers' interest groups. Assuming that within a district the union does emerge as a viable coalition, the next question to be asked is how the union goes about its task of achieving its goals and the goals of its composite interest groups. In terms of our earlier theoretical discussion that proposed viewing the union as a coalition within a political organization (that is, the school district), our specific interest is with intercoalitional mobilization, that is, with the relationships the union establishes with other key groups within the district and outside the district. If the union is to exert influence on policy matters within school districts, it may have to coalesce with other groups both within the school district and outside the school district. These relations provide the union with information and a potential source of influence over policy decisions.

Within the school district, the primary groups that must be considered are the community as represented by various interest groups (for example, PTA, citizens, tax groups, and so on), the superintendent and his administrative staff, and the school board. Outside the school district, the relationships that the local union has with the regional office (see note 3) and the state affiliate are of particular interest. In terms of potential coalitions, we may identify four distinct types of coalitions the local union can form. The first is an administrative coalition in which the union unites with the superintendent or other members of the administrative staff. The second is a political coalition, which is formed with members of the school board. Third is a grass roots coalition in which the local union combines with elements of the local community. This type of coalition appears to be of particular importance in view of the increasing demand for citizen participation in collective bargaining (Doherty, 1979; Kerchner, 1979).[4] The final possibility is an external coalition, which is formed with regional, state, or national groups outside of the local school district. The decisions made as to what types of coalition to engage in, over what issues, and at what time will have a profound impact on the effectiveness of the local union.

The art of union politics arises from the ability to form the right linkage with each group for a given issue, while at the same time not endangering the relationship established with other groups. On the local level, the union must establish effective relations with community, political, and administrative groups while avoiding antagonizing one group because of its relationship with another. The extent of this danger becomes more apparent if we consider that although we speak of coalitions as being between groups, the establishment and maintenance of a coalition generally rests on individuals as representatives of groups. For example, in one of our field sites, a proposal was under discussion concerning laying off teachers. The union was opposed to any layoffs and managed to obtain information on projected class sizes from an administrative subordinate. This information was released publicly by the union, catching the superintendent unaware and endangering the relationship between the union and the administration. The point is that in any interaction between two or more groups, the unity of each group becomes a key variable determining how that interaction will proceed.

The balancing of different coalitions is a key point deserving attention. For example, if the union requires the support of a given community group on a specific issue, but that group has in the past antagonized the school board, an affiliation with that group may endanger the union's relations with the school board. While the specific nature and content of such interactions will depend upon the case under investigation, the general phenomenon can be observed in all school districts. Any exploration of local teachers' unions must attend to these problems.

Regarding external coalitions, the local teachers' union is faced with the dilemma of balancing the demands and pressures that arise on the local level with the institutional demands that arise from the regional and the state affiliates of the union. In essence, the dilemma centers on a view of the union as a grass roots movement versus a view of the union as an institution (for example, Edelstein and Warner, 1975; Getman et al., 1976; Kochan, 1974; Strauss, 1977). While many teachers value the legal advice and services provided by either the regional or the state affiliate, as well as the state affiliate's effective lobbying on the state level, they are also wary of undue infringement by the regional and state affiliates on their autonomy. Past research (Coles, 1969; Zeigler, 1967) and comments from teachers in our current research indicate that the political views and aspirations of the state and national affiliates are also a cause of dissatisfaction with the union. Because of this, it is important to examine the services provided by the state and national affiliates, the demands made by these external groups on the local union, and the members' views of the role of the state and national affiliates. It seems probable that the aspiration of the local president for a potential career in the union would be one variable affecting this relationship. For all locals, however, the question of how to balance the demand for a grass roots union with the external demand for the institutionalization of the union is of great concern.

An important question concerns the stability of the relationship between the union and other groups, that is, do emergent coalitions form around a specific issue or are they based on some more permanent linkage (for example, ideological bonds across issues)? As an example, in one of our case studies, the teachers' union had a good relationship with the superintendent, who was ideologically supportive of teachers. However, the superintendent proved to be ineffective in getting the school board to meet particular teachers' demands. The union, despite its ideological bond with the superintendent, cooperated in ousting the superintendent from office, purely on pragmatic grounds. Another example, this one regarding the local union's relationship with its regional and state affiliates, can be cited. Based on preliminary field observations, it appears that some local unions rely on the support of their affiliates only when it pertains to salary issues; whereas other local unions accept the advice and support of the regional and state affiliates on all policy issues that potentially affect their membership. The point is that the dynamics of union involvement in school district policy are due, in large part, to the shifting basis of the union's intercoalitional mobilization. Any investigation of the intercoalitional mobilization of the local teachers' union must try to account for these changes.

Insofar as the shifting bases of intercoalitional mobilization are a result of maneuvering on the part of interest groups or coalitions to obtain more influence or to maximize their chances of achieving their goals, any investigation of the stability of coalitions formed by local teachers' unions must focus on exactly what each party in a coalition gives to and receives from partaking in that coalition (Bacharach and Lawler, 1980). Such an investigation must also examine the opponents of the coalitions. Thus we assume that any coalition (administrative, political, grass roots, or external) exists in opposition to some countercoalition (even when a coalition comes into existence to push for a specific issue, we assume that in the majority of cases some countercoalition will be formed). Whether we are examining the dynamics of a single coalition or the battle between coalitions, we are concerned with the process of bargaining (Bacharach and Lawler, 1980). It is through a thorough consideration of the dynamics of the bargaining process that an understanding of the stability of coalitions will develop. This means that our concern with coalitional stability must include an analysis of the strategies and tactics of bargaining within and between coalitions.

Question 4: What Effect Does the Local Teachers' Union Have on School District Policies ?

Having considered the potential of the union to emerge as a viable coalition, the union's efforts to mobilize intracoalitional solidarity, and the union's strategy in regard to intercoalitional mobilization, we must now turn to a consideration of the effectiveness of union action, as well as the specific areas in which action is undertaken. From a political perspective, the dynamics of organizational processes may be best observed by focusing on the decision-making process. Decisions are the arena in which resources are distributed and through which individuals and groups are able to achieve representation. Every individual or group can be expected to approach a decision with the objective of maximizing their specific interests or goals rather than the maximization of some general organizational objective. Adopting this perspective requires that we view the organization as a system in which the main issue is the mobilization of power for either achieving or blocking the achievement of a particular task (Bacharach and Lawler, 1980). Applied to local teachers' unions in school districts, this entails examining the behavior of the union as they attempt either to initiate or block decisions regarding policy issues.

Of particular interest is the range and content of issues in which the local union seeks representation. Several attempts have been made to develop a typology of issues in which unions become involved. For example, Rosenthal (1969) draws a distinction between position issues (that is, those that deal with economic and working conditions, reflect a high degree of self-interest, and represent concrete gains) and style issues (that is, those that tend to be impersonal, less immediate, and generally concerned with broad statements of policy). Perry (1979), in examining collective bargaining agreements, distinguishes between wage bargains (salary issues), effort bargains (issues such as preparation time, class size, nonteaching responsibilities, and so on), and rights bargains (relating to such issues as evaluation, layoff, assignments, policy consultation committees, and so on). Drawing on these typologies, we find it convenient for our purposes to distinguish between economic work issues and participation issues. By economic work issues, we mean those issues that relate to salary and working conditions. By participation issues, we mean those that deal with teachers' rights to participate in the making of policy or with the delineation of specific areas of authority and influence for teachers. Based on our field work, we believe that the majority of issues confronting local teachers' unions can be divided into these two categories.

As of 1969, little progress had been made by local teachers' unions in terms of participation issues (Coles, 1969; Rosenthal, 1969), although recent studies suggest that this may be changing (for example, Perry, 1979). The extent to which teachers today turn to their locals over issues involving participation is an empriical question that deserves attention. Several reasons can be given for the apparent lack of success in these areas. The first reason centers on the strategies and tactics that are appropriate to participation issues. Initially, one of the primary splits between the National Education Association (NEA) and the American Federation of Teachers (AFT) focused on the use of militant tactics and collective bargaining by teachers. The NEA, which identified itself as a professional association, felt that militant tactics and collective bargaining were unbecoming to professionals.[5] They chose instead to emphasize informal influence, professional negotiations, and working within formal channels. The AFT, for its part, utilized militant tactics to push for collective bargaining of its demands, arguing that it was possible to bargain over participation issues. Despite this stance, the success of the AFT stemmed primarily from its ability to gain concessions over economic issues. Indeed, this success forced the NEA to adopt a more militant stance and to push for positions very similar to those of the AFT (Rosenthal,

1969). The point to be emphasized is that while militant strategies and collective bargaining have been linked to participation issues in rhetoric, there is little evidence of success through the use of these mechanisms. Instead, these mechanisms have proved successful for achieving gains over economic issues.

Empirically, it is important to investigate the actions of the local teachers' unions in regard to these questions. Thus, we must ask whether the union focuses on participation issues, economic issues, or both; and whether the strategies and tactics utilized to deal with these two domains are similar. Based on our field observations and comments obtained on our surveys, this distinction seems to be important to teachers, although there is a broad range of opinion as to the role of the union. Some teachers feel that the union is strictly an economic organization that operates through collective bargaining and that participation issues are handled by individual teachers through direct contact with the administration. Others feel that the union should bargain for economic and participation issues; while still another group believes that while the union should be involved in both sets of issues, the tactics employed should vary, with the union working both through collective bargaining and other mechanisms. Some research suggests that economic matters are, indeed, best handled in collective bargaining, while participation issues are better suited to other mechanisms, such as joint committees (Love, 1969). However, it may be that collective bargaining is the best means available to the teacher for achieving participation (Belasco and Alutto, 1969). Hellriegel, French, and Peterson (1969) present data that suggest that many teachers believe this is true. In any given union, how the members and leadership feel on these matters will determine what issues the union becomes involved in and the tactics employed, and therefore it will have a significant impact on the effect of the local union on school district policy.

To date, the majority of research undertaken to assess the effect of local teachers' unions on school district policy has focused exclusively on collective bargaining. There has been little, if any, investigation of the effect of the union on school district policy outside of the collective bargaining arena. Based on our field observations, we believe that the effect of the union outside of collective bargaining is potentially extensive and deserves examination. Of particular interest is the degree to which the influence of unions outside of the collective bargaining agreement is related to their success in the collective bargaining agreement. That is, are unions who are effective in collective bargaining also effective outside of bargaining, or are the two tactics independent?

The work on collective bargaining has focused primarily upon the economic gains teachers have achieved. While there have been mixed results, the general conclusion has been that collective bargaining has resulted in an increase in teachers' salaries, although the overall gain has not been substantial (Hall and Carroll, 1973; Holmes, 1976; Kasper, 1970; Lipsky and Drotning, 1973; Moore, 1976). Work conditions, which we linked to economic issues in our typology, have also been improved by collective bargaining (Flango, 1976; Hall and Carroll, 1973; Perry, 1979). In regard to participation issues, while there has been progress in this area, particularly as the time period over which collective bargaining has been in effect within a district increases, a substantial increase in teachers' rights remains more of a desire than a reality (Belasco and Alutto, 1969; Love, 1969; Perry, 1979). The importance of assessing the range of issues selected as appropriate for bargaining and the changes in bargaining issues over time should be apparent.

Empirically, the effect of the local teachers' union on school district policy may be examined in terms of two dimensions: the scope of its involvement and the impact of its involvement. By scope, we mean the number of policy issues in which the union becomes involved. It is in this dimension that our differentiation of economic from participation issues becomes salient. A narrow scope of involvement may imply that the union becomes involved only with those issues that pertain to the salaries and fringe benefits of its members. A narrow scope may also mean strict adherence to presidential guidelines. Each year, the president of the state teachers' union establishes guidelines that indicate the minimum number of issues that should be covered in collective bargaining by local unions. A number of unions in their negotiations exceed the minimum number of issues required by the guidelines, whereas other unions fail to meet the required minimum. A broad scope of involvement may mean exceeding the presidential guidelines with respect to collective bargaining. However, a broad scope of involvement may also refer to a union's involvement in policy issues that lie outside the realm of collective bargaining.

The impact of a local teachers' union may be defined as its ability to insure that its position on an issue or a number of issues becomes a part of school district policy. In the area of collective bargaining, impact may refer to the number of concessions the local union was capable of obtaining from the district. Outside the area of collective bargaining, impact refers to the degree of success that the teachers' union, once involved in an issue or a set of issues, has in getting its viewpoint adopted as official district policy. One variable that would appear to have a significant effect on the impact of the union is the extent to which the union undergoes a "narrowing of vision" (see question 2). Generally we would expect that where a narrowing of vision occurs, the hard-nosed position that results would lead to a greater impact on school district policy. We recognize, however, the possibility that compromise and flexibility may, in the long run, prove to be a better policy for the union to adopt.

Rosenthal (1969) suggests that where participation issues are deemed important, militant tactics and a hard-nosed approach are likely to occur. These results require further testing.

The interaction between scope and impact as presented in Figure 15.1 categorizes the effect of local union on school district policy.

FIGURE 15.1

Interaction between Scope and Impact

SCOPE

		Narrow	Broad
I M P A C T	Low	Weak Effect on School District Policy	Diffuse Effect on School District Policy
	High	Focused Effect on School District Policy	Strong Effect on School District Policy

Source: Compiled by the authors.

Question 5: How Does the Nature of the Local
Environment and the Organizational Structure
of the School District Relate to Union Activity
and the Union's Effect on School District Policy?

Our first four research questions have approached the local teachers' union without consideration of the environment in which it is embedded. While there have been several areas where some mention has been made of the role of the local environment and the school district structure, no explicit questions have been posed relating these factors to union activity. Our final research question examines this relationship. We recognize the importance of both environmental factors and school district structure on union activity and will attempt here to outline some of the variables that need to be included in examining the specific nature of this relationship.

While there are numerous dimensions of environmental heterogeneity that can be examined, our primary concern is with the political, economic, and social composition of school districts (see Chapter 1).

We argue that the workings of the local teachers' union will be directly affected by the instability of the general social, political, and economic environment, or, more specifically, the relative number and strength of organized interest groups in the community vying for control over school decisions.

What research has been done on the effects of the environment on teachers' union activity has focused either on teacher characteristics related to militancy or on the relationship between the environment and collective bargaining outcomes. Zeigler (1967) found that small-town locals were more likely to adopt a professional stance and stress formal channels than were urban locals, which tended to be more politically active. We would expect, therefore, that locals in small towns would bargain primarily over economic issues and not get the union involved in participation issues. Urban locals, however, would involve the union in the full range of issues and would tend to be more militant. Watkins (1972) and Gerhart (1976) provide some empirical support for these expectations. They found that bargaining outcomes were greater in urban areas and, in Gerhart's study, for politically active unions. Both of these authors, as well as Moore and Newman (1976), cite a number of other environmental variables related to collective bargaining outcomes. These include racial balance, percent of work force in industry, legal sanctions, per capita revenue, strike activity, the public policy environment, and unemployment rates.

In general, we expect the environment to affect the union in two ways. The first is through the individual teachers. The environment may tend to produce a militant teacher either through specific characteristics of the population or through economic deprivation (here factors such as the consumer price index become important, for example, Weintraub and Thornton, 1976). In either case, environmental factors can be related to the tendency of teachers to favor the union. The environment also acts directly upon the union insofar as legitimating itself in the community is a critical part of a union's effectiveness. This is important both in terms of obtaining general community support and for the formation of grass roots coalitions (see question 3). Both of these activities will be easier in certain environments that tend to favor union activity, as opposed to environments that tend to be antiunion.

consideration of these contextual factors will it be possible to pin-point the constraints that determine what specific union action will be observed.

UNIFYING THE FIVE RESEARCH QUESTIONS:
A PRELIMINARY MODEL

Figure 15.2 summarizes the content of these five research questions and the relationships between them. The figure is not intended to be a path diagram. The numbers in the figure refer to the research question that addresses that part of the diagram.

Our first research question attempts to specify the conditions under which an individual teacher or a group of teachers will turn to the union as their representative. Specifically, under what conditions does the local teachers' union serve as the main representative for various teachers' interest groups? Focusing on the subjective costs and benefits of utilizing the union, we outlined a number of factors that were likely to affect teachers' perception of this situation. Most of these factors have been previously cited by the literature as correlates of teacher militancy, and we assume that they will bias the teacher in favor of the union. To the degree that the environment determines the likelihood of teachers having these characteristics, and insofar as some of these traits are related to the structure of the school district, it is necessary to link these two variables to the teachers' predisposition to view the union as a viable coalition. The teachers' predisposition to view the union as a viable coalition is also affected by the cohesiveness of the teachers as a group and the attitudes of their primary reference group. Both of these variables will be affected by environmental constraints and the structure of the school district.

Having outlined the components that contribute to the teachers' predisposition to view the union as a viable coalition, our second research question inquired into how the union coalesces its members, that is, what actions could the union undertake to increase the probability of their being chosen by teachers as their representative? Specifically, how does the local teachers' union ensure the involvement of the various teachers' interest groups, or, how does it maintain intracoalitional solidarity? A series of processes and mechanisms was presented, including the use of information control to determine sources of dissatisfaction, the importance of union structure to communication, the role of union leadership, the union's need to balance the types of issues they deal with, and the use of normative mechanisms for maintaining intracoalitional solidarity. Many of these processes and mechanisms will be affected by

The organizational structure of the school district wo appear to impact on union effectiveness. We are concerned with such variables as the size of the district, the number the number of departments, the administrative/teacher rati student/teacher ratio, and so on. Again, the effect of stru erates on teachers and on union activity. We have seen tha schools tend to be more militant (Rosenthal, 1969). We ha seen that high school teachers tend to be more militant tha tary teachers (Coles, 1969; Rosenthal, 1969). The point is structural factors affect the attitudes of groups of teachers and Belasco, 1976). The structure of the district also affe union as a whole. We expect that the more complex the st of the school district, the more complex the structure of tl Part of this expectation would appear to be a necessity: If trict has 40 schools, the union must have 40 building repre Increasing complexity requires greater efforts to maintain tion flow and communication, factors crucial to union succ question 2). Greater complexity also produces a greater interest groups with whom to form potential coalitions (se 3). The structure of the district also affects the collectiv ing arena (Baird and Landon, 1977). It is imperative that of organizational structure on union activity be examined i to gain an adequate understanding of the role of the local t union in school district governance and administration.

Taking account of the effects of the social, economi political environmental and organizational structure on un ity is an attempt to lay out the context in which union oper occur. In this regard, any investigation of the local teacl must also concern itself with the specific historic context the data are collected. By this we mean not so much nati state affairs, although some of these must undoubtedly be ered, as much as the specific historic background of the l the issues it becomes involved in. This includes such ite ber of previous strikes, number of grievances, past coali havior, and some specification of issue development.

Taken together, the environment, organizational st and historic context specify the arena in which union acti and occurs. These factors establish the social context fr organizational opportunities for action spring. Rosenthal remarks that these opportunities are a critical factor in tion of any union activity. (On a broader theoretical leve similar to Cohen, March, and Olsen's [1972] notion of a can"). Through the presentation of our research questio specified several areas in which variation in union organ action may be expected. It is our belief that only throug

FIGURE 15.2

A Preliminary Schematic Model for the Analysis of Local Teachers' Union Activity

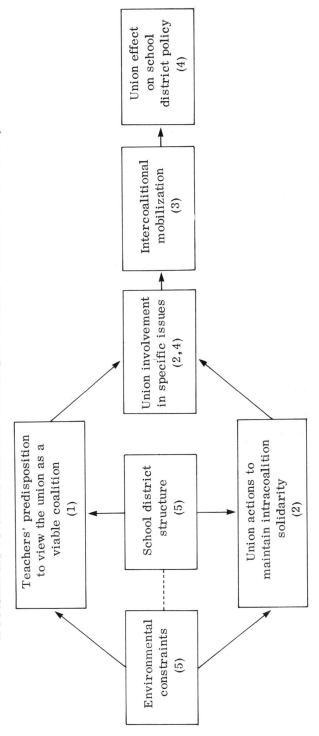

Source: Compiled by the authors.

environmental constraints and the structure of the school district, as indicated by Figure 15.2. The success that the union has in utilizing these various processes and mechanisms will result in some level of intracoalitional solidarity. A continuum of intra-coalitional solidarity was presented on which the local union can be located.

Taken together, the first two research questions outline the principal components that will determine the capacity of the union to emerge as a viable coalition. As a viable coalition, the union will involve itself in specific issues, as indicated in our preliminary schematic model. Once involved in an issue, union activity focuses on obtaining the backing and resources necessary to ensure that the union view will have an impact on that area. This entails inter-coalition mobilization, that is, forming coalitions with different groups, both locally and outside the school district. This activity is the focus of our third research question: What is the relationship of the union with other key groups within the district and outside the district, or, who is involved in the union's intercoalitional mobilization? Four different types of coalitions were presented: administrative, political, grass roots, and external. Particular emphasis was placed on the bargaining that goes on within and between coalitions as a determinant of intercoalition stability.

The intercoalition behavior of the union impinges directly on the effect the union will have on school district policy. Our fourth research question addresses this issue: What effect does the local teachers' union have on school district policies? We argued that the effect on the union can be measured by the scope and impact it has on school district policy. In investigating the union's effect on policy, it is important to consider the type of issues (we argued for a typology based on economic versus participation issues), as well as the arena through which the effort is generated (that is, via collective bargaining or outside of collective bargaining).

Our final research question sought to pinpoint the factors that make up the social and historical context in which union activity occurs. Specifically, how does the nature of the local environment and the organizational structure of the school district relate to union activity and the union's effect on school district policy? The role of these factors in our preliminary model has been outlined in presenting the preceding questions.

CONCLUSION

We began by arguing that a common dilemma in much of the research on school districts has been defining the appropriate unit of analysis. Drawing on Chapter 1, this chapter has attempted to demonstrate the content and utility of a research approach that adapts the group, embedded in a theoretical perspective that views the school district as a political system, as the unit of analysis. To do so, we chose to focus on the local teachers' union as an interest group, presenting a series of five research questions that an investigation of the teachers' union as a political group would require asking. We hope that this chapter has both addressed some important substantive issues involving local teachers' unions and suggested the usefulness of a political perspective in the study of school district governance and administration. Our efforts will be rewarded if others adapt all or part of a political perspective to investigate other groups in school systems.

NOTES

1. We are not considering, for the moment, the teacher who based his decision not on self-interest but on the interests of the collectivity. While this is the ultimate goal of union activity, pragmatically most union activity is based on an appeal to self-interests.

2. We are drawing on a distinction made by Bacharach and Lawler (1980:8) between interest group politics and coalitional politics. "An interest group may be defined as a group of actors who are aware of the commonality of their goals and the commonality of their fate beyond simply their interdependence in regard to work." A coalition is a "grouping of interest groups who are committed to achieving a common goal." The union is considered a coalition of teacher interest groups.

3. The state affiliates divide the state into regions, with a regional coordinator in charge of all the locals in the region. The coordinator holds regional meetings for the locals.

4. In this regard, the union must also strive to legitimate itself within the larger community in which the school district is located. To the degree that it succeeds in this task, the potential outside social pressures on members from friends and neighbors, as well as possible antiunion pressure on the administration and school board, will be decreased, thereby enhancing the union's position. While many of these attempts may be issue specific, that is, may seek to present the union's view of a current issue in hopes of forming a grass roots coalition, a substantial portion of these attempts will be unrelated to any current issue. Instead, they will be used to enhance the image of teachers in general, to show how professional and effective they are, or to show how concerned they are with the larger community. Included here are such devices as

press releases concerning teachers' awards or students' awards, fund raising drives for local charities, the establishment of scholarship funds, and so on.

5. In this regard, it is important to note that the quest for participation rights is related to professionalization. Teachers have always suffered from low pay and a lack of prestige, two issues that unionization sought to redress (Doherty and Oberer, 1967). Emphasizing teaching as a profession was a means of increasing teachers' prestige. In general, the desire for recognition as a profession involves an emphasis on expertise. It is on the basis of expertise that demands for participation rights are based. Because of their expertise, teachers should be given authority and influence over those areas in which their expertise is relevant. The problem arises in defining those areas of relevance (for example, see Lortie, 1977).

REFERENCES

Alutto, J., and J. Belasco. 1976. "Determinants of Attitudinal Militancy among Teachers and Nurses." In Education and Collective Bargaining: Readings in Policy and Research, edited by A. Creswell and M. Murphy. Berkeley: McCutchan.

Bacharach, S., and E. Lawler. 1980. Power, Coalitions and Bargaining: The Social Psychology and Organizational Politics. San Francisco: Jossey-Bass.

Baird, R., and J. Landon. 1977. "Teachers' Salaries and School Decentralization." In Education and Collective Bargaining: Readings in Policy and Research, edited by A. Creswell and M. Murphy. Berkeley: McCutchan.

Belasco, J., and J. Alutto. 1969. "Organizational Impacts of Teacher Negotiations." Industrial Relations 9, no. 1:67-79.

Cohen, M., J. March, and J. Olsen. 1972. "A Garbage Can Model of Organizational Choice." Administrative Science Quarterly 17, no. 1:1-25.

Coleman, J. 1973. "Loss of Power." American Sociological Review 38:1-17.

Coleman, J. 1966. "Foundations for a Theory of Collective Decisions." American Journal of Sociology 72, no. 6:615-27.

Coles, S. 1969. The Unionization of Teachers. New York: Praeger.

Corwin, R. 1970. Militant Professionalism: A Study of Organizational Conflict in High Schools. New York: Appleton-Century-Crofts.

Corwin, R. 1965. A Sociology of Education. New York: Appleton-Century-Crofts.

Crozier, M. 1964. The Bureaucratic Phenomenon. Chicago: University of Chicago Press.

Cyert, R., and J. March. 1963. A Behavioral Theory of the Firm. Englewood Cliffs, N.J.: Prentice-Hall.

Dahl, R. 1961. Who Governs? New Haven, Conn.: Yale University Press.

Doherty, R. 1979. Public Access. Ithaca, N.Y.: Industrial and Labor Relations, Cornell University Press.

Doherty, R., and W. Oberer. 1967. Teachers, School Boards, and Collective Bargaining. Ithaca, N.Y.: Industrial and Labor Relations, Cornell University Press.

Dreeben, R., and N. Gross. 1967. The Role Behavior of School Principals. Cambridge, Mass.: Harvard University, Graduate School of Education.

Edelstein, J., and M. Warner. 1975. Comparative Union Democracy. New York: John Wiley.

Flango, V. 1976. "The Impact of Collective Negotiations on Educational Policies." Journal of Collective Negotiations 5, no. 2: 133-55.

Fox, W., and M. Wince. 1976. "The Structure and Determinants of Attitudinal Militancy among Public School Teachers." Industrial and Labor Relations Review 30:47-58.

Freeman, R., and J. Medoff. 1979. "The Two Faces of Unionism." Harvard University and the National Bureau of Economic Research.

Geertz, C. 1974. The Interpretation of Cultures. New York: Basic Books.

Gerhart, P. 1976. "Determinants of Bargaining Outcomes in Local Government Labor Negotiations." Industrial and Labor Relations Review 29:331-51.

Getman, J., S. Goldberg, and J. Herman. 1976. Union Representation Elections: Law and Reality. New York: Russell Sage Foundation.

Glassman, A., and J. Belasco. 1976. "The Chapter Chairman and School Grievances." In Education and Collective Bargaining: Readings in Policy and Research, edited by A. Creswell and M. Murphy. Berkeley: McCutchan.

Goode, W. 1978. The Celebration of Heroes. Berkeley: University of California Press.

Gouldner, A. 1954. Patterns of Industrial Democracy. Glencoe, Ill.: The Free Press.

Gross, N., W. S. Mason, and A. W. McEachern. 1958. Explorations in Role Analysis. New York: John Wiley.

Hall, W., and N. Carroll. 1973. "The Effect of Teachers' Organizations on Salaries and Class Size." Industrial and Labor Relations Review 26:834-41.

Hellriegel, D., W. French, and P. Peterson. 1969. "Collective Negotiations and Teachers: A Behavioral Analysis." Industrial and Labor Relations Review 22, no. 3:380-96.

Holmes, A. 1976. "Effects of Union Activity on Teachers' Earnings." Industrial Relations 15, no. 3:328-32.

Hunter, F. 1953. Community Power Structure. Chapel Hill: University of North Carolina Press.

Kasper, H. 1970. "The Effects of Collective Bargaining on Public School Teachers' Salaries." Industrial and Labor Relations Review 24, no. 1:57-72.

Kerchner, C. 1979. "An Edited Proposal: The Impact of Citizen Participation on Collective Bargaining and School Governance." Claremont Graduate School working paper.

Kochan, T. 1978. "Contemporary Views of American Workers toward Trade Unionism." Report prepared for the Office of the Assistant Secretary for Policy, Evaluation and Research, U.S. Department of Labor.

Lipsky, D., and J. Drotning. 1973. "The Influence of Collective Bargaining on Teachers' Salaries in New York State." Industrial and Labor Relations Review 27, no. 1:18-35.

Lortie, D. 1977. "The Balance of Control and Autonomy in Elementary School Teaching." In Educational Organization and Administration, edited by D. Erickson. Berkeley: McCutchan.

Love, T. 1969. "Joint Committees: Their Role in the Development of Teacher Bargaining." Labor Law Journal, March, pp. 174-82.

Mintzberg, H. 1973. The Nature of Managerial Work. New York: Harper and Row.

Mitchell, S. 1978. "Organizing Behavior." Talk presented at the New York State School of Industrial and Labor Relations, Cornell University, November.

Moore, G. 1976. "The Effect of Collective Bargaining on Internal Salary Structures in the Public Schools." Industrial and Labor Relations Review 29:352-62.

Moore, W., and R. Newman. 1976. "The Influence of Legal and Nonlegal Factors on the Bargaining Status of Public School Teachers." Journal of Collective Negotiations 5, no. 2: 97-112.

Newton, K. 1976. Second City Politics. Oxford: The Clarendon Press.

Perry, C. 1979. "Teacher Bargaining: The Experience in Nine Systems." Industrial and Labor Relations Review 33, no. 1:3-17.

Pettigrew, A. 1973. The Politics of Organizational Decision-Making. London: Tavistock.

Rockwell, R. 1979. "Interlocking Crisis in a Suburban School System." Samson/Rockwell Cybernetics working paper.

Rosenthal, A. 1969. Pedagogues and Power. Syracuse, N.Y.: Syracuse University Press.

Selznick, P. 1957. Leadership in Administration. Evanston, Ill.: Row, Peterson.

Selznick, P. 1949. TVA and the Grass Roots. Berkeley: University of California Press.

Strauss, G. 1977. "Union Government in the U.S.: Research Past and Future." Industrial Relations 16:215-42.

Thompson, J. 1976. Policymaking in American Public Education. Englewood Cliffs, N.J.: Prentice-Hall.

Vidich, A., and J. Bensman. 1960. Small Town in Mass Society. New York: Doubleday.

Watkins, T. 1972. "The Effects of Community Environment on Negotiations." Journal of Collective Negotiations 1, no. 4: 317-27.

Weick, K. 1976. "Educational Organizations as Loosely Coupled Systems." Administrative Science Quarterly 21 (March):1-19.

Weintraub, A., and R. Thornton. 1976. "Why Teachers Strike: The Economic and Legal Determinants." Journal of Collective Negotiations 5, no. 3:193-206.

Wirt, F., and M. Kirst. 1972. The Political Web of American Schools. Boston: Little, Brown.

Zeigler, H. 1967. The Political Life of American Teachers. Englewood Cliffs, N.J.: Prentice-Hall.

Zeigler, H., and M. Jennings. 1974. Governing American Schools. North Scituate, Mass.: Duxbury Press.

ABOUT THE EDITOR
AND CONTRIBUTORS

SAMUEL B. BACHARACH is an Associate Professor in the Department of Organizational Behavior within the New York State School of Industrial and Labor Relations at Cornell University. He received his B.S. degree in Economics from the Washington Square College of Arts and Sciences of New York University and his Ph.D. in Sociology from the University of Wisconsin in 1974. He has been at Cornell University since 1973. He has served on the Editorial Board of Administrative Science Quarterly and is currently the Book Review Editor of that journal. With Edward J. Lawler he has written a book entitled Power, Coalitions, and Bargaining: The Social Psychology of Organizational Politics and is completing a second entitled Tactical Bargaining: Structure, Cognition, Action. He has published articles in such journals as Administrative Science Quarterly, Journal of Personality and Social Psychology, Industrial and Labor Relations Review, The Academy of Management Journal, and Social Forces. His current projects include an experimental investigation of power in bargaining being made jointly with Edward J. Lawler under a grant from National Science Foundation and on investigation of school district governance and administration by the National Institute of Education.

VIRGINIA D. ABERNATHY is a professor of Psychiatry (An thropology), Vanderbilt University School of Medicine. She is the author of Population Pressure and Cultural Adjustment (1976) and editor of and contributor to Frontiers in Medical Ethics: Application in a Medical Setting (1980).

MARTIN BURLINGAME is Professor of Educational Administration and Supervision at the University of Illinois at Urbana. He began his career in education as a public school teacher in Oregon and earned a Ph.D. at the University of Chicago with an emphasis on the politics of education. He served on the faculty of the University of New Mexico and as a senior research assistant at the National Institute of Education in Washington, D.C. His interests center on school-community relations and power in educational organizations.

W. W. CHARTERS received his Ph.D. in Social Psychology from the University of Michigan in 1952. He spent six years in the

Bureau of Educational Research, University of Illinois, and ten years at the Graduate Institute of Education, Washington University, St. Louis. For the past fifteen years, he has been Professor of Education in the University of Oregon's Federal Research and Development Center for Educational Policy and Management, formerly the Center for the Advanced Study of Educational Advancement.

In 1963, Professor Charters was a Fellow at the Center for Research on Careers, Harvard University, and from 1972 to 1974, he was a Fellow at the Center for Advanced Study in the Behavioral Sciences, Palo Alto, California.

His specialties include research on careers and the organizational behavior of school boards, administrators, and teachers; organizational theory in relation to educational innovation; and sex equity in education.

MARGARET S. CROWDES is a candidate for a Ph.D. in Sociology at the University of California, San Diego. Her research interests concern the connections between critical theory, feminism, and interactional approaches to social action.

JOSEPH J. CUNNINGHAM is Associate Professor of Special Education, George Peabody College for Teachers, Vanderbilt University. He is the author of papers and articles on labeling for mental retardation, the institutionalization of mildly retarded individuals, and special education teaching.

DANIEL L. DUKE is Assistant Professor of Education at Stanford University and a former school administrator and teacher. His research deals with teacher leadership, school control structure, and educational growth and decline. He is the author of numerous articles and books, including The Retransformation of the School, Managing Student Behavior Problems, and Classroom Management.

DAVID DWYER is finishing his Ph.D. at Washington University with a dissertation entitled "The New Leadership: Complexities of a Participative Ideology in Two Innovative Educational Organizations." Recently he and Louis Smith finished a major case study, Federal Policy in Action. Prior to this he taught junior high school science and directed an alternative high school.

SCARLETT G. GRAHAM is a Research Associate at the Institute for Public Policy Studies, Vanderbilt University. She is Associate Editor of The Journal of Politics, coeditor and author of Founding Principles of American Government: Two Hundred Years of

<u>Democracy on Trial</u> (1977), and the author of articles on evaluation in policy analysis.

E. MARK HANSON is Professor of Educational Administration at the University of California, Riverside. He has published extensively on issues of school organization and governance in the United States as well as on management reform in Latin American ministries of education. Professor Hanson is a consultant to the World Bank on issues of educational management in developing countries.

ERWIN C. HARGROVE is Director of the Institute for Public Policy Studies and Professor of Political Science, Vanderbilt University. He is the author of <u>Presidential Leadership</u> (1966), <u>Professional Roles in Society and Government: The English Case</u> (1972), <u>The Power of the Modern Presidency</u> (1974), and <u>The Missing Link: The Study of the Implementation of Social Policy</u> (1975).

ALMA HERTWECK is a candidate for a Ph. D. in Sociology at the University of California, San Diego. Her research interests concern the structure and consequences of educators' attribution for students' careers in schools.

MICHAEL IMBER is an Assistant Professor at the University of Kansas and a former counselor and alternative school director. His interests include curriculum reform, sex education, and school retrenchment.

STEPHEN T. KERR is an Associate Professor in the Department of Curriculum and Teaching at Teachers College, Columbia University. He taught for four years in the School of Education at the University of Puget Sound in Tacoma, Washington, where he also served as coordinator of faculty and instructional development. He has also worked as director of a study on facilities utilization for the Seattle Public Schools, as managing editor in charge of multimedia materials for a New York publisher, and as an instructor of sociology and psychology at Sheldon Jackson College in Sitka, Alaska. He obtained his undergraduate degree in 1967 from Princeton University in Slavic Languages; he also holds an M. A. from Columbia in Sociology. He received his Ph. D. in Education from the University of Washington in 1975. His current research and writing centers on issues in educational technology, the sociology of education, and comparative education.

JOHN M. KOMOCAR (M.S., 1980, University of Illinois) is a doctoral candidate in Organizational Psychology at the University of Illinois. He has done research on organizational effectiveness and job satisfaction. His current research interests focus on cognitive sense-making in organizations.

HUGH MEHAN is Associate Professor of Sociology at the University of California, San Diego, and Director, Teacher Education Program. He received his Ph.D. in Sociology from the University of California, Santa Barbara, in 1971. His principal works are Learning Lessons (Harvard University Press, 1979) and The Reality of Ethnomethodology (with Houston Wood, Wiley Interscience, 1975). He has examined the social organization of concerted activities in educational settings including classrooms, educational testing encounters, and decision-making groups. He is currently attempting to link the interactional analysis of social action to issues of social policy and social structure.

J. LEE MEIHLS is a candidate for a Ph.D. in Sociology at the University of California, San Diego. Meihls is investigating the symbolic representations constructed about students labeled learning disabled.

MARY HAYWOOD METZ received a Ph.D. in Sociology from the University of California at Berkeley in 1971. She has been Assistant Professor of Sociology at Earlham College, Richmond, Indiana, and a Lecturer in Sociology at Mount Mary College, Milwaukee, and Marquette University. Currently, she is Assistant Professor of Educational Policy Studies at the University of Wisconsin, Madison. Professor Metz's areas of interest include the sociology of education, complex organizations, and the family.

JACOB B. MICHAELSEN is Professor of Economics at the University of California, Santa Cruz. He is currently developing an economic analysis of decision making in public school districts. He has published a number of articles on schooling that reflect this interest.

STEPHEN M. MITCHELL received a B.A. from Harvard University and an M.S. and Ph.D. from Cornell University. He has been a visiting instructor at Carnegie-Mellon University and is currently a research associate in the New York State School of Industrial and Labor Relations at Cornell University. His theoretical interests center on the relationship between individual and collective action and the mechanisms that constrain this relationship. This concern has resulted in investigations of such areas as subjective methodologies, the symbolic aspects of organizational design, and the political aspects of school district governance and administration.

JOHN PRUNTY is finishing his Ph.D. at Washington University with a dissertation entitled "A Participant Observation Study of a Public Alternative High School: An Analysis of Factors Influencing Organizational Effectiveness." Prior to this he taught junior and senior high school science in St. Louis County and also served as a community youth director.

BRIAN ROWAN is Assistant Professor of Sociology at Texas Christian University. He is currently involved in two projects concerned with educational organizations. One project is an investigation of the relations between children's friendship groups and students' academic performances in elementary schools. A second project is a time-series investigation of the conditions promoting the adoption and retention of educational innovations. Professor Rowan received his Ph.D in Sociology from Stanford University.

BEVERLY K. SHOWERS is an Assistant Professor at the University of Oregon and a former teacher and staff development expert. Her work has focused on teacher involvement in school decision making, teacher self-efficacy, and teacher effectiveness.

LOUIS SMITH took his Ph.D. in Psychology at the University of Minnesota in 1955 and has been at the Graduate Institute of Education, Washington University, since then. He has coauthored Educational Psychology, The Complexities of an Urban Classroom, and Anatomy of Educational Innovation. Currently, with Prunty, Dwyer, and Kleine, he is completing an NIE project, Kensington Revisited: A 15 Year Follow-up of an Innovative School and Its Faculty.

LEE SPROULL is Assistant Professor of Social Science at Carnegie-Mellon University. She is coauthor, with Stephen Weiner and David Wolf, of Organizing an Anarchy (1978). Her current work, supported by the National Institute of Education, focuses on how local school districts respond to federal regulation. She received her Ph.D. from Stanford University in 1978.

JAMES R. TERBORG received his Ph.D. from Purdue University in 1975. He is Associate Professor of Management at the University of Oregon. He has done research on employee motivation and occupational sex discrimination. His current research is on organizational effectiveness and is being supported by the Office of Naval Research.

WILLIAM K. VAUGHN is Associate Professor of Biostatisics and Director of the Division of Biostatistics, Department of Preventive Medicine, Vanderbilt University. He has written articles and papers on such topics as sampling human populations, epidimiology, and the development of large data bases for research purposes.

LESLIE WARD is a Research Assistant in the Institute for Public Policy Studies, Vanderbilt University.